Library of Congress Cataloging in Publication Data

Hutchinson, Harry D.
  Money, banking, and the United States economy.

  Includes bibliographical references and index.
  1. Banks and banking—United States.   2. Money.
3. International finance.   4. Monetary policy—United
States.   I. Title.
HG2491.H8   1984   332.1'0973   83-11052
ISBN 0-13-600262-5

Editorial/production supervision and interior design: Barbara Grasso
Cover design: Lundgren Graphics, Ltd.
Manufacturing buyer: Ed O'Dougherty

Printed in the United States of America

10   9   8   7   6   5   4   3   2

ISBN 0-13-600262-5

Prentice-Hall International, Inc., *London*
Prentice-Hall of Australia Pty. Limited, *Sydney*
Editora Prentice-Hall do Brasil, Ltda., *Rio de Janeiro*
Prentice-Hall Canada Inc., *Toronto*
Prentice-Hall of India Private Limited, *New Delhi*
Prentice-Hall of Japan, Inc., *Tokyo*
Prentice-Hall of Southeast Asia Pte. Ltd., *Singapore*
Whitehall Books Limited, *Wellington, New Zealand*

5th edition

MONEY, BANKING, AND THE UNITED STATES ECONOMY

Harry D. Hutchinson

University of Delaware

PRENTICE-HALL, INC., Englewood Cliffs, New Jersey 07632

Contents

iii

Part Two

MONETARY AND INCOME THEORY

Part Three

MONETARY POLICY: WEAKNESSES AND ALTERNATIVES

Preface

This book is intended for use in undergraduate or survey M.B.A. courses in the economics of money and banking. Its scope and approach are more or less traditional. Part I, consisting of twelve chapters, is primarily institutional and historical in content. It deals with the definition and determinants of the money supply, an overview of the nation's financial system including financial markets and the activities of nonbank financial institutions, an in-depth discussion of commercial banking and the banking system, and a complete coverage of the structure and functions of the Federal Reserve System.

Part II, consisting of Chapters 13 through 19, is devoted to a consideration of monetary theory beginning with the early (pre-1930s) version of the quantity theory, progressing through a four-chapter development of an essentially Keynesian income-expenditure model, continuing with a discussion of the views of the modern monetarists, and concluding with a chapter on the stagflation problems of the 1970s and 1980s including some of the theoretical devices that have been developed to explain them.

Part III includes only two chapters. The first, Chapter 20, deals with the transmission mechanisms connecting the money supply with economic activity as well as with a number of alleged weaknesses of monetary policy. Chapter 21, then, deals with the prime alternatives to monetary policy, fiscal policy, debt management, and incomes policies.

Part IV, Chapters 22 through 24, covers international finance, possible alternative international monetary systems, the structure and history of the International Monetary Fund, and the enormous changes that have affected international monetary affairs in the 1970s and 1980s.

Every textbook writer claims that his book is "written for the student." I can think of no way to vary this familiar theme. Throughout, I have assigned the highest priority to keeping the discussion as clear and simple as the subject and my expository ability permit. Whether this effort will be a success, of course, only the student can judge. I simply attest that clarity has been my most important objective.

All teachers labor under certain preconceptions regarding the needs of their students. Mine include the belief that repetition of many fundamental principles already covered in the standard introductory course is a desirable and, indeed, necessary technique. For those students who really learned these basic tools in their first course, the cost involved in reviewing them once again is slight. For those (who I believe constitute the majority) who got through their principles course satisfactorily, but didn't quite fully grasp (or have already forgotten) such concepts as multiple credit expansion, the multiplier, or the balance of payments, repetition at this level is absolutely essential. Basically, I have tried to start "from scratch" in all areas, first recapitulating what is normally taught in the introductory course and then superimposing more advanced material on that base.

This edition includes substantial revision in a number of areas. Perhaps most fundamental is the incorporation of the wide ranging and extremely important provisions of the Depository Institutions Deregulation and Monetary Control Act of 1980 as well as those of the Depository Institutions Act of 1982. Another area of substantive change is that of financial innovation, its causes, and its effects on the definition of money. In addition, the section on monetary targets and the process of monetary policy formulation has been completely rewritten to incorporate very significant changes since the last edition. An entirely new chapter on the purposes and characteristics of financial markets has been added to strengthen that aspect of the discussion. Throughout the book, of course, every effort has been made to bring data, theory, and policy discussions up to date.

It has always been difficult to cover all of the topics one might like to consider in a single semester. The financial innovation, new legislation, and theoretical developments of recent years have simply made this problem even more intense. For those instructors for whom semester or quarter time constraints make coverage of the entire book impossible, I would suggest the following as a "core" that can easily be used without loss of continuity:

Chapters 1, 2, 3, the last half of 5, 6, 7, 8, 9, 10, 11, 14, 15, 16, 17 (omitting the section on IS-LM curves and the appendix), 18 and 19.

I am indebted to many people for support, encouragement, and valuable suggestions for improvements. Especially helpful have been two old friends, Professor Harold Wolf of the University of Texas at Austin and Professor Bill Reher of the University of Texas at Arlington. *Ite Caerulei.* In addition, Professor Dale F. Kuntz has offered a number of extremely useful comments and suggestions. As always, my colleagues at Delaware in both economics and finance have been extremely generous with their time and expertise. To all of them, as well as to Prentice-Hall's Barbara Grasso, who, with exceptional efficiency and professional competence, handled the production, I am very grateful.

Though all these people have contributed much to the book, since I did not, in all cases, accept their advice, I must absolve them from any responsibility for its errors of omission and commission. For those, I alone am responsible.

1

What Is Money?

This is a book about money. Accordingly, logical order and the dictates of tradition require that we begin our discussion by defining the subject. *What,* precisely, *is money?*

On its face, the question may seem to be an absurdity and, indeed, something of an insult to the intelligence of the reader. "Surely," as one of my more outspoken students informed me recently, "everyone knows what money is. Is it really necessary to waste valuable class time discussing the obvious?"

The question is, of course, rhetorical. It is never necessary to "discuss the obvious." But that which appears obvious to some may not be so clear-cut to others. It is not a fact that "everyone knows what money is." For even if no one else had any doubts about it, monetary economists have been struggling for a number of years now to arrive at some consensus on the definition of money.

The problems show up at two levels. On the one hand, there are long-standing philosophical differences as to what constitutes the true "essence" of money. One group—undoubtedly the majority—argues that the distinguishing characteristic of money is its capacity to serve as a "generally accepted medium of exchange." Another group, however, sees the essential feature of money as its ability to serve as a "temporary abode of purchasing power—in which sellers of goods, services, or financial assets hold the proceeds in the interim between sale and subsequent purchase of other goods, services or assets."[1] This difference of opinion has never really been settled, but it has been neatly side-stepped by the monetary authorities who regularly collect and publish several different money supply series (labeled M1, M2, etc.), each aimed at satisfying the members of one of the two groups.

---

[1] *Improving the Monetary Aggregates,* report of the Advisory Committee on Monetary Statistics (Washington, D.C.: Board of Governors of the Federal Reserve System, 1976), p. 9.

The other problem—recently a much more vexing one—is that of deciding precisely where to draw the line separating those financial instruments that are money and those that are not. This task would be difficult enough to undertake in a static economy without change. But the unprecedented rate of financial innovation in the last decade has so severely magnified the problem that one high Federal Reserve official was led recently to observe, "I have concluded, most reluctantly, that we can no longer measure the money supply with any precision."[2]

In light of all this, we must recognize at the outset that defining money and agreeing on the financial assets that shall be "counted" as money is a complex and challenging task. Yet if we are to speak of "the money supply," as indeed we must, meaningful communication requires that we agree on a single definition. The remainder of this chapter is aimed at that objective.

How Money Contributes to the Economy

Despite their many differences, virtually all economists agree that money must be defined functionally. That is, items that are to be considered money should be selected on the basis of the functions they perform rather than on such alternative characteristics as the identity of the issuer or the commodity of which they are made. We need, then, to consider carefully the particular functions that money does perform. Before doing so, however, it should be revealing to consider the difficulties inherent in an economy without money.

The Problems with Barter

If no money at all existed, each income recipient would necessarily have to be paid "in kind"—that is, in the form of his or her share of the actual goods that he or she had helped produce. If, for instance, one worked for a brewery, one's weekly paycheck might consist of 50 cases of beer.

Sounds great, you say? Don't be so sure. After the first couple of six-packs were consumed, most people would find it necessary to start bartering their remaining beer to others who happened to possess the food, clothing, and fuel and myriad other goods and services most of us choose to consume on a regular basis. The process of barter without money to serve as a common medium for which anything can be bought or sold would surely turn out to be a nightmare.

The problems encountered would be enormous. Not only would our beer peddler have to search out others who wished to trade off the things he or she wanted, but for a direct deal to be struck, these people would have to be people who desired to trade what they had for beer. To put it in the terms most commonly employed, exchange under barter conditions would require a *double coincidence*

---

of wants. Not only must we find people who want our beer, but these same people must possess the things we want to trade for. Even if some sort of downtown marketing system were arranged to facilitate such exchanges, one can easily imagine the trading process taking as much of one's time as earning the beer in the first place.

But that is not the end of it by any means. In a money economy, we tend to take for granted the role that money plays as a *numeraire*—a measuring device in terms of which the market worth of all goods and services is evaluated and can be compared. If there is no money to serve this function, the exchange value of every good or service must be expressed in terms of a certain number of units of every other one. If, for example, there were 1,000 different goods and services on the market, instead of 1,000 dollar prices being available to measure their relative market worth, *499,500 exchange ratios would be required*! Such a system would not only be a consumer's and accountant's nightmare—it would make efficient use of an economy's scarce resources a near impossibility.

It is fruitless to continue beating a dead horse. The inefficiency of an economy without money is probably quite obvious. To put the whole issue in a more positive vein, what are the social *merits* of money? In a phrase, an efficiently operating money system is a *sine qua non* for economic development and high living standards. It underlies and facilitates both specialization and capital formation—two essential ingredients of economic growth.

More than two centuries ago, Adam Smith emphasized the contribution that specialization can make to production levels. But specialization is the antithesis of self-sufficiency. As such, it makes *exchange* essential. Each specialist becomes dependent, not only upon all other specialist-producers, but upon the system that facilitates exchanging goods and services among them. Therefore, in a very real sense, money is an essential prerequisite to extensive specialization.

Capital formation, the process whereby new capital goods are produced, also depends heavily on a money system. Fundamentally, capital formation requires saving to release productive resources from the production of consumer goods and transference of those released resources to the building of plants, equipment, and other capital goods. All this could, conceptually, be accomplished without money, but it would be extremely difficult. In a barter system, the savers would be required to accumulate stocks of consumer goods and somehow make them available to investors who, in turn, would use them to "pay" the workers who build the capital goods. It could be done, but hardly extensively. How much simpler it is for the savers to save money income and lend that to the investors!

All this should make it clear why money was first created. It did not originate centuries ago with some farsighted government that saw the need for money and responded by offering it. Rather, it arose spontaneously out of the sheer necessity for a money substance to facilitate economic exchange. Governments now control the issuance of money, but they did not invent it, and some form of money would continue to be used with or without government involvement. In this area as much as in any other, "necessity" was truly the "mother of invention."

The Functions of Money

What, specifically, are the functions performed by money? They consist, of course, essentially of overcoming the difficulties of a barter system. Traditionally, three main functions are considered.

Medium of Exchange. First and perhaps most important, money serves as a medium of exchange—as a vehicle through which the process of exchange among interdependent specialists is made possible. In this role, money serves as an essential lubricant that permits highly industrialized, intricately specialized economies to operate smoothly and effectively.

Unit of Account. In addition to its medium-of-exchange function, money serves as a *numeraire,* a sort of "value measuring rod," in terms of which the values of millions of goods and services can be expressed and compared. Students should recognize that this function is different from that of medium of exchange. Although in the United States today the dollar fulfills both roles simultaneously, this need not be the case. There have been a number of examples in history of one form of money fulfilling the medium-of-exchange function while an entirely different instrument played the role of unit of account in the public's calculations of value.[3]

Store of Value. Money that is spent is, of course, fulfilling the medium-of-exchange function. Obviously, however, a holder of money is free to "not spend" it—to retain it for any period of time desired as a store of value or a generalized, uncommitted claim to wealth.

Money shares this role with a long list of other assets: stocks, bonds, real commodities, and many other items may also be considered appropriate forms in which to "store value." Sometimes (as in periods of falling prices), money is an extremely appropriate form in which to hold one's wealth. In inflationary periods, it is generally much less so. As we shall see, a significant portion of monetary theory and policy revolves around the public's decisions as to what portion of the money stock it chooses to hold as a store of value.

The Current Official Definition of Money in the United States

As noted earlier, most economists consider the medium-of-exchange function to be the critical one for distinguishing money from nonmoney claims. For them, the so-called "narrowly defined money stock" series entitled M1 is collected and reported on a regular basis.

---

[3]Some economists choose to list money's role as a *standard for deferred payments* as a separate function. Since this may be treated as simply a subfunction of its role as a unit of account, we do not list it separately here.

For those who consider the essence of money to be its capacity to serve as a "temporary abode of purchasing power," broader series focusing more on the store of value function are needed. To satisfy this view, the Federal Reserve System regularly reports an M2 and M3 money stock.

Let us consider each of these in turn.

The Narrowly Defined Money Stock: M1

By all odds, the most widely used definition of money is *anything generally accepted as a medium of exchange*. Although in other times and other cultures many items have fulfilled this definition (such as, for example, gold, beads, cigarettes, and even millstones), until quite recently in the United States the only things generally accepted as payment media were currency and coins in addition to demand deposits (i.e., checking accounts) held by the public at commercial banks.[4] But although these items still dominate the M1 money supply (constituting almost 80 percent of the M1 total in early 1983), financial innovation and regulatory changes in the past decade or so have complicated the issue markedly.

The Development of "Other Checkable Deposits." In brief, what we have seen is the following. Unprecedented and persisting inflation throughout the 1970s and early 1980s was accompanied by (indeed, in large part, *led* to) unprecedented rises in interest rates. These high interest rates sharply raised the opportunity cost of holding money (noninterest-earning) balances. That, in turn, led financial institutions, ever alert to the public's desire to minimize the cost of holding transactions balances, to seek new financial arrangements that could accommodate such desires. Finally, these efforts at financial innovation tended to induce governmental regulatory reforms that have had the effect of legalizing several new types of "checkable deposits."

Perhaps the most important of these are the so-called "NOW accounts." Technically speaking, NOW accounts (or negotiable orders of withdrawal) are interest-earning savings accounts on which checks can be written.[5] The first NOW accounts were issued in 1972 by mutual savings banks in Massachusetts and New Hampshire where, under state law, they were declared legal.

After being upheld by the courts, the issuance of NOW accounts spread rapidly throughout New England. Within two years, to prevent a competitive advantage to mutual savings banks, all depository institutions in Massachusetts and

---

[4]Until recently, the law forbade any institution other than commercial banks to issue demand deposits, so that it was convenient to define commercial banks as "financial institutions that issue demand deposits." Unhappily, recent changes have made the definition of a commercial bank just about as fuzzy as the definition of money.

[5]For all practical purposes, NOW accounts could be considered checking accounts that pay interest, but since federal law still forbids payment of interest on checking accounts, they are technically considered savings accounts on which checks can be written. Earlier NOW accounts were subject to interest rate ceilings but beginning in January, 1983, depository institutions have been authorized to issue so-called *Super Now's* with no interest rate ceilings.

New Hampshire except credit unions were authorized by Congress to issue NOW accounts. Then, in 1976, the same authority was granted to depository institutions in all New England states. Finally, after being legalized in still more states, Congress, in the Depository Institutions Deregulation and Monetary Control Act of 1980 (D.I.D.M.C. Act), authorized their issuance by all federally insured commercial banks, savings banks, and savings and loan associations throughout the country beginning in January 1981.

A second development of note was the authorization of so-called "ATS accounts" at commercial banks. ATS accounts (bank accounts offering "automatic transfer service") are arrangements whereby banks automatically transfer funds from interest-bearing savings accounts to checking accounts as checks are written. This, of course, permits the account owner to earn interest on his or her account— but to have it as readily available for spending purposes as a checking account. ATS accounts were initially authorized by bank regulatory agencies in 1978, challenged in the courts, but then made legal by the same 1980 D.I.D.M.C. Act that permitted nationwide NOW accounts.

Third, there was the development and subsequent legalization of "share draft accounts" issued by credit unions. These are arrangements whereby owners of interest-earning shares (accounts) at credit unions can write checks on them. They, too, were challenged in the courts, but ultimately they were made legal by the D.I.D.M.C. Act of 1980.

The Specific Components of M1. Following a revision in 1980 that properly recognized the development of these new payment media, the M1 money supply currently includes the following:

1. **Currency and coins held by the nonbank public;** *not* included in M1 are currency and coins held by the U.S. Treasury, the Federal Reserve banks, and commercial banks.
2. **Demand deposits owned at commercial banks by the nonbank public;** *not* included in M1 are demand deposits owned by commercial banks that are issued by other commercial banks, the U.S. Treasury, and foreign banks and official institutions as well as cash items in process of collection and Federal Reserve float.[6]
3. **Other checkable deposits, which include**
   a. All NOW accounts.
   b. Automatic transfer service accounts at banks and thrift institutions.
   c. Share draft accounts held at credit unions.
   d. Demand deposits (and outstanding traveler's checks) owned by the nonbank public and issued by depository institutions other than commercial banks.[7]

---

[6]Cash items in process of collection plus Federal Reserve float represents checks that have been deposited in one bank but have not yet been collected from the bank on which they are written. They are, of course, excluded to avoid double-counting a single demand deposit at two different banks.

[7]Mutual savings banks and savings and loan associations were authorized to issue demand deposits when related to newly authorized commercial loans in the D.I.D.M.C. Act of 1980 and in the Depository Institutions Act of 1982.

Continuing Financial Innovation and the M1 Concept. Certainly the addition of these ''other checkable deposits'' to the M1 money series represented a much needed improvement. But the economic environment that fostered these financial innovations has not disappeared since the major revisions of 1980. And, as a result, other, newer financial innovations continue to pop up, threatening the meaningfulness and inclusiveness of the current M1 definition.

Most important among these has been the development of the *money market mutual fund* and its more recent clone, the *money market deposit account.* A money market mutual fund, as we shall learn in more detail in a later chapter, is a specialized type of investment company that collects householders' savings via sale of ''shares'' and then uses the proceeds to purchase large denomination short-term I.O.U.'s issued by business and governments. During periods of rampant inflation such as the past decade, money market mutual fund shares have tended to pay their owners much higher rates of return than were typically available on ordinary depository institution savings accounts (which, as we shall see, have, until recently, been forbidden by law from paying competitive rates).

The enormous popularity of money market mutual funds is evidenced by their meteoric growth from total assets of $4 billion as recently as 1978 to over $230 billion in late 1982. The attractive features which led to this growth—in addition to the high rate of return—have included their availability in relatively modest (usually $1,000) denomination sizes, the fact that they can be cashed in without penalty at any time, and the fact that most funds offer their share holders limited (normally in amounts of $500 or more) check-writing privileges.

It is this latter feature that creates problems with their classification. Undoubtedly most MMMF owners look upon their shares more as financial investments similar to savings accounts or certificates of deposit than as true transactions accounts fitting the ''medium of exchange,'' M1 concept. But the fact that checks *can* be written on them leaves substantial room for doubt.

Even more perplexing is the proper classification of the much newer *money market deposit account.* Authorized initially in December of 1982 (as a result of the Depository Institutions Act of 1982) these accounts are specifically intended to permit depository institutions to compete for funds which had been drained off into the money market mutual funds. Specifically, they are a special type of savings account issued by commercial banks, mutual savings banks, and savings and loan associations which pays depositors interest returns comparable to those offered by money market mutual funds (the legal limit having been removed in the case of MMDAs). These accounts are available in initial minimum denominations of $2,500, are immediately withdrawable without penalty, and offer the advantage (over money market mutual funds) of federal government insurance up to $100,000 per account. In addition, account holders are permitted to write up to three checks per month on them.

So what about money market deposit accounts? Should they be treated as a part of M1 because they are indeed—at least to some extent—transactions accounts which serve as a medium of exchange? Or should they be relegated to the broader

M2 category because, in the main, most account holders consider them financial investments similar to savings accounts? Obviously, they present serious classification problems and, although at the time of this writing they are being included entirely as a part of M2, a case could be made for different treatment.

And if the conceptual problems created by money market accounts aren't enough, consider the recent practice of "deposit sweeping." Under this arrangement, owners of large accounts (primarily corporations) have their entire accounts available to them for check writing purposes up to a certain hour each day. At that hour, the bank automatically "sweeps" the bulk of the account into an interest-earning asset for the rest of the day. The result is that, while the entire account may be considered a part of the firm's spendable transactions balances, when M1 figures are collected (at the *end* of the day), only a small part of it gets included.

We could go on, but the point is simple. So long as the incentive is there, financial innovation is likely to continue. And as has been the case in the past, such changes have the capacity to alter drastically the items that satisfy the requirements of a claim "generally accepted as a medium of exchange."

The upshot is a problem much more profound than that of posing mere difficulties with definitions. For if the narrow M1 money supply is an important determinant of economic welfare, the fact that we can't even measure or define it adequately bodes ill for efforts to promote economic welfare via its control. In short, if we don't even know what the money supply is, it is going to be pretty hard to control.

More Broadly Defined Money Stocks: M2 and M3

For those who consider the essence of "moneyness" to be a claim's capacity to serve as a "temporary abode of purchasing power," and to serve not only as a store of value but also to be readily convertible into a medium of exchange, additional claims must be included. To those who hold this view, the essence of an instrument's moneyness is thought to be its *liquidity,* which, in turn, largely determines its suitability as a store of value.

What is liquidity? An asset is said to possess *perfect* liquidity if it can be immediately converted into a fixed number of dollars without risk of loss.[8]

Now if our money concept were to be limited to assets possessing absolutely *perfect* liquidity, the items included would be precisely the same as those identified earlier as generally accepted media of exchange—coins, currency, and checkable deposits. Such a limitation would, of course, have the virtue of providing a not entirely unreasonable distinction between "money" and "nonmoney" assets. But

---

[8]The phrase "without risk of loss" refers to dollars, not real purchasing power. For example, if a particular asset is of such a nature as to guarantee the holder immediate access to, say, $100, it has perfect liquidity even if the $100 may, as a result of inflation, have less real purchasing power than when the asset was initially purchased.

the line of demarcation—if "degree of liquidity" is to be considered the distinguishing characteristic—is inevitably an arbitrary one. Consider, for example, the following list of assets:

1. Coins and currency
2. Demand deposits (checking accounts)
3. Passbook savings deposits at commercial banks
4. Savings deposits at savings and loan associations and mutual savings banks
5. Time certificates of deposit
6. Money market deposit accounts at depository institutions
7. Money market mutual funds
8. U.S. government savings bonds
9. Marketable U.S. government securities

As noted, only items 1 and 2 qualify as possessing perfect liquidity. Coins and currency *are* dollars, and checking accounts obligate the depository institution to pay out cash at the owner's demand. But classifying these assets as money because they possess 100 percent liquidity while excluding several others that offer liquidity at somewhere around the 99 percent level certainly seems to involve drawing indefensibly fine distinctions.

Ordinary savings accounts at commercial banks, mutual savings banks, savings and loan associations, and credit unions are, in practice if not in law, as liquid as checking accounts. Although savings institutions have the legal right to make depositors wait for up to 14 days after a withdrawal request before receiving cash, this right is almost universally waived.[9] The result is that both the depositors and the savings institutions have come to look upon these accounts, in practice, as being just as much "withdrawable on demand" as checking accounts.

In addition to regular savings accounts, the depository institutions also issue time certificates of deposit (CDs).[10] These certificates, which usually offer a higher interest rate than do regular savings accounts, are most commonly sold in units of $1,000 or more and carry fixed maturity dates varying from 30 days to 6 years or more from date of issue. Of special note here are *money market certificates*. These are offered in denominations of $10,000 with maturities of 26 weeks. They pay a maximum interest rate that is no more than 0.25 percent higher than the interest paid on the most recent 6-month U.S. Treasury bill issue. Also, depository institutions issue certificates in smaller denominations that have a 30-month maturity and pay interest rates tied to the yield currently being earned on U.S. government securities with an average of 30 months to maturity.

---

[9]Indeed, savings institutions are *required* to reserve this right but are under no obligation to enforce it.

[10]For purposes of simplification, we shall omit explicit consideration of time deposits, open account, under which the depositor agrees in a written contract (though not a certificate) not to withdraw his or her funds before a specified maturity date at least 30 days hence. In cases of emergency, such funds can be withdrawn before the maturity date, but only after payment of a stiff penalty.

The larger CDs (denomination sizes of $100,000 or more), designed primarily for business firms, are generally negotiable (i.e., can be sold from one owner to another). Holders of nonnegotiable CDs who find that they need their money in advance of the specified maturity date can normally get it from the issuer, though only at the sacrifice of part of their interest income.

How liquid are such time deposits? Not quite as liquid as regular savings accounts, of course, but nevertheless very highly liquid assets.

In practice, assets held in the form of shares of money market mutual funds or as money market deposit accounts are every bit as liquid as ordinary savings accounts. Indeed, along with the higher interest return they offer, their most attractive feature to most savers has been their high degree of liquidity. They even have an edge over certificates of deposit since, unlike most certificates, there is no "penalty for early withdrawal."

The last two items—U.S. savings bonds and marketable U.S. government securities—are similar in that both are obligations of the U.S. Treasury and part of the national debt, but they are different in degree of liquidity. U.S. savings bonds (of which about $68 billion were outstanding in early 1983) are issued in the name of the initial purchaser and, as such, are nonmarketable; that is, they cannot be sold to someone else. On the other hand, savings bonds possess the unique advantage of being cashable (turned in to the government for repayment of principal plus a fixed amount of interest) at any time (after a short initial waiting period) before the actual maturity date. These bonds, then, would appear to be just about as liquid as regular savings accounts.

Marketable U.S. government securities, on the other hand (of which over $900 billion were outstanding in early 1983), are substantially less liquid.[11] These obligations cannot be "cashed in" until their fixed maturity date. A holder of a marketable U.S. security who needs his or her money before the maturity date must sell it to someone else at the going market price. The market price of such securities is a variable amount that can, at any given time (depending largely on the behavior of interest rates and the length of time till maturity of the instrument), be above or below the par value of the asset. Marketable U.S. securities therefore, although still very liquid assets, are much less so than are U.S. savings bonds or time and savings deposits.

So where is all this leading us? Where do those who consider an asset's liquidity—or suitability as a "temporary abode of purchasing power" as the essence of its moneyness draw the line between money and nonmoney items? What must be obvious by now is that *any* specific dividing line is bound to be somewhat arbitrary, and, indeed, in defining M2 and M3, the authorities were required to draw somewhat arbitrary distinctions.

---

[11]Marketable U.S. government securities include such instruments as (1) Treasury bills, with maturities varying from 91 days to 1 year; (2) Treasury notes, with maturities from 1 to 7 years; and (3) Treasury bonds, with maturities up to 30 years. In addition to savings bonds, over $200 billion of Treasury securities designed for government trust funds were also nonmarketable as of December 1982.

The Specific Components of M2 and M3. The M2 money stock series includes all the instruments found in M1 plus the following highly liquid claims:

1. *Money market mutual fund shares.* The nature of these assets has been discussed and, as noted, increased dramatically from 1978 to late 1982. (Included here are only those MMMF available for individuals).
2. *Savings deposits and "small" certificates of deposit* (in denominations of less than $100,000). These claims are issued by all depository institutions. Money market deposit accounts are included as a part of this total.
3. *Overnight repurchase agreements* (typically referred to as RPs). These assets are issued by commercial banks to companies other than depository institutions and money market mutual funds. Repurchase agreements typically arise in the following way. A corporation may have funds on deposit at a bank that it does not expect to need until the following day. It then arranges to use these funds to "purchase" a U.S. security from the bank with the understanding that the bank will "buy" the security back on the following day. Such RP transactions are usually carried out in units of $1 million or more, and the corporation earns interest on the funds for a day at a rate approximately equal to the current federal funds rate.[12] Obviously corporations owning RPs consider them exceptionally liquid assets, since they guarantee a fixed amount of funds the following day.
4. *Overnight Eurodollars.* These claims are issued by Caribbean and London branches of U.S. banks to U.S. residents other than depository institutions and money market mutual funds. These particular Eurodollars are liabilities of banks located in the Caribbean and in London, the liabilities being denominated in dollars and payable in dollars on the following day. In effect, they represent readily available savings accounts that some U.S. residents hold there.

The M3 money stock includes all the instruments included in M2 plus

1. *Time deposits in denominations larger than $100,000* issued by depository institutions to anyone other than depository institutions, money market mutual funds, the U.S. government, or foreign banks and official institutions.
2. *Repurchase agreements with maturities of longer than one day* (usually called "term RPs").
3. *Money market mutual funds* available to institutions only.

Recent Money Supply Data

To provide a better perspective on the relative proportions of the components of M1, M2, and M3, we turn now to consider some recent data (see Table 1-1).

As indicated in this table, about 72 percent of the M1 money supply consists of liabilities of commercial banks and other privately owned depository institutions

---

[12]The federal funds market will be discussed shortly. In actuality, the U.S. security simply serves as collateral for a loan that the corporation is making to the bank.

TABLE 1-1

The U.S. Money Supply (M1), January 1983
(billions, seasonally adjusted)

1.	Currency and coins held by the nonbank public	$134.2
2.	Demand deposits owned by the nonbank public	239.3
3.	Other checkable deposits[a]	108.9
	Total M1	$482.4

[a]Includes traveler's checks issued by nonbank institutions.

Source: Federal Reserve System, Statistical Release H.6 (508).

on which checks can be written.[13] The other 28 percent consists of currency and coins.

Some Details on the Currency and Coin Component

Table 1-2 provides a breakdown of the currency and coin component of the M1 money supply as of September 1982. It is, however, not completely comparable with the currency and coin total in Table 1-1. This is because the currency and coin entry in Table 1-1 includes only cash held by the nonbank public. That is, it excludes currency and coins held by the U.S. Treasury, the Federal Reserve banks, and the commercial banks. Unfortunately, the only readily available detailed breakdown of types of currency and coins in circulation includes cash held by commercial banks as well as by the nonbank public, so the total of $149.2 billion listed in Table 1-2 includes about $19 billion held by commercial banks themselves (and not a part of the money supply).

Several matters regarding Table 1-2 are worthy of note. First, it should be stressed that nearly 90 percent of the value of currency and coins in circulation is in *Federal Reserve notes*—a form of paper currency issued by the nation's 12 Federal Reserve banks. This fact, taken together with our earlier recognition that about three-quarters of the total money supply is composed of demand and other "checkable" deposit liabilities of depository institutions leads us to the astounding discovery that the Federal Reserve banks and privately owned depository institutions issue *well over 97 percent of the nation's money supply.*

It may seem surprising that the U.S. Treasury issues less than 3 percent of the nation's money supply and that virtually all of it consists of coins. Indeed, except for a ragtag collection of types of paper currency originally issued by the Treasury but currently in the process of being retired (and destroyed), the Treasury now issues only coins and a small fixed dollar amount of U.S. notes.[14]

---

[13]The "other" depository institutions referred to include savings and loan associations, mutual savings banks, and credit unions.

[14]The first five types of Treasury currency listed in Table 1-2 are currently being retired whenever they come into Treasury possession. Incidentally, for U.S. history enthusiasts, U.S. notes have a most interesting origin. They were originally issued during the Civil War, at which time they carried the nickname "greenbacks."

TABLE 1-2

Types of Currency and Coins in Circulation in the United States,
September 1982
(millions)

Federal Reserve notes		$135,174
Treasury currency		14,031
Silver certificates	$ 204	
Federal Reserve bank notes	48	
National bank notes	19	
Gold certificates	3	
U.S. notes	303	
Other[a]	1	
Dollar coins	1,504	
Fractional coins	11,949	
Total currency and coins in circulation		$149,205

[a]Includes Federal Reserve notes issued prior to July 1, 1929 and Treasury notes of 1890.

Source: Treasury Bulletin, November 1982.

Incidentally, U.S. coins, which, with the exception of the silver dollar, have been minted with a metal value well below their face value for many years, are now virtually silverless as a result of the rising market value of silver. Eisenhower "silver" dollars minted for general circulation, half-dollars, quarters, and dimes consist of a copper center covered by the same silver-looking alloy used to produce nickels—25 percent nickel and 75 percent copper.

Federal Reserve notes, the backbone of the nation's currency supply, are no longer issued in denominations larger than $100. Still outstanding as a result of past issue, however, are many Federal Reserve notes of larger denomination, including (as of 1982) 340 $10,000 bills!

The Current Components of M2 and M3

Table 1-3 reports the components of M2 and M3 as of January 1983. Here again, the effects of financial innovation in the past decade show up dramatically. Note, for example, that although M2 grew by just over 90 percent from 1975 through 1982, some of its newer components grew much faster. Overnight RPs went up by about 500 percent over the same period, overnight Eurodollars shot up from *zero* in 1975 to about $6 billion by the end of 1982, and, most important of all, money market mutual funds skyrocketed from $3.6 billion in 1975 to $230 billion in 1982—an astounding sixty fold increase in just seven years!

Relative Changes in the Narrowly Defined and Broadly Defined Money Stock Series

Figure 1-1 shows the growth in the M1, M2, and M3 series since 1959. What stands out in this graph is the tendency of the more broadly defined series,

TABLE 1-3

The Components of M2 and M3, January 1983
(billions, seasonally adjusted)

Components of M2	
M1	$ 482.4
Money market mutual funds	186.7
Savings and "small" time deposits	1,132.0
Overnight RPs	41.1
Overnight Eurodollars	6.0
Total M2[a]	$2,007.1
Components of M3	
M2	$2,007.1
Large time deposits (over $100,000)	310.8
Term RPs	40.1
MMM funds (for institutions only)	46.0
Total M3[a]	$2,399.7

[a]Totals for M2 and M3 differ from the sum of components because of a consolidation adjustment that represents the estimated amount of demand deposits and cash held by thrift institutions to service time and savings deposits and another that represents the estimated amount of RPs held by money market mutual funds for institutions only. Data are preliminary.

Source: Federal Reserve System, Statistical Release H.6 (508).

M2 and M3, to grow much more rapidly than M1. But Figure 1-1 really *understates* this trend because the M2 and M3 series include the slower-growing M1 total. If, for example, one compares the growth of M1 with the parts of M2 not included in M1 (i.e., with the growth of money market mutual funds, overnight RPs, and Caribbean Eurodollars and "small" savings accounts and time deposits), we see that whereas M1 slightly more than tripled, the "M2 minus M1" total shot up more than three times that fast—a nearly tenfold increase.

What are the causes of this relatively greater rate of growth in M2 and M3? It seems pretty clear that once again high interest rates, financial innovation, and regulatory changes play the lead role. High interest rates, of course, have lessened the attraction for noninterest-bearing cash and demand deposits, and although interest is paid on the "other checkable deposit" portion of M1, governmental regulation has, over these years, held down the maximum interest rates payable on them to levels far below what has been available elsewhere.[15] This tendency for spenders to economize on the traditional M1 type of transactions balances is evidenced by the fact that during the 1970s households cut "the ratio of their checkable deposits to their consumption spending by 18 percent," while "corporations reduced their checkable deposits relative to gross national product by 38 percent."[16]

---

[15]It should be noted that under current law, the regulation responsible for this—Regulation Q—is in the process of being phased out. Indeed, with implementation of the Depository Institutions Act of 1982, it was all but eliminated by 1983.

[16]See the excellent article, "Innovations in the Financial Markets," by Marcelle Arak in *Quarterly Review,* Federal Reserve Bank of New York, Winter 1981–1982.

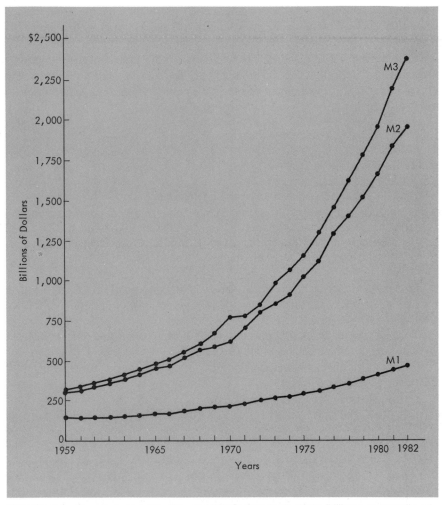

FIGURE 1-1 Growth in the M1, M2, and M3 Series, 1959–1982 (billions, seasonally adjusted)

Source: Federal Reserve System.

On the other hand, financial innovations, made possible in many cases by regulatory change, have provided savers instruments offering them much higher interest along with a very high degree of liquidity. Examples abound, but the authorization of the money market certificate and the growth of RPs, money market mutual funds, and money market deposit accounts provide excellent illustrations. Incidentally, these developments have tended to increase the rate of growth of the M2 money stock in two ways. Not only have funds tended to flow out of M1 to M2, but also, funds that—prior to these innovations—had been used to purchase instruments not included in M2 or M3 (such as Treasury bills) began to flow back through the financial institutions, further pumping up the M2 and M3 totals.

But what difference do these changes make? How important is it that financial innovation and regulatory change have caused M2 and M3 to grow relative to M1? If the changes were regular and predictable, their impact might not be of major significance. But unhappily they have not been in the past, and there appears to be no reason to expect them to be in the future. The real problem is that they create serious problems for the conduct of monetary policy, a topic we shall consider in detail in Chapter 11.

Review Questions

1. Carefully discuss the disadvantages of a barter economy.
2. "If Ms. Brown deposits $100 of cash into her checking account at a commercial bank, the effect on the M1 money supply is different from that which will result if she deposits the $100 into her savings deposit at a commercial bank. The two transactions, however, have the same effect on the M2 money supply." Explain.
3. If money is to be defined in accordance with the degree of liquidity of the asset, it is exceptionally difficult to draw the line between "money" and "nonmoney" assets. Discuss carefully.
4. What are the differences between U.S. savings bonds and marketable U.S. securities, and how do these differences affect their degree of liquidity?
5. Specify those checking accounts and currency that are *not* included in the M1 money supply definition.
6. Carefully identify "share draft" accounts.
7. If one wishes to study the M1 money supply, one must devote far more attention to the operations of banks than to the U.S. Treasury. Carefully explain why this is the case.
8. Nationwide authorization of NOW accounts and their inclusion into the M1 money supply definition tended to make M1 grow faster in recent years, relative to M2. Explain.
9. Identify the components of M2 and M3.

2

Finance and Nonbank Financial Institutions

"Economics," a student observed one day, "wouldn't be so bad if they'd get out of that oversimplified dream world they're always assuming and deal more directly with the real world we all live in."

Just so. It would indeed be nice to be able to start right off discussing the "real world" as it is, without reliance on the host of simplifying assumptions and models that appear to be the economist's stock in trade. But, of course, the modern industrialized economy is just too intricate and complex a mechanism to comprehend if approached directly "as is." The result is that students find themselves confronting a whole series of "dream worlds" in which intentionally unrealistic simplifying assumptions have been made to bring out general relationships and principles that could not otherwise be understood.

The Circular Flow Diagram

One outstanding example of this technique of successive approximations of reality is the standard circular flow diagram of an economy encountered in nearly every introductory course. Figure 2-1 is such a diagram.

The purpose of this diagram is to present a bird's-eye view of how an economy gets real goods and services produced and purchased. Pedagogically, it is not only a perfectly valid device for its purpose but extremely useful.

But of course this diagram certainly does not claim to depict the "real world." Rather, its prime function is to eliminate much of the complexity of reality, isolating the essence of the process whereby consumer goods (and government services) are purchased by households in return for the income earned from productive services sold by households to the business sector (and government).

17

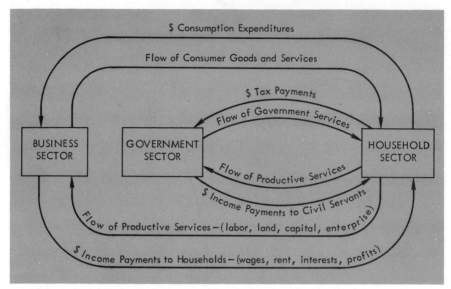

FIGURE 2-1   Circular Flow Diagram

The list of simplifying assumptions implied in such a diagram is truly imposing. Those of most direct interest for our purposes include the following:

1. It implicitly assumes no **saving** by households (or anyone else, for that matter). All the income earned via the provision of productive services is assumed to be spent to buy consumer goods or to pay taxes (that is, to purchase the services of government).
2. It allows for no **investment spending** by business to purchase newly produced plants and equipment.

Now such glaring omissions from the "real-world" scene are entirely appropriate when one's purpose is to emphasize only the direct processes whereby final consumer goods and services are produced and purchased. But it must be kept in mind that doing so ignores altogether that vast and intricate structure sometimes referred to as the "financial sector" on which much of the success of the goods-producing sectors heavily depends.

What the Financial Sector Does

The financial sector of the U.S. economy of the 1980s is a truly imposing one. As of early 1982, it employed over 5 million people, a work force larger than the entire agricultural industry, about six times the size of the primary metals industries and over eight times the size of the automobile industry.[1] What do all the people

---

[1] U.S. Department of Labor, *Employment and Earnings* (Washington, D.C.: Government Printing Office, December 1982).

not directly involved in the making of final goods and services do? How can we justify the diversion of such a large segment of our limited human resources to "mere financial" dealings?

The answer of course is that an efficient financial industry is an essential prerequisite to a modern, highly specialized, mechanized economy. It provides the medium of exchange without which specialization could hardly exist. It provides a mechanism whereby any spending unit that does not choose to spend all its current after-tax income on consumer goods (that is, chooses to save) may conveniently make it available to other spending units who prefer to spend more than their current incomes. And, finally, in the process of accomplishing the latter, it makes available a procedure through which much of the nation's vital capital formation is financed.

We shall have much more to say in upcoming chapters about the process and effects of providing money for the economy. Let us turn now, however, to a brief consideration of the implications of the other functions of the financial sector.

Transferring Purchasing Power from Surplus Spending Units to Deficit Spending Units

In the circular flow diagram depicted in Figure 2-1, a closed and complete circle was accomplished by merely assuming that nobody chooses to save. Therefore, by assumption, if $1 trillion of income is received by households in income payments for productive services rendered, $1 trillion is spent by those households to buy all the output of business firms (and government). Production at the $1 trillion level can therefore presumably be assured indefinitely, as we have simply assumed that whatever is produced is willingly purchased.

A nice world perhaps, but not a world even remotely close to current reality. Pedagogical assumptions notwithstanding, everyone knows full well that some income recipients do save (spend less than their after-tax income) while others dissave, or deficit spend (spend more than their income). Within the household sector, young families and older, retired families typically dissave, while middle-aged families generally are net savers. On balance, the household sector as a whole typically saves, the business sector typically dissaves, and the government sector typically dissaves (although on those infrequent occasions when the government achieves a budget surplus, it is a net saver).

If, for example, the household sector in our circular flow diagram in Figure 2-1 should choose to save 10 percent of its $1 trillion of income, this means that only $900 billion is spent to buy the output of business (and the government). Taken by itself, the "leakage" in the income stream that this saving represents would tend—because of the unintended accumulation of $100 billion worth of business inventories it would cause—to lead to cutbacks of production, unemployment, and declining incomes.

But this result of saving is by no means inevitable. If by chance (and there is certainly no guarantee that this will happen) the business sector wishes to deficit spend by exactly $100 billion to purchase new capital goods (that is, to invest), and if, to finance such a venture, businesses are prepared to borrow the $100 billion that households have saved, then the potential unemployment may be avoided.[2] Indeed, in these fortuitous circumstances, *two* positive benefits to the economy will result from bringing the savers and investors together and permitting the former to finance the planned investment spending of the latter. Not only can this forestall potential unemployment, but it also can provide the economy with a larger stock of capital goods that, other things being equal, will expand productive potential in the future.

Clearly, the task of bringing together savers (those with surplus funds to lend) and investors (those who plan to deficit spend to purchase new capital goods) is an absolutely vital one. It is this extraordinarily important function that the financial sector performs. **The basic economic role and justification of financial institutions, then, is to serve as middlemen between savers and investors.**

The Capital Formation Process

Before we proceed to a more detailed discussion of just how financial institutions carry out this basic function, it will be useful to digress briefly to consider further the capital formation process.

In the highly artificial Robinson Crusoe–type economy often visualized to simplify or throw into sharp relief some basic theoretical ideas, there is no financial mechanism to complicate the issue. Indeed one of the main purposes of such abstractions is to sweep aside the "veil" with which money and a financial system seem to distort and conceal the "real" economic developments underneath.

In the Crusoe–type economy where there is no money, the capital formation process is a very simple one. If Crusoe and Friday desire to raise their production of fish, they may consider it worthwhile to take several days off from actually fishing to produce a fishing net (a capital good). They realize, however, that they must continue eating while they construct the net. Consequently, they must produce an excess of consumer goods (fish, coconuts) to sustain themselves while working on their net. The act of building up this reserve stock of food is, in the purest sense, an act of *saving*—consuming less than the full amount of their income. It is this abstention from consumption that permits them to devote several days of their scarce labor supply to the construction of their net—an act of *investment*.

The fundamental "real" effect of saving, then, is **the release of productive resources from the production of consumer goods.** Investment, on the other hand, is the use of those released resources to produce a new capital good. In the Crusoe case, there is no money or financial structure to "muddy up the water" or obscure our vision of what goes on. The saving consists of stocking up real con-

---

[2]Note that it is "ex ante" or "planned" investment that is referred to here, not "ex post" or "realized" investment. The latter equals saving, by definition, but planned investment and saving are equal only in equilibrium.

sumer goods, and the investment consists of building the capital good while living off these previously saved stocks.

In a money-using economy, things are more complicated. Suppose that we have an economy in which many people are specializing, so that exchange—and therefore money—is essential. In such a case, saving takes the form of people not spending all their money income to buy consumer goods. To keep it simple, let us assume that there are still no banks, so that each saver amasses, at least temporarily, a pile of cash.

Does this kind of saving have the same real effects as that of Crusoe? Of course. People who do not spend all their money incomes to purchase consumer goods thereby *release some productive resources,* which they *could* have tied up producing more consumer goods, for other purposes. Now if the money savings are lent to business firms that desire to purchase more capital goods, they may spend the savings to hire these released resources to build them. On the monetary level, money is saved, lent to investors, and spent by them to purchase capital goods. On the real level, productive resources are released by the savers' act of abstention, but they are rehired by the investors' act of investing.[3]

Incidentally, let us make one crucial distinction clear. Throughout this book, the word *investment,* as is customary in economics, is used to mean the *production of new capital goods.* Investment spending, then, consists of *expenditures to buy* newly produced capital goods. The purchase of securities such as stocks and bonds, on the other hand, is *not,* by our terminology, investment. However, since it is a common practice in everyday speech to refer to the purchase of securities as investment, we shall distinguish security purchase by calling it "financial" investment. But the word *investment* without a qualifying adjective should always be taken to mean the production of new capital goods.

Now, as far as it goes, the preceding is all perfectly correct. But it glides over one major problem that cannot legitimately be ignored. Note that in an earlier paragraph we glibly stated that if the money savings are lent to business firms, all will be well. The extent to which, the ease with which, and the manner in which savings are made available to investors have to do largely with the development of the financial system.

Direct Finance via Sale of "Primary Securities" from Deficit Spending Units to Surplus Income Units

The simplest way in which a deficit spending unit (such as a business that needs to borrow to finance investment spending) can acquire the funds needed from surplus income units (savers) is by selling *primary securities* to them. Primary

---

[3]Note that we continue, for the present, the assumption that there is sufficient investment spending to absorb all the resources released by the saving, and thereby prevent unemployment.

securities may be defined as liabilities issued directly by the deficit spending unit (the business firm in most cases). They consist primarily of equities (stocks, which provide the buyer a part ownership in the firm), bonds (IOUs of the borrowers), and mortgages.

The Middleman Role of Brokers, Dealers, and Investment Banks

Such primary securities could, of course, be exchanged directly between the ultimate borrower and lender with no middlemen whatever involved. This, however, is not the usual procedure, for the rather obvious reason that the "search time" that might be involved in getting specific borrowers and specific lenders together would normally be prohibitive. Rather, primary securities are typically sold through *brokers* and *dealers* whose function it is to "make a market" and facilitate the transfer.

Brokers play more of a "pure middlemen" role in that they simply bring the buyer and seller of the primary security together (for a fee, of course) but do not themselves ever acquire legal title to the securities. Dealers, on the other hand, purchase primary securities outright from their issuers and then sell them to the ultimate lenders, bearing, in the process, the risk that they may not be able to find surplus income units willing to pay a price that guarantees them a profit.

Brokers and dealers operate in both the primary securities market and the secondary securities market. The *primary securities market* involves the initial sale of new securities by the deficit spending unit to the surplus income unit whereby the deficit spenders (e.g., investors) acquire the funds needed to purchase the desired capital goods. The *secondary securities market,* on the other hand, involves only the resale of securities (which have already been sold on the primary market) from one surplus income unit (saver) to another. A security sale on the secondary market simply transfers ownership of already outstanding securities, but provides no funds to deficit spending units.[4]

One type of broker-dealer firm of significance is the *investment bank.* Although investment banks now operate extensively in both the primary and secondary securities markets, their prime original function was in the primary market. That function is to aid the issuers of *new* primary securities such as corporations or governments in distributing them to surplus income units. The initial distribution of a block of new securities is a highly specialized business requiring sales outlets, capital, and expertise not normally possessed by the issuing organization. The natural result is to call in a specialist—the investment banker.

---

[4]The student must be cautious here, not to confuse "primary securities" with the "primary securities market." Primary securities, as noted, are instruments such as stocks, bonds, and mortgages that are originally issued by deficit spending units. When initially sold (by the issuer), they are sold on the primary securities market. If they are subsequently sold by the initial buyer (a surplus income unit) to another surplus income unit, the sale is on the secondary securities *market* even though the securities *themselves* are still primary securities.

The investment banker acts as adviser to the security issuer as well as its retailer. At the outset he solicits business by going directly to those who need new capital and suggesting means of raising it, as well as negotiating for the right to handle the account. The firm or syndicate of firms that obtains the privilege of distributing the borrower's securities will usually "underwrite" the sale of the entire issue, assuring the issuer of the funds sought. When underwriting an issue, the investment banker purchases it outright, relying on his or her ability to resell the securities promptly to individuals and other financial institutions at a price high enough to cover the full original cost plus a return for services rendered. In this case, of course, the investment banker is performing as a dealer.

In other cases, such as when the security issuer is new and unknown or if for other reasons the resale of all the securities appear to be in some doubt, the investment banker may refuse to underwrite, agreeing instead to make a "best effort" to find buyers for the securities, but not purchasing them independently or making any guarantee of disposing of all of them. If the banker handles the distribution in this manner, the service performed is only that of a broker.

Success for an investment banking concern thus depends heavily upon two factors: the strength of its sales force and the extent of its access to short-term capital to enable it to "carry" a large issue until it is finally distributed.

The industry includes a number of firms that specialize solely in the investment banking business, plus a number of the larger commercial banks that, in addition to their other activities, operate investment banking departments. The latter obviously have some advantage in the matter of short-term capital support.

The Supporting Role of Stock Exchanges

The willingness of savers to purchase new securities on the primary securities markets depends, in large measure, on the facilities available for selling them to someone else in the future, should the need arise. Providing these facilities (and thereby indirectly promoting the raising of new capital) is the function of over 6,000 broker-dealer firms who participate on the securities exchanges and the over-the-counter market. Investment bankers help to raise new capital for firms and governments. The securities exchanges and over-the-counter markets provide a marketplace wherein "old" securities may readily change hands on the secondary market.

Fundamentally, securities exchanges differ from the over-the-counter market only in that trading in securities listed on the exchange is carried out at auction at a central geographical location, whereas over-the-counter deals—primarily sales of the many securities that are not listed on the exchange—take place through brokers and dealers scattered throughout the nation.

A transaction on the floor of the exchange is initiated by a security owner who, desiring to buy or sell, contacts his or her broker. If the broker's firm is one of the hundreds of members of the exchange, the order is transmitted to the firm's representative on the floor. The representative then goes to the "post" on the floor, where securities are continuously auctioned off between buyers and sellers, and carries out the purchase or sale. If the broker is not a member of the exchange, the actual transaction must be carried out through a firm that is.

Over-the-counter transactions are often facilitated by the dealer's practice of carrying, on his own account, inventories of securities for sale, at a price, to the public. A few of the larger broker-dealer firms, primarily in New York City, act as "wholesalers" of over-the-counter securities, making continuous markets by standing ready to buy and sell at any time.

The Need for Financial Intermediaries

"Direct finance"—whereby brokers and dealers help to bring together surplus income units and deficit spending units—plays a very large role in the American economy. But if it were the only available method of bringing savers and investors together, there can be little doubt that a sizable proportion of the nation's savings would never find its way to the investors desiring to borrow it.

Why not? Think about it. If you save some money out of your income and the only avenue available to you to "put your savings to work for you" to earn some income is through purchase of stocks and bonds, how much of it would you commit in this manner? All of it? Careful now, you may want to give that a little more thought. What we are visualizing here is a world in which savers have only three forms in which they may hold their savings—money itself, stocks, and bonds.[5] Under such circumstances many savers might find it in their interests to hold a much larger proportion of their savings in money form than they do currently.

Why hoard money that pays no interest at all rather than lend it out and realize the interest, dividends, and possible capital gains that purchase of stocks and bonds would make possible? There are a number of rational reasons for such a course.

First, there's the matter of *liquidity*. Many people would like to have their savings in a form readily convertible to a more or less fixed number of dollars in case an emergency need or some special bargain opportunity arises. Stocks and bonds, which normally involve some default risk and also have widely varying market values, are usually fairly illiquid.

Second, there's the matter of *costs*. Brokers and dealers charge a fee for their services as middlemen. The minimum fee is often so high that small savers with minimal amounts to lend out would find a significant part of their interest and dividends absorbed by it.

Third, there may easily be a problem with the *minimum denomination sizes* in which stocks, bonds and other income earning assets are available. The saver with only a few dollars per week available might have a difficult time finding

---

[5]They may, of course, choose to hold real wealth also, instead of claims to wealth, but we are restricting the discussion here to claims only.

desired shares of stock at a small enough unit price to permit purchase. And bonds, which typically carry par values of $1,000 or more, may be totally out of reach.[6]

Fourth, sheer *lack of knowledge* about how to go about purchasing stocks and bonds, coupled with inability to evaluate the varying degrees of *risk* involved in the myriad stocks and bonds available, may lead to considerable reluctance on the part of many savers.

Given a choice of holding their wealth only in the forms of money, stocks, and bonds, many savers—especially the millions of smaller savers—would undoubtedly opt to hold large portions in cash form. And such a development could make those savings unavailable to many potential investors who would like to use them to purchase additional capital goods. For the economy, as we have seen, such a situation could be extremely costly in terms of higher unemployment and lower capital formation rates.

The Specific Functions
of Financial Intermediaries

Fortunately the surplus income unit (saver) in the U.S. economy of the 1980s is not restricted to choosing between nonincome-earning money and direct ownership of primary securities as forms of wealth to hold. In addition, the saver can choose from among a wide range of asset forms issued by the *financial intermediaries*.

Financial intermediaries, as the name suggests, take a position between the ultimate lender (saver) and the ultimate borrower (investor). They acquire the savings of surplus income units by offering them *claims on themselves* (sometimes called "indirect" or "secondary" claims) that are of greater appeal to many (in terms of liquidity, denomination size, cost of acquisition, default risk, and so on) than primary securities. Then they use the funds thus acquired to purchase the primary securities (stocks, bonds, mortgages) issued by the deficit spending units (the investors).

The student must be careful with the terminology here. Brokers, dealers, and investment banks are financial *institutions* that serve only as middlemen to bring savers and investors together. Financial *intermediaries*, on the other hand, are financial institutions that provide savers with claims more suited to their needs and tastes than primary securities.

A wide range of financial intermediaries exists that is designed to appeal to savers of practically any taste pattern. Those primarily interested in liquidity and safety will likely find such savings institutions as savings departments of commercial banks, mutual savings banks, savings and loan associations, and credit unions most attractive because the savings accounts they offer are highly liquid and, for the most part, insured against loss by the federal government. Having acquired the

---

[6]This, of course, is not the case for U.S. savings bonds, which were specifically created for the small saver.

funds, these so-called "thrift institutions" then use them to purchase mortgages, bonds, and some stocks issued by investors.

Savers less concerned with liquidity and safety who have shied away from direct purchase of primary securities—because of lack of expertise, fear of the risk of "putting all their eggs in one basket," or prohibitive denomination sizes—may find mutual funds (a form of investment company) the type of financial intermediary that meets their needs. These institutions issue shares that constitute a claim against themselves (usually making it easy to purchase in small denomination sizes) and then use the proceeds to buy primary securities issued by a wide range of investors.

Then, too, there are the financial intermediaries that offer savers specialized protection against the twin risks of dying too soon or living too long beyond their prime earning ages. In the former category are the life insurance companies that collect savings in the form of premium payments and then financially invest them in primary securities. In the latter category are pension plans, which collect savings via contributions from covered employees and their employers and then purchase a variety of primary securities.

The Growth of Intermediation

The process whereby a growing proportion of financing between deficit spending and surplus income units is carried out via financial intermediaries is often referred to as *intermediation*.[7] The increase in intermediation, as measured by the growth in assets of selected financial intermediaries since 1950, is striking—as Table 2-1 and Figure 2-2 make clear.

Note, first, that commercial banks still dominate the financial industry, although the degree of dominance has been undercut somewhat by more rapid growth of some of the nonbank intermediaries in the past quarter-century. Whereas in 1950 the commercial bank assets substantially exceeded the total assets held by all six of the nonbank financial institutions listed, by 1981 the commercial banks' total was only about 80 percent of the combined assets of their six competitors. Although still relatively small in absolute terms, the rate of growth achieved by credit unions and private noninsured pension funds is especially striking.

An Overview of the Financial System

Before we look at the major characteristics of some of the more important financial intermediaries, let us step back at this point and attempt to visualize the overall U.S. financial mechanism we have been discussing. A diagram illustrating the flow of credit is presented in Figure 2-3.

---

[7]This is in contrast to *disintermediation* wherein there is a decline in the role of financial intermediaries. As we shall see, government controls over the interest rates that intermediaries were permitted to pay to attract funds led to some substantial short-run disintermediation in the late 1960s and the mid-1970s.

TABLE 2-1

Total Assets of Selected Financial Institutions, 1950–1981[a]
(billions of dollars)

Year	Commercial Banks	Savings and Loan Associations	Life Insurance Companies	Private Noninsured Pension Plans	Mutual Savings Banks	Investment Companies	Credit Unions
1950	$ 168.9	$ 16.9	$ 64.0	NA	$ 22.4	$ 3.4	$ 1.0
1955	210.7	37.7	90.4	$ 18.1	30.4	7.4	2.7
1960	257.6	71.5	119.6	37.1	39.6	19.5	5.7
1965	377.3	129.4	158.9	72.9	58.2	38.7	10.6
1970	576.2	176.2	207.3	104.7	79.0	54.7	17.8
1975	964.9	338.2	289.3	145.2	121.1	54.6	38.0
1980	1,537.0	630.7	479.2	286.1	171.6	138.3	71.7
1981	1,651.8	663.8	521.4	279.5	175.7	230.4	77.7

NA – Not available.

[a]Figure for private pension plans is for third quarter, 1981. Investment company data include money market mutual funds.

Source: Federal Reserve Bulletin; U.S. League of Savings Associations; SEC *Statistical Bulletin;* and *Weisenberger Investment Companies Service,* 1981.

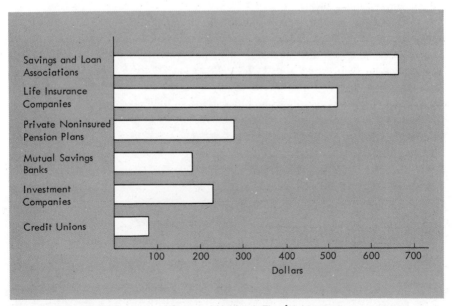

FIGURE 2-2 Value of Assets of Selected Nonbank Financial Institutions, 1981 (billions of dollars)

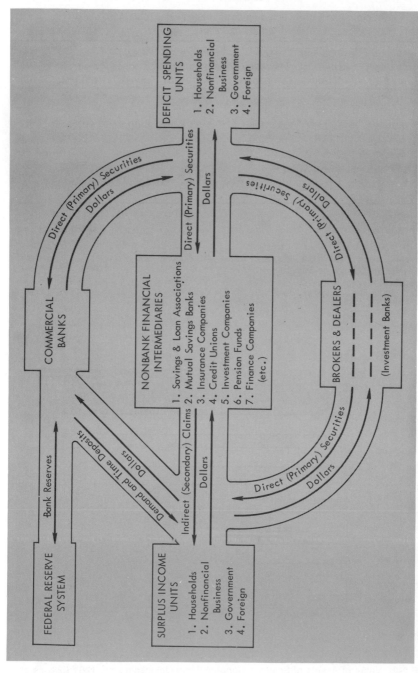

FIGURE 2-3 The Flow of Credit in the United States

Source: Adapted from a similar diagram in "Impairment in Credit Flows: Fact or Fiction?" by William N. Cox III, *Monthly Review*, Federal Reserve Bank of Atlanta, February, 1970.

Funds flow from surplus income units (savers) within all sectors on the extreme left of the diagram in three different directions. Some (at the bottom of Figure 2-3) flow, with the assistance of brokers and dealers, directly to deficit spending units who, in return, issue primary securities (stocks, bonds, mortgages). Another sizable portion goes through financial intermediaries (middle of Figure 2-3). Here the surplus income units make their funds available to the financial intermediaries in return for indirect, secondary claims (savings accounts, insurance protection, pension claims, and so on) issued by the intermediaries themselves. The intermediaries then make these funds available to the deficit spending units in return for primary securities.

Finally, a portion of the available funds of surplus income units flows to commercial banks in return for demand and time deposits there. As do nonbank financial intermediaries, commercial banks then purchase primary securities from deficit spending units. Unlike nonbank financial intermediaries, however, commercial banks' capacity to purchase primary securities is directly influenced by the amount of reserves made available to them by the Federal Reserve System. In addition, the commercial banking system possesses the power to purchase primary securities in amounts equal to several times the "reserves" it acquires. We shall be considering these peculiarities of the commercial banks in some detail in upcoming chapters.

Review Questions

1. What economic functions are performed by the "finance" industry?
2. Despite their key role in the capital formation process, the financial intermediaries carry out a relatively small proportion of the nation's investment. Do you agree? Explain carefully.
3. Carefully explain why, in a fully employed economy, saving is an essential prerequisite to capital formation.
4. Distinguish "direct finance" from financing through financial intermediaries.
5. "If there were no financial intermediaries, it is likely that a substantial amount of the money saved would be hoarded rather than made available to investors." Do you agree? Explain carefully.
6. Carefully and completely explain *how* financial intermediaries help to prevent unemployment and increase the rate of capital formation.

3

The Purposes and Characteristics of Financial Markets

Financial markets exist to facilitate the purchase and sale of financial assets. It has become customary to draw a distinction between the *capital market* and the *money market*. The purpose of this chapter is to discuss the characteristics, participants, and functions of these two important types of financial markets.

Capital Market

Capital markets exist to facilitate the exchange of long-term financial assets. Traditionally, "long-term" has been taken to mean financial claims with maturity dates more than one year from the date of issue.

Actually most of our discussion in Chapter 2 was couched in terms of capital market transactions. It is in the capital market that deficit spending units in need of long-term funds find—directly or indirectly—surplus income units who can meet their needs.

Participants in the Capital Market

On one side of the capital market are those deficit spending units that need to obtain funds for periods longer than one year to finance spending in excess of their current incomes. In the main, these units include nonfinancial business firms (desiring to finance the purchase of plant and equipment), the federal government (that borrows to finance budget deficits), and state and local governments (that borrow to finance the building of such social capital as schools, roads, etc.).

On the other side are the surplus income units with funds available to lend out. The overwhelming majority of these funds, in the U.S. economy, come from the household sector. It is true, of course, that households also borrow—to purchase

30

houses and consumer durables. But even after allowing for this, the household sector as a whole is a net saver. Indeed, the household sector is the dominant supplier of funds on the capital market.

But as noted in the preceding chapter, only part of these household funds are *directly* made available to the deficit spending units on the other side.[1] Others come indirectly, through a variety of financial intermediaries. This is the case, as we have seen, because many householders find the "secondary" claim (time deposits, mutual fund shares, pension rights, etc.) issued by the intermediaries better suited to their needs. What happens here, of course, is that the intermediaries act as a conduit through which to pass these funds on to the deficit spending units.

Financial Instruments on the Capital Market

The financial instruments employed on the capital market are the "primary" securities referred to in Chapter 2. They are issued by the deficit spending units in return for the funds being raised. Specifically, they include corporate bonds, federal government securities, state and local government securities, corporate equities (or stock), and mortgages.

Table 3-1, which lists the estimated market value of the capital market's outstanding financial instruments as of the end of 1982, provides some perspective on its overall size.

Corporate Bonds. A corporate bond is a formal IOU of a corporation that guarantees its holder a fixed periodic interest payment plus repayment of the principal on a stated maturity date. The owner of a bond is a creditor of the corporation, and the corporation is required by law to pay all interest due each time period and to repay the full principal at the maturity date.

TABLE 3-1

Capital Market Financial Instruments
Outstanding, December 1982
(billions of dollars)

U.S. government securities[a]	$ 885.3
State and local government securities	450.5
Corporation bonds	567.7
Mortgages	1,654.4
Corporation stock	1,816.1

[a]The figure for U.S. securities omits Treasury bills. Also omitted are securities issued by U.S. government agencies.

Source: Federal Reserve System, *Flow of Funds Accounts,* February 1983 and *Federal Reserve Bulletin*, April 1983.

---

[1]And even then, the middleman services of brokers and dealers are generally required.

TABLE 3-2

Holders of Corporation Bonds, December 1982
(billions of dollars)

Households	$ 72.7
Life insurance companies	199.7
Pension funds	174.1
Property and casualty insurance companies	26.0
Mutual savings banks	18.6
Other	76.6
Total	$567.7

Source: Federal Reserve System, Flow of Funds Accounts, February 1983.

As with other securities, most corporate bonds are initially sold through brokers and dealers to individuals or financial intermediaries.[2] Although bonds can be, and are, resold on the secondary market, this is done rather infrequently. Most bonds are held to maturity by their original purchasers.

From the corporation's point of view, bonds have several advantages over stock as a source of external funds. One obvious one is the fact that interest paid to bondholders is treated as a cost and thereby deductible for purposes of computing the corporate profits tax. This has an advantage over stocks, the dividends on which are not deductible. Second, when inflation is expected, the commitment to make fixed dollar interest payments plus a fixed dollar principal repayment in the future means making progressively lower payments in real terms.

In recent years, as Table 3-2 makes clear, corporate bonds have had special appeal for life insurance companies, pension funds, and individuals.

U.S. Government Securities. There are three main types of U.S. government securities: Treasury bills, notes, and bonds. Treasury bills are short-term instruments with maturities between 90 days and 1 year and, as such, will be discussed later as money market instruments. Notes and bonds, on the other hand (which in mid-1983 totaled over $600 billion, or about two-thirds of the federal government's marketable debt) have maturities from 1 to 30 years.

Their advantage to buyers, of course, is the fact that they are free of default risk and that they are highly liquid. As Table 3-3 makes clear, the market for U.S. securities is a very broad one.[3]

State and Local Government Securities. State and local government securities are of two different types: general obligation bonds and revenue bonds. General obligation bonds are "backed" by the full taxing power of the issuing government.

---

[2]Those not distributed this way are "privately placed." This means that the entire issue is sold directly to a financial intermediary rather than being advertised for public distribution.

[3]It should be noted that the data in Table 3-3 include holdings of all federal government debt, including Treasury bills. Also, it includes nonmarketable as well as marketable securities.

TABLE 3-3

U.S. Government Securities, by Holder, July 1982
(billions of dollars)

U.S. government agencies and trust funds	$ 206.3
Federal Reserve banks	132.6
Commercial banks	110.0
Mutual savings banks	5.6
Insurance companies	22.6
Other companies	39.9
State and local governments	88.7
Individuals	146.4
Foreign	143.3
Other	193.1
Total	$1,083.3

Source: Treasury Bulletin, November 1982.

Revenue bonds, on the other hand, are generally issued to raise funds for a specific project that earns its own revenue. An example is a toll highway. These bonds are technically "backed" only by the revenue-earning capacity of the project being financed and not by the full taxing power of the issuing government.[4]

The chief attraction of state and local government securities (popularly referred to as "municipals") is the fact that the interest earned on them is exempt from federal tax. This tax-exempt feature permits them to be sold at interest rates lower than those required to sell taxable securities, thereby lowering state and local government borrowing costs. At the same time, however, it tends to limit the market for them to buyers who can benefit most from the tax-exemption feature. As Table 3-4 demonstrates, this has meant that commercial banks, property and

TABLE 3-4

Holdings of State and Local Government
Securities, December 1982
(billions of dollars)

Commercial banks	$153.9
Property and casualty insurance companies	86.8
Households	161.8
Life insurance companies	8.0
Mutual funds (investment companies)	21.1
Nonfinancial corporations	3.4
State and local governments	11.4
Savings and loan associations	.8
Mutual savings banks	2.2
Brokers and dealers	1.0
Total	$450.4

Source: Federal Reserve System, Flow of Funds Accounts, February 1983.

---

[4]Many governments, however, will choose to bail out a revenue bond issue with tax funds if revenues fall short rather than see it defaulted so the risk may not be as great as on first appearance.

TABLE 3-5

Holdings of Corporate Stock, December 1982
(billions of dollars)

Households	$1,310.8
Pension funds	260.6
Life insurance companies	59.4
Mutual funds	51.2
Property and casualty insurance companies	41.5
Other	92.6
Total	$1,816.1

Source: Federal Reserve System, Flow of Funds Accounts, February 1983.

casualty insurance companies, and high-income individuals have pretty much dominated the market for municipals.

Common Stocks. A holder of the common stock of a corporation, unlike a bondholder, is a part-owner of the firm. As an owner, the stockholder is in the residual position with no fixed claims to either dividends or repayment of principal.

Common stock, of course, is a much riskier asset than a bond. If the corporation is highly profitable, the return to stockholders (in the form of both dividends and capital gains) can be much higher than that of bondholders. If it is unsuccessful, however, stockholders may get no return at all and even lose their original investment. In recent years, as is clear from Table 3-5, households and pension funds have been the dominant holders of corporate stock.

Although there is a secondary market for all capital market securities, that for equities—primarily the stock exchanges—is by far the most complete. As noted, this well-developed secondary market adds immensely to the attractiveness of stock. It must be remembered, however, that while the stock exchanges offer a ready market for the trading of stock of a listed corporation *at some price,* they do not protect the owner from the risk of substantial loss if the corporation itself has been unsuccessful.

Mortgages. A mortgage, of course, is a contract whereby the lender provides funds to finance the purchase of real estate in return for the borrower's promise to pay back the principal plus interest over a number of years.

As Table 3-6 indicates, the majority of mortgages are to finance the purchase of single-family homes. As of December 1982, over three-fourths of single-family home mortgages had been issued by commercial banks, savings and loan associations, and mutual savings banks. Commercial mortgages, on the other hand, are issued primarily by life insurance companies and commercial banks, which, as of the end of 1982, held almost two-thirds of the total outstanding.

For many years the dominant suppliers of mortgage funds have been savings and loan associations and commercial banks. This is still the case, as a glance at

TABLE 3-6

Mortgages Outstanding, by Type, December 1982
(billions of dollars)

Single-family home mortgages	$1,104.5
Multifamily residential mortgages	148.2
Commercial mortgages	294.6
Farm mortgages	107.1

Source: Federal Reserve System, *Federal Reserve Bulletin,*
April 1983.

Table 3-7 makes clear. However, recent problems in the housing market and (*not* coincidentally) severe difficulties for many savings and loan associations have generated changes in practices and in regulation that may well be harbingers of change for the future. We shall delve into some of these issues in Chapter 4.

Money Market

The so-called "money market" serves a much different function from that of the capital market. While it still involves bringing together deficit spending and surplus income units, it does so for very different reasons.

Whereas the capital market exists primarily to assist the long-term financing of capital (and social) goods, the money market is a short-term market where economic units with temporary surpluses of money are brought together with units incurring temporary shortages.

Families, businesses, and governments all find it necessary to hold a certain amount of money to bridge the gap between the receipt and the expenditure of income so as to permit a planned rate of expenditure unrestrained by the pattern of receipts. In the normal course of events, however, some units periodically find that they have accumulated more than they need for this purpose, while others periodically encounter temporary shortages. The prime function of the money market is to facilitate transactions between these two groups.

TABLE 3-7

Holdings of Mortgages, December 1982
(billions of dollars)

Savings and loan associations	$ 484.3
Commercial banks	301.7
Life insurance companies	141.3
Mortgage pools	214.4
Mutual savings banks	93.9
U.S. government	139.3
Households and all other	279.5
Total	$1,654.4

Source: Federal Reserve Bulletin, April 1983.

The transfer is accomplished via the use of a variety of short-term financial instruments issued by the borrowers. It has become customary to consider financial claims with a maturity of 1 year or less to be money market instruments, although the vast majority are 90 days or less. Among the more important money market instruments are U.S. Treasury bills, federal funds, negotiable certificates of deposit, banker's acceptances, commercial paper, and Eurodollars. These instruments are primarily the liabilities of the government, banks, or large business firms and, hence, involve only minimal default risk. Their liquidity is further enhanced by the fact that their short term forestalls major changes in value due to interest rate swings and that their markets are sufficiently broad to permit a large volume of transactions with only small effects on rates.[5]

Participants in the Money Market

The borrowers on the money market (sellers of money market instruments) include, among others, the U.S. Treasury, nonfinancial corporations, finance companies, commercial banks, and other depository institutions. The lenders (buyers of money market instruments) include some of the same institutions—such as commercial banks and nonfinancial corporations, plus such others as state and local governments, foreign banks, financial intermediaries, and (in large part, indirectly through financial intermediaries) individuals. Likely to appear on either side of the market depending upon the direction of monetary policy and a truly dominant factor on the market is the Federal Reserve System.

"Making the market," or playing the role of middleman, are a host of institutions including some of the largest commercial banks in New York, a group of 30-odd government securities dealers, a number of commercial paper dealers, and a variety of other specialized dealers and brokers.

Financial Instruments on the Money Market

As noted, money market instruments consist of a variety of claims with less than one year to maturity. As a rule, they are also easily marketable so that, to a holder, both their short term and their ready marketability provide them a very high degree of *liquidity*. In this section, we shall briefly discuss the major characteristics of some of the more important money market instruments.[6]

U.S. Treasury Bills. Without question, the most important money market instrument of all is the U.S. government *Treasury bill*. Treasury bills are the shortest-

---

[5]This entire section owes a heavy debt to that excellent publication, *Instruments of the Money Market*, 5th ed., edited by Timothy Q. Cook and Bruce J. Summers and published by the Federal Reserve Bank of Richmond, 1981.

[6]Although they constitute an important money market instrument, because they were discussed in Chapter 1, we will not reconsider RPs here.

term U.S. security, and they, together with notes and bonds (discussed earlier under capital market instruments), make up the U.S. national debt.

Treasury bills are issued weekly in denominations of no less than $10,000 (although above the $10,000 minimum, they can be acquired in multiples of $5,000). At the weekly offerings, both 91-day and 182-day bills are offered, while on a monthly basis, bills with a 1-year maturity are offered.

The interest rate paid on a Treasury bill issue is determined via competitive bidding. Persons or institutions desiring to make competitive bids state, in advance of that week's auction, the quantity of bills desired and the price they will pay. Since the bills always return $10,000 at maturity, the difference between that and the amount bid constitutes the interest earned for successful bidders.

Individuals desiring to purchase Treasury bills may do so on a noncompetitive basis by agreeing to accept the average interest yield arrived at by competitive bidders. Such noncompetitive purchases may be obtained directly from a Federal Reserve bank (where the auctions are held) by filing the appropriate form prior to the auction itself.

As of December 1982, some $312 billion worth of the $882 billion of marketable U.S. debt outstanding—over one-third—consisted of Treasury bills. Although no record is kept of the identity of holders of Treasury bills as such, 1980 data on private domestic holders of all types of Treasury securities with less than one year till maturity showed households with about 45 percent, commercial banks with 23 percent, other financial institutions with 18 percent, and state and local governments with about 12 percent.[7]

Federal Funds.   Depository institutions are required to maintain reserves to "back up" their outstanding deposit liabilities in the form of vault cash and/or as deposits at their district Federal Reserve banks.[8] Many years ago commercial banks with "excess reserves" (i.e., deposits at the Federal Reserve bank in excess of those required to back up their own outstanding deposit liabilities) began the practice of making overnight loans of excess reserves to other banks needing them. This was the beginning of the federal funds market.

Since these beginnings, the market has expanded enormously to include short-term loans of all "immediately available funds." Such immediately available funds include not only accounts at Federal Reserve banks but also "collected liabilities of commercial banks and other depository institutions."[9]

The majority of federal funds loans are overnight, with, for example, the Federal Reserve bank transferring ownership of the funds from the lending bank

---

[7]Federal Reserve System, *Flow of Funds Accounts.* Not only Treasury bills but also notes and bonds within one year of their maturity dates are included in the figures given.

[8]The depository institutions subject to these reserve requirements are commercial banks, savings and loan associations, mutual savings banks, and credit unions.

[9]Seth P. Maerowitz, "Federal Funds," *Instruments of the Money Market,* Federal Reserve Bank of Richmond, 1981, p. 42.

to the borrower for one day. On the following day, the transaction is reversed and the borrower pays interest at the federal funds rate.

The market now includes a number of large commercial banks with a standing offer to purchase all federal funds offered. Consequently, a ready market always exists for any such "immediately available funds."

Negotiable Certificates of Deposit. Negotiable certificates of deposit (CDs) are short-term certificates in denominations of $100,000 or more issued by commercial banks primarily to nonfinancial businesses who deposit funds with them.[10] These certificates, which are really a special form of time deposit, have maturities of from a minimum of 2 weeks to 12 months, with an average of around 3 months.

Certificates of deposit emerged as a significant source of bank funds and as an important money market instrument in the 1960s after an efficient secondary market for their resale developed. To be eligible for trading on the secondary market, CDs must be in minimum denominations of $1 million or more. As of December 1982, negotiable CDs issued by commercial banks totaled over $260 billion.

Banker's Acceptances. Banker's acceptances most commonly are created in the process of financing international trade. For example, a U.S. bank may issue a "letter of credit" on behalf of an American company planning to import goods. The letter of credit authorizes a foreign exporting company to draw up a "bill of exchange," calling for payment for the goods being sold, by the bank rather than the importing company. This bill of exchange is then sent to the U.S. bank that "accepts" this obligation to pay for the goods—usually within 90 days—by signing its acceptance on the face of the instrument. At this point the bill of exchange becomes an acceptance—a valuable document that is salable in the secondary market for acceptances. Although acceptances are much less important in the U.S. money market than the instruments thus far discussed, they had increased to a total of over $75 billion in early 1983.

Commercial Paper. Commercial paper consists of short-term, unsecured IOUs issued by large, well-known corporations that are sold to dealers or directly to financial institutions. Among the issuers, totaling about 1,200 as of mid-1982, finance companies, bank holding companies, and large nonfinancial corporations dominate.

Commercial paper is generally offered in denominations of $100,000 and has a maturity date averaging about 30 days. While the issuers must be reasonably large and well known to command a market, the buyers include money market mutual funds, large commercial banks, pension funds, state and local governments,

---

[10]We ignore here CDs issued by thrift institutions, most of which are nonnegotiable, and Eurodollar CDs. For an interesting account on them, see Bruce J. Summers, "Negotiable Certificates of Deposit," in *Instruments of the Money Market*, pp. 73–93.

individuals, and—since the easing of regulations in 1980—savings and loan associations and mutual savings banks.

Prior to 1966 the most important issuers of commercial paper were finance companies. An exceptionally tight money policy during 1966, however, sharply limited bank loans and forced business firms to seek other sources of funds. As a consequence, many of the larger and more creditworthy industrial corporations and utilities turned to issuance of commercial paper for the first time. In addition, especially in 1969 and early 1970, commercial banks themselves became important commercial paper issuers as they, too, sought alternative means of raising funds.

Except for temporary setbacks caused by Penn Central's default on over $80 million of its paper outstanding and the 1973–1975 recession, the commercial paper market has grown dramatically in the past couple of decades. Indeed, from December 1974 to April 1982, the volume outstanding expanded by a remarkable 243 percent and by mid-1982 had reached a total of over $170 billion.[11]

Eurodollars.   As stated in Chapter 1, Eurodollars are deposits, denominated in dollars, but held in banks outside the United States. For example, suppose that an Englishman is paid for goods sold to the United States via a mechanism that gives him a checking account in a U.S. bank. If he does not wish to convert this dollar deposit to pounds immediately, he may transfer ownership of it to his London bank in exchange for a dollar-denominated deposit claim against that bank that pays him interest. The London bank now possesses the deposit in the U.S. bank and may lend it out to any bank, foreign or American, or to any nonbank borrower. Although exact figures regarding the net size of the Eurodollar market are not available, estimates in 1980 put it far over the $500 billion level.

Review Questions

1. Carefully distinguish between the "capital" market and the "money" markets.
2. On the capital market, who are the most important participants and what are the major types of financial instruments used?
3. Distinguish among U.S. Treasury bonds, notes, and bills. Which type of U.S. security fits best in the money market?
4. Identify
    a. Federal funds
    b. Negotiable certificates of deposit
    c. Banker's acceptances
    d. Commercial paper
    e. Eurodollars

---

[11]See Evelyn M. Hurley, "The Commercial Paper Market Since the Mid-Seventies," *Federal Reserve Bulletin,* June 1982.

4

Problems and Characteristics of Selected Nonbank Financial Institutions

Although our major emphasis in the remainder of this book will be on the nature, functions, and control of commercial banks, it will be useful to acquire at least a superficial understanding of the chief characteristics of some of the more important nonbank financial institutions. To that end, this chapter examines several of them.

To distinguish between commercial banks and the other major financial institutions used to be quite a simple matter. Although all perform the crucial role of middlemen between savers and investors and despite the fact that commercial banks have always carried out many of the same specific functions as other intermediaries, one function could always be singled out as being unique to commercial banks. That was the authority to accept and create demand deposits—money itself. Prior to the 1970s, exceptions to the rule that "only commercial banks can offer checking accounts" were so rare and unimportant that one could comfortably distinguish between commercial banks and other financial institutions on that criterion alone.

But all that began changing dramatically in the 1970s. NOW accounts were first issued in 1972 by a mutual savings bank in Massachusetts and soon spread to other states and other depository institutions. Technically, of course, these are classified as "savings accounts on which checks can be written" rather than as "checking accounts that pay interest," but this is strictly legal semantics. Shortly thereafter, in 1974, share draft accounts first appeared at credit unions and spread rapidly. Clearly, with developments such as these, the monopoly that commercial banks once had on the issuance of checking accounts has long since disappeared. These innovations, along with some others to be discussed in the paragraphs that follow, have been part of an ongoing process whereby all the depository institutions have tended to become more alike.

Despite these important changes, however, commercial banks still remain sufficiently dominant in the provision of checking accounts to set them apart. For

40

example, on January 12, 1983, commercial banks were responsible for $336 billion of the total $362 billion of checking accounts and other checkable deposits in circulation—just about 93 percent of the total. We shall rely on their continued dominance in this area as a distinguishing characteristic that still sets commercial banks sufficiently apart from the other financial institutions to warrant separate coverage. Here we consider some major characteristics of seven nonbank financial institutions.

The Thrift Institutions

There are three major financial institutions that are classified as "thrift" institutions. These are savings and loan associations, mutual savings banks, and credit unions. The common characteristic of the three is the fact that all collect the savings of surplus income units primarily through issuance of time and savings deposits.[1] They diverge sharply, however, in the usage of the funds so collected. Whereas credit unions lend the bulk of theirs out to their members in the form of consumer loans, savings and loan associations and, to a somewhat lesser degree mutual savings banks, specialize primarily in mortgages. And it has been this feature— the dominance of mortgages in their portfolios of earning assets—that has been the source of a serious crisis in the early 1980s.

The Crisis of the "Mortgage Specializing" Thrifts

As noted, savings and loan associations and mutual savings banks, have long specialized heavily in mortgages. Indeed, in 1980 mortgages constituted about 80 percent of the total assets of savings and loan associations and just under 60 percent of those of mutual savings banks.

There is nothing particularly surprising about this extreme degree of specialization, especially on the part of savings and loan associations. After all, the savings and loan "industry" originated for the purpose of financing mortgages. The idea was, and is, that these institutions could attract a pool of savings by paying a moderate interest return to its owners and then lend out the funds to prospective home buyers at sufficiently higher rates to provide an adequate return to the associations themselves. It seemed an eminently reasonable arrangement. Savers got the liquidity they desired along with a satisfactory interest income, and the nation's housing industry was supplied with the financing it needed to move forward. Few noticed, and for years few complained, when government regulations

---

[1] Although accounts held with credit unions and those held at savings and loan associations are often referred to as "shares" rather than as deposits, they are not in any significant sense different from deposits.

sharply limited the permissible portfolio investment of these institutions, thereby *requiring* them, as a matter of law, to become mortgage finance specialists.

But when another kind of government regulation—ceilings on the amount of interest that thrift institutions were permitted to pay to depositors—was applied to them beginning in 1966, problems began to appear.[2] Way back in 1933, federal monetary authorities had been given the power to limit the interest rate that commercial banks were permitted to pay to owners of time and savings deposits. This power, implemented through the Federal Reserve System's *Regulation Q*, had had little or no impact prior to 1966 because the interest rate ceilings it authorized had not really been set below-market interest rates.

But starting in 1966, and again in 1969 and 1974, Regulation Q ceilings were held down well below other short-term rates. This meant that savers who kept their savings at commercial banks or thrifts were forced to accept interest returns well below those available on the unregulated parts of the money market. And, as should not have been surprising, many of them began to look elsewhere for the higher returns available on unregulated markets.

This phenomenon—the diversion of funds away from their normal path (financial intermediaries such as commercial banks, mutual savings banks, and savings and loan associations) toward direct "financial" investment in securities with higher yields—has come to be called *disintermediation*.

What were the effects of this episode of flight from the savings institutions? Obviously the savings institutions, deserted by many of their normal depositors, were seriously hurt. This, in turn, had more profound effects on the allocation of credit and on borrowers who rely most heavily on these institutions for credit. The housing industry, for example, which normally relies upon savings institutions for most of its financing, was very severely hampered during each of the periods of severe disintermediation.

Even more obvious, however, have been the *income distribution* effects of Regulation Q. Professor James Tobin has put the issue as follows:

> One of the least attractive features of recent policy has been discrimination against the small saver. He cannot earn market interest (although the small borrower must pay it). . . . The small saver cannot easily go into the open market in search of higher yields. He is impeded by the significant minimum denominations and lot sizes of market instruments, by brokerage fees, by his own unfamiliarity and ignorance.[3]

When interest returns available on government securities and other unregulated instruments rise well above those that Regulation Q ceilings permit savings institutions to pay, the well-informed, high-income saver can be expected to quickly divert his or her funds out of the regulated intermediaries to the unregulated se-

---

[2]This extension of Regulation Q–type controls to thrifts occurred as a result of the Interest Rate Control Act of 1966.

[3]James Tobin, "Deposit Interest Ceilings as a Monetary Control," *Journey of Money, Credit and Banking,* February 1970, p. 9.

curities markets. In late 1969, for example, a switch from passbook savings accounts to short-term U.S. securities meant an *increase* in interest return of nearly 4 percent, while in 1974, the differential was about 3 percent.

Such action was fine for the large saver, but it was not available for most small savers, partly because the small saver often lacks adequate information about the alternatives to savings institutions as a repository for his savings. But even given perfect information, most small savers could not have taken advantage of the much higher interest available in the securities markets because of brokerage charges and minimum denomination requirements.

What does all this add up to? Let us take January 1970 as an example. At that time the saver who had $100,000 available could have earned 8.8 percent by buying commercial paper, 8.6 percent by buying banker's acceptances, or 7.9 percent by buying new U.S. government Treasury bills. To add insult to injury, the saver could also have received 7.5 percent from a commercial bank *if he or she held a one-year certificate of deposit in the amount of $100,000 or more.* But if the saver was "small," with savings of less than $10,000, he or she probably had to be content with the 4.5 percent return permitted by Regulation Q on regular savings accounts at commercial banks or 4.75 percent at savings and loan associations or mutual savings banks.

Informed opinion regarding the effects of Regulation Q ceilings on the allocation of credit and on the small saver has long been almost unanimously critical. In response to this criticism, significant steps toward reform have been taken. First, in 1978, commercial banks, savings and loan associations, and mutual savings banks were authorized to issue *money market certificates of deposit.* These, as noted, offer interest yields essentially equal to that on the most recently issued six-month Treasury bills and come in minimum denomination sizes of $10,000. Following up on this was the authorization, in 1979, of the so-called "small saver certificate"—with maturities of 30 months or more, interest yields approximating those on U.S. securities of equivalent maturity, and *no* governmentally imposed minimum denomination sizes.

These two measures went a long way toward removing the most serious effects of Regulation Q. But the true death knell of the Regulation Q episode was rung with the passage of the Depository Institutions Deregulation and Monetary Control Act of 1980. In that law, a Depository Institutions Deregulation Committee was established with the assignment of phasing out all Regulation Q–type interest rate ceilings by March 1986.[4] And in the Depository Institutions Act of 1982, the process was speeded up even more so that by the beginning of 1983, most Regulation Q effects were already gone.

As a result of these measures, we have probably just about seen the last of the Regulation Q–induced problems of disintermediation and discrimination against the small saver. But with interest rates reaching record levels in the early 1980s,

---

[4]The prohibition against the payment of interest on checking accounts, however, was not affected by the D.I.D.M.C. Act.

the thrift institutions found that the much heralded deregulation had brought with it—at least initially—some truly serious problems.

The virtual end of Regulation Q-type ceilings revealed a severe mismatch between the maturities of thrift liabilities and assets. The government had authorized the thrifts to pay the very high interest rates needed to attract savings in the early 1980s, but it, of course, did not guarantee that they could do so at a profit. And therein lay a very large problem.

As institutions specializing in mortgages, savings and loan associations and mutual savings banks own primarily long-term assets that "turn over" only very slowly over time. The result is that when interest rates rise sharply, these institutions find themselves loaded down with long-term mortgage commitments made in the past when interest rates were lower, with only a small proportion being paid off each year. They can, of course, issue new mortgages at the current, higher interest rates to replace those few reaching maturity, but since this constitutes only a very small proportion of their assets, it raises their total interest income only slightly.

And so they are caught in a squeeze created by their practice of "borrowing short and lending long." While their asset structures permit only modest increases in their interest *income* in the short run, remaining sufficiently competitive to retain their accustomed share of depositors requires that the interest rates they *pay* be increased on *all* deposits in line with those of rival lenders. All this has meant a profit squeeze of such imposing proportions as to constitute a threat to the very existence of a large part of the industry.

Evidence of these problems abounds. For example, as Table 4-1 shows vividly, both savings and loan associations and mutual savings banks suffered (on average) sizable losses in 1981. A similar fate befell them in 1982. The cause of these heavy losses, as we have seen, is not hard to pinpoint. Although the average interest rate charged on *new* conventional home mortgages in 1981 was 14.39 percent, the average interest return on *all* mortgages (both new and old) held by insured savings and loan associations during the year was only 9.87 percent. When

TABLE 4-1

Profitability of Thrift Institutions, 1961–1981
(retained earnings as percentage of average total assets)

Year	Savings and Loan Associations	Mutual Savings Banks
1961–65	0.80%	0.45%
1966–70	0.56	0.30
1971–75	0.65	0.47
1976–79	0.74	0.51
1980	0.14	−0.12
1981	−0.49	−0.64

Source: Andrew S. Carron, *The Plight of the Thrift Institution* (Washington, D.C.: The Brookings Institution, 1982), p. 12.

it is recognized that the average "cost of funds" for the same institutions in the same year was 10.92 percent, the source of the loss is clear. Perhaps the following statement by the chairman of the Federal Home Loan Bank Board expresses the dimensions of the problem best as it applied to savings and loan associations.

> It is no secret that the thrift industry in the United States is experiencing a severe financial crisis. For the year 1981, the industry recorded a net loss of $1.52 billion, representing a negative 0.49 percent net return on assets. Net deposit outflows reached a record $25.5 billion and the industry's net worth declined steadily each month of 1981. Mortgage commitments for 1981 were 44 percent lower than those made just two years ago, and the number of associations facing potential insolvency over the next twelve months continues to grow.[5]

Without question the thrift industry has undergone a severe test in the early 1980's. It has seen an inordinate number of failures and/or consolidations of "problem" institutions with stronger ones. And it will undoubtedly see more.

But in the long run—once the transition costs of deregulation have been paid—the outlook is less bleak. Time alone will bring improvements as 4, 5, and 6 percent mortgages granted many years ago under vastly different circumstances are paid off and average earnings rise. And of course, as we learned in late 1982, significant interest rate declines can swiftly and markedly improve thrift profit prospects by lowering current payments to depositors relative to the income from mortgages.

Then too, profound differences can be expected to result from fuller exploitation of broadened powers granted to thrifts in recent years. In the Depository Institutions Deregulation and Monetary Control Act of 1980 as well as the Depository Institutions Act of 1982, thrifts were given significant new powers to diversify their activities.

Federally chartered savings and loan associations, for example, were authorized to commit up to 20 percent of their assets to consumer loans, commercial paper, or corporate debt securities, to purchase shares of certain investment companies, and to issue credit cards. Federally chartered thrifts were given the power to commit up to 10 percent of their assets to commercial loans and to purchase a limited quantity of state and local government securities. Federally chartered thrifts were also authorized to accept demand deposits "in connection with a commercial, corporate, or business loan relationship." Both types of institutions, along with all other depository institutions, were authorized to issue NOW accounts starting in 1981 and money market deposit accounts beginning in late 1982.

The main impact of these changes will be to make these two thrifts less dependent on mortgages, thereby shortening somewhat the average maturity of their portfolios. Indeed, there is ample evidence that that change is well under way. For example, whereas in 1978, savings and loan associations provided 42

---

[5]Richard T. Pratt, "Fifty Years of Service," *Federal Home Loan Bank Board Journal,* June 1982, p. 1.

percent of all funds made available to households for home mortgages, by 1981 that percentage had fallen to 23.[6]

Another very significant change that has worked to ease the pressure on the "mortgage specializing thrifts" has been the marked swing toward *adjustable rate mortgages* (ARMs) in recent years. Until quite recently, virtually all mortgages granted in the United States were fixed rate mortgages under which the rate of interest agreed upon at the time of the granting of the mortgage was kept constant throughout its term. This, of course, worked to the benefit of the borrowers and to the detriment of the lenders during periods of generally rising interest rates.

The most common type of adjustable rate mortgage currently in use in the United States is a long-term contract on which the interest rate payable is adjusted once or twice per year. Typically, an increase in the rate increases the number of payments required before the mortgage is paid off instead of increasing the size of the monthly payment. To protect the home buyer partially, many contracts place an upper limit on the amount that the interest rate may be increased each year and over the life of the mortgage.[7]

It was not until around the middle of the 1970s that adjustable rate mortgages began to be used on a significant scale in this country, and even then, their use was largely confined to state-chartered institutions in California and New England. In 1979, however, the Federal Home Loan Bank Board authorized the use of ARMs at federally chartered savings and loan associations throughout the country. Since that time, their use has spread rapidly as lenders have sought to protect themselves against rising interest rates. Indeed, it is estimated that by late 1982, over 40 percent of all new conventional mortgages were of the adjustable rate variety.[8] It seems likely that that proportion will increase as borrowers and lenders learn to live with a less stable environment. As it does, the financial situation of the thrifts will surely improve.

Savings and Loan Associations

Although we have already considered some of the recent problems of savings and loan associations, it will be useful, at this point, to step back and take a broader look at the history and characteristics of this, the largest of the thrift institutions.

---

[6]See Charles Luckett, "Recent Developments in the Mortgage and Consumer Credit Markets," *Federal Reserve Bulletin,* May 1982. It should also be pointed out that savings and loan associations increased their relative share of consumer installment credit financed from $\frac{1}{2}$ of 1 percent in 1978 to 9 percent in 1981.

[7]Another version of adjustable rate mortgage is a long-term contract with a provision to alter the interest rate payable every three to five years. For an interesting article on this issue, see Bronwyn Brock, "Mortgages with Adjustable Interest Rates Improve Viability of Thrift Industry," *Voice,* Federal Reserve Bank of Dallas, February 1981.

[8]See Marcell Arak, "Innovations in the Financial Markets," *Quarterly Review,* Federal Reserve Bank of New York, Winter 1981–1982. See also Michael J. Moran, "Thrift Institutions in Recent Years," *Federal Reserve Bulletin,* December 1982.

Savings and loan associations first appeared in the United States in 1831 and were, for many years, truly voluntary associations devoted to the financing of home building. As they prospered, their numbers grew and their operations formalized. Over the years, they came under regulations and controls set up, first by the states and then later, starting in 1933, by the federal government. At the end of December 1982, there were 3,833 savings and loan associations located, unlike mutual savings banks, in every state in the union.

A savings and loan association may receive its charter to do business from a state or from the federal government. A majority—nearly 60 percent of them— are state chartered, but since these are, on average, smaller than the federally chartered associations, the latter control about 60 percent of the industry's total assets.

The federal government agency charged with overseeing and assisting the savings and loan "industry" is the Federal Home Loan Bank System. The FHLB System is headed by a three-member Board in Washington, D.C., and its operating arm includes the 12 regional Federal Home Loan Banks spread throughout the country. The relationship between the FHLB System and the nation's savings and loan associations is not unlike that between the Federal Reserve System and its member commercial banks. All federally chartered associations are required to join the System (and purchase stock in their regional Home Loan bank), while those with state charters may join or not as they see fit. As of late 1982, the some 3,400 member associations were about half federal and half state.

Depositors at savings and loan associations have their deposits insured up to a maximum of $100,000 if their association subscribes to the insurance coverage offered by the Federal Savings and Loan Insurance Corporation (FSLIC). As of March 1983, deposits of 3,256 associations, possessing about 98 percent of the industry's total assets, were insured.[9]

The FSLIC has built up a "reserve fund" of some $6.5 billion over the years through premiums charged to member associations and interest earnings. In addition, should circumstances warrant, the Corporation is currently authorized to borrow $750 million from the U.S. Treasury and to increase the insurance premiums charged. Although these resources are formidable, the FSLIC's reserves totaled only 1.229 percent of the accounts at all insured associations in March 1982. This percentage has fallen consistently since the late 1960s, and there has been concern regarding its adequacy in light of the serious reverses suffered by many savings and loan associations in the early 1980s.

Several things are worthy of note in the consolidated savings and loan association balance sheet shown in Table 4-2. First, the dominance of mortgages in their portfolio of earning assets is striking, although as a fraction of total assets, mortgages had fallen from about 85 percent to 66 percent since 1978. This *decline*

---

[9]The associations whose accounts are not insured by the FSLIC are located in Maryland, Massachusetts, North Carolina, and Ohio. In these states, private companies offer insurance to all but a small minority of associations.

TABLE 4-2

Consolidated Balance Sheet of All Savings and Loan Associations, March 1983
(billions of dollars)

Assets		Liabilities and Net Worth	
Cash and securities	$ 97.7	Savings and time deposits	$600.7
Mortgage loans	479.4	Borrowings	86.1
Other assets	151.9	Other liabilities	15.2
		Net worth	27.0
Total	$729.0	Total	$729.0

Source: Statistical Division, Federal Home Loan Bank Board.

in the relative dominance of mortgages is almost exactly matched by the *rise* in the relative proportion of "other assets" since 1978 from 9 percent to 21 percent. It is likely that the relative growth in "other" assets has resulted from broadened portfolio investment authority granted the associations in the Depository Institutions Acts of 1980 and 1982. Noteworthy also is the fact that net worth in October 1982 was just over 3.7 percent of total assets, a considerable drop from the 5.5 percent figure obtained in 1978. This drop, of course, reflects the heavy losses suffered by the associations in the early 1980s.

Savings and loan associations, as is true for all depository institutions, are subject to reserve requirements behind their transactions accounts and any time deposits owned by businesses. These requirements were initiated in 1980 with the passage of the D.I.D.M.C. Act and are being "phased in" over a seven-year period for savings and loan associations. When fully phased in (in 1987), they will call for a required reserve ratio of approximately 3 percent on the first $26 million of transactions accounts and a ratio of between 8 and 14 percent on transactions accounts in excess of $26 million. Nonpersonal time deposits with an original maturity of less than three and a half years will have a required reserve ratio of between 0 and 9 percent.[10] The only assets that "count" to meet the legally required reserve ratio are currency and coins and checking accounts held at a Federal Reserve bank.[11]

Mutual Savings Banks

The first of the purely savings institutions, mutual savings banks, appeared on the American scene in 1816. Fulfilling a need for a thrift institution aimed primarily at the small saver that the then-existing commercial banks had not met,

---

[10]The law permits the Federal Reserve System's Board of Governors to vary these required reserve ratios, from 0 to 9 percent on nonpersonal time deposits and from 8 to 14 percent on transactions accounts over $26 million.

[11]The law permits savings and loan associations to keep required reserves on deposit with their district Federal Home Loan bank, provided that the Federal Home Loan bank keeps an equivalent amount on deposit at a Federal Reserve bank. The latter is called a "passthrough" account.

savings banks were an early success and spread rapidly. By 1875, there were 674 mutual savings banks serving over 2 million depositors.

In a rapidly developing industrial power, one might well have expected a mushrooming growth of savings banks after 1875. But quite the reverse occurred. Faced with increasingly greater competition from savings and loan associations and from commercial banks—both of which were better able to expand in the newer, developing sections of the nation—mutual savings bank expansion stopped, and the succeeding years witnessed a steady decline in the number of banks until, by late 1981, only 442 were still in existence. Of these, only 36 began business in the twentieth century, and fully 80 percent were established prior to 1875!

Mutual savings banks have lost ground, relative to the other savings institutions, for a number of reasons. Chief among these has been their inability to expand, along with competing institutions, into the newer, more rapidly growing areas of the nation. They are concentrated almost entirely in New England and the Middle Atlantic states and do not exist at all in 33 of the 50 states. In fact, as of the end of 1981, almost 75 percent of them were concentrated in New York, Massachusetts, and Connecticut.

Mutual savings banks, as the term *mutual* indicates, are run for the mutual benefit of the depositors, with policy determined by a board of trustees, which often serves without pay. All are state-chartered institutions, and although they have been eligible to belong to the Federal Reserve System since 1933, only three have chosen to join it. The accounts of depositors are insured by the Federal Deposit Insurance Corporation up to $100,000 per account at approximately three-fourths of the banks holding over 90 percent of the assets. Almost all of those that do not subscribe to FDIC coverage are located in Massachusetts, where mutual savings bank deposits are fully insured by a special state agency.

As thrift institutions, almost all their funds come from their depositors, with outstanding deposits constituting about 90 percent of their liabilities in early 1983. As with most savings accounts, depositors may be required by law to wait 14 days to withdraw funds, but this is seldom enforced.

Portfolio practices usually reflect the nature of the business. These banks had about 3 percent of their assets in cash form in early 1983, about 54 percent in mortgages, and most of the rest in high-grade corporate or government securities.

All but two of the mutual savings bank states have passed a *legal list* of assets to which mutual savings banks must restrict themselves. In general, these permit the purchase of any government securities, certain high-grade corporate securities, and mortgages. The legal restrictions imposed on savings banks are generally less restrictive than are those imposed on savings and loan associations, but considerably more so than those for life insurance companies and commercial banks.

Some indication of the effects of legal restrictions as well as the requirements of their respective businesses can be obtained by comparing the relative proportions of assets held in different forms by the three largest nonbank institutions. Such a comparison is provided in Table 4-3.

TABLE 4-3

Percentage Distribution of Assets of Three Financial Institutions, March 1982

Assets	Mutual Savings Banks	Savings and Loan Assoc.	Life Insurance Companies
Cash	3.0%		NA
U.S. securities	5.8	10.0%	1.9%
State and local government securities	1.3		1.3
Corporate and other securities	21.4		50.5
Mortgages	55.8	76.1	26.5
Other loans	9.5	—	13.1
Other assets	3.2	13.9	6.7

NA – Not available.

Source: Federal Reserve Bulletin, November 1982.

Mutual savings banks, as indicated in Table 4-4, lean heavily toward mortgages as earning assets, though not nearly so heavily as do savings and loan associations. On the other hand, regulations permit savings banks substantially more diversification than is the case for savings and loan associations—especially as regards the purchase of corporate securities.

Among recent regulatory changes affecting mutual savings banks are broadened authority in the area of consumer loans in some states as well as authorization for the issuance of nationwide credit cards. And, of course, as noted, the D.I.D.M.C. Act of 1980 authorized some commercial loans and NOW accounts while applying the same reserve requirements to transactions accounts and nonpersonal time deposits as are applied to other depository institutions.

The student may well have noted strong similarities between mutual savings banks and savings and loan associations. In truth, they *are* very much alike. Both collect the bulk of their funds via time deposits, and both use the preponderant amount of them to finance home construction. Moreover, both were in trouble in the early 1980s for essentially the same reasons.

TABLE 4-4

Consolidated Balance Sheet for All Mutual Savings Banks, January 1983
(billions of dollars)

Assets		Liabilities and Reserve Accounts	
Cash	$ 6.3	Time deposits and savings	
U.S. securities	10.2	accounts	$157.2
State and local government		Other liabilities	8.3
securities	2.5	Reserve accounts	9.2
Corporate and other securities	36.4		
Mortgages	93.9		
Other loans	17.5		
Other assets	7.9		
Total	$174.7	Total	$174.7

Source: Federal Reserve Bulletin, April 1983.

If they are all this much alike, what distinguishes them? One savings and loan official has put it this way:

> Savings and loan associations differ from other deposit-type savings institutions in one very important respect. The other deposit-type institutions have as one of their primary objectives the mobilizing of funds (savings) and the providing of a return to depositors and shareholders. They are thrift institutions first and they hold themselves to be simply that. The attitudes of such institutions toward diversification in risk assets, liquidity, borrowing from reserve pools of credit, such as the Federal Home Loan System and the Federal Reserve, are a reflection of their concern for depositors and shareholders and for the safety of their investments. In contrast, savings and loan associations, as specialized institutions, hold quite different attitudes toward diversification of risk assets and borrowing from central credit pools. Although they, too, are concerned about the welfare of savers, their concern is prompted by the need to secure funds to support home financing and home ownership in this nation. Simply, if the home financing element were eliminated from savings and loan activity and the general investment market were made its province, there probably would not be so great an economic and social justification for the existence of these associations. Savers and thrift could be served readily by any of a number of other institutions.[12]

In other words, the first concern of the savings and loan association is the financing of home construction while, at least in the opinion of this official, mutual savings banks are primarily concerned with the encouragement of thrift.

Credit Unions

Credit unions are nonprofit, voluntary associations of people with some "common bond" that organize to collect savings deposits (more technically, "shares") from their members and put these deposits to work primarily via consumer loans to their own members. Originally organized in Germany as institutions to encourage thrift and to make available inexpensive loans to lower- and middle-income people, credit unions, while still small in absolute size, have shown the most rapid rate of growth of all the financial institutions in the past quarter-century.

The members of a credit union must share some "common bond," such as working for a common employer, belonging to the same labor union or religious group, or living in the same area, although recently authorities have broadened the definition of "common bond" substantially.[13]

Credit unions can operate with either a federal or a state charter. Federal credit unions, which in recent years have controlled about two-thirds of the industry's total assets, are regulated and assisted by the National Credit Union Administration, a federal government agency set up for this specific purpose. Insurance,

---

[12]Leon T. Kendall for the United States Savings and Loan League, Commission on Money and Credit, *The Savings and Loan Business: Its Purposes, Functions, and Economic Justification,* © 1962. Reprinted by permission of Prentice-Hall, Inc., Englewood Cliffs, N.J.

[13]For example, "Today, Groups from Feminists to Former Drug Addicts Have Their Own Credit Unions," *The Wall Street Journal,* June 22, 1977, p. 22.

up to $100,000 per account, is provided by the National Credit Union Share Insurance Fund. Federally chartered credit unions are required to subscribe for this insurance, and, while many state CUs do also, many others are insured by agencies set up by the state that chartered them.

As noted, many credit unions offer their shareholders checking accounts in the form of *share draft accounts*. Share draft accounts are considered to be interest-earning savings accounts on which checks can be written, although, as are NOW accounts, they are subject to the reserve requirements applied to transactions accounts by the D.I.D.M.C. Act of 1980.

Credit unions, while in the aggregate still the smallest of the thrift institutions, have been growing more rapidly than the others in recent years. There are a number of reasons for this rapid growth.

First, credit unions are no longer subject to any Regulation Q–type controls on the interest paid on regular savings accounts, and they have, in fact, tended to pay more than have competitive thrifts. But more than that, they have tended to charge somewhat lower rates on consumer loans to their members.

How can they do this? Credit unions have a number of cost advantages over their rivals. First, they often operate with significant subsidies, ranging from free services from volunteer officers to free office space and services such as payroll deduction provided by an employer. Second, their small, homogeneous size often sharply reduces the cost in checking on the credit rating of prospective borrowers. Third, and perhaps most important, because of their nonprofit status, they pay no federal taxes.

Despite their impressive growth in recent years and recent legislation authorizing them to diversify greatly their activities, it does not seem likely that credit unions will ever challenge their rival thrifts in size. This is the case because, despite the fact that the law now authorizes them to offer share drafts and credit cards and to finance mortgages, relatively few of them do so. Most credit unions continue to function in accordance with their major original purpose—to serve small savers.

TABLE 4-5

Consolidated Balance Sheet for Credit Unions, 1981
(billions of dollars)

Assets		Liabilities and Equity	
Cash	$ 1.4	Savings accounts (shares)	$57.8
U.S. securities	0.9	Notes payable	2.4
Federal agency securities	3.0	Reserves	2.8
Time deposits and savings accounts	13.1	Other	1.5
Loans	42.5		
Other	3.6		
Total	$64.5	Total	$64.5

Source: National Credit Union Administration, *Year-End 1981 Statistics of the National Credit Union Administration,* May 1982.

Some Other Important Financial Institutions

Life Insurance Companies

Life insurance companies, which in the United States date back to 1759, sell substantially more than liquidity and an income on savings. It seems safe to argue that the vast majority of the savers who channel large portions of their incomes each year to life insurance premium payments do so more for risk protection than for direct income or liquidity.

To the policyholder, life insurance represents a type of protection, especially in the early years of family formation, that savings accounts normally cannot provide. His or her savings, sent to the insurance company in the form of premium payments, do provide some liquidity for emergencies in the form of the policy's accumulated cash value or policy loans against it. But the prime motivating factor is undoubtedly the much greater face value of the policy available for the policyholder's dependents in the case of his or her untimely death.

This fact, plus the contractual nature of most of the premium payments and the substantially more liberal regulatory legislation, permits the insurance company portfolio manager a great deal more discretion than his counterpart in a mutual savings bank or savings and loan association.

Liquidity is a much less restraining influence. This is due partly to the fact that policyholders do not normally look upon their accumulated cash value as liquid savings to be drawn upon except in the direst of emergencies and partly to the fact that the annual inflow of funds to an insurance company is largely in the form of contractual premium payments—an inflow that can be depended on much more confidently than an inflow of savings deposits in other savings institutions.

As Table 4-6 indicates, life insurance companies are heavy purchasers of corporate bonds, with some 40 percent of their total assets committed to such securities. The other major component of their portfolios is mortgages, which constituted about one-quarter of their 1983 assets. Unlike the other major mortgage-granting institutions, it is interesting to note that life insurance companies specialize

TABLE 4-6

Assets of Life Insurance Companies, February 1983
(millions of dollars)

U.S. government securities	$ 17,877
State and local government securities	8,333
Foreign government securities	10,736
Corporation bonds	213,838
Corporation stock	58,051
Mortgages	142,683
All other	144,441
Total	$595,959

Source: American Council of Life Insurance.

primarily in financing multifamily and commercial construction rather than single-family home building.

Investment Companies (Mutual Funds)

Investment companies sell shares to savers and then use the proceeds to purchase a wide variety of primary securities. To the saver, investment company shares constitute something of a middle ground between savings accounts on the one hand and the direct purchase of corporate or government securities on the other. As compared with savings accounts, investment company shares have recently offered a substantially higher return with little loss of liquidity. Similarly, as compared with the direct purchase of securities, investment company shares offer a degree of diversification of risk that the small saver could hardly obtain on his or her own, plus the experienced market knowledge of a specialized management that makes the basic financial investment decisions.

There are two kinds of investment companies—closed end and open end. A closed-end company generally issues only a certain fixed amount of its own common stock and uses this, plus whatever additional capital is raised by borrowing, to purchase operating company securities. Its common stock is then bought and sold on the stock exchange, and the individual saver who wants to purchase more of it must do so from somebody else on the exchange. Similarly, a present owner of a share of a closed-end investment company can only "get his money out" by selling it to someone else on the exchange. Closed-end companies constitute only a very small fraction of the investment company "industry," however, and we shall consequently ignore them in the remaining discussion.[14]

An open-end investment company (popularly referred to as a "mutual fund"), on the other hand, will issue new shares of its own stock to anyone who desires to purchase them. Consequently, the total assets of a successful open-end company tend to grow at the discretion of savers in contrast to the closed-end company, which maintains only a fixed amount of stock outstanding. A second major difference is that owners of open-end stocks may redeem them for cash at any time by turning them in to the company. The amount paid for redemption depends upon the market value of the company's portfolio of securities at the time, which may be greater than or less than the amount originally paid in.

There is a mutual fund to suit almost any saver's tastes. For those more interested in long-run growth of their wealth than in current return, there are a large number of *growth* funds that specialize primarily in common stock considered likely to provide significant capital appreciation. For savers looking for a bit less risk, there are what are called *balanced* funds with portfolios split between stocks and bonds. Those to whom a relatively high current income is paramount would

---

[14]As of the end of 1980, assets held by closed-end investment companies constituted only about $5\frac{1}{2}$ percent of the total held by the industry.

TABLE 4-7

Assets of Money Market Mutual Funds,
December 1982
(billions of dollars)

U.S. Treasury bills	$ 37.9
Other U.S. securities	16.7
Repurchase agreements	16.2
Certificates of deposit	59.8
Commercial paper	50.3
Banker's acceptances	18.8
All other	6.9
Total	$206.6

Source: Investment Company Institute, *1983 Mutual Fund Fact Book.*

find *income* funds an appropriate choice. Income funds, as might be guessed, tend to purchase stocks and bonds offering relatively high current dividends and interest but possessing relatively lower growth potential. And some high-income taxpayers would be likely to find the *municipal bond* (or *tax-exempt*) funds to their liking. These, as the name implies, specialize in the purchase of state and local government securities, the income from which is exempt from the federal income tax.

But by any standard the most popular form of mutual fund in recent years has been the *money market mutual* fund. Money market mutual funds, as we have seen, use savings made available to them to purchase a wide variety of money market instruments. Table 4-7 shows the portfolio of money market fund assets as of the end of 1982; Table 4-8 shows the decidedly different composition of assets held by all other types of mutual funds. Note that money market fund assets are very short term (with an average maturity of 34 days as of the end of 1981), whereas common stocks dominate the portfolios of the other mutual funds.

TABLE 4-8

Assets of All Mutual Funds Except
Money Market Funds, December 1982
(billions of dollars)

Cash and equivalent	$ 6.0
Corporate bonds	10.8
Preferred stock	1.6
Common stock	47.7
Municipal bonds	6.8
Long-term U.S. securities	3.8
Other	0.0
Total	$76.8

Source: Investment Company Institute, *1983 Mutual Fund Fact Book.*

The growth of money market mutual funds in the early 1980s has been so spectacular as to almost defy description. The first MMMF was instituted in 1972, and by the beginning of 1978 total MMMF assets had reached about $4 billion. From that point on, they literally took off. Indeed, by mid-1982 their assets were well over the $200 billion mark, a fiftyfold increase in just over four years! What had started back in 1972 as just another new variety of mutual fund had grown within a decade to a point where it was about four times the size of all other mutual funds combined.

What explains this remarkable performance? Without question, Regulation Q–type interest rate ceilings have played a very important role. Prior to the advent of money market mutual funds, as we have seen, Regulation Q ceilings discriminated sharply against small savers. For savers in sufficiently high income brackets to permit purchase of unregulated short-term instruments despite their imposing minimum denomination sizes (generally $10,000 and up), the governmentally imposed ceilings represented no barrier to the higher market returns available elsewhere in the money market. But for the majority of smaller savers who were unable to come up with such large sums, few alternatives to the artificially low returns available at savings institutions existed.

Money market mutual funds offered small savers a way around these Regulation Q barriers. Generally speaking, one can join a MMMF for an initial minimum outlay of $500 to $2,000, after which additions can be made in very small amounts. In most cases, there is no charge for getting into or out of a fund. Once acquired, an account at a MMMF is exceptionally liquid. Not only can it be "cashed in" at any time without penalty, but, in most cases, shareholders are permitted to write checks on their accounts.[15]

But Regulation Q is not the only reason for the growth of MMMFs. Even without Regulation Q ceilings (and, indeed, the nation *is* largely without them as we enter 1984), it seems likely that money market funds would have grown and prospered, though surely not as spectacularly as they have.

There is evidence, for example, that many "large" savers—people and institutions well able to afford the $10,000 minimum denomination size required to purchase U.S. securities directly—chose instead to purchase MMMF shares.[16] This may have been because money market fund shares seemed to offer greater liquidity or a higher return than do U.S. securities or, possibly, to take advantage of the added risk protection made possible by the funds' ability to diversify. Whatever the reason, this behavior provides clear-cut evidence that the growth of money market funds is not attributable to Regulation Q alone.

Also, it should be recognized that technological developments, especially in the computer and telecommunications areas, have played a not insignificant role

---

[15]Most money market funds limit check writing privileges to checks in excess of $500.

[16]See, for example, Timothy Q. Cook and Jeremy G. Duffield, "Money Market Mutual Funds," *Economic Review,* Federal Reserve Bank of Richmond, July–August 1979.

in the timing of the money market fund explosion. Money market funds depend heavily on computers to administer accounts of shareholders and provide services. A dramatic reduction in computer costs plus the widespread use of ''800'' numbers for customer contact has sharply lowered costs for money market funds and surely played an additional role in their growth.[17]

In conclusion, the following seems reasonably safe. With Regulation Q largely ''phased out,'' one important source of rapid growth by money market funds has been essentially eliminated. But the money market fund is a viable institution performing a unique and valuable intermediary service. It is quite likely to stay with us, although on a smaller scale, even without Regulation Q.

Pension Funds

In terms of total assets as well as rate of growth, pension plans rank among the most important of the financial institutions. As of the beginning of 1981, the book value of the assets held by private and governmental pension funds exceeded $700 billion.

Pension funds can be conveniently divided into three categories. As Table 4-9 indicates, as of the end of 1980, those administered by the federal and state and local governments held $279 billion of assets, private funds administered by insurance companies held just under $165 billion, and private ''noninsured'' funds, managed by trustees, held over $286 billion.

The federal government funds devote the majority of their assets to U.S. government securities, but all the others concentrate most heavily on corporate securities. The distribution of assets of the private noninsured funds as of September 1981 is shown in Table 4-10.

TABLE 4-9

Total Assets of Public and Private Pension Funds,
December 31, 1980
(billions, book value)

All private pension funds		$450.7
Insured funds	$164.6	
Noninsured funds	286.1	
All public pension funds		279.1
U.S. government	76.4	
State and local governments	202.7	

Source: Securities and Exchange Commission, *Statistical Bulletin,* September 1981.

---

[17]For an interesting discussion on this point, see Timothy Cook and Jeremy Duffield, ''Short-Term Investment Pools,'' *Economic Review,* Federal Reserve Bank of Richmond, September–October 1980.

TABLE 4-10

Assets of Private Noninsured Pension
Funds, Book Value, September 1981
(millions)

Cash and deposits	$ 9,014
U.S. government securities	34,739
Corporate and other bonds	65,824
Preferred stock	1,340
Common stock	139,180
Mortgages	4,389
Other	25,043
Total	$279,529

Source: Securities and Exchange Commission, *Statistical Bulletin*, February 1982.

Finance Companies

Finance companies operate primarily at two levels. Consumer finance companies make personal loans directly to individuals, whereas business finance companies do their lending to, or on behalf of, business firms.

Consumer loans are generally quite small, with short maturities. A 1973 survey revealed their average size to be just over $1,000 and the average maturity about 30 months.[18] Because the average size of a loan is so small, creating significant diseconomies of scale in terms of administration costs, and because the risk is large, consumer finance loans typically carry high interest charges. For example, the average interest rate charged by consumer finance companies on personal loans in November 1980 was over 21 percent per year.

In addition to making personal loans, finance companies work through business firms to finance the sale of large consumer durables. In the sale of an automobile, for example, the finance company specifies the required down payment, the maturity, and the interest rate but allows the car dealer to draw up the necessary papers with the car buyer when an automobile is bought on credit. If the car buyer fails to keep up the payments, the most common procedure is for the finance company to repossess the car and resell it to the dealer for the unpaid balance of the loan.

Finance companies also provide funds directly to businesses to help them to "carry" their accounts receivable. This can take the form of a loan to the business firm, with its (the borrowing firm's) accounts receivable serving as collateral. In some cases, however, the finance company simply purchases the right to collect the borrowing firm's accounts receivable and then collects them itself. The cus-

---

[18]See Doris C. Harless, *Nonbank Financial Institutions*, Federal Reserve Bank of Richmond, 1975, p. 32. This section draws heavily on this excellent publication.

tomers who owed the borrowing company are generally notified that their obligation is now to the finance company.

In mid-1982, the assets of all finance companies totaled over $170 billion, with about half being loans to business and the other half loans to consumers. Of the latter, more than half the total were for the purchase of automobiles.

Finance companies acquire most of their funds through the sale of long-term bonds but also rely heavily on the issuance of their own commercial paper and on bank loans. In mid-1982, for example, their liabilities included about $60 billion in long-term bonds issued and $46 billion in commercial paper, with $15 billion borrowed from banks. These sources were, of course, liberally supplemented by capital and surplus accounts of about $23 billion.

Review Questions

1. What are the common characteristics of the so-called "thrift" institutions?
2. Carefully explain how Regulation Q led to disintermediation problems for the thrift institutions in the 1960s and 1970s.
3. "Although Regulation Q ceilings created problems for thrift institutions, in the short run at least, their removal created other problems." Comment. Do you believe that elimination of Regulation Q–type ceilings will help or harm the housing industry? Explain.
4. How might an increase in the use of adjustable rate mortgages help to ease the problems of U.S. thrift institutions?
5. Why has the mutual savings bank industry lost ground (relatively) to many other financial industries during the past 50 years?
6. How might the spectacular recent growth in credit unions be explained?
7. Carefully distinguish between investment companies and investment bankers.
8. How might one explain the rapid growth of money market mutual funds in the late 1970s and early 1980s? Do you believe that the removal of Regulation Q–type ceilings will eliminate the money market funds? Why or why not?

5

Early U.S. Banking Legislation and the Commercial Banking Business

Despite the growing importance of some of the nonbank financial institutions, the commercial bank is still the bellwether of the financial industry, and in this and succeeding chapters, we shift our focus to it alone.

The commercial bank has often been referred to as the "department store" of finance. And it is an apt title. The typical commercial bank is far more than a mere safekeeper of liquid funds for its customers. Indeed, it often performs the functions of several of the financial institutions discussed in the preceding chapter in addition to its own more or less unique activities.

For example, its savings department performs functions that are substantially similar to those of a mutual savings bank or savings and loan association. If it operates a trust department, it acts in a fiduciary capacity to administer the portfolios of wealthy individuals in a manner not too different from that of an investment company. If it is one of the larger commercial banks, it may operate an investment banking business along with its other responsibilities. If it is close enough to a financial center to do so effectively, it may be a foreign exchange dealer, offering to buy or sell foreign money to all comers. And, of course, in all these roles as well as others, the commercial bank shares with the other financial institutions the fundamental task of bringing together surplus income units (savers) and deficit spending units (investors).

But while it is similar to many of the nonbank institutions in these and other ways, one characteristic sets it aside from the other financial institutions. That characteristic is its dominant role in creation of the nation's money supply in the form of demand deposits and other checkable deposits. It is true, of course, that recent changes such as the spread of the NOW and share draft account have weakened this dominance somewhat. The fact remains, however, that as of early 1983, only about 7 percent of the M1 money supply was the liability of the thrift institutions. Clearly, the commercial bank remains unique as the nation's major money creator.

In essence, what the other financial institutions do is collect portions of the *existing* money supply from surplus income units and then make them available to deficit spending units. Commercial banks not only *create* much of the money they make available to ultimate borrowers, but (because of the fractional reserve system) they possess the power to do so in amounts much greater than what is deposited with them by surplus income units.

It is because of this key role in the determination of the money supply, rather than simply because of the commercial banking sector's overhelming size, that we choose to concentrate so heavily on this segment of the financial structure. In what follows we shall all but ignore the many other functions of the commercial bank to focus as completely as possible on its central role as a money creator.

History of U.S. Commercial Banking Legislation Prior to the Federal Reserve Act

Before we discuss the nature of the commercial banking business, let us consider briefly how we got where we are. The history of commercial banking in the United States prior to the passage of the Federal Reserve Act in 1913 can most conveniently be divided into three subperiods: from 1791 to 1836, from 1836 to 1863, and from 1863 to 1913.

In the earliest days of the republic, around the 1780s, states began to charter banking companies. The federal government provided no paper currency, so early state banks did a flourishing business of granting loans in the form of bank notes—IOUs of issuing banks promising to pay specie to the holder on demand. These notes made up, at the time, our only domestically issued paper money.

In 1791, in response to the recommendations of Alexander Hamilton, the federal government chartered our first truly national bank—the First Bank of the United States. It was a large bank relative to the size of the economy, and it dominated the banking scene from 1791 to 1811. Partially owned by the federal government, it performed some of the functions of a central bank and it competed with state banks for ordinary commercial business. It handled the deposits of the federal government and also took upon itself the task of helping to ensure the convertibility of state bank notes. The latter function consisted of presenting state bank notes to the issuer with a demand for immediate payment in gold.

The First Bank of the United States went out of existence in 1811 when Congress failed to renew its charter, but five years later, in 1816, the Second Bank of the United States was chartered for an additional 20-year period. The Second Bank followed policies similar to those of its predecessor, but some mismanagement, coupled with an unfortunate involvement in political matters, earned it the enmity of President Jackson as well as the state banks. The result was that the bank's charter was allowed to lapse in 1836. For almost the next 30 years, the nation was served exclusively by state-chartered banks.

The Era of State Banking—1836 to 1863

The period from 1836 to 1863, often referred to as the "era of state banking," was, from the viewpoint of sound banking principles, a disastrous one. Despite two constructive developments early in the period, the general character of banking quickly degenerated to perhaps the lowest level in our history.

On the good side of the ledger were the first, faltering attempts at state regulation of banks and the introduction of the *free banking* principle. The free banking principle—first introduced in 1837 in the state of Michigan—permitted chartering of any banking company that could meet certain specified minimum conditions. Previously, a special act of the state legislature had been required for the chartering of any bank, a process obviously subject to the abuses of favoritism and political intrigue.

Despite these advances, the banking system, plagued with mismanagement, corruption, and just plain bad banking, sank to new depths. Banks with insufficient capital, overly speculative loans, and inadequate management were commonplace. Bank notes, promising to pay specie on demand, were often all but impossible to redeem as unscrupulous operators located "redemption centers" deep in the wilderness. As a consequence, such notes circulated at substantial and varying discounts; and the failure rate was abysmally high. With the nation's currency supply consisting almost entirely of state bank notes issued by banks scattered throughout the country, conditions were ideal for counterfeiters; and merchants found it necessary to purchase special compilations called "Counterfeit Detectors" to attempt to determine what currency was good and what was not.

The nation's monetary "system" was clearly a chaotic, deplorable shambles when the Civil War broke out. Indeed, it is something of a misnomer to call it a system at all. A significant proportion of the country's commercial banks were simply unsafe, and, although some states did attempt to exercise some restraint on their activities, the federal government had no control whatever. As a consequence, the nation's paper currency supply, which consisted primarily of state bank notes, was largely outside the control of federal authorities. And to top it all off, the bitter and costly war that began in 1861 not only had to be fought but also had to be financed. All these conditions combined to precipitate a major change in the nation's banking system with the passage of the National Bank Act of 1863.

The National Bank Act of 1863 and the 1863–1913 Period

The National Bank Act of 1863 did three things of significance. First, it authorized the establishment of nationally chartered banks, to be approved and regulated by the newly established Comptroller of the Currency. Second, the newly authorized national banks were given the privilege of issuing, under strictly regulated conditions, a new form of paper currency called the National Bank note.

Third, a prohibitive 10 percent tax was levied on the issuance of state bank notes by state-chartered banks.

The new national banks were, in general, much more strictly regulated than were state banks. To obtain a charter from the Comptroller of the Currency, a bank was required to meet minimum capital requirements, to refrain from making many loans then considered too speculative and risky, to subject itself to regular examination by the Comptroller of the Currency, and to maintain, at all times, specified reserves behind its deposits.[1]

The reserve requirements established were fixed by law (unlike today's situation whereby the Federal Reserve Board may vary the requirements within specified legal limits) and were higher for national banks located in large cities than for those in smaller localities. Specifically, national banks located in New York City, Chicago, and St. Louis were required to maintain a 25 percent reserve behind deposits, all in cash; national banks located in approximately the next 50 largest cities also had to meet a 25 percent reserve ratio but were permitted to hold half of it in checking accounts at national banks in New York, Chicago, or St. Louis; all other national banks—the so-called "country banks"—had a 15 percent reserve requirement, three-fifths of which could be held on deposit at national banks in the larger cities.

The regulations governing the issuance of National Bank notes, the new paper currency authorized by the act, reflected the deep concern for safety that had been generated by conditions during the 1836–1863 period. Banks issuing National Bank notes were required to own, and pledge as security, U.S. government securities of at least equal value.[2] This requirement not only guaranteed the safety of these notes but, as we shall see, it severely limited the amount that could be issued.

The requirements for national banks, although hardly severe by today's standards, were in most cases substantially more rigorous than were those of the states, and it was all too apparent to Congress that the more lenient standards of the states would place nationally chartered banks at a serious competitive disadvantage. Consequently, it was decided to counter the threat of state banks by means of a 10 percent tax on their bank notes.

It seems likely that the real intent of Congress was the elimination of state banks, as such, because the issuance of bank notes (as the proceeds of loans granted) was their main source of income. And a 10 percent tax made further issuance virtually prohibitive. Indeed, state bank notes did quickly disappear from circulation, and the number of state banks in existence fell from about 1,500 in 1862 to less than 250 by 1868.[3]

But the state banks themselves were saved from extinction, if that indeed

---

[1]There was, in those days, no distinction between demand and time deposits, so that all deposits were subject to the same reserve requirements.

[2]In fact, initially National Bank notes could be issued in amounts equal to only 90 percent of the value of U.S. securities possessed by the issuer.

[3]*Banking Studies* (Washington, D.C.: Federal Reserve System, 1941).

TABLE 5-1

Quantities of Bank Notes and Bank Deposits in
Circulation, Selected Years, 1834–1890
(millions of dollars)

Year	Bank Notes	Deposits
1834	$ 95	$ 76
1849	115	91
1855	187	190
1861	202	257
1870	336	775
1890	126	4,576

Source: American Bankers Association, *The Story of American Banking* (New York: American Bankers Association, 1963).

was intended, by a fortuitous quirk of circumstances. Whereas, in earlier years, borrowers from banks had generally insisted on currency and had received it in the form of bank notes, by the time the National Bank Act was passed, the advantages of deposits over currency had taken firm hold in the public's mind. And state banks found that they could continue to earn income by providing borrowers with newly created checking accounts rather than the bank notes that the new law virtually forbade. As a result, many state banks managed to continue to operate alongside the growing number of national banks, and within a few years, they once again exceeded the national banks in numbers.

The astonishingly rapid spread of the deposit banking habit among the American public in the latter nineteenth century is clearly revealed in Table 5-1.

Deficiencies of the National Bank Act of 1863

The National Bank Act of 1863 solved some of our monetary problems, but, as is so often the case, it led to still others. On the positive side, it did provide for the development of a more carefully controlled system of national banks, and it did, for the first time, concentrate control over the circulating currency in federal hands. And these were truly significant improvements. But as the nineteenth century drew to a close, it was clear that serious problems remained, some of them directly attributable to the act itself.

Four quite specific problems became increasingly evident as the twentieth century neared. It was these deficiencies that led to the passage of the Federal Reserve Act in 1913.

Rigidity and Inelasticity of the Currency Supply. The deplorable situation that had been created by the widespread overissue of state bank notes was effectively eliminated by the 10 percent issue tax, but it soon became clear that the provisions for the issuance of National Bank notes were, in themselves, not entirely adequate.

The bank note problem under the National Bank Act, unlike in the earlier years, was not a matter of overissue. If anything, it was the other way around. National banks issuing notes were required to purchase and deposit, with the Comptroller of the Currency, U.S. government securities as "backing" for their outstanding notes. They were permitted to issue notes up to an amount equaling 90 percent of the par or market value (whichever was lower) of U.S. securities so deposited.

This requirement provided admirably for the safety of National Bank notes. However, by tying the quantity that could be issued directly to U.S. securities, the act overlooked the necessity of providing a currency supply that could expand and contract as the "needs of trade" required. When a bigger currency supply was needed, but no more U.S. securities were available, the economy's requirements could not be met.

And that is just about what happened. The value of U.S. securities outstanding fell from about $2.8 billion in 1866 to about $1.6 billion in 1890 as the federal government steadily reduced its debt during the period. Consequently, the "base" on which more National Bank notes could be issued was steadily declining at a time when the nation's economy was growing by leaps and bounds. In addition, during much of the period, U.S. securities were selling at substantial premiums and hence were not particularly desirable for bank purchase. The number of National Bank notes, which had totaled about $300 million in 1870, fell precipitously during the next 20 years.[4]

Nor was the long-run decline in the absolute volume of notes the only problem. A properly functioning currency supply should also expand and contract in volume in response to seasonal, cyclical, and panic-induced demands by the public. To employ the word that was popular then, the currency supply should be "elastic" with respect to the public's demands for it. Based as it was on U.S. securities, the supply of National Bank notes was, unfortunately, highly inelastic. In the words of the Comptroller of the Currency in 1914,

> Under the conditions existing, and which have existed for years past, the currency of the country under our national banking system has been entirely lacking in the element of elasticity which is so necessary to meet the requirements of business and the periodical demands for money and currency which come, especially in the great agricultural sections of the West and South.[5]

Problems Arising Out of Reserve Requirements. In addition to the currency issue problems, reserve requirements for deposits under the National Bank Act were the source of considerable trouble. As noted, the act permitted "country" banks to keep three-fifths of their reserves on deposit in large-city banks and so-

---

[4]It should be noted that the rapid switch in public taste from notes to deposits during the same period kept this decline in currency supply from creating the havoc it might otherwise have caused.

[5]*Annual Report of the Comptroller of the Currency* (Washington, D.C.: Government Printing Office, 1914), p. 9.

called reserve city banks (those located in the approximately 50 largest cities other than New York, Chicago, and St. Louis) to keep half of theirs on deposit in national banks in New York, Chicago, or St. Louis.

The problem these reserve arrangements created is perhaps best put in the words of the Comptroller of the Currency at the time of the passage of the Federal Reserve Act:

> A further weakness of the system which developed—and, with the expansion of our trade and industries, had become more evident and threatening—was the imperfect, inefficient, and unscientific method of handling our bank reserves. Under the national banking system the banks throughout the country have been accustomed to accumulate their reserve balances in the central cities of New York, Chicago, and St. Louis, where the national banks usually have allowed interest at the rate of 2 per cent per annum, and sometimes more, to their correspondent national banks. To avoid loss from idle funds, these depository banks employed to a large extent the balances thus kept with them by putting the money out in call loans on bond and stock collateral. . . .
>
> When the banks throughout the country found it necessary to draw on their reserves in the large cities to meet the recurring seasonal demands of business, these large city banks, in turn, were forced to call in the broker's call loans, these calls resulting frequently in high money rates and declining security values, and sometimes in serious stringency, disturbance and panic, or alarm.[6]

Thus, shortsighted reserve requirement arrangements contributed mightily to periodic financial panics. Ordinary seasonal demands for credit in the agricultural interior led to pressure on large-city banks, especially in New York City, which, in turn, created pressure on the stock market and all too often degenerated into an all-out financial panic. Allowing banks to hold required reserves on deposit at other commercial banks, it seemed, only provided a conduit through which disturbances in one sector could be transmitted to others with, all too often, disastrous results.

Lack of a "Lender of Last Resort."   As the problems with reserve requirements made clear, one portion of the commercial banking system cannot readily "bail out" another part needing reserves, without risking its own liquidity position. Prior to the Federal Reserve System, banks under pressure in periods of crisis had no place to go other than to other banks under equivalent pressure to obtain needed funds.

What was sorely needed was a *central bank*—an institution in a position to make added reserve funds available to commercial banks in need, without draining funds from other banks. A "lender of last resort" to which the individual commercial banks or the banking system as a whole could turn was a vital necessity.

An Inefficient Check Collection System.   A fourth significant problem of the pre–Federal Reserve days was the extremely inefficient check collection system employed. Completed collection of checks written on out-of-town banks often took a week or more.

---

[6]Ibid., pp. 9–10.

The procedure was often quite complicated. Smaller banks normally kept reserve and clearing balances on deposit at a "correspondent" commercial bank in a nearby large city. When a check written on a bank in another city was deposited, the recipient bank would normally send it to its correspondent for collection. If it happened that the big-city correspondent bank also held a clearing balance for the bank on which the check was written the process was simple: the clearing balance of one was increased and that of the other was decreased. But if, as was more often the case, the bank on which the check was written had clearing balances at a different correspondent bank, more complicated and more time-consuming methods were necessary.

Contributing greatly to the problem was the then-common practice of many banks of deducting an *exchange charge* from the face value of all checks presented against them through the mails from out-of-town banks. Suppose, for example, that Mr. Jones wrote a $100 check on Bank X, payable to Mrs. Smith, who deposited it in Bank Y in a different city. Bank Y would then send the check in (through its big-city correspondent) for collection from Bank X. If the check were presented to Bank X by another bank in the same city, no exchange charge could be deducted. If, however, the check were received through the mails, from an out-of-town bank, Bank X might pay up only $99, keeping the $1 as an exchange charge, ostensibly to reimburse it for the cost and trouble of settling through the mails.

Naturally, banks with checks to be collected found it in their interest to seek means of avoiding the deduction of exchange charges. As one way to avoid them was to find a correspondent bank located in the same city as the payee bank, great efforts were made to do so. This sometimes meant a check would go through 6 or 8 or even 10 banks before completing the clearing process.

It was certainly an inefficient system, and one of the first actions of the Federal Reserve was to set up its own check collection facilities and to deny their use for checks written on banks that deducted exchange charges.

Although the nation suffered from these four problems for a number of years, it took the severe financial panic of 1907 to call forth positive steps toward fundamental reform. That experience led to a stopgap measure in 1908, the Aldrich-Vreeland Act, which set up, in turn, an important study group, the National Monetary Commission. Five years later, after much debate, the deliberations of the commission provided the basis for the Federal Reserve Act. We shall postpone consideration of that act and the central bank it set up until Chapter 7. Let us now take a closer look at the nature of the commercial banking business.

The Balance Sheet of a "Typical" Commercial Bank

Table 5-2 depicts a consolidated balance sheet for all commercial banks in the United States as of September 30, 1982. We shall use this picture of the entire banking system to get some feel for what a commercial bank does and for the

TABLE 5-2

Consolidated Balance Sheet for All U.S. Commercial Banks, September 30, 1982
(millions of dollars)

Assets		
Currency and coins		$ 19,194
Deposits at other U.S. banks		31,724
Federal Reserve account		21,250
Loans, total		1,094,389
Commercial and industrial	372,135	
Real estate	295,313	
Consumer	188,152	
Brokers, dealers, financial institutions	80,693	
Federal funds sold and repurchase agreements	90,580	
All others	67,516	
Securities, total		349,470
U.S. government[a]	180,195	
State and local government	149,425	
Other	19,850	
All other assets		257,758
Total assets		$1,773,785
Liabilities and Capital Accounts		
Demand deposits, total		$ 338,108
Individuals and businesses	271,678	
U.S. government	2,261	
State and local governments	14,651	
All other	49,518	
Savings deposits		231,128
Time deposits		752,505
Individuals and businesses	648,464	
State and local governments	66,794	
Other	37,247	
Borrowings		211,045
All other liabilities		114,576
Capital accounts		126,423
Total liabilities and capital accounts		$1,773,785

[a]Includes $68.8 billion of U.S. agency securities.

Source: Federal Reserve Statistical Release E.3.4, January 28, 1983.

relative importance of the various assets and liabilities to an "average" or "typical" commercial bank in this country.

One can obtain a superficial understanding of the basic nature of the commercial banking business simply by examining Table 5-2. Aside from their capital accounts and a limited amount of borrowing, commercial bank funds are raised by the issuance of two major liabilities—demand deposits and time and saving deposits.

From the individual banker's point of view, demand deposit liabilities have the advantage of requiring payment of no explicit interest to their owners, but the disadvantage of being legally payable in cash at the demand of the account holders or transferable by check at any time to anyone else.[7] Thus the main attraction of demand deposits to their owners—their perfect liquidity—represents a constant threat to the banker issuing them. He must at all times be prepared to pay out whatever amount of cash the owners choose to withdraw or transfer to another bank. For if at any time he is unable to do so, his bank can legally be closed.

Time and saving deposits are a more costly source of funds to the banker in that they do call for explicit interest payment to their owners. As we have seen, although the law requires bankers to reserve the right to withhold payment on regular savings accounts for up to 14 days, the waiting period is almost universally waived, making savings accounts almost as severe a liquidity constraint on commercial bankers as are checking accounts. Time deposits, on the other hand—especially certificates of deposit—can only be cashed in before their maturity dates if an interest penalty of some significance is paid. They therefore constitute slightly less of a withdrawal threat.

The exceptional degree of liquidity of their prime sources of funds distinguishes commercial banks from most other financial institutions and, rather obviously, involves a severe constraint on their use. Turning to the asset side of Table 5-2, it should not be surprising that commercial banks hold a much larger percentage of their assets in cash or near-cash form than the institutions considered in the preceding chapter. In September 1982, their *primary reserves*—the sum of their vault cash, checking accounts at other commercial banks, and checking accounts at district Federal Reserve banks—totaled $72,168 million, just over 4 percent of their assets.

Although these primary reserves are large in comparison with other financial institutions, when compared with commercial bank demand liabilities they are less impressive. In 1982, for example, they constituted less than one-quarter of demand deposits outstanding and less than 6 percent of total deposit liabilities. Clearly, the strongest of banks had nowhere near enough cash on hand to meet withdrawal demands had *all* its depositors chosen to demand payment at the same time.

Were the commercial banks therefore skating on thin ice in 1982 when these data were collected? By no means. Although the law requires payment of cash on demand to demand deposit owners, relatively few people exercise the privilege at any one time. A significant part of the art of commercial banking consists of knowing the habits of depositors (and the law) sufficiently well to keep the bank's primary reserve portion of its assets down to the minimum possible levels. For primary reserves, essential though they are for meeting the bank's liquidity re-

---

[7]Commercial banks have been forbidden by law from paying explicit interest on demand deposits since the 1930s. However, a sizable amount of implicit interest has been paid to checking account owners, primarily in the form of free services.

And, since the legalization of NOW accounts, the "prohibition" of interest on checking accounts is of little significance.

quirements, are nonincome-earning assets. And as private business concerns, commercial banks are understandably interested in putting all the assets they can into income-earning form.

The two basic types of *earning assets* of a commercial bank are loans and securities. In 1982, approximately 80 percent of bank assets were earning assets. We shall have more to say on this topic shortly. For the moment, let us simply note that a sizable amount of these—especially the $180 billion worth of U.S. government securities—are held partly as a sort of second line of defense against the possibility of unexpectedly large cash withdrawals (or losses to other banks). Assets held for this purpose are called *secondary reserves*. Although they normally yield somewhat lower interest returns than other earning assets, U.S. securities have the virtue of being quickly salable for cash should the amount of primary reserves on hand prove to be insufficient.

The Use of the T-account

One all but indispensable tool in the study of commercial banks is the T-account, and, as we shall rely upon it heavily in future chapters, the student should take pains to see that he or she understands it thoroughly.

A T-account is intended to reflect the change in a bank's (or in the banking system's) balance sheet as a result of a single transaction. It is, of course, not the only way to show this. One could, by depicting a full balance sheet before, and a full balance sheet after, a transacton, accomplish the same purpose. And we shall, in some cases, use this more time-consuming method. But in most situations the T-account is preferable, and we shall employ it extensively in this section.

A few examples should reveal the nature of this important tool. Suppose that Bank A, initially, is in the position reflected here:

Initial Balance Sheet of Bank A
(thousands of dollars)

Cash	$ 100	Demand deposits	$4,000
Deposits at other banks	1,000	Time deposits	2,100
Loans	3,000		
Securities	2,000		

Now we are concerned with showing the effects of a single transaction on Bank A's balance sheet. Suppose, for example, that a depositor places $100 cash in his checking account. We could reflect the result of this transaction in either of two ways—by laboriously making up an entirely new balance sheet to incorporate the changes caused by the deposit or by using a T-account.

If we take the long way around, we would construct a balance sheet like the following:

Balance Sheet of Bank A After $100 Cash Deposit
(thousands of dollars)

Cash	$ 200	Demand deposits	$4,100
Deposits at other banks	1,000	Time deposits	2,100
Loans	3,000		
Securities	2,000		

If we want to show the same thing in the simpler form of a T-account, however, we have simply

Bank A

Cash	+ $100	Demand deposits	+ $100

Note that in a T-account, only the asset or liability accounts affected by the transaction are written down, and each is accompanied by a plus or a minus sign to indicate whether the account was increased or decreased. Since a T-account shows changes in a bank's balance sheet, it must be balanced itself, with equal pluses (or minuses) on opposite sides, or with offsetting plus-minus entries on the same side.

To solidify the idea of the T-account and to provide some practice for the reader before we get to some more complicated uses, the following additional examples may be of some benefit.

1. Depositor withdraws $100 cash from his checking account in Bank A.

Bank A

Cash	− $100	Demand deposits	− $100

2. Bank A purchases a $100 U.S. security from a customer, paying the seller in cash.

Bank A

Cash	− $100		
U.S. securities	+ $100		

3. Bank A makes a $100 loan to a borrower, granting the proceeds in the form of an addition to his checking account.

Bank A

Loans	+ $100	Demand deposits	+ $100

4. A depositor at Bank A writes a $100 check on his checking account and deposits it in his time deposit at Bank A.

Bank A

		Demand deposits	− $100
		Time deposits	+ $100

5. Bank A borrows $100 of reserves from its Federal Reserve bank.

Bank A

Federal Reserve account	+ $100	Borrowings (notes payable)	+ $100

6. A borrower from Bank A pays back a $100 loan from the bank by writing a check on his account there.

Bank A

Loans	− $100	Demand deposits	− $100

The Business of Commercial Banking

Much of our ensuing consideration of commercial banks will center on the activities and control of the banking system as a whole, as this more "global" approach seems the relevant one for our purposes. We would, however, be remiss if we were to turn directly to the subject of the control of the banking system without at least some preliminary comments on the banking business, as such, from the individual banker's vantage point.

Commercial banking, more so than many businesses, is an art that requires a peculiar blend of experience, insight, intelligence, and prudence. It is an exacting profession that requires successful practitioners to satisfy not only their own stockholders and depositors but also an imposing network of governmental regulatory agencies, as well as a general public that often looks with a jaundiced eye upon the caretaker of "other people's money." In no other business is a public image of integrity and prudence of greater importance.

At the risk of oversimplifying the problems confronting bankers, their primary responsibility might be viewed as maintaining a careful balance among *solvency, liquidity,* and *profitability.* This is a task of no small magnitude because, as is so often the case, there are inherent conflicts among the three objectives.

A bank is *solvent* if, given time, it can convert its assets into sufficient cash to meet at least all its outstanding liabilities. *Liquidity,* however, requires that it be able to pay cash *immediately,* when called upon to do so, for all of its demand liabilities. It is this latter requirement that forces the commercial banker into a pattern of portfolio management that is notably different from that of the other financial institutions. Although other institutions often *do* pay on demand, only commercial banks are faced with a preponderance of liabilities that are *legally* payable on the demand of the holder.

It should be made clear that a bank may be perfectly solvent without being sufficiently liquid. Given several weeks or months in which to dispose of its assets in an orderly fashion, it may be able to raise more than enough cash to meet all its liabilities. But the liquidity problem is a different kind of constraint. Claims for cash by its demand depositors must be met in full *immediately*, not within several weeks or months. And a bank that is perfectly solvent, in the sense that it could in time pay off all claimants, could easily be forced to close its doors because of illiquidity—inability to honor its promise to pay cash *on demand* to any checking account owner.

The third requirement, *profitability*, introduces new complications. Certainly a bank can maintain its solvency by purchasing only the safest of financial assets. At the same time it must make sure that a sufficient number of these safe assets are also liquid enough, that is, quickly convertible into a fairly fixed amount of cash, to meet the likely demand for cash. But it is precisely these assets, the safest and most liquid, that will earn the bank the lowest rates of return. After all, the safest, most liquid asset of all is cash, but a bank that held a portfolio composed entirely of cash would earn no income whatever and would quickly disappear from the scene.

The commercial banker, therefore, must walk a narrow line. He must balance his asset portfolio in such a way as to satisfy all three basic requirements. This is an essential part of the skill, the knowledge, the central art of banking.

The Task of Asset Management

Given a certain amount of funds, how does the commercial banker go about deciding how to use them? How, that is, does he distribute those funds among the assets available to him so as to assure his firm of adequate profits along with liquidity and solvency? The question is a complex one, and, as Table 5-3 makes abundantly clear, the proportions of assets held in different forms have changed greatly over the years.

In 1947, shortly after World War II, commercial banks held an astonishing 64 percent of their assets in the form of primary and secondary reserves! Thirty-five years later, in 1982, that percentage had dropped to 14. In 1947, the security

TABLE 5-3

Percentage of Total Commercial Bank Assets Held
in Various Forms, 1947 and 1982

	1947	*1982*
Primary reserves	19%	4%
Securities, total	50	20
U.S. securities	45	10
Loans, total	25	62

Source: Computed from data from *Federal Reserve Bulletin.*

portion of earning assets was twice as large as commercial bank loan portfolios; by 1982 loans were three times as large as securities.

Which pattern of asset management is more "typical" for commercial banks, the 1947 pattern or the 1982 pattern? No doubt neither is truly typical, but there are sound grounds for arguing that the 1982 distribution was closer to the long-run mean. The year 1947 was atypical in a number of respects. During the depression of the 1930s and World War II, there had been relatively little private demand for credit compared with the enormous needs of the federal government. Consequently, commercial banks came out of the period with their portfolios overstocked with U.S. securities. In addition, exceptionally high legal reserve requirements and painful memories of the bank panic during the 1930s combined to keep primary reserves at abnormally high levels during the late 1940s.

Although changing circumstances inevitably alter the patterns of bank asset management over the years, the following generalizations would appear to be reasonably safe in describing the climate of the early 1980s.

Assuring Liquidity.   The first priority is to guarantee adequate liquidity. As we have seen, this means committing a certain proportion of assets to the nonincome-earning, primary reserve category and a certain proportion to the highly liquid, but relatively low-yielding, form of secondary reserves—U.S. government securities.

Once adequate liquidity has been established, the banker is free to turn toward the more agreeable job of maximizing profits. In 1982, as Table 5-2 shows, this consisted primarily of making over $372 billion of loans to business, over $295 billion to finance the purchase of real estate, and over $150 billion each for loans to consumers and the purchase of state and local government securities.

The Loan Portfolio.   Once liquidity considerations have been taken into account, one might reasonably expect commercial banks to turn to the highest-yielding assets consistent with legal restrictions and the minimization of default risk. Why, then, are business loans, which often yield a stated return somewhat lower than mortgages and consumer loans, still the dominant asset in commercial bank portfolios?

There are several sound reasons for this. In the first place, commercial banks are almost unique in their suitability for serving the local business loan market. Most commercial banks are one-office, local institutions geared to specialize in loans to local business. They, better than almost any other lender, are in a position of knowing the credit needs of their locality. They, perhaps more so than any other lenders, feel it their purview—indeed, their responsibility—to fill those needs.

But there are sounder reasons than mere tradition for their concentration on business loans. Business firms typically keep their checking accounts at those banks that take care of their credit needs and these accounts are a most important source of funds for the bank.[8]

---

[8]As of June 1982 the nonfinancial business sector held over 50 percent of the outstanding demand deposits at commercial banks.

In fact, it is a common practice for banks making such loans to require the borrower to maintain what is generally referred to as a *compensating balance* in its checking account as a precondition for granting the loan. For example, business borrowers are commonly required to maintain a checking account balance in the neighborhood of 10 percent of their unused credit line and 15 percent of the amount borrowed.[9] The effect of such a requirement, of course, is to increase the effective yield on the loan well above the stated interest rate charged because the borrower is required to pay interest on the full amount of the loan even though he cannot use it all.

In recent decades, real estate and consumer loans have been competing with the business loan for space in the commercial bank loan portfolio. Increasing commitments in these areas, the latter greatly enhanced by the widespread adoption of bank credit card plans with a national interchange, have provided healthy diversification in commercial bank portfolios and seem destined to continue.[10]

The Securities Portfolio.   Commercial bank security portfolios, as noted, consist almost entirely of securities issued by the federal government and those issued by state and local governments.

Because they are the most liquid of all the earning assets, U.S. securities are held primarily as a secondary reserve, even though their interest yield is less than that of most loans. In addition, U.S. securities serve an important role as acceptable collateral for commercial bank borrowing from the Federal Reserve banks as well as required security for the acquisition of government demand deposits.[11]

Although, as noted in Table 5-3, U.S. securities equaled almost half of commercial bank assets immediately after World War II, they have fallen off steadily over the years. This decline represents, in large part, a return to more usual portfolio practices as the abnormal accumulation of governments acquired during that war have been replaced by loans. It reflects also the development of newer, more attractive sources of short-term funds, such as the federal funds market for liquidity purposes. Clearly, U.S. securities currently seem to represent a "second-choice" asset, since they tend to rise only in periods where bank reserves are plentiful and the demand for loans has fallen off.

State and local government securities, on the other hand, constituted a rapidly growing proportion of commercial bank assets—at least prior to the 1980s. First, the interest earned on these "municipals" is exempt from federal taxation. To

---

[9]For an interesting discussion of recent practice in this area, see Henry G. Hamel and Francis J. Walsh, Jr., *Commercial Banking Arrangements* (New York: The Conference Board, 1968).

[10]A useful account of the extent of credit card plans is provided in "Credit-Card and Check-Credit Plans at Commercial Banks," *Federal Reserve Bulletin,* September 1973.

[11]See Thomas E. Davis, "Bank Holdings of U.S. Government Securities," *Monthly Review,* Federal Reserve Bank of Kansas City, July/August 1971.

commercial banks they therefore represent an important means of lowering the burden of the corporate income tax.[12] Indeed, the evidence is clear that state and local securities have been the most important mechanism for tax avoidance employed by commercial banks in recent years.[13]

Tax avoidance, however, is not the sole reason that commercial banks have expanded their portfolios of municipals. Commercial banks look upon it as something of an obligation to support area governments and generally will at least offer a bid on new issues. Such support, of course, is not entirely unrelated to the banks' desire to attract state and local government deposits. Second, as commercial banks are authorized to underwrite and deal in general obligation issues of state and local governments, those who do are in a strategic position to acquire attractive offerings for their own account. Finally, as the supply of municipals has increased, the secondary market for them—the market in which they may be resold before maturity—has improved substantially. This, of course, has made them much more liquid than they were previously.

Since the early 1970s, however, the commercial bank appetite for state and local government obligations appears to have tailed off somewhat, as indicated by the fact that from 1971 to 1982, municipals as a fraction of total commercial bank assets declined from a high of 13 percent to about 8 percent. One of the reasons for this decline is that banks are currently making fuller use of such alternative tax-avoidance devices as leasing operations and foreign tax credits.[14]

The Task of Liability Management

For many years commercial banks were relatively passive about the acquisition of funds. Of course they made the obvious efforts to attract demand and time deposits, but most of the "business of banking" was viewed as properly allocating the funds available among competing assets.

This rather passive approach to the liability side of their balance sheets was possible and perhaps even appropriate in the first decade and a half after World War II. For during that period, demand deposits constituted a very large part of

---

[12]For interesting discussions of financial institution tax-avoidance techniques, see Ralph C. Kimball, "Commercial Banks, Tax Avoidance, and the Market for State and Local Debt Since 1970," *New England Economic Review*, Federal Reserve Bank of Boston, January–February 1977; and Margaret E. Bedford, "Federal Taxation of Financial Institutions," *Monthly Review*, Federal Reserve Bank of Kansas City, June 1976. See also Bedford, Income Taxation of Commercial Banks," *Monthly Review*, Federal Reserve Bank of Kansas City, July–August 1975.

[13]It is interesting to note that via this and other tax-avoidance measures (as well as some changes in tax laws), commercial banks managed to reduce their federal taxes from over 30 percent of their net incomes in the 1950s to below 15 percent in 1975. Over the same period, changes in tax laws applying to savings and loan associations and mutual savings banks have raised their liabilities sharply. Indeed, in 1975, savings and loan associations paid a substantially higher percentage of net income to the federal government than did the commercial banks.

[14]See Bedford, "Income Taxation of Commercial Banks."

financial assets held by business, and bank portfolios were sufficiently overstocked with U.S. securities to permit the financing of much of the expanding private demand for credit by unloading them.

By 1960, however, it was clear that commercial banks were failing to attract funds at a rate commensurate with the rest of the economy. Increasing sophistication and response to generally rising interest rates by corporate financial managers had led them to sharply reduce their holdings of demand deposits. Time deposits, on the other hand, were expanding rapidly, and commercial banks were falling behind, relative to the other financial institutions, in attracting them. To combat this development the commercial banks launched a massive and innovative campaign, beginning during the 1960s, to attract a larger share of the funds available. They did it by more extensive use of existing sources of funds, by developing new liability instruments with which to attract funds, and by competing vigorously, on a price basis, to attract a larger share. This effort has come to be called *liability management.*

Liability management has featured the development and refinement of a number of money market instruments discussed earlier. These include the broadening of the federal funds market, the borrowing of Eurodollars, and the development of the negotiable certificate of deposit and repurchase agreement, among others. This much more aggressive approach to commercial bank management has continued right on into the mid-1980s.[15]

Review Questions

1. Identify the First and Second Banks of the United States.
2. Discuss the problems with the nation's banking system that led to passage of the National Bank Act of 1863.
3. Identify the three main provisions of the National Bank Act of 1863 and then discuss the four major deficiencies of the act.
4. Identify "exchange charges" and explain how their widespread use under the National Bank Act of 1863 affected the check collection process.
5. "The exceptional degree of liquidity of their prime sources of funds distinguishes commercial banks from most other financial institutions and involves a severe restraint on their use." Explain.

---

[15]Evidence of this continued aggressiveness includes an attempt, in late 1982, to induce state banking authorities to authorize state-chartered banks to issue "Super-NOW" accounts on which interest rates comparable to those paid by money market funds were offered on amounts beyond a certain minimum balance. Although declared illegal by the FDIC, the state of South Dakota authorized such accounts in 1982 with the explicit intent of permitting banks to compete more effectively with money market funds in attracting deposits. These individual state efforts became moot, however, when the Depository Institutions Deregulation Committee authorized Super-NOW accounts nationwide in January, 1983.

6. Distinguish
   a. A T-account from a balance sheet.
   b. Liquidity from solvency.
   c. Primary reserves from secondary reserves.
   d. Asset management from liability management.
7. What are "compensating balances"? How might they affect the interest cost of a loan?
8. What are several reasons why commercial banks are heavy purchasers of state and local government securities?

6

Over the years it has become customary to characterize the U.S. commercial banking system as unique in two important respects. First, it is a *dual banking system* wherein some banks are chartered and regulated by state governments while others are chartered and regulated by the federal government.[1] Second, it is often described as a *unit banking system,* composed of many individual, one-office banks, rather than a few mammoth banking companies controlling extensive, nationwide systems of branch offices. Let us consider these two aspects of the nation's banking system in turn.

A Dual Banking System

As noted in the preceding chapter, there are strong grounds for the belief that Congress's real purpose in levying a 10 percent tax on the issuance of state bank notes as part of the National Bank Act of 1863 was the elimination of state-chartered banks themselves. If so, as Table 6-1 makes clear, the effort failed.

Immediately after passage of the National Bank Act, the number of state banks in existence fell off precipitously. Within 10 years, however, saved from extinction by the public's widespread adoption of the checking habit, they began an impressive comeback. Before the turn of the century, state-chartered banks once again outnumbered national banks, and by 1920, they numbered well over 20,000. Although the number of national banks also grew rapidly through the early 1920s, they reached their high watermark at a level less than half that of state banks. Even

---

[1] Our discussion will omit reference to the 14 unincorporated so-called "private banks" that remained in existence in 1977. New unincorporated banks are now illegal in all states.

TABLE 6-1

Number of State and National Commercial Banks in the United States, 1860–1980

Year	State Banks	National Banks	Total
1860	1,562	—	1,562
1865	349	1,294	1,643
1870	325	1,612	1,937
1875	586	2,076	2,662
1880	650	2,076	2,726
1885	1,015	2,689	3,704
1890	2,250	3,484	5,734
1895	4,369	3,715	8,084
1900	5,007	3,731	8,738
1905	9,018	5,664	14,682
1910	14,348	7,138	21,486
1915	17,748	7,597	25,345
1920	20,635	8,024	28,659
1925	19,573	8,066	27,639
1930	15,798	7,247	23,045
1935	9,752	5,425	15,177
1940	9,181	5,164	14,345
1945	8,994	5,017	14,011
1950	9,163	4,958	14,121
1955	9,024	4,692	13,716
1960	8,942	4,530	13,472
1965	8,989	4,815	13,804
1970	9,066	4,620	13,686
1975	9,888	4,744	14,632
1980	10,411	4,425	14,836

Source: Federal Reserve System, *Annual Statistical Digest,* various issues.

though the total number of commercial banks has fallen off sharply since that time, state banks continue to outnumber national banks by over two to one.

One can, however, reach erroneous conclusions about the importance of state banks in the current banking scene by considering the number of banks alone. Despite the numerical dominance of state banks, the national banks are, on the average, much larger. The result, as is evident in Table 6-2, is that national banks

TABLE 6-2

National and State Banks, Number of Banks and Deposits, December 31, 1982

	National	State
Number of banks	4,579	9,857
Percentage of banks	32%	68%
Value of deposits	$779.1 billion	$614.6 billion
Percentage of total commercial bank deposits	56%	44%

Source: *Federal Reserve Bulletin.*

currently control nearly 60 percent of the total deposits at all U.S. commercial banks.

"Why," one might reasonably ask, "should the United States have a dual banking system anyway?" What advantage can there possibly be in maintaining two entirely different sets of regulatory agencies with different standards for chartering as well as for supervision?

One defender of the dual banking system puts it this way:

> Critics of the dual banking system sometimes regard it as little more than an arrangement under which commercial banks seek to play off one supervisory authority against another—or to escape strict regulation implemented at either level—and thereby to derive advantages which other highly regulated industries do not have.
>
> Such a criticism ignores the fact that the historic value of dual banking lies in its ability to provide an escape valve from arbitrary or discriminatory chartering and regulatory policies at either the state or Federal level. The possible intrusion of such inequities into either the chartering of banks or their regulation, with consequent implications for the allocation of credit among prospective borrowers, is an eventuality against which the strongest public safeguards should be erected.[2]

Critics of the system, on the other hand, see the dual banking system as an outmoded relic from the nation's past whose continued existence is explainable only on grounds of legislative inertia and the political power of states and state-chartered banks. In their view, protection for depositors, equity as between banks, and the nation's economic welfare would all be better served by subjecting all commercial banks in the nation to a common set of federal government standards.

A Unit Banking System

Another distinguishing characteristic of the U.S. commercial banking system is the fact that it is primarily made up of many single-office, "unit" banks, rather than the small group of vast branch systems typical in many other countries. It is not at all uncommon elsewhere for a mere handful of banking companies, each with hundreds of branches throughout the country, to dominate the entire nation's banking system. England, for example, has fewer than two dozen banks and, of them, 5 do most of the banking business. Canada, our closest neighbor, operates with a total of 11 domestic chartered banks to serve the whole dominion.[3] In sharp contrast, about 8,000 of the 14,836 U.S. commercial banks in operation on December 31, 1981, had no branches at all, and the average number of branches per banking company for the nation as a whole was just over two and one-half per bank!

---

[2]William J. Brown, *The Dual Banking System in the United States* (New York: American Bankers Association, 1968), p. 59.

[3]Under the 1980 Bank Act, a number of foreign banks have also received charters to do business in Canada.

The major reason for the limited development of branch banking and the resultant decentralized U.S. commercial banking industry is legislative restriction. At the state level, many states, especially those in the Midwest, have either forbidden branching altogether or have allowed it on only a limited basis. At the federal level, two laws—the *McFadden Act* and the *Douglas Amendment* to the Bank Holding Company Act of 1956—have, for many years, more or less effectively barred interstate banking. The McFadden Act requires national banks to adhere to the branching laws of the state in which their home office is located. The Douglas Amendment prohibits holding companies from owning more than 5 percent of the stock of a bank in a different state unless the legislature of the host state specifically authorizes it.

This legislative antipathy to the development of branch banking in the United States is rooted in our national heritage. Decentralization has long been considered a major virtue in economic life, for good or ill, and no potential concentration of power has been more feared by the American people and their representatives than that of the financial community—the "money lenders."

But although legislative prohibition has limited the development of branch banking and molded our banking system into a unique, many-firm industry, it would be a mistake to conclude from this that the American banking industry is a real-world model of the economist's textbook version of pure competition. Let us turn now to consider the structure of the U.S. commercial banking industry in more detail.

Concentration in the U.S. Commercial Banking Industry

Just how competitive is the U.S. banking system? Numbers alone shed little light on the issue. What had been a banking system of over 30,000 banks in 1921 had shrunk, largely as a result of failures in the 1920s and 1930s, to about 14,000 by 1940. It has fluctuated around that level ever since.

Now 14,000 firms in a single industry is an enormous number by almost any standard. It is far more than most other countries have. And, in comparison with other large industries in the United States, it is an equally impressive number. But the degree of competitiveness in an industry depends also on such matters as the size distribution within the industry and the size of the market within which competition can be effective. On both these grounds, the U.S. commercial banking system is less atomistic than the 14,000-firm figure might imply.

As is clear from Table 6-3, a relatively few large banks dominate the industry. For example, in 1982 the 164 largest banks, constituting only 1.6 percent of the nation's insured commercial banks, held almost half the deposits of the entire system! At the other end of the spectrum, we find the smallest 50 percent of the banks—those with total assets of less than $25 million—held just over 7 percent

TABLE 6-3

Size Distribution of Insured U.S. Commercial Banks, June 30, 1982

Size Class (value of assets)	Number of Banks	Percentage of Banks	Percentage of Total Deposits Held
$1,000 billion or more	164	1.6%	45.6%
$500 billion to $999.9 billion	152	1.6	8.0
$100 billion to $499.9 billion	1,269	8.8	18.6
$50 billion to $99.9 billion	1,989	13.8	10.6
$25 billion to $49.9 billion	3,616	25.0	9.9
$10 billion to $24.9 billion	4,644	32.1	6.0
$0 to $9.9 billion	2,601	17.1	1.3

Source: Banks and Branches Data Book, June 30, 1982, Federal Deposit Insurance Corporation.

of the deposits. Clearly within this industry there are significant differences in size and economic clout.

National data such as these, however, shed relatively little light on the degree of competition within the banking industry for the simple reason that the relevant market for many of the services of commercial banks is essentially local. It matters little that there are over 14,000 banks unless something can be said about the extent to which they compete directly with one another in the attraction of deposits and the making of loans.

What evidence do we have regarding the degree of competitiveness of the industry in this more specific, localized sense? One could show, for example, that in most metropolitan areas in the United States, three banks control a majority of the total deposits. And one might also present evidence showing a sizable number of "one-bank" towns in this country. But such evidence, while not without interest, fails to reflect the equally significant impact of such structural factors as the degree of branch banking and the extent of bank holding companies. And it also overlooks entirely the growing competition from the thrift institutions for the "one-stop" banking business, which used to be almost the sole preserve of commercial banks.[4]

Branch Banking

As noted, the McFadden Act, which required national banks to observe the branching restrictions of the state in which they were located, has long been considered the major barrier to the spread of branch banking in the United States. For

---

[4]There are those who would argue that the spread of checking account authority and the liberalization of thrift institution portfolio regulations have all but wiped out the commercial banking industry as an identifiable group of firms offering a common and unique bundle of services. Such a position implies that we should now consider all the depository institutions as the "industry" and measure competitiveness accordingly.

since no state had the power to authorize banking in another state, the effect of the McFadden Act was to outlaw interstate branching.

Within state borders, sharp differences are discernible. State laws run the gamut from outright prohibition of any branch banking to the privilege of statewide branching. As of June 30, 1982, 22 states permitted statewide branching, 19 permitted limited branching (such as within a city, within a county, or within contiguous counties), while 9 states forbade branching altogether. States on the West Coast and along the Eastern Seaboard typically permit statewide branching; the majority of the unit banking states, on the other hand, are located near the middle of the nation.

For many years the trend has consistently been toward more liberal branching laws, and there is little doubt that it will continue. Evidence to this effect includes the fact that, whereas in 1960 only 16 states permitted statewide branching and 18 allowed no branching at all, by 1982 the statewide branching total had grown to 22 while the number of unit banking states had declined to 9. The number of branches in operation increased from less than 4,000 at the end of World War II to over 40,000 by the beginning of 1982.

How might we evaluate the trend toward more extensive branch banking in the United States? The alleged advantages of a branch operation over a one-unit bank are rather obvious. If a bank is allowed to become larger, it can obtain certain economies of scale in its operation.[5] In addition, branches can offer small communities some banking services that self-sufficient unit banks cannot afford. Finally, diversification permitted by branching enhances the safety of the bank.

It is not possible to settle the issue of branch versus unit banks here. Certainly our experience with the failure rate of very small unit banks argues persuasively for "large" banks. But the advantages of size, as such, and of branch structure must be distinguished. We face here the same type of dilemma as is faced by our antitrust authorities—how far should we go in sacrificing the advantages of size and diversity to combat the disadvantages of concentration? Nonetheless, it seems evident that most experts would look favorably upon a further extension of branch banking.

Commercial Bank Holding Companies

The fact that 9 states prohibit branch banking entirely may well lead to the conclusion that in these states, at least, concentration of control over the banking industry is minimal. Such a conclusion, however, would be unwarranted because

---

[5]The quantitative importance of these advantages, at least for very large banks, is doubted by some. It is also argued that the branch bank structure, as distinct from size itself, has certain offsetting disadvantages. See P. M. Horvitz, "Economies of Scale in Banking," *Private Financial Institutions* (Englewood Cliffs, N.J.: Prentice-Hall, 1963). For more recent views on the same topic, see Alan S. McCall, "Economies of Scale, Operating Efficiencies and the Organizational Structure of Commercial Banks," *Journal of Bank Research,* Summer 1980. See, also, Stephen Mathis and Thomas Ulrich, "Small Business Credit: The Competitive Factor," *The Bankers Magazine,* January–February 1982.

FIGURE 6-1 Percentage of Commercial Banking Deposits Held by Multibank Holding Companies

Source: Federal Reserve Bulletin, February 1982, p. 81.

in many of the unit banking states, the holding company device provides a degree of concentration of control comparable to that in many branch banking states. Indeed, of the unit banking states, only 4—Kansas, Nebraska, Oklahoma, and West Virginia—are without significant concentration via the multibank holding company device.[6] This fact is illustrated in Figure 6-1.[7]

The holding company device has a long history in the United States commercial banking industry, but it was of relatively little significance until the late 1960s. The basic law under which the federal government controls bank holding companies is the Bank Holding Company Act of 1956. Under that law, the Board of Governors of the Federal Reserve System was granted the power to regulate bank holding companies. It explicitly exempted one-bank holding companies from regulation and—via the aforementioned Douglas Amendment—made it illegal for a holding company to control a bank in a different state,

---

[6]For an excellent review see Donald T. Savage, "Developments in Banking Structure, 1970–81," *Federal Reserve Bulletin*, February 1982.

[7]In interpreting Figure 6-1, it should be noted that Illinois passed a law authorizing multibank holding companies as recently as 1981.

unless the acquisition of such shares or assets of a State bank by an out-of-State bank holding company is specifically authorized by the statute laws of the State in which such bank is located.

Until recently, the Douglas Amendment has been about as effective in forbidding interstate banking via the holding company device as the McFadden Act has been in preventing interstate branching directly.

In 1956 there were a total of 53 multiple-bank holding companies, which controlled 428 banks possessing 7.5 percent of total commercial bank deposits. By 1965 those totals had increased only slightly—there were still 53 holding companies, and they then controlled 468 banks with just under 8 percent of total deposits. Beginning in 1966, however, multiple-bank holding companies entered into a period of very rapid growth, swelling their ranks—as of the end of 1981—to 407 holding company groups, controlling 2,607 banks and 38 percent of all commercial bank deposits. Much, but by no means all, of this growth represented an effort to "get around" the restrictions on branching imposed by unit banking and limited branching states.

But multibank holding companies were not the only ones showing remarkable growth during these years. One-bank holding companies also spread rapidly, starting in the late 1960s. In 1965, there were some 550 one-bank holding companies controlling only about 4.5 percent of the nation's deposits. By 1981, this had grown to 3,093 banks, controlling 36 percent of all deposits. Indeed, partly in reaction to this startling growth, Congress amended the Holding Company Act in 1970 to extend the Federal Reserve Board's control over one-bank holding companies as well as multibank companies.

One-bank holding companies have several advantages. First, they permit a holding company to engage in banking as well as in certain other related financial activities so long as the Board of Governors approves. Second, there are certain tax benefits to the one-bank holding company form. If at least 80 percent of the stock of the bank is owned by the holding company, the income of the bank that is subject to tax can be reduced by the amount of interest paid by the holding company on its debt.

Whatever the reasons, the dominance of the holding company device is a clear-cut fact in the 1980s, with holding companies (both one-bank and multibank) controlling about 75 percent of all commercial bank assets. On the surface, one might well assume that the effect of this rapid spread in bank holding companies would invariably be to increase the concentration of control in banking and therefore—in line with traditional monopoly theory—lead to increased prices and/or reduced services to the community. But this has by no means always occurred, as a number of studies have shown. Where a bank holding company opens a new bank or strengthens a small existing one because of acquisition, it may well result in *increased* competitiveness in an area, rather than the reverse. For example, in the opinion of one expert,

The holding company movement has increased competitiveness in banking, both at the national banking level and within numerous specific states (many more than those, *if* any, in which competitiveness may have been reduced). Indeed, much of the criticism of holding companies is an understandable reaction to the breaking down of anti-competitive state-line barriers. . . .[8]

Correspondent Banking

Another method of overcoming some of the limitations imposed by restrictive branching laws and obtaining some of the advantages of large-scale operation for small banks is the extensive use of correspondent banking arrangements. The correspondent banking system is less formal than the holding company approach and is sometimes credited with overcoming many of the alleged disadvantages of a unit banking structure.

For many years, smaller unit banks around the nation have maintained checking accounts in nearby large-city banks in return for a variety of vital services. This practice, of course, had a legal origin extending all the way back to the National Bank Act, under which smaller national banks were permitted to keep part of their required reserves on deposit in larger banks. And, although the legal reserve provisions of the National Bank Act have long since disappeared, even in the 1980s reserve requirements imposed by states on state-chartered (nonmember) banks have been met with deposits in other commercial banks.

Even in the absence of state reserve requirements, however, there is little doubt that the nation's smaller banks will continue to maintain sizable deposits at big-city correspondents. They benefit in a number of ways from such arrangements.

First, virtually all smaller banks clear nonlocal checks through their big-city correspondents. Although the Federal Reserve System offers check-clearing services to any bank willing to hold a deposit in a Federal Reserve bank, smaller banks generally prefer to rely on their big-city correspondents. This preference results from the following considerations: (1) big-city correspondent banks are often closer than the appropriate Federal Reserve facility, and (2) the requirements for sorting checks sent in for collection are generally less stringent at correspondent banks than at the Federal Reserve.

A second important service performed by big-city correspondent banks is loan participation. When a small country bank receives an application for an un-

---

[8]Roy A. Scholland, testimony before the House of Representatives Committee on Banking, Currency, and Housing, 94th Cong., 1st sess., December 8, 1975. On the bank holding company issue, see also David D. Whitehead and B. Frank King, "Multibank Holding Companies and Local Market Concentration," *Monthly Review,* Federal Reserve Bank of Atlanta, April 1976; and Dale S. Drum, "M.B.H.C.'s: Evidence After Two Decades of Regulation," *Business Conditions,* Federal Reserve Bank of Chicago, December 1976. The most thorough recent survey is Board of Governors of the Federal Reserve System, *The Bank Holding Company Movement to 1978: A Compendium* (Washington, D.C.: Federal Reserve System, 1978).

usually large loan, its big-city correspondent will often help out by taking on that portion of the loan that the smaller bank cannot handle. Sometimes, too, loan participation runs in the other direction.

In addition to check clearing and loan participation, big-city correspondent banks provide a wide range of other services for their smaller "respondents." These include reports on the state of the economy, advice on portfolio management, borrowing federal funds in small lots, arranging international transactions, sharing computer facilities, and a wide array of other activities.[9]

The Current Trend
Toward Interstate Banking

As this is being written, interstate banking—with the exception of those institutions already involved in it before restrictive laws were passed—is still essentially illegal. But there can be no doubt that full-scale interstate banking is just around the corner.

There are many forces pushing in this direction. In the first place, a not insignificant number of banks is already legally participating in interstate banking. These include holding companies involved in interstate banking before passage of the Douglas Amendment to the Bank Holding Company Act of 1956. They were permitted to continue via "grandfather" clauses in the law. The largest of these is the First Interstate Bancorporation, which operates in 11 western states and ranks in size among the 10 largest banks in the country. In addition, numerous foreign-owned banks also operate across state lines. Foreign banks were not subject to the McFadden Act prior to passage of the International Banking Act in 1978, and those already engaged in interstate banking prior to July 1978 were also "grandfathered."[10]

Other developments tipping the balance toward interstate banking are state laws regarding holding companies. As noted earlier, the Douglas Amendment permits a holding company to operate across state lines if the state to which it expands specifically authorizes it to do so. Until recently, only Maine authorized out-of-state bank holding companies to operate within its borders, but such authorization was limited to holding companies from states offering reciprocity to Maine holding companies.[11] Since no other state offered such reciprocity, until very recent legislation by New York, the Maine law has not had much impact. More recently,

---

[9]For an informative discussion of correspondent banking, see Robert E. Knight, "Correspondent Banking, Part I: Balances and Services," *Monthly Review,* Federal Reserve Bank of Kansas City, November 1970.

[10]On this and many other issues having to do with bank regulation, see the excellent publication by Carter H. Golembe and David S. Holland, *Federal Regulation of Banking* (Washington, D.C.: Golembe Associates, Inc., 1981).

[11]Iowa also has a law that permits one specific out-of-state holding company to operate there but since that company was operating there prior to 1956, its existence was "grandfathered" by the Bank Holding Company Act of 1956 in any case.

however, South Dakota (in 1980) and Delaware (in 1981) have passed laws inviting out-of-state bank holding companies in under specified conditions. Since a number of holding companies have already begun operations in these two states, it seems likely that other states may well "enter the competition" to attract out-of-state banks.

The trend toward interstate banking is also being helped along by growing acceptance of the notion that financial institutions in difficulty might often best be merged with stronger companies from other states. A notable example of this was the approval, in 1982, of a takeover by a New York commercial bank holding company of a troubled California savings and loan association. A clear signal that more such interstate mergers are to be expected was the explicit approval of them in the Depository Institutions Act of 1982 in cases where satisfactory intrastate mergers are not viable options.

But the real force that appears destined to break down the barriers against interstate banking is surely competition from less regulated rivals. For commercial banks and thrifts have not only been struggling from their battles with the money market funds—which have had the advantages of no reserve requirements, no Regulation Q ceilings, *and* no restrictions on interstate operations—but they are now being challenged by nonbank competitors operating on a nationwide scale.

A recent press report citing the potential effects of a legal loophole in the Bank Holding Company Act provides evidence of this phenomenon. That Act defines a commercial bank as an institution that "accepts deposits that the depositor has the legal right to withdraw on demand and engages in the business of making commercial loans." Interpreting this definition literally, it may be possible for a bank to practice all phases of banking except the making of commercial loans and thereby not be legally considered a bank for purposes of the Bank Holding Company Act. The implications of this for interstate banking are enormous. If an institution is not legally a bank as defined by the Bank Holding Company Act, the Douglas Amendment—which severely limits interstate banking via the holding company device—does not apply. And that opens the door wide to interstate banking.

According to the *American Banker*, "A broad array of companies, including a furniture store and Parker Pen Co., have used the loophole to purchase banks that have shed their commercial lending services."

"There have also been recent reports that a group of investors will ask the Comptroller of the Currency for permission to start a 26-state, 32 bank operation under the loophole."[12]

As Frederick Dean, Jr., chairman of a task force of the Association of Bank Holding Companies, has observed:

> Consider: *Sears* has 3,600 nationwide officers, thousands of EFT-access terminals, and extensive consumer and business credit mechanisms in place; the nation's largest

---

[12]"Volcker Hits Loophole Letting Commercial Firms Own Banks," *American Banker*, December 2, 1982.

credit base, and the capacity to provide funds transaction services and to gather "deposits" in the form of consumer debt notes. *Beneficial Finance* has 2,600 offices worldwide that already are linked electronically to grant credit; they can sell insurance; they can make both first and second mortgages; and they also possess the potentiality for funds transfer and funds gathering activity (indeed, in 26 states they have direct deposit-gathering authority, and in one—California—they exercise it to a limited degree). *Merrill Lynch* et al. are truly full service institutions parked on our doorsteps right now. They are nationwide and electronically linked.[13]

Given competition of this magnitude, further lifting of the barriers against interstate banking in the near future seems inevitable.

Regulation of Commercial Banks

For many years U.S. commercial banking has been subjected to a far more extensive and complex degree of governmental regulation than have most other industries. This should not be surprising; as the issuer of the bulk of the nation's money supply, the banking industry's soundness and success are almost indispensable prerequisites for the soundness of the economy itself.

Although the justification for special regulatory procedures in an industry so vital to the health of the entire economy seems self-evident, the appropriate specific form and direction of those regulations are often less clear. This has been the case partly because of differing notions as to how to ensure adequate competition in the industry and partly because of an apparent conflict between the measures needed to ensure safety and those required to promote efficiency.

As a recent presidential study commission puts it,

> The system did not evolve through happenstance. For well over a century the American public has insisted that its financial institutions be both competitive and sound. The two objectives are not easily reconciled, and yet both must be achieved if we are to avoid, on the one hand, a highly concentrated financial structure and, on the other, a system unable to withstand the vicissitudes of economic change. The public is entitled to the benefits of a dynamic and innovative system responsive to shifting needs. Yet the public also should be able to rely on the strength and soundness of the system.[14]

Who does the regulating and what is the purpose of specific regulatory measures? Let us consider these questions in turn.

---

[13]Quoted in Raoul D. Edwards, "Interstate Banking: The Debate Begins," *The Bankers Magazine,* September–October 1980, p. 68.

[14]*Report of the President's Commission on Financial Structure and Regulation* (Washington, D.C.: Government Printing Office, December 1971), p. 7.

Who Are the Regulators?

The four main commercial bank regulatory agencies are the Comptroller of the Currency, the Federal Reserve System, the Federal Deposit Insurance Corporation, and 50 state regulatory commissions. In addition, on questions of bank merger, consolidation, and holding company acquisitions, the U.S. Department of Justice often exercises its considerable antitrust authority.

The Comptroller of the Currency. The Office of the Comptroller of the Currency, as noted, was established more than a century ago as an integral part of the National Bank Act. Technically, the Comptroller's office is a part of the Treasury Department, but it operates pretty much as if it were an autonomous agency. The Comptroller himself for instance is appointed by the president to a five-year term from which, like the Board of Governors of the Federal Reserve, he may not be removed except for "cause."

Unlike the FRS and the FDIC, the Comptroller of the Currency operates strictly as a regulator—chartering national banks and examining and supervising those already chartered. The Fed, of course, is only a part-time regulator, being primarily occupied with the conduct of monetary policy. The FDIC, on the other hand, is a regulator only to the extent that its prime responsibility as an insurer demands it.

As a representative of the generally larger national banks, it should perhaps not be surprising that the Comptroller's office has tended to favor interstate banking and freer mergers while opposing such restrictions as the McFadden Act.[15] In these respects, the other regulations tend to differ markedly.[16]

The Federal Reserve System. The Federal Reserve System, about which we shall have much more to say in the next chapter, controls and supervises the activities of all commercial banks belonging to the system. As a matter of law, all national banks must join the Federal Reserve (thus making them subject to control by both the Comptroller of the Currency and the FRS). State banks may join the Federal Reserve System if they choose. The approximately 1,000 state banks that have chosen to join are thereby subjected to the regulatory power of both the FRS and the state banking agency in their state.

The Federal Deposit Insurance Corporation. The Federal Deposit Insurance Corporation was established in 1933 in the wake of the wholesale bank failures of the 1920s and early 1930s to offer insurance protection to depositors in any covered

---

[15]See Leonard Lapidus, *The Report of the Study of State and Federal Regulation of Commercial Banks* (Washington, D.C.: Federal Deposit Insurance Corporation, 1980), pp. 19–20.

[16]Ibid., p. 20.

bank or trust company receiving deposits. Membership in the FDIC requires a bank to pay an "insurance premium" based on the size of its deposits and to subject itself to the regulations and supervision of the corporation.[17] Included among the regulations are limits on the amount of loans to any one borrower, minimum capital-to-asset ratios, and a variety of restrictions on the type of assets considered acceptable.

Depositors in insured banks have their deposits insured up to $100,000 per deposit.[18] As of late 1982, 99 percent of the nation's banks with 99 percent of total deposits subscribed to FDIC protection. Indeed, all national banks and most state banks are required to subscribe. Because more than half the deposits are owned by businesses, however, many accounts exceed the $100,000 limit, and it is estimated that only about 70 percent of *deposits* are fully covered by the insurance.

The protection of individual depositors is the most obvious and visible effect of the FDIC's existence. But more fundamental from the social viewpoint is the vast improvement it has brought about in the condition of the banking system as a whole. There are two important aspects to this more basic achievement.

First, because of the corporation's regulatory requirements and supervisory activities, the preponderant majority of the nation's commercial banks are probably much safer than they might otherwise be. This is especially important because most of the nation's banks do not belong to the Federal Reserve System and, therefore, are not directly subject to that form of federal government regulation. The regulatory standards of the states vary widely, and it is fortunate that all but a handful of the nonmember state banks must meet the basic requirements of the FDIC in order to offer their depositors the advantage of deposit insurance.

Second, the very existence of deposit insurance has effectively eliminated, at its source, the bank panic and "run-on-the-bank" psychology that was so damaging to the entire economy in the 1920s and early 1930s. Bank panics are peculiar phenomena. In normal times, depositors prefer keeping the majority of their money balances in deposit form for the simple reason that payment by check is much more convenient. If, however, doubts develop regarding the basic soundness of the banks, depositors naturally become concerned. If a few banks fail and their depositors are unable to redeem their deposits at full value, general concern rapidly deteriorates into panic. Depositors line up at their own banks in ever-increasing numbers, withdrawing cash to be sure that they "get theirs" before their bank too is forced to close its doors. And such panic philosophy tends to spread like wildfire until—as happened in the early 1930s—all banks, sound and unsound alike, find themselves facing liquidity crises that threaten their very existence.

---

[17]The "insurance premium" amounted to about 0.07 percent of assessable deposits in 1981. FDIC inspectors actually examine all insured nonmember banks at least once every two years, relying on Federal Reserve System inspections in the case of member banks.

[18]The $100,000 maximum applies to the sum of all deposits owned by any one individual or business depositor in any insured bank. Accounts by the same depositor in different insured banks are each insured up to $100,000.

But panics of this sort are entirely avoidable catastrophes. Ironically, the public only wants to withdraw cash at such times because it has developed the fear that it cannot get it. If people can be assured that they *can* convert their deposits to cash easily, they will not want the cash. The prevention of panics, then, is absurdly simple. Convince the public that it can always get its money and it will not rush to get it in the first place. This, without question, has been the major accomplishment of the FDIC.

When, despite all efforts to avoid them, bank failures do occur, the FDIC has several options open to it.[19] Once the chartering agency has declared a bank insolvent (and named the FDIC as receiver), it can step in, take over the assets, and immediately begin paying off the insured deposits. Or, if it considers this approach inappropriate, it may assist a sound bank in absorbing both the sound assets and the deposits of the failed bank. Of the 620 bank failures requiring FDIC disbursements between 1934 and 1982, depositors were simply paid off in 319 cases, and the deposits were assumed by other banks in 301. Total losses to the FDIC over the entire 48-year period were just under $2 billion.[20]

The choice between paying off insured depositors and arranging a takeover has important implications. If insured depositors are paid off, those with deposits over $100,000 stand to incur losses, whereas if all deposits are simply taken over by another bank, the effect is 100 percent insurance protection. The FDIC defends the deposit assumption (and consequent 100 percent insurance) approach as the best means of ensuring that bank failures do not undermine the public's confidence in the banking system. On the other hand, it has been argued that this produces a "large bank bias." Whereas small banks can be allowed to disappear with only relatively minor losses due to uninsured deposits (and, consequently, a relatively minor effect on public confidence), the same is not true of large banks.[21] The result is that large depositors who might stand to suffer losses in case of failure will have a natural tendency to patronize only large banks where the FDIC is less likely to permit the losses to occur.

Some concern has been raised in recent years about the safety of the banking system as a result of an increase in the number of failures and of the size of the banks that have gone under. The facts have been expressed succinctly by the chairman of the FDIC:

More bank failures occurred in 1976 than in any year since 1942. The eight largest bank failures in the FDIC's history took place in the 39-month period from October,

---

[19]In addition to its normal supervisory and regulatory activities, the corporation may attempt to forestall actual failure by a "problem" bank by insisting upon merger with a stronger bank and/or making large loans to tide the bank over until major corrective measures can be carried out.

[20]*Annual Report of the FDIC, 1982.* A third possibility, resorted to only infrequently, is to set up a "Deposit Insurance National Bank"—a bank run by the FDIC itself for up to two years.

[21]That this has tended to be the case is indicated by the fact that the value of deposits assumed by other banks in the failures of 301 banks has been almost 20 times the size of deposits in the 319 failed banks in which the deposit payoff route was chosen. *Annual Report of the FDIC, 1982.*

1973 to December, 1976—banks whose assets aggregated over $3\frac{1}{2}$-times as many assets as all the other insured banks that have been closed during the entire history of the FDIC.[22]

And these worries have not really abated during the 1980s. Indeed, the stresses associated with serious recession, coupled with the severe financial difficulties confronted by the nation's mutual savings banks (most of which are insured by the FDIC), led to more failures in 1982 than in any year since 1940!

Just how serious are these problems? Conversely, how sound is the FDIC? Despite problems, it appears in pretty good shape. As of the end of 1982, FDIC assets totaled $13.8 billion, an amount equal to about 1.21 percent of total insured deposits. Although the latter figure may seem small, it was higher than during much of the 1970s.[23] In addition, current law authorizes the fund to borrow $3 billion from the U.S. Treasury should it ever be needed. Finally, should the FDIC's needs ever exceed these resources, it is difficult to imagine Congress failing to act to provide whatever is needed. Insured bank deposits, it would seem, are a pretty secure asset.

State Bank Regulatory Commissions.   State-chartered banks that do not choose to join the Federal Reserve System—and as we have seen this constitutes a majority of the banks—are subject to the control and regulation of the state that issues their charter. Although it is difficult to generalize about 50 different sets of regulations, we can say that—in the main—state control is less stringent than is that of the Federal Reserve System.

There are, of course, minimum capital requirements and controls over acceptable earning assets, accounting statements, structure, and management. In addition, with one exception, there are legal reserve requirements behind deposits. Prior to the passage of the Depository Institutions Deregulation and Monetary Control Act of 1980 (which imposes similar reserve requirements on all depository institutions), the difference between state reserve requirements and those of the Federal Reserve System was a matter of real significance. The difference was that, whereas the Federal Reserve permitted only vault cash and accounts held at Federal Reserve banks to "count" to fulfill required reserve ratios, states permitted non-member banks to count accounts at other commercial banks and—in more than half the states—government securities and other income-earning assets. Since this made state reserve requirements substantially less onerous than those of the Fed, it was quite natural for banks to leave the Federal Reserve System. The effect of this membership drain, a major reason for passage of the DIDMC Act of 1980, is depicted in Figure 6-2.

---

[22]*Annual Report of the FDIC, 1976,* p. xi.

[23]It should be pointed out that the Depository Institutions Deregulation and Monetary Control Act of 1980 authorizes the FDIC Board of Directors automatically to raise assessments imposed on insured institutions whenever the fund-to-insured deposit ratio falls below 1.10 percent.

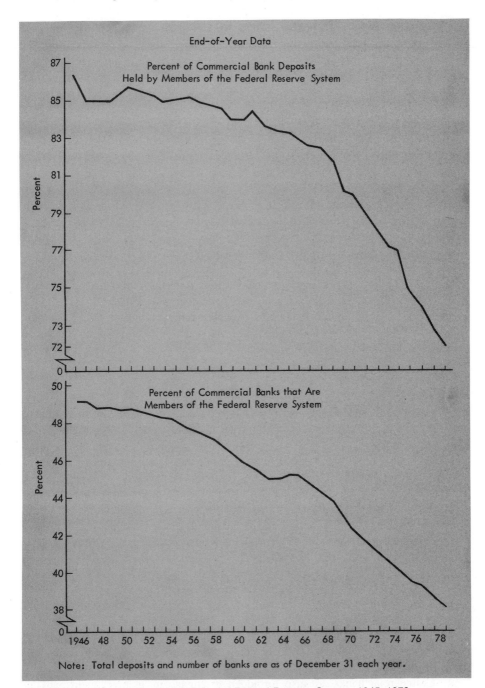

FIGURE 6-2 Decline in Membership in the Federal Reserve System, 1945–1978

Source: Review, Federal Reserve Bank of St. Louis, August 1977; and *Federal Reserve Bulletin.*

Avoiding Unnecessary Duplication in Bank Regulation. It should be obvious from the foregoing discussion that not only is bank regulation a complex business in the United States but authority and responsibilities overlap in a number of areas. National banks, for example, are required to belong to the Federal Reserve System and to subscribe to FDIC coverage. They are thus subject to the regulations and supervision of three different agencies: the Comptroller of the Currency, the FRS authorities, and the FDIC authorities. State member banks are controlled by the Federal Reserve, the FDIC, and the regulations of the banking commission of the state in which they are chartered. Nonmember state banks are subject to regulation by their state banking commission and (except for the few who do not carry insurance coverage) the FDIC.

To minimize duplication of effort, especially with respect to actual examination of the banks themselves, a system has been worked out whereby bank examinations of one agency are accepted by others. The Comptroller of the Currency bears the brunt of examining national banks, making its findings available to the Federal Reserve and the FDIC. The Federal Reserve System carries out the actual examination of state member banks (along with the state banking commission, if they choose). These reports are also made available to the FDIC. The FDIC examines all insured nonmember banks (often in conjunction with the appropriate state authorities). Finally, state authorities alone are responsible for supervision and inspection of uninsured state banks.

What Is Regulated?

Bank regulation is obviously too complex a matter to deal with in any detail in a textbook such as this one. Therefore, we shall only touch on the highlights in this brief section.

To start a new bank, a charter from either the state bank commissioner or the federal Comptroller of the Currency is required. Among other things, minimal capital requirements for obtaining a charter have been established. In addition, the applicant must generally be able to convince the chartering agency that a "need" for more banking facilities exists in the intended area of operation. This latter requirement has been the subject of considerable dispute because it obviously could have the effect of protecting existing banks from added competition. Its ostensible purpose is to prevent "overbanking" and the development of too many small, weak banks, such as is thought to have been the case in the 1920s.

The authority to establish branches is also regulated by state law. The right to merge with other banks is subject not only to approval by the authorities discussed earlier but also to review by the Department of Justice to ensure that antitrust laws are not being violated. Holding companies, as previously pointed out, are similarly regulated.

Commercial banks are also forbidden to engage in an investment banking business (except in government securities), to purchase common stock for their own portfolios, to lend more than a specified percentage of their capital to any one borrower, to lend more than a specified amount to borrowers seeking credit for security purchase, to pay interest on checking accounts, to pay more than a specified interest rate on most savings accounts, and a whole host of other matters.

There is little question that banks are subject to a wide range of controls and restrictions. What *is* at question is the extent to which the current regulations protect the public as opposed to merely limiting competition and protecting existing banks. This topic will continue to receive careful consideration in the future.

Review Questions

1. Examine the pros and cons of the maintenance of the "dual banking" system.
2. Do you believe that the McFadden Act and other laws limiting branch banking in the United States contribute to a more competitive U.S. banking system? Why or why not?
3. What is the effect of the "Douglas Amendment" to the Bank Holding Company Act?
4. Discuss carefully the development of federal law regulating bank holding companies in the United States.
5. Write an essay discussing the nature of, and reasons for, the current trend toward interstate banking. Do you believe that it is a healthy trend? Why or why not?
6. Explain the ways in which the FDIC has improved the U.S. commercial banking system.
7. It has been argued that the FDIC's policy of arranging assumption of the deposits of large failed banks while simply paying off on insured deposits at smaller failed banks provides a competitive advantage to the larger banks. Explain this viewpoint.
8. Passage of the Depository Institutions Deregulation and Monetary Control Act of 1980 probably has put an end to the long-standing tendency for commercial banks to leave the Federal Reserve System. Explain why this should be expected.

7

The Federal Reserve System—
Structure and Functions

About 60 percent of the commercial banks in the United States are not members of the Federal Reserve System and, therefore, are not directly subject to the authority of that federal government agency. It would, however, be a gross error to conclude from this fact that the Federal Reserve authorities lack the power to exercise wide-reaching control over the nation's banking and monetary system. Not only do the banks that belong to the System hold almost 75 percent of the nation's deposits, but Federal Reserve actions have powerful direct and indirect effects on all banks—member and nonmember alike. For these reasons, as well as for the sake of brevity, we shall concentrate almost solely on the Federal Reserve System and its member banks in the remaining chapters of our institutional discussion.

The Evolution of the Federal Reserve System

The Original Federal Reserve Act—1913

As we have seen, the inelastic currency supply, inefficient check collection facilities, ill-designed reserve requirements, and other deficiencies of the National Bank Act of 1863 combined to produce a series of financial panics throughout the latter decades of the nineteenth century and on over into the first decade of the twentieth. This experience, in turn, prompted a searching study by the National Monetary Commission, whose report ultimately led to the passage of the Federal Reserve Act in 1913.

The Federal Reserve System originally established by that act was a far cry from the powerful central bank we know today. It consisted of 12 district Federal Reserve banks with considerable autonomy, along with a fairly weak seven-member coordinating group—the Board of Governors. As we shall see shortly, time and painful experience have since shifted the locus of power almost entirely out of the hands of the individual Federal Reserve banks into those of the Board.

More remarkable than the changes in structure, however, has been the evolution of the philosophy and objectives of the System. Whereas we now take for granted the goals of full employment, economic growth, and stable prices as almost the *sine qua non* of monetary policy, the framers of the original Federal Reserve Act made no mention of any of them. The act was intended, in its own words, "to furnish an elastic currency, to afford means of rediscounting commercial paper, to establish a more effective supervision of banking in the United States, and for other purposes."[1] It seems clear from this statement that the act was aimed primarily at the specific weaknesses that had cropped up under the national banking system rather than at the creation of a powerful new agency to stabilize the economy.

What were its specific provisions? It did require, as today, that all national banks join, while making membership voluntary for state banks. It borrowed from the National Bank Act the concept of differing reserve requirements for member banks in different-sized cities, but it specified that required reserves must be kept on deposit in district Federal Reserve banks.[2] There was no provision for discretionary alteration in required reserve ratios by the Board. Open-market operations—today, by any measure, the most important of all monetary policy weapons—were essentially unknown.[3] For all practical purposes, the only discretionary monetary policy tool initially established by the act was the power to alter the Federal Reserve "discount rate"—the interest rate charged by Federal Reserve banks on short-term loans of reserves to member banks.

The Commercial Loan (or "Real Bills") Theory

This limited reliance on discretionary monetary tools is explainable partially by the then widespread faith in a doctrine called the **commercial loan** (or "real bills") **theory.** The commercial loan theory centered on the belief that both the quantity and the quality of bank credit could be satisfactorily controlled if the basic legislation encouraged banks to restrict themselves largely to short-term (90 days in the general case) loans to business for the purpose of purchasing inventories. Such legislation, it was felt, would guarantee that banks would lend only for

---

[1]*Preamble*, the Federal Reserve Act.

[2]This was the case following a 1917 amendment. In the original act, vault cash also could be counted. From 1917 till late 1959, only deposits at the Fed could be counted. Since 1959, both vault cash and the member bank's Federal Reserve account have been acceptable.

[3]The Federal Reserve banks were given the power to purchase U.S. securities, but this was thought of primarily as a measure to permit them to earn income. The vastly more important effects of security purchases on member bank reserves, interest rates, and the money supply were simply not widely recognized or understood at the time.

productive rather than speculative purposes and that an expansion in the quantity of bank credit would only occur when such an increase was needed to finance expanded trade. It was a soothing theory. Not only could we ensure that bank loans were sound and that bank credit would not expand to an inflationary level, but we could do so by law, thereby avoiding any heavy reliance on the discretion of policymakers.

The original Federal Reserve Act attempted to implement the commercial loan theory primarily through the discount mechanism.[4] It required member banks desiring to borrow reserves from their district Federal Reserve bank to turn over— as collateral for the loan—IOUs of businesses arising out of short-term loans the member banks had made to finance inventory purchases. Such IOUs came to be called "eligible paper," denoting the fact that they were initially the only assets eligible at the Federal Reserve's "discount window." The idea was, of course, to restrict access to the discount window—and hence to the added reserves available there—to those member banks who "behaved themselves" by making loans consistent with the commercial loan theory.

The notion that it was possible to control both the quality and the quantity of credit automatically through laws requiring commercial banks to specialize in short-term inventory loans to business—the commercial loan theory—soon proved to be a fallacious one. For example, commercial loan adherents argued that restricting bank assets to short-term inventory loans would ensure the liquidity of banks because of the alleged *self-liquidating* character of loans secured by a firm's inventories. The idea was that a firm that borrowed to finance the purchase of its stock-in-trade would be in a position to repay the bank as soon as it had turned over that portion of its inventory. What was overlooked in the argument was the possibility of an economywide collapse of economic activity that would make it difficult or impossible for the borrower to sell his goods. In such a situation, short-term inventory loans derive their liquidity only from the fact that they can be discounted at the central bank—not through any inherently self-liquidating features.

Even more seriously misleading was the argument that tying discounts to short-term inventory loans would guarantee that the money supply could not be excessive. Commercial loan advocates argued that as long as access to the discount facility was limited to banks possessing "productive" short-term inventory loans, bank reserves and the money supply could only increase as the volume of physical production itself increased. Inflation, then, need not be a matter of concern.

But this, of course, misses the very essence of excess demand inflation. Once full employment is reached, firms bid against one another to obtain a larger share of the fixed supply of productive resources. As no more is to be had, the bidding simply forces prices up. As prices rise, the *dollar value* of each inventory acquisition necessarily rises. Firms, then, come to banks for ever-larger amounts of

---

[4]In addition, Federal Reserve notes, the new currency authorized by the act, could originally only be issued with a backing not only of gold but also of "eligible paper"—short-term IOUs of businesses acquired from member banks by the Federal Reserve banks through the discount facility.

credit, and bank portfolios become stocked with more and more short-term commercial paper "eligible" for discount. The flaw in the commercial loan idea, of course, is that the quantity of short-term commercial loans does not only rise when real production rises; it also increases when the money value of production rises via inflationary price increases. And when this happens, far from preventing inflation, the commercial loan theory provisions actually feed it.

Changes in the Federal Reserve System Since 1913

It is perhaps one measure of the strength of the Federal Reserve Act that it has been able to weather successfully the test of time and evolve to handle ideas and objectives not even conceived of at the time of its passage.

The elements of the commercial loan theory embedded in the act disappeared fairly quickly, as did the notion of a decentralized system with 12 semiautonomous district banks.

It was in the 1930s, however, that the most far-reaching overhaul occurred. The agonizing experience of mass unemployment during the Great Depression and the spectacular bank panic of the early 1930s provided the impetus. Legislation enacted in the early and middle 1930s authorized variable reserve requirements, set up the FDIC, gave the Board of Governors of the Federal Reserve the power to establish margin requirements on the purchase of stock and ceilings on interest payable on savings accounts, and a host of other things. The most important change, however, was one of attitude and objective. No longer was the Federal Reserve System looked upon as an institution primarily concerned with correcting some deficiencies in the National Bank Act of 1863. It was now a powerful federal government stabilization agency charged with a crucial role in battling unemployment and inflation.

The Structure of the Federal Reserve System Today

The Federal Reserve System today consists of the rather complex structure sketched in Figure 7-1. Let us briefly discuss the various parts of the System, starting with the Board of Governors.

The Board of Governors

The Board of Governors of the Federal Reserve System consists of seven members, appointed by the president to 14-year terms. The seven governors are the top monetary authorities in the United States. Their power and prestige within the federal government are such as to rank them on a par with the most powerful

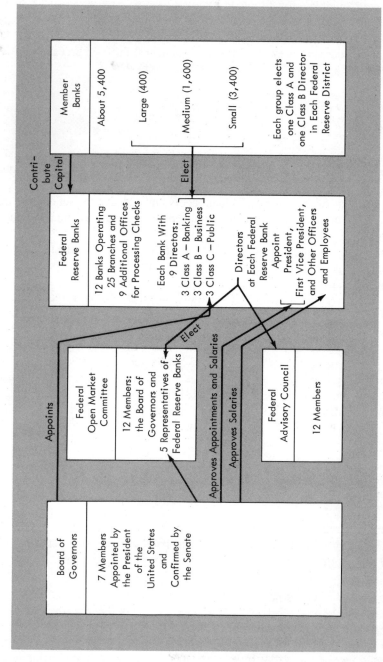

FIGURE 7-1 Structure of the Federal Reserve System

Source: Federal Reserve System.

of governmental officials. They are the architects of, and bear the final responsibility for, the nation's monetary policy.

It is they who have the power to alter reserve requirements (within the legal limits established by Congress) applying to depository institution deposits. It is they who "review and determine" (which, for all practical purposes, means "set") the discount rates charged by Federal Reserve banks on loans to depository institutions. It is they who set margin requirements on the purchase of securities. And it is they who compose a majority of the Open Market Committee, which determines the extent and direction of the most effective monetary policy weapon of all—open-market operations. Without question, the governors are the nation's most powerful monetary authorities, and it is they who direct and control the activities of the rest of the "System."

The "Independence" of the Federal Reserve.   The Board of Governors is a strictly governmental agency concerned solely with the public interest. It does, however, maintain a somewhat unique status among governmental agencies in that it is, to a degree, insulated from, and "independent" of, much of the direct control by the president and Congress to which most other agencies are subject.

The 14-year terms, for example, guarantee any member a tenure in office of longer duration than that of the president who makes the appointment. A member of the Board of Governors—not unlike a federal judge—may only be removed from office before the end of his or her term for "cause." Once appointed, he or she does not—as do cabinet members and other high officials—serve at the pleasure of the president. Consequently, in case of a difference in policy views, a Federal Reserve governor is free to pursue a monetary policy to which the president may be opposed without fear of dismissal.

In addition to this degree of protection from control by the executive, the Board of Governors also possesses an element of independence from legislative dictation that most other government agencies lack. This should certainly not be interpreted as implying that the Federal Reserve is *totally* independent of Congress. The System was established by congressional action, and its structure, powers, and indeed its very existence are subject at all times to the legislative will.

Within the confines of existing law, however, the Federal Reserve System possesses a unique degree of freedom from congressional pressures simply because it earns its own income. Congress's power over the purse strings is, of course, among its most basic instruments of control. The majority of governmental agencies are required to come to the Congress each year to request continuing financial support through appropriations. Officials of the Federal Reserve System also are obligated to appear regularly before various congressional committees to report on its activities. But unlike most others, they do not come, hat in hand, requesting the funds required to carry on for another year. Such humility is unnecessary because the 12 Federal Reserve banks earn far more than enough income from their operations to pay all the Fed's expenses as well as all those of the Board of Governors. This, quite clearly, provides them with additional degrees of freedom.

The justification for this unusual degree of "independence" is a subject of some dispute. On the one hand, it is argued that some such independence is needed to ensure that monetary policy and the public interest in a stable dollar are not dominated by the political interests of the executive departments, especially the Treasury. On the other hand, it is stressed that a sound governmental approach to cyclical and growth problems requires a degree of coordination among the various policy agencies, which the Federal Reserve System's "independence" may not always permit. Those who would reduce this "independence" argue that democratic society requires that all elements of government entrusted with the determination of basic policy should be made directly responsible to the electorate or elected officials rather than insulated from such responsibility.

A note of caution, however, is in order here. It is true that the members of the Board of Governors and the Federal Reserve System as a whole possess a unique degree of independence within the government. It is also true that the independence they possess has, in the past, permitted them to defy the wishes of presidents as well as some powerful congressional leaders. But one must be careful not to carry the independence aspect to extremes. The Fed is certainly *not* an "autonomous fourth branch of government," wholly impervious to pressures from the executive and legislature. Indeed, some authorities have argued that, despite its technical independence, the Board of Governors tends to do pretty much whatever the incumbent administration wants. And even if that is not quite true, one can hardly ignore the fact that the Federal Reserve System with all its powers is the result of an act of Congress. It can hardly behave as if it were really independent of Congress when it knows that that body can take away all its authority whenever it chooses. Uniquely independent, yes. Completely independent, by no means.

The Federal Reserve Banks

When the Federal Reserve System was established, congressional fear of concentration of power led the legislature to set up 12 regional Federal Reserve banks rather than the single central bank typical of most other nations. The distribution of these banks within the 12 geographical Federal Reserve districts is depicted in Figure 7-2.

Ownership and Control of Federal Reserve Banks. The 12 Federal Reserve banks themselves are often referred to as "quasi-public" institutions. This phrase means that, although they are entirely privately owned, they are operated with a view solely to public, governmental objectives.

All the stock issued by a Federal Reserve bank is owned by the privately owned member banks of its district. In addition, six of the nine members of each district bank's board of directors are selected by their member bank owners. But despite this 100 percent private ownership and seemingly effective private control of a majority of their directors, Federal Reserve banks today are, in most important respects, subject almost completely to the dictates of a strictly governmental agency, the Board of Governors in Washington.

FIGURE 7-2 The Federal Reserve System: Boundaries of Federal Reserve Districts and Their Branch Territories

Source: Federal Reserve Bulletin.

The Board of Governors, for example, appoints the three remaining members (the so-called "Class C directors" mentioned in Figure 7-1) of each Federal Reserve bank's board of directors, one of whom is selected to be chairman of the Board. In addition, the individual Reserve banks' directors have little direct say about such important matters as the setting of their own discount rates or the composition of their own security portfolios. Discount rates, though nominally set by the individual Reserve bank, are subject to review and determination by the Board of Governors. In actual practice, this results in the Board of Governors rather than individual Federal Reserve banks determining the rate. Similarly, the purchase and sale of U.S. securities, which make up nearly the whole of Federal Reserve bank earning assets, is subject to the complete control of the Open Market Committee, a group dominated by the Board of Governors. As a result, the private owners and their six representatives on their Reserve bank's board of directors have little control over the most fundamental policy matters.

Earnings of Federal Reserve Banks. The public status of Federal Reserve banks is further reflected in their attitude toward, and disposition of, profits. Unlike other privately owned institutions, the Federal Reserve banks are governmentally oriented

TABLE 7-1

Sources and Disposition of Federal Reserve Bank
Earnings, 1982
(millions of dollars)

Income, by source	
Interest on U.S. securities	$15,493
All other income	1,027
Gross income	16,520
Net expenses	1,155
Net income	15,365
Disposition of net income	
Dividends to member banks	79
Transferred to surplus	78
Paid to U.S. Treasury	15,208

Source: Federal Reserve Bulletin, February 1983, p. 91.

and thus view the making of a profit on their operations as an objective that is distinctly secondary to the goal of carrying out their public function. This is not to say that Federal Reserve banks do not attempt to minimize their operating costs and to "buy low and sell high" when altering their portfolio of assets. They do, and, as we shall see, the result of their efforts yields them very large profits indeed. The point is that making a profit is not their goal. If faced with a choice between making a profit on a transaction and carrying out their public responsibilities as executors of the nation's monetary policy at a loss, they would unhesitatingly choose the latter course.

Be that as it may, the Federal Reserve banks actually do earn very substantial profits from their operations—a fact that, as noted, insulates the System somewhat from congressional dictation. Data for Federal Reserve bank earnings in 1982 are presented in Table 7-1.

As the table shows, most of the income of the System accrues from interest earned on U.S. securities that have been acquired in the process of implementing open-market policy. Included in the "other income" category was $390 million earned during the year from the sale of Federal Reserve services. This is a relatively new source of income that results from the requirement in the Depository Institutions Deregulation and Monetary Control Act of 1980 that previously free services henceforth be explicitly priced.

It is very important for the student to realize that, although U.S. securities *are* the source of the bulk of Federal Reserve bank earnings, these assets were not acquired for this reason. Rather they were acquired in the process of carrying out monetary policy, and the purpose of their acquisition was to exert influence on the cost and availability of credit in the economy. The profit earned is purely a side effect of measures carried out for other reasons.

Nevertheless, substantial profits are regularly made by Federal Reserve banks, and it is interesting to note how they are distributed. In 1982, after paying $79 million in dividends on Federal Reserve bank stock owned by the member banks and adding $78 million to their capital surplus, the System returned the rest—some $15 billion—to the U.S. Treasury.[5]

"How," one might reasonably ask, "can they make so much income that, after paying all their expenses, all their dividends, and adding to their surplus, they still have about 90 percent of their *gross* revenue left to turn over to the Treasury? That sort of thing would be a startling accomplishment for any firm, let alone one that isn't even motivated by profit maximization."

The answer is a simple one. You too could show billions in profits if you had the powers of the Federal Reserve banks. Almost all their revenue was interest on their $100-plus billion portfolio of U.S. securities. These securities—accumulated over the years through open-market purchases by the System—are acquired almost without cost because they, as the nation's ultimate monetary authority, possess the power to simply *create* whatever money is needed to buy them. We shall see how this is done later on in our discussion.

Balance Sheet of Federal Reserve Banks. Probably the most fruitful way of learning about what Federal Reserve banks do is to study their balance sheets. For example, see Table 7-2.

TABLE 7-2

Consolidated Balance Sheet of All 12 Federal Reserve Banks, February 23, 1983
(billions of dollars)

Assets		Liabilities and Capital Accounts		
Gold certificates	$ 11.1	Federal Reserve notes		$139.7
Cash	.5	outstanding		
Loans	.5	Demand deposits, total		31.6
U.S. securities	138.1	Depository institutions	28.3	
Uncollected cash items	12.4	U.S. Treasury	2.6	
All other assets[a]	23.2	Foreign	.2	
		Other	.5	
		Deferred availability cash items		9.8
		Other liabilities[b]		1.6
		Capital accounts		3.1
Total assets	$185.8	Total liabilities and capital accounts		$185.8

[a]"Other assets" not separately listed include the special drawing rights certificate account, which is a claim on the International Monetary Fund transferred to the Federal Reserve banks by the U.S. Treasury; federal agency obligations, issued to aid farm and home loan programs, that are purchased by the System's open-market account; and a small total of banker's acceptances.

[b]"Other liabilities" include liabilities for dividends on member-bank-held stock accrued but not yet paid and unearned discounts on securities purchased at discount.

Source: Federal Reserve Statistical Release H.4.1, February 25, 1983.

---

[5]This payment to the Treasury is technically referred to as payment of "interest on Federal Reserve notes outstanding." Federal Reserve bank profits have regularly been so embarrassingly large that it was necessary to find a technicality in the law to authorize their return to the Treasury. Note what this means, however. Almost all the Fed's income comes from the Treasury in the form of interest on U.S. securities owned by Federal Reserve banks. The bulk of it, however—over 90 percent—is returned to the Treasury as "interest on Federal Reserve notes!" In a sense, then, one might argue that the portion of the national debt owned by the Federal Reserve System is virtually costless.

The first asset, *gold certificates,* represents an item of considerable historical importance, although it currently has little significance to Federal Reserve banks. Gold certificates are issued by the U.S. Treasury, which is authorized by present law to print up one dollar in gold certificates for each dollar of gold owned. The gold certificates are then deposited in the Federal Reserve banks by the Treasury in return for an increase in the Treasury's checking account there.[6]

Until 1968 these gold certificates served as "legal reserves" for the issuance of Federal Reserve notes by the Federal Reserve banks. Under the law at that time, Federal Reserve banks were required to "back up" each dollar of Federal Reserve notes issued (remember, Federal Reserve notes make up the preponderant majority of the nation's currency supply) with 25 cents worth of gold certificates. Technically, then, the gold supply—which limited the gold certificate supply—placed an outside limit on the amount of Federal Reserve notes that could be issued.

In practice, however, the technical limit implied by that law was never permitted to become operable. Each time the limit was approached, Congress (wisely, it should be noted) changed the law, lowering the requirement.[7] In 1968 the last remaining legal tie between the U.S. gold supply and its money supply was abolished when the 25 percent gold certificate collateral requirement behind Federal Reserve notes was dropped.[8]

Consequently, the Federal Reserve's gold certificate account today has little meaning—legally or otherwise. The amount held is strictly a function of the size of the U.S. gold stock, and it has almost no significance for domestic policy considerations.[9]

The *cash* asset account includes all currency and coins in the possession of the Federal Reserve banks, which are issued by, and are the liability of, the U.S. Treasury. This small account consists primarily of coins, although it also includes a limited amount of Treasury-issued currency such as U.S. notes. It is important for the reader to recognize that the bulk of the nation's currency supply—Federal Reserve notes—is *issued* by the Federal Reserve banks and, hence, shows up on the liability side of their balance sheet as "Federal Reserve notes outstanding."

Discounts and advances consist primarily of IOUs of member banks who have borrowed reserves from their district Federal Reserve banks via the "discount window." Such loans are normally made for 15 days, on the borrowing bank's

---

[6]When the Treasury sells gold, it must withdraw an equivalent amount of gold certificates from the Federal Reserve banks. Actually these gold certificates currently are simply bookkeeping credits, not physical pieces of paper.

[7]In 1945, the requirement of a 40 percent gold certificate behind Federal Reserve notes and 35 percent behind member bank deposits was reduced to 25 percent behind both. In 1965 the 25 percent gold certificate requirement behind member bank deposits was dropped. Then, in 1968, the 25 percent requirement behind Federal Reserve notes was also abolished.

[8]A glance at Table 7-2 will confirm the reason for this change. Federal Reserve notes outstanding in 1983 were far more than four times the gold certificate total.

[9]Although no longer required, all the gold certificates were being used as collateral for Federal Reserve notes as of February 1983. If necessary, these could be replaced by U.S. securities at any time.

own promissory note, secured by U.S. securities.[10] Although seldom used in recent years, Federal Reserve banks may also make loans for up to 90 days to member banks by discounting "eligible" paper or by accepting any other asset satisfactory to the Federal Reserve as security.

The largest and most important of Federal Reserve bank assets is the $138 billion portfolio of *U.S. securities*. These securities are, of course, initially issued by the U.S. Treasury to finance deficit spending by the federal government. Those held by the Federal Reserve banks are acquired as a result of the Fed's open-market operations, about which we shall have much more to say shortly. It should be noted, however, that the Fed's portfolio of U.S. securities is *not* generally purchased directly from the U.S. Treasury. Rather, the Federal Reserve buys them through middlemen securities dealers, from individuals or financial institutions that have previously acquired them from the Treasury. The Federal Reserve is limited by law in its ability to purchase securities directly from the Treasury, and it does so only very infrequently.[11]

The final asset account, *uncollected cash items,* arises out of the check collection process, which we shall consider in detail shortly. In essence, this $12 billion account represents checks written on member banks that have been received and/or sent out by the Federal Reserve but have not yet been received by, or collected from, the payee banks.

On the liability and net worth side, the $140 billion of *Federal Reserve notes outstanding* represents the majority of the nation's currency supply. It is a liability of the Federal Reserve banks, of course, because they are the issuing agents.

Among the demand deposits outstanding, those owed to the member banks and the other depository institutions constitute the bulk of the legal reserves that they, in turn, use to "back up" the demand and time deposits of their customers. The *U.S. Treasury demand deposit* is the checking account on which the Treasury writes virtually all the checks with which it makes payment for the goods and services it purchases. The *other demand deposits* liability includes, among others, deposits held in Federal Reserve banks by nonmember banks for check-clearing purposes and deposits of certain international organizations.

The *deferred availability cash items* is, like uncollected cash items on the asset side, a temporary account that arises in the process of check clearing and collection. We shall deal with it shortly. Finally, the *capital accounts* represent the equity that the member bank owners have built up in their Federal Reserve banks by virtue of the requirement that they purchase stock in them.

---

[10]Actually, since 1971, such loans may be made even without the physical transfer of a promissory note, simply by a verbal agreement over the telephone. Member banks often store stocks of U.S. securities at their Federal Reserve bank so that they will be available to serve as security when borrowing becomes necessary.

[11]The U.S. securities purchased by Federal Reserve banks are usually short-term obligations. As of February 1983, for example, $74 billion of the $138 billion total were within one year of maturity and only about $29 billion had maturity dates greater than five years.

The Member Banks

The base of the Federal Reserve System is composed of the member banks, consisting in December 1982 of 4,579 national banks, which are required to belong, plus 1,039 of the larger state banks that have voluntarily chosen to join. The member bank undertakes certain responsibilities in return for the privileges of membership.

It is required to subscribe to stock in the Federal Reserve bank of its district in an amount equal to 6 percent of its own capital and surplus, although, to date, only half that amount must be paid in. The rest is subject to call. It must abide by a list of System regulations regarding its capital structure, its loans and investments, its branch operations, its holding company operations, and the activities of its directors. It must submit, at the discretion of the System, to supervision and examination by Federal Reserve authorities. Finally, it must observe the reserve requirements set by the Federal Reserve for depository institutions with its deposit size.[12]

In return for these obligations, the member bank enjoys certain privileges. Its ownership of Federal Reserve bank stock entitles it to participate in the selection of six of the nine members of the board of directors of its Federal Reserve bank. In addition, it receives a safe 6 percent dividend on such stock owned.

Prior to passage of the DIDMC Act of 1980, other unique advantages of membership in the System included the availability of emergency loans of reserves through the Fed's so-called "discount window" and access to the extensive check-clearing and collection facilities and the sophisticated wire transfer system of the System. While those services still exist, they are no longer either free or exclusively made available to member banks. For since all depository institutions have been made subject to the same reserve requirements, all now have equal access, at a price, to Fed services.

The Federal Open Market Committee

If there is any one group within which the basic decision of monetary policy is made, it is in the 12-member Federal Open Market Committee. Its membership consists of the 7 members of the Board of Governors plus 5 presidents of Federal Reserve banks. The president of the New York Federal Reserve Bank is a permanent member, and the 4 remaining positions are rotated among the presidents of the other Federal Reserve banks.

The Open Market Committee has sole responsibility for determining the direction and extent of the System's open-market operations. After carefully considering the economy's needs, it decides upon the type and scale of operations, and

---

[12]Of course, since the passage of the DIDMC Act of 1980, all depository institutions have the same reserve requirements, whether members of the Federal Reserve or not.

its decisions are binding on all Federal Reserve banks. If the Open Market Committee decides to sell, each Federal Reserve bank is *required* to make available for sale its proportionate share of the securities. Conversely, if the committee decides to buy, each Federal Reserve bank is required to make payment for its proportionate share of the total purchase.

We shall delve more deeply into the mechanics of open-market operations later. For the moment, it should simply be recognized that, as the one dominant tool of monetary policy is open-market operations, the Open Market Committee is an extremely important group.

The Federal Advisory Council

Of substantially lesser importance in terms of the actual determination of basic policy is the 12-member Federal Advisory Council. It consists of one representative from each Federal Reserve district, usually a commercial banker. It meets quarterly in, as its name indicates, a purely advisory capacity. It is intended to provide the Board of Governors direct access to the viewpoints of representative private bankers from around the country.

Functions and Objectives of the Federal Reserve System

Large governmental agencies generally do not have the privilege of working toward one single objective. The Federal Reserve System is no exception.

Its functions might most usefully be categorized into three groups. First, it carries out a variety of activities aimed at maintenance of a sound and effectively functioning money supply and commercial banking industry. Second, it acts as "fiscal agent" for the U.S. Treasury, aiding in the handling of Treasury cash balances, the collection of taxes, the sale and redemption of bonds, and the expenditure of funds.[13] Finally, and of greatest importance, it uses its arsenal of monetary policy weapons to pursue directly the basic social, but sadly, often conflicting, objectives of full employment, price stability, rapid economic growth, and balance-of-payments equilibrium.

Promoting Efficient Banking System and Effective Exchange Media

Included in the group of activities aimed at facilitating the effective operation of banks and the money supply are the following.

---

[13]Acting as "fiscal agent" is *not* the same as carrying out fiscal policy. The latter is done by Congress.

1. Clearing and Collecting Checks.   A healthy proportion of the checks that are not strictly local are collected via the Federal Reserve banks, which make their collection facilities available to all depository institutions at a price covering cost. The result is a highly efficient mechanism that greatly enhances the effectiveness of our main payments media. In addition to carrying out a major portion of the actual collecting chores, the System has also added immeasurably to the acceptability of demand deposits by requiring that all checks collected through its facilities be remitted at par by the bank on which they are written. This requirement has finally eliminated the practice of deducting exchange charges in the United States.

In the next chapter, we shall consider check collection procedures in some detail. For the moment it is sufficient to point out that the primary vehicles used by the Federal Reserve in the collection procedure are the member banks' reserve accounts. The bank in which a check is deposited sends it in to its Federal Reserve bank, which completes the collection process by adding the amount of the check to that bank's reserve account, subtracting an equal amount from the reserve account of the bank on which it is written, and mailing the check on to the latter bank.

2. Providing an Outside Source for Borrowing Additional Reserves.   One of the prime functions of a central bank is the provision of a source from which individual commercial banks in need can borrow additional reserves without, at the same time, reducing the reserves of some other commercial bank. The Federal Reserve's facilities for discounts and advances, popularly called the "discount window," provide such a source. Indeed, as we have seen, this was one of the original purposes of the Federal Reserve Act.

Now that the restrictive notions involved in the commercial loan theory have been abandoned, a depository institution can borrow additional reserves from the Federal Reserve by offering virtually any sound asset it possesses as collateral. This is especially helpful to individual banks or groups of banks in particular areas that may be under some temporary but extreme pressure, as, for example, during a bank panic. It also helps banks that may have some difficulties immediately meeting changed conditions in the economy, or in the Federal Reserve's own regulations, make, with time, an orderly transition to the new circumstances.

3. Issuance of an "Elastic" Currency—the Federal Reserve Note.   The Federal Reserve banks, as we have seen, provide the overwhelming majority of the nation's currency supply in the form of Federal Reserve notes. In doing so, they respond in an almost completely passive manner to the desires of the public for currency. That is to say, the quantity of Federal Reserve notes issued by the System tends to expand and contract as the public's desire for currency rises and falls.

A note of caution is in order here. The Federal Reserve System is by no means passive with respect to the total supply of *money*. Indeed, its main mission is to actively control this strategic quantity. If it passively permitted the total supply of money to expand and contract according to public desire, it would be defaulting on its primary task of stabilization.

It can, however, passively permit an expansion in the supply of Federal Reserve notes whenever the public desires to hold more currency *and fewer demand deposits,* without in any way abandoning its control over the total size of the money supply. And this is precisely what present law regulating the issuance of Federal Reserve notes permits.

When, as is true during the holiday season in December, the public develops a need for relatively more currency and relatively fewer demand deposits, checks are written at commercial banks for cash. The currency paid out, primarily Federal Reserve notes, comes, of course, directly from the vaults of commercial banks. These banks, however, must now replenish their vault cash to be prepared for further cash withdrawals. They do so, by going to their district Reserve bank.

The banks obtain their needed supplies of currency by writing checks themselves, for cash, on their reserve accounts. If they possess sufficient excess reserves to do so without reducing their reserve accounts below prescribed levels, that is the end of the matter. If they do not have an adequate amount of excess reserves, they may, by pledging an "acceptable" asset as collateral, borrow the needed amount through the Federal Reserve's discount window.

Such borrowing for predictable seasonal needs is not often required, however, because the Federal Reserve authorities normally take steps through open-market purchases to provide added reserves in advance of the need.

From the Fed's point of view, requests from depository institutions for more currency are easily accommodated. As they are the issuers of Federal Reserve notes, they need only to have more of them printed. It is true that the law requires the Federal Reserve to "back up" Federal Reserve notes with collateral. This, however, presents no immediate problem. The collateral required may be "eligible paper," gold certificates, or U.S. securities.[14] As Table 7-2 makes clear, the Fed currently holds almost enough U.S. securities to satisfy all collateral requirements. And if more were needed for such a purpose, almost any amount could be effortlessly acquired.

Conversely, when the public's desire for currency abates, such as normally occurs after the holiday season, the reverse process occurs. The public deposits the unwanted currency in checking accounts at depository institutions, and they, in turn, send the plethora of Federal Reserve notes back to the Federal Reserve banks in exchange for an increase in their reserve accounts there.

This high degree of elasticity of our currency supply represents a marked improvement over the stringent note-issue restrictions existing under the National Banking System and is one of the major accomplishments of the Federal Reserve Act.

4. Supervision and Examination of Member Banks. In addition to concerning itself with the *quantity* of member bank assets, a concern through which it

---

[14]Of the $134 billion in Federal Reserve notes outstanding as of June 1982, $119 billion of the collateral was in the form of U.S. securities, $11 billion was in the form of gold certificates, and the remaining $4 billion was "eligible" paper and special drawing rights certificates.

controls the quantity of money, the Federal Reserve System must also consider the *quality* of these assets. It must be concerned not only with the extent of bank operations but with their soundness and prudence.

As we have seen, Federal Reserve authorities regularly examine the state-chartered banks that belong to the System to determine and evaluate their assets and liabilities, their liquidity, their solvency, the quality of their management, and their compliance with established laws and regulations.

This function also includes supervising and overseeing the operations of bank holding companies within the district, analyzing their annual reports, and passing on applications for new branches or mergers.

Aiding the Treasury

A somewhat different hat is worn by the Federal Reserve in its role as "fiscal agent" for the Treasury Department. In this capacity, the System performs many direct services for the Treasury, as well as aiding it in a more substantive manner when it offers a new issue of U.S. securities.

The services performed for the Treasury are many. The Federal Reserve banks hold Treasury checking accounts out of which most of the government's bills are paid. In addition, they supervise the *tax and loan accounts*, which are additional Treasury checking accounts held at a large number of commercial banks and savings institutions throughout the country. When the Treasury offers a new block of securities for sale, the Federal Reserve banks "receive the application of banks, dealers and others who wish to buy, make allotments of securities in accordance with instructions from the Treasury, deliver the securities to the purchasers, receive payment for them, and credit the amounts received to Treasury accounts."[15] When government securities mature, Federal Reserve banks redeem them. When U.S. savings bonds are issued, it is the Federal Reserve banks that do the job, and when they are cashed in, the Reserve banks handle the necessary transaction. It is evident that these direct services to the Treasury make up, in and of themselves, a formidable task.

But that is not the whole of the Federal Reserve System's responsibility vis-à-vis the Treasury Department. In addition to the preceding list of essentially administrative tasks, the System also undertakes to facilitate, in a more substantive way, the flotation of new Treasury securities. Specifically, it is its job to see to it that a new Treasury securities issue "succeeds" in the sense that there are sufficient buyers to take up the entire issue.

A responsibility of this type is extremely difficult to spell out specifically. Generally, it has required that the Federal Reserve act to maintain "orderly conditions" in the government bond market when new borrowing is under way. The

---

[15]*The Federal Reserve System, Purposes and Functions* (Washington, D.C.: Government Printing Office, 1954), p. 160.

meaning of "orderly conditions" is vague at best. The Federal Reserve usually offers a partial and temporary "support" to the government bond market at such times, perhaps involving the purchase of enough old U.S. securities to keep prices from being forced down too sharply by the new issue.

The very vagueness of this commitment to orderly conditions in the government bond market has, however, led to disagreement and friction between the two agencies that, in at least one famous incident, grew into a full-fledged public dispute.

Monetary Policy and Credit Control

Important as the other two groups of functions are, they are decidedly less important, in a relative sense, than the credit control function. When one thinks of monetary policy, one thinks not so much of *serving* the banking system as of *controlling* it. Here is the real *raison d'être* of the Federal Reserve System. This is its major function.

To put it all into one sentence, the primary function of the Federal Reserve System is **to control the supply of money and credit and thereby regulate the cost of credit (the interest rate) in a manner that will affect aggregate demand in a direction that will contribute to the achievement of full employment, stable prices, rapid economic growth, and balance-of-payments equilibrium.**

The means available to System authorities for the pursuance of these goals are, of course, the traditional tools of monetary policy. They include such general credit control weapons as the power to alter required reserve ratios and discount rates and the authority to engage in open-market sale or purchase of U.S. securities. In addition, selective control over the use of credit for the purchase of stocks in the form of margin requirements is available as well as the somewhat vague and ill-defined policy popularly called *moral suasion.*

We shall postpone detailed consideration of these monetary policy tools to a later point. To provide a more thorough grounding for this task, let us turn once again to a discussion of some of the more technical aspects of commercial bank operations.

Review Questions

1. Explain and evaluate the commercial loan theory.
2. The Board of Governors of the Federal Reserve System is often said to be uniquely "independent" of both the executive and the legislature. Carefully explain the nature of this alleged "independence" and comment on its justification. Do you believe that the Fed should be made more accountable to the president than is currently the case?
3. "The Federal Reserve banks are privately owned institutions that operate as if they were governmentally owned." Explain.

4. The Federal Reserve banks are permitted to earn enormous profits as a result of special powers granted them by the Congress. Comment. Can you think of any problems that this arrangement might cause?

5. "Part of the nation's currency supply is an asset of the Federal Reserve banks, but even more of it is a liability." Explain.

6. Carefully explain how the nation's *currency* supply is determined. How would your answer differ if the question referred to the nation's *money* supply?

7. What is the composition of, and chief responsibility of, the Federal Open Market Committee?

8. Aside from carrying out monetary policy, what are the other functions of the Federal Reserve System?

9. Define monetary policy.

8

Check Collection
and Reserve Requirements

Any further description or evaluation of the credit control powers of the Federal Reserve System must be postponed until we learn more about the origin of that credit at the commercial bank level. This, in turn, requires familiarity with check collection procedures and some specifics of member bank reserve requirements, the tasks to which this chapter is devoted.

Check Collection

The simplest check collection procedure, of course, is that of a check that is written on and deposited in the same bank. In this case, all that is necessary is for the single bank involved to increase the account of the check depositor and decrease that of the check writer. No mechanism or collection agency is required because only one bank is involved. In the majority of cases, however, wherein the check writer keeps his or her account at one bank and the check depositor banks at another, some procedures for settling the debt that arises between the two banks become necessary.

We shall consider, in turn, the means used to collect checks (1) written on one bank and deposited in a different bank in the same city; (2) written on one member bank and deposited in a different member bank in the same Federal Reserve district; (3) written on one member bank and deposited in a different member bank located in a different Federal Reserve district; and (4) written on an out-of-town bank, and collected through facilities other than the Federal Reserve. Then, following a brief discussion of *Federal Reserve float,* we shall conclude the section

117

with some observations on recent efforts to improve check collection procedures and the payments mechanism generally.

Check Collection Between Banks Located in the Same City—The Local Clearinghouse

Purely local checks, written on accounts at one bank and deposited in a different bank located in the same city, are collected at least once daily via the local clearinghouse.

A local clearinghouse is a voluntary organization of all the commercial banks in a particular community, set up for the express purpose of facilitating the clearance and collection of such purely local checks.

Its method of operation is quite simple. Each day at an agreed-upon hour, each local bank sends a messenger, armed with all checks written on other local banks but deposited in his bank, to the clearinghouse. Physically, the clearinghouse may be simply an office in one of the more conveniently located banks or, in the case of larger cities, a separate facility. Each bank messenger turns the checks collected over to the manager of the clearinghouse, whose function it is to make up a statement on the basis of which most of these interbank claims are canceled out.

Suppose, for example, in a three-bank town that the messenger from Bank X presents checks written on other local banks totaling $10,000, $7,000 of which are written on Bank Y and $3,000 of which are written on Bank Z; the messenger from Bank Y presents $4,000 of checks drawn on Bank X and $2,000 on Bank Z; and the messenger from Bank Z brings $5,000 worth of claims on Bank X and $3,000 on Bank Y. The clearinghouse manager would then make up a clearing statement resembling that in Table 8-1.

In this situation, as can be readily observed, Bank X has $10,000 of claims on other local banks, and other local banks have $9,000 on Bank X. Bank X is therefore said to have a *favorable clearing balance* amounting to $1,000. Similarly, Bank Z, which presents $8,000 of claims on the other two banks but has only $5,000 presented against it, has a $3,000 favorable clearing balance. Bank Y

TABLE 8-1

Local Clearinghouse Statement

	Checks Written on			Total Checks Brought
	Bank X	Bank Y	Bank Z	
Bank X brings	—	$7,000	$3,000	$10,000
Bank Y brings	$4,000	—	2,000	6,000
Bank Z brings	5,000	3,000	—	8,000
Total checks written on	$9,000	$10,000	$5,000	$24,000

presents claims on Banks X and Z totaling $6,000 but is, in its turn, confronted with claims on it of $10,000. Bank Y, therefore, has an *unfavorable clearing balance* totaling $4,000.

Note that $24,000 of local checks are involved here but that a payment of $4,000 from Bank Y—$1,000 to Bank X and $3,000 to Bank Z—will be sufficient to settle accounts. The rest disappears through the simple process of cancellation. Bank X, for example, has given credit to its depositors for the $10,000 in local checks deposited there. It is compensated by marking down other depositors' accounts by $9,000 (the checks presented against it at the clearinghouse) and receiving the $1,000 from Bank Y.

If all three banks are members of the Federal Reserve System, the $4,000 payment can be made quite simply by a telephone call to the Federal Reserve bank requesting an increase in Bank X's reserve account by $1,000, an increase in Bank Z's by $3,000, and an offsetting decrease in Bank Y's by $4,000.[1]

Collection of a Check Between Two Member Banks in Different Cities, but the Same Federal Reserve District

Only local checks can be collected through a local clearinghouse. When banks in different cities are involved, a different collection agency is required. For member banks, the prime collection agency is their district Reserve bank.

Suppose that Mr. Jones writes a $100 check on his account in a Reading, Pennsylvania, member bank, payable to Firm X, which banks at a Philadelphia member bank. How is this check collected?[2]

The check, deposited by Firm X in its Philadelphia member bank, is sent by that bank to the Philadelphia Federal Reserve Bank, which serves both it and the Reading member bank. The Philadelphia Federal Reserve Bank *collects* the check by increasing the reserve account of the Philadelphia member bank by $100 and decreasing the reserve account of the Reading bank by a similar amount. The check is then sent to the Reading bank, which completes the collection process by marking down Mr. Jones's checking account by $100 and, at the end of the month, sending him the canceled check along with his monthly statement.

In terms of T-accounts, the transaction has the following effects:

---

[1]Settlement of the balance is just as simple even if all local banks are not members of the Federal Reserve System. One common practice, for example, is for all local banks to maintain a checking account at a single agreed-upon local bank (or out-of-town large city correspondent). Again, settlement can be completed via a single telephone call from the clearinghouse manager.

[2]The process to be described in this section is an oversimplified version of the actual process. Despite its oversimplification, we shall use it as the basis for future examples that involve check collections. A more complete discussion of the actual process, including the complications introduced by time lags in the collection process, will be presented in the section entitled "A More Detailed Discussion of Check Collection—Federal Reserve Float."

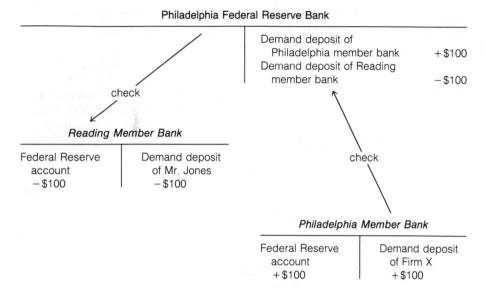

Collection of a Check Between Two Member Banks in Different Federal Reserve Districts

Things become a bit more complicated when two different Federal Reserve districts are involved, for the rather obvious reason that the member banks concerned do not carry Reserve accounts at a common Federal Reserve bank.

Suppose, for example, that our Mr. Jones in Reading (Philadelphia Federal Reserve district) makes out a check to pay a bill to Firm Y, located in New York City (New York Federal Reserve district). In this case, when Firm Y deposits the check in its New York member bank, this bank sends it to the New York Federal Reserve Bank to initiate the collection process. The New York Federal Reserve Bank, as before, increases the reserve account of the New York member bank, but this time it cannot collect from the bank on which the check is written. What solution exists for this problem?

For just such cases, the Federal Reserve System maintains an office in Washington called the *Interdistrict Settlement Fund*. Each of the 12 Federal Reserve banks maintains an Interdistrict Settlement Account at the Interdistrict Settlement Fund. Although strictly paper entries, these accounts function exactly as if they were checking accounts owned by the Federal Reserve banks whose function is to settle claims between districts.[3]

On receipt of the check from Firm Y's New York member bank, the New York Federal Reserve Bank would, after increasing the member bank's reserve

---

[3]Prior to April 1975, Federal Reserve bank "deposits" at the Interdistrict Settlement Fund consisted of gold certificates, which thus were shifted among Federal Reserve banks in accordance with interdistrict claims.

account, send a wire to the Interdistrict Settlement Fund stating that it had received a check for $100 written on a bank in the Philadelphia Federal Reserve district. The Interdistrict Settlement Fund would respond to this by increasing the New York Federal Reserve Bank's Interdistrict Settlement Account and decreasing that of the Philadelphia Federal Reserve Bank.

In the meantime the check would be sent directly from the New York Federal Reserve Bank to the Philadelphia Federal Reserve Bank where the latter would reduce the Reading bank's reserve account, as well as its own claim on the Interdistrict Settlement Fund, and then send it, at long last, to Reading.[4]

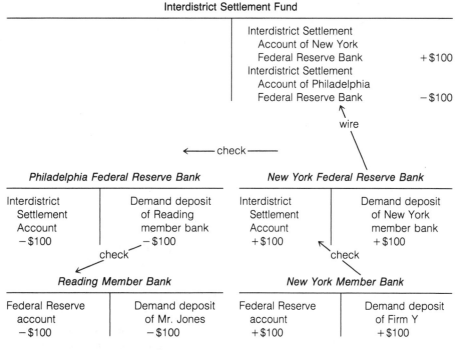

Collection of Nonlocal Checks Through Correspondent Banks

Although the Federal Reserve System clears billions of checks each year, an even greater number are collected outside the facilities of the System through correspondent banks. In 1981, for example, 16.6 billion checks were cleared through

---

[4]Each year Federal Reserve banks having had more claims on other district banks than have been presented against them at the Interdistrict Settlement Fund are "paid" for them by having U.S. securities shifted away from the other Reserve banks to them. It should be noted that an alternative procedure is for the member bank in which the check is deposited to send it directly to the Federal Reserve bank of the bank on which the check is written.

the Fed, but this figure represented less than half the estimated annual total of around 40 billion.

There are a number of reasons for this extensive reliance on correspondent banks for check collection, many of which were commented on in our earlier consideration of correspondent banking. These include the fact that correspondent banks are often closer and offer more rapid clearance than the appropriate Federal Reserve facility and that correspondent banks sometimes do not require their "respondents" to sort, code, and process checks as extensively as does the Fed. Thus, despite the fact that nonmember banks and other depository institutions may have checks collected via the Federal Reserve mechanism by maintaining a clearing balance at a Federal Reserve bank, relatively few do so.

Nonlocal checks collected through correspondents can be handled in a variety of ways. If the bank on which the check is written and the bank in which it is deposited happen to have a common correspondent bank, collection simply requires the correspondent to shift its deposit obligation from the former to the latter bank. If the correspondent bank receives a check from one of its respondents written on a bank that does not have an account with it, it may give deposit credit to its respondent bank and send the check on to its own district Federal Reserve bank for collection. Or the correspondent bank may send it on to another commercial bank in which it and the bank on which the check is written both carry correspondent accounts.

A More Detailed Discussion of Check Collection—Federal Reserve Float

The preceding examples are perfectly adequate descriptions of the check collection process for most purposes. Indeed, in any future examples we may use in this book, we shall rely on them fully.

However, they are oversimplified rather than exact descriptions. And the oversimplification involved, although justified as a means of cutting out unnecessary detail, is seriously deficient in that it excludes explicit recognition of a rather significant concept—**Federal Reserve float.** This section is aimed at correcting that deficiency.

Let us refocus on the case of the check written on Member Bank Y but deposited in Member Bank X in the same Federal Reserve district.[5] In our earlier example of this case, we assumed that the bank sending the check in immediately got an addition to its reserves and that the bank on which it was written lost reserves as soon as the check reached the Federal Reserve bank. Now we must recognize that, strictly speaking, neither of these assumptions is correct.

---

[5] Once again, to avoid unnecessary complication, we take an oversimplified example. The majority of checks cleared within the same Federal Reserve district currently provide credit within one day. Most of the Federal Reserve float we shall be concentrating on here arises out of interdistrict checks. Because such a transaction combines the complications of time lags with that of the Interdistrict Settlement Fund, our example will be restricted to an intradistrict transaction.

When a member bank in which a check is deposited sends it to the Federal Reserve bank, it does *not* immediately increase its Federal Reserve account but instead marks it up to a *temporary* account called its *Federal Reserve Collection Account.*

Thus the initial T-account effect would actually be

Member Bank X

Federal Reserve Collection Account	+$100	Demand deposit of check depositor	+$100

The important difference here is that the bank may *not* count its Federal Reserve Collection Account as a part of its legal reserves. When the check is received by the Federal Reserve bank, it, instead of immediately altering the reserve accounts of the two member banks involved, will indicate its receipt of the check by entering that amount in two temporary accounts entitled *uncollected cash items* and *deferred availability cash items.* The T-account effects would be

Federal Reserve Bank

Uncollected cash items	+$100	Deferred availability cash items	+$100

The *uncollected cash item* entry is a temporary account to allow for the fact that the Federal Reserve bank will shortly (as soon as Bank Y receives the check) have a claim on Bank Y. When the bank on which the check is written receives it, the Federal Reserve bank will remove the *uncollected cash item* entry and, at that time, mark down the reserve account of Bank Y. Then, and only then, does that bank lose reserves from the check.

The *deferred availability cash items,* on the other hand, is a temporary account that recognizes that the Federal Reserve bank owes that amount to Member Bank X but that credit for additional legal reserves is being temporarily withheld— deferred—for a certain period of time.

Now the Federal Reserve bank maintains a time schedule for each member bank in its district. This schedule categorizes each bank according to the *usual time it takes for a check to go from the Federal Reserve bank to each particular member bank.* If, for example, the normal time for mail delivery to Bank Y in our example were two days, Bank Y would be in the "two-day" category. The significance of this category lies in the fact that any bank sending in a check written on Bank Y would know that, *whether the check was actually delivered to Bank Y in the usual time or not,* it could take credit for additional reserves automatically after waiting the prescribed two-day period.

In the usual case, the check *would* be received by Bank Y at the end of two days, in which case the following T-account entries would be appropriate:

Federal Reserve Bank

(5) Uncollected cash items −$100	(3) Deferred availability cash items −$100 (4) Demand deposits of Bank X +$100 (6) Demand deposits of Bank Y −$100

Bank Y		Bank X
(7) Federal Reserve account −$100	(8) Demand deposit of check writer −$100	(1) Federal Reserve collection account −$100 (2) Federal Reserve account +$100

Entries (1), (2), (3), and (4) are necessary to recognize that, the scheduled time having elapsed, Bank X eliminates the temporary *Federal Reserve Collection Account* and takes credit for a $100 addition to its legal reserves, while the Federal Reserve bank eliminates the temporary *deferred availability item* account because the reserve credit to Bank X is no longer deferred.

Entries (5) and (6) are to take note of the fact that, as Bank Y has now actually received the check, the temporary *uncollected cash item* account can be eliminated and collection actually made by marking down Bank Y's reserve account.

There is, however, another possibility. If, after the scheduled two-day period has elapsed, Bank Y has for some reason *not yet* received the check, Bank X will automatically get its additional reserves (because the scheduled time period is up), but Bank Y will not yet lose any (because it has not yet, in fact, received the check).

In this case the T-account entries at the end of this two-day period would be

Federal Reserve Bank		Bank X	
	Deferred availability cash item −$100 Demand deposit of Bank X +$100	Federal Reserve Collection Account −$100 Federal Reserve account +$100	

For the moment (and until the check *is* actually received by Bank Y), the Federal Reserve's balance sheet still shows a $100 uncollected cash item, but no deferred availability cash item for this check. Also, for the same time period, *both banks are entitled to claim that $100 as a part of their legal reserves.* What has happened is that, because of the methods it uses to collect checks, the Federal Reserve has added to the volume of member bank legal reserves just as surely as if it had made a loan to a member bank for $100. In this case, Federal Reserve float has arisen.

As this example illustrates, Federal Reserve float increases whenever a bank that has sent in a check for collection receives an addition to its reserves before the check actually reaches the bank on which it was written and its reserves are correspondingly reduced. Such an increase, raising as it does the total legal reserves of the system, is conceptually precisely the same as a very-short-term loan of reserves by the Fed.

For the System as a whole, the amount of Federal Reserve float can always be determined from the balance sheets of all Federal Reserve banks, as the excess of uncollected cash items over deferred availability cash items. For example, in August 1982, uncollected cash items totaled $8.1 billion and deferred availability cash items totaled $5.5 billion. As of that date, therefore, Federal Reserve float totaled $2.6 billion.

Because they necessarily involve increases in the total of member bank reserves, and therefore in those banks' lending capacity, rises in Federal Reserve float are watched closely by Federal Reserve officials. Anything that slows down the normal delivery of the mails—a rail strike, a crippling storm—can markedly raise bank reserves at least temporarily via this rather involved route and may require offsetting action.

It is important that the student familiarize himself or herself with the nature of Federal Reserve float and with the actual details of check collection. However, as specific detail can sometimes be a burden when considering other matters, we shall, in the remainder of this book, revert to the more simplified versions covered in the preceding sections. Specifically, in any future examples involving check collections, we shall ignore the "temporary" accounts just discussed and assume that reserve changes take place immediately.

Check Collection, Float, and the Monetary Control Act of 1980

As we have seen, prior to the Monetary Control Act of 1980, member banks of the Federal Reserve System were subjected to substantially more rigorous reserve requirements than were applied to nonmember banks and other depository institutions. In an attempt to recompense them partially for this added expense, member banks were provided a number of services free of charge by the Federal Reserve System. When, however, the Monetary Control Act extended the same reserve requirements to all depository institutions, the main justification for these subsidized services to member banks was eliminated. As a result, the Monetary Control Act specifically required the Fed to (1) make such services as check collection, currency and coin provision, wire transfer, and securities safekeeping available to all depository institutions and (2) to sell such services to all users (including member banks) at prices that cover all costs including an estimate for the taxes and profits of a private supplier.

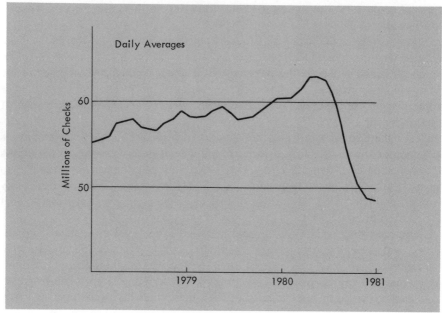

FIGURE 8-1   Number of Checks Processed by the Federal Reserve System, 1979–1981

Source: Board of Governors of Federal Reserve System, *1981 Annual Report.*

The most obvious result of this requirement is increased equity. If all depository institutions are to meet the same reserve requirements, all should have access to the discount window and to other Fed services on the same terms. But, in addition, charging explicit prices for such resource-using activities of the Fed will permit competition between the Fed and private sellers (e.g., correspondent banks) for the business and will require member bank buyers to economize on the use of services heretofore considered "free goods." This should promote a more efficient use of resources in this area.

Charges for Federal Reserve check collection were introduced in mid-1981, and, as Figure 8-1 makes clear, the effect was as might have been expected: a significant reduction in checks processed through the Fed. Indeed, between 1980 and 1981, the number of checks collected via the Federal Reserve fell off by about 22 percent.

Another requirement of the Monetary Control Act was that, as soon as possible, the Federal Reserve should begin to charge for the heretofore interest-free loan of reserves provided the banking system when float arises. The Federal Reserve's initial response to this requirement has been an intensive effort to reduce the size of the float. Beginning in 1980, the Board of Governors launched a program to reduce the level of float through improvements in the collection process. This plan reduced the size of float from a daily average of $4.2 billion in 1980 to a daily average of $1.8 billion during the second quarter of 1982. Further changes authorized during 1983 were expected to reduce the float total by an additional 80 percent. Then starting in October 1983, the Fed was to begin charging interest (at the Federal Funds rate) on the small amount of float remaining.

Improving the Nation's Payment Mechanism: The Growth of Electronic Funds Transfer Systems

The sheer magnitude of the task of processing around 40 billion checks each year, plus the realization that this total has tended to double each decade, has forced the nation's monetary authorities into a series of measures aimed at speeding up the collection process and at reducing its enormous cost.[6]

The process of modernizing the check collection process began many years ago with the development of magnetic ink encoding of checks—an innovation that made possible the now almost-universal practice of machine processing of checks. It has continued more recently with the establishment of a number of regional check processing centers throughout the nation, and it goes forward at the moment with a series of efforts at the ultimate solution—replacement of paper checks altogether by systems permitting transfer of funds solely by electronic means.

What Is EFT?

In general terms, the movement toward development of an electronic funds transfer (EFT) system involves the substitution of electronic data processing and transmission for the current manual processing laboriously carried out primarily through paper checks. Preliminary steps toward establishment of a full-blown EFT system have included such measures as eliminating charges for, and expanding access to, the Federal Reserve's existing wire facilities for the transfer of funds. But the heart of the movement involves the spread of automated teller machines, point-of-sale systems, and automated clearinghouses.[7]

An *automated teller machine* (ATM) performs a number of banking services automatically either on or off the bank's premises. Among these services are the

---

[6]According to one recent estimate, the volume of checks collected in the U.S. tends to increase by 7.3 percent per year. See R. William Powers, "A Survey of Check Volumes in the U.S.," *Journal of Bank Research,* Winter 1976. Back in the mid-1970s, it was estimated that the direct costs of processing a single check averaged around 20 cents per check, producing a total annual tab, even in 1975 prices, of around $6 billion. See Arthur D. Little, *The Consequences of Electronic Funds Transfer* (Arthur D. Little, 1975).

[7]For discussions of the EFT development, see William C. Niblack, "Development of Electronic Funds Transfer Systems," *Review,* Federal Reserve Bank of St. Louis, September 1976; Charles J. Smaistra, "Current Issues in Electronic Funds Transfer," *Review,* Federal Reserve Bank of Dallas, February 1977; and *The Economics of a National Electronic Funds Transfer System,* Federal Reserve Bank of Boston Conference Series, No. 13, October 1974. For more recent references, see N. Sue Ford, "Electronic Funds Transfer: Revolution Postponed," *Economic Perspectives,* Federal Reserve Bank of Chicago, November–December 1980; and "Federal Reserve and the Payments System," *Federal Reserve Bulletin,* February 1981.

receipt of deposits, the dispensing of cash from demand and savings deposits, and making advances on credit cards. Access to the machine is via a card with magnetic strip and secret code number. Often the ATM is tied in to the bank's computer, permitting immediate alterations in the customer's account.

Point-of-sale systems (POS) are located in retail establishments and facilitate payment for goods purchased electronically. Also operated by the customer's card, these facilities perform services ranging from the authorization of checks or credit cards to transferring funds instantaneously (through the use of terminals tied in to the bank's computer) from the customer's to the store's account.

Automated clearinghouses (ACH) permit electronic clearing between banks. One of their most common uses is to make payroll payments directly to employees' banks without the use of checks. In this case, the employer places the payroll data on a computer tape and sends it to the (employer's) bank. Employees who are customers of the same bank have their accounts increased directly. Data as to amounts and banks of employees who bank elsewhere are then put on a magnetic tape that is delivered to the ACH. There a computer sorts out the information, bank by bank, and each other bank receives a computer tape listing the employees and the amount of their payment.

The Problems and Prospects of EFT Development. Several years ago it was generally thought that EFT systems would develop rapidly and smoothly, dramatically changing the nature of the nation's payments mechanism in short order. Indeed, if one considers the *value* of transactions, over 80 percent are already completed by some form of electronic funds transfer. On the other hand, if one focuses on the *number* of transactions, it is apparent that EFT has not yet really won the day, for as recently as 1980, paper checks still accounted for about 85 percent of transactions. While EFT steadily gains wider acceptance, one is forced to the conclusion that the long-heralded "checkless society is still some distance away."[8]

The hurdles to more rapid development have included a mixed bag of technological, cultural, and regulatory factors. While it seems clear that, given sufficiently extensive use, the electronic devices are capable of substantially reducing the average costs of payment, the initial outlays required are enormous. A large share of these costs would, of course, be fixed costs, so that—given very intensive use by the public—the cost per unit could be brought down to levels well below those of more conventional methods.

But the public's reception of EFT has been lukewarm, forestalling full realization of the significant economies of scale that are available. The reasons for

---

[8]A good illustration of the change is provided by the following two quotations from *Business Week* magazine. On August 4, 1975, *Business Week* reported, "Faster than any but the most optimistic thought possible, electronic banking is sweeping the country. . . ." Less than two years later, on April 18, 1977, the same magazine observed, "Suddenly it appears that the great electronic banking revolution that has been 'just around the corner' for a decade may never arrive at all."

public resistance are varied. Customs change slowly, and many people simply do not trust computers. In addition, there is considerable reluctance to give up the tried and true financial record that canceled checks provide. And many have expressed real concern that EFT data banks might ultimately collect so much personal information as to constitute a serious threat to privacy.

In one important respect, however, banking law has, at least up until quite recently, tended to "stack the deck" against EFT and in favor of paper checks. As we noted earlier, it has long been illegal for banks to pay explicit interest on checking accounts. But, especially with the Federal Reserve System offering check collection free of charge to its member banks, checking accounts have tended to be real money makers for banks. So they have proceeded to subsidize checking accounts with *implicit* interest payments—not the least of which has been the provision of "free" checking.

But, as we have seen, the Monetary Control Act of 1980 has instituted some important changes. Now that banks must pay for the Fed's check collecting services, checking accounts are more expensive to administer and "free" checking may very well be on the way out. If these changes signal an end to the practice of subsidizing paper checks, and if EFT really can accomplish check collection at a much lower per unit cost than can the current manual system, the lower charges may well provide the incentive needed to change the public's attitude toward EFT markedly. It is not possible at this point to predict how rapidly EFT will grow. One can, however, be certain that it *will* continue growing.

Federal Reserve System
Reserve Requirements

Under current law, all depository institutions are required to "back up" their transactions accounts and their "nonpersonal" time deposits with a specified fraction of *total* or *legal* reserves. This requirement is, without question, the cornerstone of the System's power to control the money supply.

The applicable current law (the Monetary Control Act of 1980) identifies the depository institutions subject to reserve requirements as commercial banks (member and nonmember), mutual savings banks, savings and loan associations, and credit unions.[9] The "transactions accounts" behind which reserves are required include checking accounts, NOW accounts, ATS accounts, and share draft accounts. The "nonpersonal time deposits" subject to reserves are time deposits with maturities of less than two and a half years owned by anyone other than natural persons or sole proprietors.

---

[9]Technically, the law covers all these institutions covered by, or eligible to apply for, federal insurance. See Charles R. McNeill, "The Depository Institutions Deregulation and Monetary Control Act of 1980," *Federal Reserve Bulletin,* June 1980.

TABLE 8-2

Legal Limits to Board of Governors' Authority
to Vary Required Reserve Ratios[a]

Transaction Accounts[b]	Minimum	Maximum
0 - $2 million[c]	0	0
$2 - $26 million[c]	3%	3%
Over $26 million	8	14
Nonpersonal savings and time deposits	0	9

[a]If five members of the Board of Governors vote to declare the existence of "extraordinary circumstances," the Board may impose any reserve ratio on any liability of depository institutions for 180 days.

[b]If five members of the Board of Governors vote affirmatively, the Board may impose supplementary reserve requirements up to 4 percent on transactions accounts.

[c]The amount to which the zero and 3 percent bracket applies grows each year by 80 percent of the percentage change in total transactions accounts at all depository institutions.

The Monetary Control Act specifies the assets that qualify as "total" or "legal" reserves to include vault cash or checking accounts held at a district Federal Reserve bank.[10] Finally, the law sets up limits within which the Board of Governors of the Federal Reserve System may alter the *required reserve ratio*. These limits are reported in Table 8-2.[11]

There is, of course, nothing in the law to prevent a depository institution from holding *more* total reserves (i.e., vault cash and Federal Reserve account) than its outstanding deposits and required reserve ratios dictate. The institution that does so is said to have *excess* reserves—total legal reserves that exceed the minimum amount required to back up present deposit liabilities.

Perhaps a numerical example will help to clarify the terminology here. Suppose that Bank A happens to be a member bank for which the applicable required reserve ratios average out to 12 percent for transactions accounts and 3 percent for nonpersonal time deposits. Assume further that Bank A's balance sheet is

---

[10]Accounts held by depository institutions at Federal Home Loan banks, the National Credit Union Administration Central Liquidity Facility, or correspondent banks count toward satisfying the reserve requirement if those institutions "pass through" such reserves to a Federal Reserve bank. Reserves are "passed through" if the correspondent bank or other authorized institution opens a dollar-for-dollar account at a Federal Reserve bank "on behalf of" its respondent bank.

[11]The legal limits reported in Table 8-2 are those included in the MCA of 1980 and the Depository Institutions Act of 1982. Actually they are being phased in over time. Member banks (which have been subject to higher ratios) were scheduled to have their requirements "phased down" to these levels by late 1983. Other depository institutions (which have previously had no federal reserve requirement to meet) are scheduled to have requirements "phased up" to the legislated requirements by September 1987.

Bank A

Cash	$ 100	Transactions accounts (demand deposits plus NOW and ATS accounts)	$2,000
Federal Reserve account	250		
Loans and securities	3,500		
Other assets	1,150	Nonpersonal time deposits	2,500
		Other liabilities and net worth	500

In that case its *total* reserves are $350 (the sum of its cash and Federal Reserve account). Its *required* reserves (the amount of total reserves the law requires it to have to "back up" its current outstanding transactions accounts and nonpersonal time deposits) equal $315—the sum of .12 × $2,000 and .03 × $2,500. Its *excess* reserves, therefore, equal $35.

The student should always remember the following simple relationship:

$$\text{Total reserves} \equiv \text{Required reserves} + \text{Excess reserves}$$

Given sufficient information to compute any two of these totals, the third is obvious.

Reserve requirements need not be met on a daily basis. Member banks have a two-week "reserve period" within which they are required to maintain *average daily total reserves* equal to the required percentage of *average daily deposits* outstanding during that period.[12] If, for example, average daily deposits during the period require average daily total reserves of $4 million, the requirement could be satisfied by a bank's holding average daily total reserves of $3 million for the first nine business days, so long as it had the $13 million needed on the tenth day to achieve the required $4 million average for the period.

And what happens if a depository institution fails to meet the requirement? If the deficiency is minor—no more than 2 percent of the reserves required for the period—no penalty is assessed if it carries an equivalent amount of excess reserves the following period.[13] And even in the case of larger deficiencies, the Federal Reserve bank may waive any penalty depending on the circumstances. Where a penalty is assessed, the usual practice is to charge the offending institution a fine on the amount of the deficiency at a rate that is 2 percent higher than the current Federal Reserve discount rate. For more serious violators, the System may invoke "cease-and-desist" orders or, where appropriate, assess civil money penalties.

---

[12]Prior to a change to be effective in February, 1984, the reserve calculation was made on a *lagged* basis. That is, required reserves for any week were based upon the quantity of deposits outstanding *two weeks previously*. The change from *lagged* reserve accounting to the present *contemporaneous* reserve accounting came after sharp criticism of the former practice. Reserves behind nontransactions deposits are still computed on a lagged basis.

[13]Similarly, excess reserves in any period, up to a maximum of 2 percent of required reserves in that period, may be "carried forward" to apply to the following week's required reserves.

One final word of caution about the purpose of reserve requirements may be appropriate before we proceed. It is perhaps natural to think of required reserves as primarily a source of liquidity for the bank. Indeed, there can be little doubt that earlier reserve requirement legislation *was* aimed largely at providing liquid funds in case of sudden unexpected withdrawals. But those days have long since passed. Such a view constitutes a serious misconception regarding the major role of reserve requirements. After all, if the law requires that an institution *hold* a certain quantity of reserves, those reserves certainly are not available to pay out to meet cash demands.

Far from providing for bank liquidity needs, reserve requirements are the fulcrum or cornerstone on the basis of which our monetary authorities limit the supply of money and credit in the economy. And this is a much more important function than partially providing for bank liquidity.

Review Questions

1. Explain the operation of local clearinghouses. Why must the total of unfavorable clearing balances at any clearinghouse always equal the total of favorable clearing balances?

2. Carefully explain how the collection of a check written on a member bank in one Federal Reserve district and deposited in a member bank in a different district affects the balance sheets of the Federal Reserve banks involved.

3. Explain how Federal Reserve float arises. What is the significance of a sudden large increase in float?

4. Identify
   a. Interdistrict Settlement Fund.
   b. Deferred availability cash items.
   c. Point-of-sale systems.
   d. Uncollected cash items.

5. Explain carefully how the Monetary Control Act of 1980 has affected check collection and Federal Reserve float.

6. "In one important respect banking law has, at least up until quite recently, tended to stack the deck against EFT and in favor of paper checks." Why is this the case? What has happened "recently" to reduce this bias?

7. Carefully explain the reserve requirements applied to depository institutions including (a) the assets that can be counted as "total" reserves, (b) the legal limits to required reserve ratios, (c) the deposit liabilities behind which reserves must be maintained, (d) the "reserve period" over which the legal requirement is computed, and (e) the fundamental purpose of legally required reserves.

9

The Creation and Destruction of Money by Commercial Banks Under Simplified Conditions

In this chapter, we consider the process whereby commercial banks create and destroy money under the assumptions that no one withdraws cash, that no time deposits exist and that the banks do not willingly keep excess reserves. These assumptions are, of course, far removed from reality, but they do serve the important function of providing us with the clearest possible preliminary view of the money creation process. A more realistic and much more complex discussion of the money supply expansion issue will be presented in Chapter 10.

The Fundamental Nature and Origin of Demand Deposits as Money

In one way, at least, it is unfortunate that the demand deposit portion of the money supply bears the name "deposit." The word *deposit* carries with it a connotation that can be seriously misleading to the introductory student. He or she is all too likely to leap to the seemingly logical conclusion that all demand deposits must necessarily have originated with the *deposit* of cash in a checking account somewhere, some time in the past.

Such a "money in the bank" view of demand deposits not only misconstrues their origin but also often leads to a distorted idea of the essence of demand deposits as money. The fundamental essence of demand deposits is the *debt of a bank*. It is the bank's debt that goes from person to person—settling transactions. The debt of the bank *is* the medium of exchange that performs the essential task of money regardless of its origin or the amount of currency involved.

Of course, demand deposits *can* originate from a depositor placing currency in a checking account—but this is the exception. Think for a moment about your own checking account. How often is it replenished by a direct deposit of currency?

For most people, the answer is, "Seldom." Most people build up their balances by deposit of a check on another bank—the weekly paycheck from their employer or the student's monthly check from home. This simply consists of a transfer of a demand deposit from one bank to another. But where did that demand deposit really *originate?* Is it likely that the check writer—your employer or your parents— originated it by depositing cash in their accounts? Not really. Chances are that they too received it in the form of a check.

The truth is, of course, that the bulk of the demand deposit portion of our money supply originates not from the deposit of currency but, rather, from commercial bank lending. It can, in fact, be said that *whenever a commercial bank makes a loan or purchases a security (from the nonbank public), it creates new money and thereby expands the nation's money supply.* Similarly, whenever a loan at a commercial bank is paid off or a security is sold (to a member of the nonbank public), money is thereby destroyed and the money supply cut. Let us see why this occurs.

How Banks Create and Destroy Money

Whenever a commercial bank makes a loan, it accepts the borrower's IOU, in return for which it makes available the proceeds of the loan in money form. Similarly, when a bank purchases a security from a member of the nonbank public, it adds the security to its portfolio and pays the seller with newly created money. In either case, the borrower (or the seller of the security) acquires claim to a new checking account, which the bank creates by simply writing it up on its books.[1] The T-account effects in these cases would be

Bank X Makes a Loan		Bank X Buys a Security	
Loans (borrower's IOU) +$100	Demand deposits (owed to borrower) + $100	Securities +$100	Demand deposits (owed to seller of security) +$100

In each case, the demand deposit created by the bank to complete the transaction constitutes a net addition to the nation's money supply, raising M1. Indeed the majority of the U.S. money supply originates in just this fashion.

Exactly the reverse occurs whenever bank loans mature and are paid off or

---

[1] Obviously the bank must possess sufficient reserves to permit this. The proceeds of a loan or the payment for a security *could*, of course, be made in the form of cash rather than a newly created demand deposit. This would be a most unusual procedure, since borrowers generally prefer the safety and convenience of a deposit. Even in this case, however, the money supply would rise, since cash that had been in bank vaults would then be in circulation.

when banks sell securities to members of the nonbank public. In this case, the borrower (or the purchaser of the security) must pay money into the bank, thereby removing it from circulation and reducing M1. In the most common situation, where payment is effected via a check written on an account at the bank being paid, the T-account effects are[2]

Loan at Bank X Paid Off		Bank X Sells a Security	
Loans −$100	Demand deposits (of borrower) −$100	Securities −$100	Demand deposits (of buyer of security) −$100

The important thing for the student to bear in mind from all this is the simple fact that **commercial banks cannot avoid raising the nation's money supply when they acquire more earning assets from the public.**

The Limits to Commercial Bank Money Creation, Assuming No Cash Drain, Time Deposits, or Desired Excess Reserves

At first glance, commercial banking would appear to be an absurdly lucrative business. After all, where else can a business manager create the "product" that provides his or her income—money for loan—by the mere stroke of a pen? What a wonderfully simple means of amassing profits! "Mr. Businessman, you give me your IOU for $100,000 and I shall reciprocate by giving you mine—in the form of a checking account—for the same amount, *provided* that you agree to pay me back an additional $10,000 in interest for doing so." What a seemingly effortless way of earning a living!

But alas, the road to riches for the commercial banker is not really all that easy. It is true that the banker has every reason for desiring to expand his loans, thereby expanding the money supply by an equivalent amount—for when he can do this, he does indeed raise his income. But his ability to do so is limited on a number of fronts and for a variety of reasons. We turn now to a consideration of the limits to the lending (and money creating) capacity of commercial banks. We shall approach this topic in three steps. First, our focus will be restricted to the individual commercial bank and the limitations on its ability to create more money. Then, we shall switch to a consideration of the banking system as a whole under the highly oversimplified assumptions of no cash drain and no time deposits and no desired excess reserves. Third, in the next chapter, we shall attempt a closer approach to reality by relaxing our assumptions and admitting cash drain, time

---

[2]If the borrower pays off the loan with cash—an unlikely possibility—the money supply is still reduced by the amount of the payment, since cash that was in the public's hands then disappears into bank vaults (where it is no longer counted as part of M1).

deposits, and desired excess reserves into the picture. Throughout this chapter and the next, to keep the discussion as simple as possible, we shall focus only on commercial banks and only on the demand deposit component of transactions accounts.

The Single Commercial Bank

The individual commercial bank, as a profit-seeking institution, has a natural desire to maximize its ownership of earning assets—loans and securities. Because, as we have just seen, such assets can be readily acquired by the simple act of creating more demand deposits, an obvious question arises. What keeps commercial banks from expanding the money supply to infinite proportions in their quest for added profits? What limits the individual bank's money creation?[3]

To begin with, any issuer of demand deposits must be prepared as a matter of law, to pay *cash on demand* to any depositor who requests it. Consequently, *even if there were no required reserve ratio at all,* commercial banks could not freely expand loans (and demand deposits) without limit. As long as people desire to hold their money partly in the form of demand deposits and partly in the form of cash, any expansion in the former will surely induce an increase in the latter. If, for example, a bank possesses $1 million in cash and has, at the moment, $40 million of demand deposits outstanding, the $1 million may be just adequate to meet usual demands for cash on the part of the holders of the $40 million. Any increase in loans (and therefore in demand deposits) in this case would consequently raise the demand deposit total, and the attendant risk of cash withdrawal, to a level at which $1 million in cash would be insufficient. Such a bank, then, would be unable to grant more loans.

The risk of cash withdrawal, however, is not the most important limitation on the single bank's loan expansion potential. Far more confining is the restriction that is imposed by the combination of the *required reserve ratio* and the *likelihood that borrowers of newly created deposits will write checks on them that will be deposited in other banks.*

Let us revert, once again, to an example. Suppose that member Bank X, subject to a required reserve ratio of 20 percent, has the following assets and liabilities:

Bank X

Cash	$ 10,000	Demand deposits	$600,000
Federal Reserve account	125,000	Other liabilities and net worth	100,000
Loans and securities	560,000		
Other assets	5,000		

---

[3]While the physical act of creating added deposits *is* essentially costless, servicing those deposits (and attracting the reserves that permit them) does, of course, involve real marginal costs, which certainly could make some loans losing propositions. If such costs were to be the effective limit on loans, however, they would result in banks retaining excess reserves—a possibility that we have assumed away.

Assuming no nonpersonal time deposits, Bank X has excess reserves totaling $15,000 ($135,000 minus 20 percent of $600,000). The very existence of excess reserves indicates unused lending power available to the bank. We can assume that, as a profit-maximizing institution, Bank X will want to exploit its full lending (and interest-earning) capacity. Just how far can it go?

If the required reserve ratio were the only limitation, it seems clear that, at least initially, it could *legally* lend an additional $75,000—for if a 20 percent required reserve ratio means anything, it signifies that each dollar of reserves can, at maximum, back up $5 of demand deposits. Therefore $15,000 of excess reserves can be used *legally* to back up $75,000 of additional demand deposits. But hold on a bit!

No banker can afford to be satisfied with considering only what is legal today without some concern with what is likely tomorrow. And the truth is that if Bank X *should* lend out an additional $75,000 on the basis of its present $15,000 of excess reserves, it will certainly be in trouble tomorrow.

Let us take a long look at the consequences of a single bank lending out, as in this case, an amount equal to five times its excess reserves. Immediately after the loan is granted, Bank X's balance sheet would be altered to look like this:

Bank X

Cash	$ 10,000	Demand deposits	$675,000
Federal Reserve account	125,000	Other liabilities and net worth	100,000
Loans and securities	635,000		
Other assets	5,000		

Bank X is, for the moment at least, within the limits of the law, as its $135,000 of total legal reserves are exactly 20 percent of its outstanding demand deposits. But it had better beware the future.

The borrower of the $75,000 can certainly be expected to begin writing checks on his newly created account almost immediately. After all, who borrows money at interest without the intent of spending the money? Bank X must count on $75,000 worth of checks being written in short order.

Now the important question is, "Where will those checks end up?" If they are redeposited by the check recipient into accounts at Bank X, Bank X will lose no reserves and be in no difficulty. If, however, they are deposited in a *different* member bank, then Bank X can expect to lose $75,000 of reserves as a result of their collection through the Federal Reserve.

Which eventuality is most likely? The answer is obvious. Bank X is only 1 out of more than 14,000 commercial banks in this country—any of which might receive a check—so the odds on its returning to Bank X are prohibitively small. And if the likely thing happens and $75,000 of checks are written, deposited in a different bank, and collected via the Federal Reserve, Bank X will quickly find itself in the following position:

Bank X

Cash	$ 10,000	Demand deposits	$600,000
Federal Reserve account	50,000	Other liabilities and net worth	100,000
Loans and securities	635,000		
Other assets	5,000		

Its total legal reserves are reduced to $60,000, while its required reserves are $120,000. It has a $60,000 deficiency, which, if not made up shortly, will lay it open to fines or other penalties. Clearly no single bank would knowingly place itself in this situation.

For the reasons just discussed, individual commercial banks making loans must *expect* to lose reserves shortly in the amount loaned. Consequently, the prudent banker must limit his or her lending (and money creating) activities to a scale that will preclude the embarrassment and expense of a reserve deficiency. The only completely safe practice is to limit new loans to the *amount of the bank's excess reserves* rather than a multiple of them. This is, in fact, the usual custom of commercial bankers.

If Bank X should follow the "working rule" of lending just the amount of its excess reserves, $15,000, the expected loss of reserves that follows the granting of the loan will not leave it with a reserve deficiency. Immediately after making the loan, its balance sheet would be

Bank X

Cash	$ 10,000	Demand deposits	$615,000
Federal Reserve account	125,000	Other liabilities and net worth	100,000
Loans and securities	575,000		
Other assets	5,000		

Then, after the borrower writes checks, the recipient deposits them in a different bank, and they are collected via the Federal Reserve, it would be left with

Bank X

Cash	$ 10,000	Demand deposits	$600,000
Federal Reserve account	110,000	Other liabilities and net worth	100,000
Loans and securities	575,000		
Other assets	5,000		

Its remaining reserves of $120,000 are just sufficient to meet the requirements of the law, and it can go on about its business. Its prudence, in limiting its loans to the amount of its excess reserves, has paid off.

Summing up, the individual commercial bank is limited in its lending and money-creating activities by **(1) the likelihood of cash withdrawal and (2) the legal reserve requirement, coupled with the likelihood that it will quickly lose**

reserves (to other commercial banks) in the full amount of any loan it makes.
To protect against either or both of these threats, the single commercial banker in
a many-bank system can safely lend out only **the amount of his or her excess
reserves.**

The Commercial Banking System,
Assuming No Cash Withdrawal,
Time Deposits,
or Desired Excess Reserves

No one bank can safely expand the money supply by more than the amount
of its excess reserves. But if we widen our horizon to encompass all 14,000-plus
commercial banks—the banking system as a whole—we find, not surprisingly, that
potential expansion is considerably enhanced. With each single bank along the way
expanding to its safe maximum, the sum created by all is bound to be greater.

In this section, for simplicity, we assume that banks have no desire to hold
on to any excess reserves and that depositors are satisfied to keep checking accounts
in that form—withdrawing no cash and converting no demand deposits to time
deposits. Once a demand deposit is created via the loan process, it is assumed to
stay in that form.

With these simplifications, which will be dropped in the next chapter, the
results are apparent. Unlike the single-bank case, when loans are made and checks
are written on the newly created deposits, there is no loss of reserves *for the system
as a whole*. This is because the loss of reserves by the bank that made the loan is
exactly offset, from the vantage point of the system as a whole, by the gain of
reserves on the part of the bank in which the checks are deposited.

If, in this case, the banking system starts out with excess reserves of $15,000,
and none of these reserves can be lost *to the system* through cash withdrawal,
through conversion to time deposits, or through transfer to another bank, then the
maximum possible expansion of deposits and loans is only reached when every
dollar of excess reserves is used to support its maximum permissible amount of
demand deposits.

If, for example, the required reserve ratio is 20 percent (one-fifth), this means
that at maximum each $1 of reserves may support $5 of deposits. Consequently,
$15,000 of excess reserves could, at the extreme, back up five times that amount,
or $75,000 of new demand deposits. If the required reserve ratio were 10 percent
(one-tenth), each dollar of reserves would back up $10 of deposits, and $15,000
of excess reserves would not be "used up" until $150,000 of demand deposits had
been created. Finally, a 25 percent (one-fourth) required reserve ratio would imply
that each dollar of reserves can support $4 of deposits, so that $15,000 of excess
reserves would be sufficient to back up $60,000 of additional deposits.

It is not coincidental that in each of the preceding examples, the maximum
possible expansion of demand deposits by the banking system as a whole equals
the *reciprocal of the required reserve ratio times its excess reserves*. Under the

assumptions we have made, that is the formula for computing maximum potential deposit (and loan) expansion for the banking system as a whole.

To compute maximum potential deposit and loan expansion by the entire commercial banking system (no cash withdrawal and no conversion to time deposits),

$$\frac{1}{\text{Required reserve ratio}} \times \frac{\text{Excess reserves}}{\text{of system}} = \frac{\text{Maximum possible}}{\text{expansion of demand}} \\ \text{deposits and loans}$$

Some memorization of pat formulas is useful for handling economic issues, but memorization alone is sterile without a thorough understanding of the logic that lies behind the formulas. Let us take a brief look beyond the mere mathematics of the final outcome, to the *process* whereby this result may be achieved.

Suppose, for example, that we have a banking system in which no bank has excess (or a deficiency of) reserves except Bank A, which, at the moment, is in the following condition:

Bank A

Cash	$ 50,000	Demand deposits	$2,000,000
Federal Reserve account	380,000	Other liabilities and net worth	300,000
Loans and securities	1,800,000		
Other assets	70,000		

If the required reserve ratio for all banks is 20 percent, Bank A (and the banking system as a whole) has $30,000 of excess reserves. Of course, we know immediately that, given these facts, the banking system as a whole can increase loans and demand deposits by $150,000 before the expansion limit is reached. Then, and only then, will every dollar of reserves be backing up its legal limit of $5 of deposits. Then, and only then, will every dollar of excess reserves have been "used up" in the sense that it will have become part of the required reserves.

But our interest here is in the *process* by which this limit is approached. It all starts, of course, in Bank A, the only bank with the present capacity to grant additional loans. As a single bank, Bank A, for reasons discussed earlier, will find its ideal combination of profitability and safety by following the working rule of lending out an amount just equal to its excess reserves. The T-account effects of its doing so will be

Bank A

Loans	+ $30,000	Demand deposits	+ $30,000

It is to be expected that the borrower will then write checks on his or her newly acquired account and that the recipient of those checks will deposit them in another bank. If the other bank is Bank B (and, to simplify, a member bank), it will immediately send the checks in for collection via the Federal Reserve. The effects of this step are

Bank A		Bank B	
Federal Reserve account −$30,000	Demand deposits −$30,000	Federal Reserve account +$30,000	Demand deposits +$30,000

Now the wisdom of Bank A's forbearance in lending only the amount of its excess reserves becomes evident. The expected has happened, and it has lost reserves equal to the loan granted. But, because it retains $400,000 of legal reserves, it is still able to support the remaining $2 million of demand deposits. It has done all the money creating it could and is now safely out of the picture.

But whereas Bank A has lost all its excess reserves, the banking *system* has not. The $30,000 of reserves, lost by Bank A, have been gained by Bank B. And now Bank B is in a position to grant a loan.

Bank B, which started with no excess reserves, has now received a $30,000 boost in its total reserves and an equivalent increase in its demand deposit liabilities. Remembering that $6,000 of the added reserves are required to back up the added deposits, we see that Bank B now has excess reserves of $24,000. It can, therefore, safely lend that amount.

Bank B		
Loans	+$24,000	Demand deposits +$24,000

At this point, $54,000 of newly created money exists. The $30,000 created by Bank A is still held as a deposit in Bank B, and an additional $24,000 has just been created by Bank B. As before, the borrower can be expected to write checks on the $24,000, and the checks will in all likelihood be deposited in a different bank (Bank C), which will, in turn, send them through the Federal Reserve collection facilities.

Bank B		Bank C	
Federal Reserve account −$24,000	Demand deposits −$24,000	Federal Reserve account +$24,000	Demand deposits +$24,000

Bank B loses $24,000 of the $30,000 of reserves it originally acquired, but the $6,000 it retains is sufficient to back up the $30,000 demand deposit that is still there. As before, however, another bank has gained the lost reserves. And, as the $24,000 of added total reserves provides Bank C with $19,200 of *excess* reserves (added total reserves, $24,000, minus 20 percent of added demand deposits, $4,800), this bank can now add further to the credit and money supply:

	Bank C	
Loans	+$19,200	Demand deposits	+$19,200

At this point, $73,200 of new money exists, $30,000 created by Bank A and still in Bank B, $24,000 created by Bank B and now in Bank C, and $19,200, just created by Bank C. Bank C will shortly lose $19,200 of reserves and deposits and Bank D will gain them. Bank D will then have excess reserves of $15,360 and will lend that much. It, in turn, will lose that amount to Bank E, which will then be in a position to create an additional $12,288, and so on. It is hardly necessary to continue with this description, the future course of which must be obvious by now.

Note that at each step along the way, individual commercial banks add to the money supply 80 percent of the amount added by the preceding bank. What we have, then, is a process in which, if the original excess reserves is represented by x, money is created in the following amounts:

	Bank A		*Bank B*		*Bank C*		*Bank D*	
Amount of new money created	x	+	.8x	+	.8(.8x)	+	.8[.8(.8x)]	etc.

This series of money supply additions clearly make up an infinite geometrical series, the formula for the addition of which is

$$\frac{1}{(1 - \text{The common multiple})} \quad \text{times} \quad \text{The first term in the series}$$

or, in this case,

$$\frac{1}{(1 - .80)} \times \begin{matrix} \text{Initial} \\ \text{excess} \\ \text{reserves} \end{matrix} = \frac{1}{.20} \times \$30,000 = 5 \times \$30,000 = \$150,000$$

Since, in this simplified case of banking system expansion, the denominator—1 minus the common multiple—must always equal the required reserve ratio, the mathematics and logic underlying the formula used earlier become clearer. What we now know is that the formula

$$\frac{1}{\text{Required reserve ratio}} \times \begin{matrix} \text{Excess} \\ \text{reserves} \end{matrix} = \begin{matrix} \text{Maximum possible expansion} \\ \text{of demand deposits} \\ \text{and loans} \end{matrix}$$

TABLE 9-1

Summary of Process of Demand Deposit Expansion by Entire Banking System, No Cash or Time Deposits

Banks	New Money Created by	New Loans Made by	Newly Created Demand Deposits Retained by	Original Excess Reserves Retained as Required Reserves by
A	$30,000	$30,000	—	—
B	24,000	24,000	$30,000	$6,000
C	19,200	19,200	24,000	4,800
D	15,360	15,360	19,200	3,840
E	12,288	12,288	15,360	3,072
F	9,830	9,830	12,288	2,458
G	7,864	7,864	9,830	1,966
H	6,291	6,291	7,864	1,573
I	5,033	5,033	6,291	1,258
J	4,026	4,026	5,033	1,007
K	3,221	3,221	4,026	805
L	2,577	2,577	3,221	644
M	2,062	2,062	2,577	515
N	1,650	1,650	2,062	412
O	1,320	1,320	1,650	330
P	1,056	1,056	1,320	264
Q	845	845	1,056	211
All other	3,377	3,377	4,222	845
Total by banking system as a whole	$150,000	$150,000	$150,000	$30,000

is simply the formula for summing the additions to the money supply that occur over time at Banks A, B, C, D, and so on, in amounts making up a geometric progression. The process of expansion just described is depicted in tabular form in Table 9-1.[4]

Commercial Bank Adjustment to Reserve Deficiencies

As we have just seen, commercial banks typically respond to excess reserves by acquiring more earning assets, thereby raising the money supply to the limit imposed by the required reserve ratio.[5] Let us now consider the other side of the coin. How do commercial banks adjust to reserve deficiencies?

---

[4]Some students may recognize the arithmetical equivalence of the so-called "money multiplier" (1/RRR) with the expenditure multiplier (1/MPS) normally encountered in introductory courses. The two are arithmetically identical—both being the formula for summing an infinite geometric series.

[5]Under the conditions assumed in this chapter.

A Single Bank with a Reserve Deficiency

We begin with the case of a single bank. Assume, for example, that Bank A is currently in the following position:

Bank A

Cash	$ 50,000	Demand deposits	$2,250,000
Federal Reserve account	375,000	Other liabilities and net worth	750,000
Loans and securities	2,200,000		
Other assets	375,000		

If the required reserve ratio is 20 percent for demand deposits, Bank A clearly has a reserve deficiency totaling $25,000. Such a situation cannot be permitted to continue indefinitely. If it should threaten to do so, Bank A will be forced to take action.

Now it must be remembered that the reserve requirement is a *ratio*. A $25,000 deficiency can be eliminated either by obtaining $25,000 of additional legal reserves or (if RRR = 20 percent) by reducing demand deposits by $125,000, or by some combination of the two. Of course, the acquisition of more reserves is normally preferable, and a commercial bank can opt for this solution in a number of ways. It could sell some of its U.S. securities, borrow reserves on the federal funds market, or borrow them through the Fed's discount window. Let us consider these options in turn.

Sale of U.S. Securities. One possible method is via the sale of some of its secondary reserves—its short-term U.S. securities. If our Bank A can find a buyer for $25,000 worth of U.S. securities, its reserve deficiency will probably be erased. Three possible sales must be considered—to another member bank, to a member of the nonbank public, and to a Federal Reserve bank.

If another member bank should purchase them, the normal means of payment between member banks will provide Bank A with additional reserves at the expense of the purchasing bank, as the following T-accounts illustrate.

Bank A		Member Bank Purchasing Securities	
U.S. securities −$25,000		U.S. securities +$25,000	
Federal Reserve account +$25,000		Federal Reserve account −$25,000	

If the purchaser is a nonbank financial institution such as an insurance company, or any member of the nonbank public, payment would normally be made by a check written on an account at another member bank, the collection of which would, once again, raise Bank A's reserve account by the requisite amount while lowering that of the other bank.

Bank A		Member Bank on Which Check Is Written to Purchase Securities	
U.S. securities −$25,000 Federal Reserve account +$25,000		Federal Reserve account −$25,000	Demand deposits −$25,000

Finally it is conceivable that Bank A might sell its U.S. securities to a Federal Reserve bank. If so, the T-account effects would be

Bank A		Federal Reserve Bank	
U.S. securities −$25,000 Federal Reserve account +$25,000		U.S. securities +$25,000	Demand deposit of member banks +$25,000

Of course it must be remembered that this last transaction constitutes a Federal Reserve open-market purchase, which would be available only when the Fed *desires* to increase bank reserves. Bank A cannot count on selling to the Federal Reserve System, but if the Fed *is* in the market to buy, Bank A may be in luck.

Borrowing Federal Funds.   An attractive alternative to the sale of U.S. securities would be borrowing the needed reserves on the *federal funds* market. Federal funds, as noted earlier, consist of excess reserves in the form of deposits in the district Federal Reserve bank, which are lent by one member bank to another. Typically, federal fund transactions take the form of an unsecured 24-hour loan.[6] Arrangements are agreed upon by telephone between the lending bank and the borrowing bank (often referred to as the "buying" bank and the "selling" bank) and confirmed later by mail. The actual transfer of the reserves is normally accomplished

---

[6]Although most federal funds transactions are still of a specified, very-short-term maturity, recent years have seen increasing use of open-ended transactions wherein the borrowing bank is authorized to continue to use the funds for an indefinite period until notified to the contrary by the lending bank. In addition, some federal fund transactions have had specified maturity dates of up to one year. See Donald C. Miller, "Bank Asset and Liability Management," *The World Banking Challenge* (Washington, D.C.: American Bankers Association, 1972), p. 102. For a more recent discussion, see C. M. Lucas, M. T. Jones, and T. B. Thurston, "Federal Funds and Repurchase Agreements," *Quarterly Review,* Federal Reserve Bank of New York, Summer 1977.

via a phone call or telegram from the lending bank to the Federal Reserve bank, instructing the latter to transfer the agreed-upon amount from its reserve account to that of the borrower. In the most usual case (a one-day loan), the Federal Reserve bank will reverse the transaction on the following day. Payment of interest for the loan—at the going *federal funds rate*—is normally made later by separate check.

The T-account effects of borrowing federal funds, for Bank A, might thus be

Bank A		Member Bank That Lends Excess Reserves	
Federal Reserve account +$25,000	Notes payable +$25,000	Federal Reserve account −$25,000 Loans +$25,000	

The federal funds market has grown rapidly in size and sophistication in the past decade. Originally, a market only among larger banks, it has more recently expanded to include most of the nation's banks. The increasing participation of smaller banks is partly a result of the development of large-bank intermediaries or brokers that "make a market" in federal funds for those who wish either to borrow or to lend. The reduction in the minimum-size transactions unit from $1 million to as little as $25,000 has also helped to open the market to much wider participation.

In addition, the essentially short-term nature of the market makes it almost ideal for handling many of the day-to-day changes involved in bank reserve management. Most small banks could not afford the skilled and specialized personnel required to keep their reserves fully used at all times by purchasing other earning assets. The federal funds market, therefore, provides access to income that might otherwise be forgone.

For a bank with a reserve deficiency, the short term of federal funds transactions has a special appeal. U.S. securities, although highly liquid, are generally sold through dealers who charge a commission for the service. Often it is cheaper to pay a federal funds rate that is higher than the interest forgone on the U.S. security if the added reserves are only needed temporarily, for the full cost of the security sale includes not only the interest forgone but the commission charge by the dealer.[7]

Borrowing Through the Federal Reserve Discount Window. A third source of funds for a bank with a reserve deficiency is the discount window of its Federal Reserve bank. It will be recalled that one of the original purposes of the Federal Reserve was to set up a "lender of last resort" to which individual member banks in temporary need could turn.

---

[7]For an excellent survey of the federal funds market, see Parker W. Willis, *A Study of the Market for Federal Funds,* a Federal Reserve Board publication, which is part of the Federal Reserve study, *Fundamental Reappraisal of the Discount Mechanism,* 1967.

Although on the surface this might well seem the most attractive "way out" of all for our Bank A, it has not been of great significance in recent years. We shall dig more deeply into this issue in Chapter 11. For our present discussion, we need only note that two reasons for the relative unattractiveness of the discount window have been advanced. On the one hand, it has long been argued that member banks are traditionally reluctant to be in debt to the central bank and only turn to the Fed as a last resort. On the other hand, it has been persuasively argued more recently that the Federal Reserve's Regulation A, which has governed the administration of the discount window, has worked so as to, in effect, refuse many potential member bank borrowers access to loans. In any case, borrowing from the Federal Reserve has not been of great importance in recent years.

The Banking System
with a Reserve Deficiency

Just as there is a difference in the expansion potential of a single bank and the entire banking system when excess reserves exist, so too there is a difference in the alternatives available to the single bank and the system when reserves are deficient.

Suppose, for example, that we once again start with the assumption that Bank A has a $25,000 reserve deficiency but now add the assumption that *no other bank in the system has any excess reserves*. This gives us a case where the banking system as a whole has a $25,000 reserve deficiency.

Bank A must now eliminate its deficiency. Under the assumed conditions, it cannot borrow federal funds because no excess reserves exist at other banks. For the same reason, it cannot expect to bail itself out by the sale of some of its U.S. securities to other member banks. Finally, as a reserve shortage such as this would normally only occur when the Federal Reserve was following a restrictive monetary policy, Bank A almost surely can forget any ideas of selling securities to the Federal Reserve itself.

This leaves Bank A with only two remaining options for obtaining the necessary $25,000 of reserves. It can sell U.S. securities to a member of the nonbank public, or it can apply for a loan at the Federal Reserve discount window.

Now suppose for the moment that the Federal Reserve is so intent on implementing a "tight money" policy that it refuses to lend any reserves to Bank A. This assumption is decidedly *not* a realistic one. Although the Fed does have the right to refuse a request for a loan, it would be very unlikely to do so under the conditions we have described. We make the assumption only to illustrate the power that the Federal Reserve *does* have—if it should ever choose to use it—to force a multiple contraction of credit and money supply.

If a loan from the discount window is ruled out, Bank A has only one way in which to acquire more reserves—it can sell U.S. securities to the nonbank public. Suppose that it does so, selling $25,000 of U.S. securities to an insurance company that pays by a check written on its account at Bank B. The T-account effects, the reader will recall, would be

Bank A	
Federal Reserve account +\$25,000 U.S. securities −\$25,000	

Bank B	
Federal Reserve account −\$25,000	Demand deposit of insurace co. −\$25,000

So where does this leave us? Bank A has eliminated its reserve deficiency. But what of the system as a whole? Specifically, what about Bank B, which had neither an excess nor a deficiency of reserves before this transaction? Clearly, Bank B has inherited most of the reserve deficiency Bank A has just escaped. Its *required* reserves are reduced by \$5,000 (20 percent of \$25,000) because its demand deposits are down by \$25,000; but its *total legal* reserves are down by a full \$25,000, so it now has a \$20,000 reserve deficiency.

Now of course Bank B can get out from under the same way Bank A did— by selling a \$20,000 U.S. security to a member of the public. But when it does so, assuming that the buyer of the securities pays by check on his or her account at Bank C, Bank C ends up with \$20,000 fewer demand deposit liabilities and \$20,000 less reserves—a reserve deficiency of \$16,000.

If this game of "hot potato" is carried on until no bank in the system has any reserve deficiency, we end up with a multiple contraction that is exactly the reverse of the multiple expansion discussed earlier. The end will only come when the banking system has unloaded a total of \$125,000 of U.S. securities to the public so that demand deposits are reduced by a full \$125,000. *Not* coincidentally, that represents the reciprocal of the required reserve ratio (5) times the original reserve deficiency (\$25,000).

Before leaving this subject, it should be pointed out that selling securities is not really the only out. The same general result could be achieved if banks with reserve deficiencies would reduce their loans. There are two ways in which this might be done. To the extent that they have made loans that are subject to *call* (broker's loans are often call loans, which must be paid back at the discretion of the bank), they can call for their payment. If these are repaid by checks written on accounts at Bank A, the effect, of course is

Bank A	
Loans −\$125,000	Demand deposits −\$125,000

In the event that the quantity of call loans outstanding is insufficient to do the job, Bank A can obtain the same sort of result by simply refusing to renew other loans that reach their maturity date and must be paid off. One of the techniques of bank portfolio management is to arrange for a maturity structure of earning assets such that some are coming due, if not every day, at least on some regular basis. Consequently, although under happier circumstances the loans that are coming due would be immediately reissued, under the assumed stress of a persistent reserve deficiency, they must be permitted to disappear.

Summary

This chapter has endeavored to explain how—under the unrealistic assumptions of no cash drain, no time deposits, and no desired excess reserves—commercial banks expand and contract the nation's money supply as they go about their business of attempting to maximize profits. Given the assumptions made, we have seen that the only limit on money supply expansion by the banking system as a whole is the required reserve ratio. Further, we have learned that the existence of fractional (below 100 percent) reserve requirements permits the banking system as a whole—though not any one bank—to create new money in an amount that is a multiple of excess reserves.

Specifically, we have seen that, given the simplifying assumptions used,

1. A *single bank* with excess reserves can make new loans and create new money in an amount equal to

$$1 \times \frac{\text{Excess}}{\text{reserves}} = \frac{\text{Maximum safe increase}}{\text{in loans and demand deposits}}$$

2. The *banking system* with excess reserves can make new loans and create new money in an amount equal to

$$\frac{1}{\text{RRR}} \times \frac{\text{Excess}}{\text{reserves}} = \frac{\text{Maximum possible increase in}}{\text{loans and demand deposits}}$$

3. A *single bank* with a reserve deficiency has a variety of means of eliminating its deficiencies without the necessity of a reduction in the money supply.

4. The *banking system* with a reserve deficiency must reduce its loans or securities to eliminate the deficiency if the Federal Reserve System will not provide it more reserves. This must be done by an amount equal to

$$\frac{1}{\text{RRR}} \times \frac{\text{Reserve}}{\text{deficiency}} = \frac{\text{Necessary reduction in loans}}{\text{or securities and in demand deposits}}$$

Review Questions

1. Show appropriately labeled T-accounts depicting the effect on commercial banks (and the money supply) of a commercial bank
   a. Making a loan to a member of the public.
   b. Purchasing a U.S. security from a member of the nonbank public.
   c. Having a loan made earlier to a member of the public paid off via a check.
   d. Selling a U.S. security to a member of the nonbank public.
2. Explain carefully why a single bank in a many-bank system cannot safely make new loans in an amount larger than its excess reserves.

3. Assume that the banking system as a whole has the following consolidated balance sheet and that the required reserve ratio for demand deposits is 15 percent while that for time deposits is 5 percent.

Cash	$ 50,000	Demand deposits	$1,000,000
Federal Reserve account	180,000	Time deposits	1,000,000
Loans	1,500,000	Other	250,000
Securities	500,000		
Other	20,000		

   a. What are the excess reserves of the banking system?
   b. Assuming no cash drain, no change in time deposits, and that the banks do not willingly hold any excess reserves, what is the maximum increase in the money supply that the system can now create?

4. Carefully discuss the avenues open to a single bank with a reserve deficiency for eliminating that deficiency.

5. "If a single bank has a $100,000 reserve deficiency, the sale of $100,000 of U.S. securities to the nonbank public will normally (but not always) eliminate the deficiency. Such action will not, however, eliminate a $100,000 reserve deficiency of the banking system as a whole."
   a. Using T-accounts, show how such a sale by Bank A would normally eliminate its deficiency. Under what circumstance would it not do so?
   b. Explain carefully why such a sale could not eliminate the banking system's deficiency.

6. "If the banking system as a whole has a reserve deficiency and cannot acquire more total reserves, the result must be a multiple contraction of demand deposits and loans or securities." Explain.

10

The Determinants
of the Money Supply

A solid basis for understanding complex institutions sometimes necessitates suppression of the detail of the "real-world" situation to isolate and magnify main underlying causal mechanisms. Such is the case with commercial banking.

For purposes of throwing into bold relief the central fact that multiple credit creation results from fractional reserve banking, the oversimplified version presented in the preceding chapter probably does a better job than a more detailed, "realistic" discussion. But if the ultimate objective is to consider practical policy measures in a going economy, some of the more important complicating factors must be reinjected into the picture.

The Federal Reserve's Board of Governors, for example, can hardly carry out its real-world obligations by blandly assuming—without further concern for what, in fact, *will* happen—that with a 20 percent required reserve ratio, $1 billion of excess reserves will produce a $5 billion rise in the money supply. This result will be realized only if the public withdraws no cash and converts no demand deposits to time deposits, and if the banks are unwilling to carry any excess reserves. If the public or the commercial banks should happen to be so uncooperative as to violate these assumptions, then the $5 billion money supply increase simply will not come about. The Board of Governors must be concerned not with what "would be if the world fit the assumptions," but with what *will* happen in the world that exists.

The fact is that people *do* typically desire to hold more currency when their checking accounts increase. They *do* tend to convert some of their added demand deposits into time deposit form as their wealth grows. And banks *do*, depending on conditions, sometimes willingly retain some excess reserves rather than lend "up to the hilt." Our task in the first section of this chapter is to take explicit account of these complexities and their effect on the system's credit potential.

The Money Creation Capacity of the Banking System Under More Realistic Conditions

Given excess reserves, commercial banks, as we have seen, have every incentive to expand their earning assets. In the process, the borrowing members of the public receive, as the proceeds of the loans, newly created demand deposits. But once the loans are made and the new checking accounts are credited to the public, it is the public and not the banks who will determine, according to its preferences, whether those funds will remain in demand deposit form, be converted to currency, or be transferred into some such near-money form as time deposits.

The public, of course, has its preferences and freely exercises them. While most transactions are settled by check, currency or coin is more convenient for a wide variety of others, and depositors quite naturally have no compunction about withdrawing the amount required to meet such needs. Similarly, even though checking accounts may well possess superior liquidity, they pay no explicit interest. Depositors consequently regularly transfer some funds out of checking and into savings accounts to bolster their incomes.

Both these actions, of course, reduce the banking system's money-creating powers. If the system starts with $100,000 of excess reserves and a 20 percent required reserve ratio, it can create new demand deposits totaling $500,000, *provided that each dollar of those excess reserves is available to back up its full complement of $5 worth of demand deposits*. But if, along the way, the public is going to take actions that "use up" those reserves in other ways, the result will be quite different. After all, a dollar withdrawn in cash form takes away a reserve dollar that *could have* supported $5 in demand deposit form. And a dollar required to "back up" time deposits is simply not available to back up demand deposits. Allowing for cash drain and conversion to time deposits can only reduce the size of the system's so-called "money multiplier" to something less than the reciprocal of the required reserve ratio.

A Numerical Example of the Process of Expansion, Assuming Cash Drain and Time Deposits

Let us assume the following conditions hold in the banking system:

1. The banking system has $100,000 of excess reserves, all initially held by Bank A. (We retain, for the moment, the assumption that banks will not willingly keep excess reserves in that form.)
2. The required reserve ratio for demand deposits—henceforth symbolized as R_d—is 16 percent.
3. The required reserve ratio for time deposits—henceforth symbolized as R_t—is 5 percent.
4. The public's relative preference for the three assets—demand deposits, cash, and time deposits (which we shall henceforth refer to as the public's "preferred asset ratio")—

is such that for every added $5 worth of demand deposits willingly held, it insists upon holding an additional $4 of time deposits and an additional $1 of currency and coins. In essence, this means that when the banks provide the public with $10 of new demand deposits, the public will withdraw $1 in cash and transfer $4 into savings accounts, retaining only $5 of the demand deposits initially received in that form.

Now let us trace through a few steps of the process whereby expansion might occur under such conditions. Initially, Banker A, with $100,000 of excess reserves, will—as before—lend the maximum safe amount, $100,000. In doing so, of course, $100,000 of new demand deposits are created as the proceeds of the loan:

Bank A		
Loans	+$100,000	Demand deposits　　　+$100,000

Again, precisely as in the preceding chapter, the borrower can be expected to' write $100,000 of checks payable to a creditor, who will deposit them in his or her bank (Bank B). When Bank B sends them through the Federal Reserve for collection, the effects will be

Bank A		Bank B	
Federal Reserve account −$100,000	Demand deposits −$100,000	Federal Reserve account +$100,000	Demand deposits +$100,000

Up to now nothing is altered from the simpler case in Chapter 9. Now, however, we must introduce the effects of the new assumptions implied by the public's preferred asset ratio. If the depositor in Bank B is an "average" member of the public, he or she is unwilling to keep all the new funds in demand deposit form. Rather, $10,000 will be withdrawn in cash and $40,000 will be transferred to a time deposit account (leaving only $50,000 in demand deposits). The effects on Bank B of this transaction are

Bank B		
Cash	−$10,000	Demand deposits　　　−$50,000
		Time deposits　　　　+$40,000

And what is Banker B's reserve position now? Notice that, whereas he originally received a $100,000 increase in his total reserves, the cash withdrawal has reduced that by $10,000. And of the $90,000 remaining, $8,000(.16 × $50,000) is required to back up the $50,000 of demand deposits still there and $2,000(.05 × $40,000) is required to back up the $40,000 time deposit. Consequently, Banker B now has *excess* reserves of $80,000 on the basis of which he can make more loans. Banker B can now safely lend that amount.

Bank B

Loans	+$80,000	Demand deposits	+$80,000

If, as before, checks are written on the full $80,000, deposited in another bank (Bank C), and collected via the Federal Reserve, the effects are

Bank B		Bank C	
Federal Reserve account −$80,000	Demand deposits −$80,000	Federal Reserve account +$80,000	Demand deposits +$80,000

Once again, at this point the owner of the $80,000 deposit in Bank C converts it to the forms and in the proportions desired. He withdraws $8,000 in cash and transfers $32,000 to his savings account (leaving himself exactly $40,000 of demand deposits).

Bank C

Cash	−$8,000	Demand deposits	−$40,000
		Time deposits	+$32,000

And now what is Bank C's reserve position? The net addition to its total reserves is $72,000 ($80,000 minus the cash withdrawal of $8,000). Its added required reserves are $8,000 (.16 × $40,000 plus .05 × $32,000). Consequently, Bank C now has $64,000 of excess reserves to support another loan of that amount.

There is no point in continuing this example. Obviously the same process repeats itself over and over again until ultimately, at the limit, all the original $100,000 of excess reserves is "used up"—either by becoming required to back up the growing demand and time deposit liabilities or by being lost entirely to the banking system via cash withdrawals. But how can we add up the results of this more complex series of events?

The "Demand Deposit Multiplier" with Cash Drain and Time Deposits

What we need is a "demand deposit multiplier"—an expression that tells us the maximum number of dollars of new demand deposits that can be supported by each dollar of excess reserves. In the simpler case considered in the preceding chapter, we came up with a demand deposit multiplier equal to $1/R_d$. If R_d (the required reserve ratio applying to demand deposits) is 20 percent, this multiplier simply recognizes that for each $1 of demand deposits created, 20 cents worth of the original excess reserves are "used up" by becoming reserves.[1] This, of course, produces a "multiplier" of 5.

---

[1] In the simplified case from Chapter 9, what we have termed the *demand deposit multiplier* is also the *money multiplier*, since under the assumptions employed, there the entire money supply was demand deposits!

The situation is more complex, but the principle is the same where cash drain and time deposits are admitted. Here, for each added dollar of demand deposits created and held by the public, excess reserves are "used up" as required backing not only for demand deposits but also for time deposits. And still more is lost to the system altogether via the cash withdrawal. In the example used in the preceding section, for instance, for each additional dollar of demand deposits created and held, 16 cents of the original excess reserves is shifted to the required reserve category to back it up (R_d = 16 percent). And since the public adds 80 cents to its time deposits for each added \$1 of demand deposits (recall the assumption that the public insists upon \$4 in added time deposits for each \$5 in added demand deposits—80 percent as much) and the required reserve ratio for time deposits, R_t, is assumed to be 5 percent, another 4 cents (\$.80 × .05) of the original excess reserves is required to back up the new time deposits. Finally, with the public desiring to add to its cash an amount equal to 20 percent of its added demand deposits, the creation of an added dollar of demand deposits generates a 20 cent loss of reserves via cash withdrawal. So how does all this add up? Each one dollar of new demand deposits created and held leads to the "using up" of a total of 40 cents worth of the original excess reserves. It follows from this that each \$1.00 of excess reserves is sufficient to permit the addition of \$2.50 to the quantity of demand deposits. The "demand deposit multiplier," then, is $2\frac{1}{2}$.

All this can, of course, be more simply represented in arithmetic terms. The formula for the demand deposit multiplier is

$$\frac{1}{R_d + c + (R_t \times t)}$$

where

R_d = required reserve ratio behind demand deposits

R_t = required reserve ratio behind time deposits

c = the amount of added cash desired by the public, *for each added dollar of demand deposits*

t = the amount of added time deposits desired by the public, *for each added dollar of demand deposits*

In the example used in the preceding section R_d = 16 percent; R_t = 5 percent; $c = \frac{1}{5}$, or .20; and $t = \frac{4}{5}$, or .80. We thus have a demand deposit multiplier equal to[2]

$$\frac{1}{.16 + .20 + (.05 \times .80)} = \frac{1}{.40} = 2\frac{1}{2}$$

---

[2]Note particularly that c and t are *fractions* that must be computed from the public's preferred asset ratio. In the example employed, we assume that the public chose to hold demand deposits, time deposits, and cash in a 5-4-1 ratio. Thus, since it chooses to hold \$1 in cash for each \$5 in demand deposits, c equals \$1/\$5, or .20. And since it chooses to hold \$4 of time deposits for each \$5 of demand deposits, t equals \$4/\$5, or .80.

Now to compute the maximum increase in demand deposits created and held by the public, we merely need multiply the "multiplier" by the excess reserves possessed by the system;

$$\frac{1}{R_d + c + (R_t \times t)} \times \begin{array}{l} \textbf{Excess} \\ \textbf{reserves} \end{array} = \begin{array}{l} \textbf{Maximum possible} \\ \textbf{increase in demand} \\ \textbf{deposits by the banking} \\ \textbf{system}^3 \end{array}$$

From this result, it is a simple matter to compute the other changes of interest to us. The demand deposit multiplier, $2\frac{1}{2}$, times the initial excess reserves of \$100,000 tells us that when the expansion process is completed, the demand deposit liabilities of the banking system will be increased by \$250,000.

To compute the added time deposits resulting, we merely multiply t (desired added time deposits as a fraction of added demand deposits) by the amount of additional demand deposits:

$$t \times \Delta \text{ Demand deposits} = \Delta \text{ Time deposits}$$
$$.80 \times \$250,000 = \$200,000$$

Total cash withdrawn by the public is simply c (desired added cash as a fraction of added demand deposits) times the amount of additional demand deposits:

$$c \times \Delta \text{ Demand deposits} = \Delta \text{ Cash held by public}$$
$$.20 \times \$250,000 = \$50,000^4$$

And what about the change in the money supply? If we assume, for simplicity, that none of the time deposits created are "checkable deposits" (such as NOW accounts or ATS accounts) so that changes in the M1 money supply must be composed of changes in demand deposits or cash held by the public, the money supply increases by \$300,000. This, of course, is simply the sum of the increase in demand deposits and cash in the hands of the public.

Finally, we can compute the change in loans of the banking system by adding

---

³This, of course, is the maximum demand deposits *after* the public has put its assets in the desired proportion. Many more demand deposits are actually created when loans are made, but many of them are given up in favor of cash or time deposits.

⁴Note that when demand deposits have risen by \$250,000, time deposits by \$200,000, and the publicly held currency supply by \$50,000, all the \$100,000 of excess reserves we started with have been "used up" either as required reserves to back up deposits or withdrawn altogether from the banks. The cash drain "uses up" \$50,000 of it, and the other \$50,000 [(.16 × \$250,000) + (.05 × \$200,000)] has become "required" to back up the new deposits.

together the changes in demand deposits, time deposits, and cash—a total of $500,000.[5]

The effects of the entire process on the banking system's balance sheet in T-account form would be

Banking System			
Cash	−$50,000	Demand deposits	+$250,000
Loans	+$500,000	Time deposits	+$200,000

The Effect of Desired Excess Reserves

Up to now we have assumed that banks do not willingly hold on to any excess reserves—preferring instead to maximize their earning assets and the deposit liabilities that come along with them. But this may not always be the case.

Why might banks choose to retain some excess reserves, thereby forgoing potential income? Because the commercial bank operates in an uncertain world in which contingencies abound. It must be ready to pay cash on demand to any of its depositors, and required reserves are not available for that purpose. It may quite reasonably feel that the greater its deposit liabilities, the greater its exposure to sudden, unexpected cash withdrawals. And, of course, it may be that the added revenue derivable from further loans does not justify the added costs incurred in the process.

Whatever the reason for holding them, what is the effect of desired excess reserves on the system's expansion potential? Simply to reduce it by precisely the same degree as would an equivalent required reserve ratio. After all, whether reserves are held as a matter of law or of bank preference, their limiting effects are similar. Suppose, for example, that we assume that the banks in the case considered choose to hold excess reserves equal to 10 percent of any increase in their demand deposit liabilities, and we symbolize that desire as x. Then the demand deposit multiplier would become

$$\frac{1}{R_d + c + (R_t \cdot t) + x}$$

where x = the number of dollars of excess reserves willingly held by banks, expressed as a fraction of the change in demand deposits.

Substituting in the numbers assumed, we have

$$\frac{1}{.16 + .20 + (.05 \times .80) + .10} = \frac{1}{.50} = 2$$

---

[5]What really happens here is that, during the process expansion, banks lend $500,000 and create a full $500,000 of demand deposits. But the public, unwilling to hold all its added assets in demand deposit form, withdraws $50,000 in cash and transfers $200,000 to time accounts.

Inclusion of the desired excess reserve variable reduces the demand deposit multiplier from $2\frac{1}{2}$ to 2. Clearly the same result would have been produced by an increase in the required reserve ratio to 26 percent.

The "Money Multiplier" with Cash Drain, Time Deposits, and Desired Excess Reserves

The expression we have derived thus far

$$\frac{1}{R_d + c + (R_t \cdot t) + x}$$

tells us the increase in *demand deposits* that can be obtained from each dollar of excess reserves possessed by the system. It is but a short step from this to derive a "money multiplier"—an expression for the increase in the *money supply* derivable for each dollar of excess reserves.

The change in the money supply, of course, is simply the sum of the change in demand deposits and the change in cash held by the public.[6] The cash component, we have seen, can easily be computed by c times ΔDD, which is equivalent to

$$c\left[\frac{1}{R_d + c + (R_t \cdot t) + x} \times \text{Excess reserves}\right]$$

or

$$\frac{c}{R_d + c + (R_t \cdot t) + x} \times \text{Excess reserves}$$

The change in the entire money supply then equals

$$\overbrace{\frac{1}{R_d + c + (R_t \cdot t) + x} \times \text{Excess reserves}}^{\text{Change in demand deposits}} \quad \text{plus} \quad \overbrace{\frac{c}{R_d + c + (R_t \cdot t) + x} \times \text{Excess reserves}}^{\text{Change in cash}}$$

which combines to

$$\boxed{\frac{1 + c}{R_d + c + (R_t \cdot t) + x} \times \text{Excess reserves} = \text{Change in money supply}}$$

---

[6]This is true, of course, only if we once again assume no NOW or ATS accounts.

The expression on the left—the *money multiplier*—can be used to compute the change in the money supply that results from any dollar of excess reserves obtained by the banking system. Obviously it constitutes a powerful tool of analysis in that it reveals much about the determinants of the nation's money supply.

The Money Multiplier and the Monetary Base

Since the commercial banking system can only create new money on the basis of excess reserves, it is important that the student understand the logic and limits of the expansion process in those terms. But necessary as it is, the "money multiplier times excess reserves" formulation is something less than an ideal device for revealing the specific role played by the monetary authorities in control of the money stock.

The point is that although the monetary authorities do not really *directly* determine the banking system's excess reserves, they *are* directly responsible for issuing the nation's entire stock of currency and coins and for altering the size of member bank Federal Reserve accounts. But when they raise either of these, there is no assurance that the total effect of their efforts will be reflected in increased excess bank reserves, primarily because some of them may immediately be required reserves and others may be withdrawn from the system altogether. Clearly we will be better able to evaluate the role of government in the money determination process if we can recast the terms of our money expansion formula in such a way as to permit us to apply the money multiplier directly to specific actions of the monetary authorities themselves.

This we can do by employing the concept of the *monetary base*. **The monetary base includes all currency and coins in circulation—in the hands of the nonbank public as well as the vaults of depository institutions—plus the sum of Federal Reserve accounts owned by depository institutions.**[7] The monetary base, or "high-powered money" as it is sometimes called, not only is directly controllable by the monetary authorities (the Federal Reserve System and, to a much lesser extent, the U.S. Treasury) but is the ultimate base of the nation's money supply. Indeed, the money multiplier times the monetary base always, by definition, equals the money supply.[8] That is,

---

[7]Some economists prefer to call this total the "source base." To the total of currency in circulation and Federal Reserve accounts, they would add a small additional total called the "reserve adjustment." The reserve adjustment is intended to permit changes in required reserve ratios to be reflected not only in the size of the money multiplier but also in the size of the monetary base. See Leonall C. Andersen and Jerry L. Jordan, "The Monetary Base—Explanation and Analytical Use," *Review,* Federal Reserve Bank of St. Louis, August 1968. For an updating of the concept, see also R. A. Gilbert, "Revision of the St. Louis Federal Reserve's Adjusted Monetary Base," *Review,* Federal Reserve Bank of St. Louis, December 1980.

[8]The careful reader will no doubt have noticed that we refer to "depository institutions" rather than commercial banks. This is a result of changes instituted by the Monetary Control Act of 1980. Liabilities of institutions other than commercial banks are now a part of the money supply, and they, like commercial banks, are required to maintain reserves behind transactions accounts and nonpersonal time deposits.

$$\frac{1 + c}{R_d + c + (R_t \cdot t) + x} \times \frac{\text{Monetary}}{\text{base}} = \text{Money supply}$$

Let us see why this must be so. The monetary base, B, consists of total depository institution reserves, TR, plus cash in the public's hands, C. By definition, therefore,

$$B = TR + C$$

Now, in equilibrium, all depository institution reserves are either required or willingly held as excess reserves. That is,

$$TR = (R_d \cdot DD) \quad + \quad (R_t \cdot TD) \quad + \quad (x \cdot DD)$$

| Required reserves behind demand deposits | Required reserves behind time deposits | Desired excess reserves |

where DD stands for transactions accounts and TD stands for nonpersonal time deposits.

Substituting the second expression into the first, we have

$$B = (R_d \cdot DD) + (R_t \cdot TD) + (x \cdot DD) + C$$

Now, defining t and c as before, we know that

$$TD = t \cdot DD$$
$$C = c \cdot DD$$

Therefore, we can say,

$$B = (R_d \cdot DD) + (R_t \cdot t \cdot DD) + (x \cdot DD) + (c \cdot DD)$$

Factoring out the DD, this becomes

$$B = [R_d + (R_t \cdot t) + x + c]DD$$

If we now divide both sides by the term in the brackets, we get

$$\frac{1}{R_d + c + (R_t \cdot t) + x} \cdot B = DD$$

To put this in terms of the money supply, rather than demand deposits, we must recall that the money supply, M, equals transactions deposits, DD, plus cash in the hands of the public, C. Therefore,

$$M = DD + C$$

and, since $C = cDD$, we have

$$M = DD + cDD$$

and, factoring out the DD

$$M = (1 + c)DD$$

Now, multiplying both sides of the expression derived by $(1 + c)$, we have

$$\frac{1 + c}{R_d + c + (R_t \cdot t) + x} \cdot B = M$$

That is, the money multiplier times the monetary base equals the money supply. And if this is correct, the same thing must hold for *changes* in the monetary base:

$$\frac{1 + c}{R_d + c + (R_t \cdot t) + x} \cdot \Delta B = \Delta M$$

An Aside: The Difference Between the Money Multiplier Related to Changes in Excess Reserves and Related to Changes in the Monetary Base

It may seem incongruous to the reader that, whereas earlier we stated that the money multiplier times excess reserves produces the change in the money supply, we are now saying that the same multiplier times the change in the monetary base (clearly a total that can be quite different from excess reserves) equals the change in the money supply. Can both these uses of the money multiplier possibly be correct? Indeed they can.

Consider what each form tells us. The ''money multiplier times a change in excess reserves'' formulation tells us how much new money the banking system is capable of creating if it is provided with a given amount of excess reserves. The ''money multiplier times an increase in the monetary base'' formulation, on the other hand, tells us how much new money will result (whether directly created by the banking system or not) from a given increase in the monetary base!

Many Federal Reserve monetary actions affect excess reserves and the monetary base identically, so that no conflict arises. This is true, for instance, of an open-market purchase from the member banks and of a Federal Reserve discount. In both cases, the Fed provides the selling (or borrowing) member bank an increase in its Federal Reserve account in the amount of the purchase (or discount), and since there is no accompanying change in the bank's deposit liabilities, the entire rise in the monetary base takes the form of excess reserves. Any increase in the money supply that results in these cases must come from the banking system creating new money on the base of its newly acquired excess reserves.

In other cases, though, there appears to be a difference. By way of example, let us assume that the Federal Reserve purchases $120 million of U.S. securities from members of the nonbank public, paying by check. When the check is deposited in the seller's account at a member bank and collected via the FRS, the T-account effect on that member bank will be

Member Bank of the Seller of the Securities

Federal Reserve account	+$120 million	Demand deposit	+$120 million

Now assume that R_d = 20 percent and c = .20 (and, for simplicity, that there are no time deposits or desired excess reserves, so that t and x are both zero).

Under these assumptions, the money multiplier—$(1 + c)/(R_d + c)$—equals 3. The open-market purchase has increased the monetary base by $120 million, so that the "money multiplier times an increase in the monetary base" formulation tells us that the Federal Reserve's action will ultimately lead to a rise in the money supply of 3 × 120, or $360 million.

But what about the "money multiplier times a change in excess reserves" formulation? With a required reserve ratio of 20 percent, the increase in excess reserves resulting from the open-market purchase is $96 million ($24 million being required to back up the new $120 million deposit acquired by the seller of the securities). But the money multiplier—3—times the increase in excess reserves—$96 million—seems to say that the increase in the money supply will be only $288 million.

Which formulation is wrong? Neither. They simply represent different answers to different questions. The "money multiplier times a change in excess reserves" formulation tells you, quite correctly, how much new money the banking system can create *if given $96 million of excess reserves*. The "money multiplier times a change in monetary base" formulation, on the other hand, tells you, quite correctly, how much new money will ultimately result from a $120 million open-market purchase.

Notice that if one follows the assumptions throughout, there is no conflict. Assuming that the original seller of the securities is an average member of the public (with c = .20), she will not be willing to keep all her $120 million proceeds in checking account form. Rather, she will write a $20 million check for cash, leaving herself with the desired $100 million of demand deposits and $20 million of cash. This action would reduce the bank's excess reserves to $80 million ($120 million minus $20 million lost via cash withdrawal and another $20 million required to back up the remaining $100 million of deposits). On the basis of these excess reserves, the banking system can create new money equal to 3 × $80 million, or $240 million. And that $240 million created by bank loans, added to the $120 million still possessed by the seller of the securities, gives us the same $360 million total money supply change the other formulation gave us.

What it comes down to is this. If one is interested in the amount of new money that the banking system can create, given a certain amount of excess reserves, the "money multiplier times excess reserves" formulation will do the job nicely. If, however, one is interested in the amount of new money likely to result from specific actions taken by the monetary authority, then the "money multiplier times monetary base" formulation is the one that is needed. And since much of our upcoming concern is with monetary policy, it is the version that is likely to be most useful.

Summary

The formula derived in this chapter,

$$\left(\frac{1 + c}{R_d + c + (R_t \cdot t) + x} \times \begin{array}{c}\text{Change in the}\\ \text{monetary}\\ \text{base}\end{array} = \begin{array}{c}\text{Change in the}\\ \text{money supply}\end{array} \right)$$

is an exceptionally effective mechanism for organizing discussion of the determinants of the nation's money supply. The next two chapters will focus on the methods whereby the nation's monetary authorities attempt to control the money supply—through altering the monetary base or the money multiplier.

Review Questions

1. Briefly explain how cash drain, an increase in time deposits, and the holding of "desired" excess reserves reduces the maximum demand deposits a banking system can support.

⁂2. Carefully explain *why* the sum of the increase in demand deposits and time deposits, plus the cash withdrawn from the banking system, necessarily equals the maximum possible increase in loans for the system.

3. What are the components of the "monetary base"? What is the significance of the monetary base?

4. Assume an economy in which R_d = 13 percent and R_t = 7 percent. The public insists upon holding $.75 in cash and $5.00 in time deposits for each $5.00 of demand deposits, and the banks insist upon holding excess reserves equal to

$2\frac{1}{2}$ percent of *all* outstanding demand deposits. Assume further that the initial balance sheet for the commercial banking system is as follows:

Cash	$ 30,000	Demand deposits	$1,000,000
Federal Reserve account	165,000	Time deposits	1,000,000
Loans and securities	1,900,000	Other	100,000
Other	5,000		

Compute the changes the banking system would be required to make to fit the conditions given and show the banking system's balance sheet after it has completed all necessary adjustments.

5. Assume a banking system in which the following conditions hold:
   a. R_d = 15 percent and R_t = 5 percent.
   b. The people insist upon holding $3.00 in time deposits and $.50 in cash for $5.00 in demand deposits they will hold.
   c. The banks insist upon holding $2 in excess for every $100 *increase* in demand deposit liabilities above $400,000 (but none for the first $400,000).
   d. The banking system's initial balance sheet is

Cash	$ 12,000	Demand deposits	$400,000
Federal Reserve account	69,000	Time deposits	240,000
Loans and securities	600,000	Other liabilities	60,000
Other assets	19,000		

Compute the data required to show the position of the banking system after it has expanded to the limits permitted it by the given conditions. Enter the appropriate figures for each account in a balance sheet for the banking system after it has adjusted to the conditions given. Prove that your answer is correct by showing that all the initial excess reserves are now "used up" as required reserves, desired excess reserves, or withdrawn from the banks in cash. .

6. Assume an economy in which R_d = 16 percent and R_t = 5 percent, and in which the public chooses to hold $1.00 in currency and $4.00 in time deposits for every $5.00 in demand deposits it will hold. Assume further that banks choose to hold no excess reserves (x = 0). Now the Federal Reserve carries out an open-market purchase from the nonbank public in the amount of $100 million. This initially raises the banking system's total reserves by $100 million and its outstanding demand deposit liabilities by $100 million.
   a. Using the change in the monetary base resulting from this open-market purchase and the demand deposit multiplier, compute the change in the banking system's demand deposits that will result.
   b. Assuming that the member of the nonbank public who sold the securities to the Fed subsequently converts the $100 million into the proportions indicated by c and t, compute the excess reserves available *after* this conversion. Then multiply the demand deposit multiplier times the result. Add this to the demand deposits retained by the seller of the securities.

   Your answer for the total demand deposit expansion should be the same for (a) and (b).

11

The Major Monetary Policy Tools

Even a casual inspection of the money supply formula derived in the preceding chapter reveals that if the Federal Reserve System is to control the nation's money supply, it must do so via alterations in the monetary base and/or the required reserve ratios, since the remaining elements of the money multiplier, c, t, and x, are directly determined by the public and the commercial banks.

This chapter considers the tools of monetary policy available to the Fed and their implications for control of the nation's money stock.

General versus Selective Controls

It has become customary to separate the various monetary policy tools into two categories, general and selective. *General* (or *quantitative*) *credit controls* are those that, when implemented, alter the total supply of credit available to borrowers in general without singling out for discriminatory treatment (intentionally at least) any particular group of borrowers that desires credit for a specific purpose. The total supply of credit may be cut, for example, but it is the "credit market" rather than the monetary authorities that determines which particular potential borrowers are rationed out. *Selective* (or *qualitative*) *credit controls,* on the other hand, are specifically aimed at altering the quantity of credit available for specified groups of borrowers that are borrowing to finance the purchase of a particular item, or selected group of items.

Included in the Federal Reserve's arsenal of general credit controls is the power to alter required reserve ratios and discount rates, as well as open-market operations. At the present time, there is only one specifically selective control on the books—the power to set margin requirements on the purchase of stock. However, in the past, the purchase of real estate and of selected consumer durable goods on credit has been controlled, and we shall comment briefly on those efforts at selective control.

General Credit Controls

The Power to Alter Required Reserve Ratios

The original Federal Reserve Act allowed the Board of Governors no discretion in the area of reserve requirements. It set up fixed required reserve ratios for the member banks in each group and specified the member bank assets that could be counted as legal reserves.

It was in 1933 that Congress first gave the Board of Governors temporary authority to alter required reserve ratios, and in 1935 this temporary power was granted on a permanent basis. But prior to 1980, the Fed's reserve requirements applied only to commercial banks that were members of the Federal Reserve System (FRS).

With the passage of the Monetary Control Act of 1980, as we have seen, FRS reserve requirements were extended to all depository institutions issuing transactions accounts or nonpersonal time deposits.[1] Table 11-1 repeats the current legal limits on the Board of Governors' authority to alter required reserve ratios.

The specific procedures for computing reserve requirements have recently been changed and are quite complex. Starting in February 1984, depository institutions with over $15 million in total deposits outstanding are required, every other Monday, to compute their average daily outstanding transactions accounts for the preceding two weeks. Given the required reserve ratio, this permits them to com-

TABLE 11-1

Legal Limits to Board of Governors' Authority to Vary
Required Reserve Ratios

	Minimum	Maximum
Transactions accounts		
0 to $2 million	0	0
$2 to $26 million	3%	3%
Over $26 million	8%	14%
Nonpersonal savings and time deposits	0	9%

---

[1]This means all commercial banks, mutual savings banks, savings and loan associations, and any credit union that is insured or is eligible for federal insurance. U.S. agencies and branches of foreign banks are subject to the same requirements in accordance with the International Banking Act of 1978. As already noted, the new requirements, as applied to depository institutions other than member banks, will not be fully phased in until 1987.

pute their *required* reserves for the period. The law then requires them to have maintained average daily total reserves (vault cash plus Federal Reserve account) of the prescribed minimum amount for the two-week period ending on the Wednesday two days after the end of their two-week "computation period."

An example may help to clarify this procedure. Suppose that on Monday, June 28, depository institutions report their average daily transactions accounts for the preceding two weeks to have been $350 billion. If the required reserve ratio applicable to these accounts is 10 percent, this means that the average daily sum of vault cash and Federal Reserve account of these institutions for the two-week period prior to Wednesday, June 30, must be at least $35 billion to satisfy the reserve requirement law.[2]

The Effects of Altering Required Reserve Ratios.   A numerical example may help to illustrate the potency of this credit control tool. To keep things as simple as possible, let us assume that commercial banks are the only depository institutions, that demand deposits are the only transactions accounts, and that all time deposits are nonpersonal so that reserve requirements apply. Assume further that initially the consolidated balance sheet of all commercial banks is as given here:

All Commercial Banks

Cash plus Federal Reserve		Demand deposits	$400
account	$ 80	Time deposits	400
Other assets	920	Other liabilities and net worth	200

Now, suppose that R_d = 14 percent, R_t = 6 percent, and the public's preferred asset ratio is $1 in time deposits ($t$ = 1.0) and $.20 in cash ($c$ = .20) for each $1 in demand deposits. Finally, let us assume that banks desire to hold no excess reserves (x = 0).

Given all these assumptions, we know that (1) the public must currently be holding $80 of cash (since that is 20 percent of its demand deposit holding); (2) the monetary base is $160 (sum of total bank reserves and cash held by public);

the "money multiplier" must be $3 \left(\dfrac{1.20}{.14 + .20 + (1 \times .06)} \right)$; and (4) the max-

---

[2]This constitutes a substantial change from the procedure in effect from 1968 until 1984. During that period, reserves for any period were only required to be the specified percentage of average daily deposits outstanding *two weeks previously.* This procedure, with its two-week lag, drew sharp criticism from some who felt that it measurably weakened monetary control.

Required reserves for other liabilities against which reserves must be maintained—such as nonpersonal time deposits—will also be computed by figuring average daily nonpersonal time deposits outstanding for the preceding two weeks every other Monday. Reserves behind these, however, will be lagged by two weeks much like the system in effect for all deposits prior to 1984. See *Federal Reserve Bulletin,* October 1982, p. 625.

Depository institutions with less than $15 million of deposits are required to report deposits only once per quarter and have the option of a different method of reserve computation. See *Federal Reserve Bulletin,* October 1982, pp. 625–26 and November 1982, pp. 707–9.

imum possible money supply is $480 (money multiplier times monetary base), which just equals the current money supply. Under current conditions, in other words, the money supply cannot be increased.[3]

But suppose now that Fed economists determine that a recession is developing and that moderating its effects requires an increase in bank loans and the money supply. What could the Board of Governors do?

It could, if it chose, cut the required reserve ratio for demand deposits from 14 percent to 8 percent and also cut that for time deposits from 6 percent to 2 percent. Let us consider the effects of such a change.

Employing the assumptions already made, such action would raise the money multiplier from 3 to 4 (new multiplier equals $\dfrac{1.2}{.08 + .20 + (1 \times .02)}$). This larger multiplier times the monetary base of $160 produces a possible money supply of $640—a money stock increase of $160.[4]

But this increase in the money supply and in bank lending capacity is not the only effect of lower required reserve ratios, for increasing the supply of bank credit (i.e., loanable funds) will tend to affect the *price of loanable funds* in the same direction as would any increase in supply. The price of loanable funds—the interest rate—will tend to *fall*. And such reductions in interest rates will tend to encourage prospective investors to borrow and spend. Thus, we see, cuts in required reserve ratios tend to affect demand in two ways. Not only do they make loanable funds more readily available for investors, but they tend to make them cheaper as well.

The reverse, of course, is also true. *Increases* in required reserve ratios tend to *reduce* the size of the money multiplier (and *cut* excess reserves) leading to *reductions* in the availability of loanable funds, *reductions* in the potential money supply, and *increases* in interest rates. All these effects, in turn, tend to cut, or hold down on, spending with borrowed funds.

Evaluation of Variable Reserve Ratios as a Stabilization Device. Whatever else might be said about it, one thing is clear: the power to alter required reserve ratios is a very potent weapon. With demand deposits and other checkable deposits currently over the $300 billion mark, each 1 percent cut in the ratio releases over $3 billion of excess reserves, thereby providing the basis for an expansion in loans and money supply several times that amount. Although the numerical example considered in the preceding section is an extreme one (in practice, the Fed would be more likely to alter reserve ratios by 1 or 2 percent at most), it does serve to illustrate the potency of this particular element of monetary policy.

But despite its power, the Fed has not tended to rely heavily on variable

---

[3]Put another way, since there are no excess reserves, the banks can make no further loans.

[4]Note that the effect could also be put in terms of excess reserves. With $R_d = 8$ percent and $R_t = 2$ percent, required reserves are $40, so that excess reserves are $40. The money multiplier (four) times the excess reserves created by the cut in R_d and R_t equals $160.

reserve ratios to combat the ups and downs of the regular business cycle. Why is this the case? The Commission on Money and Credit made the following observation more than two decades ago:

> While changes in reserve requirements are a powerful instrument of credit control, they are awkward and cumbersome in comparison with open market operations and present difficult problems of adjustment for many medium-sized and small banks. . . . The Commission believes that the power to change reserve requirements should be used only sparingly and favors major reliance on the use of open market operations for countercyclical adjustments.[5]

There have been several major objections to relying on changes in reserve requirements for the day-to-day implementation of monetary policy. First, this particular credit control tool lacks flexibility. Unlike open-market operations, which can be carried out every day and easily reversed when necessary, changing reserve ratios is only feasible several times per year at best. And precisely because they are changed only infrequently, reserve ratio changes tend to receive considerable press and public notice. Thus they carry with them definite so-called "*announcement effects*"—psychological reactions by the banks and the public to Federal Reserve actions. We shall have more to say about announcement effects in discussing discount rate changes. For the moment, it should be noted that some authorities feel that such reactions to monetary policy moves may tend to undercut the intent of the policy.

Finally, prior to the Monetary Control Act of 1980 extending uniform reserve requirements to all depository institutions, the Board of Governors tended to be extremely sensitive to the likelihood that raising required reserve ratios for member banks would cause even more state-chartered banks to leave the System.

In light of all these problems, the Fed has tended to rely more heavily on its other general credit controls—especially open-market operations—for the implementation of the bulk of its contracyclical monetary policies. The power to alter reserve ratios (especially to *raise* them) has, despite its acknowledged potency, been held largely in reserve in case a real emergency requiring restriction arises. It will be interesting to see what effect the uniform reserve requirements of the Monetary Control Act will have on this pattern of use.

The "Discount Window" and the Power to Alter the Federal Reserve "Discount Rate"

As we have seen, one major reason for establishing the Federal Reserve System in the first place was to provide an "outside" source of reserves from which banks in temporary need might borrow. The facility set up to serve this purpose has come to be called the Fed's "discount window" and the interest rate

---

[5]Commission on Money and Credit, *Money and Credit* (Englewood Cliffs, N.J.: Prentice-Hall, 1961), p. 67.

charged on such loans, the "discount rate." Although the power to alter the discount rate is generally considered to be the monetary policy weapon, let us first consider the evolution of the discount facility itself.

The Evolution of the FRS Discount Mechanism.   In accordance with the framers' faith in the commercial loan theory, the original Federal Reserve Act attempted to tie member bank borrowing from the Fed directly to the volume of short-term commercial loans. This was accomplished by requiring that member banks desiring to borrow reserves from their district Federal Reserve bank pledge, as collateral for the loan, the IOUs that they (the member banks) had acquired from businesses that had borrowed from them. Such short-term IOUs—dubbed "eligible paper" in the original act—were initially the only form of collateral that a member bank was entitled to use to borrow through the Fed's discount window. The thought was, of course, that all would be well if the acquisition of additional reserves through the discount window was limited by the volume of short-term commercial loans that the banks had made.[6]

As we have seen, the commercial loan theory was ill-conceived and did not last long. Indeed, within a very few years, the collateral eligible for borrowing through the discount window was broadened to include U.S. securities and then later—in the 1930s—further liberalized to include "any asset acceptable to the lending Federal Reserve bank."[7]

This liberalization of collateral requirements for discounts did much more than sound the death knell of the commercial loan theory. More germane to our current topic, it brought to an end the early practice of relying on collateral "eligibility requirements" as the prime means of limiting access to the discount window.

It was clear, of course, that *some* method was required to limit member bank borrowing from the Federal Reserve—unrestrained, easy access to borrowed reserves could not be permitted to offset completely efforts at restrictive monetary policies. In the years since "eligibility requirements" were abandoned as the prime rationing device, the System had depended in varying degrees on two means of limiting access to the discount window—the discount rate and authoritative, nonprice rationing. We shall consider the discount rate shortly; let us look now at the nonprice rationing methods used by the System.

---

[6]Originally, the common practice was for a district Federal Reserve bank to actually purchase a business's IOU from the borrowing bank by "rediscounting" it. This consisted of giving the borrowing bank the face value of the IOU minus the discount rate charged. In recent years, all discount window borrowing has been via an *advance,* where eligible paper is merely pledged as collateral rather than purchased.

[7]Until the Monetary Control Act of 1980 authorized elimination of the penalty, discount window borrowing collateralized with any asset other than short-term commercial loans or U.S. securities carried a discount rate one-half a percentage point higher.

Loans from Federal Reserve banks have always been clearly designated as a privilege of member banks, not a right. Over the years, the System has made various efforts to spell out the circumstances under which a member bank might expect to be accommodated at the discount window and the circumstances under which it should not. Currently these conditions—the rules under which the discount window is administered—are spelled out in the System's *Regulation A.*

Under Regulation A any depository institution subject to the uniform reserve requirements established in the Monetary Control Act of 1980 may borrow through the Fed's discount window.[8] It is expected, however, to do so only as a last resort, after all "reasonable alternative sources of funds . . . have been fully used." Federal Reserve credit is *not* to be used as a substitute for capital, nor is undue use to be made of such credit "for the speculative carrying of, or trading in securities, real estate, or commodities or for any other purpose inconsistent with the maintenance of sound credit conditions."[9]

On a more positive note, discount window credit is available for two main purposes. Most is *short-term adjustment credit,* which is made available on a very-short-term basis to assist a depository institution "to meet temporary requirements for funds, or to cushion more persistent outflows of funds pending an orderly adjustment of the institution's assets and liabilities." In addition, the Fed offers *extended credit,* which is made available for longer periods to smaller institutions suffering from regular seasonal drains of funds or in exceptional circumstances arising from "sustained deposit drains, impaired access to money market funds, sudden deterioration in loan repayment performance . . . or difficulties adjusting to changing money market conditions over a longer period, particularly at times of deposit disintermediation."[10]

The T-Account Effects of a Federal Reserve Discount or Advance. Once the Federal Reserve agrees to a member bank's application for a loan, the procedures are simple. Normally the borrowing bank signs an IOU, pledging some of its U.S. securities as collateral for the loan.[11] The proceeds of the loan, of course, take the form of an increase in the borrower's Federal Reserve account. If the borrower is a member bank, the T-account effects are as follows:

---

[8]It should be noted that Regulation A also permits a Federal Reserve bank, after consultation with the Board, to extend credit to individuals or nondepository business firms "in unusual and exigent circumstances" where it is clear that "credit is not available from other sources and failure to obtain such credit would adversely affect the economy."

[9]Board of Governors of the Federal Reserve System, "Advances and Discounts by Federal Reserve Banks—Regulation A," *Federal Reserve Bulletin,* September 1980, p. 757.

[10]For both adjustment and extended credit, a surcharge above the basic discount rate may be charged under certain circumstances.

[11]Actually, this degree of formality is not really required. A request to borrow can be made by letter, wire, or telephone. In addition, many banks have their district Federal Reserve bank hold some of their U.S. securities for safekeeping so that the needed collateral is already there.

Federal Reserve Bank		Borrowing Member Bank	
Discounts and advances (the IOU signed by member bank) +$100	Deposit of borrowing member bank +$100	Federal Reserve account +$100	Notes payable +$100

The major effect of the transaction is to increase the monetary base (and the borrowing bank's excess reserves) by the full amount of the discount. Temporary though it is, the result is to permit a potential money stock increase equal to the money multiplier times the increase in base that it generates.

Altering the Discount Rate as a Stabilization Weapon.   As noted, the interest rate charged for these loans of reserves is called the Federal Reserve *discount rate*. Technically, each district Federal Reserve bank sets its own discount rate, and the Board of Governors "reviews and determines" the rates set. In fact, however, the individual Reserve banks have relatively little autonomy in this decision. In practice, the Board of Governors really sets the rates.[12]

System authorities are free to set whatever discount rate seems appropriate. Discount rate increases are generally considered contractionary monetary measures (holding down on spending for new goods and services), while decreases are thought of as expansionary (encouraging an increase in such spending). To understand better the issues involved, let us consider the likely transmission mechanism between a rise in the Fed's discount rate and its intended cut in aggregate demand. How, in other words, are discount rate increases expected to "work"?

First, since the increase makes reserves borrowed from the Fed more expensive than before, it may be that some banks that would have borrowed before the rise will decide not to now. If this is the case, the discount rate increase will have prevented the increase in the system's reserves (or in the monetary base) that would have occurred in its absence.

But that isn't all. If the banks that refrained from borrowing because of the higher discount rate still need additional reserves, they will have to turn elsewhere to get them. They may, for instance, attempt to borrow federal funds instead. But if they do, they are adding to the demand for an existing supply of federal funds and the result will surely be a rise in the federal funds rate. Or they may raise the reserves needed by selling a short-term U.S. security—part of their secondary reserves. But this approach, by adding to the supply of such securities seeking a buyer, will lower the price of U.S. securities, thereby raising the effective interest

---

[12]Changes in the discount rate are generally discussed and agreed upon at regular meetings of the Open Market Committee in which the Board of Governors as well as the presidents of all 12 Federal Reserve banks have the opportunity to participate. Of course, only the 5 Federal Reserve bank presidents currently serving on the FOMC have the right to vote, but all Federal Reserve bank presidents can attend and participate in the discussions.

TABLE 11-2

Comparative Short-Term Interest Rates, 1966–1982
(percentage)

Year	Banker's Acceptances	Federal Funds	U.S. 91-day Treasury Bills	Federal Reserve Discount Rate[a]
1966	5.36	5.11	4.85	4.50
1967	4.75	4.22	4.29	4.50
1968	5.75	5.66	5.34	5.50
1969	7.61	8.22	6.67	6.00
1970	7.31	7.17	6.39	5.50
1971	4.85	4.66	4.33	4.50
1972	4.47	4.44	4.07	4.50
1973	8.08	8.74	7.03	7.50
1974	9.92	10.51	7.84	7.75
1975	6.30	5.82	5.80	6.00
1976	5.19	5.05	4.98	5.25
1977	5.59	5.54	5.27	6.00
1978	8.11	7.93	7.19	9.50
1979	11.04	11.19	10.07	12.00
1980	12.72	13.36	11.43	13.00
1981	15.32	16.38	14.03	12.00
1982	11.89	12.26	10.61	8.50

[a]Discount rate in effect at end of year. All other figures are averages for the year.

Source: Federal Reserve Bulletin, various issues.

yields being earned on *them.*[13] Either way, the increase in the Fed's discount rate has led to increases in *other* short-term interest rates. And since, via arbitrage, such a change will tend ultimately to raise all short-term rates, prospective spenders may be induced to cut back on their spending with borrowed money because of the higher cost.

That, at least, is how a discount rate increase is *supposed* to work and, indeed, to some degree it probably does. But even if it does, there are solid reasons for doubting its potency as a stabilization weapon.

One problem with the scenario just sketched is its implication that—in periods of rising interest rates—it is the rises in the Fed's discount rate which cause other short-term rates to rise. But a check of the record quickly refutes this. In recent years, most discount rate increases have been technical adjustments to bring the discount rate into line with other short-term rates. Instead of the discount rate forcing other rates upward, the direction of causation has been pretty much the other way around. The comparative data in Table 11-2 show essentially the same story. Instead of *leading* other interest rates, the discount rate has tended to *lag* behind.

----

[13]We shall see in Chapter 16 why a fall in the market value of a bond necessarily implies a rise in the interest yield earned on it.

Note one final point about the data in Table 11-2. In years when short-term interest rates were peaking (check, for example, 1969, 1974, 1981), discount rates not only lagged other rates but show up as a real bargain. What, one is tempted to ask, kept member banks from taking advantage of these "bargain" rates and borrowing heavily from the Fed rather than obtaining their reserves at higher cost elsewhere?[14]

First, it should be recognized that member bank borrowing did, indeed, rise during these years to take advantage of the spread. But "excessive" borrowing was probably prevented by Regulation A and by the alleged reluctance of commercial bankers to be in debt to the central bank.

According to the "reluctance" theory, bankers will normally only borrow from the Federal Reserve as a last resort when other, more desired sources of funds are relatively inaccessible. Its prime implication is that the discount rate need not be above other rates to prevent overuse of the discount facility.

There is undoubtedly real substance to the reluctance theory, but it is difficult to conceive of that alone as being sufficient to prevent overuse of Fed credit when the spread is as large as it was in 1974 and 1981. Undoubtedly, the nonprice rationing implied by the rules of Regulation A played a major role also.

Announcement Effects.   Most authorities are agreed that discount rate increases, though working in the proper *direction* to restrain excessive spending, probably make only a very slight contribution toward combating inflationary pressures. Somewhat more emphasis has been placed by some upon the psychological "announcement" effects of a change in the discount rate.

The argument runs something like this. Unlike open-market operations, which are being carried on continuously, discount rate changes are only made periodically. When such changes are made, especially when they involve a change of *direction,* they are widely interpreted as a signal or indication of the Board of Governors' thinking and of the future course of monetary policy. A rise in the discount rate after a series of reductions, for example, may well indicate that the Board foresees some inflationary pressure and can be expected to use its general credit controls to make credit (and bank reserves) harder to get in the near future.

The effect of such a "signal" of the Federal Reserve's future intentions will depend upon a number of factors. Those who would rely on it as a helpful development see bankers reacting to the likelihood of a shortage of reserves in the future by slowing down on current loans in order to conserve some "elbow room" for making loans to important customers later on when additional reserves will be difficult to obtain and when the interest return will be more favorable than it is

---

[14]It should be pointed out that Table 11-2 overstates the spread to a degree, especially in 1969, 1974, and 1982, because the discount rate figure is an end-of-year figure rather than an average for the year.

today. If this is the reaction of lenders, the announcement effect of the rise in the discount rate does promote the objectives of the Federal Reserve. Credit extension is slowed down, as is desired.

Critics, however, see some potential problems with this mechanism.[15] If bankers interpret the increase in the discount rate as a "one-shot" affair, to be followed in the future by lower rates, it will be in their interest to lend more now, taking advantage of the temporarily higher return available. And if they do so, the expectational effects of the discount rate rise are perverse, encouraging rather than restricting current inflationary pressure.

Nor is that the end of it. There is no reason to assume that reaction to the announcement of a discount rate increase will be restricted to lenders. After all, borrowers and spenders, also armed with expectations about the future, read the newspapers too. And if borrowers and spenders interpret a rise in the discount rate as a heralding of future inflationary pressure, they may well borrow and spend more now because of it to beat the rise in borrowing costs and prices that is coming in the future.[16] To the degree that this is the case, the discount rate signal has even more seriously perverse effects.[17]

Conclusion—Evaluation of the Discount Mechanism. As these comments indicate, the power to alter the discount rate is regarded as an extremely weak stabilization weapon by the majority of authorities. Indeed one distinguished economist some years ago was so disenchanted with the whole mechanism as to propose outright elimination of the discount window itself.[18]

Although most economists share the conviction that the power to alter the discount rate is an exceptionally ineffective weapon in the monetary policy arsenal, few would concur in the proposal to close the window altogether. It can still be argued that the discount facility is an important guarantor of the banking system's liquidity, especially in a major bank panic. Second, some have argued, the fact that individual banks have a temporary source of borrowed reserves permits the Federal Reserve to make freer use of more powerful tools of credit restraint, such as open-market operations, than might be the case if the discount window, serving as a sort of "safety valve," did not exist. Finally, alterations in the discount rate are sometimes useful to deal with *balance-of-payments* problems. That is, a rise in the discount rate may be used not just to reduce domestic demand, but also to

[15]See, for example, W. L. Smith, "The Instruments of General Monetary Control," *National Banking Review,* September 1963, pp. 59–64.

[16]At least this would be rational behavior to the degree that they doubt the Federal Reserve's ability to combat the inflation.

[17]Discount rate increases are sometimes used as a signal for a quite different purpose—to indicate to other countries and speculators the nation's intention to clamp down on domestic inflation for balance-of-payments reasons. Discussion of international factors is postponed until later chapters.

[18]M. Friedman, *A Program for Monetary Stability* (New York: Fordham University Press, 1959).

raise short-term interest rates generally as a means of attracting short-term foreign capital to this country (or keeping that which is already here from leaving).[19]

Open-Market Operations

Open-market operations are, by a wide margin, the most important of the arsenal of monetary policy weapons. *Open-market operations,* for our purposes can be defined as *the purchase or sale of U.S. securities by the Federal Reserve System* **for the purpose of altering the amount of member bank reserves.**

Policy in this area is determined by the Federal Open Market Committee, which normally meets about every six weeks in Washington. The committee, as noted earlier, includes the 7 members of the Board of Governors plus 5 Federal Reserve bank presidents. It should be noted that although only the official committee members can vote, all 12 Federal Reserve banks normally send representatives who participate in the discussions. Once the FOMC has reached a consensus, it transmits its orders to an official with the title of *system account manager,* who operates out of the New York Federal Reserve Bank.

The basic responsibility of the system account manager is to carry out the directives of the Federal Open Market Committee—to do the buying when purchases are decreed and to do the selling when the reverse is called for. Put this way, the account manager may appear to have a purely perfunctory task, that of buying or selling when he is told to do so. Actually this is far from the truth; his is an exacting position requiring an inordinate amount of skill and knowledge of the securities market, in addition to considerable discretion and judgment.

Some indication of the degree of discretion required of the system account manager can be gleaned from the general nature of the instructions passed on to him by the Federal Open Market Committee. For example, part of the directive issued as a result of the Committee's meeting on May 18, 1982 stated

> The Federal Open Market Committee seeks to foster monetary and financial conditions that will help to reduce inflation, promote a resumption of growth in output on a sustainable basis, and contribute to a sustainable pattern of international transactions. At its meeting in early February, the Committee agreed that its objectives would be furthered by growth of M1, M2, and M3 from the fourth quarter of 1981 to the fourth quarter of 1982 within ranges of 2½ to 5½ percent, 6 to 9 percent, and 6½ to 9½ percent, respectively. The associated range for bank credit was 6 to 9 percent.
>   In the short run, the Committee seeks behavior of reserve aggregates consistent with growth of M1 and M2 from March to June at annual rates of about 3 percent and 8 percent, respectively.[20]

---

[19]For recent commentaries on the discount mechanism, see Daniel L. Thornton, "The Discount Rate and Market Interest Rates: What's the Connection?" *Review,* Federal Reserve Bank of St. Louis, June–July 1982; and Gordon H. Sellon, Jr., "The Role of the Discount Rate in Monetary Policy: A Theoretical Analysis," *Economic Review,* Federal Reserve Bank of Kansas City, June 1980.

[20]"Record of Policy Actions of the Federal Open Market Committee," *Federal Reserve Bulletin,* July 1982, p. 421.

In the concluding section of this chapter, we shall return to the issue of FOMC policy directives, concentrating specifically on the committee's designation of "targets" for the system account manager. For the present, let us ignore this issue and concentrate on the mechanism through which the directives are implemented.

If the Federal Open Market Committee has given orders that require the purchase of securities, their intent is to increase the quantity of member bank reserves. The account manager, who operates in New York for the obvious reason that it is the location of the market for U.S. securities, carries out his orders through 30-odd major government securities dealers in the city.

The government securities dealers are middlemen who bring together buyers and sellers of U.S. securities. They offer a ready market for government obligations by regularly quoting "bid" and "ask" prices on federal government obligations. As middlemen, they purchase securities with the intent of reselling them to institutions and individuals who desire them as a part of their regular portfolios, although they also hold some for their own accounts; when they sell, they acquire most of the securities ultimately from the same types of institutions and individuals. Their income is earned primarily for their services of bringing buyer and seller together.

When the Federal Reserve's system account manager is given orders requiring purchase of securities, he contacts, usually via telephone, all the major government securities dealers and obtains comparative bids. The dealer or dealers offering the lowest price then are generally awarded the business. Conversely, in the case of an open-market sale, the dealer or dealers offering the highest price would normally be the successful bidders.

The system account manager acts on behalf of all 12 Federal Reserve banks, which have no discretion regarding their own individual participation in the operation. When the account manager buys securities, the total increase in the System's portfolio of securities is apportioned among all the Reserve banks. Similarly, if he, in pursuance of orders from the Open Market Committee, sells securities, the individual Federal Reserve banks' portfolios of U.S. securities will each be proportionately reduced, regardless of their own desires in the matter.

On the other hand, it is important to understand that no compulsion whatever applies to the member banks. The term "open market" implies that the Federal Reserve buys or sells at a price that is attractive enough to convince someone to enter into a deal voluntarily. If the Fed is buying and the member banks do not choose to sell, they cannot be compelled to do so. In such a situation the system account manager would simply have to offer a high enough price to convince a member of the nonbank public to sell. Who the seller happens to be is a matter of little moment to the Federal Reserve, for, as we shall see, the monetary base (and total bank reserves) will be increased by the amount of the purchase regardless.

Mechanics of an Open-Market Purchase. The actual mechanics of the purchase go something like this. The dealer purchases the U.S. securities from the ultimate seller by means of a check written on his account at a member bank. The Federal

Reserve, in turn, pays the dealer for the securities via an officer's check, which it makes up on itself and which the dealer can be expected to deposit in his checking account at a member bank. The result is that the Federal Reserve has the securities, the ultimate seller of the securities has an increase in his checking account, and the member banks have more reserves.

The U.S. securities purchased to carry out open-market policy, it should be understood, are *not* "new" U.S. securities issued by the U.S. Treasury to finance current deficit spending. The Federal Reserve System is constrained by law from purchasing more than a small amount of such "new" securities directly from the Treasury.[21] Rather, open-market purchases are carried out in the "secondary" market and the securities are bought, through dealers, from commercial banks or the nonbank public (individuals, nonbank financial institutions, other corporations, and so on). Such transactions, then, simply involve a transfer of ownership of already existing U.S. securities, and the U.S. Treasury (though it is, of course, the original issuer) does not enter into the picture at all.

The immediate result of an open-market purchase differs slightly, depending on whether the ultimate seller of the securities is a member bank or a member of the "nonbank public." If we ignored the intermediate role played by the dealer, the T-account effects of a purchase from a member bank would be as follows:

Federal Reserve		Member Bank	
U.S. securities +$100	Demand deposits of member banks +$100	U.S. securities −$100 Federal Reserve account +$100	

In this case, the monetary base (and total member bank reserves) have gone up by the amount of the purchase (making possible, of course, a future expansion in the money supply by some multiple of this amount). Member bank *excess* reserves also rise by the amount of the purchase, but the purchase itself (as distinct from subsequent actions banks may take as a result of it) has no immediate effect on the money supply.

If, on the other hand, the ultimate seller is a member of the nonbank public (say, for example, an insurance company), the T-account effects, again ignoring the transactions of the dealer middleman, would be

---

[21]The law currently forbids the Federal Reserve System from owning more than $5 billion worth of U.S. securities that have been purchased directly from the Treasury. The Treasury can borrow directly from the Fed only after five of the seven members of the Board of Governors declare the existence of "unusual and exigent circumstances." In addition (although it, along with direct borrowing, cannot exceed the $5 billion legal limit), the Fed stands ready to lend up to $2 billion of its existing portfolio of U.S. securities to the Treasury in emergencies. In such cases, the Treasury would be expected to sell the securities for cash and to buy new ones to return to the Fed within six months.

Federal Reserve		Insurance Company's Member Bank		Insurance Company	
U.S. securities +$100	Demand deposits of member banks +$100	Federal Reserve account +$100	Demand deposit of insurance company +$100	U.S. securities −$100 Checking account at member bank +$100	

In this case, it is assumed that the Federal Reserve pays the insurance company (the ultimate seller) with a $100 check (written on itself). The insurance company then deposits its check in its account at a member bank, which sends it in for collection to the Federal Reserve and receives payment in the form of an increase in its Federal Reserve account.

As before, the monetary base (and, of course, total member bank reserves) are increased by the full amount of the purchase. In this case, however, the immediate effect on *excess* reserves and the money supply is somewhat different from that when member banks were the sellers. For here the money supply is increased by $100 as a direct result of the purchase itself (the new demand deposit obtained by the insurance company). And since this new demand deposit necessitates setting aside part of the bank's new Federal Reserve account as required reserves, *excess* reserves go up by something less than $100. (For example, if R_d equals 20 percent, the increase in excess reserves is only $80.)

The differences in the two cases, however, are of no real significance. What really matters is that, no matter who the seller is, a **Federal Reserve open-market purchase always increases the monetary base (and total member bank reserves) by the amount of the purchase.** This, in turn, provides the basis for an increase in the money supply equal to the money multiplier times the change in the monetary base. And that expansion in money and loans, in its turn, leads to lower interest rates.

The interest rate effects of an open-market purchase are twofold—an initial reduction caused by the purchase itself plus further cuts later caused by the expansion in credit permitted by the increased reserves.

The initial cut comes about as a direct result of the purchase of securities. If the account manager sets out, for example, to purchase $2 billion of U.S. securities during a given week, he is not likely to find sellers willing to offer such a large amount at the current market price. This is no problem for the account manager, of course; all he needs to do is pay a slightly higher price to induce enough sellers to part with the necessary volume.

Such action, of course, tends to raise the market value of U.S. securities. If a security has been selling for $1,000 and paying the holder an interest return of $100 per year, its effective yield was 10 percent per annum. If a Federal Reserve open-market purchase now raises that market value to, say, $1,050 (still paying the holder the fixed $100 per year), the yield, expressed as a percentage of its new, higher market value is now closer to 9.5 percent. Interest returns on Treasury securities are thus immediately reduced by the purchase.

Ultimately, further interest rate cuts can be expected as the banks make use of their now more plentiful reserves to expand the money and credit supply. Such an increase in the supply of credit—or, alternatively, in the supply of "loanable funds"—together with an unchanged demand for loanable funds will quite naturally lead to a fall in the price of loanable funds—the rate of interest.

Mechanics of an Open-Market Sale. If the Open Market Committee sees a need for credit restraint and calls, accordingly, for a policy involving open-market sales, the reverse of this operation is in order. The system account manager would contact all government security dealers asking for the prices they would offer to take the quantity of securities for sale. The dealers, in turn, would quote prices that would seem to them low enough to enable them to resell the securities to ultimate holders and still earn a return for their intermediary service. When the sale is made, the dealers would pay the Federal Reserve with checks on their accounts at member banks but would then be repaid by checks written by the ultimate purchasers on their own checking accounts.

If the T-account effects involving the security dealers' role were once again ignored, the effect of a Federal Reserve sale to a member bank would be

Federal Reserve		Member Bank	
U.S. securities −$100	Demand deposits of member banks −$100	U.S. securities +$100 Federal Reserve account −$100	

The monetary base and total as well as excess reserves are reduced by the full amount of the sale, while, for the moment at least, there is no effect on the money supply.

If the ultimate purchaser turns out to be a member of the nonbank public (once again we will assume it to be an insurance company), the T-account effects of the sale are

Federal Reserve		Insurance Company's Member Bank		Insurance Company	
U.S. securities −$100	Demand deposits of member banks −$100	Federal Reserve account −$100	Demand deposits of insurance company −$100	U.S. securities +$100 Checking account at member banks −$100	

In this case, it is assumed that the insurance company pays the Federal Reserve with a check written on its account at a member bank. The Federal Reserve then collects the check by marking down the Reserve account of the member bank on which it is written by $100. The monetary base and total reserves are cut by the full amount of the sale; but here the money supply is immediately cut by $100), so excess reserves go down by only $80 (assuming a 20 percent reserve ratio, required reserves are reduced by $20 because of the elimination of the insurance company's checking account). In both cases, however, the removal of $100 of total reserves from the member bank reduces the (potential) money supply by the money multiplier times the amount of the sale.

In summary, **when the Federal Reserve sells U.S. securities, the monetary base and total bank reserves are cut by the amount of the sale no matter who buys.** This cut reduces the (potential) money and credit supply by that amount times the money multiplier. Finally, there is upward pressure on interest rates—initially because the open-market sale lowers U.S. security prices and later because the supply of credit (or loanable funds) is reduced relative to the demand.

The Advantages of Open-Market Operations. Open-market operations unquestionably bear the bulk of the burden of carrying out monetary policy. The main reasons for their primacy are clear. To begin with, the initiative for their implementation is entirely in Federal Reserve hands and not, as with the discount mechanism, partly with the member banks. Second, with the U.S. security portfolio of well over $100 billion and the ability to purchase many more if conditions warrant, the System has sufficient power to alter bank reserves within any desired limits via the weapon. Third, the open-market device is a model of flexibility. Because it is used continuously, it does not carry with it the psychological "announcement effects" that accompany alterations in the discount rate or required reserve ratios. Consequently, it is entirely feasible to "operate by feel," buying today and then reversing to a sale tomorrow if conditions warrant. Open-market operations can be made as powerful as a sledge hammer or as discriminating as a surgeon's scalpel. In an area replete with controversy, there is remarkable unanimity with respect to the preeminence of open-market operations among monetary policy weapons.

Selective Credit Controls

If the government should take some action to reduce sharply the supply of eggs produced in the United States, the price of eggs would have to rise, assuming a free, competitive market. As fewer eggs would be available, some people who would have eaten them under the old conditions would now be unable to do so. But the mechanism for determining which particular consumers get "cut out" of the egg market would be the impersonal one of the price system. Those who are unwilling (or unable) to pay the higher price, we say, are "rationed out" by the increase in price.

Contrast this situation to one in which the government simply decreed that all consumers living in New York City would have to go without eggs next year. Here, as before, government action has had the effect of cutting out certain people from egg consumption; but whereas in the former case, the government does not specify the particular individuals who will do without (leaving it to the forces of the market to determine that), in the latter case it does.

This comes pretty close to illustrating the difference between general credit controls and selective ones. Under general credit controls, government action may be taken to reduce the total supply of credit available, but the credit "market" determines which particular credit users will have to do without. Under selective credit controls, government takes action to alter the amount (or terms) of credit available for specific groups of people who desire to use it for a particular purpose.

In past years Congress has given the Board of Governors authority to impose selective credit controls on three different groups of credit users: those who purchase securities on credit, those who purchase consumer durables on credit, and those who buy real estate with borrowed funds. As of today, the authority with respect to real estate and consumer durables has lapsed, leaving margin controls on the purchase of stock as the only selective control now available to the Board.[22]

The Power to Set Margin Requirements on the Purchase of Stock

In 1934 the Securities Exchange Act gave the Federal Reserve's Board of Governors the authority to set margin requirements on the purchase of stocks. Acting on this basic legislative authority, the Board of Governors subsequently issued Regulations T and U, specifying the details of the control. Briefly, the Board is empowered to specify what proportion of the purchase price of stocks may *not* be borrowed from brokers or commercial banks.[23] If, for example, the margin requirement is at 65 percent, banks and brokers that lend money for the purpose

---

[22]This represents a quite narrow view of selective credit controls. One might reasonably call any policy that attempts to channel credit into, or out of, a particular use a selective credit policy. Such a definition would therefore include many other measures, such as several mortgage interest subsidy programs, portfolio limitations restricting savings and loan associations primarily to mortgages, ceilings on FHA and VA mortgage interest, and usury laws. For an excellent survey of the entire subject, see *Studies in Selective Credit Policies,* edited by Ira Kaminov and James M. O'Brien, Federal Reserve Bank of Philadelphia, 1975.

[23]More specifically, Regulation T controls loans for stock purchase from security brokers and dealers to purchasers; Regulation U has to do with loans from *any* commercial bank (member or nonmember) to either brokers or purchasers of stock. In addition, Regulations X and G place limitations on credit granted for security purchase by lenders other than banks, brokers, and dealers as well as on the borrowers themselves.

of financing stock purchases may only lend 35 percent of the purchase price. Alternatively, a 65 percent margin requirement indicates that the buyer of stock must put up 65 percent of the purchase price in cash.

Experience in the 1920s and early 1930s, of course, provided the background and impetus to the initial margin requirement legislation. The stock market boom of the 1920s was generously fed by bank credit. Purchases of stock on very thin margins (with the bulk of the purchase price borrowed) were common. Inevitably, this meant that the safety of a significant proportion of bank loans depended on fluctuations in stock prices. When the stock market crash came in 1929, the rapid decline in market prices quickly wiped out the equity of many owners, leaving the banks (and many brokers who had in turn borrowed from banks) with collateral that was decreasing in value at an alarming rate. Chaos followed. Banks were forced to sell the securities to attempt to meet their commitments to depositors, with the effect of depressing the stock market still further while pouring more fuel on the fires of the bank panic that ensued. It was indeed a time for action, and among the many laws passed in response to the crisis was the one granting the authority to set margin requirements any place between zero (no cash required to purchase stocks) and 100 percent (banks and brokers may not lend anything to finance stock purchases).

Entirely aside from the general philosophical issues regarding selective controls, a number of problems have emerged concerning the implementation of margin requirements. In theory, at least, control is effected through the lender, who is expected to determine the intended use of the funds that he or she is lending. Generally this problem is simplified by the fact that when stocks are to be purchased, the stock itself composes the collateral for the loan.

Weaknesses of Margin Requirements. A number of leakages in the network of control have appeared over the years. To begin with, a borrower may deny any intention of purchasing stocks with his or her borrowed funds, pledge other assets as collateral for the loan, but then go ahead and buy stocks anyway. Or the borrower may purchase stocks with cash he or she would normally use to purchase materials and supplies and then borrow money to finance the materials and supplies purchased, pledging the stocks he or she already has as collateral for the loan. In addition, lenders other than commercial banks and brokers, who are not subject to margin requirements, may increase their security loans when brokers and commercial banks are being held down by high margin requirements. And, indeed, some of these nonregulated lenders may be getting the funds they lend to finance security purchases from commercial banks themselves.

Despite these weaknesses in practice, many authorities feel that margin requirements serve a useful purpose.[24] That purpose, however, is not the same as

---

[24]Approval, however, is far from unanimous. See, for example, Thomas G. Moore, "Stock Market Margin Requirements," *Journal of Political Economy,* Vol. 74, No. 2 (1966).

for general credit controls. Although a tightening of general credit controls may combat rises in the *general* price level, there is considerable doubt that increases in margin requirements accomplish the same results, for they are aimed, as their name indicates, *selectively* at one segment of the economy. If they are successful, they clamp down on excessive speculation in the stock market and stock price increases, but there is little reason to believe they have much effectiveness in combating general inflation of the prices of goods and services. After all, holding down on the use of credit to purchase stocks does not in any way cut the quantity of credit available to buy other things. And it is quite likely that the credit that would, in the absence of margin requirements, have been used to purchase stocks may now be used to purchase something else.

The Power to Limit the Use of Credit
by Buyers of Real Estate
and Consumer Durable Goods

During World War II, the Board of Governors was given the power to limit the credit that could be granted on the purchase of a number of major consumer durable goods. Although this authority ended in 1947, it was granted again during the Korean war, starting in 1950. In addition, 1950 saw the first grant of authority to the Board of Governors to control credit used to finance the purchase of real estate.[25] Authority for both controls lapsed in mid-1952, and the Board now has no power in either area.

Consumer credit controls were enforced on a specific list of major consumer durable goods. They took the form of minimum down payment requirements coupled with maximum repayment periods for the amount borrowed. For example, during much of World War II, minimum down payments of $33\frac{1}{3}$ percent and maximum repayment periods of 12 months were enforced on an extensive array of consumer durables. Controls over the use of credit in the purchase of real estate limited the size of the mortgage that could be granted to a specified percentage of the market value of the home and also set up maximum terms for the length of the mortgage.

Although both these efforts at selective controls now fall in the category of history, debate over the wisdom of their possible use in peacetime continues. This is especially true with respect to controls over consumer credit, which some feel should be given to the Federal Reserve on a standby basis, to be used when conditions warrant. Those favoring such authority cite the destabilizing role that they believe consumer credit has played in business cycles in recent years. Opponents counter with the arguments that extension of selective controls in peacetime

---

[25] Actually the control over real estate credit was shared by the Board of Governors and the Housing and Home Finance Administration.

is inimical to the philosophy of a free enterprise, consumer-directed economy and that they are unlikely to accomplish their intended goal in any case.[26]

Moral Suasion

In addition to the general and selective credit control devices, some notice should be taken of the rather vague, ill-defined area usually referred to as *moral suasion*. Properly speaking, moral suasion is not really a *control* device at all, as it involves voluntary cooperation by, rather than coercion of, the member banks. It might be described best as an attempt, on the part of Federal Reserve authorities, to persuade banks to voluntarily tailor their lending policies to the desires of the System, thereby reducing the need for more overt credit control measures.

This attempt to persuade comes through many channels. During the periodic examinations made of state member banks, discussions with bank officers often turn to the System's overall aims in credit policy. At periodic banquets and meetings held for bankers in their district, representatives of the Reserve bank hammer away at the reasons for, and wisdom of, recent policy actions. In their frequent publications, the Board of Governors and the 12 Federal Reserve banks carry the message very much farther. Much of this, it is true, might well be put under the heading of mere public relations, but the most sanguine supporters of moral suasion claim that it accomplishes much more. If bankers do respond to these many appeals to "do right" as far as credit is concerned, the burden that must be borne by the other tools of monetary policy is proportionately reduced.

For all the natural appeal of the voluntary way of doing things, it seems fair to observe that, barring some unusual and compelling incentive to cooperate, the moral suasion approach probably, in and of itself, accomplishes little. However, our experience with it during the Korean war provides some basis for optimism in times of national emergency.

At that time, at the urging of the Federal Reserve, the credit industry, including nonbank leaders as well as commercial banks, set up the National Voluntary Credit Restraint Committee. The purpose of the committee was to draw up a set of standards, specifying those uses of credit that were in the national interest and those that were not. The entire approach was voluntary, but there is considerable evidence that the committee elicited widespread cooperation among lenders and that the Federal Reserve's task of controlling credit expansion was thereby measurably relieved.

---

[26]For excellent brief surveys of selective credit controls, see James M. O'Brien, "Can Credit Controls Be Controlled?" *Business Review,* Federal Reserve Bank of Philadelphia, January 1972; and Arnold Dill, "Selective Credit Controls: The Experience and Recent Interest," *Monthly Review,* Federal Reserve Bank of Atlanta, May 1971. For a more thorough review of the entire area, see Kaminov and O'Brien, *Studies in Selective Credit Policies.*

However, this experience cannot be taken as evidence of the peacetime effectiveness of moral suasion. The Korean war provided a sufficient sense of national emergency and patriotic fervor to partially overcome the normally powerful drive to maximize profits. It is impossible to say what the future will hold, but there can be little question that the voluntary approach is less effective without some special incentives to help modify actions aimed at profit maximization.

The Process of Monetary Policy Formulation

The fundamental decisions that establish the direction and extent of the nation's monetary policy are hammered out at the regular meetings of the Federal Open Market Committee. As noted, these meetings are attended not only by the 12 voting members of the committee but also by officials from the 7 Federal Reserve banks not currently represented on the FOMC. Although the future course of open-market operations is the prime concern, decisions regarding the use of all the monetary policy tools are made during the course of their deliberations.

At the meetings, participants are provided with extensive background data, including forecasts of production, prices, employment, and so forth, arrived at by a combination of the judgment of the Board's staff and the output of the Fed's large econometric model of the economy. With this impressive array of information as the basis, the committee then sets out to determine policy.

The System's ultimate targets are clear enough, of course. "Success" requires policy measures that will result in favorable effects on production, employment, and prices. But since none of the Fed's policy tools works *directly* on these ultimate policy variables, the policymakers are forced to rely upon intermediate targets that (1) they feel they *can* control tolerably well with the instruments at their disposal and (2) they feel are reasonably closely linked, through some logical cause-and-effect transmission mechanism, to the ultimate production, employment, and price-level targets.

The intermediate targets toward which Fed policy has been directly aimed have changed markedly over the years. Throughout the 1950s and much of the 1960s, System authorities tended to characterize their immediate objective as stabilizing "money market conditions." Translated into lay terms, "money market conditions" is technical jargon referring to an array of key short-term interest rates that the FOMC was attempting to manipulate.[27] During this period, low and/or falling short-term interest rates were interpreted as evidence of an "easy" or expansive monetary policy, whereas high and/or rising rates were accepted as evidence of a "tight" or contractive monetary policy.

---

[27]In addition to short-term interest rates, money market conditions were also often taken to include the banking system's "free reserves" (excess reserves minus borrowed reserves). See Benjamin M. Friedman, "The Inefficiency of Short-Run Monetary Targets," *Brookings Papers on Economic Activity,* Vol. 2, 1977, pp. 297–98.

In retrospect, it seems clear that this early preoccupation with interest rates as the intermediate target for monetary policy resulted partly from concern for the stability of financial institutions and partly from early "Keynesian" views on the efficacy of monetary policy as a weapon in the nation's stabilization arsenal. Since some early Keynesians viewed fiscal policy as very potent and monetary policy as "working" (altering aggregate demand) only as a consequence of very large changes in the interest rates, it was hardly surprising that the former was relied upon to control aggregate demand, whereas the latter was looked upon more as a device for maintaining stability in financial markets.[28]

By the latter 1960s, however, an unfortunately pro-cyclical fiscal policy along with accelerating rates of inflation forced a reevaluation of the practice of relying solely on interest rate behavior as the intermediate target to guide monetary policy. Although other issues played a role in this change, the most important was probably that played by inflationary expectations.[29]

The point here is a simple one. If rising market interest rates are accepted as evidence that a restrictive monetary policy has been implemented, policymakers may interpret what is actually an expansionary (inflationary) monetary policy as a contractionary one. This is because, when lenders have come to expect a rise in the price level, they will tack an "inflationary premium" on to the "real" rate of interest that they will accept. If, for instance, the market rate of interest rises from 10 percent to 12 percent such behavior could very well signify (or, indeed, result from) an *expansionary* monetary policy. This would be the case if, at the same time, the expected inflation rate rose by 5 percent, implying that the "real" rate of interest actually *fell* by 3 percent.

As a result of considerations such as these, significant changes began to appear in FOMC directives to the system account manager. First, in 1966 the Open Market Committee, though still couching its directives primarily in terms of effects on money market conditions, began to add a "proviso clause" to take explicit account of money supply changes. For example, the directive from the FOMC meeting of July 18, 1967, stated that open-market operations were to be conducted

---

[28]See Gordon H. Sellon, Jr., and Ronald L. Teigen, "The Choice of Short-Run Targets for Monetary Policy," *Economic Review,* Federal Reserve Bank of Kansas City, May 1981, for an especially lucid account. See, also, Stephen H. Axilrod, "Monetary Policy, Money Supply, and the Federal Reserve's Operating Procedures," *Federal Reserve Bulletin,* January 1982; and Benjamin M. Friedman, "Time to Reexamine the Monetary Targets Framework," *New England Economic Review,* March–April 1982.

[29]A factor of real significance in the movement away from interest rates and toward the money stock as the appropriate target for monetary policy was the opposition of the monetarists, who gained considerable strength during the 1960s. Although we shall consider the monetarist viewpoint in some depth in Chapter 18, it should be noted at this point that one need not subscribe to the entire monetarist position to accept their belief that the prime monetary policy target should be a money aggregate rather than interest rates. See William Poole, "Rules of Thumb for Guiding Monetary Policy," *Open Market Policies and Operating Procedures,* Board of Governors of the Federal Reserve System, 1971; and Richard G. Davis, "Implementing Open Market Policy with Monetary Aggregate Objectives," *Monthly Review,* Federal Reserve Bank of New York, July 1973.

with a view to maintaining about the prevailing conditions in the money market; but operations shall be modified insofar as the Treasury financing permits to moderate any apparent tendency for bank credit and money to expand more than currently expected.[30]

Then, in 1970, a further shift in emphasis appeared wherein directives began to be written primarily in terms of effects on the money supply and bank credit, with "money market conditions" in the secondary, or proviso, role. For example, the directive of April 7, 1970, stated that

> To implement this policy, the Committee desires to see moderate growth in money and bank credit over the months ahead. System open market operations until the next meeting of the Committee shall be conducted with a view to maintaining money market conditions consistent with that objective.[31]

It was not, however, until the mid-1970s that the Congress made this movement toward explicit recognition of monetary aggregates as intermediate targets for monetary policy mandatory. First, in a 1975 Congressional Resolution and, then, in the Full Employment and Balanced Growth Act of 1978, Congress required the Fed to publicly announce its targets explicitly in terms of annual percentage rates of growth in the money supply. For nearly a decade, then, the Federal Reserve System has been announcing and pursuing explicit money supply growth rates. But this has not really meant that interest rate targets have been altogether abandoned. In fact, until October 1979, the System saw fit to pursue its money supply growth targets indirectly via control of the federal funds interest rate.

What this amounted to was a "two-stage" targeting procedure.[32] First, the Fed recognizes that it cannot directly control output and prices, so it selects (indeed, is required by law to select) the rate of growth in the money supply as an "intermediate target" thought to be reasonably closely linked to output and prices. But then, knowing that it cannot directly control the rate of growth in the money supply either, the FRS selects an "operating target" that it considers to be closely linked to its intermediate target and over which it feels it *does* have adequate direct control. In oversimplified terms, monetary policy formulation then looked much like that in the following schematic sketch:

| FRS monetary policy tools | directly control $\rightarrow$ | Federal funds rate | Which is closely related to $\rightarrow$ | Rate of money supply increase | Which is closely related to $\rightarrow$ | Prices and output |

---

[30]"Record of Policy Actions of F.O.M.C.," *Federal Reserve Bulletin*, November 1967.

[31]"Record of Policy Actions of F.O.M.C.," *Federal Reserve Bulletin*, July 1970.

[32]See Sellon and Teigen, "The Choice of Short-Run Targets for Monetary Policy."

How well did this approach work? Not well enough, as its abandonment in October 1979 clearly attests. The problem was that although control of the operating target (the federal funds rate) was quite good, its influence on the intermediate target (money supply growth rate) was much less precise. For striking evidence of this result for the year 1977, see Figures 11-1 and 11-2.

It was the Fed's inability to keep the rate of money supply growth within its target ranges plus the widespread belief that this excessive monetary growth was contributing heavily to the accelerating inflation of the late 1970s that led to the significant change in monetary policy targeting that took place in October 1979. Table 11-3 provides evidence of the nature of the problem.

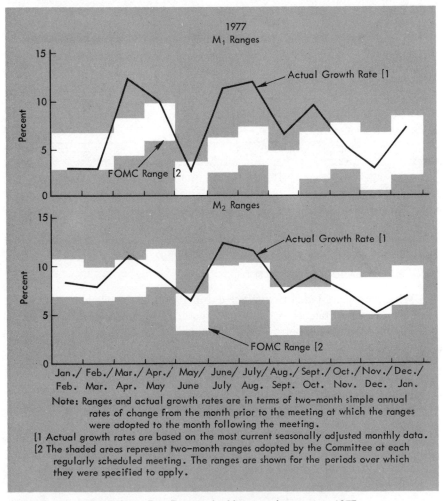

FIGURE 11-1 FOMC Short-Run Ranges for Monetary Aggregates, 1977

Source: Review, Federal Reserve Bank of St. Louis, March 1978.

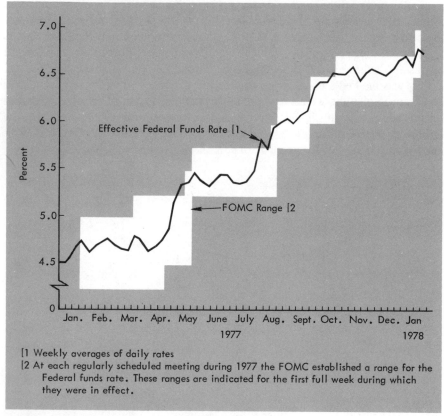

[1 Weekly averages of daily rates
[2 At each regularly scheduled meeting during 1977 the FOMC established a range for the
Federal funds rate. These ranges are indicated for the first full week during which
they were in effect.

FIGURE 11-2   FOMC Ranges for Federal Funds Rate, 1977

Source: Review, Federal Reserve Bank of St. Louis, March 1978.

What the Open Market Committee did in 1979 was to switch away from the federal funds interest rate as its operating target to "nonborrowed reserves" (total reserves minus the amount borrowed through the discount window). This has meant that, since October 1979, targeting for monetary policy formulation has been

FRS monetary policy tools	$\xrightarrow[\text{control}]{\text{Directly}}$	Nonborrowed reserves	$\xrightarrow[\text{related to}]{\text{Which is closely}}$	Rate of money supply increase	$\xrightarrow[\text{related to}]{\text{which is closely}}$	Prices and output

TABLE 11-3

Money Supply Growth and Inflation, 1977 and 1978

Year	FRS Target Range for M1	Actual % Change in M1	% Rise in Consumer Price Index
1977	4.5–6.5%	7.9%	6.8%
1978	4.0–6.5	7.2	9.0

The upshot of all this is that monetary policy formulation in the mid-1980s works as follows. The Federal Reserve System establishes target ranges for the rate of growth in M1, M2, and M3 from the fourth quarter of each year to the fourth quarter of the next year.[33] Subsequently, at each Open Market Committee meeting, the FOMC establishes "short-run" (two- to three-month) targets for M1 and M2 that are considered appropriate to stay within (or return to) the annual growth rates established. In essence, the system account manager is then directed to aim at maintaining a level of nonborrowed reserves sufficient to achieve the desired short-run rate of growth in M1 and M2. The federal funds rate, which previously was constrained within a very narrow range, is now permitted to vary as much as 4 to 5 percent during the month, and even if it strays outside this range, the account manager is advised only to "consult" with the committee. An example is the policy directive issued as a result of the FOMC meeting held on March 29–30, 1982:

> At its meeting in early February, the Committee agreed that its objectives would be furthered by growth of M1, M2, and M3 from the fourth quarter of 1981 to the fourth quarter of 1982 within ranges of $2\frac{1}{2}$ to $5\frac{1}{2}$ percent, 6 to 9 percent, and $6\frac{1}{2}$ to $9\frac{1}{2}$ percent, respectively. . . .
>
> In the short run the Committee seeks behavior of reserve aggregates consistent with growth of M1 and M2 from March to June at annual rates of about 3 percent and 8 percent, respectively. . . .
>
> The Chairman may call for Committee consultation if it appears to the Manager for Domestic Operations that pursuit of the monetary objectives and related reserve paths during the period before the next meeting is likely to be associated with a federal funds rate persistently outside a range of 12 to 16 percent.[34]

Following these procedures from 1979 through 1982 the Federal Reserve System was able to bring down the annual rate of growth of the money supply quite substantially. As a partial consequence (although the absence of massive supply shocks such as rocked the economy in the mid and late seventies helped enormously too) the rate of inflation as measured by the consumer price index fell dramatically to under 4 percent for 1982.

But despite the apparent success of their anti-inflation strategy, the Open Market Committee saw fit to diverge from it in the last half of 1982. First, about midyear, the FOMC announced their willingness to permit M1 to grow at rates "somewhat above the targeted ranges" for the rest of the year. Then in their October, 1982 meeting the committee went further by failing to specify *any* short run target for M1.

---

[33]A target is also set for the rate of growth of a broader aggregate called "bank credit."

[34]"Record of Policy Actions of the Federal Open Market Committee," *Federal Reserve Bulletin,* June 1982, pp. 368–69. The Manager for Domestic Operations referred to in the directive is the official we have called the system account manager. The reader should note that despite the Fed's significant movement toward the monetarist position over the years, monetarists were not ready to applaud the result as of 1982. See, for example, Milton Friedman, "Monetary Policy: Theory and Practice," and Robert Rasche and Allan Meltzer, "Is the Federal Reserve's Monetary Control Policy Misdirected?" Both articles are in the *Journal of Money, Credit, and Banking,* February 1982.

This notable deemphasis of the M1 target was a result of two considerations. On the one hand, as the recession deepened during 1982, the economy experienced a rare decline in the velocity of spending.[35] Accordingly, it was determined that a somewhat more rapid rise in M1 would not only not rekindle inflation but might indeed help arrest the increasingly serious recession.

A second reason had to do with uncertainty as to the effects on M1 of the maturing of a very large amount of so-called "all-savers" certificates and the initiation of the money market deposit accounts in December of 1982. As the Open Market Committee put it in its October, 1982 meeting:

> Specification of the behavior of M1 over the balance of the year is subject to unusually great uncertainties because it will be substantially affected by special circumstances— in the very near term by reinvestment of funds from maturing all-savers certificates and later by the public's response to the new account directly competitive with money market funds mandated by recent legislation. The probable difficulties in interpretation of M1 during the period suggest much less than usual weight to be placed on move- ments in that aggregate during the current quarter. These developments are expected to affect M2 and other broader aggregates to a much smaller extent.[36]

The effect of this change in policy was marked. Whereas the M1 total had risen by only 2.3 percent in 1981, and the target range set for its growth in 1982 was 2.5 to 5.5 percent, its actual growth rate for 1982 was over 8.5 percent!

By early 1983, however, both the apparent bottoming out of the recession and the assimilation of the newly authorized accounts led the Committee to reassert an M1 target range of from 4 to 8 percent for the calendar year 1983. This wider and higher range "reflects allowance for a possible change in cyclical behavior as well as for the evolving character of M1 as a more important repository for sav- ings. . . ."[37]

Review Questions

1. a. Assume that initially the banking system has total reserves of $30 billion and that outstanding demand and time deposit liabilities are $100 billion each. If R_d = 25 percent and R_t = 5 percent, confirm that there are no excess reserves.

   b. Now, assuming that c = .20 and t = 1.0, compute the monetary base.

---

[35]"The velocity decline for M1, which is likely to amount to about 3 percent from the fourth quarter of 1981 to the fourth quarter of 1982, stands in sharp contrast to the average yearly rise in velocity of 3 to 4 percent over the past decade; it will be the first significant decline in velocity in about 30 years." Statement by Paul M. Volcker, Chairman, Board of Governors of the Federal Reserve System before the Joint Economic Committee of the Congress, November 24, 1982.

[36]"Record of Policy Actions of the Federal Open Market Committee," *Federal Reserve Bulletin,* December 1982, p. 766.

[37]"Monetary Policy Report to Congress," *Federal Reserve Bulletin,* March 1983, p. 137.

    c. If R_d is now reduced to 15 percent, use the (new) money multiplier to compute the change in money supply made possible by the required reserve ratio change.

2. If the required reserve ratio is raised, trace through, in step-by-step fashion (i.e., via the transmission mechanism), exactly how such a measure would be expected to affect aggregate demand.

3. Specifically, how *might* an increase in the discount rate tend to cut aggregate demand?

4. "In the early days of the Federal Reserve System, authorities relied upon eligibility requirements to limit access to the discount window. More recently, Regulation A has been relied on to do this job." Explain.

5. The "announcement effects" of discount rate changes may either reinforce or work against the intent of the policy. Explain.

6. Explain *two* ways in which an open-market purchase may affect interest rates.

7. Show, by the use of appropriately labeled T-accounts for the member banks and the Federal Reserve banks, the effects of a $100 million open-market purchase from the member banks and from the nonbank public. In each case, indicate the effect *of the purchase alone* on member bank total reserves, excess reserves, and the money supply.

8. Write an essay comparing the relative advantages and disadvantages of the three general credit controls of the Federal Reserve.

9. "All Federal Reserve open-market operations are carried out in the secondary, rather than the primary, securities market." Why is this the case?

10. Opponents of selective credit controls often argue that such controls interfere with consumer choice in the allocation of the nation's resources. Develop this point.

11. Carefully explain the circumstances that led the Federal Reserve System to abandon direct attempts to control short-term interest rates in favor of directly controlling nonborrowed reserves.

12. Explain, as completely as you can, the Fed's current procedures for formulating monetary policy.

12

Other Determinants of the Money Supply

The money supply, as we have seen, depends upon the size of the money multiplier $\dfrac{1 + c}{R_d + c + (R_t \cdot t) + x}$ and of the monetary base. The essence of monetary policy is the Federal Reserve's power to alter the size of the multiplier (by varying R_d and R_t) and/or the monetary base (by implementing any of its three general credit controls).

But while the Fed is the sole institution whose main responsibility is control of the money supply, it by no means is the only one whose actions actually *do* affect it. There are three other groups in the economy whose activities, though primarily motivated by other considerations, do, in fact, affect the money supply—the nonbank public, the commercial banks, and the U.S. Treasury Department.

It should already be clear how the nonbank public can do this. Any change in its so-called "preferred asset" ratio will, by altering c or t, obviously affect the size of the money multiplier and, therefore, the size of the money supply a given monetary base can support. Similarly, any change in the banking system's desire for excess reserves (i.e., in x) will alter the money multiplier.

The effects of Treasury actions on the money supply are somewhat more complex, and most of this chapter will focus on them. All of the factors affecting the size of the monetary base will then be summarized at the end of the chapter.

Effects of Treasury Activities

The U.S. Treasury, of course, is primarily charged with meeting the nation's fiscal needs. At the risk of oversimplifying what is actually a monumental task, this responsibility might be said to boil down to seeing to it that the federal government always has on hand the funds that are necessary to carry out the spending programs set up by Congress.

This alone involves a number of fundamental duties, including collection of taxes, borrowing by sale of government securities when required spending exceeds tax revenue, handling the cash balances of the federal government including those arising from a tax surplus, and refunding the outstanding federal debt when necessary. Each of these duties provides the Treasury with major areas of discretion, such that the impact on the economy of handling the job one way or the other must be given careful consideration.

For example, if a deficit must be financed, it makes a difference what type of securities is sold. If a tax surplus is in the offing, different ways of handling it will have substantially different impacts on the economy. If a sizable portion of the national debt is approaching maturity and there is no tax surplus available to meet the bill, the choice of the type of obligation to sell to obtain the needed funds can be crucial. And even the apparently simple decision of determining the location of the Treasury's cash balances involves matters that are by no means inconsequential.

In this section, we shall consider the consequences for bank reserves and the money supply of several of the more important Treasury activities. Specifically, we shall look at the effects of changing the location of Treasury cash balances, the effects of financing deficits and disposing of surpluses in various ways, and the effects of refunding the existing national debt.

The Location of Treasury Cash Balances— Tax and Loan Accounts

One very important task of the Treasury, the handling of which can markedly affect commercial bank reserves, is the management of its cash balances. These balances consist, beyond a small amount held in the form of currency and coins, primarily of checking accounts at the 12 Federal Reserve banks and at some 13,000 commercial banks designated as special depositories.[1] In addition, in accordance with legislation that became effective in 1978, the other major depository institutions—mutual savings banks, savings and loan associations, and credit unions— are also eligible to hold Treasury balances.

Treasury deposits held at commercial banks and the other depository institutions are called *tax and loan accounts*. As the name implies, these accounts are used to receive funds being paid in to the federal government by taxpayers as well as by those who, through the purchase of U.S. securities, are lending money to the government.

---

[1] A depository institution can qualify as a "special depository," thereby becoming eligible to hold tax and loan accounts, by pledging certain specified securities as collateral and by being recommended by the Federal Reserve bank in its district.

Why, the reader may ask, does the Treasury keep checking accounts at commercial banks and other depository institutions *as well as* at Federal Reserve banks? Why not simplify matters by keeping all its demand deposits at the Federal Reserve? A moment or two of reflection will clear up this matter.

When taxes are paid in by the public or when loan funds are made available to the government, the taxpayer (or security purchaser) generally writes a check on his or her account at a commercial bank to make payment. If these funds were deposited directly into the Treasury's accounts at the Federal Reserve, the immediate effect would be to reduce bank reserves and the money supply by that amount, as the following T-accounts indicate:

Federal Reserve Banks		Member Banks	
Demand deposits of member banks −$100 Demand deposit of U.S. Treasury +$100		Federal Reserve account −$100	Demand deposit of taxpayer −$100

When the Treasury spends out of its accounts at Federal Reserve banks, the effects on the money supply and bank reserves are, of course, the other way around. The Treasury makes out a check payable to some member of the public who deposits it in his or her account at his or her commercial bank and the collection process raises bank reserves:

Federal Reserve Banks		Member Banks	
Demand deposits of member banks +$100 Demand deposit of U.S. Treasury −$100		Federal Reserve account +$100	Demand deposit of person paid by Treasury +$100

If the money collection and money disbursement sides of Treasury operations were always perfectly coordinated, their opposing effects on reserves and the money supply would offset one another, so that no major disturbance would be forthcoming. But, unfortunately, no such neat offset occurs. Treasury receipts, both from taxes and from security sales, arrive in an uneven pattern throughout the year, bulking particularly large on April 15 when settlement for the personal income tax is due and at the end of each quarter when corporate payments come in. Treasury spending patterns, on the other hand, are much more evenly distributed throughout the year. Without tax and loan accounts this failure of Treasury income and outgo to mesh perfectly would subject the banking system to constant disruption in the form of substantial net losses of reserves around the end of each quarter, offset only over time by government spending.

It was for the purpose of minimizing the disturbing effects of Treasury operations on the banking system that the tax and loan accounts were established. Under this arrangement, most taxes (and loan funds) are paid in initially to a tax and loan account, usually at a commercial bank. As this simply represents a change in the ownership of demand deposits still in commercial banks, no loss in bank reserves results.

The Treasury, however, does not choose to subject itself to the administrative chaos that might be involved in making its disbursements directly out of the tax and loan accounts located at over 13,000 different commercial banks plus many other eligible nonbank depositories. Its expenditures, therefore, with rare exceptions, are made through checks written on its accounts at Federal Reserve banks, a source that is regularly replenished, as expenditures are planned, by transfer of the necessary amount from the tax and loan accounts to accounts at the Fed.

For example, suppose $10 billion in taxes is collected on April 15, and the funds are spent at a rate of $500 million per day thereafter. On April 15 the T-account effects of collection would be

Commercial Banks	
	Demand deposits of taxpayers −$10 billion Demand deposits of U.S. Treasury +$10 billion

On April 16 and each day thereafter for 20 days, funds are transferred to Federal Reserve banks,

Federal Reserve		Commercial Banks	
	Demand deposits of member banks −$500 million Demand deposits of U.S. Treasury +$500 million	Federal Reserve account −$500 million	Demand deposits of U.S. Treasury −$500 million

and the Treasury then immediately spends the funds:

Federal Reserve		Commercial Banks	
	Demand deposits of U.S. Treasury −$500 million Demand deposits of member banks +$500 million	Federal Reserve account +$500 million	Demand deposit of those paid by the Treasury +$500 million

For many years commercial banks with tax and loan accounts were permitted to hold the large Treasury deposits without payment of interest on the assumption that the value of services performed by the banks for the Treasury was approximately equivalent to the interest that might have been earned on deposits. This arrangement was changed as a result of a Treasury study in 1974, which concluded that the value of the balances to the depositories far exceeded the value of services rendered by the banks.[2]

The result was an act of Congress that took effect in 1978, under which

1. Nonbank depository institutions were given the right to hold Treasury tax and loan accounts.

2. All institutions holding Treasury balances are required to pay interest on them if held for more than one day.[3]

3. In return for the payment of interest, the Treasury now pays for services rendered by depository institutions on a per item basis.[4]

4. The Treasury is authorized to use its cash balances to purchase its own securities as well as those issued by federal government agencies.[5]

The Monetary Aspects of Fiscal Policy: Effects on Bank Reserves and the Money Supply of Alternative Means of Financing Deficits and Disposing of Tax Surpluses[6]

A common practice in introductory economics courses is to distinguish sharply between monetary policy and fiscal policy. The former is generally defined as action by the Federal Reserve System to alter the quantity of bank reserves and the potential money and credit supply so as to ultimately affect the level of aggregate

---

[2]Report on a study of tax and loan accounts, U.S. Department of the Treasury, June 1974.

[3]Actually, depositories must choose one of two options. If they choose to keep the Treasury funds beyond one day, they must transfer them to an interest-bearing note account that is callable by the Treasury on demand. If they choose not to pay interest, they must transfer the funds to the Treasury's account at the Federal Reserve within 24 hours.

[4]For example, the Treasury originally agreed to pay 50 cents for each processing of a Treasury deposit, 70 cents for each savings bond sold over the counter, and 30 cents for each savings bond redeemed. See "Interest Authorized on U.S. Treasury Demand Deposits at Commercial Banks," *Voice,* Federal Reserve Bank of Dallas, January 1978.

[5]For more detail on this change in procedures, see William N. Cox, "Changes in the Treasury's Cash Management Procedures," *Economic Review,* Federal Reserve Bank of Atlanta, January–February 1978; and Elijah Brewer, "Treasury to Invest Surplus Tax and Loan Balances," *Economic Perspective,* Federal Reserve Bank of Chicago, November–December 1977.

[6]In this section, we shall oversimplify by ignoring the tax and loan accounts, assuming for the moment that both tax and loan funds are deposited directly in the Treasury's Federal Reserve account. The complexity that this simplification overcomes is considerable and the final effects on bank reserves and the money supply of each operation are unchanged in any case.

demand in the necessary direction for stability and growth. Fiscal policy, on the other hand, is usually described as alterations in tax and/or expenditure programs by Congress, also aimed at promoting stability and growth via effects on aggregate demand.

Thus the two sets of policy tools are seen to be distinctly different means for achieving the same final objectives. Fiscal policy "works" (affects aggregate demand) largely through altering the income available to spending groups. Monetary policy, on the other hand, works primarily through a change in the degree of liquidity of the wealth held by the community.

Such distinctions are useful for throwing into broad relief the central difference between two techniques. But, valuable though it may be to emphasize the conceptual differences between them, it is important to recognize that a single policy action can often involve them both.

This is particularly true of fiscal policy, the execution of which is the particular responsibility of the Treasury Department. If, for example, Congress cuts taxes to raise demand, the *fiscal* policy effects of the action have to do with increased consumption and investment spending by those groups whose disposable incomes have been increased by the tax cut.

But that is not all there is to it. If the tax cut has reduced governmental revenue below its expenditures, it is the task of the Treasury to raise the funds needed to cover the deficit. The particular means it chooses to carry out this responsibility, whether it prints new money or borrows, and if the latter, from whom it borrows, are matters that can also affect the money supply and bank reserves. And the overall effect of the deficit on aggregate demand will depend, to some extent, on these decisions.

The Financing of a Budget Deficit.   When the expenditure and tax laws enacted by Congress result in a budget deficit, it is the Treasury's responsibility to provide the money not raised by taxation. Although in theory small deficits might be financed on a very-short-term basis by drawing down balances already held by the Treasury at its special depositories or at Federal Reserve banks, such expedients are, for obvious reasons, strictly limited. Financing deficits of any significance requires the Treasury to sell new U.S. securities to borrow the needed funds. And the monetary effects of such security sales will differ, depending upon the identity of the purchasers.

Borrowing by Sale of New U.S. Securities to the Nonbank Public.   If the Treasury should finance a deficit by sale of securities to members of the nonbank public, the operation (once the funds are spent) has no net effects on the money supply, bank reserves, or monetary base.

Although the sale of the securities and transfer of the proceeds into the Treasury's Federal Reserve account reduces both the public's money supply and the banking system's reserves, the subsequent deficit spending pumps the money right back out into the public's hands and the reserves right back to the commercial banks. Consequently, we can conclude that *financing deficit spending via sale of U.S. securities to the nonbank public has no net monetary effects.*

Borrowing by Sale of New U.S. Securities to the Commercial Banks. The monetary effects are only slightly different if the securities are sold to commercial banks. In this case, the T-account effects of the sale of the securities are

Federal Reserve		Commercial Banks	
	Demand deposits of commercial banks −$100 Demand deposits of U.S. Treasury +$100	U.S. securities +$100 Federal Reserve account −$100	

When the borrowed funds are subsequently spent, the effects are

Federal Reserve		Commercial Banks	
	Demand deposits of U.S. Treasury −$100 Demand deposits of commercial banks +$100	Federal Reserve account +$100	Demand deposits of those paid by the government +$100

Here, when the banks buy the securities, they pay the Treasury with a check on their Federal Reserve account. This half of the transaction cuts the banking system's total reserves but has no effect on the money supply. However, when the funds are spent by the Treasury (assuming that those paid by the government deposit their checks in commercial banks), the banks' total reserves are restored to their original level while the money supply is increased.

One would be tempted to conclude that this method of financing a deficit is more expansionary than the preceding example because it increases the money supply. Such a conclusion, however, does not really seem warranted. Note that there is no change in the monetary base involved here. The transaction does not really put the banking system in a position to create any more money than it could have before. All that has happened is that excess reserves that the banking system already had have been "used up" (i.e., turned into required reserves) by the expansion in demand deposits.

Borrowing by Sale of New U.S. Securities to the Federal Reserve System. If the Treasury should borrow the funds needed to finance the deficit by selling new U.S. securities to the Federal Reserve banks the effects would be as follows:

Sale of the securities:

Federal Reserve		Commercial Banks
U.S. securities +$100	Demand deposits of U.S. Treasury +$100	No effect

Treasury spends the proceeds:

Federal Reserve		Commercial Banks	
	Demand deposits of U.S. Treasury −$100 Demand deposits of commercial banks +$100	Federal Reserve account +$100	Demand deposits of those paid by the government +$100

This procedure is emphatically more expansionary than the two preceding cases. Because the Treasury would be borrowing new money created by the Federal Reserve, neither bank reserves nor the money supply would be cut by the sale of the securities. Both, however, would be increased by the expenditure of the funds. Clearly, deficit spending financed by borrowing from the Federal Reserve would be very expansionary. But the whole thing is more academic exercise than practical possibility. The reader must be very careful to note the following reservations regarding this case:

1. Strictly speaking, what is described here is *not an open-market purchase* in the sense in which that phrase is used in this text. The careful reader will remember that open-market purchases were limited earlier to purchases of "old" U.S. securities (on the secondary market) rather than to "new" ones just issued by the Treasury (on the primary market).

2. What is envisaged here—the purchase of new U.S. securities by the Federal Reserve System—is limited by law to an amount no larger than $5 billion, as noted in the preceding chapter. The reason for this limitation should be easy to see. The fact is that there is no real difference between financing a Treasury deficit by sale of securities to the Federal Reserve and running the printing presses. In either case the Treasury is simply obtaining its spending money from another government agency. Why should it make a difference whether the money creator is the Federal Reserve or the Bureau of Engraving?

All in all, we must conclude that while the Treasury *could* conceivably cause substantial monetary effects in financing deficits, such effects, in practice, are likely to be minor.

The Disposition of a Tax Surplus. On those rare occasions when tax revenues are in excess of government expenditures, the Treasury's area of discretion has to do with the handling of the tax surplus. Two major possibilities present themselves.

The Treasury might simply hoard the surplus, either in its commercial bank tax and loan accounts or in its checking account at the Federal Reserve. Or it may use it to retire a portion of its outstanding debt.

If a tax surplus is held in the tax and loan accounts at commercial banks, its collection will reduce the money supply but leave the monetary base, total bank reserves and excess reserves unaffected.[7] If, however, the surplus is transferred to the Treasury's Federal Reserve account, and hoarded there, its effect will be to lower the money supply, bank reserves, and the monetary base by the amount of the surplus and excess reserves by a lesser amount, the magnitude of which depends on the required reserve ratio. Clearly the second alternative is more contractionary than the first.

The hoarding of tax surpluses is reasonable economically, depending on the state of the economy, but this practice could be hazardous politically. When a large national debt on which interest is accruing exists, it is extremely difficult to justify holding a tax surplus when it might be used to reduce the level of debt. Consequently, the usual practice of the Treasury is to employ surpluses to retire outstanding securities.

Using Tax Surplus to Retire Securities Held by Nonbank Public. None If a tax surplus is used to retire maturing U.S. securities held by the nonbank public, neither the money supply nor bank reserves are altered. The collection of the tax surplus cuts both the money supply and the total reserves, but the use of it to retire securities held by the public pumps that money and those reserves right back to the public and the banks.

We can therefore conclude that *whenever the Treasury collects a tax surplus and uses it to retire U.S. securities held by the nonbank public, the net effect—considering both tax collection and security retirement—is to leave total member bank reserves, the monetary base, and the money supply unchanged.*

Using Tax Surplus to Retire Securities Held by Commercial Banks. A tax surplus used to retire maturing U.S. securities held by the commercial banks would reduce the money supply but would leave total member bank reserves and the monetary base unchanged. That is, the collection of the tax surplus reduces demand deposits of taxpayers and (when the Treasury deposits the funds in its Federal Reserve account), total member bank reserves by the full amount of the surplus. Subsequently, when the surplus is spent to retire bank-held securities, the total reserves are restored to the banks, but demand deposits remain below their original level. In T-accounts we have the following:

1. Collection of tax surplus and deposit in Treasury's Federal Reserve account:

---

[7]Because the money supply excludes Treasury deposits, it is reduced by the collection of the surplus. However, the amount of demand deposits behind which commercial banks are required to maintain reserves is unchanged, so that, despite the drop in the money supply, as defined, required reserves are unchanged.

Federal Reserve	Commercial Banks	
	Federal Reserve	Demand deposits
Demand deposits of	account	of taxpayers
member banks	−$100	−$100
−$100		
Demand deposits of		
Treasury		
+$100		

2. The tax surplus is used to retire maturing securities held by commercial banks:

Federal Reserve	Commercial Banks	
	U.S. securities	
Demand deposits of	−$100	
U.S. Treasury	Federal Reserve	
−$100	account	
Demand deposits of	+$100	
commercial banks		
+$100		

Note once again that, despite the fact that the money supply is reduced in this case, it is hardly more contractionary than the preceding example where the money supply was unaffected. The difference is that, in this case, since demand deposits (and, therefore, required reserves) are reduced while total reserves are unchanged, *excess* reserves are *increased*. By any reasonable assumptions, one would have to expect the banking system subsequently to make new loans (creating new money) on the basis of these excess reserves, thereby restoring the money supply to its original size.   *reduce money sup of mB*

Using Tax Surplus to Retire Securities Held by the Federal Reserve Banks. Finally, a tax surplus could be used to retire U.S. securities held by the Federal Reserve banks themselves. This approach, as the following T-accounts demonstrate, will result in a reduction of both the money supply *and* total commercial bank reserves (as well as the monetary base) by the amount of the surplus. It does so because this use of the surplus funds restores neither the public's demand deposits nor the commercial banks' reserves that were drained away in tax collection.

1. Collection of tax surplus and deposit in Federal Reserve:

Federal Reserve	Commercial Banks	
	Federal Reserve	Demand deposit
Demand deposits of	account	of taxpayers
commercial banks	−$100	−$100
−$100		
Demand deposit of		
Treasury		
+$100		

2. Use of tax surplus to retire U.S. securities owned by the Federal Reserve banks:

Federal Reserve		Commercial Banks
U.S. securities −$100	Demand deposits of U.S. Treasury −$100	No effect

Note that the monetary effects of this method of handling a tax surplus are exactly equivalent to those that would result from the Treasury's collecting the tax surplus and hoarding it all in its checking account at the Federal Reserve. Clearly, if the purpose of collecting the tax surplus is to reduce an excessive level of aggregate demand to combat inflation, using it to pay off Federal Reserve–held securities or hoarding it in the Treasury's Federal Reserve account will be preferable (cut aggregate demand more) to the other possibilities discussed. This is so because both the fiscal *and* the monetary effects of the action are contractive.

Treasury Debt Refunding

One of the Treasury Department's weightier responsibilities is the refunding of debt that matures each year when no tax surplus is available to retire it. This, of course, requires the sale of new securities to raise the funds with which to retire those coming due. The Treasury, as the issuer, is free to tailor the type and maturity of the new issue to its desires. Certain types of securities especially appeal to particular groups of lenders, so the Treasury, in designing the nature and special characteristics of the new issue, can reasonably effectively determine the security's purchaser.

This, too, provides a means of altering the monetary base and the money supply, and the possibilities are many. By way of example, assume that $100 million of securities held by the Federal Reserve are approaching maturity and that the Treasury chooses to raise the funds to pay them off by selling an equivalent amount of new securities to the nonbank public. The effects of these transactions are shown as follows in T-account form.

1. Sale of new U.S. securities to nonbank public and deposit of funds in the Treasury's Federal Reserve account:

Federal Reserve		Commercial Banks	
	Demand deposits of commercial banks −$100	Federal Reserve account −$100	Demand deposits of security purchasers −$100
	Demand deposits of U.S. Treasury +$100		

2. Use of the newly borrowed funds to retire maturing U.S. securities held by the Federal Reserve:

Federal Reserve		Commercial Banks
U.S. securities −$100	Demand deposits of U.S. Treasury −$100	No effect

The result of this particular refunding operation is to reduce both the money supply and the monetary base by the full amount of the refunding operation, a monetary effect that is sharply contractionary.

We shall not take the time here to go through the monetary effects of all possible refunding combinations. This is an exercise that the student might prefer to work out on his or her own. It is clear, however, that substantial increases or decreases in the economy's liquidity are possible via the debt refunding mechanism.

Defensive versus Dynamic Monetary Policy

Monetary policy, as one authority put it, has its *defensive* and its *dynamic* aspects.[8]

Defensive policy is under way when the Federal Reserve System, for example, employs open-market operations to combat or offset an undesired change in the monetary base or money supply that has come about as a result of activities by the public, the commercial banks, or the Treasury such as those just described. *Dynamic* policy, on the other hand, involves the use of monetary policy weapons, not just to prevent unfavorable changes but rather to promote actively desired positive changes. Many of the more serious problems encountered by the Fed in achieving its short-run money supply targets arise out of its inability to anticipate changes in conditions originating with actions by the public or Treasury and calling for defensive policy.

It cannot be overemphasized, however, that, despite all this, it is still the Fed that holds the whip hand in determination of the money supply. It is true, for example, that alterations in the location of Treasury checking accounts *can* affect commercial bank reserves, but the very existence of the tax and loan accounts represents an attempt by the Treasury to *avoid* such changes. The monetary base *can* be increased in cases of deficit spending, but this will only happen if the Federal Reserve itself decides to be the buyer of the securities. Total bank reserves *can* be decreased if a tax surplus is collected and used to retire securities held by

---

[8]Robert V. Roosa coined these appropriate terms in his excellent monograph entitled *Federal Reserve Operations in the Money and Government Securities Markets,* published by the Federal Reserve Bank of New York in 1956.

the Federal Reserve, and a variety of effects on bank reserves is possible with debt refunding. But the Fed can, whenever it chooses, offset such results with open-market operations. Clearly, despite the wide-ranging capacities of the public and the Treasury to affect the size of the nation's money stock, the ultimate monetary power rests with the Fed.

Summary—Sources and Uses of Bank Reserves and the Monetary Base

In the past few chapters, we have considered a wide range of activities—by the public, the commercial banks, the Treasury, and the Federal Reserve itself—that affect the nation's money supply. Obviously, it would be convenient if we could consolidate all these into a single neat statement that summarizes all the factors affecting bank reserves and the monetary base. Fortunately such a statement exists, and Table 12-1 reports the data for March 2, 1983.

Table 12-1, the result of a complex process of consolidation and cancellation of all the items in the balance sheets of the Federal Reserve banks and the Treasury monetary accounts, itemizes all the factors affecting depository institution reserves at the Federal Reserve. On the left side, under the heading "Factors Supplying

TABLE 12-1

Factors Affecting the Reserves of Depository Institutions and the Monetary Base, March 2, 1983 (millions of dollars)

Factors Supplying Reserve Funds			Factors Absorbing Reserve Funds	
1. Federal Reserve credit			5. Treasury cash	463
outstanding		155,821	6. Treasury deposits	
U.S. securities[a]	143,728		at Federal Reserve	
Loans	710		banks	2,896
Float	2,387		7. Other deposits	
Other Federal			at Federal Reserve	
Reserve			banks (except	
assets	8,996		member bank	
2. Gold stock		11,139	deposits)	1,331
3. Special drawing rights			8. Other Federal	
certificate account		4,618	Reserve liabilities	
4. Treasury currency			and capital	4,882
outstanding		13,786	9. Currency in	
			circulation	151,945
			10. Depository institutions	
			reserve balances	23,847

[a]Includes federal agency securities.

Source: Federal Reserve Statistical Release H.4.1, March 4, 1983.

Reserve Funds,'' are reported all the items whose increase (decrease) raises (lowers) the size of depository institutions' Federal Reserve accounts. On the right—above the double line and entitled ''Factors Absorbing Reserve Funds''—appear all the items whose increase (decrease) lowers (raises) depository institution reserves. The sum of items 1 through 4 on the left side minus the sum of items 5 through 9 on the right, then, equals depository institution deposits at Federal Reserve banks (item 10).

If one's concern is with factors affecting the monetary base, only a slight change in focus is required. Since the monetary base equals the sum of items 9 and 10 in Table 12-1, it is clear that any increase (decrease) in items 1 through 4 will increase (decrease) the monetary base, while any increase (decrease) in items 5 through 8 will decrease (increase) the monetary base.

The appendix to this chapter contains a detailed explanation of the derivation of this table. For those who choose not to become involved in this much detail, a few definitions of the items listed may suffice to bring out its essence.

Federal Reserve credit outstanding reflects the sum of the items that supply bank reserves that are under the direct control of the Federal Reserve System. Dominant, of course, is the System's portfolio of U.S. securities resulting from open-market purchases.

The *gold stock* constitutes the total gold supply owned by the U.S. Treasury.[9]

The *special drawing rights certificate account* is an asset of the Federal Reserve banks that results from the Treasury ''monetizing'' special drawing rights received from the International Monetary Fund. From the Fed's point of view, this account has the same source and significance as gold certificates. (Special drawing rights are more fully explained in Chapter 24.)

Treasury currency outstanding includes all the U.S. currency and coins held by the nonbank public, the commercial banks, the Federal Reserve banks, and the Treasury itself, except Federal Reserve notes.

Treasury cash constitutes all currency and coins (including any uncoined silver bullion) held by the Treasury in its own vaults.

Currency in circulation consists of all currency and coins held outside the Treasury and the Federal Reserve banks. It therefore includes Federal Reserve notes and currency and coins issued by the Treasury that are held by the commercial banks and by the nonbank public.

So much for definitions. How does one read and interpret such a table as that presented in Table 12-1? Let us use the changes from October 14, 1981 to October 13, 1982 as an example with the data as reported in Table 12-2. What does this tell us about the changes over that 12-month period?

Note that the dominant factor supplying additional reserve funds for depository institutions during that year was open-market operations, which provided

---

[9]Valued at the ''official'' gold price of $42.22 per ounce rather than at the free market price many times higher.

TABLE 12-2

Factors Affecting Depository Institution Reserves and the Monetary Base,
October 1981 and October 1982
(billions of dollars)

Factors Supplying Reserve Funds	October 1981		October 1982		Change
1. Federal Reserve credit outstanding		$146.3		$153.6	+7.3
U.S. securities	$131.9		$140.3		+8.4
Loans	1.2		0.4		−0.8
Float	3.0		2.3		−0.7
Other Federal Reserve assets	9.2		9.6		+0.4
2. Gold stock		11.1		11.1	—
3. Special drawing rights certificate account		3.3		4.2	+0.9
4. Treasury currency outstanding		13.7		13.8	+0.1
Factors Absorbing Reserve Funds					
5. Treasury cash		0.4		0.4	—
6. Treasury deposits at Federal Reserve banks		2.9		2.8	−0.1
7. Other deposits at Federal Reserve banks (except member banks)		0.7		1.1	+0.4
8. Other Federal Reserve liabilities and capital		5.2		5.0	−0.2
9. Currency in circulation		139.4		149.8	+10.4

Source: Federal Reserve Statistical Release H.4.1.

over $8 billion of added reserves. With one exception, most of the other factors changed only slightly. That one exception, however, was a whopping $10 billion increase in currency in circulation.

The upshot is that, from October 1981 to October 1982, reserve balances held with Federal Reserve banks actually *fell* by some $2 billion.[10]

And how about the change in the monetary base? Since it consists of the sum of the change in depository institution Federal Reserve accounts (negative $2 billion) and the change in currency in circulation (positive $10.4 billion), the monetary base rose by slightly over $8 billion—virtually all of which was attributable to

---

[10]Since about $0.8 billion of the increase in currency in circulation consisted of an increase in the vault cash of depository institutions, total reserves fell by only about $1.2 billion.

open-market purchases. Once again we see the dominance of open-market operations in controlling the money supply, bank reserves, and the monetary base.

Review Questions

1. What is the fundamental purpose of Treasury tax and loan accounts?
2. When the Treasury sells U.S. securities to finance a deficit and then spends the proceeds, the national debt increases and the money supply may also increase. When the Federal Reserve sells U.S. securities, however, the national debt is unaffected and the money supply normally falls. Carefully explain the difference in these two cases.
3. When the Treasury sells U.S. securities to finance deficit spending, the effects on bank reserves and the money supply will differ depending on to whom the securities are sold. Using appropriately labeled T-accounts, illustrate these differences when the securities are sold to the public, the commercial banks, and the Federal Reserve.
4. If the Congress raises taxes to produce a budget surplus, contrast the monetary effects involved when the surplus is (a) hoarded in tax and loan accounts, (b) hoarded in the Treasury's account at Federal Reserve, (c) used to retire maturing securities held by the nonbank public, (d) used to retire maturing securities held by the commercial banks, (e) used to retire maturing securities held by the Federal Reserve banks.
5. If, as during World War II, we are already at full employment but the Treasury is required to finance large budget deficits, what method of financing the deficits seems most appropriate? Explain carefully.
6. Using appropriately labled T-accounts for the member banks and the Federal Reserve banks, illustrate the effects of the Treasury borrowing $100 million from the nonbank public and then using the proceeds to retire maturing securities held by the Federal Reserve banks. What is the effect of this on the monetary base and the money supply?
7. Suppose you know that during a certain period Federal Reserve float rose by $1 billion, U.S. securities held by the Fed rose by $5 billion, Treasury currency outstanding went up by $1 billion, Treasury deposits at the Fed rose by $3 billion, and currency in circulation went up by $3 billion. What would be the net effect of all this on member bank deposits at the Fed? How about the net effect on the monetary base?

Appendix

Derivation of the "Factors Affecting Bank Reserves" Statement

The "Factors Affecting Bank Reserves" statement is published weekly by the Federal Reserve System as Release H.4.1 and appears monthly in the *Federal Reserve Bulletin*.[11] As noted, it results from a process of consolidation and cancellation of the items in the consolidated balance sheet of all Federal Reserve banks and of a partial balance sheet containing the U.S. Treasury's monetary accounts. Let us trace through the derivation of this very important statement for September 30, 1976.

The consolidated balance sheet for all Federal Reserve banks for September 30, 1976, was as follows:

Consolidated Federal Reserve Bank Balance Sheet, September 30, 1976
(millions of dollars)

Assets		Liabilities and Capital Accounts	
1. Gold certificates	$ 11,598	8. Federal Reserve notes outstanding	$ 79,674
2. SDR certificate account	800	9. Deposits of member banks	26,220
3. Cash	370	10. Deposits of U.S. Treasury	13,296
4. Loans (discounts and advances)	322	11. Deposits of others	1,417
5. U.S. securities[a]	103,507	12. Deferred availability cash items	4,771
6. Cash items in process of collection	7,768	13. Other liabilities	1,205
7. Other assets[b]	4,638	14. Capital accounts	2,420
	$129,003		$129,003

[a]Includes federal agency securities held.
[b]Includes acceptances held.

---

[11]Actually, the current statement is entitled "Factors Affecting Reserves of Depository Institutions" since the Monetary Control Act applied reserves to all depository institutions. The changes in the statement, however, are very slight so that the derivation given here, even though it is from the late 1970s, does little violence to current reality.

The Treasury monetary accounts as of the same date were

Treasury Monetary Accounts, September 30, 1976
(millions of dollars)

15. Gold stock	$11,598	18. Gold certificates	$11,598
16. Treasury currency		19. Treasury currency outside	
outstanding	10,742	Treasury	10,380
17. Federal Reserve notes		20. Treasury cash	496
held in the Treasury	134		
	$22,474		$22,474

To aid the reader in understanding the following derivation, it may be useful to begin with some definitions.

Treasury currency outstanding (item 16), it will be recalled, includes all paper currency and coins issued by the Treasury that are held by anyone in the economy, including the nonbank public, the member banks, the Federal Reserve banks, and the Treasury itself. (Except for some $300-odd million of U.S. notes, all paper currency issued by the Treasury is currently in process of retirement.) Of the $10,742 million of Treasury currency outstanding, for example, $362 million is held by the Treasury itself (item 16 minus item 19), $370 million is held by the Federal Reserve banks (item 3), and the remaining $10,010 million is held by the member banks and public.

Treasury currency outside the Treasury (item 19) includes, as its title indicates, all Treasury currency outstanding not held by the Treasury. It includes the $10,010 million held by the member banks and public plus the $370 million held by the Federal Reserve banks.

Treasury cash measures the amount of funds the Treasury has at its disposal without writing checks on its Federal Reserve or tax and loan accounts. Thus it is composed of the $362 million of Treasury currency held by the Treasury plus the $134 million of Federal Reserve notes in Treasury vaults.

Deriving the "Factors Affecting Bank Reserves" statement first requires combining the statements of the Federal Reserve banks and of the Treasury monetary accounts. This, of course, can be simply done by listing all the assets from both statements on one side and all the liabilities and capital accounts from both on the other. That is,

a. $(1) + (2) + (3) + (4) + (5) + (6) + (7) + (15) + (16) + (17) \equiv (8) + (9) + (10) + (11) + (12) + (13) + (14) + (18) + (19) + (20)$

Since we are interested in isolating the determinants of member bank reserve accounts at the Fed, it will be useful to rearrange the preceding definitional identity to read

b. $(9) \equiv [(1) + (2) + (3) + (4) + (5) + (6) + (7) + (15) + (16) + (17)] - [(8) + (10) + (11) + (12) + (13) + (14) + (18) + (19) + (20)]$

From here on the procedure is simply to consolidate the items in the awkward expression (b) so as to reduce them to the minimum number of basic determinants. This involves four operations:

1. Consolidating items 6 and 12 and replacing them with the positive item "float."
2. Consolidating items 3, 8, 17, and 19 and replacing them with the negative item "currency in circulation."
3. Eliminating gold certificates from each side, items 1 and 18.
4. Consolidating items 13 and 14 into "other Federal Reserve liabilities and capital."

Let us run through these four adjustments, one by one. Since Federal Reserve float is the difference between cash items in process of collection and deferred availability cash items, we can easily amend expression (b) by subtracting item 12 from item 6 and entering the positive result as float—a factor supplying reserve funds.

c. $(9) \equiv [(1) + (2) + (3) + (4) + (5) + (7) + (15) + (16) + (17) + \text{F.R. float}]$
    $- [(8) + (10) + (11) + (13) + (14) + (18) + (19) + (20)]$

Next we can consolidate four more of our original items into a single entry entitled "currency in circulation" if we add items 8 and 19 and subtract from this the sum of items 3 and 17. What this step gives us is the amount of currency and coins held outside the Treasury and Federal Reserve banks. This, of course, is currency and coins held by the nonbank public and the member banks—a total defined earlier as currency in circulation. With the adjustment, we have

d. $(9) \equiv [(1) + (2) + (4) + (5) + (7) + (15) + (16) + \text{F.R. float}] - [(10) + (11)$
    $+ (13) + (14) + (18) + (20) + \text{Currency in circulation}]$

Next, since items 1 and 18 both represent gold certificates, with opposite signs, they can be eliminated, producing:

e. $(9) \equiv [(2) + (4) + (5) + (7) + (15) + (16) + \text{F.R. float}] - [(10) + (11) +$
    $(13) + (14) + (20) + \text{Currency in circulation}]$

Finally, we replace the sum of items 13 and 14 with the single item "other Federal Reserve liabilities and capital" on the negative side and wind up with

f. $(9) \equiv [(2) + (4) + (5) + (7) + (15) + (16) + \text{F.R. float}] - [(10) + (11) +$
    $(20) + \text{Other F.R. liabilities and capital accounts} + \text{Currency in circulation}]$

Expression (f) represents the irreducible list of factors affecting member bank reserve accounts, which makes up the statement we set out to derive. When the positive factors on the right side of the identity sign in expression (f) are listed on the reserve-supplying side and the negative factors are listed on the reserve-absorbing side, we have

Factors Affecting Member Bank Reserves, September 30, 1976
(millions of dollars)

Factors Supplying Reserve Funds		*Factors Absorbing Reserve Funds*	
5. U.S. securities owned by Federal Reserve banks	$103,507	20. Treasury cash	$ 496
4. Loans to member banks by Federal Reserve banks	322	10. Treasury deposits at the Federal Reserve	13,296
7. Other Federal Reserve assets	4,638	11. Other deposits at Federal Reserve banks (except member banks)	1,417
15. Gold stock	11,598		
2. Special drawing rights certificate account	800	Other Federal Reserve liabilities and capital accounts	3,625
16. Treasury currency outstanding	10,742	Currency in circulation	89,549
Federal Reserve float	2,997		

What specifically does the table tell us? Since the sum of the "Factors Supplying Reserve Funds" was $134.6 billion and the sum of the "Factors Absorbing Reserve Funds" was $108.4 billion, it tells us that on September 30, 1976, the value of member bank deposits at Federal Reserve banks was $26.2 billion.[12] In addition, it tells us that the monetary base as of September 30, 1976 was $115.7 billion, a figure easily computed by adding the currency in circulation item to member bank deposits at the Fed.

---

[12]Total member bank reserves on September 30, 1976 were $34.6 billion, since, in addition to the $26.2 billion of deposits at the Fed, member banks held vault cash (which is a part of the currency in circulation total in the table) totaling some $8.4 billion.

13

Early Attempts to Explain the Value of Money— The "Old" Quantity Theory

In this section, we switch our focus from institutional to theoretical matters. Armed with our technical knowledge of what *makes* the money and credit supply change, we must now come to grips with the far more significant question of what *difference* it makes if the money and credit supply *does* change. To be more specific, to what degree and in what circumstances do changes in the money and credit supply affect, for good or ill, our major economic goals of maximum production, full employment, stable prices, and rapid economic growth?

The answer to this question lies squarely within the bailiwick of economic theory, the subject of Chapters 13 through 19. To deal adequately with the effect of changes in the money supply on our economic goals, we will, in the following chapters, be concerned with building up—via income determination, monetary, and interest rate theories—a ''model'' of the economy through which we can trace the effect of changes in monetary and other variables.

We begin, in this chapter, by considering two earlier attempts to explain the determinants of the value of money. Ever since certain items became generally acceptable as mediums of exchange, people have been curious about the determinants of their acceptability and purchasing power. If a tailor sells a suit for $100, he is giving up an item with obvious utility in return for what may be a few scraps of paper. Why should he be willing to do this? What determines how many ''scraps of paper'' he can get for the suit? Why are people willing to accept money for goods and what determines the value of this money (or its reciprocal, the price level)?

The Commodity Theory

One early answer to questions such as these came from the so-called "commodity theorists." In their view, the source of money's acceptability and value was the commodity value of the money substance itself. Money was freely accepted because the commodity of which it was made (or into which paper money was convertible) had significant value in some nonmoney use. Our tailor willingly gives up the suit because he receives in its stead a commodity (gold perhaps?) of equal (or greater, to the tailor) value.

Specifically, the value of money (or its reciprocal, the price level) was said to vary directly with the quantity of the commodity of which it was made (or "backed"). Hence to the commodity theorist, the more gold there was in or "be-hind" each dollar, the greater the value of the dollar and the lower the price level.

Now to the modern reader, long since accustomed to nonconvertible paper money, such a theory may sound incredibly naïve. And though it would, indeed, be naïve to apply it in this form to today's world, some defense of the earlier commodity theorists seems in order.

It should be noted that the first monies *were* commodities—commodities that evolved naturally to their money use. There can be little doubt that these commodity monies *were* acceptable in exchange largely because of the nonmoney value of the commodity itself. And it seems reasonable to assume that their purchasing power— the amount of goods and services obtainable for each money unit—*would* tend to vary directly with the quantity of the commodity. Consequently, *many years ago* the commodity theory undoubtedly was a fairly reasonable and at least partly valid hypothesis.

But time and changing customs have a sneaky way of playing tricks on long-established "truths." A combination of government issue, the legal tender power, and, most important of all, a growing willingness among the public to accept certain tokens at an exchange value far exceeding their commodity value, has long since cut the ground out from under the commodity theory. It is certainly no longer true, and has not been so for many years, that the acceptability or value of money is determined by the commodity of which it is made (or backed).

But the idea died hard and, indeed, in the general public's mind is probably not completely dead yet. How often does one hear, even today, statements that imply that the value of the American dollar is somehow directly and fundamentally derived from the gold held in Fort Knox?

These myths from the past appear to possess remarkable staying power, the facts notwithstanding. Even though the U.S. Treasury has refused to exchange gold for dollars held by Americans since 1933, the idea that the Treasury's gold hoard "gives the dollar value" has persisted. Let us be done with this fiction. The dollar today is a *fiat* currency, the acceptability (domestically) and value of which depends in no way on a commodity backing, gold or otherwise. The value of the dollar depends on a far more substantial foundation than that relatively insignificant stock of glittering yellow metal stored in Fort Knox.

The Basis of Money's Acceptability

But all this is simply negative. If people do not accept money because of the commodity value of the substance of which it is made, why do they accept it? Why should people be willing to give up goods and services of obvious utility and value in return for mere "scraps of paper"? The answer seems obvious. These "scraps of paper," if they function as an effective money, must also have utility.[1]

The seller of goods is a demander of money. If Mr. Jones is willing to part with x bushels of wheat for $100, he is not only supplying x bushels of wheat; he is also demanding $100 of money, which he is willing to hold for some period of time. Hence we can reasonably speak of a demand for money that, as in the ordinary theory of demand, is based on utility.

What utility does the possession of money provide? First, and most distinctive, money acts as a *medium of exchange*. Mr. Jones will accept $100 for his wheat because he knows that the $100 is generally acceptable to other sellers who have goods and services he wants to purchase. Possession of the $100 permits him to obtain what he wants when he wants it without all the inconvenience of barter.

But that isn't all. Money also serves reasonably well, along with a number of other items, as a *store of value*. Mr. Jones may not, at the moment, desire to purchase any goods and services. He may prefer to bid his time, retaining *command* over goods, without any immediate commitment to one or another. In this case, he may choose to hold on to the money rather than some other form of wealth.[2]

The "Old" Quantity Theory

Although the commodity theory explanation of the value of money long seemed to have strong appeal for the general public, it never attracted substantial support from economists. For many years, the majority of economists espoused a quantitative rather than a qualitative explanation of the value of money. This took the form of the time-honored **quantity theory of money.**

As does the commodity theory, the quantity theory traces its origin back many years. Unlike the commodity theory, however, the quantity theory has been able to adapt itself over the years. As cruder versions have been challenged and discredited, newer, more sophisticated hypotheses have been developed to replace the old. If long survival under constant attack can be taken as a measure of the strength of an idea, the quantity theory must be awarded an honored position in economic thought. For, albeit in a form much altered from that of its origin, the quantity theory continues today to be a lively source of debate among monetary theorists.

---

[1]Of course, to function as an effective money, the legal tender power helps, custom helps, and limitation of supply is absolutely essential.

[2]As we shall see, holding wealth in money form has certain advantages over holding it in other forms. It also has its disadvantages.

As its name implies, the quantity theory, in all its versions, looks to the quantity of money as the main causal determinant of changes in the price level. If the theory is valid, its implications for monetary policy are indeed enormous. For, as we have seen, the quantity of money is subject, given sufficient skill by the monetary authorities and a stable institutional environment, to reasonably precise control. If the price level should be responsive in a predictable degree to the supply of money, knowledge of the relationship would obviously be invaluable to policymakers.

Of course, none of the versions of this theory has been so naïve as simply to posit the proposition that, without some logical behavioral process, prices automatically follow the money supply, willy-nilly. Developed by brilliant theorists, all quantity theories worthy of the name have attempted to explain the process— the causal sequence—whereby a larger money supply leads to higher prices.

But theorizing about relationships in a complex economy requires order and simplification to avoid a hodge-podge of confusing detail. It requires, among other things, a simplified framework of the economy within which the important variables stand out as clearly as do superhighways on a large-scale road map. In a phrase, what is needed is a "way of looking" at the economy that will screen out the unnecessary detail and provide the foundation for the construction of a cause-and-effect theory.

Each version of the quantity theory has relied upon a variant of either the *equation of exchange* or the *cash balance equation* as its way of looking at some of the important variables in the economy. As these equations are the frameworks upon which the quantity theory is built, we shall consider them in the next section before discussing the theory itself.

The Equation of Exchange

The *equation of exchange* is simply a complicated way of stating an obvious truth. Starting from the unassailable proposition that for every dollar spent by a buyer, a dollar is received by a seller, we can proceed without difficulty to the equally obvious statement that, for any given group (assuming, of course, no transactions outside the group) during any given time period, the dollar value of all newly produced goods and services purchased equals the dollar value of all newly produced goods and services sold.

Although it may seem absurd to stress such an obvious identity as "amount bought equals amount sold," that is really all the equation of exchange says. The equation itself is

$$MV \equiv PQ$$

where

    M = the average supply of money during the period

    V = the number of times per period (i.e., the rate at which) the average dollar is

spent to purchase newly produced goods and services (for short, V can be called
the actual velocity)

P = the average price of all newly produced goods and services sold during the period

Q = (quantity) the number of physical units of newly produced goods and services
sold during the period

So what does this fancy equation really say? The left side, MV, clearly equals
the dollar amount spent on newly produced goods and services during the period,
whereas the right side, PQ, just as clearly equals the dollar amount received for
selling them. Because the equation is a truism—true, by definition, under any and
all conditions—we have used an identity sign ($\equiv$) rather than a simple equals sign.

But, the reader may be thinking, of what use is it to dress up an obvious
identity in this form when everyone already grants that the amount bought equals
the amount sold? The answer to this question is very simple. When we break total
expenditures down into the two components M and V, we have spotlighted two
variables—the money supply and the rate of spending it—that do fluctuate and that
do affect the level of expenditures. And when we break down the other side (which
obviously is equal to GNP) into a P and a Q component, we are separating out
two variables—the price level and the level of physical output—that have obvious
implications for economic welfare.

But it is nevertheless a fact that the identity MV $\equiv$ PQ is, as such, merely
a sterile framework. It is not a theory. It does not say that MV *causes* PQ, nor
does it imply the reverse causation. The quantity theory, as we shall see, *is* a cause-
and-effect theory that uses the equation of exchange as a framework. But the
equation itself says no more than that the amount bought equals the amount sold.[3]

The Cash Balance Equation

While most earlier American economists were looking at things in terms of
the equation of exchange, their counterparts in England, especially at Cambridge
University, were coming to essentially similar conclusions by the use of a slightly
different equation. This has come to be called the cash balance equation (sometimes
referred to as the Cambridge equation).

The cash balance equation is

$$M \equiv kPQ$$

where M, P, and Q are defined exactly as in the equation of exchange and k is *the
period of time (expressed as a fraction of the time period) people hold on to the
average dollar before spending it to purchase newly produced goods and services*.

Obviously the only difference between the cash balance equation and the

---

[3]Another version of the equation of exchange is the so-called "transactions" version wherein
all transactions are considered rather than just spending on newly produced goods and services. In this
case, the equation is usually written as MV $\equiv$ PT, and V, P, and T are defined in terms of all transactions
rather than restricted to expenditures on GNP.

equation of exchange is the use of k instead of V. Let us look at the relationship between these two variables. Algebraically, the relationship is a simple one. Since $MV \equiv PQ$, $V \equiv PQ/M$; and since $M \equiv kPQ$, $k \equiv M/PQ$. Clearly, V and k are simply reciprocals of one another.

But arithmetic aside, what is the *logic* of the relation between the two? Suppose, for example, that the time period is one year and V is 4. This means, of course, that the average dollar is spent four times per year on new goods and services, or every three months. That in turn means that the average dollar is *held* for three months before it is spent. And if it is held for three months, it is held for one-quarter of the time period. Clearly, k therefore equals one-fourth.

The equation of exchange, as we have seen, is an identity that merely expresses the fact that the amount spent on new goods and services equals the amount received from selling them. Is there a similar commonsense explanation of the identity expressed by the cash balance equation?

Indeed there is. The left side, M, of course, equals the average supply of money in existence during the period. But what about the right side, kPQ? Although it may not be intuitively obvious, this expression measures the amount of money people actually held during the period. So the equation itself simply states the obvious truism that the amount of money in existence during the period was equal to the amount people and institutions actually held.

Equilibrium Conditions versus Definitional Identities

As definitional identities, neither the cash balance nor the equation-of-exchange approach adds much of significance to our understanding of the working of the economy. As long as V and k are defined in terms of what people *do* with money rather than with what people *desire* to do with it, the equations are sterile truisms offering, in and of themselves, no insight into the forces that lead to economic change. Unless we know whether or not people are actually spending money at the rate they desire to (or actually holding the size of money balances they wish to), we cannot say whether we have an equilibrium situation that will tend to be maintained or a disequilibrium situation that portends change.

Consider, for example, an analogous case familiar to all students of introductory economics—the case of the market for a single good. Suppose the demand for and supply of Product X are as follows:

Market for Product X

Quantity Demanded	Price	Quantity Supplied
10	$5	50
20	4	40
30	3	30
40	2	20
50	1	10

If the market price is at $3, we say we have equilibrium because the quantity demanded equals the quantity supplied. Or, alternatively, $3 is the equilibrium price because at that price what people *desire to do,* they *do do.* The quantity that buyers *want* to buy is 30 units, and they do so. The quantity that sellers *want* to sell is 30 units, and they do so. Since neither buyers nor sellers are forced to do something they do not want to do, there is no force (in the form of frustrated buyers or sellers) tending to cause a change. This is the essence of equilibrium.

But what is the situation if the market price is, say, $4? At that price the amount sellers *desire* to sell is 40 units, but the amount they actually do sell is only 20, since that is all buyers will take at $4. At $4, then, even though the quantity *actually sold* equals the quantity *actually bought* (as, of course, it always must by definition), the quantity that sellers *desire to sell* exceeds the quantity that buyers *desire to buy.* We have, therefore, a disequilibrium situation in which sellers—barred from doing what they want to do at the market price—will take action that will tend to change the price.

In the case of the market for a single good, to say that the quantity bought equals the quantity sold is to state a **definitional identity** that holds at any price, equilibrium or not. To say that the quantity demanded equals the quantity supplied, however, is to state an **equilibrium condition**—one that holds only at the equilibrium price where buyers and sellers can do what they desire to do.

Now all of this is perfectly analogous to the equations just introduced. If MV equals PQ (or M equals kPQ), all we know is that the amount spent equals the amount received (or that the supply of money in existence was held by someone). But that situation holds for *any* values of the variables in the equations. What it does not tell us is whether this is an equilibrium situation that can be expected to continue or a disequilibrium one in which spenders (or money holders) are being frustrated. If one of disequilibrium, dissatisfied spenders (or money holders) will take action (just as dissatisfied sellers did in the Product X case at the $4 price), which will tend to change the values of some of the variables (just as the price fell in the Product X case).

How can we change our equations so as to put them in the form of *equilibrium conditions* rather than mere *definitional identities?* What we need is a behavioral variable couched in terms of what people *desire* to do rather than what they *actually* do. *Equilibrium* can then be defined as a situation in which people are actually doing what they desire to do, so that there is no dissatisfaction causing changes.

To put our equations in the form of equilibrium conditions, what we need is to redefine V in terms of the rate people *desire* to spend on new goods and services and to redefine k in terms of the fraction of the time period people *desire* to hold the average dollar before spending it. This is done now with a prime added to distinguish desired V and k from actual. That is,

V' = (desired velocity) the number of times per period people *desire* to spend the average dollar on newly produced goods and services

k' = the fraction of the time period people *desire* to hold the average dollar before spending it on newly produced goods and services

Using these new definitions for V' and k', we now have two new equations, each of which is an equilibrium condition rather than a mere definitional identity. What does MV' = PQ say? It says that "equilibrium will be reached when desired spending on newly produced goods and services equals the amount produced." And note that this is nothing more than a restatement of the old, familiar equilibrium production condition—aggregate demand equals aggregate supply.[4]

And what about the cash balance equation presented in the form of an equilibrium condition? What does M = k'PQ say? Now that k' has been defined in terms of money holders' *desires*, the right side of this equation can quite properly be labeled the demand for money. So the equation M = k'PQ says that "in equilibrium the supply of money (M) equals the demand for money (k'PQ)."

Let us illustrate what we have via an arithmetical example, using the cash balance form of equation. Suppose that initially M = $200, k' = 1/5, P = $2.50, and Q = 400. Under these conditions, we are at equilibrium because

$$M \text{ equals } k'PQ$$

which means → the supply of money equals the demand for money which requires also that → actual k equals desired k'.

Now suppose the Federal Reserve authorities make use of their monetary policy weapons to increase the supply of money to $240. Immediately after such action we have a disequilibrium situation wherein

$$M > k'PQ$$

which means → the supply of money exceeds the demand for money which requires that → actual k > desired k'.

Now, how can people respond to a disequilibrium situation in which the supply of money they *must* hold (and cannot change) exceeds the quantity they *desire* to hold under current circumstances? They will respond, of course, by

---

[4]For future reference, let us establish one more point about the left-hand side of the equation of exchange, if V' is defined as desired velocity:

$$MV' = \frac{\text{Total intended expenditures on newly}}{\text{produced goods and services}} = C + I + G$$

Total spending on new goods and services can be broken down in two different ways. In the equation of exchange, it is broken down in a way that spotlights the money supply and the rate at which it is spent. Another method of breaking down the same total is by spending groups—consumption spending, investment spending, and government spending on goods and services. Although we shall not make much of this relationship now, the student should bear it in mind when we come to the next chapter and the Keynesian theory of income determination. As we shall see, the basic difference between those who choose to use the income version of the equation of exchange and those who adhere to the theory to be discussed in Chapters 14 through 17 is that while the former find it more useful to emphasize the money supply—velocity breakdown of total expenditures—the latter group considers a breakdown by spending groups more fruitful. We shall return to this comparison later. Let it simply be observed at this point that both approaches are useful; neither is "wrong."

attempting to unload the unwanted, excess money balances. This, of course, does not imply that they will act irrationally by throwing unwanted money balances away. Rather, they will "unload" them by spending them to buy products or securities.

The reader should note, however, that while such spending gets rid of the unwanted money balances of the spender, it in no way reduces the money supply the community as a whole holds. This is so, of course, because any money spent by Mrs. A is necessarily acquired by Mr. B (the seller of the goods or securities).

Despite this, as we shall see, these efforts to unload unwanted money balances *will* lead to changes in the economy that ultimately must move it toward a new, different equilibrium position.

The Advantages of the Cash Balance Equation

It should be clear by now that there is no fundamental difference between the equation of exchange and the cash balance equation approaches. V and k are simply the reciprocals of one another. It is, as one distinguished authority once put it, merely the difference between "money resting" and "money on the wing."

Yet despite their formal similarity, the cash balance approach seems to have been the forerunner of many more pathbreaking ideas in monetary economics than its alter ego, the equation of exchange. The reasons for this are not altogether clear, but in retrospect it seems apparent that the cash balance way of looking at the economy led to the asking of more fruitful questions.

The velocity concept has always seemed somewhat mechanistic. It was rather difficult to conceive of people spending their money at a rate other than that desired. On the other hand, it was much easier to imagine people having cash balances larger or smaller than desired. Similarly, although the reasons for changes in desired velocity proved difficult to come up with, it was just a bit easier to conceptualize changes in desired cash balances.

Perhaps the most important difference between the two is that the cash balance equation is conveniently arranged in supply and demand terms, which provided a better "mesh" with general economic theory. For the left-hand side, M is the supply of money while the right, $k'PQ$ is just as surely the demand for money. This format led theorists of the cash balance orientation to focus on the question, "What determines the demand for money?" It has turned out to be a most useful approach.

The Essence of the "Old" Quantity Theory

Whatever the relative merits of the different equations, one point should be clearly understood. Neither of them is a theory. Neither of them, in and of itself, sheds any light on cause and effect in the economy. They do provide a useful means of organizing some of the economy's key variables, but it remains for the theoretician to provide hypotheses regarding the nature of cause-and-effect relationships between the variables. To say that MV *equals* PQ is merely to present an obvious truism. No theory is involved. To say, however, that MV *causes* PQ is to promulgate a theoretical hypothesis arguing that M and/or V are active variables but that P and/or Q are passive ones; that although a change in MV can cause a change in PQ, no change in PQ can come about without alterations in MV being the causal force.

All versions of the quantity theory have argued that M is a key causal variable and that P (or PQ) is a passive one that "results" from the level of M. All have also looked upon V' (or k') as being, if not absolutely fixed, at least quite stable. Over the years, however, the several versions of the quantity theory have differed notably in detail and degree of sophistication. In this chapter, we shall deal only with the older (pre-1930s) versions of the quantity theory. The "modern" quantity theory associated most prominently with the name of Professor Milton Friedman and the "monetarist" school will be discussed in a later chapter.

The Key Assumptions for the "Old" Quantity Theory.   The usefulness and relevance of a theory depend upon the simplifying assumptions underlying it as well as upon the internal logic of the reasoning involved. In the case of the older versions of the quantity theory, the underlying assumptions are absolutely crucial to the argument, and we must look at them carefully.

In the first place, in complete accord with other elements of classical employment theory, it was assumed that a free enterprise economy contains within it a mechanism that will reasonably promptly restore those conditions necessary for full employment when any tendency toward a deficiency of demand arises. Full employment was considered the "norm."

Temporary divergences from the full-employment state were admissible, of course, but these were looked upon as so readily correctable that major periods of long-run mass unemployment need not be a source of concern.

The important significance of the full-employment assumption for our purposes is its effect on the level of production. If we can count on reasonably full employment most of the time, the main reason for short-run, drastic changes in output (Q in the equation of exchange) is removed. Over time, of course, output will grow as the labor force, capital equipment, and technology grow, but these factors take effect slowly and rather steadily over longer time periods. Output may grow at 3 to 4 percent per year, but this kind of change is both steady and predictable. The likelihood of shorter-run drastic changes in Q, such as the 25 percent reduction that occurred during the Great Depression of the 1930s, was ruled out by assumption. Hence it was argued that Q, although not absolutely fixed, would change very little, and predictably from year to year.

Second, the quantity theory rested on some key assumptions regarding the nature and determinants of V′ (or k′). It too was considered to be a constant, or nearly so. The logic behind this assumption merits rather careful consideration.

Let us first look at it from the cash balance approach:

$$M = k'PQ$$

Because the right side of this equation denotes the demand for money, the cash balance theorists focused on the question, "Why should rational people demand money? They can't eat it. It pays them no interest return. What rational reasons are there for people willingly accepting and holding money?"

One answer was easy to come up with. People are willing to accept and hold money because it facilitates exchange. Barter—the exchange of goods for goods— is unwieldy and difficult. It is much simpler to accept income in the form of a medium of exchange and then spend it gradually throughout the pay period to acquire the goods and services one desires.

People, in other words, willingly hold some money to finance transactions— consumer expenditures—that they need to make between paydays. There is, to put it in the terminology of one famed Cambridge economist, a *transactions* demand for money.

Now what determines the size of this transactions demand for money? Pretty clearly, the level of income itself. If the only reason for willingly holding money is to finance consumer expenditures between paydays, the level of consumer expenditures dictates the amount of money that will be held. And the level of income pretty well determines the amount of consumer expenditures.

People, then, do willingly hold money, but only to bridge the gap between paydays. What they hold, they intend to spend before the following paycheck gives them a new supply. If Mrs. Jones receives $500 on the first of each month, she holds that money only to finance expenditures during the month so that by the end of the month she has no money left. Indeed, if the only reason for holding money at all is to finance expenditures, it would be irrational not to spend it all before the next check comes in. Holding money *during* the month makes sense because it is needed to facilitate transactions, but holding it longer than that is irrational.

Now all this may bother the alert reader. Suppose that Mrs. Jones wants to spend only $400 of her $500 paycheck on consumer goods and save the extra $100. Isn't it possible that she may choose to keep the $100 saved in money form? Isn't it conceivable, in other words, that money may be demanded as an asset—as one way in which wealth may be held over time? If so, there would be *two* sources of demand for money. Some would be held to facilitate transactions during the pay period, and an additional amount could be kept—perhaps over a number of pay periods—as a means of storing wealth along with stocks, bonds, and other assets.

Although some earlier economists did recognize the possibility of an asset demand for money, the strict quantity theorists considered this irrational behavior.

If a person is accumulating wealth, they reasoned, and has a choice between holding it in the form of securities on which interest is earned and holding it in the form of money, which pays no interest, he or she would be foolish to choose money. Holding money as a store of wealth seemed irrational, as doing so meant sacrificing the income that could be earned by purchasing securities.

The result was that to these quantity theorists *the only rational demand for money was a transactions demand.* People will accept and hold only as much money as they need to facilitate upcoming expenditures.

The implications of all this for V′ (or k′) were profound, for it led the quantity theorists to look upon V′ as pretty much of a constant also—changing little in the short run.

If people hold money only to finance expenditures, what can cause changes in the quantity demanded? Except over the long run, only changes in the level of income itself. It was recognized that changes in the financial structure, in the efficiency of check collection, and in payment habits *could* alter the amount of money needed to finance transactions of a given size, but these things change only slowly over long periods and in a shorter-run context could be properly ignored. The demand for money, then, was thought to be a constant fraction (k′) of the level of income (PQ). If it takes $100 of money balances to finance the purchase of $300 of goods and services, it will take $200 of money to finance a $600 income. (k′ is a constant fraction, one-third.)

Let us now sum up this section. The key assumptions of the older quantity theory were

1. *The level of income (and, hence, Q in the equation) was considered essentially a constant in the short run.*
2. *Desired velocity, V′ (and its reciprocal k′) was considered essentially a constant in the short run.*

Following directly from the two assumptions just discussed, the quantity theory argues that

---

The price level is determined by the money supply. Changes in the money supply cause equal proportionate changes in the price level in the same direction.

The Approach to a New Equilibrium Under a Crude Version of the Old Quantity Theory.   Let us return to a numerical example to illustrate the process through which the quantity theory conclusion might be reached. Assume, as before, that we start from an equilibrium position in which M = $200, k′ = 1/5, P = $2.50, and Q = 400. Now suppose that the Fed upsets this equilibrium by increasing the money supply to $240. That is,

Initial Equilibrium Situation	Situation Immediately After Money Supply Increase
M = $200 k' = $\frac{1}{5}$ P = $2.50 Q = 400	M = $240 k' = $\frac{1}{5}$ P = $2.50 Q = 400

Immediately after the Federal Reserve increases the money supply, the demand for money is $200 ($\frac{1}{5}$ · $2.50·400) and the supply is $240. People, therefore, are currently holding $40 more in money balances than they desire to hold under these conditions. What can they do about this unsatisfactory situation?

Individuals can, of course, attempt to correct it by unloading some of their excess money balances—by, for one example, spending them on consumer goods. If they should do this, note again that the entire community's money supply does not change, since the excess balances have merely been transferred to the sellers of the consumer goods. And if the quantity theorists' assumptions about the stability of Q and k' hold, they do not change either.

What does? The price level, of course. If the initial disequilibrium *does* generate a rise in consumption spending (as the way of unloading excess money balances), the result must be a rise in aggregate demand. And if, in accordance with the quantity theorists' assumption, we are already at full employment so that Q cannot rise in response, P must rise.

By how much must the price level rise? It must continue rising so long as the disequilibrium situation created by excess money balances remains. But note that the rise in prices itself will ultimately wipe out the disequilibrium. As prices rise, the money value of income (PQ) rises. Since more money is needed to finance a higher dollar value of transactions, eventually the rise in prices transforms the new money into *desired* money balances. This will be the case when P has risen to $3, at which point

New Equilibrium	
M = $240 k' = $\frac{1}{5}$ P = $3.00 Q = 400	i.e., M = k'PQ 240 = $\frac{1}{5}$ × 3 × 400

At this point the quantity theory has worked itself out. A 20 percent rise in the supply of money has led to a 20 percent rise in the price level, just as the theory says.

A More Realistic Explanation of the "Old" Quantity Theory Process. Even if one should grant the key quantity theory assumptions of stable V' and Q, the preceding explanation is excessively oversimplified. It does not necessarily follow that a public that holds excess money balances will choose to spend the excess on added consumer goods.

People generally increase their purchases of consumer goods only when an increase in their income or wealth permits it and excess money balances are *not* the same as excess wealth or income. The money supply, for example, may have been increased through a Federal Reserve System open-market purchase that does not directly and immediately change the public's wealth or income. Is there a more realistic means of tracing through the process of the quantity theory working itself out?

Of course there is. People with excess money balances may choose to buy existing securities rather than consumer goods. But this does not change the quantity theory conclusion in any way. The increased demand for securities will raise security prices, and this, in turn, lowers interest rates.[5] Lower interest rates will permit an increase in spending on those goods most dependent on borrowed money, especially capital goods.

So we are back where we were before. The rise in the money supply ultimately causes a rise in the demand for goods and services, which, in turn, raises prices. And once again, a new equilibrium will only be reached when prices have risen by the same percentage as did the money supply.

The Validity and Importance of the "Old" Quantity Theory

How valid is the "old" quantity theory as an explanation of actual price-level movements in the United States? Although over time the money supply and prices have tended to move generally in the same direction, the relationship is far from the close one the theory would imply.

First, contrary to the key assumption of a relatively stable Q over time, we observe that real GNP (the closest approximation of Q available) has tended to vary markedly in both the short and the long run, especially during the Great Depression of the 1930s and during a number of Post World War II recessions.

Second, the assumption of a relatively stable desired velocity (or k′) seems also to be at variance with the facts, especially if the money measure employed is the narrowly defined M1 variant. As Table 13-1 clearly reveals, V not only has risen dramatically since World War II, but it has tended to level off or fall during most post–World War II recessions. Such behavior hardly supports the contention that M alone causes P![6]

All in all, although there is a very rough similarity between money supply

---

[5]The inverse relationship between bond prices and interest rates will be examined in Chapter 16.

[6]It should be noted, however, that if the M2 money definition is used, the resulting velocity figure is far more stable, at least during the last two decades.

TABLE 13-1

Income Velocity Since World War II[a]

Year	V	Year	V
1947	2.04	1965	4.08
1948	2.30	1966	4.35
1949	2.31	1967	4.32
1950	2.46	1968	4.37
1951	2.67	1969	4.58
1952	2.73	1970	4.58
1953	2.83	1971	4.66
1954	2.77	1972	4.70
1955	2.94	1973	4.98
1956	3.06	1974	5.16
1957	3.24	1975	5.31
1958	3.17	1976	5.52
1959	3.46	1977	5.70
1960	3.56	1978	5.92
1961	3.58	1979	6.18
1962	3.78	1980	6.32
1963	3.85	1981	6.61
1964	3.94		

[a]Figures prior to 1959 are computed from a slightly different definition of money.

and price-level movements over time, the "fit," as illustrated in Figure 13-1, is sufficiently imprecise as to invalidate the "old" quantity theory.

Finally, it should be made clear that even a much closer correlation between the money supply and the price level than has actually existed would not "prove" the quantity theory. For the quantity theory not only says that money and prices will move together but also says that the money supply is the *causal* factor. A quantity theorist of the vintage discussed in this chapter must show not only that the price level rises by 20 percent when the money supply goes up 20 percent but also that the latter *causes* the former. If it could be shown that a rise in the price level makes necessary, and therefore " calls forth," equivalent increases in the stock of money, the quantity theory is in trouble.

Few, if any, economists today subscribe to the quantity theory as discussed in this chapter. Yet, as noted earlier, the quantity theory has displayed remarkable resilience. Just as many were prepared to retire it permanently to a place in history, a new version, in very much altered form, has arisen to challenge economists and policymakers.

The "modern" quantity theory, originally fostered primarily by a highly respected group of economists at the University of Chicago, has become a center of controversy in the past two decades. In a sense, it and its policy conclusions are a reaction to the "new orthodoxy" that has come along with the Keynesian "revolution," just as Keynes's momentous contributions represented an attack on the classical theory of which the "old" quantity theory was a part.

In deference to the actual chronological development of these ideas, we shall

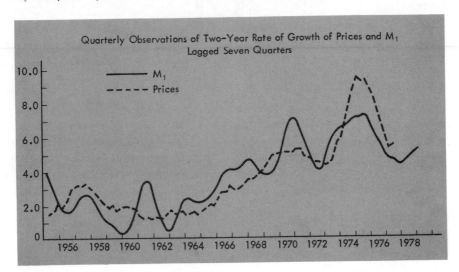

Figure 13-1 M1 and Prices, 1956–1978

Source: Robert L. Hetzel, "A Primer on the Importance of the Money Supply," *Economic Review*, Federal Reserve Bank of Richmond, September–October 1977.

not go into the "modern" quantity theory at this point. Instead, let us turn now to the Keynesian "revolution," returning later, in Chapter 18, to consider the rebirth of the quantity theory philosophy.

Review Questions

1. "To say that MV ≡ PQ is simply to state an obvious truism; to say that MV′ = PQ, however, is to state an equilibrium condition." Explain carefully.

2. Contrast the equation of exchange and the cash balance equation when each is stated in the form of an equilibrium condition. In this form, what does each equation "say"?

3. Carefully explain the logic of (as distinct from the algebra of) the relation between V and k.

4. Identify and explain the two key assumptions underlying the conclusions reached by the "old" quantity theorists.

5. What is the basic conclusion of the "old" quantity theory?

6. "If M = $200, k′ = 1/5, P = $2.00, Q = 400, and we know that 400 is the full-employment level of production, we must expect inflation to result." Explain carefully.

7. If M = $500, k′ = 1/4, P = $2.00, and Q = 1,000, how would you characterize the situation of the economy? Now if the Fed should carry out open-market purchases that increase M to $600, what is the situation immediately after the money supply has been increased? Explain, using quantity theory assumptions, what people are likely to do about this disequilibrium situation that will ultimately produce a new equilibrium. What will be the sizes of the four variables in the new equilibrium situation?

14

The Simplified Theory
of Income Determination

Introduction: The Classical Backdrop
and Its Overthrow

Besides the quantity theory, classical economic theory (pre-1935) contained a body of reasoning that led many of its earlier followers to believe that there existed, within a free enterprise economy, a mechanism that would swiftly, surely, and automatically restore full employment whenever the ugly specter of involuntary unemployment reared its head. Hence the long-cherished philosophy of *laissez-faire*—let the economy alone.

The Classical Theory

The main mechanism involved was thought to be the rate of interest. Briefly, and in highly oversimplified form, the classical argument ran this way:

1. The very process of producing any given value of goods leads to an equivalent amount of income being earned by *someone* for producing them. (If $500 billion worth of goods are produced, $500 billion of income is earned for producing them.)

2. Ignoring government and foreign trade, the recipients of this income must dispose of it either by spending it to buy consumer goods or by not spending it on consumer goods. If we define *saving* as income received but not spent on consumer goods, all income is either consumed or saved. (Suppose, of the $500 billion income, that $400 billion is spent on consumption and $100 billion is saved.)

3. What is needed to keep the following period's production at the same high $500 billion level is for everything produced this period to be sold. Demand, therefore, must total $500 billion.

4. In addition to the $400 billion of consumer expenditures, the other element

of demand that is needed to ensure that there is the $500 billion of total spending required to purchase all $500 billion of goods produced is *investment spending,* that is, spending by business to purchase newly produced capital goods. In our example, $100 billion of investment spending—along with the $400 billion of consumer spending—would be required to produce the needed $500 billion of demand. Note that as long as spending by investors just equals the saving ("not spending" by consumers), we can be sure that there is sufficient total spending to purchase everything produced.

5. What is needed then is something that will cause investment spending to be as large as saving. The required mechanism is the rate of interest.

a. The rate of interest is determined where the quantity of funds supplied by savers equals the quantity of funds demanded by investors.

b. Because people only save money (refrain from consumption) in order to receive the reward of interest (hoarding is irrational), the higher the interest rate, the larger the quantity that will be saved. (The savings *schedule* will be positively sloped with respect to the rate of interest.)

c. Because interest is one of the costs that a business must incur to invest, the quantity invested will be larger, the lower the rate of interest. (As shown in Figure 14-1, the investment schedule will be negatively sloped with respect to the rate of interest.)

6. With this setup (and assuming that the interest rate is a flexible price), a deficiency of demand to buy what has been produced cannot exist for long. For, if saving *should* exceed investment, the rate of interest will be bid down, and this movement in the interest rate will at one and the same time expand the quantity invested and lower the quantity saved until the two come together.

Consequently, movements in the rate of interest will keep investment equal to saving, which, in turn, guarantees that everything produced is bought, so that

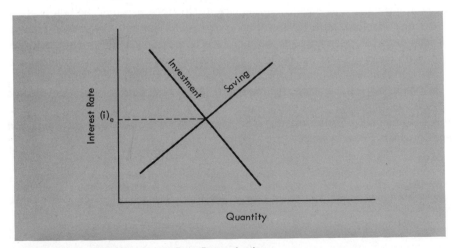

FIGURE 14-1 Classical Interest Rate Determination

producers need not lay off workers because of unsold inventories from this period's production.[1]

Keynes and His Attack on the Classicals

It was a rosy picture. But it turned out to be a misleading theory, because it did not really "fit the facts." It did not accord with our experience in the "real world." Through the many years during which the classical theory dominated thinking, there were challengers, some of them very important. But the final overthrow of the heart of the structure, at least in England and the United States, awaited the Great Depression of the 1930s and the publication of J. M. Keynes's *General Theory of Employment, Interest and Money* in 1936.

It did not take an economist to recognize, in the early 1930s, that something *must* be wrong with a theory that argues that full employment is the "norm" and unemployment simply a temporary interruption that will soon be automatically eliminated by movements in the interest rate. When upwards of one-fourth of the labor force is pounding the pavements seeking nonexistent jobs, the man on the street, being unencumbered with the niceties of theory, saw clearly that something pretty fundamental was wrong. So, too, did the already famous British economist, John Maynard Keynes.

After a long struggle to break out of the well-worn track of classical reasoning, Keynes consolidated his new ideas into his now renowned *General Theory*. In it he confessed that his work was the result of "a struggle of escape from habitual thoughts and modes of expression. . . . The difficulty lies, not in the new ideas, but in escaping from the old ones, which ramify, for those brought up as most of us have been, into every corner of our minds."[2]

Keynes leaves no doubt about the purpose of his study. It is, on the one hand, to expose the fallacies of the classical theory and, on the other, to construct a new framework, a new theory, to replace it. No fence straddler, he boldly states in his first chapter that the classical analysis is valid only in very special circumstances "which happen not to be those of the economic society in which we actually live, with the result that its teaching is misleading and disastrous if we attempt to apply it to the facts of experience."[3]

With this statement as a springboard, Keynes goes on to point out specific fallacies in the classical reasoning and to develop his own framework of analysis. It is essentially this framework that we call here the *theory of income determination* and to which we shall shortly turn.

---

[1] This description of the classical ideas is admittedly highly oversimplified and should not, by any means, be taken as a complete evaluation. It is included here for pedagogical, rather than analytical, reasons, and it omits much of the classical argument, not the least of which is the assumption of flexible wages and prices.

[2] J. M. Keynes, *General Theory of Employment, Interest and Money* (London: Macmillan, 1936), p. viii.

[3] Ibid., p. 3.

Before doing so, it should be pointed out that the theory that will be developed in Chapters 14 through 17 should not be taken to be an exact reproduction of Keynes's *General Theory*. His famous volume is now almost 50 years old and has had to weather the storm of controversy its author expected. As is true of all new ideas, substantial portions of what Keynes said have been deleted, and many things he did not foresee have been added. What we will be exploring, then, is not *Keynes's theory* but what has now come to be accepted as an important, integral part of economic theory. We are concerned, not in evaluating Keynes, but in making use of his major contributions to our discipline.

One final word before proceeding. Although the fact that Lord Keynes made the most vital contributions to the theory of income determination hardly seems debatable, it would be less than just to leave the impression that his was the only voice raised in opposition to classical economics. Although many names might be mentioned, it seems clear that that of Knut Wicksell, a giant among the impressive list of outstanding Swedish economists, deserves a special place of honor. Written many years before the *General Theory,* Wicksell's work in many ways anticipates a great deal of the substance of what has since been referred to as the *Keynesian revolution.*

Let us now turn from the background and the developers of the theory of income determination to the theory itself.

The General Approach

The *theory of income determination* is just what its name implies—an attempt to say something about how the level of income and production gets determined in a modern capitalistic economy. But its implications run deeper. If we can develop a theory that tells us how the level of production is determined, and what can make it change, we shall be in a position to go further and say something about what determines the level of employment, prices, and the like. Our goal, then, is to develop a theoretical framework that will permit us to discuss, in an organized fashion, the factors that affect our ability to achieve the generally accepted economic goals of full production, full employment, and stable prices.

We start off with the rather commonsense view that, because in a free enterprise economy, producers can only be expected to produce that which they can sell, the level of intended expenditures on newly produced goods and services is the main direct determinant of the level of production.[4]

Now, as pointed out earlier, there are two alternative ways of looking at total expenditures on newly produced goods and services, or *aggregate demand* as we

---

[4]This is, of course, a relatively short-run viewpoint. In the longer run, one would have to consider not only the determinants of the level of aggregate demand but also the quantities and qualities of productive factors available and the state of technology. We are, in what follows, assuming these factors to be essentially fixed, thereby bypassing discussion of the area that has come to be called economic growth.

shall refer to it. One could take the equation of exchange approach and break aggregate demand down into the components of M and V. Or, if it appears to provide a better insight into the causation involved, the alternative of subdividing total expenditures by spending group can be adopted. The "Keynesian" theory of income determination is built around the latter alternative.

Simplifying Assumptions

To keep our analysis within manageable proportions, some simplifying assumptions are necessary. For the time being, we will be talking about an economy in which the following complications are ruled out by assumption:

1. There are no exports or imports. (We deal with a "closed" economy.)
2. There is no business saving. (There are no depreciation allowances or corporate retained earnings.)
3. All taxes are personal taxes and all are "lump-sum" taxes, which do not vary as income varies. (There are no business taxes, no income taxes, and no social security taxes.)
4. The government makes no transfer payments. (All government expenditures are to purchase newly produced goods or current productive services.)
5. Neither investment spending nor government spending varies with the level of income. (The size of each is determined "autonomously"—by something other than the level of income—and changes in the income level have no effect on the amount of either.)
6. If the economy is at less than the full-employment level of output, increases in aggregate demand will raise only production and employment, but not prices. (This, of course, is by no means true of the "real world" and we assume it for pedagogical reasons only.)
7. The rate of interest is assumed to be fixed and invariant.[5]

Definitions and Symbols

It is essential that the student be completely familiar with the definitions and symbols that will be employed. The most important of these are

1. *Consumption expenditures* (C)—spending by households to buy newly produced consumer goods and services.
2. *Investment expenditures* (I)—*intentional* spending, primarily by business, to buy newly produced capital goods and additions to inventory.

Note two things about this definition. First, expenditures to buy already

---

[5]The significance of this assumption will be made clear later on, in Chapter 17.

existing capital goods or to buy stocks and bonds (sometimes referred to as *financial investment*) are *not* investment as we are using the term. Second, increases in inventories that were *unintended* (those that arise simply because everything produced could not be sold), are not a part of investment. In other words, when the word "investment" appears without a qualifying adjective, it refers to *planned* or *intended* investment, not *actual* or *realized* investment.

3. *Government expenditures* (G)—spending by all levels of government to purchase newly produced goods or current productive services. This would include purchasing government goods from private business firms as well as purchasing the current productive services of government employees. It would *not* include government transfer payments, which are ruled out by assumption.
4. *Taxes* (T)—the portion of personal income received by individuals that must be paid to the government in taxes. (Remember, these are *not* income taxes.)
5. *Saving* (S)—that portion of income received by individuals (personal income) that is neither paid in taxes nor spent by consumer goods during the period. Alternatively, because personal income minus taxes equals disposable income, saving can be defined as that portion of disposable income not spent to buy consumer goods during the period.

It is extremely important that the student recognize that we are defining *saving* negatively. Saving is not something individuals *do* with their income; it is something they do *not* do.

Perhaps this point can best be illustrated by example. Suppose that an individual receives $5,000 of personal income. Out of this he is required to pay $800 in taxes, leaving him $4,200 in disposable income. If he now decides to spend $3,500 to purchase consumer goods, his saving, *by definition,* is $700. This is the amount of his personal income he does *not* spend on taxes or consumption. (Or, again, it is the portion of disposable income not spent on consumption.)

What *does* he do with the $700 that we are calling saving? We do not know, but he may do *anything* with it except pay taxes or buy consumer goods. He may, for example, put it in a savings account at a bank. He may lend it to someone in return for an IOU. He may buy stocks or bonds. He may simply hoard it in money form, either in the cookie jar at home or in a checking account at his bank. He could use it (although this is rare) to buy a piece of equipment for his business. In this case he is both a saver *and* an investor. Or, to carry the illustration to absurd lengths, he may even *lose* the money. The point is, so long as he receives income that he does *not* use for taxes or consumption spending, no matter what he *does* do with it, that portion of his income is, *by definition,* saved.[6]

---

[6]The use of money that has been saved to purchase securities or capital equipment does not constitute dissaving. The student must be careful not to equate saving with hoarding.

6. *Total production* or *total income* (Y)—the total value of new goods and services produced during the period. Alternative terms for this concept are *aggregate supply* or *gross national product*. (It should be noted that, because of the simplifying assumptions under which we are working, personal income is also equal in amount to GNP.)

The Nature of the Economy
Being Considered

It does very little good to simply memorize definitions and simplifying assumptions and attempt to go on from there with the analysis. Much more fruitful is a careful attempt to conceptualize the nature of the economy that the simplifying assumptions produce. What is the nature of the economy we are considering?

First, it is an economy in which all the income resulting from production (GNP) is received by individuals as personal income in the form of wages, rent, interest, or profits.

$$Y \equiv GNP \equiv PI$$

This results from assumptions 2, 3, and 4. It will be remembered that, in the national income accounts, GNP and PI are related in the following manner:

	Gross national product
minus	Depreciation allowances
equals	Net national product
minus	Indirect business taxes
equals	National income
minus	Social security taxes Corporate profits taxes Corporate retained earnings
plus	Government transfer payments
equals	Personal income

Simplifying assumption 2 eliminates depreciation allowances and corporate retained earnings. Assumption 3 rules out indirect business taxes, social security taxes, and corporate profits taxes; and assumption 4 eliminates government transfer payments. The result is that there is no difference in amount between GNP and PI. If $500 billion of production takes place, $500 billion is assumed received by individuals as personal income.

Now, since disposable income is defined as personal income minus personal taxes, the following relationship also holds, by definition:

$$Y \equiv GNP \equiv PI \equiv DI + T$$

All disposable income is (as a result of our definition of saving) either spent on consumption or saved. Consequently, as $DI \equiv C + S$ and $Y \equiv DI + T$, by substitution we have

$$Y \equiv C + S + T$$

or, alternatively,

$$\text{Aggregate supply} \equiv C + S + T$$

This simply says that we have defined things so that all the income earned from production in any time period is spent on consumption, saved, or paid in taxes to the government.

When goods are produced and put up for sale, they meet a demand. Demand (aggregate demand) in our economy is composed of three kinds of spending: consumption, investment, and government. A fourth potential demand—by foreigners—is ruled out by the first simplifying assumption. Consequently, we can say

$$\text{Aggregate demand} \equiv C + I + G$$

The Definition of the Time Period

One final conceptual problem must be cleared up before we can proceed. This concerns the definition of the time period. In the "real world," of course, production, the receipt of income, and the spending of it make up a continuous process not really divisible into discrete, finite time periods. Nevertheless it will be convenient to break up this "real-world" sequence into arbitrary time periods.

We shall assume that the first thing that happens during our time period is that producers turn out the period's output of new goods and services—GNP. Second, during the same period, an equivalent amount of personal income is paid out in the form of wages, rent, interest, and profits. Third, the recipients of this income split it up among consumption, saving, and taxes. Finally, at the end of the period, the goods produced at the beginning are put on the market for sale. There they are met with a demand composed of consumption, investment, and government spending.

This marks the end of the first time period. The second period begins once again with the production of goods and services. The amount produced in the second period depends, however, on the sales experience of producers in the previous period.[7] Time, in other words, is arbitrarily being broken down as follows:

Period 1

$$\overbrace{\text{Production}_1 \rightarrow \text{Income}_1 \rightarrow \text{Spending}_1}$$

Period 2

$$\overbrace{\text{Production}_2 \rightarrow \text{Income}_2 \rightarrow \text{Spending}_2}$$

The more detailed schematic picture of all this contained in Figure 14-2 may be helpful in visualizing it. Note that although production, income, and C + S + T are all equal by definition, aggregate demand does not have to equal aggregate supply. That, indeed, is why production levels change from period to period.

Conditions for Stable, Rising, and Falling Production

Now that the nature of the model is clear (if it is not, go back over the preceding section carefully before going on), we can proceed to consider the circumstances under which production will rise, fall, or stay the same from period to period. Actually, this is a simple, commonsense matter.

Aggregate Supply and Aggregate Demand

Under what circumstances will the level of production set in period 1 be continued in the following period?[8] The answer results from simple logic. It makes sense to argue that if the goods and services produced in period 1 are all sold to buyers (consumers, investors, and the government) during the period, producers have reason to be satisfied with period 1's production level and to continue it in

---

[7]Technically speaking, we are relying on a "production lag" to separate our time periods. We shall be assuming that the production that takes place in period 2 is determined on the basis of sellers' experience during period 1. An alternative method would involve reliance on an "expenditure lag" wherein, as is indicated,

Period 1

$$\overbrace{\text{Expend}_1 \rightarrow \text{Production}_1 \rightarrow \text{Income}_1}$$

Period 2

$$\overbrace{\text{Expend}_2 \rightarrow \text{Production}_2 \rightarrow \text{Income}_2}$$

income earners are assumed to be paid for work done in period 1 in that same period but cannot use their income until the following period.

[8]It should be repeated here that we assume that idle resources are available and that prices are rigid. In addition, it is assumed for this chapter that interest rates are fixed at a given level.

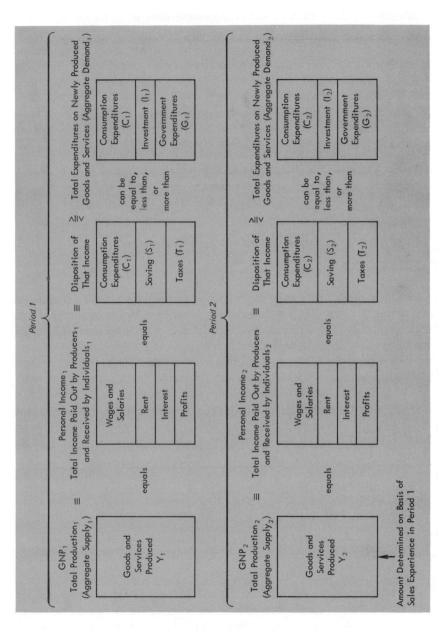

FIGURE 14-2 Conceptual Picture of Production, Income, Expenditure Process

239

the following period. If, in other words, aggregate demand in period 1 ($C_1 + I_1 + G_1$) just equals aggregate supply (the level of production), everything produced is bought. Producers' inventories neither rise because of a disappointing sales experience nor fall because of an unexpectedly heavy demand. There is, therefore, no reason to alter production schedules for the next period. The *equilibrium* level of production has been achieved.

Equilibrium, of course, means a stable situation—a position *toward which* forces are pushing the production level.[9] It is a production level that, once achieved, will tend to maintained.

Equilibrium Condition (condition under which production will stay the same in period 2 as in period 1):

$$\text{Aggregate demand}_1 = \text{Aggregate supply}_1$$

But now suppose that sales experience is disappointing. What if aggregate demand during the period is *less* than enough to buy everything produced? If, for example, producers set their production schedules at a $500 billion level but find that the three spending groups purchase at only the $450 billion level, what then? If this is the case, producers find themselves with an unintended rise in their inventories amounting to $50 billion worth of unsold goods. It is certainly not difficult to predict the result. Production in period 2 will undoubtedly be scaled down to permit a "working off" of these excessive inventories. To state it more specifically,

---

Condition for Falling Production (condition under which production will be reduced from period 1 to period 2):

$$\text{Aggregate demand}_1 < \text{Aggregate supply}_1$$

Finally, what is to be expected if demand exceeds producers' expectations? What if $500 billion of goods and services are produced in period 1, but buyers purchase $550 billion? Such an experience is a happy one for sellers who find that they have sold not only everything produced during the period but $50 billion more out of their inventories on hand. The only logical response to this "sellers' market"

---

[9]This is true, at least, of a *stable* equilibrium position, which is the only case we shall consider.

situation is to raise production schedules in the following period to meet the higher demand.[10]

Condition for Rising Production (condition under which production will be raised from period 1 to period 2):

Aggregate demand$_1$ > Aggregate supply$_1$

Fundamental Conditions in Terms of I + G and S + T

Now it is sometimes useful to state these three conditions in a different way. The student should learn both, but it is important that he or she recognize that they are simply alternative ways of saying the same thing. The logic—the "why"—of the three conditions, however they are stated, remains the same as that just discussed.

Let us use a numerical example to illustrate the alternative approach. Suppose that production in period 1 (aggregate supply$_1$) is $500 billion. It is then definitionally true that the total income earned is $500 billion. It is also definitionally true that the sum of $C_1 + S_1 + T_1$ is $500 billion. Finally, let us suppose that taxes equal $70 billion and consumption spending, $380 billion, so that saving, by definition, is $50 billion. We have, then, a situation such as:

GNP$_1$ (Production, aggregate supply$_1$) $500 billion		PI$_1$ (Income earned$_1$) $500 billion			
	$\equiv$		$\equiv$	C_1	$380 billion
				S_1	50 billion
				T_1	70 billion
					$500 billion

As $C_1 + S_1 + T_1$ is, by definition, always equal to aggregate supply in period 1, there is no reason why we cannot use the former total, rather than the latter, in our fundamental conditions. And, as aggregate demand in period 1 is nothing but the sum of expenditures by the three spending groups, it is optional whether we use the total figure and call it aggregate demand or the sum of its components, $C_1 + I_1 + G_1$.

We can, then, restate our fundamental conditions in the following way:

1. Condition for stable production as between periods 1 and 2—when $C_1 + I_1 + G_1 = C_1 + S_1 + T_1$

---

[10]In fact, of course, they may be raised further than that. Producers may choose not only to meet the demand but also to build their depleted inventories back to the desired size.

2. Condition for rising production as between periods 1 and 2—when $C_1 + I_1 + G_1 > C_1 + S_1 + T_1$

3. Condition for falling production as between periods 1 and 2—when $C_1 + I_1 + G_1 < C_1 + S_1 + T_1$

Indeed, we can go one step farther. Recognizing that the same quantity on each side of an equality or inequality sign can be dropped without altering the sense of our statements, we can eliminate consumption spending and end up with

> **1. Equilibrium condition** $\rightarrow I_1 + G_1 = S_1 + T_1$
> **2. Condition for rising production** $\rightarrow I_1 + G_1 > S_1 + T_1$
> **3. Condition for falling production** $\rightarrow I_1 + G_1 < S_1 + T_1$

One fact here can hardly be overemphasized. The student who commits these three conditions to memory without taking the slight time and trouble required to understand their commonsense logic is doing himself or herself a great disservice. If the student does not "see" that the condition $I_1 + G_1 > S_1 + T_1$ is simply another way of expressing the condition aggregate demand exceeds aggregate supply, which, in turn, is simply the economist's way of saying more was bought than was produced, he or she is missing, at the outset, the fundamental commonsense logic of the entire theory of income determination. If the student simply memorizes, he or she ends up with a strictly mechanistic picture of our theory, which bars him or her from a true appreciation of its value.

The Determinants of Consumption and the Consumption Schedule

Demand, it would seem, plays the key role. If aggregate demand exceeds aggregate supply, production (and employment along with it) will rise; aggregate demand lower than aggregate supply means falling production (and, presumably, increasing unemployment). If C, I, and G can be kept at appropriate levels, some of our more serious economic maladies can be kept under control.

The logical next step in our inquiry seems clear. We must give some consideration to the determinants of the components of aggregate demand. What causes C, I, and G to be high or low—to rise or fall?

Actually in the present chapter we shall attempt only a part of the job. We shall deal with the determinants of consumption but, for the present, treat investment and government spending as "given." To employ the usual economist's parlance, we shall assume that both investment and government spending are "autonomous" variables, dependent on determinants other than the level of production and income with which we are primarily concerned.

We might, for example, assume that government spending depends entirely on the state of the nation's foreign affairs, without any relationship whatever to the level of income within the country. Similarly, it could be argued that investment spending depends completely on future expectations and not at all on the present income level.[11]

The result is that frequent statements, such as the following, will be encountered: "Investment is $100 billion and government spending, $85 billion." The student should interpret this as meaning that future expectations cause I to settle at $100 billion while foreign affairs cause G to be $85 billion; that changes in the nation's income level will in no way affect these figures; and that they will remain "fixed" at these levels until expectations and/or foreign affairs change.

The Determinants of Consumption Spending

What determines the nation's total consumption spending? Why does Country A spend $500 billion to purchase consumer goods while Country B spends only $100 billion? Why does Country A spend $500 billion on consumption in one year and then $550 billion in the next year?

Our concern here is for the determinants of the nation's *total* consumption spending, but any individual consumer could, from personal experience, come up with an acceptable list. To some degree, our knowledge of these determinants depends on commonsense reasoning from individual experience and to some degree on careful statistical investigation of the past. In any case, it seems clear that the following are among the most important:

1. Level of Income. One of the cornerstones of Keynesian theory is the observation that the most important determinant of consumption spending (and of saving) is the current level of income received and available to spend. The importance of this to Keynes was twofold. First, it denied the classical assumption that the interest rate was the major factor determining the quantity saved (and consumed). Second, much of the usefulness of the Keynesian multiplier rests on the stability of the relationship between income and consumption.

A priori, it seems obvious that consumption should vary with income. And the relationship, statistical investigation shows, *is* very strong. But it is not perfect. One explanation for the imperfect correlation of consumption and income is that other factors besides income influence consumption spending. Some of these "other factors" are listed in the discussions that follow.

A second possible explanation, put forth by a number of economists, is the possibility that it may not be so much the current, *absolute* level of income that determines consumption as some *relative* or *permanent* concept of income.[12] Per-

---

[11]Neither of these assumptions is completely realistic, of course. They are made only to simplify the analysis.

[12]See, for example, J. S. Duesenberry, *Income, Saving and the Theory of Consumer Behavior* (Cambridge, Mass.: Harvard University Press, 1949), M. Friedman, *A Theory of the Consumption Function* (Princeton, N.J.: Princeton University Press, 1957), and A. Ando and F. Modigliani, "The Life Cycle Hypothesis of Saving: Aggregate Implications and Tests," *American Economic Review,* March 1963.

haps consumers respond more to their income relative to others or to their income relative to the income they have become accustomed to in the past. Perhaps they decide their consumption spending more on the basis of what they consider to be their lifetime, "permanent" income than on current short-run changes therein. We shall not delve further into these theories here, but they are of great importance in modern consumption theory.

2. Consumer Expectations Regarding Future Prices, Incomes, and Availability of Goods. A rational person who confidently expects future prices to be higher will have a strong incentive to spend a larger percentage of his or her income on consumer goods now, while prices are still relatively low, than he or she would in the absence of such an expectation.

Similarly, a person who expects his or her income to be higher in future years would be quite within the bounds of logic to spend a larger percentage of his or her income on consumption now than he or she would if such a rise in income were not expected.

And, finally, if people expect, as appears to have been the case in past wartime periods as well as during energy shortages, that, because of wartime priorities or foreign embargos, such things as automobile tires and gasoline may not be freely available for some time, they are motivated by personal self-interest to "stock-up" now on those goods they expect to need.

3. Real Value of Consumers' Liquid Wealth. Other things equal, the person (or society) who possesses a large amount of liquid wealth will be free to spend a larger percentage of his or her income on consumption than he or she would if it were necessary to build up, via saving, a contingency reserve fund.

4. Community's Present Stock of Consumer Durables. Presumably the greater the stock of consumer durables now held by the public, and the newer these goods are, the less the need for consumers to buy more. This, then, would be a negative variable, causing consumption spending to vary inversely to it, other things being equal.

5. The Age Composition of the Population. Since it is a well-known fact that, on average, younger people (just establishing family units) and older, retired people are—by necessity—relatively heavy spenders with little opportunity to save while middle-aged people (who have already paid for their homes and/or have educated their children) tend to be relatively heavy savers, the age composition of the population goes a long way toward determining the split between consumption and saving.

6. Social Customs and Attitudes Toward Saving. Other things being equal, the attitude of the public toward the virtues of saving will certainly matter. One would expect, for example, a community whose social mores classify saving as a highly ranked virtue to spend less on consumption than another community similar in all respects except this sociopsychological bent toward saving.

7. Level of Personal Taxes. The total income earned (or GNP) is not all available to be spent as the income earners choose. Out of gross income (which, recall, equals personal income in our oversimplified world), the government takes a chunk in the form of taxes. Thus the higher the level of personal taxes, the lower the level of consumption and saving (and vice versa).

The Consumption Schedule Defined

As is true for all economic variables, the nation's consumption spending is affected by many factors. Yet, if we are to deal with consumption analytically, we must devise a method of expressing these many interrelationships in a simplified manner. The method traditionally used in economics is the consumption schedule (or function).

A nation's consumption schedule presents *the amounts that will be spent on consumption at all possible levels of income, other determinants (besides income) being considered fixed.* In short, the consumption schedule shows how the national total of consumption spending will change if the nation's income (and nothing else) is varied.

How might one obtain the data for a consumption schedule? Because it deals with what people *will* do in the future, the only fully appropriate technique available would be a survey—asking people what their intentions are.

Suppose, for example, that we have a nation of 1 million families and we ask each family (or some statistically appropriate sample) the following questions: "Assuming that your expectations, wealth, ownership of consumer durables, taxes, and attitude toward thrift (the *non*income determinants of consumption) stay as they are now, how much will you spend to buy consumer goods next week if your income is 0? How much will you spend if your income turns out to be $100? How much if it is $200? $300? $400? $500?"

Now such a survey is conceivable, but almost surely our respondents would want to know whether the reference is to income before or after taxes. Let us take care of that problem first by assuming that the government collects $100 in taxes, leaving the people with disposable income exactly $100 less than GNP. Now we can put our survey question in terms of after-tax income (that is, in terms of consumption spending out of disposable income).

When the survey is completed, we could then total up the responses received for each income level and draw up a table such as Table 14-1.

The consumption schedule—the relation between income and consumption—could be either columns 1 and 4 (relation between GNP and consumption) or columns 3 and 4 (relation between DI and consumption). Although either relationship could be used, let us concentrate on the relation between GNP and consumption.[13]

---

[13]A word of interpretation is in order here. A consumption schedule shows the relation between various possible amounts of total (national) GNP and total (national) consumption. The numbers in the schedule are presumed to be national aggregates. They do *not* compare the consumption spending of different families at different income levels.

If it seems strange to single out one determinant of consumption—income— and hold all others fixed, the student might well recall the concept of the market demand for a single product. Whereas the quantity consumers are willing and able to take of a good depends not only on its price but also on consumer tastes, incomes, expectations, and the like, the demand curve assumes that all the determinants except price are fixed and then shows the relation between price and the quantity demanded. A change in any of the determinants other than price, we say, will shift the demand curve itself.

This concept, familiar in the case of the market demand for a good, is precisely paralleled by the consumption schedule. Here, too, we select the one determinant that seems most important and assume the others fixed. Here, too, a change in the main variable (income) will lead to a different amount consumed but will not change (shift) the consumption schedule itself. This is perfectly analogous to a change in price changing the quantity demanded but not shifting the demand curve itself. It will be well worth the reader's time to think through the similarities in these two important economic tools before proceeding.

Methods of Expressing a Nation's Consumption Schedule

Assuming that we have made our survey and have aggregated the responses received, there are three alternative methods for expressing the consumption schedule. We can (1) report the data, as in Table 14-1, in tabular form, (2) show the results geometrically as a line in a graph, or (3) express the relationship algebraically in an equation.

TABLE 14-1

Numerical Example of Consumption Schedule
(millions)

1 Possible Alternative Levels of GNP	2 Taxes	3 Possible Alternative Levels of Disposable Income	4 C	5 S
$ 0	$100	−$100	$ 50	−$150
100	100	0	100	−100
200	100	100	150	− 50
300	100	200	200	0
400	100	300	250	50
500	100	400	300	100
600	100	500	350	150
700	100	600	400	200

Consumption Function as a Table—The APC, APS, MPC, and MPS

Using the data from Table 14-1, the consumption (and saving) schedule could simply be reported as follows:

GNP	C	S
$ 0	$ 50	−$150
100	100	− 100
200	150	− 50
300	200	0
400	250	50
500	300	100
600	350	150
700	400	200

If one already has all the figures that make up the consumption and saving schedule, one needs nothing else for a full picture. However, there are several expressions that partially reflect the *nature* of the relation between income and consumption which may be used to describe that relationship. These are the average propensity to consume, the average propensity to save, the marginal propensity to consume, and the marginal propensity to save.

1. Average Propensity to Consume.   This may be defined as "consumption expressed as a fraction of income."

$$\text{APC} = \frac{\text{C}}{\text{GNP}}$$

In the example, the figures are such that the APC is different at each level of GNP. For instance, when GNP is 200, the APC is $\frac{3}{4}$; when GNP is 400, the APC is $\frac{5}{8}$; and when GNP is 600, the APC is $\frac{7}{12}$. As common sense would seem to dictate, the APC (fraction of GNP consumed) falls as income rises.

2. Average Propensity to Save.   The APS is "saving expressed as a fraction of income."

$$\text{APS} = \frac{\text{S}}{\text{GNP}}$$

It, too, changes as income changes, becoming larger as income rises. It is $\frac{1}{8}$ when GNP is 400, $\frac{1}{5}$ when GNP is 500, and $\frac{1}{4}$ when GNP is 600.[14]

3. Marginal Propensity to Consume. The MPC is actually a more important concept for our analysis than the APC. It can be defined as "the *change in* consumption expressed as a fraction of the *change in* GNP."

$$MPC = \frac{\Delta C}{\Delta GNP}$$

We have chosen figures for our numerical example in the table that, unlike the APC, result in the same MPC at all income levels. Note that between any two GNP levels chosen, the MPC is .5. Every $100 *change in* GNP calls forth a $50 *change in* consumption spending in the same direction.

There are two reasons for the use of an example with a constant MPC. First, this comes reasonably close to reality. Attempts to measure the U.S. consumption schedule have revealed an MPC that changes little when income changes except at the highest income levels. Second, the constant MPC assumption greatly simplifies the upcoming analysis. For both reasons, we shall retain this feature in future examples.

4. Marginal Propensity to Save. The MPS is defined as "the change in saving, expressed as a fraction of any change in income." The numerical example shows that every $100 rise in GNP calls forth a $50 increase in saving. The MPS, then, is .5.[15]

$$MPS = \frac{\Delta S}{\Delta GNP}$$

Graphical Representation of the Consumption Schedule. An alternative method of representing the results of our survey is via a graph. The consumption schedule can be simply plotted in a two-dimensional diagram as in Figure 14-3.

With expenditures measured off on the vertical axis and GNP on the horizontal (the units on each axis being identical), each dot in Figure 14-3 represents the amount of consumption spending at a particular GNP level. The eight dots,

---

[14]Note that because we are using GNP as our measure of income, the APC and APS do not total to 1 as they would if we employed the relation between disposable income and C and S. This is because part of GNP goes to the government in the form of taxes.

[15]The MPC plus the MPS *do* total 1 in this case, but only because our example assumes that taxes are a lump-sum $100, not related to the income level. If there were an income tax in the picture, part of any change in GNP would be taken in this form of increased income taxes. In that case one would need the sum of the MPC, the MPS, and the marginal propensity to tax, to equal 1.

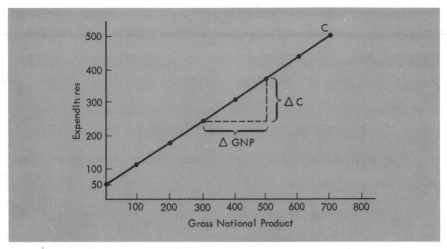

FIGURE 14-3   The Consumption Function

then, represent all the data included in the above numerical table. When they are joined together by the line labeled C, we have a complete graphical representation of the community's consumption schedule.

The dot on the vertical axis, of course, shows the amount of consumption (50) when GNP is zero. The *slope* of the line—measured as the vertical rise divided by the horizontal distance—is equal to $\Delta C/\Delta GNP$—or the MPC. Hence we can say that the larger the MPC, the steeper the consumption function.

Algebraic Representation of the Consumption Function.   Anything that can be depicted by a straight line has an equation of the form $y = a + bx$ and can be stated algebraically. For the consumption function we have been working with, the equation is

$$C = .5 \, GNP + 50$$

Obtaining the equation from the table is a simple matter. The constant term is always the amount of consumption at zero GNP. The coefficient of the GNP variable (.5 in our example) is always equal to the marginal propensity to consume.

Changes in the Equilibrium Level of Production: The Multiplier Concept

A Numerical Example

Earlier we learned that when $I + G > S + T$ (that is, aggregate demand exceeds aggregate supply), production and income must rise. We are now prepared to tackle that more difficult question of *how much* production and income will rise before equilibrium ($I + G = S + T$) is restored.

The answer is inherently tied in with the consumption function concept just discussed. That is, *because* consumption spending gets bigger when income rises, and *because* consumption spending is a part of aggregate demand requiring further rises in production and income, any initial rise in spending will set off a whole chain of events in the economy, which will raise production and income by some multiple of the original increase.

Perhaps a numerical example with two different economies is the best way to make the point. Suppose we look, simultaneously, at Economies A and B, in Tables 14-2 and 14-3.

It may help, at this point, to recall the simplifying assumptions under which we are working. Total production (aggregate supply) churns out an equal amount of income. This income is partly dispersed in the payment of taxes (which are assumed to be a fixed amount, not varying with income). The amount left after taxes is disposable income, which households either consume or save. The amount they choose to spend on consumption, together with investment and government spending, makes up aggregate demand. Consequently, for Economies A and B, column 1 is aggregate supply and the sum of columns 4, 6, and 7 is aggregate demand.

To determine the equilibrium level of production in Economy A, we can either find the place where aggregate demand just equals aggregate supply or employ the equivalent alternative of locating the point where $I + G = S + T$. The student should verify independently the fact that Economy A's equilibrium level is $300. Note also that at any level of production less than $300, more will be bought than is produced; while at any production level above $300, there will not be enough spending to purchase everything turned out.

In Economy B, for precisely the same reason, the equilibrium level of production is $400. In this case also, any level of output less than $400 will be faced with a demand that absorbs more than the amount produced, whereas a production level of over $400 will be so high that the spending propensities in the economy will not be enough to buy it all.

Finally, it should be noted that the two economies are exactly alike in all but one respect—their consumption functions. The citizens of Economy B are clearly the "bigger spenders," with a marginal propensity to consume of .75 rather than the .5 that is the case for Economy A. The explanation for this difference is to be found in the other, *nonincome* determinants of consumption discussed in the previous section.

Solving Algebraically for the Equilibrium Level

When complete tables are given, as in this case, one can simply read off the equilibrium production level by locating the point at which aggregate demand equals aggregate supply. Such a procedure is not always possible, however, espe-

TABLE 14-2

Economy A (MPC = $\frac{1}{2}$)

1	2	3	4	5	6	7	8
Possible Levels of Production (Aggregate Supply, GNP)	"Lump-Sum" Taxes Collected	Possible Levels of Disposable Income (1 − 2)	Consumption Expenditures	Saving (3 − 4)	Investment Spending	Government Spending	Aggregate Demand (4 + 6 + 7)
$100	$50	$ 50	$100	−$ 50	$45	$55	$200
200	50	150	150	0	45	55	250
300	50	250	200	50	45	55	300
400	50	350	250	100	45	55	350
500	50	450	300	150	45	55	400
600	50	550	350	200	45	55	450

TABLE 14-3

Economy B (MPC = $\frac{3}{4}$)

1	2	3	4	5	6	7	8
Possible Levels of Production (Aggregate Supply, GNP)	"Lump-Sum" Taxes Collected	Possible Levels of Disposable Income (1 − 2)	Consumption Expenditures	Saving (3 − 4)	Investment Spending	Government Spending	Aggregate Demand (4 + 6 + 7)
$100	$50	$ 50	$ 75	−$ 25	$45	$55	$175
200	50	150	150	0	45	55	250
300	50	250	225	25	45	55	325
400	50	350	300	50	45	55	400
500	50	450	375	75	45	55	475
600	50	550	450	100	45	55	550

cially in the classroom where time limitations may not permit the copying of long columns of numbers on the chalkboard.

Fortunately there is an alternative means of computing the equilibrium production level. In Table 14-2, the following information is given for Economy A:

$$C = .5 \text{ GNP} + 50$$
$$I = 45$$
$$G = 55$$

The condition for equilibrium production, we know, is aggregate supply equals aggregate demand, which can be written as

$$\text{GNP} = C + I + G$$

By substituting the given information for C, I, and G into the equilibrium condition, we can solve for the equilibrium GNP:

$$\text{GNP} = C + I + G$$

Substituting,

$$\text{GNP} = .5 \text{ GNP} + 50 + 45 + 55$$

Solving,

$$.5 \text{ GNP} = 150$$
$$\text{GNP} = 300$$

The same thing can be done for Economy B. We are given the following information:

$$C = .75 \text{ GNP}[16]$$
$$I = 45$$
$$G = 55$$

Plugging these data into the equilibrium condition, we have

$$\text{GNP} = C + I + G$$
$$\text{GNP} = .75 \text{ GNP} + 45 + 55$$
$$.25 \text{ GNP} = 100$$
$$\text{GNP} = 400$$

---

[16]In this case, because consumption falls by \$75 for every \$100 drop in GNP, consumption spending will be zero at zero GNP, so that we have no constant term in the consumption function.

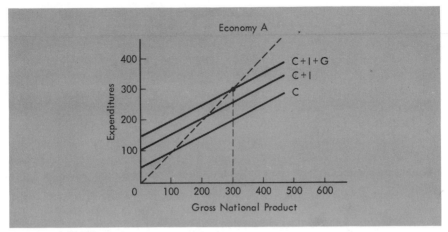

FIGURE 14-4 Determination of Equilibrium—Economy A

Graphical Presentation of the Same Data

While we are about it, let us see how the data for Economies A and B might be depicted graphically. Figure 14-4 refers to Economy A; Figure 14-5 is for Economy B.

In both diagrams, the elements of aggregate demand (C, I, and G) are measured off vertically, and the level of income earned appears on the horizontal axis. The line labeled C in each is the consumption function that corresponds to the data from columns 1 and 4 in Tables 14-2 and 14-3. The line labeled C + I results

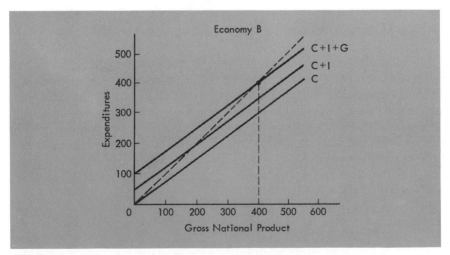

FIGURE 14-5 Determination of Equilibrium—Economy B

from adding the amount of investment spending (here, $45 at all levels of income) to the amount of consumer spending at each income level. The C + I + G, or aggregate demand line, is computed by adding the $55 of government spending to the C + I total at each level of income. The dashed 45° line is the locus of all points equidistant from the two axes. As one axis measures aggregate supply and the other aggregate demand, it should be clear the 45° line contains all points of equilibrium.

There is, in each graph, only one level of production that satisfies the conditions for equilibrium. That is where the C + I + G (aggregate demand) line crosses (equals) the 45° line. Here, and only here, the amount being produced is all bought by spenders. Here, and only here, does aggregate demand equal aggregate supply.

The Multiplier, Initiated by a Rise in Investment

Now suppose that each of our two economies has reached the equilibrium level of production—A at $300 and B at $400. What effect will a $50 rise (to $95) in the level of investment spending have?[17]

The initial impact is obvious. In each economy, aggregate demand will, in the first instance, exceed aggregate supply by $50. That is, Economy A will find that its $300 aggregate supply encounters a $350 aggregate demand, while in Economy B the $400 of goods turned out will be met by $450 worth of spending. In both cases, inventories will be drawn down, and therefore production in the following period can be expected to rise.

The question we are concerned with here is, "By *how much* must the level of production rise before it reaches a new equilibrium level?"

The Multiplier Process

It is not difficult, with the aid of Tables 14-2 and 14-3, to determine the new equilibrium levels for Economies A and B. If, in Economy A, investment rises to $95 and government spending remains at $55, their total is $150, and equilibrium requires that saving plus taxes (remember, equilibrium is where I + G = S + T) also equal $150. Such a position is only reached when production has risen by $100, to $400. Similarly, in Economy B, when the sum of investment and government spending rises to $150, what is needed to restore equilibrium is a rise in S + T to the same point. This would require a rise there by $200, to a new equilibrium production level of $600.

---

[17]The reader should note that we are referring to a permanent rise in the level of investment, not just a rise for a single period. The assumption is that investment rises to $95 and stays there rather than falls back to $45 in the following period.

Because a $50 rise in investment forces production up by $100 in Economy A, we say the "multiplier" for that country is 2. Because a $50 rise in investment spending leads to a $200 rise in Economy B's equilibrium level of output, we say that the multiplier for that nation is 4.

But this is all too automatic. Simply reading results from tables does nothing to make clear the logical causation involved in the *process* by which production is forced up. We need to take the time to ferret out the economic logic involved instead of turning the whole thing into nothing more than sterile arithmetic. We need, in other words, to deal with the "whys" of the multiplier process. *Why* does production in Country A rise by double the initial rise in investment? *Why* does production in Country B rise by twice as much as that in Country A? What is the process that we refer to as the multiplier and why does it operate as it does?

Let us concentrate first on Country A. If the only change in spending propensities that takes place is a $50 rise in investment, why is a $50 rise in production not sufficient to restore equilibrium?

Table 14-4 provides us with a period-by-period picture of the multiplier process. Within each time period, it is assumed that the total income earned from production is all disposed of by paying taxes, spending on consumption, and saving. Second, it is assumed that the level of aggregate demand (sum of C, I, and G in any period) determines the level of production in the following period. That is, we are assuming that producers always adjust their production levels to the level of the *previous* period's demand.[18]

In period 1, the production of $300 is met by an equivalent aggregate demand, so that there is no apparent reason for changing production levels in period 2. As

TABLE 14-4

The Movement Toward Equilibrium of Economy A (MPC $= \frac{1}{2}$)

| | Time Period | | | | | | New Equilibrium |
	1	2	3	4	5		
Production and income	$300	$300	$350	$375	$387.50	→	$400
C	200	200	225	237.50	243.75	→	250
I	45	95	95	95	95	→	95
G	55	55	55	55	55	→	55
T	50	50	50	50	50	→	50
S	50	50	75	87.50	93.75	→	100
Aggregate demand	300	350	375	387.50	393.75	→	400

---

[18]This is not the only possible assumption or even necessarily the most likely one, but *some* assumption must be made. The fact is that whether producers anticipate by raising production to a *higher* level than the previous period's demand, the final equilibrium level is unchanged. We adopt this assumption simply as the most convenient one for purposes of exposition.

between periods 1 and 2, Economy A is at equilibrium. In period 2, the $300 of earned income is again split among taxes ($50), consumption ($200), and saving ($50). But in this period, investors suddenly decide that they want to increase their purchases of capital goods from the old level of $45 to the higher level of $95. Thus, aggregate demand in period 2 turns out to be $350, although production was only $300 (I + G > S + T by $50). Consequently, inventories of sellers in period 2 are drawn down, and we expect them to raise production in the following period. By assumption, we take the amount of this production rise to be $50, so that production (and income earned from production) in period 3 is $350.

Up to this point, the multiplier process has not entered the picture. But it begins to show up in period 3. Here, $50 of added income is earned and, as we assume taxes do not rise, it is all available to recipients as disposable income to spend on consumption or save. How do they split this new income? The *marginal* propensity to consume of one-half tells us that half of it will be spent on consumption and half will be saved. Consequently, consumption spending in period 3 rises by $25 to $225 and saving goes up to $75. The result (of the additional consumption spending) is that once again aggregate demand ($375) exceeds aggregate supply ($350). The $50 rise in production that took place in period 3 was not enough to restore equilibrium because demand, in the form of added consumer spending, rose still higher. This is the heart of the multiplier idea.

Assuming, once again, that producers react to the disequilibrium of period 3 by raising period 4's production by the amount of the excess demand experienced in period 3, production will go up to $375. Once again, however, the $25.00 of added income earned as a result of this production boost leads to a $12.50 rise in consumption and an equal rise in saving. Aggregate demand in period 4 is thus $387.50; aggregate supply, only $375.00.

There is no need to carry the discussion further. The point is that, via some such process, *production must keep on rising until it is so high that the sum of taxes and saving is enough to equal the higher level of I + G.*

The multiplier effects show up in periods 4, 5, 6, 7, . . ., where production is pushed up beyond the $350 level, because the added income earned from additional production leads to additional consumption spending. The multiplier then results entirely from the fact that a **rise in production leads to a rise in income, which leads to a rise in consumer spending, which, in turn, causes production to be raised further in the following period, and so forth.**

Table 14-5 provides the same period-by-period picture of the rise to the new equilibrium in Economy B. Why is the multiplier larger in this case? Why does production rise further before reaching the new equilibrium? Because here, consumers who get added income spend a larger portion of it, thus adding more to aggregate demand in each period and, consequently, more to production. Or, to approach it from the other direction, saving rises less rapidly here as income rises (the MPS is smaller). As equilibrium requires that saving rise by enough to offset (equal) the higher level of investment that started it all, the lower the marginal propensity to save, the greater the rise in income required to "call forth" the necessary amount of saving.

TABLE 14-5

The Movement Toward Equilibrium of Economy B (MPC $= \frac{3}{4}$)

	Time Period						New
	1	2	3	4	5		Equilibrium
Production							
and income	$400	$400	$450	$487.50	$515.60	→	$600
C	300	300	337.50	365.60	386.70	→	450
I	45	95	95	95	95	→	95
G	55	55	55	55	55	→	55
T	50	50	50	50	50	→	50
S	50	50	62.50	71.90	78.90	→	100
Aggregate							
demand	400	450	487.50	515.60	536.70	→	600

The multiplier, and its workings, can also be visualized in graphical terms, as Figures 14-6 and 14-7 indicate. In each of these graphs, the rise in investment spending is indicated by the vertical distance between the $C + I_1 + G$ line (where $I_1 = \$45$) and the $C + I_2 + G$ line (where $I_2 = \$95$). The change in the equilibrium level of production and income is the horizontal distance between GNP_1 and GNP_2, which, in turn, are located by the points where $C + I_1 + G$ and $C + I_2 + G$ cross the 45° line. The multiplier is the horizontal distance between GNP_1 and GNP_2 in each case, divided by the vertical distance between $C + I_1 + G$ and $C + I_2 + G$.

The period-by-period working out of the multiplier presented in numerical form in Table 14-4 for Economy A is shown graphically in Figure 14-8.

In time period 2 (Table 14-4), aggregate demand turns out to be AC, but

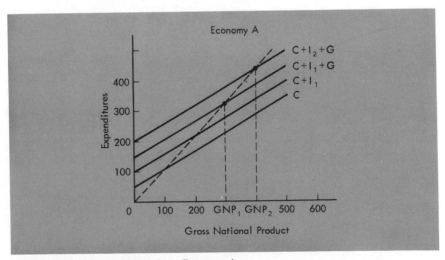

FIGURE 14-6 Effect of Multiplier—Economy A

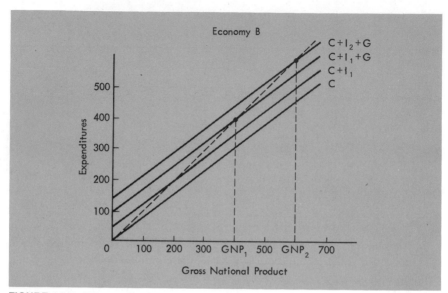

FIGURE 14-7   Effect of Multiplier—Economy B

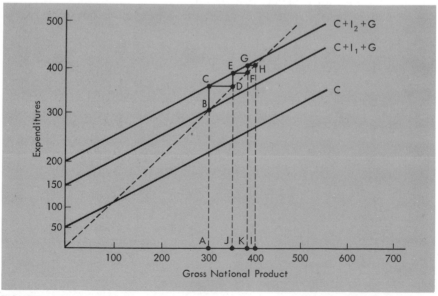

FIGURE 14-8   The Process of the Multiplier

aggregate supply is only AB. As a result, aggregate supply is pushed up in time period 3 to JD (to an amount equal to AC—the previous period's demand). Aggregate demand in period 3, however, turns out to be JE (because of the induced rise in consumption). Consequently, aggregate supply must be raised again in time period 4—to KF. This still does not produce equilibrium, however, because demand in period 4 has risen to KG. The cumulative rise continues, as in Table 14-4, until GNP reaches 400.

Multiplier Definitions

Up to this point we have been discussing the multiplier *process* without ever defining the multiplier itself. Let us turn to the definition.

The multiplier is simply a number that, multiplied times any change in aggregate demand, gives the change in the equilibrium level of production.
That is,

$$\text{Multiplier} \times \begin{array}{c} \textbf{Initial} \\ \textbf{change in} \\ \textbf{aggregate demand} \end{array} = \begin{array}{c} \textbf{Change in} \\ \textbf{equilibrium} \\ \textbf{level of production} \end{array}$$

Note two things. Although in the example for Economies A and B, it was a rise in the investment spending part of aggregate demand that "triggered" the multiplier, the same thing would have resulted had government spending or the level of the consumption function initially risen by $50. The multiplier is a general concept that "works" no matter what form the initial change in demand takes.

Second, the multiplier is reversible. An initial *decline* in C, or I, or G will set off a multiplied *decline* in GNP for reasons exactly the reverse of those just discussed.

It should be clear to the student who followed the examples given that the *size* of the multiplier is inherently tied up with the size of the MPC and the MPS in the economy. Specifically, the multiplier equals[19]

$$\frac{1}{1 - \text{MPC}} \quad \text{or} \quad \frac{1}{\text{MPS}}$$

---

[19]A little caution is in order here. In this example, *because we have assumed lump-sum taxes,* MPC + MPS = 1, so that $1/(1 - \text{MPC})$ and $1/\text{MPS}$ are simply alternative expressions of the same thing. If an income tax were included in the picture, $1/(1 - \text{MPC})$ would still be the correct formula for the multiplier, but the alternative expression would have to be $1/(\text{MPS} + \text{MPT})$, where the MPT is the marginal propensity to tax. The student will be well advised to stick to $1/(1 - \text{MPC})$, which is correct with or without an income tax (and so long as the consumption is the only expenditure element related to income).

Why does $1/(1 - MPC)$ give you the multiplier? Mathematically, the multiplier process makes up an infinite geometric series, the sum of which can always be obtained by multiplying by the reciprocal of 1 minus the common multiple.

If the MPC were .5, for example, and investment spending initially rose by $1, production would rise, over time, by the following amounts:

$$\$1 \rightarrow 50\text{¢} \rightarrow 25\text{¢} \rightarrow 12\tfrac{1}{2}\text{¢} \rightarrow 6\tfrac{1}{4}\text{¢} \rightarrow 3\tfrac{1}{8}\text{¢}, \text{ and so on}$$

Note that each additional increase in production is one-half of that of the preceding period. We thus have an infinite geometric series in which .5 is the common multiple. The *sum* of this series (at the limit) can be obtained by taking $1/(1 - \text{common multiple})$ times the initial increase. This is precisely the multiplier formula, as the MPC *is* the common multiple.

Less formally, why should the multiplier equal 1/MPS? Suppose the MPS were one-fifth. If investment spending should rise by $10 (so that I + G > S + T by $10 initially), how can the equilibrium production level be restored? Clearly, if investment is assumed to stay at its higher level and G and T are fixed, the only thing that can restore the equilibrium situation (I + G = S + T) is a $10 rise in saving. Now what does an MPS of one-fifth really mean? Simply that it takes a $5 change in income to cause people to save $1 more. So how much must income rise to induce people to save the added $10 needed to restore equilibrium? Clearly enough, it must rise by $50, or 5 × $10.

The Algebraic Solution Again

Referring once again to the data for Economy B in Table 14-3, one can easily compute the change in equilibrium production levels via simple algebra.

It will be remembered that the initial given conditions for Economy B were

$$C = .75 \text{ GNP}$$
$$I = \$45$$
$$G = \$55$$

so that the initial equilibrium GNP was $400. We are concerned with computing the change in GNP if investment should be raised to $95 (by $50).

There are two very simple methods for obtaining the answer. One may simply plug the *new* data into the equilibrium condition and solve. Thus we have

$$C = .75 \text{ GNP}$$
$$I = \$95$$
$$G = \$55$$

Equilibrium condition:

$$\text{GNP} = C + I + G$$

Substituting,

$$GNP = .75\ GNP + \$95 + \$55$$
$$.25\ GNP = \$150$$
$$GNP = \$600$$

A \$50 rise in investment spending raises the equilibrium GNP by \$200.

Alternatively, one might use the multiplier to get the answer. It will be remembered that the coefficient of the GNP term in the consumption function is the MPC. In this case the MPC is .75.

The multiplier is $1/(1 - MPC)$. The multiplier in Economy B, then, is $1/(1 - .75)$, or 4. Consequently, we can quickly compute the *change* in the equilibrium GNP by

Multiplier		Initial Change in Investment		Change in Equilibrium GNP
4	×	+ \$50	=	+ \$200

The Multiplier, Initiated by a Rise in Government Spending

Perhaps it is unnecessary to make the point specifically, but the student should keep in mind that the multiplier is a *general* concept. The multiplier process can just as readily be set off by a rise in government spending as by a rise in investment, and a cut in government spending may initiate the same sort of downward multiplied spiral as a cut in investment.

Referring once again to Economies A and B in Tables 14-2 and 14-3, a \$50 rise in government spending, rather than in investment, would, other things being equal, lead to the same final results. The only difference for Economy A would be that \$50 of the \$100 rise would be accounted for by government, rather than investment spending. The same may be said of the \$200 rise in Economy B. A student can hardly understand the theory underlining fiscal policy until he or she recognizes the part the multiplier process plays in it.

The Multiplier, Initiated by an Upward Shift in the Consumption Function

It was pointed out earlier that there are a number of determinants of consumption, including not only income but wealth, stock of consumer durables, consumer expectations, taxes, and the like. The latter are assumed constant when any consumption function is drawn and a change in any of them shifts the level of the consumption function.

Clearly, consumption spending can rise, either because income has risen, permitting increased consumption, or because one of the other determinants has changed, leading to greater consumption spending (and less saving) than before at *every* income level. It would be convenient to be able to distinguish verbally between these two possibilities.

Such a distinction is possible with the aid of the familiar economic terms *autonomous* and *induced*. An *induced* change in consumption spending may be defined as *a change in consumption spending that is caused by a change in income*. The multiplier effect is a result of induced consumption spending.

On the other hand, *an increase in consumption spending that occurs because of an upward shift of the consumption function itself* (which has, in turn, been caused by changes in consumer expectations, wealth, and so forth) may be referred to as an *autonomous* rise in consumption.

Perhaps the distinction can be made clear with an example. Suppose we are dealing with a country in which, at the moment, the consumption function is

GNP	Consumption
$ 0	$ 50
100	100
200	150
300	200
400	250
500	300
600	350

If, because of a rise in investment or government spending, income should be increased, consumption spending would also rise. Such an increase would be an induced rise in consumption caused by *a movement along a given consumption function*.

On the other hand, if consumer expectations should change so that the entire consumption function is raised, as shown in the following table, the $50 rise in consumption spending is autonomous.

GNP	Consumption (Before Change in Expectations)	Consumption (After Change in Expectations)
$ 0	$ 50	$100
100	100	150
200	150	200
300	200	250
400	250	300
500	300	350
600	350	400

The difference between an induced rise and an autonomous rise in consumption is illustrated further in Figure 14-9.

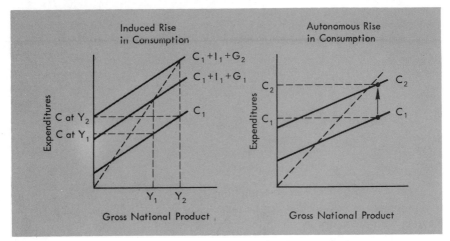

FIGURE 14-9   Autonomous versus Induced Changes in Consumption

Now although induced changes in consumption *are* the heart of the multiplier process, autonomous changes in consumption can, exactly like investment and government spending, *set off* the multiplier. Suppose we illustrate by assuming an economy whose equilibrium is upset by an upward shift of the consumption function itself from $C = .5$ GNP $+ \$50$ in period 1 to $C = .5$ GNP $+ \$100$ in period 2.

Table 14-6 and Figure 14-10 show the result. In period 1, equilibrium has been achieved. In period 2, however, there is an autonomous rise in consumption by \$50, which is the result of an upward shift of the consumption function itself (accompanied by an equivalent downward shift in the saving function). This autonomous rise in consumer spending, then, leads into the same multiplied expansion as before. The rise in consumption spending in period 2 is autonomous; the *further* rise in consumer spending in succeeding periods is *induced*.

TABLE 14-6

Movement Toward Equilibrium After Rise in Level of Consumption Function

	Time Period						New Equilibrium
	1	*2*	*3*	*4*	*5*		
Production (GNP) and income	$300	$300	$350	$375	$387.50	→	$400
C	200	250	275	287.50	293.75	→	300
I	45	45	45	45	45	→	45
G	55	55	55	55	55	→	55
T	50	50	50	50	50	→	50
S	50	0	25	37.50	43.75	→	50
Aggregate demand	300	350	375	387.50	393.75	→	400

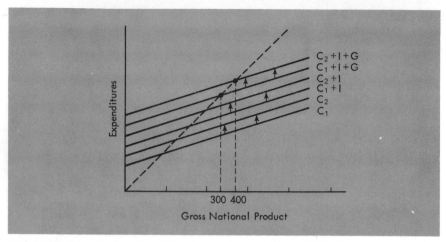

FIGURE 14-10   Effect on Equilibrium Income Level of Upward Shift of Consumption Function

Review Questions

1. What mechanism did the classical economists think would guarantee that any level of output would generate sufficient demand to buy it all? Explain.

2. What is the *significance* of the equilibrium level of production? What *conditions* must be fulfilled for the economy to be at equilibrium as it is defined in this chapter?

3. From your knowledge of recent "real-world" events, speculate on the importance of the assumptions made in this chapter of a *stable price level* and *stable interest rates*.

4. List and explain the determinants of the level of the consumption function. Is the money level of income one of them? Explain why or why not.

5. If C = .8 GNP + 30, investment spending is $80, and government spending on goods and services is $50, what is the equilibrium level of GNP?

6. Carefully, in commonsense, logical terms, explain the *process* of the multiplier.

7. Explain the difference between an *autonomous* rise and an *induced* rise in consumption.

8. For each of the following changes, indicate the effect on the equilibrium GNP and briefly explain:
   a. The MPC is .75 and G and lump-sum T are both increased by 100.
   b. Business saving is raised to a larger fraction of GNP.
   c. People decide to save $100 more than before at every level of GNP.

9. Assume an economy in which*

---

*Question 9 is based on the material in the appendix to Chapter 14.

a. Individuals dissave (negative personal savings) by $30 at zero DI and save $20 for each $100 increase in DI.

b. There is an income tax with a rate equal to 15 percent of GNP plus a lump-sum tax equal to $25.

c. Business savings is 5 percent of GNP, investment spending is $70, and government spending is $100.

   (1) Compute the equilibrium GNP.

   (2) Compute the new equilibrium GNP if now taxes are cut to .10 GNP + 20 and government spending is cut by 32 (to 68). (Can you do this by use of the multiplier?)

   (3) Draw an income determination graph that depicts the situation in (1). Indicate the amounts of the vertical intercepts of the C line and the C + I + G line. Now draw in the new C lines and new C + I + G lines for the conditions in (2). Indicate the new vertical intercepts. What are the slopes of the C + I + G lines in (1) and in (2)?

Appendix

Computing Equilibrium Income Levels
Under More Realistic Assumptions

The simplifying assumptions under which we have been operating up to now were designed to ease computational burdens while still permitting the essential structure to show through. But such oversimplification is only useful for pedagogical purposes. The very simplicity of our assumptions often disturbs the literal, practical-minded student searching for answers to "real-world" problems.

In this appendix, we shall relax some of our more unrealistic assumptions and work through a number of problems that may be of some interest. The main tool will be elementary algebra, but along the way we shall make reference to the effects of certain changes on the graphs we shall rely upon exclusively in upcoming chapters.

New Assumptions.   We shall begin with an economy in which

1. There is a personal income tax.
2. Corporations do accumulate retained earnings (i.e., there *is* business saving).

Aside from these two changes, all assumptions will remain as before.

Symbols and Definitions.   The following symbols will be employed:

Y_g = gross national product, net national product, or national income
Y_p = personal income
Y_d = disposable income
C = consumption expenditures
I = investment expenditures
G = government expenditures
T = tax revenue
S = total saving (sum of business saving and personal saving)

266

S_b = business saving (retained earnings expressed as percentage of GNP)
S_p = personal saving by households

Definitional Relationships.

$$S \equiv S_b + S_p$$
$$Y_d \equiv C + S_p$$
$$Y_p \equiv Y_d + T$$
$$Y_g \equiv Y_p + S_b \equiv Y_d + T + S_b$$
$$Y_g \equiv C + S_p + S_b + T$$
$$Y_g \equiv C + S + T$$

All these relationships follow directly from definitions used in arriving at the national income accounts aggregates. It will be easier to keep the national income account "ladder" in mind than to attempt simply to memorize these.

$$C + S + T \equiv Y_g \equiv \text{Aggregate supply}$$
$$C + I + G \equiv \text{Aggregate demand}$$

Numerical Example—Initial Conditions.   Now assume an economy in which the following conditions hold initially:

$$C = .8Y_d + 15$$
$$I = 65$$
$$G = 80$$
$$T = .2Y_g \text{ (implying an income tax rate averaging 20 percent of GNP)}$$
$$S_b = .05Y_g$$

Consumption Out of Disposable Income versus Consumption Out of Gross National Product.   The alert student will note that the consumption function given relates consumer spending to disposable income rather than to GNP, as was the case earlier in the chapter. As this may be the source of confusion, let us look at these relationships more carefully. Selected data fitting the given conditions are presented in the following table.

Y_g	$S_b(.05Y_g)$	$T(.20Y_g)$	Y_d	$C(.8Y_d + 15)$
100	5	20	75	60 + 15 = 75
200	10	40	150	120 + 15 + 135
300	15	60	225	180 + 15 = 195
400	20	80	300	240 + 15 = 255
500	25	100	375	300 + 15 = 315

By definition, Y_d equals Y_g minus business saving and taxes. Disposable income—available to people to use as they choose—is what is left out of Y_g *after* businesses take out the amount they choose to save and the government collects its tax revenue. People receive Y_d, out of which they spend a part on consumption, and save the rest (S_p).

But all this is more than a bit confusing. There are two income aggregates— Y_g and Y_d. Consumption is obviously related to both. Doesn't this give us *two* different consumption functions and *two* different MPCs? Which is the *right* one for which purpose? The question deserves careful consideration.

If the consumption function is being used as a reflection of a psychological propensity by consumers, clearly the relationship between consumption and disposable income is the appropriate one. Certainly personal behavior is better reflected by relating consumption to the income people are free to dispose of as they choose than to a more all-inclusive income concept such as GNP. So it is entirely in order to present the consumption function as it is—in terms of disposable income.

But what *about* the relation between consumption and GNP? Does it have any significance at all? Indeed it does! When one uses the conventional income determination graph, the consumption function drawn is the relation between C and GNP. When one uses the MPC to compute the multiplier, it is $\Delta C / \Delta GNP$ that is used, not $\Delta C / \Delta DI$. Finally, when one sets out to determine the equilibrium production level in a numerical problem, the first task is to convert the consumption function from its relationship to DI to a relationship to GNP.

This is not difficult. It simply requires figuring the relation between DI and GNP and then substituting in the given consumption function. For example we know that, by definition,

$$Y_d = Y_g - (S_b + T)$$

Substituting given data for S_b and T, we have

$$Y_d = Y_g - (.05Y_g + .20Y_g)$$
$$Y_d = Y_g - .25Y_g$$
$$Y_d = .75Y_g$$

Now as we know that disposable income is 75 percent of GNP, we can substitute this in the given C function and solve.

Given,

$$C = .8Y_d + 15$$

from above,

$$Y_d = .75Y_g$$

Substituting,

$$C = .8(.75Y_g) + 15$$
$$C = .6Y_g + 15$$

We now have a consumption function relating consumer spending to GNP. If we were to draw a consumption function in the conventional income determination diagram, it is $C = .6Y_g + 15$ that we would plot, *not* $C = .8Y_d + 15$.

Suppose that we want to compute the multiplier for this economy. The formula, it will be recalled, is $1/(1 - MPC)$, but *which* MPC shall we use—the .8 contained in the function related to disposable income or the .6 just computed? The MPC out of GNP, .6, is the appropriate one for figuring the multiplier.[20] Hence the multiplier in this economy is $2\frac{1}{2}$, *not* 5.

Computing the Initial Equilibrium GNP. Now that we have consumption in terms of GNP, computing the initial equilibrium in our given economy is simply a matter of substitution into the equilibrium condition.

The equilibrium condition is

$$Y_g = C + I + G$$

Substituting,

$$Y_g = .6Y_g + 15 + 65 + 80$$
$$.4Y_g = 160$$
$$Y_g = 400$$

The initial equilibrium level of GNP is 400. In graphical terms, all this would look like Figure 14-11.

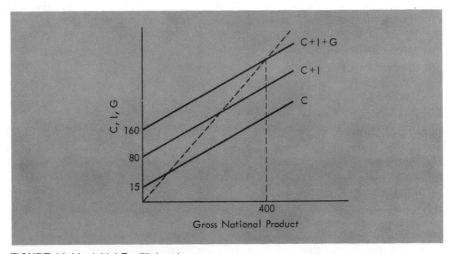

FIGURE 14-11 Initial Equilibrium Income

---

[20]Conventional symbols often used in economics are b for the MPC out of DI and t for the income tax rate. The multiplier for an economy with an income tax (but no business saving) is then $1/[1 - b(1 - t)]$. The careful reader will recognize that $b(1 - t)$ is simply the MPC out of GNP.

Effect of a Rise in Investment. Suppose that investment rises by 20 (to 85). What will be the effect on the equilibrium GNP? The answer can be obtained either by plugging the new investment figure into the equilibrium condition or by using the multiplier. We shall go through both.

We now have given

$$C = .6Y_g + 15$$
$$G = 80$$
$$I = 85 \text{ (up 20 from 65)}$$

Substituting,

$$Y_g = .6Y_g + 15 + 80 + 85$$
$$.4Y_g = 180$$
$$Y_g = 450$$

Alternatively, we could use our knowledge of the multiplier to get the answer. The multiplier equals $1/(1 - .6) = 2\frac{1}{2}$.

Multiplier		Change in I		Change in Equilibrium GNP
$2\frac{1}{2}$	×	$(+20)$	=	$+50$

The equilibrium GNP rises by 50, from 400 to 450. Graphically, this looks like Figure 14-12.

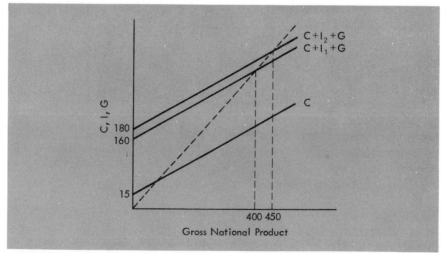

FIGURE 14-12   Rise in Equilibrium Income Resulting from Investment Increase

Effect of a Rise in Government Spending.   Going back to the original conditions with an initial equilibrium GNP of 400, what will be the effect of a fiscal policy change in which government spending is increased by 40 with no change in taxes?

Substituting into the equilibrium condition, we have

$$C = .6Y_g + 15$$
$$I = 65$$
$$G = 120 \text{ (up 40 from 80)}$$
$$Y_g = .6Y_g + 15 + 65 + 120$$
$$.4Y_g = 200$$
$$Y_g = 500$$

Using the multiplier, we have

Multiplier	Change in G	Change in Equilibrium GNP
$2\frac{1}{2}$	$\times$ $(+40)$ =	$+100$

The graph of this is given in Figure 14-13.

Effect of a Cut in Income Tax Rate.   Suppose that a different form of fiscal policy is used to raise GNP. Let us assume, again starting from the initial situation, that the income tax rate is cut in half—from 20 percent of GNP to 10 percent of GNP. What will this do?

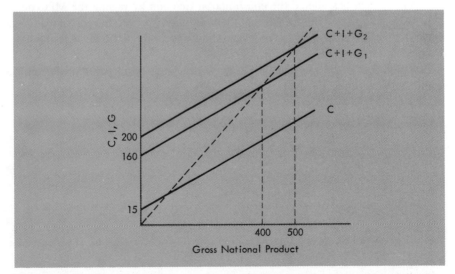

FIGURE 14-13   Rise in Equilibrium Income Resulting from Rise in Government Spending

This type of change poses a different problem. The cut in income taxes, of course, is expected to raise GNP by permitting consumption spending to rise. But how do we compute how much the initial increase is?

Clearly, as a tax cut means that the government is taking less out of GNP and leaving more money in disposable income form, the tax change alters the consumption function. The first step is to compute the *new* relation between consumption and GNP.

We have given

$$C = .8Y_d + 15$$
$$S_b = .05Y_g$$
$$T = .10Y_g \text{ (down from .20Y}_g)$$

Definitionally,

$$Y_d = Y_g - (S_b + T)$$

Substituting,

$$Y_d = Y_g - (.05Y_g + .10Y_g)$$
$$Y_d = .85Y_g$$

Substituting in the given C function,

$$C = .8(.85Y_g) + 15$$
$$C = .68Y_g + 15$$

The tax cut has altered the consumption function by raising the MPC out of GNP from .60 to .68. This means that the multiplier is larger and, graphically, the consumption line is steeper. (Remember, the slope of the C function in the graph *is* the MPC out of GNP.)

The effect of the tax cut on GNP can now be readily computed from the equilibrium condition.[21]

$$Y_g = C + I + G$$
$$Y_g = .68Y_g + 15 + 65 + 80$$
$$.32Y_g = 160$$
$$Y_g = 500$$

---

[21]It can also be computed by use of the multiplier, although with added complications. The multiplier—using the *new* MPC out of GNP—is now $1/(1 - .68)$, or $1/.32$. The initial rise in aggregate demand permitted by the tax cut is a rise in consumption spending of 32. (Under the original conditions, GNP was 400 and the tax rate was 20 percent, so tax revenue was 80. The halving of the tax rate thus initially raises disposable income by 40, out of which consumers spend 8/10, or 32, and save the rest.) The multiplier, $1/.32$, times the initial increase in consumption of 32, produces a rise in the equilibrium GNP of 100.

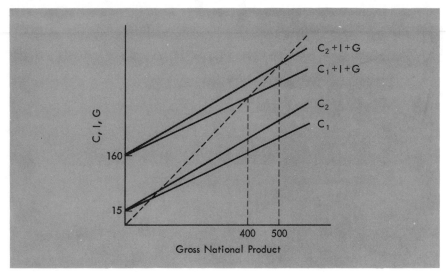

FIGURE 14-14   Rise in Equilibrium Income Resulting from Income Tax Rate Cut

Graphically, as shown in Figure 14-14, the income tax cut case is a bit different. Because the immediate effect is to raise the MPC out of GNP, the slope of the consumption function is increased. The aggregate demand line, then, is also steepened.

Summary.   Although many more examples could be worked through, what we have covered should be sufficient for our purposes. Perhaps a summary of the effects of, and approach to, other possible changes would be useful.

A change that raises (lowers) any of the constant terms (I, G, or the constant term in the consumption function) will simply raise (lower) the level of the aggregate demand line without affecting its slope (the MPC). Such problems can be solved by substituting the new data directly into the equilibrium condition or by using the (old) multiplier.

However, if the change involved affects the income tax rate, the percentage of business saving, or the MPC out of disposable income, the solution is more complicated. A cut (rise) in the income tax rate or in the percentage of business saving, or a rise (fall) in the MPC out of disposable income, will steepen (flatten) the consumption function. Consequently, in any of these cases, it will first be necessary to compute the new relation between consumption and GNP. This *new* consumption function can then be substituted into the equilibrium condition, or the *new* multiplier can be employed.

15

Investment Spending

Introduction

Mastering economic theory is not unlike erecting a building. Even the finest of superstructures will produce a faulty finished product if the foundation is weak. We should, therefore, make sure that the essence of Chapter 14 is clearly in mind before plunging more deeply into the analysis.

We have seen that the modern theory of income determination rests upon the basic assumption that it is the level of expenditures to purchase newly produced goods and services that determines how much will be produced. More specifically, we have argued that production will tend toward the level where aggregate demand just equals aggregate supply—the equilibrium level.

Of the three elements of aggregate demand—consumption, investment, and government spending—only consumption has thus far been carefully considered. We have seen that, whereas many factors affect the level of consumer spending, income is by far the most important, so important, in fact, that we refer to the relation between income and consumption as a functional relationship, the consumption function.

The existence of the so-called "multiplier" in the economy is, indeed, due primarily to the fact that consumption spending is so heavily dependent on income. Any autonomous rise in consumption, investment, or government spending, we have argued, will not only cause production to rise but, by causing rises in income, will induce further rises in consumption spending, so that before a new equilibrium position is reached, production will have risen by a multiple of the original increase.

Multiple changes in the level of production and income (and, indirectly, in employment and/or prices), then, can emanate from autonomous changes in any of the three elements of aggregate demand. What we need to know more about are the possible causes of the autonomous changes that initiate these cumulative income changes.

We already know something about the causes of autonomous changes in consumption spending. Consumer expectations, consumer wealth, the existing stock of consumer durables, taxes, and so on, all can, by changing, cause autonomous consumption changes. But in actuality, although these factors *can* be important in initiating income changes, they generally are not. Consumption spending, in the long run at least, is a relatively stable, passive portion of aggregate demand, changing in significant amount only when income does.

Not so for the other two elements. Both investment spending and government spending can be highly volatile, setting off repeated cumulative changes in the nation's income in one direction or another. We must, if we are to be able to say much about the economy, know more about them and the causes of their erratic behavior.

Unfortunately, not much can be said, from the economic point of view, about the determinants of government spending. At least not in the context in which we are considering it. The level of such spending is so heavily dependent on essentially noneconomic factors such as international affairs and domestic politics that a discussion of economic determinants hardly seems warranted. We will, therefore, pass it by, with the important and obvious reminder that, as one of the major tools of fiscal policy, government spending can and does have significant effects on the level of income.

This leaves investment, possibly the most volatile of the elements of aggregate demand. The remainder of this chapter considers the determinants of the level of investment spending, the causes of its volatility, and the effects of its erratic behavior on the level of income in the economy.

The Determinants of the Level of Investment Spending

Investment, the reader will remember, has been defined as "intentional spending to buy newly produced capital goods." The question before us is, "What causes such spending to be large or small?"

If one were to start out and, reasoning from sheer common sense, list the factors that would appear to affect the level of investment spending, the list would be imposing. Among others, the following would certainly be included:

1. Expected future levels of demand (to buy products produced on machines bought today).
2. Expected future wage and material costs (to purchase the labor and materials needed to operate the machine, or to use instead of the machine).
3. Expected future added tax liability to be incurred as a result of selling the goods produced by the machine.

4. The current price of the machines to be bought.
5. The interest cost of borrowing the money to buy the machine (or to forgo the potential interest return on one's own money to buy the machine).
6. Future consumer tastes (Will they shift away from products that can be produced on the machines available to be purchased?).
7. The pace of technological change (Will a better machine soon make those available now obsolete?).
8. The "gambling spirit" of entrepreneurs.
9. The existing stock of capital goods.

There can be no doubt that each of the factors on this partial list plays a role in the determination of the level of investment spending in any period. The problem that confronts us is, "How can all these factors be organized to develop a reasonably accurate, yet not too unwieldy, theory?"

Essentially what economists have done is to cover almost all these individual determinants under the unquestionably vague phrase "business managers' expectations of future profits." We say that the level of investment spending today depends upon "business managers' expectations of future profits," which, in turn, depends on almost all the factors in the foregoing list. But such sweeping generalities, though formally correct, are not very helpful for purposes of analysis. We need to see how all these variables can be systematically handled.

The Investment Decision— The Variables Involved

It should help to clarify matters if we attempt to follow through the logical thought process of an individual business manager considering the purchase of a particular machine.

Suppose that Mr. Jones is trying to decide whether to buy a certain machine, the price of which is $21,000, for his business. If he is a profit maximizer, what does he consider in arriving at his decision?

He knows that if he buys the machine and uses it in production, his total revenue will increase. The machine will add to his ability to produce and, assuming that he can sell this added output, its use adds to his firm's gross income. That's the good side of it. On the negative side, he realizes that certain added costs will accrue from buying and using it. His costs will be increased not only by the initial price of the machine but also by the interest cost he incurs to finance the purchase and by the added labor, material, and tax costs that will necessarily be encountered to operate it. Presumably, his decision on whether to purchase it will rest on the balance of good versus bad. If it is expected to add more to his revenue than to his costs, he can increase his profits by buying it. On the other hand, if expected costs from buying and using it exceed expected added revenue from selling the goods produced on it, he will forgo the opportunity.

It is apparent that the investment decision is full of "ifs." Our business manager must first estimate the expected added revenue as a result of purchasing the machine. What does such an estimate entail? It requires that he "guess" at

1. The physical productivity of the machine per year.
2. The economic life of the machine (which involves a guess at how soon his competitors may come up with a better machine which will make this one obsolete).
3. Consumer demand for the product produced on the machine (which involves not only a forecast of consumer tastes but also an estimate of the course of the business cycle).

Fraught with difficulty though it may be, no investment will be made by a profit maximizer without, explicitly or implicitly, considering all these imponderables. Let us assume that our Mr. Jones has done so and has come up with a "best guess" that the annual added total revenue he will derive from selling products produced on the machine is $25,000. Furthermore, he expects this added revenue to continue for two years, the expected useful life of the machine.

Now let us consider the negative side. Mr. Jones *knows* that buying and operating the machine will add to his yearly costs by the following amounts:

1. The initial cost of the machine, $21,000, spread over two years, or $10,500 per year.
2. The interest cost involved in financing the purchase, which we shall for the moment assume to be $2,100 per year. Note that he bears this cost whether or not he pays that amount out of pocket to a lender from whom he borrows. For if he uses his own funds, tying them up in the purchase of this machine means he is forgoing that amount of interest income he *could earn* by lending his money to someone else.

In addition to evaluating these known costs, he will have to resort once again to his engineers, accountants, or crystal ball to obtain a best guess at others. Suppose that he does so and comes up with the following estimates:

1.	Labor cost incurred to operate and maintain the machine each year	$5,000
2.	Cost of material fed into the machine each year	$3,500
3.	Increased annual taxes incurred as a result of added goods sold and/or profit made	$3,400

Now if we put all his estimates together, this would appear to be the picture:

Expected added annual revenue		$25,000
Minus: Expected added annual costs		24,500
Original cost of machine (depreciation)	$10,500	
Interest cost	2,100	
Labor and material cost	8,500	
Taxes	3,400	
Expected added annual profits		$ 500

In this case the purchase of the machine would appear to be advisable, yielding an addition to profits of $500 for each of the next two years. It would seem that, to maximize his profits, Mr. Jones must make the investment.

But hold on. We have omitted something that is absolutely crucial to the investment decision. The $500 expected annual net profit figure we have come up with may be Mr. Jones's "best guess," but it is, at best, a guess. Mr. Jones *thinks* that this $500 is the greatest likelihood, but, as any business manager must, he knows that there is some (lesser) chance that if he buys the machine he will lose money. Can the risk involved be ignored altogether by assuming that Mr. Jones will always act on his best guess despite his being aware that things might turn out differently?

That depends on how much of a gambler Mr. Jones is. Let us suppose, for purposes of argument, that whereas a $500 annual profit is most likely (there being 50 chances out of 100 that this will be the result), there are also 5 chances out of 100 that he will lose $1,000 per year, 20 chances out of 100 that he will just break even, 20 chances out of 100 that he will make an annual profit of $1,000, and 5 chances out of 100 that he will make $2,000 profit per year.

If that is the case, his outlook on the likely profitability of the investment would look something like that in Figure 15-1. This, of course, is a probability distribution that, in this case, turns out to be a symmetrical curve.

The problem facing Mr. Jones has now been complicated. Would he be as willing to accept this set of probable results as a *certain* $500 profit per year? It all depends on his personality. If he is a relatively conservative man, he would

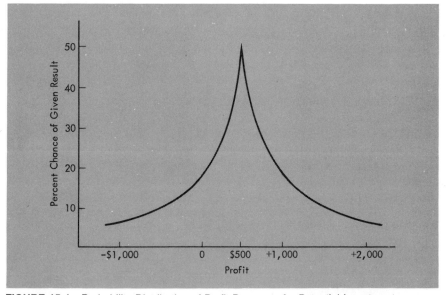

FIGURE 15-1   Probability Distribution of Profit Prospects for Potential Investment

prefer a certain $500 to this range of possibilities, even though the chances of loss may appear to be offset by equal chances of larger gain. In such a case, the risk involved is a positive detriment that would lessen the chance of his buying the machine. If, on the other hand, he is a gambler by nature, he might conceivably prefer this set of probabilities to a certain $500, putting more store in the possibilities of greater profit than in the equal likelihood of loss.

There is no safe way of characterizing all business managers with respect to their attitude toward the risk involved. However, it would seem that most would be on the conservative side, preferring a certain $500 to the range of probabilities shown in Figure 15-1. If that is the case for Mr. Jones, we had better take account of his aversion to risk in his investment decision.

Suppose that, to cover his risk, Mr. Jones insists that his best guess on the profitability of a $21,000 investment be at least $1,000 per year. If this is the case, that $1,000 *risk allowance* will have the same effect in deterring his purchase of the machine as would an additional out-of-pocket cost of $1,000. There is no reason we cannot consider it explicitly as another cost, like wages, interest, and so on, that must be covered.

Now that we have all the data needed, what about the $21,000 machine? Will Mr. Jones go ahead and buy it or not? The answer, of course, is that he will not. When the risk allowance of $1,000 is added to the other costs, totaling $24,500, we end up with expected annual costs of $25,500 and expected annual revenue of only $25,000. Purchase of the machine would be a losing proposition (or at least would not pay enough to be worth the risk involved).

The Marginal Efficiency of Investment

Logically, the investment decision in the preceding example is sound. If expected added annual revenue exceeds expected added annual cost (including risk allowance), the machine will be purchased by a profit maximizer. If cost exceeds revenue, it will not.

But economists for years have had a somewhat different way of manipulating these cost and revenue figures. It involves the concept of the *marginal efficiency of investment*. Let us see what is involved.

The marginal efficiency of investment may be defined as *the rate of discount that will equate expected annual net revenues to the present cost of the machine.* In somewhat less exact terms, the MEI may also be described as the *expected rate of return on an investment (with interest not being included as one of the costs).*

Symbolically, the MEI of any given prospective investment project can be determined from the following expression:

$$C = \frac{R_1}{(1 + r)} + \frac{R_2}{(1 + r)^2} + \cdots + \frac{Rn}{(1 + r)^n}$$

where

$$C = \text{the original cost of the machine}$$

R_1, R_2, etc. = the expected annual net revenue computed by subtracting all costs except interest and depreciation from expected annual gross revenue

$$r = \text{marginal efficiency of investment}$$

In the example, we have the following:

$C = \$21,000$
R_1 and $R_2 = \$12,100$

Expected annual gross revenue		$25,000
Expected annual costs (excluding depreciation and interest)		12,900
Labor and materials	$8,500	
Taxes	3,400	
Risk allowance	1,000	
		$12,100

Substituting these figures into the formula, we get

$$\$21,000 = \frac{\$12,100}{(1 + r)} + \frac{\$12,100}{(1 + r)^2}$$

Solving for r, we get .10. Therefore, this machine has an MEI of 10 percent.

Now all this may seem a little strange to the reader, especially the fact that interest and depreciation costs are not included in the computation of expected net revenue. Do we really ignore these costs when computing the MEI? If so, what good is it?

The answer is no and yes. We do *not* exclude depreciation when computing the MEI. After all, the full depreciation cost is simply the price of the machine, included as C in the formula.

On the other hand, the interest cost *is* excluded in the computation of the MEI. But this is not to say that it is omitted entirely from consideration in the investment decision. It is simply brought in at a different point.

In our example, the machine has an MEI of 10 percent. But this does *not* say that the machine is expected to yield a clear profit of 10 percent per year. What it says is *if you do not consider the interest cost,* the machine is expected to yield 10 percent. Consequently, we can never tell whether an investment will be profitable or not by considering the MEI alone. We must consider it *in comparison* with the one cost it does not take into account—the interest rate.

Our machine has an MEI of 10 percent. It will add to profits and be undertaken only if the only cost not yet considered—the interest cost—is less than 10 percent.

If MEI > *rate of interest,* the investment is considered profitable and will be made.

If MEI < *rate of interest,* the investment will add more to costs than to revenues and will not be made.

If MEI = *rate of interest,* the investment is a marginal one about which profit maximizers will be indifferent.

The Marginal Efficiency of Investment Schedule for the Economy as a Whole

At any point in time, many potential investments are under consideration by many different firms throughout the economy. Although the estimating approach may be different from that just described, presumably each investment project has, to the business manager considering it, some expected rate of return.

Suppose that we were to carry out a gigantic survey of all business managers asking each to list investments being contemplated and the MEI for each. If we should then "add up" all the responses received for the economy as a whole, we might end up with a result something like the following:

Dollars Worth of Investment Projects (billions of dollars)	With an MEI (Expected Rate of Return) of at Least
$10	20%
15	18
20	16
25	14
30	12
35	10
40	8
45	6
50	4
55	2

Such a result could equally well be expressed graphically, as in Figure 15-2.

Why do we end up here with a downward sloping curve? Why do we imply with our example that the marginal rate of return to be expected from $40 billion worth of investment is less than that to be expected from $20 billion worth? Because each investment figure includes the value of all the projects with a higher rate of return plus the value of additional projects that are expected to realize the lower rate. For example, when investment is pushed from $30 billion to $35 billion, the marginal expected rate of return falls from 12 percent to 10 percent. The investment projects that can be expected to yield at least 12 percent total up to $30 billion, but the total for which a return of at least 10 percent is expected is $5 billion higher because it includes both the $30 billion for which a 12 percent return is expected

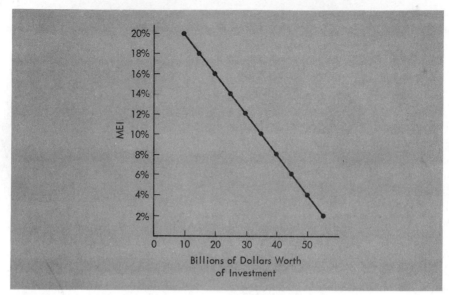

FIGURE 15-2   Array of Potential Investment Opportunities

plus the additional $5 billion worth of projects for which returns of 11.5 percent, 11 percent, 10.5 percent, and 10 percent are expected.

The curve we have in Figure 15-2, however, is not an investment demand schedule. It is nothing more than a cumulative array of prospective investment projects with their expected rates of return computed without considering the interest cost. Alternatively, it tells us that there exists at the moment $10 billion worth of potential investment projects with an expected rate of return (not deducting interest cost) of 20 percent *or more*, that there are $15 billion worth of potential investment projects with an expected rate of return (not deducting interest cost) of 18 percent *or more*, and so on.

To convert Figure 15-2 into an investment demand schedule, we need to bring in explicit recognition of the one cost not yet accounted for at all up to now. That cost, is, of course, the rate of interest. Any investment expenditure involves an interest cost—whether explicit or implicit. If the investor borrows the money to buy his machine externally from a lender on the capital market, his interest cost is, of course, the amount the lender charges him. If, however, he uses internally generated funds—such as his own retained earnings—to buy the machine, he does not avoid an interest cost. The difference is that in this case his interest cost is an implicit rather than an explicit one. It is the interest return he *could* have earned from his retained earnings had he lent them out to someone else and charged the going rate of interest, rather than tying them up to the purchase of a machine. And this form of interest cost—the opportunity cost of using his own funds—is just as real as any other.

Let us bring the interest cost into our example by using the vertical axis (which, in Figure 15-2, is already in percentage terms) to measure off *both* the MEI *and* the market rate of interest. This is done in Figure 15-3.

Note that the curve labeled MEI in Figure 15-3 is exactly the same curve (from exactly the same source) as the curve in Figure 15-2. It, like the curve in Figure 15-2, tells us the MEI of various levels of investment spending.

Now suppose that the market rate of interest (the level of which is, of course, subject to manipulation by the Federal Reserve System) happens to be 10 percent—as indicated by the dashed horizontal line at the 10 percent level. What does our Figure 15-3 tell us? It says that if the business managers in this economy are profit maximizers, they will buy exactly $35 billion worth of capital goods. That is, they will purchase all capital goods for which the MEI exceeds the rate of interest, for so long as the MEI exceeds the interest rate—a profit is realizable on the purchase. *Profit maximizers, then, must carry investment up to the point where the MEI is driven down to equal the rate of interest* to exploit all profit opportunities.

Suppose, for example, that the money to purchase machines must be borrowed externally so that there is an explicit interest payment to a lender of 10 percent. So long as buying the machine will bring in a rate of return (not allowing for interest cost) of *more* than 10 percent, a profit can be realized on the machine.

Or consider the possibility that the money needed to buy capital goods is already available in the form of accumulated retained earnings. Then what Figure

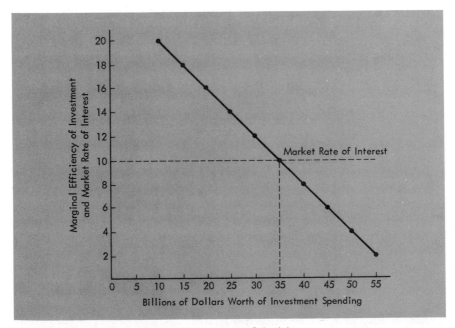

FIGURE 15-3 Marginal Efficiency of Investment Schedule

15-3 tells us is that business managers have two alternatives. They can put their money into buying machines and realize the rates of return shown on the MEI curve or put it into buying bonds or other financial assets and realize the market interest rate of 10 percent. If this is their choice, it is obvious that (with the first $35 billion of their retained earnings) they will do better to buy capital goods.

Note now the effect of a reduction in the market rate of interest to, say, 6 percent. This lower interest cost will make an additional $10 billion of investment projects profitable (that is, those between $35 billion and $45 billion). Conversely, an increase in the rate of interest from 10 to 12 percent would cut back on investment spending by $5 billion (because now the investment projects between $30 and $35 billion are not profitable enough to cover all costs including interest).

Before proceeding, one word of caution is in order. All references to the rate of interest in this chapter should be interpreted as referring to the *real* rate of interest—the rate of interest adjusted to eliminate the effects of inflation. If, for example, the market rate of interest rises from 10 to 15 percent in a year in which the rate of the price-level increase goes up 5 percent, the *real* rate of interest (the *real* cost of borrowing money) has not risen at all.

Determinants of the Level of the MEI Curve of the Economy

For the student who followed through on the logical thought process of our mythical Mr. Jones in arriving at the MEI for his particular $21,000 investment, most of the factors that determine the level of, or cause shifts in, the economy's MEI curve will be apparent. Anything that raises expected revenues would raise the MEI (and tend to shift the curve out to the right), and anything that raises costs (except the rate of interest) would lower the MEI (and tend to shift the curve to the left). Nevertheless, because we are now talking about the determinants of the level of the entire MEI curve for the economy as a whole rather than the considerations behind one prospective investment for one business manager, we had better list some of the more important determinants.

1. Technology. There can be no doubt that technological progress, whether in the form of development of new methods of production or new products, has profound effects on the level of the MEI curve. Although there may be exceptions, we will assume that improvements in the state of technical knowledge tend to raise the MEI curve—that is, shift it to the right.

2. Stock of Capital Goods on Hand. To the degree that the stock of capital goods in the economy increases more rapidly than do the other factors of production, we will, other things being equal, encounter diminishing marginal physical productivity of capital. Consequently, the larger the stock of capital goods already on hand, relative to the other productive factors, the farther to the left is the MEI curve.

3. Tax Policy. Just as our Mr. Jones's decision was affected by the level of taxes he expected to have to pay, so must the outlook of all prospective investors be influenced by tax policy. This applies not only to corporate profits tax rates, business property taxes, and excise taxes but also to less obvious factors such as changes in the rate at which depreciation is permitted for tax purposes. Clearly any tax change that has the effect of reducing taxes on the income earned from successful investment would, other things being equal, tend to shift the community's MEI curve to the right.

4. Business Managers' Psychology. Because investment spending is entirely an activity that "pays off" only in the future, its volume is inevitably influenced by the psychology of investors. Even the hard economic facts that underlie the estimate of the rate of return from an investment are colored by the psychological makeup of those who make the investment decisions, because "future expectations" involve a degree of crystal ball gazing that, by its very nature, cannot be based entirely on economic fact. If the investor group is composed primarily of "gamblers," the risk allowance will be smaller and the resulting investment larger than if investors are extremely cautious by nature.

5. Social and Political Atmosphere. Just as the interpretation of economic facts is influenced by psychology, so must it be affected by apparent changes in the social or political structure within which the economy functions. Rationally or irrationally, the illness of a president, the election of a seemingly hostile Congress, the intensification of social problems—all will affect business managers' expectations. In large part, of course, the effectiveness of such developments as determinants of investment depends upon the effect they appear likely to have on such fundamental economic facts as tax policy and the like. Nevertheless, they would seem to be sufficiently different in origin to justify a separate listing.

This is hardly an exhaustive list, but it does include some of the most important determinants of the MEI curve's level. A change in any one will alter the expectation of return from investment all along the line, thereby raising or lowering the MEI curve itself.

The Significance of the Slope (or Elasticity) of the MEI Curve

Although there can be no doubt that the MEI curve slopes downward to the right, there is considerable doubt and disagreement as to how *rapidly* it falls. In this section, we shall say what we can about the actual slope (or elasticity[1]) of the MEI curve and then explore its implications.

---

[1]Although the slope and elasticity of a demand curve are not identical, with the exceptions of the limiting cases of perfectly elastic and perfectly inelastic curves, we shall oversimplify here by ignoring the difference. Specifically, we refer to a relatively steep MEI curve (or a steep portion of an MEI curve) as inelastic and to a relatively flat curve (or portion thereof) as elastic.

Is the usual MEI curve for the American economy relatively steep or relatively flat? The truth is, we do not really know. Extensive efforts have been made to find out, but as yet there appears to be no conclusive proof one way or the other. Some scholars have attempted to get at the issue via the survey technique, in which business managers are asked the relative importance of various factors as determinants of investment. Although the survey results almost unanimously reveal the interest rate as a factor of generally minor importance, this approach falls short of conclusively demonstrating that the MEI curve is inelastic. Other investigators have employed econometric techniques with indifferent success. Others, with and without resort to empirical evidence, have theorized that such things as risk allowances, corporate profits taxes, and short payoff periods make for an inelastic investment demand curve.

Perhaps continued effort along these lines will pay off with more definitive results in the future. Until that point is reached, however, an agnostic view appears most appropriate. We just do not know how elastic or inelastic the MEI curve is.

But the question is a vitally important one, especially in its implications for the effectiveness of monetary policy. If it could be shown that the MEI curve was highly elastic (relatively flat) over most of its range, this would be equivalent to saying that slightly lowering the rate of interest (with a given MEI curve) will make profitable and call forth substantial amounts of additional investment spending. A highly inelastic MEI curve carries exactly the opposite implications. Let us look at Figure 15-4 to examine this point.

In the graph on the left, we have drawn a relatively flat MEI curve to represent a high degree of elasticity. On the right, the fairly steep curve is intended to depict an example of low elasticity. It can be seen that a reduction in the interest rate from 10 percent to 8 percent permits a relatively large increase in the volume of investment in the elastic case, but only a small increase where the MEI is decidedly inelastic. An easy money policy designed to raise aggregate demand via a lowering of interest rates would clearly be more successful, the more elastic the MEI. The

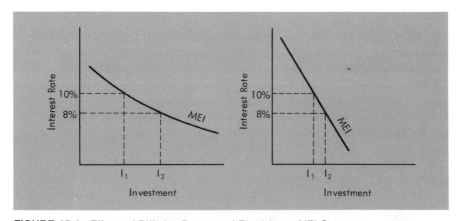

FIGURE 15-4   Effects of Differing Degrees of Elasticity on MEI Curves

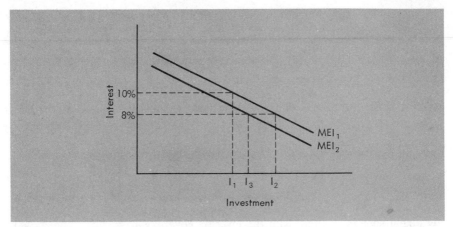

FIGURE 15-5   MEI Elasticity Partially Offset by Shift of Curve

same reasoning applies, of course, to the effectiveness of interest rate increases induced by a tight money policy.

Before leaving this area, note that the statement "investment is highly elastic with respect to the rate of interest" is not necessarily the same thing as arguing that the interest rate is *important* as a determinant of the level of investment. Perhaps another example will help to make the point.

In Figure 15-5 we have drawn a pair of MEI curves that are highly elastic over most of their ranges. Suppose that, initially, the MEI curve applicable for our economy is MEI_1 and that the rate of interest is 10 percent. This would mean that the volume of investment spending would be I_1. Now, suppose that Federal Reserve policy lowers the interest rate to 8 percent to combat a developing recession. *If the MEI curve itself does not shift,* the reduction in interest rates will permit a substantial increase in investment spending up to I_2. But, in fact, there is good reason to expect a shift in the curve itself as business managers' expectations are adversely affected by the developing recession. If the MEI curve shifts to the left to MEI_2 at the same time as the interest rate is reduced, the new volume of investment will be I_3, a very slight increase. Thus we have a situation wherein, even though investment is highly elastic with respect to the rate of interest, changes in the other factors (business managers' expectations) that affect investment work in the opposite direction and keep investment from rising substantially.

The reverse, of course, is also possible. If the MEI curve is highly elastic and monetary policy raises interest rates to combat a developing inflation (the purpose being to cut investment spending), the elasticity of the investment demand curve does not guarantee that investment spending will be diminished. For the optimism generated among business managers by the boom conditions may be reflected in an upward shift of the MEI curve itself, producing a smaller decrease in investment than a stable, elastic curve would lead one to expect. Indeed, there may even be an increase.

If, in fact, shifts in the MEI curve itself are so frequent and significant as to "swamp" the effects on investment of interest rate changes, then one must conclude that even if the MEI is elastic, interest may not be an important factor in determining investment. This possibility partially motivated our earlier statement that replies to surveys by business managers to the effect that interest was not an important factor do not necessarily prove that the MEI curve is inelastic.

Summary

We have now what amounts to half a theory. We have seen that, given the rate of interest, the marginal efficiency of investment schedule will tell us the volume of investment at which producers will maximize expected profits. This volume of investment spending, along with the level of government spending and the consumption function, will permit us to determine the equilibrium level of production and income. All this can be expressed graphically, as in Figure 15-6.

If the rate of interest is given to us as i_0, the volume of investment spending will be I_0. When this volume of investment is added (vertically) to the consumption and government spending curves, we find that the equilibrium level of income and production is Y_0.

Of course different assumptions for curves involved would give us different answers. If business managers' expectations became worse, the MEI curve itself would shift to the left, in which case an interest rate of i_0 would produce a smaller volume of investment and, consequently, a lower equilibrium level of income. If one of the determinants of the consumption schedule, such as income taxes or consumer expectations, should change from what is depicted to produce a higher or steeper consumption function, the equilibrium level of income would be higher, even with the same level of investment.

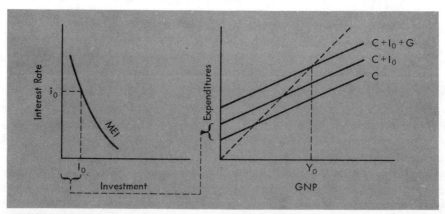

FIGURE 15-6 Combining MEI and Income Determination Diagrams

A good deal can be said about the economy with the aid of this "half model" alone. But we must go further. To complete the picture, we need to know how the rate of interest is determined. This is the subject of Chapter 16. Once it is completed, we will have covered all the pieces of our simplified model of the economy and will be in a position to go ahead in Chapter 17 and use it in its entirety.

Review Questions

1. Make up a list of all the factors discussed in this chapter, an increase in which will lower the MEI of a single potential investment project. What will these changes do to the level of the MEI curve?

2. Carefully explain why profit-maximizing business managers will carry investment spending up to the point where the MEI just equals the interest rate rather than stopping at a point where the MEI is much higher than the interest rate. Can you relate this to a single business manager's output decision and the comparison of marginal revenue and marginal cost?

3. List and explain the major factors that could cause a nation's MEI curve to shift to the right.

4. "It is a fact that in year 1 the interest rate was 8 percent and the volume of investment spending was $80 billion. Then in year 2 the interest rate was 12 percent and investment spending rose to $160 billion. This proves that the MEI curve for that nation must have had a positive slope." Do you agree? Explain why or why not. What impact would it have on your explanation if you knew that the price level rose by 50 percent from year 1 to year 2?

5. If the Fed is trying to raise aggregate demand via reductions in interest rates, would it prefer a steep or a flat MEI curve? Explain.

16

The Rate of Interest

What determines the rate of interest is a question over which economists have struggled for many years. This debate still goes on, but, fortunately, enough solid ground of agreement has been established to permit a fairly confident discussion of where we now stand and how we got there.

This chapter is divided into two main sections. After some brief introductory comments limiting the area of discussion, we shall consider the first of two current approaches to the theory of interest. Called the *loanable funds theory,* this approach is a modification of the classical explanation of the rate of interest.

Following the loanable funds discussion, we shall consider the *liquidity preference theory* of interest. This approach is another one of the contributions of J. M. Keynes, and we give it fuller consideration because of the facility with which it fits into the complete Keynesian model.

Limitations to the Area of Discussion

It is a gross oversimplification to speak of *the* rate of interest, since there are many different rates of interest ruling in any economy at any given time. What do we mean by *the* rate of interest?

The rate of interest should be taken to mean the rate of return paid to a lender who has lent his or her money for a long period of time by a borrower for whom the chances of default are extremely remote. For instance, the return on a long-term, virtually riskless security would provide a good measure of what we mean by *the* rate of interest. There is no better example than the interest paid on a long-term U.S. government security.

But what about all the other rates being paid? At any one time, even if we had already determined *the* rate of interest to be 10 percent, one could find examples of a whole structure of rates ranging from perhaps 5 percent to as high as 40 percent or more. What explains the divergencies from our "pure" 10 percent rate?

To answer such questions adequately, we would have to become deeply involved in a complicated discussion of the structure of interest rates. This, we shall not do.

Suffice it to say that interest rates above and below the "pure" rate are largely explainable by differences in the term of the loan, the costs of collection, the risk involved, and the expectations of the parties (especially in regard to future price changes). We shall, in the discussion that follows, ignore such differences and concentrate on the forces that determine the "pure" long-term "riskless" rate of interest.

The Loanable Funds Theory of Interest

The explanation of interest that has perhaps the greatest appeal to common sense is the loanable funds theory. It considers the interest rate, reasonably enough, to be simply *the price paid for the right to borrow and use loanable funds*. With this straightforward definition of interest as the focus, it then becomes necessary to consider the components that determine that price—the demand for and supply of loanable funds.

The Classical Theory Background to Loanable Funds

The loanable funds interest theory is a logical extension and modification of the much older classical theory of interest. It may therefore be useful to consider the classical theory briefly first.

One of the oldest areas of dispute in interest theory has to do with the ultimate determinants of interest. Is the interest rate a *real* or a *monetary* phenomenon? Does it depend entirely on real variables within the economy or can it be permanently altered by mere monetary manipulations?

The classical answer to this question was clear-cut. To the classical economists, money was only a "veil" that partially concealed but did not really alter any of the basic "real" forces in the economy. This was as true of their interest theory as of other elements of their elegant structure.

Their reasoning ran something like this:

> Interest is what must be paid for the right to borrow money. But this amount is a price that, like all other prices, is determined by demand and supply. The demand for borrowed money comes almost entirely from business managers, who desire to use the funds to purchase capital goods. The supply, on the other hand, comes from individuals who, having decided not to spend all their income on consumption, have some left over in the form of saving, available to lend out.

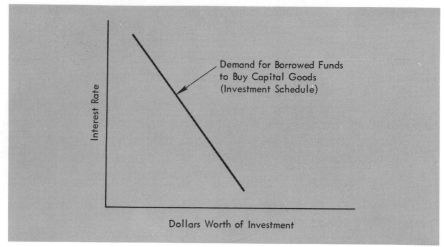

FIGURE 16-1 Demands for Funds for Investment

But we must look behind these surface phenomena for a fuller understanding. The amount of borrowed money demanded by business managers depends essentially on the marginal productivity of capital goods. If the productivity of any added machine is expected to be high enough to more than cover the interest cost of financing its purchase, it must be bought to maximize profits. However, additional capital goods, when combined with the other factors of production, will produce diminishing marginal productivity. Therefore, more such goods will be bought only at lower rates of interest because their lower productivity will not cover higher rates. That is to say, the demand for borrowed funds (reflecting, as it does, the diminishing productivity of capital) will look like that in Figure 16.1.[1]

On the other side of the market, the supply of funds made available by savers is motivated by the opportunity of receiving interest on funds not spent for consumption. Actually, as noted earlier, it was argued that it is irrational for people to refrain from spending their income on consumption (and suffer the disutility associated with such abstinence) and then hoard the saved money. For any rational person would prefer some interest return on his or her savings to none. Therefore, as it is the reward of interest that motivates saving, the higher the rate of interest, the greater the quantity we can expect to be saved. The supply of savings, then, would look like that in Figure 16-2.

As the supply of funds to be lent out at interest comes from saving and the demand for funds to borrow comes from investors, the price—the rate of interest—will settle at an equilibrium level at which saving and investment are equal. This

---

[1]The classical investment schedule is related to, but not quite the same as, the Keynesian MEI schedule discussed in the preceding chapter.

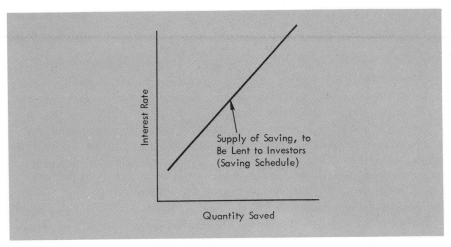

FIGURE 16-2 Supply of Funds from Saving

equilibrium rate of interest is shown in Figure 16-3 where demand and supply intersect.

In summary, then, the classical economists considered the rate of interest to be entirely a "real" phenomenon reflecting the real disutility suffered by savers as a result of their abstinence, on the one hand, and the real marginal productivity of capital goods, on the other.

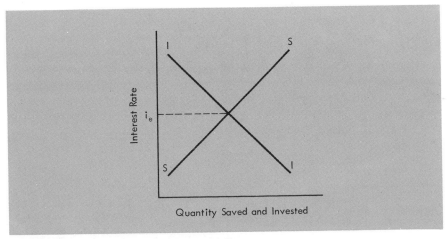

FIGURE 16-3 Classical Equilibrium Interest Rate

Reformulation into the Loanable
Funds Theory

There is much that is appealing and much that is correct in the classical interest theory. But it has not stood up under the test of time—partly because of institutional and structural changes in the economy over the years and partly because of flaws in the underlying assumptions.

In the first place, critics asked, is saving out of current income really the only source of funds to be lent out (and therefore to affect the interest rate)? What about banks? Certainly as creators of money (and not simply middlemen), they lend money *in addition* to what savers save. And while we're about it, how about those savers? Is it really true that what is saved is *always* lent out at interest? Suppose savers *do* choose to hoard part of what they save in year 1 and then lend it out (in addition to year 2's saving) in the following year? Won't this affect the interest rate in both years?

Second, what of the other side of the market—the demand side? True, business investors do borrow much of what is lent, but are they the only borrowers? Surely we know that the government has been a significant borrower in recent decades. And for that matter, consumers are by no means all net savers. They, too, borrow and pay interest.

Questions such as these led to the reformulation of the classical interest theory into a more complete explanation called the *loanable funds* theory of interest.

The loanable funds theory, as noted, takes the interest rate as "the price that must be paid for the right to borrow and use loanable funds." To explain that price, one need only look at the determinants of the demand for, and supply of, loanable funds.

On the supply side, saving is still considered an important component.[2] Now, however, the contribution of banks and the possibility of hoarding or dishoarding are also taken into account.

Components of Supply of Loanable Funds.

1. Gross saving out of current income
     plus
2. New money created by banks (or minus money destroyed)
     plus
3. Dishoarding—lending of funds saved in previous years but hoarded then (or minus hoarding)

---

[2]Unlike the classical theory, however, there is no assurance that the quantity saved is larger the higher the interest rate. Some people save without reference to the interest rate, and some may even save *more* the *lower* the rate of interest.

Let us consider a numerical example. Suppose that in year 1, the following events occur:

Total income received	$800 billion
Total consumption spending	700 billion
Therefore, total saving	100 billion
Total amount lent out by savers at interest	75 billion
Therefore, total hoarding	25 billion
Total new money created by banks in making loans	50 billion

What is the total supply of loanable funds made available in year 1? Pretty clearly it is $125 billion. Banks put in $50 billion of newly created money. Consumers saved $100 billion, but not all of it was lent out. The $25 billion that was hoarded during year 1 must be subtracted to arrive at the correct figure.

Suppose now in year 2 that

Total income received	$900 billion
Total consumption spending	800 billion
Therefore, total saving	100 billion
Total amount lent out by savers at interest ($100 billion from this year's saving, plus the $25 billion that was hoarded in year 1)	125 billion
Therefore, total dishoarding	25 billion
Total new money created by banks in making loans	50 billion

In year 2, the supply of loanable funds totals $175 billion—$100 billion from year 2 saving, $50 billion from banks, and $25 billion from lending out money saved and hoarded last year.

So much for the supply side. What makes up the demand for loanable funds? Who demands the right to borrow and use the funds that savers, dishoarders, and banks make available?

Components of Demand for Loanable Funds.

1. Business demand to finance the purchase of capital goods (investment)
   plus
2. Government demand to finance deficit spending (or minus government tax surplus)
   plus
3. Consumer demand to finance consumer purchases on credit

In essence, then, the loanable funds theory of interest concludes that, *other things equal,* the rate of interest will tend to rise as a result of an increase in business, government, or consumer borrowing; consumer hoarding; a decline in the money supply; or a shift to the left in the saving schedule (where the saving schedule involved is the relation between saving and the rate of interest). Reverse movements will tend to lower the rate of interest.

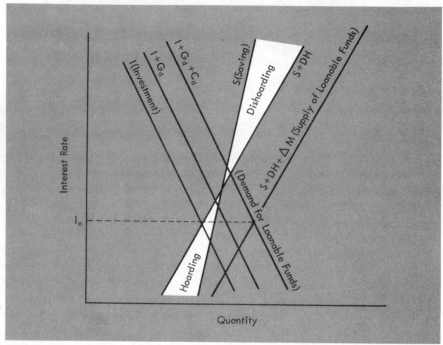

FIGURE 16-4   Graphical Representation of Loanable Funds Theory of Interest

Graphically, the loanable funds theory of interest might appear as in Figure 16-4, where S equals saving, DH stands for dishoarding, ΔM represents an increase in the money supply, I equals demand by business for funds to finance investment, G_d stands for the government budget deficit, and C_d represents gross consumer borrowing. Note that the diagram assumes that dishoarding will occur at high interest rates and hoarding will be likely at low rates. The equilibrium rate of interest, as pointed out, is determined where the *demand for loanable funds forthcoming from business, government, and consumers equals the supply of loanable funds made available by savers, dishoarders, and the banks.*[3]

The Liquidity Preference Theory of Interest

When J. M. Keynes wrote his epic *General Theory*, he concocted an interest theory with an entirely different approach. As a longtime Cambridge economist, he was

---

[3]Note that the saving schedule has been drawn here with a positive slope reflecting a higher quantity saved at higher rates of interest. This classicallike assumption is *not* necessarily descriptive of reality.

accustomed to thinking in terms of the demand for *money* rather than the quite different demand for loanable funds we have been discussing. To the Keynes of the *General Theory,* interest *is the price that must be paid to get people to forgo willingly the advantages of liquidity.*

Income recipients, Keynes pointed out, must make two decisions. First, they must decide how much they will spend on consumption and how much they will save. Then, they must decide how much of their saved funds they will lend out at interest and how much they will hold on to in the form of (perhaps temporarily) idle money.

This second decision is the crucial one for the interest rate. Lending out saved funds (such as by buying bonds) has the attraction of returning an interest income to the saver. On the other hand, giving up money in return for bonds or other IOUs has a real disadvantage—a loss of *liquidity.* Possession of money balances provides the holder advantages not available to the bondholder. The person who holds bonds but no money will have to go through the trouble, inconvenience, and perhaps risk of selling bonds to get money when he or she wants to make a purchase. The money holder is in a better position to take care of unexpected contingencies and take advantage of unexpected bargains. Consequently, the decision as to the form in which savings will be held is an economic decision in which the saver must contrast the attractiveness of an interest return and less liquidity on the one hand with perfect liquidity and no interest on the other.

The liquidity preference theorist looks upon the equilibrium rate of interest as **that rate that will cause people willingly to hold the existing supply of money.** There are, as we shall be discussing in more detail, two prime reasons for holding money. Some money must be held to finance expenditures on goods and services during the pay period. Second—and this is the crucial matter—other amounts of money will be held willingly as an asset, beyond transactions needs, because the advantages of liquidity seem to outweigh the advantages of an interest return.

Clearly, this latter portion of the demand for money will vary inversely with the current rate of interest. If the rate of interest being paid to those who give up liquidity (and buy bonds) is very low, many people will find the advantage of holding money superior to the low return paid for parting with liquidity. The quantity of money demanded will thus be large. Conversely, if the current rate of interest is relatively high, the advantage of giving up liquidity by buying bonds is relatively greater. The quantity of money demanded will be small.

But let us not overlook one fact. The supply of money that exists (and that *must* be held, either willingly or unwillingly) is determined by the monetary authorities. If the current rate of interest is quite high, people will choose to hold relatively less money and more bonds. In fact, they may not *want* to hold all the money that exists under such conditions. But they have no choice. They (as a group) *must* hold all the money that the Federal Reserve has foisted upon them. But if they do not *willingly* hold all this money, their individual efforts to get rid of the excess will tend (in a manner we shall describe shortly) to lower the rate of interest.

Similarly, suppose that the current rate of interest is very low, so that people desire to hold large amounts of money (the liquidity advantage exceeding the advantage of a small interest return). If the Federal Reserve is keeping the money supply at a low level, there may be less money in existence than people would *like* to hold. Consumers as a group cannot change the supply of money that exists, but, as individuals, each can *try* to acquire more. These efforts, we shall see, will tend to raise the rate of interest.

In essence, then, the liquidity preference theory says that **the interest rate is determined by the demand for and supply of money.** If the demand for money (the amount people would willingly hold) exceeds today's supply of money, the interest rate will rise because of people's efforts to acquire more. If the supply of money that exists is greater than the demand for money (the amount willingly held), the efforts of people to get rid of the excess will force the interest rate down. The **equilibrium** rate of interest, then, is **that rate of interest at which people willingly hold (i.e., demand) exactly the supply of money that exists.**

One word of caution before we look more deeply into the demand for money. This theory is different from the loanable funds theory. The student should be careful *not* to identify the supply of loanable funds with the supply of money. They are two different animals. Similarly, the demand for loanable funds is quite different from the demand for money.

The Demand for Money

Most of Part I was devoted to discussing the determinants of the supply of money. We need not repeat that material here. But our coverage of the demand for money thus far has been, to say the least, highly superficial. We have, as yet, done little more than allude to the fact that there is some sort of inverse relationship between the level of the interest rate and the quantity of money demanded. We must do better than that. We must know more about this demand for money.

When Keynes introduced his liquidity preference theory, he argued that there were three rational motives for holding (demanding) money. He entitled these the *transactions, precautionary,* and *speculative motives.* In our discussion, we shall ignore the precautionary motive[4] and deal separately with the transactions and speculative demands.

---

[4]The precautionary motive holdings consist of money balances held, over and above those needed to finance transactions or take advantage of speculation on movements in the interest rate, to cover contingencies such as accident and sudden illness. We do not treat this motive separately because its determinants are quite similar to the transactions demand.

The Transactions Demand for Money. All of us have some need to hold money balances for some period to cover our requirement for cash between paydays. We shall define *transactions balances* in just this way—*money, held in cash form temporarily, for the purpose of financing needed expenditures for goods and services between paydays.*

Transactions balances constitute assets held in noninterest-bearing money form simply because of *convenience*. If, for example, a person is paid $1,500 on the first of each month and has every intention of spending all that income on consumer goods during the month, it would be *most* unusual for him or her to buy a $1,500 bond with it or put it in a savings account or even a money market fund to maximize interest earnings. Why? First, because he or she is unlikely to earn any interest, even in a savings account, if the money is needed in less than 30 days. Second, even if interest *could* be earned on it, the paltry return for such a limited time period would hardly be worth the time and trouble of dealing with the savings institution every day or so to draw out what is needed to spend that day.

All of us carry *some* transactions money balances to bridge the gap between the periodic receipt of income and the more or less continual expenditure of it. *Any* person with change in pocket or purse, or a positive balance in a checking account, has a transactions demand for money if those are funds he or she counts on spending before the next paycheck arrives.

Probably the best way to look at the transactions demand for money is via the simple diagram in Figure 16-5. We depict there the transactions balances held by a man who is paid $1,500 per month, on the first of each month, and who spends that money at a constant rate throughout the month, ending up with a zero balance at the end of the month. Such a person has, on the average, $750 of transactions balances—$1,500 on the first of the month, $1,450 on the second, $1,400 on the third, and so forth, until, on the thirtieth, he spends his last $50.

If so prudent a spending pattern seems hardly applicable to anyone we know, we can just as easily depict, by the same device, the more familiar case (to most

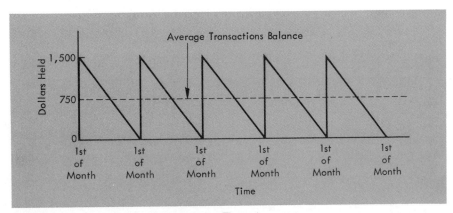

FIGURE 16-5 Transactions Balances over Time—I

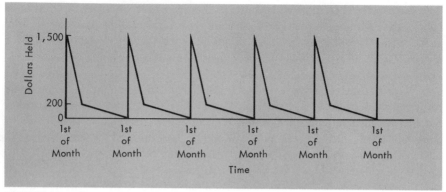

FIGURE 16-6 Transactions Balances over Time—II

of us) of the person who spends most of his income shortly after payday. Suppose that our subject receives $1,500 on the first of each month but spends $1,300 of it in the first day, spreading the other $200 out equally over the remaining 29 days of the month.

Such a person's transactions balances are depicted in Figure 16-6. He, of course, has a much smaller average demand for transactions money than does his more "prudent" counterpart. On the average he holds somewhat less than $150 for transactions purposes—$1,500 the first day, $200 on the second, about $193.10 on the third, and so forth, spending his last $6.90 (approximately) on the thirtieth day.

It should be clear that all of us have some (however small) transactions demand for money. And, although it is equally obvious that we differ widely in the size of our individual transactions demands, it is not individual differences that most concern us in the task at hand. What is more important for our purposes here are the determinants of the size of the transactions demand for the nation as a whole. What kinds of changes in the economy could significantly increase or decrease the entire nation's transactions demand?

Determinants of the Quantity of Money Demanded for Transactions Purposes in the Nation as a Whole.   The most obvious determinants are four: the public's payment habits, the degree of vertical integration of production, the development of the economy's financial system, and the level of income.[5] Let us discuss these in order.

Suppose that our prudent individual, who, it will be remembered, received $1,500 each month and spent it all with the perfect regularity of $50 per day until his balance was exhausted on the thirtieth day, is notified by his employer that henceforth he will be paid twice monthly, on the first and fifteenth. What effect, if any, will such a "speeding up" of his paydays have on his transactions demand?

---

[5] Another determinant, the rate of interest, will be considered shortly.

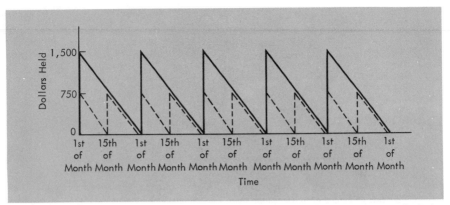

FIGURE 16-7   Transactions Balances over Time—Effect of Reduction in Payment Period

Figure 16-7 depicts the situation. His previous payment and spending pattern is shown by the solid line and the new "two paydays per month" arrangement by the broken line. Assuming that he remains "prudent" and continues to spend just $50 per day, it is readily apparent that his average transactions demand for money has been cut in half. Whereas before he held, on the average, $750 in transactions balances, now he finds he can get along just as well with a mean balance of $375.

If such a speedup in payment habits occurs throughout the economy, the result is clear. A smaller stock of money will suffice to do the same work as one twice as large. In terms of the equation of exchange, because money sits idle for a shorter period of time, on the average, the velocity of spending is raised. The same level of spending (MV) is thereby obtainable with a smaller supply of money. We can say then that *a speedup in payment habits tends to reduce the transactions demand for money,* whereas a slowdown in frequency of payment would raise the transactions demand.

The second determinant is the *degree of vertical integration of production.* If there is little vertical integration of production, each step in the productive process being carried out by separate firms, each firm must carry some transactions cash balance. If, on the other hand, production is carried on from raw material to finished product within the same highly integrated firm, there exists at least the possibility that a smaller total transactions balance will be needed to finance the entire process.

Third, the *development of the country's financial system* will certainly be a determining factor. A highly developed financial system, wherein opportunity to borrow funds to finance needed purchases is easily and economically available, will permit an individual to get along on a substantially smaller cash balance than is the case where it is very difficult to obtain credit. Consider, for example, the effects of the credit card on transactions money balances. The more highly developed the financial system, other things being equal, the lower the transactions demand for money.

Finally, *the level of income* itself appears to be a quite important determinant.

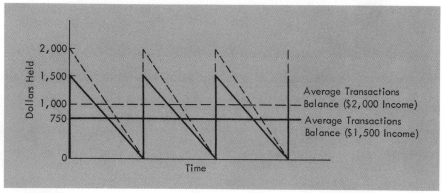

FIGURE 16-8　Transactions Balances over Time—Effect of Rise in Income

This is simply to say that the higher a person's income, the greater his transactions and therefore the greater his need for transactions cash balances. The point can perhaps be best illustrated as in Figure 16-8.

Here the solid lines, as before, indicate the fluctuation in cash balances under the assumptions that our subject's monthly pay is $1,500 and that he spends it evenly over the month. If his monthly income should now be raised to $2,000 and he should still choose to spend it all at a steady rate before his next payday, his transactions balance would behave in a manner depicted by the broken lines. Clearly the rise in income raises his transactions demand for money. With a $1,500 monthly check, his average transactions balance is $750, whereas, with $2,000, the average for the month rises to $1,000. And, in this case, what is true for the individual would appear also to be true for the nation as a whole. The quantity of money demanded for transactions purposes for the community as a whole will surely rise as the nation's income (GNP) rises. For the more income we have, the more spending we do, and hence the larger transactions balances we need to facilitate that spending.

In summary, we can say the quantity of money demanded for transactions purposes will tend to be larger

1.　The less frequently people are paid.
2.　The less the vertical integration of industry structure.
3.　The harder it is to borrow funds needed for spending.
4.　The higher the level of income.

The Transactions Demand-for-Money Curve.　Although all four of these factors affect the size of the transactions demand, the first three would appear to change only slowly over the long run. That is, a change in payment habits, degree of vertical integration, or "maturity" of the financial structure will certainly affect the transactions demand *when they change*, but all three normally change only slowly over a long period of time. Hence, within any short-run context, these three

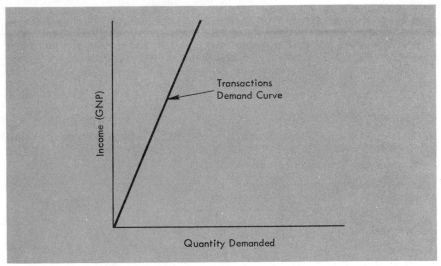

FIGURE 16-9   Transactions Demand-for-Money Curve

are not likely, *in fact,* to cause significant changes in the size of the transactions demand. The level of income, on the other hand, is subject to significant short-run as well as long-run changes. The result is that, in practice, the transactions demand for money changes, in the short run, largely in response to changes in the level of income (GNP).

To take account of these considerations, we depict the transactions demand for money graphically in Figure 16-9. Here the level of income is measured off on the vertical axis and quantity (of transactions funds demanded) on the horizontal axis. The transactions demand curve itself is upward-sloping, indicating that the quantity of transactions balances demanded rises as income rises. *The degree of slope depends on the other three determinants.* For example, the effect of a speedup of payment habits, further vertical integration, or a significant advance in the nation's credit facilities would be to steepen the curve itself. Opposite changes in any of these three would have a tendency to move the curve to a flatter position.

We have, then, in Figure 16-9, a curve that tells us how, with a given set of payment habits, vertical integration, and financial system, the quantity of money demanded for transactions purposes varies with the level of income.

The Transactions Demand and the Quantity Theory.   There was nothing revolutionary or even novel about Keynes's transactions demand for money. Indeed, if we were to stop here, we would be right back in a crude quantity theory world.

The student will remember that the early quantity theorists held that V' (or k') was essentially a constant because the only rational reason they could accept for holding money was to finance upcoming expenditures—the transactions demand, pure and simple.

True, they recognized that changes in payment habits, integration, or the

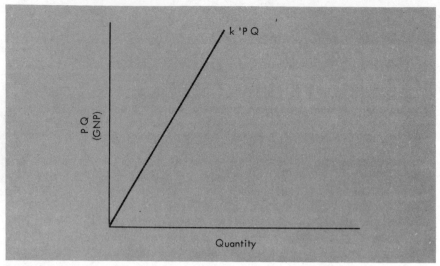

FIGURE 16-10   Transactions Demand Curve Related to Quantity Theory

financial structure would tend to change V' (k'), but only slowly in the long run. In the short run, the only factor that could change the quantity of money demanded was a change in income itself.

What Cambridge economist Keynes was arguing in his discussion of the transactions demand for money was completely in keeping with views that had held sway for years. Take, for example, the cash balance equation:

$$M = k'PQ$$

What does it really say? In equilibrium, the supply of money (M) must equal the demand for money ($k'PQ$). If we were to plot this demand for money on a graph, we would have something like that in Figure 16-10, where the line depicts the demand for money and its slope depends upon the size of k'. As k' was thought to change only when long-run determinants such as payment habits and the financial structure change, it seemed quite appropriate to assume that k' (V') was essentially a constant in the short run. And if k' is a constant (and Q is also), the crude quantity theory follows by definition.

The Keynesian Speculative (or "Asset") Demand for Money

Keynes, however, was not content with the idea that the demand for money was entirely a transactions demand. One of his major innovations in the *General Theory* was the argument that there was also a speculative demand for money—a demand for money balances in addition to the transactions demand, that results from speculation about the future course of the rate of interest.

TABLE 16-1

An Example—The Relation Between Interest Rates and Bond Prices

Date	Par Value	Coupon Rate	Coupon Payment	Market Rate of Interest	Market Value of Bond
When issued	$1,000	8%	$80	8%	$1,000
After interest rates rise	1,000	8	80	10	800
After interest rates fall	1,000	8	80	5	1,600

In explaining the speculative demand, Keynes dealt with a model in which it was assumed that savers have only two forms for holding wealth—long-term bonds and money. By so limiting the options of savers, Keynes not only departed sharply from reality as we know it but also opened himself to challenge. Later on, we shall consider some of these challenges. For the moment, however, let us accept Keynes's initial assumptions.

Relation Between Bond Prices and Interest Rates. To understand fully the speculative demand for money *à la* Keynes, we must do some preliminary spadework on the relation between bond prices and interest rates.

To keep the discussion as simple as possible without sacrificing anything fundamental, we shall work with an example in which the bonds involved are *perpetuities*—bonds that have no maturity date. The borrower (issuer of the bonds) agrees to pay interest to the holder forever, but the principal is never to be paid back. In such a case, the only way a bondholder can get his principal back (he hopes) is by selling the bond to someone else.

Suppose we take, for our example, a bond that was originally issued by the lender at a par value and purchase price of $1,000. The bond carries a coupon rate of 8 percent, which is to say that the issuer agrees to pay, in perpetuity, 8 percent of the par value of the bond ($80) annually to the holder. Let us also assume that the market rate of interest, which we shall define as the *rate of interest being paid elsewhere in the economy on securities of a risk similar to this one,* was also 8 percent when the bond was originally issued.[6] These figures are listed in the first line of Table 16-1.

Now the par value, coupon rate, and coupon payment are printed on the face of the security and, as such, cannot change while the bond is outstanding. The issuer is committed to paying $80 per year to the holder, regardless of any other changes in the economy.

---

[6]This is simply a commonsense assumption. If the market rate of interest had been 9 percent when the bond was originally issued, no rational lender would have bought it at par because, by definition, similar investments were available that paid more. On the other hand, if the market rate of interest had been 6 percent, the issuer of this bond would be foolish to attach a coupon rate of 8 percent to his obligation. Presumably he could, in such a case, attract borrowers by paying less. Simple logic leads us to expect the coupon rate of a newly issued bond to approximate the market rate of interest.

The market rate of interest and the market value of the bond, however, are something else again. The former, as we know, can easily change as a result of changes in money supply, saving, investment, hoarding, dishoarding, and the like. Our task here is to understand how such changes in interest rates relate to changes in bond prices.

Suppose, in our example in Table 16-1, that five years after the bond is issued, the market rate of interest rises from 8 percent to 10 percent. At what price can the holder of the bond sell it? Clearly, he will find no rational person willing to pay $1,000 for it, as this would be tantamount to accepting an $80-per-year income when otherwise similar alternatives are available paying $100 per year. If an actual return of 10 percent on a bond of similar risk is available elsewhere, the maximum price for which our bond can be sold to rational people is $800 (.10X = $80). That is, because $80 is all that this bond pays, the rational purchaser will be willing to pay an amount that "$80 is 10 percent of," and no more.

The holder of the bond will suffer a $200 capital loss if he sells it after the market rate of interest rises to 10 percent. A rise in the rate of interest has thus had the effect of lowering bond prices.

If we look further into the future, say, 10 years from the date of issue, and assume that by that time the market rate of interest has fallen to 5 percent, we get the reverse result. Now the holder of this bond paying $80 per year can expect to find a buyer who will pay substantially *more* than the $1,000 par value. For if 5 percent is a prospective buyer's best alternative, he should be willing to pay up to $1,600 to acquire our bond (.05X = $80). In this case, the seller of the bond realizes a handsome capital gain.

Though the case of a bond with a fixed maturity date requires more complicated arithmetic, it is no different in principle.[7] By way of summary, we can say that **whenever interest rates fall, bond prices rise, and vice versa.**

---

[7]In the case of a bond with five years until maturity, for example, the present value can be computed from the formula

$$V = \frac{R}{1 + i} + \frac{R}{(1 + i)^2} + \frac{R}{(1 + i)^3} + \frac{R}{(1 + i)^4} + \frac{R}{(1 + i)^5} + \frac{P}{(1 + i)^5}$$

where

R = annual coupon payment
V = present market value of the bond
i = market rate of interest
P = par value of the bond, to be repaid at maturity

The expression can be reduced to

$$V = \frac{R}{i}\left[1 - \frac{1}{(1 + i)^5} \right] + \frac{P}{(1 + i)^5}$$

Our example of a perpetuity, in which the interest is paid forever [so that $k/(1 + i)^5$ becomes infinitely small and the last term, $P/(1 + i)^5$, is zero], reduces the formula to $V = R/i$. As the limiting case, the change in present value resulting from any given change in the rate of interest will always be larger for a perpetuity than for the more realistic case of a bond with a fixed maturity date. Also, the closer the bond is to the maturity date, the less the change in its market price that will result from an interest rate change.

This relationship is purely arithmetical and should be interpreted as definitional rather than as a cause-and-effect proposition. To say that interest rates rise is just another way of saying that bond prices fall. To say that bond prices rise is just another way of saying that interest rates have fallen. We shall therefore proceed to use them interchangeably.

An Example of the Advantage of Holding Speculative Balances. Let us get back to the speculative demand for money. If a person confidently expects the rate of interest to rise in the near future, she is, according to Keynes, perfectly justified in holding idle (speculative) money balances over and above her needs for transactions and precautionary purposes for that period. Indeed, she would be irrational if she did not do so.

It is a simple matter to demonstrate the point. Suppose that Miss Jones expects the interest rate to rise from the present 8 percent level to 10 percent within six months. If we return to the example from Table 16-1, she would have to pay $1,000 for the bond if she should buy it today while the market rate is still at 8 percent, but if her expectations turn out to be correct, she can buy it six months from now for $800. Of course, by holding idle money for the six-month period, she would be forgoing an interest return of $40 (half a year's interest). But there is certainly nothing irrational about giving up $40 interest return to be able to save $200 on the purchase price of the bond! Clearly there is logic in a speculative demand for money.

The Community's Speculative Demand for Money. Granting that holding idle money for speculative purposes makes sense, what determines the size of this demand on the part of the community as a whole? Obviously, the more people who expect interest rates to rise, the greater the speculative demand. But this does not advance us very far, as it leaves unanswered the fundamental question, "What leads people to expect changes in interest rates?"

One way of approaching this more fundamental question is to consider people's ideas regarding the *normal range* of interest rates. Our ideas of *high* or *low* interest rates are usually formulated in light of our recent experience. If we have become "used to" interest rates that have varied from 2 to 6 percent, we tend to think of 6 percent as pretty high and 2 percent as quite low. If, on the other hand, we have become accustomed to rates varying from 5 to 15 percent, 12 or 13 percent does not seem unusually high and anything below 6 percent appears to us as quite low.

People's conceptions of what the normal range of interest rate fluctuation *is* must certainly form part of the basis for their expectations of *changes* in rates. For example, if a person, because of his recent observations, forms the judgment that interest rates normally fluctuate within a 2 to 6 percent range, the existence, now, of an 8 percent rate would lead him to expect, almost compellingly, a drop in rates. An 8 percent interest rate appears abnormally high to him and he expects a fall. Similarly, an actual 1.5 percent rate appears abnormally low, leading him to expect an increase.

The same thing applies to the whole community. If the entire community feels that 5 percent is as low as interest rates are going to get and 15 percent is as high as they are likely to go, when interest rates actually reach (or perhaps even surpass) 15 percent, everyone will expect them to fall. If, on the other hand, interest rates actually get down to (or below) 5 percent, everyone will expect them to rise.

Under such circumstances, we should expect rational people to hold *no* speculative money balances when the interest rate is 15 percent, because at such a level they unanimously expect bond prices to *rise,* and they will go out and buy them now rather than wait. Conversely, when the rate of interest is down to 5 percent, we can expect people to hold very large speculative money balances because all look for interest rates to rise (bond prices to fall), and it will be preferable to hold their saving in money form until they do.

Following this logic, it would appear that the community's speculative demand for money will vary inversely with the rate of interest. At rates that are low relative to recent experience, the quantity demanded for speculative purposes will be large; whereas at rates that are high relative to recent experience, speculative balances will be small.

Of course our discussion thus far oversimplifies greatly. No individual is quite sure just where the upper and lower interest rate limits are. Although he may feel that the normal range is 5 percent to 15 percent, he is not quite certain, for example, that rates will not start rising again after dipping to 6 percent. Therefore, instead of holding no speculative balances until a 5 percent interest rate is reached, he may hold *some* at 6 percent, but even more at 5 percent, where the likelihood of a rise is even greater. If the rate of interest should actually reach 4 percent, and

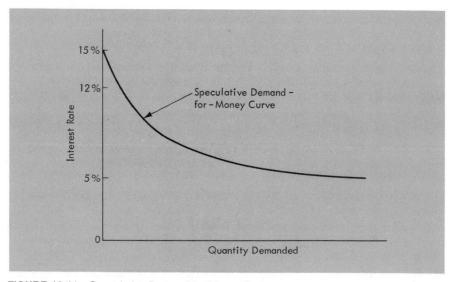

FIGURE 16-11 Speculative Demand-for-Money Curve

this is so low that he is positively convinced it *must* rise, then he will rationally hold *all* his added wealth in idle speculative balances, betting on a drop in bond prices, which appears all but certain.

Then, too, it is a gross oversimplification to talk as if all people were alike, with exactly the same interest rate expectations. Some may look upon 5 percent as the "lowest possible rate" but others may consider 6 or 7 percent as the floor and choose to hold speculative balances when those market rates are realized. Similarly, for the individual who considers an existing rate of 15 percent to be the highest possible, it would be irrational to hold any speculative money balances. Not so, however, for his neighbor who feels that interest rates may rise as high as 17 or 18 percent.

What kind of speculative demand for the nation as a whole would result if all individuals behaved this way? Clearly the quantity of money demanded for speculative reasons would vary inversely with the rate of interest. The demand for speculative balances would look something like that in Figure 16-11.

Here we depict a situation in which no speculative funds are held when the interest rate reaches 15 percent, presumably indicating that when interest rates are that high, *no one* expects a further increase and, therefore, no one holds any speculative money balances. At a rate of 12 percent, however, some few people expect a rise in interest rates, so there is a small positive quantity demanded. The lower the interest rate, the more people come to expect a rise; consequently, the greater the quantity of speculative funds demanded. By the time the rate of interest gets down to as low as 5 percent, according to Figure 16-11, everyone is convinced that interest rates must rise, so that the speculative demand becomes infinite. This area (the flat portion) of the speculative demand-for-money curve has been given the name *liquidity trap* and has a significance to which we shall return shortly.

Post-Keynesian Amendments and Additions to the Demand-for-Money Concept

Some have argued that the liquidity preference theory of interest was the key contribution of the "Keynesian revolution." Certainly it was of major significance. If the demand for money (and hence V') is subject to so unstable a determinant as people's expectations, then we must be much less certain about the effects of a change in the money supply on expenditures than were the early quantity theorists. If changes in M can be partially offset by opposite changes in V', then the money supply is a less all-important variable and monetary policy is a substantially less sure policy tool. The liquidity preference theory of interest, with the speculative demand for money playing the star role, was certainly a major Keynesian contribution.

But the *General Theory* was a pioneering work of the 1930s and Keynes's successors have had nearly a half-century to comprehend, ponder, debate, and improve upon his theoretical framework. A significant portion of all this later work has gone into amending his insights into the demand for money.

Revision in Transactions Demand.   To Keynes, as to his classical predecessors, the prime short-run determinant of the transactions demand for money was the level of income. This much is still generally accepted.

However, several writers have pointed out the importance of another determinant of transactions demand, not stressed by Keynes.[8] The new variable is the rate of interest itself.

To relate the size of transactions balances solely to the level of income to be transacted, these writers point out, is to make the determination of these "active" balances all too mechanistic. To say that there are always x dollars in transactions balances when income is y dollars is equivalent to saying that transactors have no decision to make and no alternatives to consider.

Clearly, within limits at least, this is not the case. Any money held—whether in the form of transactions or asset balances—*could* be lent out at interest. If a person has made the decision to hold an average of $500 in transactions balances— to finance upcoming consumption expenditures—she has presumably decided that the interest return she could earn on it by lending it out for a few days or so is not worth the trouble, cost, and inconvenience of doing so. To deposit one's money in a savings account on day 1 and then withdraw it for spending on day 3 or 4 is more bother than the few cents of interest sacrificed is worth.

This may be so when the rate of interest is 5 percent, but does the same thing necessarily follow when it has risen to 10 percent? And if a 5 percent return on $500 for a week doesn't seem worth two trips to the bank, would the same thing be true if what was being sacrificed was 5 percent of $1 million for a week?

Certainly rational people must consider the opportunity cost of their transactions balances. Although it may normally be convenient to hold an average of $500 in transactions balances to finance $2,000 of expenditures per month, a doubling of the rate of interest may be sufficient incentive to cause a transactor to make those two trips to the savings bank or calls to the money market fund and cut her average transactions balance substantially.

These considerations are especially pertinent in the case of huge business firms and state and local governments whose financial managers handle immense cash balances. When large transactions balances are involved, potentially large amounts of interest are being sacrificed. As interest rates rise, the sophisticated financial managers of big institutions find it more and more in their interests to take the trouble required to "economize" on their transactions balances. For, in these cases, even one day's interest lost may be a substantial amount. There is solid evidence that corporate and government financial managers do, indeed, tend to pare the size of their transactions balances when interest rates rise. And because more than half the money supply is held by business, such actions will likely have a significant impact on the community's total transactions demand.

---

[8]See, for example, A. H. Hansen, *Monetary Theory and Fiscal Policy* (New York: McGraw-Hill, 1949); W. J. Baumol, "The Transactions Demand for Cash: An Inventory Theoretic Approach," *Quarterly Journal of Economics,* November 1952; and James Tobin, "The Interest Elasticity of Transactions Demand for Cash," *Review of Economics and Statistics,* August 1956.

The upshot of all this is that it appears that the transactions demand for money varies positively with the level of income and *negatively with the rate of interest.*

The significance of this amendment to the Keynesian framework is not minor. It can affect the efficiency of monetary policy. For example, if the Federal Reserve is pursuing a "tight money" policy—raising interest rates to restrain expenditures—the fact that individuals, firms, and governments economize on their transactions balances as interest rates rise makes the Fed's job that much more difficult. For if these groups succeed in "economizing" on their transactions balances, they are enabling any given-sized money stock to "do more work." That is, their actions tend to increase the velocity of spending.

Revision in Speculative (or Asset) Demand. The Keynesian speculative money demand depended heavily on the concept of a "normal" rate of interest. Only if the interest rate was below "normal," and therefore expected to rise, was it rational to hold speculative money balances.

According to Keynes,

1. People hold speculative money balances because of expectations of interest rate increases (and accompanying capital losses on bonds).
2. The quantity of speculative money balances demanded is larger, the lower the interest rate (that is, the speculative demand curve has a negative slope) because, the lower the rate, the more intense the expectation of a rise becomes.
3. The *level* of the speculative demand curve for money depends on the range over which people consider interest fluctuations to be *normal*. If, for example, the normal range in the public's mind were from 2 percent to 6 percent, the curve would become flat at 2 percent and cut the vertical axis at 6 percent. If, on the other hand, the public's ideas of normality should change to the point where they consider 4 percent an unusually low rate and 10 percent a high one, the speculative demand curve would shift to the higher limits set by the 4 percent and 10 percent figures.

Some post-Keynesians, while accepting the validity of the concept of an asset demand for money (a demand for money in excess of that needed to finance transactions), have expressed reservations with regard to Keynes's heavy dependence on speculation as its *raison d'être.*

It has been pointed out, for example, that one can explain the existence and negative slope of the asset (speculative) demand-for-money curve without any reliance at all upon the concept of a normal range of interest rates. Even if the public has no prior conceptions of the likely direction of movement of interest rates, the mere knowledge that they are likely to change in either direction will be sufficient to produce a downward-sloping asset demand-for-money curve.[9] The argument is a fairly simple one.

When one buys a bond (instead of holding asset money balances), one obtains the advantage of interest but incurs the disadvantages of illiquidity. Among the

---

[9]See J. Tobin, "Liquidity Preference as Behavior Toward Risk," *Review of Economic Studies,* February 1958.

disadvantages of illiquidity is the risk that interest rates will rise, causing capital losses to the holder.

Now no one can be *sure* that the rate of interest will move in one certain direction, but one can be pretty confident that it will change—up or down. Even if one thinks that there is as great a chance that interest rates will fall (conferring capital gains) as that they will rise (inflicting capital losses), he can hardly be indifferent to the risk that they may rise.

Suppose, for example, that an investor is faced with the following decision. He has $100 that he can keep in money form or use to purchase a $100 bond paying 5 percent. If he keeps the $100 (and the price level is constant), he is certain of what he will have. If he buys the bond *and if the interest rate doesn't rise and cause a capital loss,* he will have $105 next year. But that "if" is not a small one.

Suppose that our investor feels that it is most likely that the interest rate will stay about where it is but that there are equal (smaller) probabilities that it will change (up or down) by 1 percent. The most likely case is that it will not change, so that the $5 of interest return will be clear gain. Does this mean that he will give up the certainty of holding money to buy the bond?

Not necessarily. The small (equal) chance of capital gain or loss arising out of an interest rate fall or rise involves some degree of risk. And although the 5 percent interest return is a "good" thing favoring purchase of the bond, the risk of interest rate change is a "bad" thing opposing its purchase (favoring the holding of idle money instead).

At low rates of interest, the "bad" thing (risk) may well be dominant, so that large money balances will be held. As the interest rate rises, however, the return compensates more and more for the risk involved, so that more bonds will be purchased and less idle money will be held. It is therefore rational to hold asset money balances even without any conception of a "normal" interest rate level. And, following this logic, the asset demand-for-money curve will be negatively sloped, indicating larger asset money balances at lower interest rates.

Nor, in the opinions of many, is the level of the asset demand-for-money curve adequately explained by the range of the public's interest rate expectations. For one thing, we could expect the quantity of money held as an asset to be smaller, at any given rate of interest, the greater the variety (i.e., for other than transactions purposes) of near-monies available. Surely, it has been argued, a community whose claims to wealth consist of nothing but money and highly illiquid bonds will find a need to hold a larger percentage of its wealth in the form of money than another community in which many diverse near-monies, issued by a variety of financial institutions, are available to compete with money as a means of satisfying this desire for liquidity. Keynes, of course, assumed a world in which the only financial assets available were bonds and money. Clearly such an assumption does not fit our current scene, and the argument here is that the existence of near-monies makes a significant difference.

Finally, it has been pointed out that the community's wealth must also be considered as a factor determining the level of the asset demand-for-money curve.

Certainly a wealthier community that is attempting to maintain a portfolio of assets that, in some sense, satisfies its relative desires for liquid and illiquid assets can be expected to demand more money (and other assets too) to hold than a poorer community with similar tastes and expectations.

Once these amendments and additions are made to the Keynesian arguments, we have an asset demand-for-money curve that will lie farther to the right:

1. The greater the community's wealth,
2. The less the variety of other liquid assets available, and
3. The higher the range of interest rates the community looks upon as normal.

The curve will be steeper,

1. The wider the range over which the average person expects interest rate fluctuation, and
2. The greater the divergence of opinion among the public as to the normal range of interest rates. For example, if half the population considers 1 percent a normal low and 6 percent a normal high, while the other half considers 5 percent the likely low and 10 percent the high, the community's asset demand for money will be steeper (stretching from 1 percent to 10 percent) than if everyone agreed on a range from 1 percent to 6 percent.

The Total Demand for Money

Now we must bring our two pieces together. The total demand for money is the sum of the transactions demand and the asset (speculative) demand, and our main task here is to combine the two, both conceptually and graphically.

We concluded earlier that the quantity of money demanded for transactions purposes changes primarily as a result of changes in the level of income.[10] The quantity demanded for asset purposes, on the other hand, varies with the rate of interest. How can we depict these two in the same two-dimensional graph?

Figure 16-12 deals with this problem. In part (a) the transactions demand is drawn; in part (b) the asset demand is reproduced. In part (c) the two are combined to form the **total** demand for money.

Because there is no way to show variations in three variables (interest rate, income level, and quantity of money demanded) in a two-dimensional diagram, explicit reference to one must be eliminated. Our choice, as indicated by Figure 16-12c, is to eliminate income and plot the total demand-for-money curve with the vertical axis measuring off changes in interest rates and the horizontal axis, quantity demanded.

How then do we take account of the unquestioned fact that changes in the

---

[10]We shall, for simplicity's sake, ignore the fact that the transactions demand is also related to the interest rate.

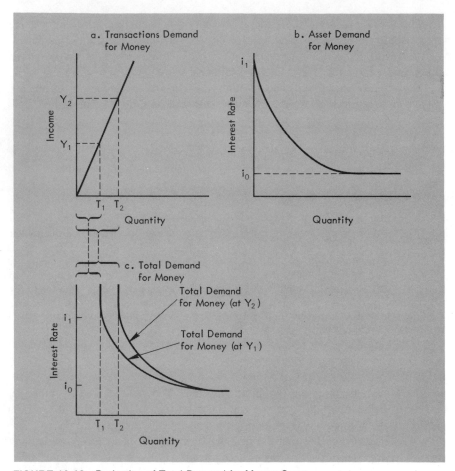

FIGURE 16-12   Derivation of Total Demand-for-Money Curve

level of income, by changing the quantity of money demanded for transactions purposes, will change the total demand for money? Very simply.

As Figure 16-12 shows, we must draw a new total demand-for-money curve for each level of income. For example, in part (a), when the level of income is Y_1, the quantity demanded for transactions purposes is T_1. For this particular income level, a fixed number of dollars is demanded for transactions purposes. We take account of that amount in part (c) by the dashed vertical line labeled T_1. Then, to form the total demand for money, we simply "add on," horizontally, the additional quantities demanded at various rates of interest for asset purposes. The result is the *total demand for money when the level of income is at* Y_1.

If the level of income should rise to Y_2, a whole new total demand-for-money curve is required. Such a change in income would raise the amount demanded for transactions purposes to T_2 in part (a), which, in part (c) is reflected by the dashed

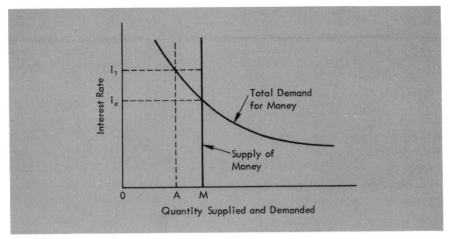

FIGURE 16-13 Supply and Demand for Money—The Equilibrium Rate of Interest

vertical line labeled T_2. When the (assumed unchanged) asset demand is added to this larger transactions demand, the result is a higher total demand-for-money curve, labeled "Total Demand for Money" (at Y_2).

We arrive then, at a diagram in which changes in the level of income shift the entire total demand-for-money curve and changes in the rate of interest (by altering the quantity demanded for asset purposes) change the quantity demanded via movements along a given demand curve.

The Demand for Money, the Supply of Money, and the Equilibrium Rate of Interest

Now that we have made our way through the reasoning that underlies the concept of demand for money, we are prepared to put it together with the supply and discuss the determination of the equilibrium rate of interest.

Supply and demand are shown together in Figure 16-13. The supply of money, being a certain number of dollars at any point in time, is shown as a vertical line.[11] In the diagram, the equilibrium rate of interest is i_e.

Why must the rate of interest tend toward the point where the demand for

---

[11]The vertical line for the supply of money implies an assumption that the supply of money is autonomously determined by the monetary authorities and does not vary with the rate of interest. Recent research indicates that this may not be entirely accurate. The monetary authorities can determine the amount of bank reserves, but the money supply depends also on what banks do with reserves. There are some indications that the money supply actually gets larger at higher interest rates as banks find lending more rewarding. This is a matter of some significance, as it tends to influence the potential effectiveness of both monetary and fiscal policy.

money equals its supply? Suppose that, for the moment, the actual market rate is i_1. At this rate, the quantity of money people *desire* to hold for transactions and asset purposes (read off the total demand-for-money curve) is less than the supply that exists (which they *must* hold). Consequently, some people hold some money *unwillingly* (specifically, the amount AM at i_1).

Now no person needs to hold on to money that he or she does not want to hold. But, short of giving or throwing it away, what can a person *do* with money he or she does not want to hold? One answer, of course, is to spend it to buy bonds.

What will be the effects of unwanted cash being spent to buy bonds? Assuming that the supply of bonds available is unchanged, the immediate result can only be a rise in their prices. But, as we have seen, higher bond prices are equivalent to lower interest rates. The market rate of interest will thus be forced down by the price rise. For how long must this process of buying more bonds with unwanted cash, raising bond prices, and lowering interest rates continue? Clearly, until there is no more unwanted cash to keep it going. A look at Figure 16-13 will show that this point will only be reached when the market rate of interest has fallen from i_1 to i_e. Here, equilibrium is restored in the sense that people willingly hold, in their transactions and asset balances, all the money that exists.

Perhaps one more example will help to clarify this point. Suppose, as in Figure 16-14, that the rate of interest is originally at the equilibrium level of i_1, and that the Federal Reserve, in pursuance of a tight money policy, upsets this equilibrium by reducing the supply of money from S of M_1 to S of M_2.

Immediately after the cut in money supply, individuals find themselves (at the relatively low i_1 interest rate) desiring to hold more money in their transactions and asset balances than there is money to be held. What can they do about this

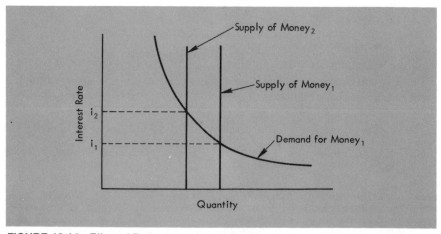

FIGURE 16-14   Effect of Reduction in Money Supply

kind of frustration? *Individuals* can accumulate larger cash balances not only by cutting back on their purchases of bonds but also by offering for sale some of the bonds they already own. Such action, of course, does nothing to increase the supply of money for the community as a whole (merely transferring the shortage from one person to another), but it will have the effect (via lowering the demand for, and raising the supply of, bonds on the market) of lowering bond prices and raising interest rates. When interest rate i_2 is reached, we again have equilibrium because, now, people only want to hold the smaller money supply that exists.

Review Questions

1. Contrast the *loanable funds* and *liquidity preference* theories of interest.
2. "An increase in dishoarding affects interest rates in the same direction as an open-market purchase by the Fed." Do you agree? Explain.
3. What are transactions money balances? Carefully explain how each of the following affect the slope of the transactions demand for money curve:
   a. Payment habits
   b. The availability of credit
   c. The degree of vertical integration of production
4. Explain carefully how and why the current rate of interest might affect the quantity of money demanded for transactions purposes. How might an inverse relation between the rate of interest and the quantity of money demanded for transactions purposes affect the degree of effectiveness of a contractionary monetary policy? Explain.
5. "If the only reason people willingly held money was for transactions purposes, and the quantity demanded was not affected by the rate of interest, one of the key assumptions of the 'old' quantity theory would be valid." Explain.
6. Verbally and graphically explain (using the liquidity preference theory of interest),
   a. How a law outlawing the credit card might affect interest rates.
   b. The process whereby the interest rate would move from the old to the new equilibrium level.
7. Verbally and graphically explain (using the liquidity preference theory of interest),
   a. How a decrease in the level of GNP would affect interest rates.
   b. The process whereby the interest rate would move from the old to the new equilibrium level.
8. Carefully explain the logic of an asset demand for money as well as why the quantity of money demanded for asset purposes would be expected to be larger at lower interest rates.
9. What would be the significance, for expansionary monetary policy, of the economy being currently in a "liquidity trap"?

10. Explain what will happen to the level of the total demand for money curve as a result of
   a. A rise in GNP.
   b. A speedup in payment habits.
   c. A reduction in the level of the range of interest rates considered normal.

11. List all the determinants of the level of the asset demand-for-money curve.

12. Speculate on the likely impact on the effectiveness of monetary policy of the quantity of money *supplied* being directly related to the rate of interest. Can you think of any reason why the quantity of money supplied *might* vary positively with the rate of interest? (Remember "desired" excess reserves?)

17

Review and Use of the Theory—
The Post-Keynesian Model

The three previous chapters were intended to serve as building blocks. Each has concentrated on developing one part of the so-called "post-Keynesian" theory of income determination. The task that remains is to assemble the pieces to construct a single, usable, theoretical framework.

Our approach will be two-pronged. First, we shall review and summarize the important ideas developed in Chapters 14, 15, and 16, winding up with a graphical model of the economy that encompasses them all. Then, we shall go to some lengths to demonstrate how such a model can be used as a framework for analyzing the effects of various changes in the economy on its performance.

Summary of the Parts and Development of the Whole

A Review

We started off in Chapter 14 with a discussion of the immediate determinants of the level of production and income. We observed first that production tends to rise whenever aggregate demand exceeds aggregate supply; that production will fall whenever aggregate demand falls short of aggregate supply; and that a change in either direction will stop only when income and production reach the equilibrium level where aggregate demand just equals aggregate supply.

When we looked at this mechanism in more detail, we saw that the all-important aggregate demand level was composed of consumption spending, investment spending, and government spending. Assuming, as a first approximation, that investment and government spending were autonomously determined by outside forces, we concentrated on the determinants of consumption. Here we con-

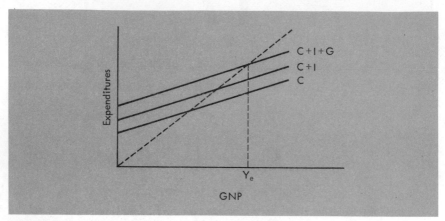

FIGURE 17-1   Equilibrium Income Determination Diagram

cluded that, given consumer expectations, wealth, and the like, consumption spending varies with the level of income. These considerations provided us with the basis for producing Figure 17-1 to depict the determination of the equilibrium level of production.

What this diagram tells us is that, given the amount spent by government and investors, if we survey the public so that we know how much it will spend on consumption at various levels of income, we can, from these three pieces of information, figure out the equilibrium level of production and income.

But, of course, the amount spent on investment is not a given datum. Consequently, we went on in Chapter 15 to investigate the investment decision somewhat more thoroughly. Here we developed an investment demand schedule, entitled

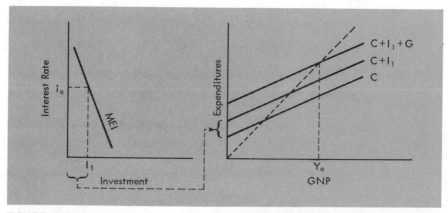

FIGURE 17-2   MEI and Income Determination Diagrams Combined

the marginal efficiency of investment schedule, the level of which depended mainly on business managers' expectations of the future profits to be had by investing. This MEI curve, we said, tells us how much investment spending there will be, at various rates of interest. The two diagrams together (as in Figure 17-2), then, provided us with a more complete picture than Figure 17-1 does alone.

Here we were able to say, given the rate of interest, that investment spending will be so and so much and that it, along with government spending and the consumption function, will determine the equilibrium income level.

This, of course, led us finally to investigate what determines the rate of interest. To fit in more easily with our analysis, we chose to emphasize the liquidity preference theory of interest, wherein interest rates depend on the demand for and supply of money. Here we saw that the demand for money is composed of two parts, the transactions and asset demands. The size of the transactions demand depends, most importantly, on the level of income, whereas the quantity demanded for asset purposes varies inversely with the rate of interest. The two together make up the total demand for money, which, along with the supply of money, determines the equilibrium rate of interest.

Thus we have made a complete circle. In Figure 17-2, constructed on the basis of Chapters 14 and 15, we say "*given the rate of interest*, the MEI schedule plus the consumption schedule and government spending *will tell us the equilibrium level of income*." In Figure 17-3, based on Chapter 16, we say "*given the level of income*, we can compute the quantity of money demanded for transactions purposes, which, along with the asset demand and the supply of money, *will tell us the equilibrium interest rate*." Clearly these two parts of the analysis are interdependent and need to be combined for a complete theory. That is precisely what we plan to do next.

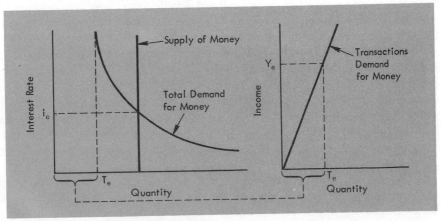

FIGURE 17-3 Interest Rate Determination

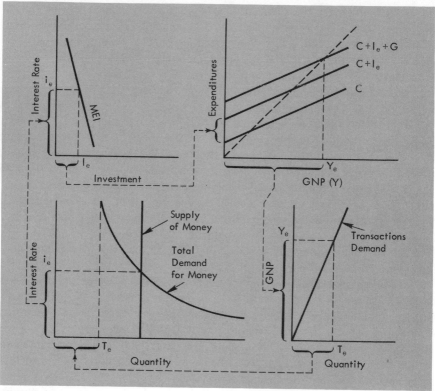

FIGURE 17-4 An Economy in "General" Equilibrium

The Four-Diagram Model

Figure 17-4 presents the full theory in diagrammatic form. It includes nothing we have not discussed before, the only new feature being the fact that we have combined it all into one four-diagram model.

Figure 17-4 is drawn to show an economy in **"general"** *equilibrium*. That is to say, the "equilibrium" level of income determined in the upper-right-hand drawing calls forth (in the lower-right-hand drawing) a quantity of money demanded for transactions purposes, which, along with the asset demand and money supply (lower-left-hand drawing), determines an "equilibrium" rate of interest that permits a level of investment (upper-left-hand drawing) consistent with the level of income with which we started. This is a long and, perhaps, tortuous statement, but it will bear study.

What we have now is a new situation. Whereas in Chapter 14 we could speak of the equilibrium level of production in terms of the single condition, *aggregate demand equals aggregate supply,* and in Chapter 16 we could consider the equilibrium rate of interest as wherever *the demand for money equals the supply of money,* now things are more complicated. Now that we are considering both the goods market and the money market in one interdetermined whole, *general* equilibrium requires that all three of the following conditions be met:

1. Aggregate demand equals aggregate supply.
2. Demand for money equals supply of money.
3. The production level and interest rate levels must be consistent with one another.[1]

If, for example, the rate of interest at which the demand for money equals the supply of money is one that will shortly cause investment spending to change, then the production level must change too. This would *not* be a state of general equilibrium. Only when there is no tendency toward change in any part of the four-diagram model do we have general equilibrium.

The Determinants of the Slopes and Levels of the Curves

The purpose of the four-diagram model is to provide us with a framework for analyzing the economic effects of any one of a large number of initial changes. The "initial changes" that this model equips us to deal with are changes in the determinants of the levels and/or slopes of the curves. To facilitate the task coming up in the next section, let us complete our review by listing, in one place, most of the determinants discussed in Chapters 14, 15, and 16. It will be convenient to handle this in outline form, starting first with the curve in the lower-right-hand sector and working our way around clockwise.

Some Major Determinants of Slopes and Levels of Curves in the Four-Diagram Model

A. Determinants of Slope of Transactions Demand-for-Money Curve
   1. Frequency of payment habits—a speedup would steepen the curve
   2. Development of financial structure—further development would steepen the curve
   3. Degree of vertical integration of industry—the greater the integration, the steeper the curve
B. Determinants of Level of (Total) Demand-for-Money Curve
   1. Transactions demand, which is larger the higher the level of income
   2. Level of speculative (asset) demand, which will be higher the higher the range of interest rates people feel is normal, the larger the community's wealth, and the smaller the choice of other highly liquid assets
C. Determinants of Position of Supply-of-Money Curve
   1. Federal Reserve policy
   2. Treasury policy
   3. Public's preferred asset ratio
   4. Commercial bank policy as to desired excess reserves

---

[1]It is implicitly assumed that when the money market is cleared (i.e., when the demand for money equals the supply of money), the bond market is also cleared.

D. Determinants of Level of MEI Curve
  1. State of technical knowledge—curve usually raised by technological innovations
  2. Stock of existing capital goods—curve is usually lower the more capital goods there are because of diminishing marginal productivity
  3. Level of business taxes—curve is generally higher, the lower the business taxes
  4. Degree of "optimism" or "pessimism" of business managers regarding future profit prospects—the more optimistic, the higher the curve
E. Determinants of Level of Aggregate Demand (C + I + G) Curve
  1. Level of investment, which depends on the MEI and interest rate
  2. Level of government spending on goods and services, which is considered autonomous—that is, determined by noneconomic factors
  3. Level of consumption function, which depends, in turn, on
    a. Consumer expectations
    b. Consumer wealth
    c. Consumer tastes (attitudes toward virtues of saving)
    d. Level of personal taxes
    e. Stock of consumer durables already on hand
    f. Age composition of the population

Examples of Use of the Complete Theory Using the Four-Diagram Approach

We are now prepared to make use of our model. Before tracing through a number of specific examples, however, it might be helpful to provide some ground rules to facilitate the use of the four-diagram framework.

We shall always start off with an economy in general equilibrium in the sense in which this condition is pictured in Figure 17-4. That is, we shall assume that prior to a change in one of the curves, the equilibrium rate of interest determined in the lower-left-hand graph is consistent with the equilibrium level of income determined in the upper-right-hand graph, and vice versa.

Then we shall assume a change in conditions that changes one of the curves and attempt to trace the effects of that change on the economy, until a new "general" equilibrium position (where once again the rate of interest is consistent with the level of income, and vice versa) is reached.

The first task will be to locate the curve (or curves) affected by the assumed change in conditions. Once the nature of this original shift is determined, its effects should be traced through the four diagrams in a *clockwise* direction. That is to say, if the initial change affects the rate of interest determined in the lower-left-hand graph, the effect of this on the volume of investment in the upper-left-hand graph should be read off next, followed by a determination of the effect of this change in investment on the equilibrium level of income in the upper-right-hand graph, and so on.

As we shall soon see, it will be necessary to "go around" our four-diagram model more than once before a new, internally consistent equilibrium is reached. To facilitate discussion, we shall refer to these circuits of our model as "rounds."

The end of a round will be assumed to have been reached each time we determine a new level of income in the upper-right-hand graph.

For example, if our initial change were in the lower-left-hand graph, the rate of interest would be affected first. This would, in turn, affect the level of investment, which would then alter the level of income in the upper-right-hand graph. At this point we have completed round 1 of the change toward a new equilibrium. The effect of this change in income on the transactions demand for money, its subsequent effect on the total demand for money and the interest rate, this secondary effect on investment, and finally on the level of income, will be referred to as round 2 of the complete change. And so on.

The Effects of an Increase in the Supply of Money

Suppose that the initial equilibrium of the economy is disturbed by a Federal Reserve open-market purchase from the nonbank public. This, of course, has the immediate effect of moving the money supply line out to the right (to S or M_1, in Figure 17-5).

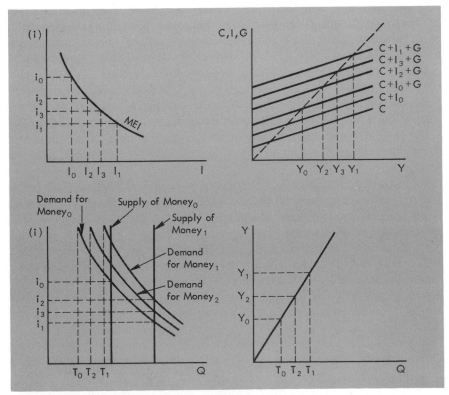

FIGURE 17-5 Effect of Rise in Supply of Money

Such a change, other things being equal, will tend to lower the rate of interest from i_0 to i_1. At this lower rate of interest, the upper-left-hand graph tells us, the amount spent on investment will rise from I_0 to I_1. Going on over to the upper-right-hand graph, we then see that, given the MPC (slope of consumption function), such a rise in investment will raise the level of income from Y_0 to Y_1. This is the end of round 1, and, as can easily be seen, the open-market operations have had the initial effect of raising the level of income.

But that is not the end of the adjustment, since a new "general" equilibrium has not yet been achieved—interest rate level i_1 and income level Y_1 are *not* consistent with one another. The increase in people's incomes (from Y_0 to Y_1) generated in our "round 1" result will mean that they will now need larger transactions money balances to finance a higher level of transactions. Consequently (in what we shall refer to as a "round 2" adjustment), the quantity of money demanded for transactions purposes must rise from T_0 to T_1. And this, in turn, will push the total demand-for-money curve (lower-left-hand graph) out to the right from D for M_0 to D for M_1. Such a shift will raise the rate of interest somewhat, from i_1 to i_2 (but i_2 will almost certainly still be lower than i_0). The higher rate of interest will cut back investment from I_1 to I_2, which, in turn, will reduce the level of income from Y_1 to Y_2 (Y_2 will still be higher than the original equilibrium of Y_0).

We have now completed round 2 and it can be seen that its effects are to offset partially the effects of round 1. The first round, considering the direct effects of the increased money supply, raised the income level to Y_1, but the second round, which takes account of the increased transactions demand called forth by that rise in income, operates, in lesser degree, in the opposite direction.

And even yet we are not through. There is a third round to be considered. The reduction in income (from Y_1 to Y_2) will lower the transactions demand once again (from T_1 to T_2), which will lower the total demand for money (from D for M_1 to D for M_2) and lower the rate of interest (from i_2 to i_3). This will permit a rise in investment (from I_2 to I_3), which will raise the level of income again, this time to Y_3.

We need go no further with the detailed description of this adjustment process, although it will be apparent to the alert reader that further rounds would be necessary before a new equilibrium in which the rate of interest and the level of income are consistent would be reached.

Indeed, if we carried on with the same approach through several more "rounds," the approach to equilibrium taken by the level of income and the rate of interest would appear to be an oscillating one such as depicted in Figure 17-6.

In Figure 17-6a, Y_0 is taken to be the initial equilibrium level of income. Y_1 depicts the rise we get in round 1 as a result of increase in money supply. Then round 2 brings us back down to Y_2, and round 3 raises income once again to Y_3. This oscillating process continues through successive rounds at lesser and lesser amplitude until, finally, a new equilibrium level of income consistent with the interest rate is approached.

Similarly, in Figure 17-6b, the route apparently followed by the rate of interest is sketched in. The increased supply of money initially lowers the rate of

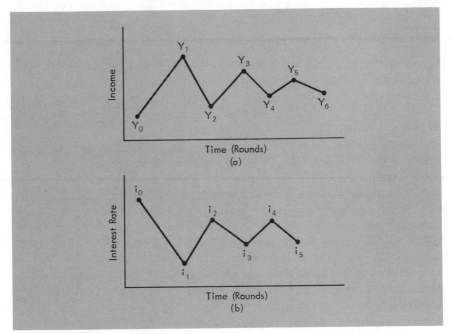

FIGURE 17-6 Path of Income and Interest Rate Changes Through Time Assumed in Four-Diagram Model of the Economy

interest from i_0 to i_1. The higher level of income permitted by i_1, however, raises the transactions demand for money in round 2, producing i_2. This then gives way in the third round to i_3, and so forth.

Now as Figures 17-5 and 17-6 make amply clear, tracing the adjustment process through all the way to a new "general" equilibrium would be a cumbersome and, indeed, impossible task. Fortunately, for our purposes, completing round after round after round is neither necessary nor desirable.

We need not go beyond two rounds to generalize about the ultimate "general" equilibrium effects on income and interest rate. If the given change in conditions is such as to raise (lower) the level of income in round 1, unless very peculiar circumstances exist, the effect of round 2 will be to lower (raise) income to a point below (above) that reached in round 1 but still above (below) the original level. Future rounds will simply cause further fluctuations *within the limits reached in rounds 1 and 2*. The new general equilibrium results then, would normally be

1. Higher (lower) than the original equilibrium.
2. Lower (higher) than the income after round 1.
3. Higher (lower) than the income after round 2.[2]

---

[2]The same generalization holds for the interest rate. If the effect in the first round is to lower (raise) it, it will be raised (lowered) somewhat in the second round and then lowered (raised) again in the third. In equilibrium, it will be lower (higher) than originally but higher (lower) than after the first round.

An Important Note of Caution

Before we proceed, it is most important that the student recognize that the "round-by-round" adjustment process just sketched is by no means a literal description of the path that the economy *actually* follows in response to a change in underlying conditions. Rather it represents a strictly pedagogical device whereby we are attempting to highlight some of the causal relationships involved in the adjustment process.

To discuss the adjustment of the economy to a change in conditions, one has essentially three choices. First, to trace the process of change, one might develop a truly dynamic analysis of the path of adjustment. Such an approach, however, would be extremely complex and well beyond the scope of this book. Second, one might largely ignore the *process* by which adjustment occurs, choosing instead to concentrate solely on the old and new equilibrium positions involved. This approach, of course, has the advantage of bypassing the complexities involved in discussing the process of change, but this very advantage necessitates the omission of explanatory causal interconnections that some would consider essential. A third approach is to create an artificial (and unrealistic) description of the adjustment process to bring out the causal interconnections that *do* exist when the economy moves from one equilibrium position to another. This, of course, is the course followed in the bulk of this chapter.

The four-diagram models' "round-by-round" approach has the advantage of showing the "whys" of change more clearly. But it carries with it the hazard of appearing to say more than it really does. Although it is extremely useful as a pedagogical device, Figure 17-6 and the "round-by-round" approach must *not* be taken as a description of reality. The level of income and rate of interest do not, in fact, bounce up and down like a yo-yo in the approach to a new general equilibrium position.

Determinants of the Effectiveness of Changes in Money Supply in Affecting the Level of Income

As we observed earlier, the main function of the Federal Reserve System is to control the supply of money to contribute to price stability and full employment. In other words, the System attempts to use its controls over the money supply to hold down on inflationary rises in income in boom periods and to contribute to increases in income (in the form of increased production and employment) during recessions.

Having just discussed the process through which changes in the money supply affect the level of income, mention of the *magnitude* of the effect of money supply changes on income levels may well be in order.

As a policy weapon, money supply changes are intended to "work" via their effect on aggregate demand. A cut in the money supply is "successful" as a contracyclical tool to the degree that it cuts or holds down aggregate demand. Conversely, an increase in the money supply, in the same context, is successful to the degree that it raises or holds up aggregate demand. Our question here is, "Under what conditions will changes in the money supply be most effective in achieving their goal of affecting aggregate demand?"

Possible Effects on Interest Rates. Let us look at it first from the point of view of antirecession monetary policy—a rise in the supply of money. If such a policy is to affect aggregate demand and income levels, it must first lower the interest rate.[3]

How effective it will be will depend, in part, on *how much* the interest rate is lowered as a result of any given money supply increase. Clearly, this in turn depends partly upon how high interest rates already are. As Figure 17-7 shows, if interest rates are currently near the top of their "normal range," that portion of the demand-for-money curve will normally be very steep and money supply increases will tend to cause relatively large interest rate declines. If, on the other hand, the interest rate is already so low that many people expect increases, the relevant portion of the demand-for-money curve may be relatively flat and money supply increases will elicit only moderate reduction in the interest rate. The extreme situation would be if there existed, and we were in, a perfectly horizontal portion of the demand-for-money curve (the liquidity trap). Here, expansionary monetary

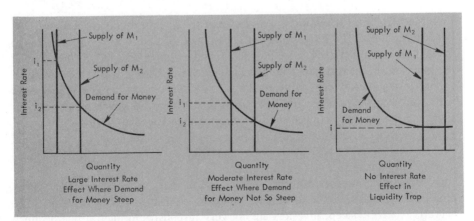

FIGURE 17-7 Effect of Slope of Demand-for-Money Curve on the Amount of Interest Rate Change

---

[3]It should be observed that, according to the modern version of the quantity theory, money supply increases may raise aggregate demand directly as asset holders seek to trade off the new, unwanted money for other assets, as well as indirectly via an initial lowering of the interest rate. This point of view will be considered in the following chapter.

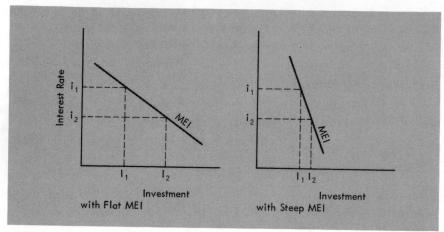

FIGURE 17-8   Effect of Slope of MEI Curve on the Amount of Change in Investment Spending

policy would be useless, since money supply increases would be completely absorbed into speculative balances, permitting no decline in interest rates whatever.[4]

We can conclude, therefore, that **money supply changes will have more effect on interest rates the steeper the slope of the total demand-for-money curve in the area affected.**

Possible Effects on Investment.   But even if the interest rate is reduced, success is not guaranteed. The drop in interest rates is not the end, but merely a means to the end. The goal here is to raise production and employment, and the hope is that the reduction in interest rates will permit such a rise. Now it is true that, to some extent, lower interest rates will encourage more spending by anyone who spends with borrowed funds. Not only business investors but also government and consumers make use of borrowed funds to finance their spending. But the latter two groups seem to be unusually insensitive to the interest rate as a cost factor, and we shall oversimplify here by assuming that they do not react at all. This leaves us with only business investors to consider.

How much more investment spending can be expected consequent to a given drop in the interest rate? It all depends on the slope of the MEI curve. If the MEI curve is relatively steep, investors are not very responsive to interest rate declines and investment will not rise much. Conversely, a flat MEI curve indicates a situation wherein an interest rate decrease will permit a sizable rise in investment spending. Figure 17-8 illustrates the two possibilities.

Our conclusion is that **money supply increases (and consequent interest**

---

[4]It should be noted that empirical investigation has found no evidence of a true liquidity trap in the United States.

rate declines) **will lead to larger increases in investment spending the flatter the MEI curve in the area affected.**

Effects on Equilibrium Income Levels. If a money supply increase has lowered interest rates and that, in turn, has raised investment spending, then we can expect (consider the upper-right-hand diagram in Figure 17-5) a rise in the equilibrium level of income. How large a rise in GNP will result from a given increase in investment spending depends, of course, on the size of the multiplier. Since the multiplier is larger, the larger the MPC, and since the MPC *is* the slope of the consumption function, we can say **the steeper the consumption function, the larger the rise in GNP that will result from a given money supply increase.**

Effect of the Slope of the Transactions Demand-for-Money Curve on the (Undesirable) "Second-Round" Effect. Finally, we must consider the potential effects of round 2. If the money supply increase has succeeded in raising GNP in the first "round," it will lead to an increase in the quantity of money demanded for transactions purposes at the beginning of the second. And since any such increase must ultimately lead to some rise in the total demand for money, some rise in interest rates (barring a liquidity trap), and some cutback in investment spending, it is an undesirable change tending to offset some of the desired effects on GNP achieved during the first round. (*The "second round" always works to undercut somewhat the effects of the "first round."*) Consequently, to maximize the desired effect of a money supply change on GNP, it is preferable to minimize the unfavorable second-round effect.

What slope of the transactions demand-for-money curve will minimize these

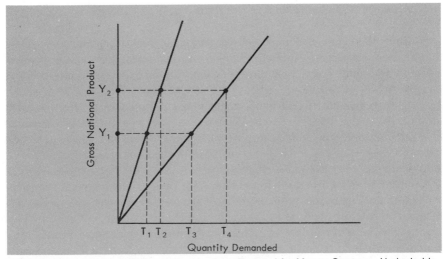

FIGURE 17-9   Effect of Slope of Transactions Demand-for-Money Curve on Undesirable "Second-Round" Effects

TABLE 17-1

Determinants of the Effectiveness and/or Ineffectiveness of Money Supply Changes

Changes in the Money Supply Will Have Greater Effects on Income If	Changes in the Money Supply Will Be Relatively Ineffective in Changing Income If
1. The total demand-for-money curve is steep in the affected area.	1. The total demand-for-money curve is flat in the affected area.
2. The MEI curve is flat in the affected area.	2. The MEI curve is steep in the affected area.
3. The consumption function is steep.	3. The consumption function is flat.
4. The transactions demand-for-money curve is steep, leading to small offsetting second-round effects.	4. The transactions demand-for-money curve is flat, causing a large offsetting second-round effect.

undesirable second-round developments? A steep curve, because the steeper the transactions demand curve, the smaller the increase in the quantity of money demanded for transactions purposes that will result from any given first-round GNP increase. We can therefore conclude **the rise in the general equilibrium GNP that will result from an increase in the money supply will be greater the steeper the transactions demand-for-money curve.** This is illustrated in Figure 17-9. Note there that with the steeper curve, a rise in GNP from Y_1 to Y_2 will increase the quantity demanded by only T_1T_2, whereas with the flatter curve, the increase is the much larger amount, T_3T_4.

The effects of the slopes of all these curves on the effectiveness of money supply changes in altering GNP are summarized in Table 17-1.

The Effects of an Improvement in Business Managers' Expectations of the Future

Suppose, because of important technological improvements, for example, that business managers' expected returns from investment are sharply increased. Other things being equal, what changes could this be expected to bring about in the economy?

Clearly the most likely initial major impact would be an MEI curve shift upward and to the right. As Figure 17-10 shows, this would permit an initial rise in investment spending from I_0 to I_1. This in turn would raise aggregate demand (from $C + I_0 + G$ to $C + I_1 + G$) and raise the level of income from Y_0 to Y_1. And this is the end of round 1.

The higher income level would then raise the quantity of money demanded for transactions purposes to T_1 from T_0. This would raise the total demand for money (from D for M_0 to D for M_1) and raise the rate of interest to i_1. A higher interest rate would cause some cutback in investment spending (from I_1 to I_2), which would, in turn, lower aggregate demand and the level of income from Y_1 to Y_2. This marks the end of round 2.

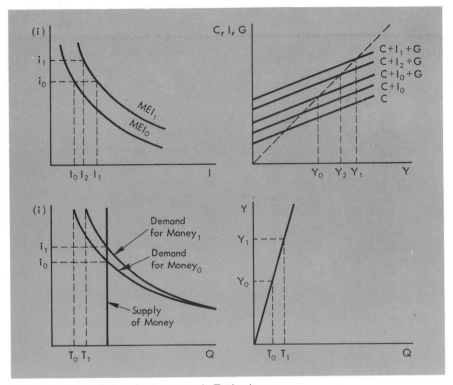

FIGURE 17-10 Effect of Improvement in Technology

If we should follow this process on to its conclusion at a new stable equilibrium, we would find that the level of income would be somewhere between Y_1 and Y_2. In any event it would be higher than Y_0. The rate of interest would finally end up higher than i_0, but somewhat lower than i_1.

The Effects of a Speedup in Paydays

Although it is hardly a very likely change in the short run, it will nevertheless be instructive to trace through the effects of a change in payment habits. Suppose, for example, that all business firms suddenly started paying weekly rather than monthly salaries.

As seen in the preceding chapter, such a change will reduce the need for transactions balances, thereby increasing the slope of the transactions demand-for-money curve in the lower-right-hand graph (from transactions demand for M_0 to transactions demand for M_1) in Figure 17-11. This, at income level Y_0, will lower the quantity of money demanded for transactions purposes from T_0 to T_1.

The result of the cut in the transactions demand will be a shift in the total demand for money to the left (to D for M_1) and a fall in the rate of interest (from

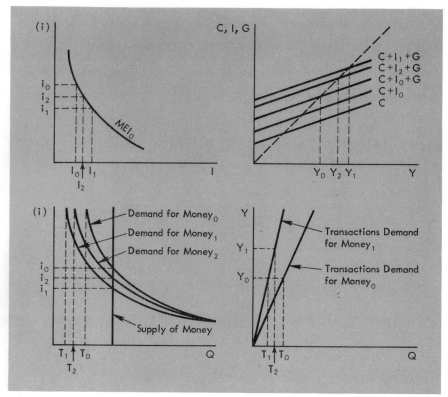

FIGURE 17-11 Effect of Speedup in Payment Habits

i_0 to i_1). The lower interest rate permits a rise in investment (from I_0 to I_1), which, in turn, raises the level of income from Y_0 to Y_1.

In round 2, the quantity of money demanded for transactions purposes rises from T_1 to T_2, the total demand for money rises from D for M_1 to D for M_2, and the rate of interest comes back up to i_2. The higher interest cuts back investment to I_2, which lower the level of income from Y_1 to Y_2. If this were followed through, the general equilibrium level of income would be between Y_1 and Y_2 (and definitely higher than Y_0), whereas the final equilibrium interest rate would be between i_1 and i_2, definitely lower than the initial level of i_0.

The Effect of a Cut in Personal Taxes, Creating a Government Deficit

Our four-diagram model also equips us to trace through the effects of a fiscal policy measure, but, as we shall see, the analysis can be more complicated. The additional wrinkle introduced here has to do with the method used by the government to finance the deficit that it incurs (or the means of disposing of the surplus).

We already know, from Part I, that if the Treasury finances a deficit by selling bonds to the nonbank public and then spends the proceeds, there is no net effect on the money supply, whereas borrowing from the banks will increase the stock of money. And we noted then that the latter course would be the more expansionary of the two. With the aid of our theoretical model, we are now in a position to be more specific about the implications of these two alternatives.

Treasury Deficit Spending Financed by Borrowing from the Nonbank Public—No Change in Money Supply. Suppose that a government deficit is created by means of a (lump-sum) cut in personal taxes (assuming unchanged government spending) and the amount of the deficit is raised by sale of U.S. securities to members of the nonbank public.

In such a case, the sale of the bonds cuts the public's money supply, but immediate spending by the government will raise it again by an equivalent amount. Hence, on balance, the supply of money is unaffected.

But, of course, aggregate demand *is* affected by the tax cut. By cutting personal taxes, the government permits a larger slice of gross income to go to individuals in the form of disposable income. They, in turn, can be counted on to spend a substantial part of it on additional consumption. Graphically, then, the first important effect on our four-diagram model will be to shift the consumption function and the aggregate demand line to the higher level of $C_1 + I_0 + G$,[5] as in Figure 17-12. The upward shift will be by somewhat less than the amount of the tax cut so long as (as we assume) that the MPC is less than 1.[6]

The initial rise in consumption permitted by the tax cut, plus the additional "induced" rises in consumption caused by the multiplier, will drive income up form Y_0 to Y_1. In short order, then, we complete round 1. The fiscal policy has had its desired effect by raising aggregate demand and income (and, it is hoped, employment along with them).

But, unfortunately, round 2 will have effects on the rate of interest that will, to some degree, offset part of the rise in income. The increase to Y_1 will raise the quantity of money demanded for transactions purposes from T_0 to T_1; this will raise the total demand-for-money curve to D for M_1 and raise the interest rate from i_0 to i_1. The higher interest rate will cut investment spending back to I_1, which will lower aggregate demand from $C_1 + I_0 + G$ to $C_1 + I_1 + G$ and reduce the income level to Y_2. Further revolutions will culminate in a new equilibrium level somewhere between Y_1 and Y_2 and a new equilibrium interest rate between i_0 and i_1.

---

[5]As we are not assuming that taxes are related to income, we can show this effect with a parallel upward shift of the consumption schedule. If the cut had been in income taxes, the consumption schedule would become steeper, with a larger multiplier.

[6]In cases of fiscal policy, confusion can be avoided by starting the analysis in one of the two top diagrams—with the initial effects of the tax or government expenditure change, and then considering the effects on the money supply, if any, in round 2.

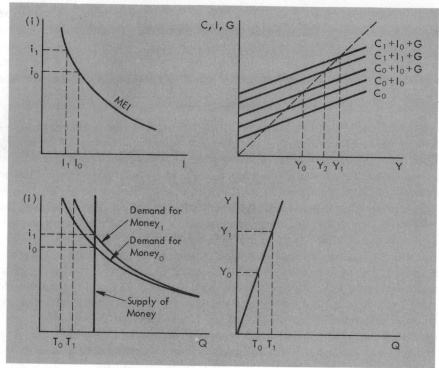

FIGURE 17-12 Effect of Deficit Spending—Deficit Borrowed from Nonbank Public

What are the implications of all this in so many words? Simply this. The reduction in taxes is successful in raising the level of income, but part of the "good" effects on aggregate demand are undercut because the government has financed its deficit in a manner that raised interest rates and cut back on private investment. This tendency for the intended effects of a fiscal policy measure to be undercut because the interest rate changes induced by the financing of the government's deficit affect investment spending in the opposite direction has come to be called the **crowding out** effect of fiscal policy. Its magnitude is the subject of substantial current debate. Although the majority of the economics profession appears to retain the conviction that it does not eliminate all the intended effects of a fiscal policy measure (as we have depicted it in Figure 17-12), some of the so called "modern monetarists" maintain that it does and that, consequently, fiscal policy measures that involve no money supply changes are totally ineffective.

We shall have more to say about this issue in the next chapter. For now, it is important for the student to recognize that the conclusion generally reached in the introductory macroeconomics course to the effect that "if the multiplier is 4 and government spending is raised by 10, the equilibrium GNP will rise by 40"

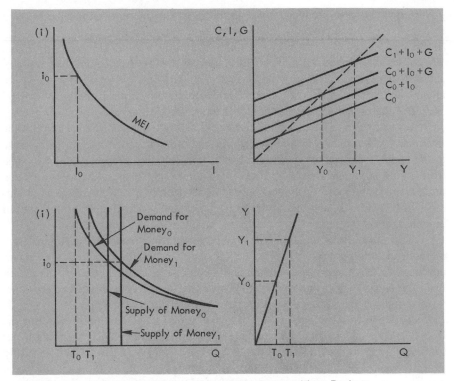

FIGURE 17-13 Effect of Deficit Spending—Deficit Borrowed from Banks

only holds if the effects on aggregate demand of financing the deficit (our "second-round" effects) are ignored.[7]

Treasury Deficit Spending Financed by Borrowing from the Banks—Rise in Supply of Money. Suppose, in contrast to the case just discussed, that the deficit created by the tax cut is financed by sale of U.S. securities to the banks rather than to the public. In this case, as pointed out earlier, the money that the government borrows is newly created by the banks and, when spent, the money supply of the public rises.

In terms of our four-diagram model, we again start in the upper-right-hand graph, showing the upward shift in aggregate demand and the rise in income caused by the tax cut. In Figure 17-13, income rises initially from Y_0 to Y_1.

As before, the higher income level will require more money for transactions purposes, which, in turn, will raise the demand for money from D for M_0 to D for M_1. But here we encounter something new. By selling bonds to the banks, the

---

[7]That is, as we shall see in the following section, unless the deficit is financed in a manner that increases the money supply.

government has also produced a rise in the supply of money—from S of M_0 to S of M_1. Unlike the situation in which the bonds were sold to the public, the effect (if any) on the rate of interest during this second round is indeterminate. In Figure 17-13, we have drawn the relevant schedules so that the changes in the supply of and demand for money exactly offset one another, but, of course, this need not always be the case. The interest rate could rise slightly if the increase in demand exceeded that in supply or fall slightly if the reverse occurred.

So far as general conclusions are concerned, one thing can be said with some assurance. When the deficit is financed via sale of bonds to the banks, the increase in the supply of money that accompanies it will certainly keep the rate of interest from rising as much as it would have had the bonds been sold to the nonbank public with the money supply unchanged. Consequently, private investment spending will be cut back less than in the former case and the final equilibrium level of income *must* be higher. "Crowding out," in other words, must be less.

This, then, tells us something more specific about the merits of different methods of handling fiscal policy. If deficit spending is carried out with the express purpose of raising aggregate demand and income, it is better to borrow the deficit from the banks than from the public because the former course will be less likely to raise interest rates and cut back on private investment spending.

These results also permit us to make some generalizations regarding the "best" means of financing deficits when the purpose of the deficit spending is *not* to raise aggregate demand. Take the case of an all-out war effort (such as World War II) where we are already at full employment but the government deems it necessary to operate at a substantial deficit because of very heavy military expenditures.

In such a situation, increases in aggregate demand drive money income up by means of inflationary price rises (in the absence of direct controls over prices). Anything that can be done to hold down on the inflationary rise in aggregate demand will be helpful.

Clearly the inflationary pressure will be lessened if the deficit is financed by borrowing from the nonbank public rather than the banks. Why? Because that course will result in a rise in the rate of interest (demand for money rises but supply does not), which will have the favorable effect of cutting private investment somewhat. If the deficit were financed via sale of bonds to the banks, the increased demand for money, caused by the rise in income, might well be offset by the increase in the supply of money, forestalling any rise in interest rates. Borrowing from the nonbank public is, thus, less inflationary.

The Effect of a Reduction in Government Expenditures, Creating a Tax Surplus

One further example of the operation of our model may be useful. Suppose that the government, to combat inflationary pressures, cuts government spending without reducing taxes, thereby creating a tax surplus. As in the previous case (where we had to specify how the deficit was financed), we cannot really spell out the effects unless we are told what the government does with its tax surplus. The purpose of the policy is presumably to cut aggregate demand and prevent further price increases, but its effectiveness will depend partly on the disposition of the surplus.

Normally, such tax surpluses are used to retire part of the existing national debt. But it makes a difference whether the securities retired are those held by banks or those held by the nonbank public.

Treasury Tax Surplus Used to Retire Securities Held by the Nonbank Public— No Change in Money Supply.

The reduction in government spending affects the upper-right-hand graph by reducing aggregate demand and, hence, the money level of income (from Y_0 to Y_1 in Figure 17-14). This, in turn, reduces the quantity of money needed for transactions purposes and cuts the total demand for money (from D for M_0 to D for M_1).

As the paying off of bonds held by the public places the surplus money collected in taxes back into circulation, the money supply is unaffected and the rate of interest must fall. Such a fall will permit more investment spending (from

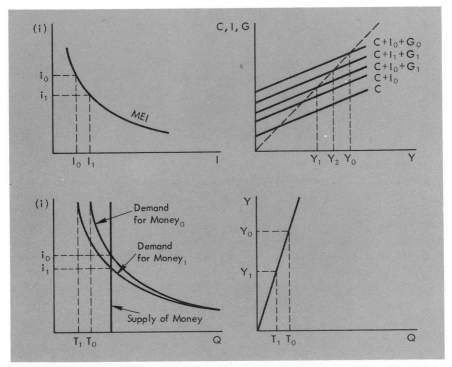

FIGURE 17-14 Effect of Tax Surplus—Surplus Used to Retire Bonds Held by Nonbank Public

I_0 to I_1), and this increase will raise aggregate demand back up a bit, offsetting, to some degree, the intended contractionary effects of the surplus.

Treasury Tax Surplus Used to Retire Securities Owned by the Banks—Money Supply Is Cut.   Where the intent of the policy is to cut aggregate demand and combat inflation, more desirable results will be forthcoming from using the tax surplus to retire securities held by the banks. This is because, in this case, the money supply is reduced (see Figure 17-15).

Once again the cut in government spending reduces aggregate demand and the money level of income. This will lower the need for transactions balances and lower the demand for money. In contrast to the previous case, however, the lower demand for money need not lead to a reduction in interest rates and an undesirable rise in investment spending. For here the cut in the demand for money may be completely offset by the cut in the supply of money, and interest rates can thus remain unchanged. The result must be a greater total reduction in aggregate demand (and, presumably, in inflationary pressure) than is obtainable where the surplus is used to retire publicly held securities.

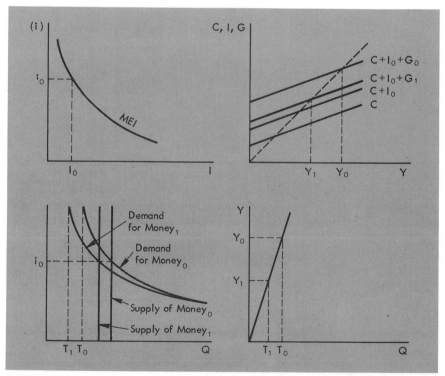

FIGURE 17-15   Effect of Tax Surplus—Surplus Used to Retire Bonds Held by Banks

Determinants of the Effectiveness
of "Pure" Fiscal Policy in Altering GNP

The examples considered in the last few pages provide an ideal background for some summarization regarding the conditions most favorable to effective fiscal policy measures. These, then, can be readily compared with those pertaining to monetary policy, as listed in Table 17-1.

For this purpose, "pure" fiscal policy measures will be defined as alterations in government expenditures and/or taxes *without any change in the money supply*. The creation of budget deficits financed by sale of securities to the public or budget surpluses used to retire securities held by the public would consequently fill the bill as "pure" fiscal policy measures.

As fiscal policy is most commonly aimed at affecting the nation's GNP, we shall use the change in GNP as the measure of effectiveness. The greater the ultimate effect on aggregate demand and GNP, the more "successful" the fiscal policy measure.

With these guidelines in mind, what conditions—what slopes of curves—will be most conducive to an effective fiscal policy measure? For purposes of illustration, we shall restrict our discussion to fiscal policy (cut in taxes and/or rise in government expenditures) aimed at raising GNP. (The student should then think through, on his or her own, the reverse case where the aim is to cut aggregate demand.)

Consider first the upper-right-hand, income determination diagram of any of the four-diagram models where fiscal policy has its first impact. Here a **steep consumption function is desirable.** A steep consumption function indicates a larger MPC, which, in turn, means a large multiplier. The larger the multiplier, the larger the change in GNP resulting from an initial rise in G or cut in T. So much for round 1.

In round 2, the student will recall, developments will be unfavorable, partially diminishing the first-round, desired rise in GNP. Consequently, the smaller the second-round effects, the more effective the fiscal policy measure.

A steep transactions demand-for-money curve will be most favorable. This is because the steeper the transactions demand curve, the smaller the increase in quantity of money demanded for transactions purposes as a result of the first-round rise in GNP. The smaller this increase is, the less the rise in the total demand-for-money curve in the lower-left-hand diagram and the smaller the unfavorable second-round effects.

With any given rise (shift to the right) in the total demand-for-money curve, **the interest rate will rise less, the flatter the total demand-for-money curve.** This is illustrated in Figure 17-16.

Here, if the demand-for-money curve should shift to the right from relatively flat D_1 to D_2, the interest rate rises only from i_1 to i_2. If, however, the original demand-for-money curve were the relatively steep D_3 curve, a shift to the right (equivalent to the shift between D_1 and D_2) to D_4 would raise the interest rate all

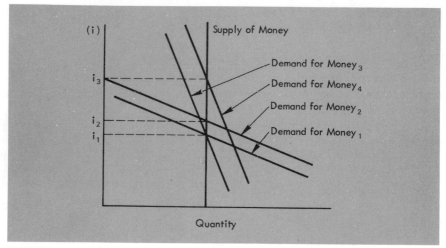

FIGURE 17-16   Effect on Interest Rate of Slope of Shifting Demand-for-Money Curve

the way up to i_3. As a rise in the interest rate has unfavorable effects, a flat demand-for-money curve is preferable.

Finally, turning to the upper-left-hand diagram of any of the four-diagram models, **fiscal policy will be more effective the steeper the MEI curve.** Any change in investment will come in round 2, and the effects on aggregate demand will be the opposite of those desired. A steep MEI curve will mean very little cutback in investment spending because of a rise in interest rates. For an expansionary fiscal policy measure, this is desirable. All this is summarized in Table 17-2.

Note that in comparing Table 17-2 with Table 17-1, monetary and fiscal policy are both more effective the steeper the consumption function and the steeper the transactions demand-for-money curve. Monetary policy, however, requires a steep total demand-for-money curve and a flat MEI curve; fiscal policy is most effective if these two curves are of the opposite slopes. These differences should be kept in mind in the next chapter, when we consider the modern quantity theory.

TABLE 17-2

Determinants of the Effectiveness of "Pure" Fiscal Policy Measures

Fiscal Policy Will Have Greater Effects on GNP If	Fiscal Policy Will Have Smaller Effects on GNP If
1. The consumption function is steep.	1. The consumption function is flat.
2. The transactions demand-for-money curve is steep.	2. The transactions demand-for-money curve is flat.
3. The total demand-for-money curve is flat.	3. The total demand-for-money curve is steep.
4. The MEI curve is steep.	4. The MEI curve is flat.

An Alternative Geometric Approach—
IS and LM Curves

In attempting to illustrate a complicated set of relationships geometrically, one is often confronted with difficult choices. On the one hand, it is useful to have all the "pieces" of the theory explicitly exposed so that changes and interconnections can be clearly seen. This is the virtue of the four-diagram approach.

But virtue has its price, and the student who has carefully worked through the examples presented in the preceding section will be keenly aware of the "price" of the four-diagram framework. It is a most cumbersome apparatus, hardly efficient for repeated chalkboard use in the classroom.

Is there a simpler geometric construct that can be used to represent all this? There is indeed. All the curves involved in the upper two diagrams can be collapsed into a single line, typically designated as an IS curve. Similarly, all the curves included in the bottom two diagrams can be represented by a single "LM" curve. In fact, the IS–LM method is, by all odds, the dominant geometric representation of the Keynesian theory now commonly employed.

Our task in this section is twofold. First, we shall investigate the derivation of IS and LM curves; then, we shall illustrate their use.

Derivation of IS and LM Curves

IS Curves. An IS curve may be defined as **a curve that shows the various possible equilibrium levels of income that would result from various given rates of interest.**

It should be clear by now, focusing on the top two diagrams of the four-diagram framework, that each rate of interest permits a given level of investment spending, which, along with C and G, leads to a certain "equilibrium" level of income. In Figure 17-17, for example, relatively low interest rate i_1 produces investment spending I_1, which, along with C and G, establishes income level Y_1. Higher interest rate i_2 permits less investment, I_2, which in turn leads to lower income level Y_2. And so on.

The IS curve involves no more than a line that shows all the possible interest rate-income combinations. Its derivation can be shown as in Figure 17-18.

Here the MEI curve (with a lump-sum amount of government spending added to it) is shown in the lower-right diagram. The upper-right diagram is simply a 45° line with I + G on the horizontal axis and S + T on the vertical. The upper left is the saving plus taxes schedule related to the income level.

Starting in the lower-right corner, if the interest rate is i_1, this will permit I + G_1. Going up to the upper right, we know that, in equilibrium I + G equals S + T, so that we will have to have saving plus taxes of S + T_1. Finally, in the upper left, for saving plus taxes to be at the S + T_1 level, we must have an income level of Y_1. (The S + T schedule is, of course, directly derived from the consumption function. In this example, we simply use the I + G = S + T form of

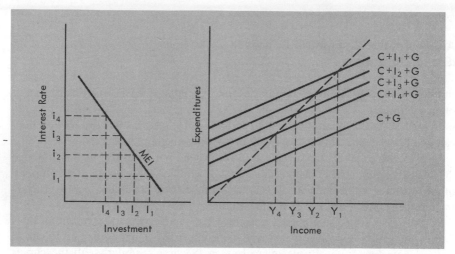

FIGURE 17-17 IS Curve—Interest Rates and Income Levels

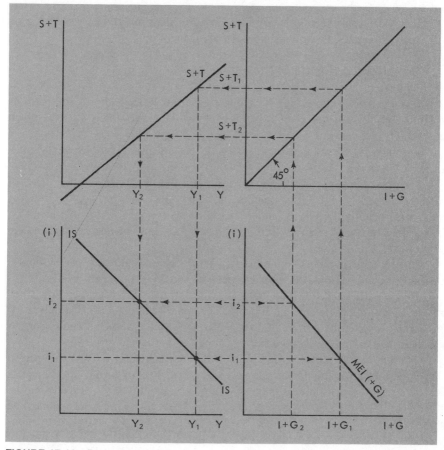

FIGURE 17-18 Derivation of IS Curve

TABLE 17-3

Some Major Causes of Shifts in IS Curve

Initial Cause	Effect on IS
1. Rise in G or parallel rise in MEI curve	1. Shifts to right by initial amount times multiplier
2. Fall in G or parallel fall in MEI curve	2. Shifts to left by initial amount times multiplier
3. Parallel rise in consumption function (fall in S + T function)	3. Shifts to right by initial amount times multiplier
4. Parallel fall in consumption function (rise in S + T function)	4. Shifts to left by initial amount times multiplier
5. Steepened (flattened) slope of MEI curve	5. Steepens (flattens)
6. Steepened (flattened) slope of consumption function	6. Flattens (steepens)

the equilibrium condition rather than aggregate demand equals aggregate supply condition used in the upper-right-hand part of the four-diagram model.) This gives us the first dot on the IS curve—interest rate i_1, which will lead to income level Y_1.

The same procedure is then followed starting from interest rate i_2. This produces $I + G_2$, which means that we must have saving plus taxes equal to $S + T_2$. This level is only reached when income is at level Y_2. We have a second dot depicting another interest-income relation. When these dots (and, conceptually, many more similar ones) are joined together in a line, we have an IS curve.

Now, before proceeding, the student should think through what we have done. This IS curve "represents" the results of a given MEI curve, a given quantity of government spending, and a given consumption schedule (which implies a given tax rate). A change in any of these underlying functions will change the IS curve itself.

For example, a lump-sum rise in government spending or a parallel shift to the right in the MEI curve will shift the MEI ($+ G$) curve (Figure 17-18) to the right by that amount. If the effect of this is followed through Figure 17-18, it will be apparent that the original change, plus the effects of the multiplier that enter the picture in the upper-left diagram, will shift the IS curve to the right by an amount equal to the original change in G (or I) times the multiplier.

To shorten the discussion, some of the main causes of shifts in the IS curve are listed in Table 17-3. The student should be cautioned, however, that this is not a table simply to memorize. If the IS–LM framework is to be used, it will be well worth the effort to trace through the derivation in each case.

LM Curves. The LM curve shows **various possible equilibrium rates of interest that would result from alternative given levels of income.** This curve represents everything in the two bottom diagrams of the four-diagram framework. It recognizes, as in Figure 17-19, that for every level of income there is a different transactions demand, which, in its turn, produces a different rate of interest.

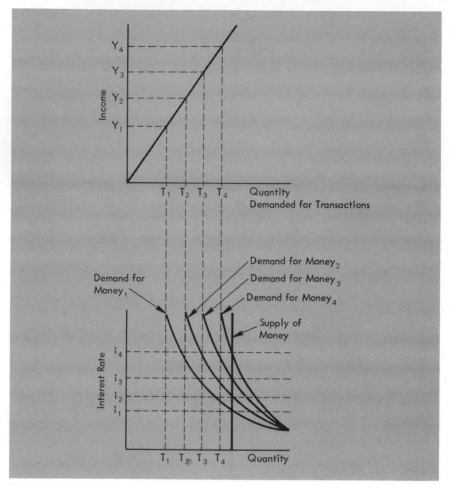

FIGURE 17-19   LM Curve—Income Levels and Interest Rates

The complete derivation of an LM curve is depicted in Figure 17-20, which can perhaps most logically be interpreted as starting in the upper-left diagram where a transactions demand-for-money curve is depicted. (Note that the axes are reversed compared with earlier transactions demand curves used.) The upper-right diagram depicts (by its distance out from the origin) the given supply of money. The lower right, of course, is the asset demand-for-money curve.

If the level of income is Y_1, then OM_{dt1} of the money supply is needed for transactions purposes, leaving OM_{da1} available as asset balances. For people willingly to hold that amount of asset money, the asset demand curve tells us that the interest rate must be as low as i_1. If income is Y_2, on the other hand, OM_{dt2} of the given money supply is used up as transactions balances, leaving only OM_{da2} to be absorbed for asset purposes. This will be accomplished at interest rate i_2.

The LM curve, like the IS curve, rests on a complicated base. The underlying

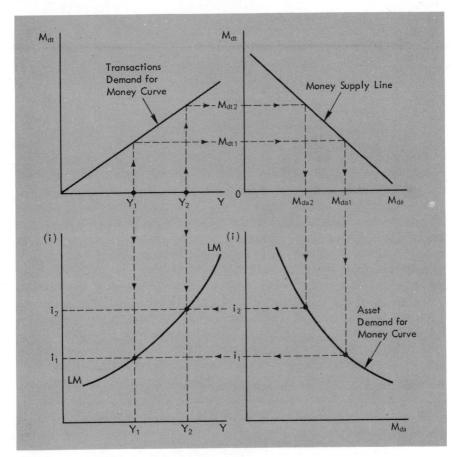

FIGURE 17-20   Derivation of LM Curve

curves in this case are the transactions demand-for-money curve, the asset demand-for-money curve, and the supply of money. If any of these changes its level or slope, the LM curve changes also. Some possible causes of shifts in the LM curve are listed in Table 17-4.

TABLE 17-4

Some Major Causes of Shifts in LM Curves

Initial Cause	Effect on LM
1. Rise (fall) in supply of money	1. Shift to right (left)
2. Rise (fall) in level of asset demand-for-money curve	2. Shift to left (right)
3. Steepening (flattening) of transactions demand-for-money curve (as drawn in Figure 17-19)	3. Flattening (steepening)
4. Steepening (flattening) of asset demand-for-money curve	4. Steepening (flattening)

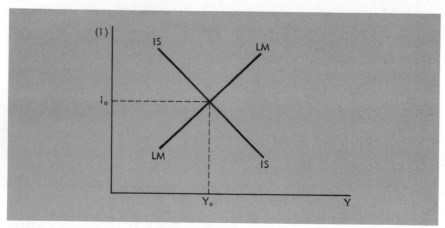

FIGURE 17-21   Equilibrium with IS–LM Curves

Use of IS–LM Curves

When the IS and LM curves are drawn together, their intersection shows the level of income and rate of interest needed to produce "general" equilibrium. In Figure 17-21, then, the equilibrium level of income is Y_e, and the associated equilibrium rate of interest is i_e.

Effect of Rise in Supply of Money.   If the Federal Reserve institutes an "easy money" policy, raising the money supply while everything else is unchanged, the results are routinely shown in IS–LM terms. In Figure 17-22, the money supply increase shifts the LM curve to the right and this lowers the rate of interest from i_1 to i_2 while raising the level of income from Y_1 to Y_2.

Note, however, the effects of a different situation. If the asset demand-for-money curve had had a liquidity trap in it, the LM curve would have been horizontal

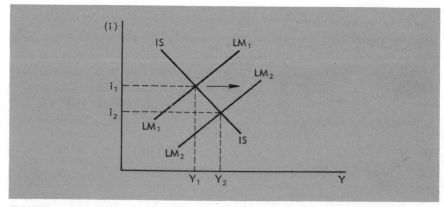

FIGURE 17-22   Change in Equilibrium from Shift in LM Curve

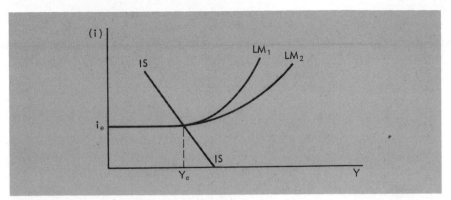

FIGURE 17-23 Equilibrium in the Liquidity Trap

over that range of interest rates too. (Trace it through and see for yourself.) In that case, as Figure 17-23 illustrates, the easy money policy would fail to affect interest rates or the income level.

Effect of a Cut in the Income Tax Rate with the Deficit Financed by Sale of Bonds to Public.   Suppose that the income tax rate is cut (with government spending unchanged) and the deficit thereby created is financed by borrowing from the nonbank public (so that there is no change in money supply). How is this shown with IS and LM curves?

It will be recalled that a lower income tax rate produces a steeper consumption function. Such a change (because it increases the multiplier) would flatten (and raise) the IS curve. This would tend to raise the equilibrium income level (from Y_1 to Y_2 in Figure 17-24) and raise the equilibrium rate of interest. Note that the "round 1" increase in Y (labeled Y, round 1) is cut back in succeeding rounds by interest rate increases, to Y_2.

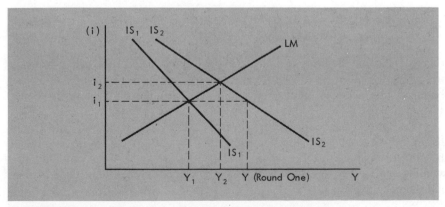

FIGURE 17-24 Income Tax Cut—No Change in Money Supply

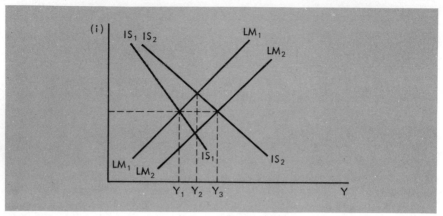

FIGURE 17-25   Income Tax Cut with Money Supply Increase

Effect of Cut in Income Tax with Deficit Financed by Sale of Bonds to Banks.   Once again, let us contrast the fixed money supply case to one depicting an increase in money. If the government deficit created by the cut in income taxes were financed by sale of securities to the banks, the supply of money would be raised.

The IS–LM result is shown in Figure 17-25. Again, the IS curve flattens (and rises) as a result of the tax cut. Here, however, the money supply increase shifts the LM curve to the right also, producing a larger rise in income (from Y_1 to Y_3) and, in this particular case, no rise whatever in the rate of interest. The money supply increase, by keeping the rate of interest down, permits a larger increase in income than if the money stock were held constant. The increase is larger by an amount equal to Y_2Y_3.

Conclusion

The four-diagram framework and the IS–LM approach are alternative means of presenting the same ideas. The former has the advantage of revealing more clearly the underlying interconnections that lead to change, although the latter is geometrically simpler.

One should not be misled, however. Geometrical simplicity does not imply theoretical simplicity. The innocent-appearing IS and LM curves involve exactly the same complexities as their components. To use IS and LM curves with understanding and facility, one must already have worked through their underpinnings quite thoroughly.

Review Questions

1. Indicate the slopes (flat or steep) of the MEI curve and of the total demand-for-money curve that are most conducive to money supply changes having a large effect on aggregate demand, and, in each case, briefly explain why.

2. If it is desired to raise GNP by $25 billion and the MPS is .4, explain the circumstances that must hold for a $10 billion rise in government spending on goods and services to accomplish the desired goal. (Assume that the government budget is balanced before the rise in G.)

3. Carefully explain *why* fiscal and monetary policy require different slopes in some of the curves in the four-diagram model to have the greatest effect on GNP.

4. Explain the significance of the slope of the transactions demand-for-money curve to the effectiveness of money supply changes aimed at raising GNP.

5. Explain what would be the implications for expansionary "pure" fiscal policy if bond prices were already at the lowest levels the public considers possible.

6. In the context of the four-diagram model of the economy, carefully explain how the method used to dispose of the tax surplus will affect the effectiveness of a fiscal policy measure aimed at cutting aggregate demand.

7. Assume that initially we are at general equilibrium. Then the Fed carries out open-market sales to the banks. This produces an initial disequilibrium in the money market that will cause money holders to react in such a way as to cause changes that will—ultimately—restore equality between the demand for, and supply of, money.

   Using only the liquidity preferences theory of interest, explain the process whereby people may react to the initial disequilibrium as well as why they will be satisfied when the new equilibrium is reached.

8. "Contractionary fiscal policy is less effective, the higher the interest rates already are and the more responsive investors are to changes in interest rates." Do you agree? Explain carefully why this is or is not the case.

9. Using the full four-diagram model of the economy as a framework for your reasoning, indicate in each case (a) the curve (or curves) initially affected by the changes given, (b) the type of effect on the curve or curves (i.e., steepened, flattened, shifted right or left, shifted up or down), and (c) the effect on the general equilibrium GNP and rate of interest (i.e., increased, decreased, indeterminate).

   a. The public's conception of the normal range of interest rate fluctuation changes from a range of 3 to 8 percent to a range of 6 to 11 percent.

   b. The personal income tax rate is reduced and the budget deficit thereby created is financed by selling new U.S. securities to the banks.

   c. Corporate profit taxes are cut and the budget deficit created is financed by sale of new U.S. securities to the public.

   d. Personal taxes are raised from .15 GNP + 20 to .20 GNP + 30 and the tax surplus thereby created is used to retire maturing U.S. securities held by the banks.

e. A natural disaster destroys half the nation's stock of capital goods and consumer durable goods.

f. The government lowers business taxes and finances the deficit thereby created by selling U.S. securities to the nonbank public.

g. Government spending is raised by $20 billion and lump-sum taxes are increased by $20 billion to finance it.

h. Businesses increase the fraction of GNP that they withhold in the form of business saving.

10. "If government spending is raised by $10 billion, it will cause the IS curve to shift to the right by $10 billion." Do you agree? Explain why or why not.

11. Using IS and LM curves, illustrate and discuss the effects on GNP and interest rates of an increase in lump-sum taxes with the tax surplus used to retire securities held by the banks.

12. What would be the effect on the slope of its LM curve if, in a particular economy, a liquidity trap existed at interest rates below 4 percent? Using IS and LM curves, illustrate the comparative effectiveness of pure fiscal policy and monetary policy if carried out within the liquidity trap.

13. What is the connection between the slope of the total demand-for-money curve and the slope of the LM curve; between the slope of the MEI curve and the slope of the IS curve? In both cases, explain carefully.

Appendix

Algebraic Presentation

As every line has an equation, the theoretical model sketched out in this chapter can also be presented algebraically. This appendix may be looked upon as simply a continuation of the appendix to Chapter 14, supplemented by the material added in Chapters 15 and 16.

Let us begin by assuming an economy in which the following conditions hold initially:

$C = .625Y_d + 100$	(The consumption function in terms of disposable income)
$T = .2Y_g$	(An income tax with an average tax rate equal to 20 percent of GNP)
$I = 40 - 200i$	(A straight-line MEI curve negatively sloped with respect to the interest rate)
$G = 60$	(Government spending a constant, autonomously determined)
$M_s = 91$	(The money supply a constant, autonomously determined)
$M_{dt} = .2Y_g$	(The transactions demand for money equal to 20 percent of GNP)
$M_{da} = 20 - 100i$	(The asset demand for money a straight line, negatively related to the interest rate)

Equilibrium Conditions

1. Aggregate supply equals aggregate demand, or

$$Y_g = C + I + G$$

2. Supply of money equals demand for money, or

$$M_s = M_{dt} + M_{da}$$

3. Level of income and rate of interest must be the same (that is, consistent) for both.

Computing Initial Equilibrium Income
and Interest Rate Levels

Putting Consumption in Terms of GNP.   By definition,

$$Y_d = Y_g - T$$

Substituting,

$$Y_d = Y_g - .2Y_g$$
$$Y_d = .8Y_g$$

Substituting in C function,

$$C = .625(.8Y_g) + 100$$

Therefore,

$$C = .5Y_g + 100$$

Solving for Equilibrium in the Goods Market (Getting Equation for IS Curve).   The equilibrium condition is

$$Y_g = C + I + G$$

Substituting,

$$Y_g = (.5Y_g + 100) + (40 - 200_i) + 60$$
$$Y_g = .5Y_g - 200i + 200$$
$$.5Y_g = 200 - 200i$$
$$Y_g = 400 - 400i \text{ (equation for IS curve)}$$

Solving for Equilibrium in the Money Market (Getting Equation for LM Curve).   The equilibrium condition is

$$M_s = M_{dt} + M_{da}$$

Substituting,

$$91 = .2Y_g + (20 - 100i)$$
$$.2Y_g = 71 + 100i$$
$$Y_g = 355 + 500i \text{ (equation for LM curve)}$$

Solution for Initial "General" Equilibrium in Economy. The income level and interest rates are compatible only at the levels where the IS and LM curves intersect. Therefore, we have equilibrium condition

$$IS = LM$$

Substituting,

$$400 - 400i - Y_g = 355 + 500i - Y_g$$
$$900i = 45$$
$$i = .05$$

The initial equilibrium interest rate equals 5 percent.

Substituting 5 percent in LM equation (or IS),

$$Y_g = 355 + 500(.05)$$
$$Y_g = 355 + 25$$
$$Y_g = 380$$

The initial equilibrium GNP equals 380.

Computing Effect of Cut in Money Supply on GNP and Interest Rate

Now suppose that the economy has achieved its equilibrium positions of 380 and 5 percent and the monetary authorities apply a "tight money" policy consisting of a cut in the money supply to 82 (by 9). What will such a policy do to GNP and the interest rate?

Computing New LM Equation. As the only change is in the money supply, the IS curve is unchanged. Equating the new money supply with the demand for money, we have

$$82 = .2Y_g + 20 - 100i$$
$$.2Y_g = 62 + 100i$$
$$Y_g = 310 + 500i \text{ (new LM curve)}$$

Computing New Equilibriums.

$$IS = LM$$
$$400 - 400i = 310 + 500i$$
$$900i = 90$$
$$i = .10$$

The new equilibrium interest rate is 10 percent.

Substituting the 10 percent interest rate into the LM equation,

$$Y_g = 310 + 500(.10)$$
$$Y_g = 360$$

The new equilibrium GNP level is 360.

The Approach to the New Equilibrium by "Rounds"

This same change can be shown in rounds as in the early part of the chapter where the four-diagram approach was used.

Note that each value in Table 17-5 is computed directly from the given equation. The only complication is for the transactions demand for money, which is always based on the *previous* round's level of income. This treatment follows the discussion in the body of the chapter exactly.

Several significant items show up when the data are presented in this form. In the first place, note the crucial role played by asset money balances. In the new equilibrium, only $4 of the original $9 cut from the money supply comes out of transactions balances; the other $5 is drawn out of asset balances by the rise in the interest rate. If there had been no asset money balances and the entire money supply reduction had been withdrawn from transactions balances, income would have been reduced by a full 45—a figure directly reflecting the fact that each dollar in transactions balances supports 5 in income. This would be a "crude quantity theory type" world in which money supply changes lead to equal proportional income changes.

Second, the data make clear that when the money market is included in the model, the simple multiplier used in Chapter 14 is inadequate to compute the change in equilibrium GNP. Note that in round 1, the rise in interest to 14 percent cut investment spending by 18. This, in turn, led to a cut in the GNP level (after the first round) of 36. As the MPC in this economy is 0.5, the multiplier is 2, and

TABLE 17-5

Round-by-Round Approach to "General" Equilibrium

	Initial Equilibrium	End of Round 1	End of Round 2	End of Round 3	End of Round 4		New Equilibrium
M_s	91	82	82	82	82	→	82
M_{dt}	76	76	68.8	74.56	69.95	→	72
M_{da}	15	6	13.2	7.44	12.05	→	10
i	5%	14%	6.8%	12.56%	7.95%	→	10%
C	290	272	286.4	274.88	284.10	→	280
I + G	90	72	86.4	74.88	84.10	→	80
Y_g	380	344	372.2	349.76	368.20	→	360

2 times the initial cut in investment is, indeed, 36. But of course that's only the beginning of the story. The later effects on the demand for money, and hence the rate of interest, are not taken into account by the simple multiplier.[8] One of the main reasons for bringing the money market and interest rate determination into the picture is to illustrate how it operates to cut down on the size of the simple multiplier.

The note of caution made earlier regarding the "round-by-round" approach to a new general equilibrium should be repeated here. This section and the data in Table 17-5 are included for pedagogical reasons only. In no sense does the real world follow such an adjustment path.

Computing Effects on GNP and Interest Rate of Fiscal Policy Measures

Returning to the original conditions, under which, it will be recalled, the IS equation was $Y_g = 400 - 400i$, the LM equation $Y_g = 355 + 500i$, the equilibrium GNP, 380, and the equilibrium interest rate 5 percent, let us compute the effects of certain fiscal policy measures.

Rise in Government Spending Financed by Borrowing from Nonbank Public. Suppose that in an effort to raise employment and production, the government now raises its spending by $9, borrowing the proceeds from the public.

The increase in government spending changes the IS equation because, of course, government spending is now $69 rather than $60. Thus we have

$$Y_g = C + I + G$$
$$Y_g = (.5Y_g + 100) + (40 - 200i) + 69$$
$$.5Y_g = 209 - 200i$$
$$Y_g = 418 - 400i \text{ (new IS equation)}$$

As the deficit is financed by sale of bonds to the public, the money supply is, of course, not changed. The LM equation therefore stays the same:

$$Y_g = 355 + 500i \text{ (LM equation)}$$

---

[8]The multiplier that takes account of the monetary sector changes is

$$\frac{1}{1 - b(1 - t) + (x \times y/z)}$$

where b = MPC out of DI, t = income tax rate, x = coefficient of interest term in investment equation, y = coefficient of income term in transactions demand-for-money equation, and z = coefficient of interest term in asset demand-for-money equation. With the given numbers, we have

$$\frac{1}{1 - .625(1 - .2) + (-200 \times .2/-100)} = \frac{1}{1 - .5 + .4} = \text{a multiplier of } 1.0/.9$$

This multiplier times the initial cut in investment—$1.0/.9 \times 18$—gives us a cut in the GNP of 20.

Solving by means of simultaneous equations, we get new equilibrium values for GNP and the interest rate of

$$Y_g = 390$$
$$i = 7\%$$

Note that the expansionary fiscal policy has had its desired effect of raising the income level. However, in the process, the interest rate is also increased, and that holds the income expansion well below the rise of 18 that the simple multiplier would have predicted.

Rise in Government Spending with Deficit Financed by New Money. If the $9 of added government spending should be financed by sale of bonds to the banks, the effects are markedly different. For in this case the money supply goes up by $9 at the same time government spending rises. We have what is in effect an expansive fiscal policy aided by an expansive monetary policy.

Once again the rise in government spending gives us an IS equation of

$$Y_g = 418 - 400i$$

In this case, however, the LM equation is also altered by the increase in money supply from 91 to 100. To get the new LM equation, we have

$$\text{Supply of money} = \text{Demand for money}$$
$$100 = .2Y_g + (20 - 100i)$$
$$.2Y_g = 80 + 100i$$
$$Y_g = 400 + 500i \text{ (new LM equation)}$$

Solving now for the equilibrium income and interest rate levels, we get

$$Y_g = 410$$
$$i = 2\%$$

The important thing to note here is that the increase in the supply of money kept the interest rate from restricting the expansive effect of the fiscal policy, so that Y_g rose substantially more than in the preceding example. Indeed, in this example the increase in the supply of money had so much more weight than the rise in demand caused by the increase in Y_g that the equilibrium interest rate actually went *down*, permitting investment spending to rise also. This latter result should not be taken as necessarily typical. It is simply the result of the particular set of equations we chose to assume initially. The student will recall that in a case such as this—depending upon the particular circumstances—the interest rate may fall, rise, or stay the same. The important point is that it winds up at a lower level than in the preceding example and hence the income level rises more.

18

The Modern Quantity Theory and the Monetarist– Post-Keynesian Debate

It is a tribute to the genius and enduring influence of J. M. Keynes that the theoretical model presented in the preceding four chapters is, despite updating modifications, essentially the same structure as that put forth by the Cambridge master nearly 50 years ago. Surely it is not an overstatement to describe the upheaval in economic thought associated with the publication of the *General Theory* as a Keynesian ''revolution.''

But revolution sometimes begets counterrevolution. During the past 25 years, an influential group of economists, originally based primarily at the University of Chicago, has emerged to challenge some of the theory and much of the policy that—since Keynes—has become almost the accepted ''dogma'' of the economics profession. These neoclassical economists, led by Professor Milton Friedman, have reformulated and refurbished an old classical idea, which almost, but not quite, died under the Keynesian onslaught. Their special concern is with the quantity theory of money, restyled in a new theoretical format and supported by impressive new empirical data.

The Keynesian Position—A Variable Velocity and a Role for Fiscal Policy

It will be recalled that a central tenet of the older versions of the quantity theory was the assumption that the velocity of spending is essentially fixed, leading inevitably to the corollary proposition that changes in the money supply lead to equal percentage changes in aggregate demand. If MV' is equal to aggregate demand and V' is a constant, change in M is both a necessary and a sufficient condition for an alteration in total intended spending.

The fixed velocity assumption ultimately fell victim to both fact and theory.

The facts alone, which revealed velocity as a number that varied both cyclically and secularly, were enough to undermine the foundations of the old theory.

But it was left to Keynes to provide a theoretical base for a varying velocity. This he provided with his speculative demand-for-money concept. To Keynes, the reader will recall, the demand for money $(1/V')$ varied not only with the level of income (the transactions demand) but also with the rate of interest (the speculative demand). The relation to the interest rate was the crucial factor.

For if the public was now thought willing to hold essentially idle money balances for speculative purposes, as well as active transactions balances, a number of previously unexplored possibilities were opened up for investigation.

In the first place, money supply increases no longer were seen as necessarily guaranteeing aggregate demand increases. Under "normal" conditions, part (but not all) of any increase in the money supply was absorbed into idle, speculative balances. Because that portion of the money supply increase went unspent, velocity fell. If, for example, the money supply were \$100 with a velocity of 4 per year, a \$50 increase in M, half of which was spent 4 times per year in transactions balances and half of which was held idle in speculative balances, would result in a new velocity figure of $3\frac{1}{3}$. That is,

$$\frac{(100 \times 4) + (25 \times 4)}{150} = \frac{500}{150} = 3\frac{1}{3}$$

Aggregate demand would have risen (to \$500), but by a smaller percentage than the money supply.

Under "abnormal" conditions, however, money supply increases might not raise aggregate demand at all! This, of course, could happen if the "liquidity trap" had been reached. In such a case, *all* of any money supply increase is absorbed into speculative balances, leading to a reduction in velocity exactly equivalent to the rise in M.[1]

Second, and perhaps of greater significance, the introduction of a speculative money demand, with its resulting variability in velocity, provided a means by which

---

[1]Some have chastised Keynes for developing a model in which the liquidity trap is a crucial and necessary element. Such criticism has taken on added meaning in recent years when empirical investigation has been unable to locate any such "trap" in the U.S. economy.

Whatever the sins of some of his followers, Keynes himself does not appear guilty of overstressing the liquidity trap notion. Indeed, he considered an infinitely elastic demand-for-money curve as only a "possibility."

"There is the possibility, for the reasons discussed above, that, after the rate of interest has fallen to a certain level, liquidity preference may become virtually absolute in the sense that almost everyone prefers cash to holding a debt which yields so low a rate of interest. In this event the monetary authority would have lost effective control over the rate of interest. But whilst this limiting case might become practically important in the future, I know of no example of it hitherto." John Maynard Keynes, *General Theory of Employment, Interest and Money* (London and New York: Macmillan, 1936), p. 207. For a different view on Keynes's emphasis on a liquidity trap, however, see Milton Friedman, "Comments on the Critics," *Journal of Political Economy,* September–October 1972, pp. 945–46.

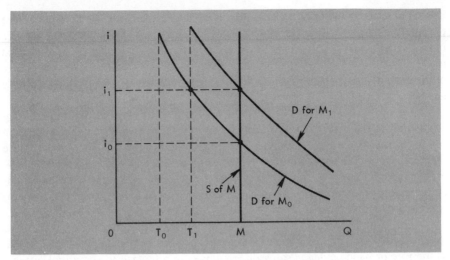

FIGURE 18-1   Increased Transactions Demand Raises Velocity

aggregate demand could be raised *without* any change in the money supply. For policy purposes, this represented a monumental change because it allowed the introduction of fiscal policy as a stabilization tool.

It is not difficult to see what is involved here. Prior to Keynes, "pure" fiscal policy—where the government's budget is altered without a change in the money supply—had not been thought capable of affecting aggregate demand. For if aggregate demand is MV' and V' is a constant, only measures that raise M can raise demand.[2]

Now, however, assuming the existence of idle, speculative money balances, things looked quite different. A rise in government spending (or a cut in taxes) *could* raise aggregate demand by the simple expedient of "pulling" that part of the existing money supply needed to finance transactions out of idle, speculative balances into active, transactions use.

Look at Figure 18-1. Suppose that government spending has been increased, raising the equilibrium income level and that that, in turn, has increased the transactions demand for money from OT_0 to OT_1. This raises the total demand for money from D for M_0 to D for M_1 and increases the interest rate from i_0 to i_1. Now, in this "Keynesian" case, the rise in interest rates will *not* be enough to cut investment spending back by as much as government spending initially rose because

---

[2]The rationale for this attitude was simple. If all existing money is already being used to finance all the expenditures it can, what can, for example, a rise in government spending without a rise in the money supply do? The added money spent by government is necessarily acquired from the public by the sale of new government bonds. This, in the classical view, merely pushes interest rates up high enough to cut back private investment spending by the amount government spending rose. Fiscal policy under these circumstances is simply a means of determining what percentage of resources will be used publicly and what percentage privately, but *not* a means of affecting the total amount actually used.

it is moderated by the existence of speculative money balances. Notice that before the interest rate rose, transactions balances totaled only OT_0, with T_0M held idle in speculative balances. After interest rises to i_1, transactions balances are increased to OT_1, with only T_1M being kept idle. What this means is that a larger percentage of the existing money supply is now being spent to buy goods and services; velocity has been raised.

Keynes's *General Theory* thus not only tended to undercut the hitherto implicit faith in the effectiveness of money supply changes but laid the foundation for fiscal policy as a potentially more useful stabilization weapon. When these theoretical developments were combined with actual experience in the 1930s— massive excess reserves, record low interest rates, but persistent widespread unemployment—the impotency of monetary policy seemed to have been clearly demonstrated in actual practice.[3]

The result of all this was that many economists, especially during the 1940s, overreacted. Fiscal policy was elevated to the throne and monetary policy demoted to the role of handmaiden. Professor Friedman, in reference to some of Keynes's followers, put it this way: "His disciples, as disciples will, went much farther than the master. The view became widespread that 'money does not matter.' "[4]

The Theoretical Foundation of the Modern Quantity Theory

While all this was going on in the majority of the economics profession, the "oral tradition" of the quantity theory continued at the University of Chicago. Finally, in the mid-1950s, Professor Friedman offered a "restatement of the quantity theory—in modern terms."[5] The result was not only a new and more sophisticated version of the quantity theory, altered from the old "crude" theory, but one set up in a form subject to empirical testing. Let us look first at the theoretical framework.

Friedman's prime concern was to show that velocity (or its inverse, the

---

[3]This interpretation of the experience of the Great Depression has been sharply challenged by the modern quantity theorists who point out that despite the low interest rates and excess reserves, the money supply was permitted to fall dramatically.

[4]Milton Friedman, *Employment Growth and Price Levels,* Hearings Before the Joint Economic Committee, 86th Cong., 1st sess., May 25–28, 1958. In some ways it is strange that this overly negative attitude toward the role of money in the economy should have developed following the *General Theory,* for Keynes himself had developed a theoretical model in which money (barring a liquidity trap) *did* play an important role. Before the *General Theory,* classical theory had relegated money to the role of determining only the price level. Keynes made it a variable that could affect production and employment also. For an excellent statement to this effect, see Lawrence S. Ritter, "The Role of Money in Keynesian Theory," in *Banking and Monetary Studies,* ed. Deane Carson (Homewood, Ill.: Richard D. Irwin, 1963).

[5]See Milton Friedman, "The Quantity Theory of Money: A Restatement," in *Studies in the Quantity Theory of Money* (Chicago: University of Chicago Press, 1956).

demand for money) was not a "will-o'-the-wisp," dancing around in unpredictable fashion to the tune of hundreds of undeterminable variables but, rather, was a stable function of a limited number of key variables. This point deserves stress. Friedman does not consider—as did some of the older quantity theorists—that velocity is a stable, predictable *number* but, rather, that it is a quantity that bears a stable, predictable *relationship* to a limited number of other important factors.

Unlike Keynes, Friedman does not begin with an analysis of the motives for holding money. He takes it as an observable fact that people *do* hold money (velocity is not infinite) and concentrates on the determinants of *how much* money will be held.

Money, to Friedman, is one of a number of forms in which people can choose to hold their wealth. An individual may decide to hold durable goods, to hold stocks, or to hold bonds, but he or she may also opt to hold money. The question is, "What determines how much money he or she will choose to hold?" "What are the determinants of an individual's demand for money?"

The approach employed should be quite familiar to economics students. The demand for money is treated in exactly the same fashion as the demand for any good. How do we approach the demand for, say, automobiles? The quantity demanded, we say, will depend on the car's price, the prices of other, related goods that might be purchased instead, the amount of income available, and consumer tastes and expectations. The ordinary, demand-for-good X function thus could be represented as

$$D_x = f(P_x, P_y, P_z, Y, t)$$

where P_x is the price of good X, P_y and P_z are the prices of alternative related goods, Y is income, which represents a constraint on the ability to purchase good X, and t represents tastes and expectations.

The almost completely analogous demand-for-money function suggested by Professor Friedman is[6]

$$M_d = f(r_b, r_e, \frac{1}{P}\frac{dP}{dt}, W, t)$$

---

[6]Actually this is an oversimplification of Friedman's function. The wealth variable preferred by Friedman is what he calls "permanent income" rather than the usually defined wealth magnitude. In addition, Friedman includes another variable that is omitted entirely. This variable is the ratio of nonhuman to human wealth.

Friedman's inclusion of this variable is based upon the totally logical position that the usual measure of wealth—nonhuman wealth—understates total wealth. If wealth is any asset on which income can be earned, then the productive capacities of human beings (present discounted value of future wage and salary payments) is just as properly considered wealth as a stock or bond. When a person is making a decision as to the form in which he or she will hold his or her wealth, that person has, in addition to the option of holding it in the form of money, stocks, or bonds, the possibility of using it (through further education or training) to enhance his or her human wealth. The logic of including it seems unassailable and it is omitted in the text solely for the sake of simplicity.

where

r_b = the interest return available on bonds

r_e = the dividends (and capital gains) available on equities or direct ownership of capital goods

$\dfrac{1}{P}\dfrac{dP}{dt}$ = the expected rate of price change

W = wealth

t = tastes and preferences

Let us see if we can put this rather imposing expression into commonsense language. It says that the quantity of money that is demanded (M_d) will tend to be

1. Lower, the higher the return that could be earned by buying bonds (r_b).
2. Lower, the higher the return that could be earned by buying equities (r_e).

3. Lower, the more rapid the rate of expected price increase $\left(\dfrac{1}{P}\dfrac{dP}{dt}\right)$.

4. Higher, the greater the amount of wealth available to be apportioned (W).
5. Higher or lower, as affected by tastes and preferences (t).

This then is the function that Professor Friedman believes to be reasonably stable. Velocity (or the demand for money) is not a fixed quantum but varies in a fairly predictable fashion with the return on bonds and stocks, price expectations, wealth, and tastes.

Now up to this point there is little dispute. Almost everyone—quantity theorist and Keynesian alike—would be likely to accept, with perhaps minor modification, such a formulation of the demand for money. To quote Friedman once again, "Almost every economist will accept the general lines of the preceding analysis on a purely formal and abstract level, although each would doubtless choose to express it differently in detail."[7]

The differences enter in when the stability of the relationship itself and the direction and degree of influence of the independent variables are considered. Some opponents of the modern quantity theory would include other independent variables in the equation and argue that their omission results in an unstable function. In addition, they would place considerable weight and significance on the relation between interest rates and the demand for money. Friedman, on the other hand, saw the function itself as stable and, barring the development of hyperinflation, only wealth as a variable likely to cause significant changes in velocity.[8]

From this beginning, the debate between the modern quantity theorists (or

---

[7]Friedman, "Quantity Theory of Money: A Restatement."

[8]Although in his earlier work Professor Friedman did argue that interest rates were of minor significance, in more recent articles he appears to have changed this position.

"monetarists") and their opponents (the "post-Keynesians") has developed over a quarter-century into a major controversy of the greatest importance for economic policy. Skipping over the decades of debate, let us attempt to abstract the essence of the monetarist position as it appears to stand today.

The Essence of the Monetarist Position

It is exceedingly difficult, if not impossible, to summarize the position of all advocates of the modern quantity theory. The monetarist "position," like its counterpart the post-Keynesian position, has been built up over the years by a large group of highly competent individual scholars who, though in general agreement regarding the basic role of money in the economy, differ in many ways as to detail and as to specific policy prescription. In the following discussion, we shall, in the main, overlook the relatively minor differences among individual monetarists to bring out the common elements that distinguish the views of the group as a whole from their post-Keynesian adversaries.[9]

The Basic Tenets of Monetarism

The fundamental convictions all the modern monetarists appear to share include the following propositions:[10]

1. The supply of money is the single most important determinant of money GNP. Specifically, the monetarists argue that the supply of money is the "dominant, though not exclusive" determinant of both the level of physical output and the price level in the short run and of the level of prices in the long run. The long-run level of physical output is taken to be uninfluenced by the supply of money but dependent, instead, on such real factors as technology and the quantity and quality of productive resources.

Now statements such as these, though perhaps formally correct, are almost devoid of significance unless something can be said about *how* "dominant" the monetarists perceive the money supply to be and *how* "nonexclusive" it is as a determinant of economic activity. Perhaps quotations from two prominent monetarist position advocates regarding the extent of their faith in the money supply as the dominant determinant can put some meat on this barebones statement.

Professor Friedman has expressed his views as follows: "I regard the description of our position as 'money is all that matters for changes in *nominal* income

----

[9]Needless to say, the post-Keynesian "group" is no more monolithic than the monetarists with regard to detail and specific policy prescription.

[10]Much of this section follows the statement by Leonall C. Andersen, "The State of the Monetarist Debate," *Review,* Federal Reserve Bank of St. Louis, September 1973.

and for *short-run* changes in real income' as an exaggeration but *one that gives the right flavor to our conclusions.*"[11]

In a similar vein, monetarist Leonall C. Andersen has concluded that "the key proposition is that changes in money dominate other short-run influences on output and other long-run influences on the price level and nominal aggregate demand."[12]

And more recently, David Laidler has put it this way.

> The characteristic monetarist belief that variations in the supply of money are the "dominant impulse" (to borrow Brunner's phrase) causing fluctuations in money income is clearly related to this traditional version of the quantity theory, but modern monetarists are more clearcut in their attribution of a dominant causative role to the money supply than were quantity theorists of earlier vintages.[13]

In short, although factors other than the money supply can have an impact on the level of GNP (that is, on the level of production, employment, and prices) in the short run, such effects are distinctly subordinate to that exerted by the supply of money. Change the supply of money, say the monetarists, and you will inevitably cause the price level and/or the level of production to rise in the short run; in the longer run, the effect will be entirely on prices.

This position would appear to go far beyond the mere denial of the more extreme early "Keynesian" arguments that a liquidity trap or an excessively inelastic MEI curve may negate the effects of money supply changes altogether. It posits not only that changes in the money supply always "work" (in the sense that they always affect aggregate demand in the same direction) but that they are the *dominant* cause of *any* change in aggregate demand. That is, not only do money supply changes inevitably (albeit with some lag) alter P and Q but, whereas other factors can have temporary and subordinate effects, *P and Q* (in the short run) *are not likely to be changed significantly without some prior change in the money supply providing the driving force.*

2. Money supply changes affect aggregate demand through effects on a range of assets much broader than that implied by the Keynesian theory. The monetarists feel that Keynesian theory involves an unnecessarily narrow transmission mechanism between money supply and aggregate demand changes. Specifically, it is argued that in the Keynesian system, money supply increases that do not, at the same time, raise income, will be spent on bonds, thereby lowering interest rates and, ultimately, permitting an increase in investment spending because of a lowered cost of borrowing.

---

[11]Milton Friedman, "A Theoretical Framework for Monetary Analysis," *Journal of Political Economy,* March–April 1970 (emphasis added).

[12]Andersen, "State of the Monetarist Debate," p. 3.

[13]David Laidler, "Monetarism: An Interpretation and an Assessment," *The Economic Journal,* March 1981, p. 5.

The monetarist position is that excess money balances produced by an increase in the money supply will lead to spending on a much broader range of assets than the "bonds-only" model of Keynes. Professor Friedman has put it as follows:

> The attempt by holders of money to restore or retain a desired balance sheet after an unexpected increase in the quantity of money will tend to raise the prices of assets and reduce interest rates, which will encourage both spending to produce new assets and spending on current services rather than on purchasing existing assets. This is how an initial effect on balance sheets gets translated into an effect on income and spending.
>
> The difference between us and the Keynesians is less in the nature of the process than in the range of assets considered. The Keynesians tend to concentrate on a narrow range of marketable assets and recorded interest rates. We insist that a far wider range of assets and interest rates must be taken into account—such assets as durable and semi-durable consumer goods, structures and other real property. As a result, we regard the market rate stressed by the Keynesians as only a small part of the total spectrum of rates that are relevant. . . .[14]

3. Fiscal policy, without changes in the money supply, has little or no effect on aggregate demand or the level of GNP. This proposition follows, of course, as a logical consequence of the first proposition. If the government raises its spending and/or reduces taxes, financing the budget deficit thereby created by sale of securities to the nonbank public, the money supply is unchanged. Such a fiscal policy measure, argue many monetarists, will have little or no effect on aggregate demand.

This extreme conclusion—that fiscal policy by itself is virtually impotent—does seem to have been reached by Professor Friedman. In a debate focusing on the relative merits of monetary and fiscal policy, Friedman says, "in my opinion, the state of the budget by itself has no significant effect on the course of nominal income, on inflation, or deflation, or on cyclical fluctuations."[15]

The Friedman position on fiscal policy is obviously of profound importance. If it is correct, much of what has been taught in economics courses and much of government policy in the past 40 years is simply wrong. A policy position of such basic significance deserves a closer look.

The "state of the budget by itself," of course, refers to tax and/or government expenditure changes that are *not* accompanied by money supply changes. Let us follow the reasoning as applied to a tax cut, with the deficit financed by sale of securities to the public.

Such a fiscal move would be intended to raise aggregate demand. As it does not involve a money supply increase, aggregate demand (MV') can only be increased if the fiscal action somehow raises velocity.

---

[14]Milton Friedman, *A Theoretical Framework for Monetary Analysis,* Occasional Paper 112 (New York: National Bureau of Economic Research, 1971), pp. 27–29.

[15]M. Friedman and W. W. Heller, *Monetary versus Fiscal Policy* (New York: W. W. Norton, 1969), p. 51.

In the simplest version of the Keynesian system, this rise in velocity is made possible by the existence of idle, speculative money balances. When consumer spending is increased as a result of the tax cut, income rises. This raises the demand for money, which, in turn, increases the interest rate. The rise in interest rates then "pulls" part of the existing money supply out of asset balances (where it had a zero velocity) into transactions balances where it is spent. It is true, of course, that the higher interest rate cuts back somewhat on investment spending, thereby partially undercutting the expansionary effects of the policy, but this (second-round) effect is thought of only as diminishing the "good" effects—not eliminating them.

Professor Friedman does not accept this line of reasoning. He would grant that a tax cut would lead to an initial increase in consumer spending. That is, to put it in the terms of Chapter 17, the "round 1" effect would be as desired. However, it is his view that the "round 2" effects—the increase in the interest rate induced by financing the deficit in a manner that creates no new money— would be likely to undo all, or almost all, the accomplishments of the first round.

To most post-Keynesians, such a position—that second-round interest rate changes would completely offset, or "crowd out," the favorable first-round effects—necessarily implied the assumption that the demand-for-money curve was perfectly inelastic (i.e., vertical). And such an assumption, if indeed it did lie beneath the Friedman conclusions, would be contrary to a very considerable amount of empirical evidence already available.[16]

Many attempts have been made to measure the relation between the rate of interest and the quantity of money demanded. In every study, with the single exception of an early one by Professor Friedman, it was determined that there was indeed a significant negative relation between interest and the demand for money. (That is, the total demand-for-money curve was found to have some degree of negative slope rather than being vertical.)

In reference to these data, Professor Lester Chandler observes that "It is highly significant that Professor Friedman stands almost alone in contending that income velocity and demands for cash balances are not significantly affected by changes of interest rates. Virtually all other investigators have found very significant effects."[17] Similarly, David Laidler reports, "there is an overwhelming body of evidence in favor of the proposition that the demand for money is stably and negatively related to the rate of interest. Of all the issues in monetary economics, this is the one that appears to have been settled most decisively."[18]

---

[16]Indeed the only empirical results that showed no relation between the interest rate and the quantity of money demanded were those of Professor Friedman himself in his earlier article, "The Demand for Money—Some Theoretical and Empirical Results," *Journal of Political Economy*, June 1959.

[17]Lester V. Chandler, "Standards for Guiding Monetary Action," Hearings Before the Joint Economic Committee, 90th Cong., 2d sess., May 1968, p. 158.

[18]David E. W. Laidler, *The Demand for Money: Theories and Evidence* (Scranton, Pa.: International Textbook Co., 1969), p. 97. For excellent reviews of the results of basic research articles on this point and others in the quantity theory area, Laidler's book is superb. See also R. L. Teigen, "The Demand for and Supply of Money," in *Readings in Money, National Income and Stabilization Policy,* ed. Ronald L. Teigen (Homewood, Ill.: Richard D. Irwin, 1978), pp. 54–81.

These empirical results are, of course, of potentially great importance. If velocity does vary with interest rates, monetary changes are not necessarily the only avenue to altering income levels. Fiscal policy can also play a role. Professor Paul A. Samuelson put it this way:

> There is every plausible reason in terms of experience, in terms of rarified neo-classical theory, for the velocity of circulation to be a systematic and increasing function of the rate of interest; and the minute you believe that, you have moved from the right of the spectrum—that of monetarism—to that noble eclectic position which I hold, the post-Keynesian position.[19]

Professor Friedman, however, is unmoved by such evidence. He has stated in rebuttal that he sees "no 'fundamental issues' in either monetary theory or monetary policy [that] hinge on whether [the demand for money depends on interest rates]."[20] Rather, he attributes his anticipated strong "second-round" reduction in spending to the fact that "the categories of spending affected by changes in interest rates are far broader than the business capital formation, housing construction, and inventory accumulation to which the neo-Keynesians tend to restrict 'investment.' "[21]

That this latter position fails to satisfy many post-Keynesians is evidenced by the following statement from two distinguished members of that school: "most monetarists disavow the interest inelasticity of the demand for money but still do not believe in the efficacy of fiscal policy. How they can have it both ways is not clear."[22]

And more recently Professor James Tobin has observed, "If monetarist propositions about the effects of monetary and fiscal policies on output and prices are at stake, the only reasonable way to make sense of this dictum is to take full employment, in the sense of cleared markets for labour and capital services, as the assumed state of the economy."[23]

4. The determinants and direction of interest rate movements are different from those stressed by Keynesians. The monetarists argue that the simple Keynesian model covered in the preceding chapter leads to erroneous conclusions regarding the effects of money supply changes on interest rates. Worse yet, they maintain,

---

[19]Paul A. Sa. uelson, "The Role of Money in National Economic Policy," *Controlling Monetary Aggregates,* Federal Reserve Bank of Boston, 1969, p. 12.

[20]Milton Friedman, "Interest Rates and the Demand for Money," *Journal of Law and Economics,* October 1966, p. 85.

[21]Milton Friedman, "Comments on the Critics," *Journal of Political Economy,* September–October 1972, pp. 915–16. In this statement Professor Friedman appears to be relating his views on fiscal policy strongly to those on the transmission mechanism discussed in proposition 2. For a similar view on this point, see Karl Brunner, "Commentary on 'The State of the Monetarist Debate,' " *Review,* Federal Reserve Bank of St. Louis, September 1973.

[22]Alan S. Blinder and Robert M. Solow, "Analytical Foundations of Fiscal Policy," *The Economics of Public Finance* (Washington, D.C.: The Brookings Institution, 1974), p. 62.

[23]James Tobin, "Comment on the Paper by Professor Laidler," *The Economic Journal,* March 1981, p. 56.

these "erroneous conclusions" have tended to cause the Federal Reserve authorities to misinterpret the magnitude, and sometimes even the direction, of the monetary policy they were implementing.

To the monetarists, money supply increases affect interest rates in three different ways. First, there is a *liquidity effect,* which causes a very short run reduction in interest rates. It is comparable to the "round 1" effect discussed in Chapter 17. Second, there is an *output effect*—a tendency for interest rates to rise because of the rise in production and demand for money resulting from the first round. This is approximately equivalent to the "round 2" offsetting effect. Finally, there is a *price expectations effect.* Because lenders come to expect a continuation of inflation, they will tend to tack on to the "real" rate of interest, a premium covering the expected rate of inflation. If, for example, lenders are willing to lend at 5 percent when they expect no inflation, they will insist on 8 percent when they come to expect a 3 percent inflation rate.

Now with the relatively short-run liquidity effect exerting a downward pressure on interest rates and both the output and price expectations effect tending to increase them, the monetarists argue that *it would not be unusual for an increase in the money supply to result in higher interest rates* rather than the lower rates the simple Keynesian model implies.[24]

The fact that the simple Keynesian model predicts interest rate decreases to result from money supply increases had led, according to the monetarists, to gross misinterpretation of monetary policies being followed. If one takes the level and/or direction of interest rate movements as the indicator of the direction of monetary policy (as, it is argued, has been typical), one is likely to view intervals of high and rising interest rates as periods of restrictive monetary policy. But such a conclusion, according to the monetarists, is apt to be quite wrong. If *increases* in the money supply lead to *increases* in interest rates, a period of rising interest rates may well be more likely an expansionary, "easy money" period caused by money supply increases. As a result, the monetarists argue that the monetary authorities should forget interest rates (which they cannot really control in the desired direction anyway) and concentrate on controlling the supply of money.

5. The economy is basically stable and, when disturbed by some change in basic conditions, will fairly quickly readjust on its own. In general, the monetarists look upon a private enterprise economy as inherently stable with a strong built-in propensity to recover quickly from disturbing forces and "naturally revert

---

[24]For an argument that the Keynesian model is perfectly consistent with the possibility of money and interest rates moving in the same direction, see Ronald L. Teigen, "A Critical Look at Monetarist Economics," *Review,* St. Louis Federal Reserve Bank, January 1972, pp. 19–20.

It should be pointed out that the higher interest rate expected by the monetarists is a higher "nominal" rate of interest; that is, a higher market rate of interest that is not adjusted to account for price change. The simple version of the Keynesian model implies that a lower "real" (adjusted) interest rate will result.

to its long-run growth path."[25] This should not be taken to mean that the monetarists visualize a completely *laissez-faire* economy as one in which disturbances can never cause disagreeable effects on output, employment, and prices. What is argued is that such disturbances, if not exacerbated by misguided government policy, will tend automatically and reasonably promptly to correct themselves.

As a corollary to this point, monetarists typically take the position that serious, long-lasting economic maladjustments in the nation's past have resulted largely from governmental mismanagement. A vivid example of this position is the claim by some monetarists that the severity of the Great Depression of the 1930s is attributable, in large part, to the Federal Reserve System's failure to keep the money supply from falling.[26]

The Monetarist Evidence

In support of the positions just sketched, the modern quantity theorists have amassed a considerable volume of empirical data. This evidence includes (1) time series data showing the relation between money and income in the United States for nearly a century; (2) extensive historical case studies purporting to show that external factors were responsible for most of the money supply changes—not the change in income itself; (3) least squares regression analysis aimed at demonstrating that monetary factors "explain" a much larger percentage of the variation in income levels than do fiscal factors; and (4) real-world experience, especially in 1966–1967 and 1968–1970, which was widely interpreted as supporting their case.

The Time Series Data.   A substantial part of the time series data cited by the monetarists comes from a prodigious work by Professor Friedman and Anna J. Schwartz, entitled *A Monetary History of the United States, 1867–1960*, and a companion piece by the same two authors, entitled "Money and Business Cycles."[27]

The impressive long-run relationship between money and money income that they have uncovered can be seen in Figures 18-2 and 18-3.

Note in Figure 18-2 that the shaded areas represent periods of business contraction and the unshaded areas show expansion periods. The similarity in the two series is clear, especially during major periods of expansion and contraction. Figure 18-3 depicts "moving standard deviations" of annual rates of change in money and income from 1871 to 1958. These are simply "measures of the variability of

---

[25]Andersen, "State of the Monetarist Debate," p. 7.

[26]Some authorities would include the concept of a "natural" rate of unemployment and the associated "accelerationist" argument as an integral part of the monetarist position. While most monetarists do appear to accept these theoretical constructs, we choose to deal with them in a later chapter.

[27]M. Milton Friedman and Anna J. Schwartz, *A Monetary History of the United States, 1867–1960* (Princeton, N.J.: Princeton University Press, 1963); and "Money and Business Cycles," *Review of Economics and Statistics*, February 1963.

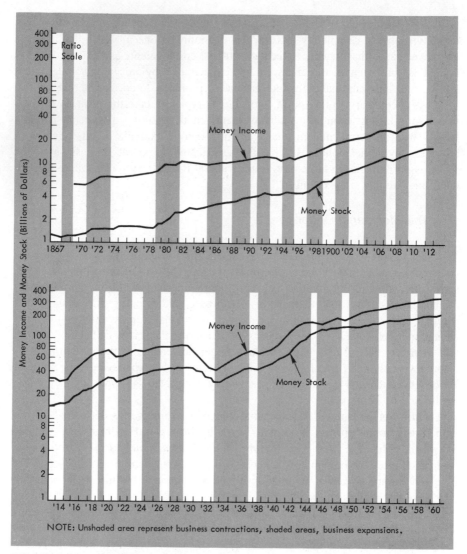

FIGURE 18-2   Money Stock and Money Income, 1867–1960

the rates of change, in the one case of money and in the other case, of income."[28]

Bringing the evidence a bit more up to date, Figure 18-4 charts comparative changes in GNP, M1, and M2 from 1960 through 1981. Two things of significance

---

[28]Friedman and Schwartz, "Money and Business Cycles," p. 40.

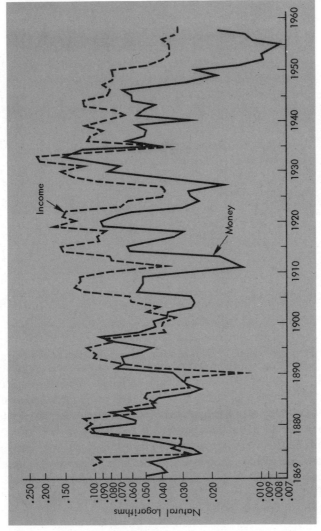

FIGURE 18-3 Money and Business Cycles: Moving Standard Deviation of Annual Rates of Change in Money, 1869–1958, and in Income, 1871–1958, Four-Term Series

Source: M. Friedman and A. Schwartz, "Money and Business Cycles." *Review of Economics and Statistics*, February 1963.

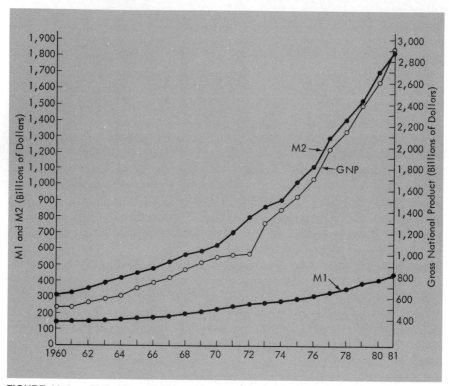

FIGURE 18-4a   GNP, M1, and M2, 1960–1981

should be noted in this graph. In the first figure (18-4a), which traces the absolute amounts of the three series, it is clear that the M2 pattern much more closely approximates that of GNP. This reflects a fact pointed out by many monetarists in recent years—that the velocity of M2 has been much stabler in the past two decades than has the velocity of the M1 money stock.[29]

Second, especially evident in the second graph (18-4b), is the apparent tendency for the change in money stock series to turn down prior to declines in the change in GNP series. This is particularly notable in 1965–1966, 1968–1969, 1972–1974, and 1978–1980. Although grossly oversimplified, this behavior coincides impressively with the conclusions of the monetarist theory.

The "Case Study" Data.   Friedman and Schwartz, as well as a number of other quantity theorists, offer a voluminous list of historical instances where observed changes in the money stock could not have been induced by the associated change in income levels. This evidence is intended to show that it has been the money

---

[29]It should be noted, however, that this impressive degree of stability of V_2 is *not* evident prior to 1960.

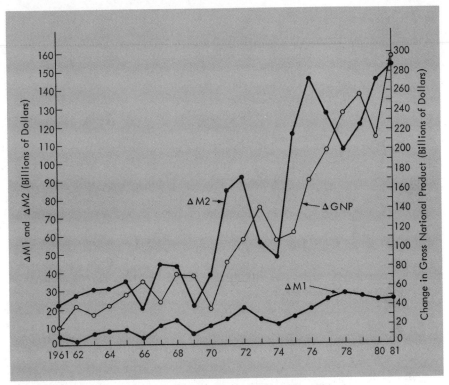

FIGURE 18-4b Annual Changes in GNP, M1, and M2, 1961–1981

variable that has been the "driving force" causing most of the major observed income changes.

For example, they point out that the long expansion from 1897 to 1914 reflected an increase in gold production. Similarly, large gold inflows to the United States during the two world wars are considered contributory to those money stock increases. In 1920, 1931, and 1936—all periods of sharp monetary and income contraction—specific Federal Reserve actions are singled out as independent causes of monetary change. In 1920 and 1931, very large increases in the discount rate are focused on; in 1936, a doubling of reserve requirements is cited as the culprit.[30]

This evidence is especially significant in light of one of the major arguments advanced by the opponents of the modern quantity theory. Known as the "reverse causation" thesis, it involves the proposition that time series data showing close relationships between M and GNP could just as easily be a result of GNP *causing* M as M *causing* GNP. The latter direction of causation is, of course, crucial for the quantity theory. We shall return to this point in the concluding section of this chapter.

---

[30]Friedman and Schwartz, *A Monetary History*, pp. 686–95.

The Regression Analysis Evidence. A somewhat different approach to illustrating and confirming the importance of monetary factors (and the alleged insignificance of fiscal factors) is the use of multiple correlation techniques. This approach was adopted first by Professor Friedman and Professor David Meiselman in a 1963 article and has since been refined and carried further in a series of papers presented by the St. Louis Federal Reserve Bank.[31]

Friedman and Meiselman regressed data for the money supply and "autonomous expenditures" against consumption for a number of years. Their results showed that the money supply was an important and statistically significant "predictor" of consumption, but not so their "autonomous expenditures." The conclusion drawn by Friedman and Meiselman was that the demand for money (velocity) was more stable than the Keynesian multiplier and, consequently, that money supply changes are a more reliable method of controlling national income than fiscal changes.

Critics found the Friedman-Meiselman paper unconvincing, partly because of the technique used and partly because of the choice of variables. Subsequently, in 1968, Leonall Andersen and Jerry Jordan of the Federal Reserve Bank of St. Louis published their own research results from an econometric model of the economy now popularly referred to as the "St. Louis model." Profiting from reviews of the Friedman-Meiselman effort, Andersen and Jordan (A–J) chose their variables carefully to avoid some of the earlier criticisms.

The A–J results, nonetheless, were in substantial agreement with the Friedman-Meiselman conclusions. Fiscal policy, the A–J model indicated, has only minor and temporary effects on GNP. For example, an early version of the model predicted that a $1 million rise in government spending would raise GNP by $400,000 in three months and by $900,000 in six months. By the end of one year, however, the "second-round crowding out" phenomenon would have reduced the increase in GNP to a mere $100,000. In other words, the "government expenditure multiplier" after one year would be a paltry one-tenth. In sharp contrast to its fiscal results, the St. Louis model predicted that a $1 million rise in the money supply would lead to a $1.6 million rise in GNP within three months, a $3.5 million increase after six months, and a full $6.6 million by the end of one year![32]

The St. Louis model created a not inconsiderable stir among economists of both the monetarist and the post-Keynesian camps. The methodology employed in

---

[31]Milton Friedman and David Meiselman, "The Relative Stability of Monetary Velocity and the Investment Multiplier in the United States, 1897–1958," in a Commission on Money and Credit Report entitled *Stabilization Policies* (Englewood Cliffs, N.J.: Prentice-Hall, 1963). The basic paper of the St. Louis Federal Reserve Bank effort is Leonall C. Andersen and Jerry L. Jordan, "Monetary and Fiscal Actions: A Test of Their Relative Importance in Economic Stabilization," *Review,* St. Louis Federal Reserve Bank, November 1968.

[32]The data cited in this paragraph are taken from the excellent review article by Richard G. Davis, "How Much Does Money Matter? A Look at Some Recent Evidence," *Monthly Review,* Federal Reserve Bank of New York, June 1969.

construction of the model has been, as we shall see shortly, severely criticized by the Keynesians. And even more significant, the model's ability to predict GNP movements, which was impressive for earlier years, deteriorated markedly during the chaotic 1970s.[33]

The Experience of the Late 1960s as Monetarist "Evidence."   It is probably fair to say that all this research left the majority of the economics profession intrigued and impressed—but unconvinced. "Of course money matters—perhaps more than we had recognized," seemed to be the general reaction, "but so do a lot of other things, including fiscal policy. We can accept much of the evidence testifying to the crucial role of money, but not the conclusions that money alone matters or that fiscal policy doesn't."

This attitude no doubt remains the dominant one today, but some events of the latter 1960s gave the monetarist case a considerable boost. It will be recalled that prices rose rapidly after 1965. In 1966, with the federal budget still in deficit, the Federal Reserve System clamped down hard on money supply increases. Some monetarists predicted that, despite the budget deficit, this monetary action would shortly produce a recession. In fact, the economy did not go into recession, but it did level off sufficiently in 1967 to produce what some have called a "minirecession." The quantity theorists pointed to this experience as evidence supporting their position; their opponents have cited the absence of a full-fledged recession as a quantity theory failure. This episode shows up clearly in Figure 18-4b.

But more was to come. Inflation accelerated once again in late 1967 and 1968. In an effort to control it, Congress at long last passed, in June 1968, a 10 percent personal income tax surcharge.

This fiscal measure, which was primarily responsible for transforming a fiscal year 1968 budget deficit of $25 billion into a fiscal year 1969 budget surplus of over $3 billion, was widely expected to dampen the inflationary pressure in relatively short order. Federal Reserve authorities, in fact, were so confident of the tax measure's contractionary impact that they—in order to avoid a feared contractionary "overkill"—allowed the money supply to be increased more rapidly in the latter part of 1968. The result was that for a number of months in late 1968 and early 1969 we had a rare "real-world" test case. Fiscal policy had turned sharply restrictive while monetary policy continued in an expansive direction.

What happened? Consumer prices rose during 1969 by 5.6 percent while the unemployment rate stayed under 4 percent for the entire year. The fiscal policy either did not work or, at best, worked only with an intolerably long lag. Finally, in early 1969, the Federal Reserve System reversed its expansionary money policy and during that year curtailed monetary expansion very sharply. By the end of

---

[33]See, for example, Stephen K. McNees, "A Comparison of the Forecasting Accuracy of the Fair and St. Louis Econometric Models," *New England Economic Review,* Federal Reserve Bank of Boston, September–October 1973.

1969 the economy began weakening, and in early 1970 the nation's fourth post–World War II recession was upon us.

The monetarists, quite naturally, claimed a major victory. Professor Friedman had stated publicly in early 1967, "I do not share the widespread view that a tax increase which is not matched by higher government spending will necessarily have a strong braking effect on the economy."[34] In summary, they pointed out that (1) when fiscal policy was restrictive and monetary policy expansive, the economy did not slow down, but (2) when restrictions were placed on the rate of growth in the money supply in 1969, it was not long before the boom ended. This, they argued, is precisely what the monetarist theories predicted.

There can be little doubt that these events gave the quantity theorists a powerful shot in the arm, and their opponents, considerable food for thought. But despite all this, the disagreement continues. The monetarists have unquestionably made real headway in convincing some of their detractors. They still represent, however, a minority within the economics profession. We shall consider the views of the unconvinced majority in the final section of this chapter. Before doing so, however, it seems appropriate to draw together the main policy prescriptions advocated by the monetarists.

The Policy Prescriptions of the Monetarists

If the monetarists had complete control of the nation's economic affairs, how would they conduct policy? The following prescriptions would no doubt be the result.

Rely on Control of the Money Supply to Stabilize Cyclical Fluctuations

In the short run, the monetarists argue, the supply of money is the "dominant" determinant of both the price level and the level of output (and along with it, presumably, the level of employment). In terms of the equation of exchange, this says that velocity (V') is, though not a constant, sufficiently stable to permit us to have great confidence that proper control of the money supply will provide reasonable stability in employment and prices. Fluctuations would still occur, but they would be relatively minor and relatively quickly corrected.

Eliminate "Pure" Fiscal Policy as a Stabilization Tool

Because fiscal policy that does not have the effect of altering the money supply cannot be expected to have much impact on aggregate demand, it should be abandoned. This does not necessarily require acceptance of the "annually bal-

---

[34]M. Friedman, *Newsweek*, January 23, 1967.

anced budget'' philosophy, as most monetarists do not appear to oppose unbalanced budgets as such. What it does mean is that if government spending is to be increased and/or taxes decreased to raise aggregate demand, the deficit thereby created must be financed with newly created money if it is to have any real impact. And even in that case, it is the increase in M rather than the fiscal actions that provides the driving force to raise aggregate demand.[35]

The Money Supply, Not Interest Rates, Should Be the Guide to Policy

As noted, the monetarists feel that the level or direction of movement of interest rates is *not* an appropriate guide for policy. In their view, high or rising interest rates may well be a reflection of an expansionary, rather than a contractionary, policy. For example, they frequently cite the experience of the Great Depression when, despite *extremely* low interest rates, the money supply was permitted to fall by about one-third. Had we focused on the supply of money rather than on interest rates, they argue, the severe income contraction of the 1930s might not have occurred.

The monetary authorities, then, should concentrate on properly controlling the supply of money and allow interest rates to do what they will.[36]

Eliminate the Discretion of the Monetary Authorities

A final most important policy position accepted by most quantity theorists has to do with time lags—the period of time between a money supply change and its resultant effect on the level of income.

One might suppose that as the quantity theorists are so confident of the potency of monetary changes, they would be ardent champions of discretionary monetary policy as the ideal stabilization device. Such a supposition, though understandable, would be quite wrong.

For a policy weapon to be an effective stabilization tool, not only must it affect income in the desired *direction* but it must do so at the right *time*. If the problem is recession and unemployment, it is not enough to know that money supply increases will, sooner or later, raise aggregate demand and income. It must do so quickly enough to raise demand while that is what is still needed. Money supply increases that do not raise demand until the recession has already ended clearly do more harm than good by adding to succeeding inflation.

---

[35]Again, not all monetarists would necessarily subscribe to this policy prescription.

[36]As we have seen, with the October 1979 change in its operating procedure, the Fed appears to have moved sharply in this direction. Despite this, however, the monetarist leader finds little to praise about the performance of the Federal Reserve System. See Milton Friedman, ''Monetary Policy: Theory and Practice,'' *Journal of Money, Credit, and Banking*, February 1982, pp. 98–118.

In their empirical work, Professor Friedman and others have found that the money supply (or the rate of change therein) affects GNP only with long and variable lags.[37] For example, in one of his works with Anna Schwartz, it was determined that the money supply series leads the GNP series by periods varying from 6 to 29 months at business cycle peaks and from 4 to 22 months at the troughs.[38]

The policy conclusion that most monetarists reach from evidence such as this is simple. Potent though monetary policy is, it is not appropriate for "fine-tuning." Discretionary monetary action taken to combat a cyclical downswing (upswing) may very easily result in an addition to (contraction in) demand in the succeeding phase of the cycle, where it simply makes matters worse. Indeed the quantity theorists feel that our past experience with discretion in monetary policy has had just this effect—causing more instability than it has combated.

In line with this view, Professor Friedman has called for an *end to discretion in monetary policy*. In place of the judgment of the monetary authorities, he would substitute a rule requiring an annual fixed percentage increase in the money supply. Although Friedman is not adamant about any exact rate of increase, he has suggested a rate in the 3- to 4-percent-per-year neighborhood as one that reasonably closely approximates the economy's past average annual rate of growth in real output.

The fixed money supply increase rule is not represented as a cure-all for the business cycle. The monetarists are quite aware that the nation would still suffer from cyclical fluctuations, even with this kind of rule. What is claimed, however, is that the more stable monetary environment produced by such a rule would provide a more stable economy than we have had (or are likely to have in the future) with discretion.

The Views of the Opposition

Without question, the modern quantity theory represents a major challenge to economic "orthodoxy." A sophisticated theoretical framework has been buttressed by an impressive array of empirical data in support of the policy positions just discussed. A distinguished group within the economics profession has been convinced of the general validity of the monetarist view. Some elements of the press and of Congress have been similarly persuaded.

And there is no doubt that they have made progress. There is, for example, rather general agreement among monetarists and post-Keynesians alike (1) that money supply changes *do* have significant effects on GNP; (2) that there is no

---

[37]This evidence is obviously in some conflict with the Andersen-Jordan "St. Louis model," which, as we have seen, forecasts not only large but very rapid response to money supply changes.

[38]Friedman and Schwartz, "Money and Business Cycles," pp. 37–38.

evidence in support of Keynes's suggestion that the demand-for-money curve may, at some low interest rate, become perfectly elastic—that is, there is no evidence of a liquidity trap; (3) that although the quantity of money demanded does, in fact, increase as the interest rate falls, the degree of elasticity is small; (4) that the so-called "crowding out" effect of the interest rate consequent to a pure fiscal policy measure is of sufficient size to markedly reduce its effect on aggregate demand; and (5) that more attention should be paid to the rate of growth of monetary aggregates such as the money supply than had been given previously.

But despite the gains of its adherents, the more extreme version of the monetarist position probably remains a minority view within the economics profession. Many distinguished economists representing the post-Keynesian viewpoint have spoken out in opposition to the basic tenets and the policy prescriptions of the monetarists. In general, these advocates have praised the monetarists for their professional skill and diligence in shedding new light on the role of money in the economy. But with regard to the key proposition of monetarism that "money is the *dominant* determinant of short run GNP changes," many would subscribe to the blunt retort of Professor Lawrence Klein—"I don't believe a word of it."[39]

The post-Keynesian counterattack has taken place on a broad front. *First,* the evidence presented by Friedman and others to the effect that historically the money supply and GNP have been closely correlated (or, alternately expressed, that velocity has been remarkably stable) has been criticized both as to the degree of correlation and as to the direction of causation. *Second,* the statistical models of the monetarists such as the Andersen-Jordan St. Louis model have been sharply criticized on grounds of methodology and challenged as to predictive capability. *Third,* the post-Keynesians have strongly supported their continuing faith in fiscal policy as, along with monetary policy, a viable stabilization weapon. *Fourth,* the monetarists have been severely chastised for their failure to provide a precise, detailed definition of the transmission mechanism they believe so powerfully transmits monetary changes to GNP.

Criticism of the Monetarists' Money-GNP Relationship

In this area, the post-Keynesians have expressed their skepticism along two different lines. In the first place, a number of critics have argued that, even using the monetarists' own data, the historical relationship between money and GNP has not been sufficiently close to support monetarist policy prescriptions. Second, it has been pointed out—via the so-called "reverse causation argument"—that mere correlation between two variables does not necessarily imply causation. Perhaps it has been GNP changes that have caused money changes rather than the other way around.

---

[39]Lawrence R. Klein, "Commentary on 'The State of the Monetarist Debate,' " *Review,* Federal Reserve Bank of St. Louis, September 1973, p. 10.

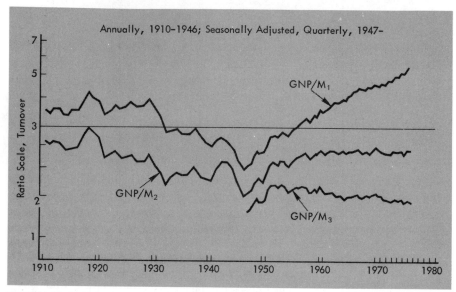

FIGURE 18-5   Velocity of M1, M2, and M3, 1910–1976

Source: Paul S. Anderson, "Behavior of Monetary Velocity," *New England Economic Review,* Federal Reserve Bank of Boston, March–April 1977.

Velocity Is Not Stable Enough.   Although it cannot be denied that the Friedman-Schwartz evidence shows that, historically, the stock of money and the level of GNP have tended to move together, the issue—if monetarist policy prescriptions are to be adopted—is, *How* close is the relationship? Or, to ask the same question the other way around, just *how* stable is velocity in fact?

As we have seen in Chapter 13 (Table 13-1), velocity in the United States has not only risen from 2.04 in 1947 to 6.61 in 1981 but has tended to vary procyclically. That is, in each postwar recession, V has declined, whereas in boom periods it has invariably increased. Post-Keynesian critics argue that this hardly represents the "extraordinary empirical stability and regularity" Professor Friedman claims income velocity demonstrates.

Nor, if a long enough period is considered, does the velocity of the more broadly defined M2 money stock seem to show "extraordinary" stability. It is true that this variable has been quite stable since 1960, but prior to that year, as Figure 18-5 makes clear, it too was subject to significant variability.

In addition, the Friedman-Schwartz data themselves have often been cited as providing evidence for the nonquantity theorists. Much stress, for example, is placed on the following statement: "the observed year-to-year change in velocity was less than 10 percent in 78 out of 91 year-to-year changes from 1860 . . . to 1960."[40] The monetarists offer this as one summary piece of evidence supporting

---

[40]Friedman and Schwartz, *A Monetary History,* p. 682.

their view that the money supply and income tend to move closely together. Many post-Keynesians read it quite the other way around. "Since a 10 percent difference in money income is the difference between inflation and recession, these figures are not very reassuring" is the opinion of one authority.[41] Another critic puts it this way: "a difference of 10 percent in the velocity of a given money stock, at today's level of the money stock, would result in a difference of about $80 billion in GNP. The Council of Economic Advisers gets roasted when errors in its annual forecasts are a fraction of that amount."[42]

The Reverse Causation Argument.   Even a closer fit of the money supply and GNP would probably not satisfy many post-Keynesians. For, as they have pointed out many times, correlation does not imply causation. Money and GNP could move together because—as the monetarists argue—the money supply basically determines GNP. But they could also move together for the reverse reason—because changes in GNP cause the money supply to move accordingly. This is the "reverse causation" argument.

The monetarists argue that the supply of money is an exogenous variable—one determined outside their model by the monetary authorities. But this need not always be the case. If the monetary authorities and the banking system follow the practice of accommodating the "demands for credit," we may find them expanding the money supply *because* production, income, and the "demand for credit" have picked up. If so, this would involve GNP changes causing money supply changes rather than the other way around.[43]

The Defense of Fiscal Policy

Post-Keynesians also reject the views expressed by Friedman and the Andersen-Jordan St. Louis model evidence to the effect that fiscal policy is virtually useless as a means of affecting GNP.

In denial, they cite the overwhelming body of evidence showing that the demand for money is negatively related to interest rates and that, therefore, aggregate demand (MV') can, indeed, vary without a change in M. In the short run at least, they contend, "pure" fiscal policy can change V enough to permit desired changes in aggregate demand.

---

[41]James Tobin, "The Monetary Interpretation of History," *American Economic Review,* June 1965.

[42]Daniel H. Brill, "Can the Government 'Fine-Tune' the Economy?" Address to American Statistical Association, February 1968, reprinted in *Standards for Guiding Monetary Action,* Hearings Before the Joint Economic Committee, 90th Cong., 2d sess., May 1968, p. 158.

[43]On this point, see Raymond Lombra and Raymond Torto, "Federal Reserve Defensive Behavior and the Reserve Causation Argument," *Staff Economic Studies,* Board of Governors of the Federal Reserve System, 1972. Lombra and Torto argue that defensive open-market operations by the FOMC "confirm the interdependence of the supply and demand for money" and provide persuasive evidence of the validity of the reverse causation argument.

The "fiscal multiplier" included in the St. Louis model (which, it will be remembered, shows the effects of fiscal measures virtually disappearing at the end of one year) are in sharp contrast to those included in many other econometric models of the economy constructed in accordance with the post-Keynesian position. As Professor Lawrence Klein puts it,

> Most American models, other than the St. Louis model, imply fiscal multipliers that rise fairly quickly to values between 2.0 and 3.0. They fluctuate in a narrow range for a number of years and then decline. . . . For the only period of policy relevance (before many other changes besides the original fiscal policy change, have taken place) the fiscal multipliers are estimated to be substantial by a broad consensus.[44]

As noted, the monetarist camp itself is divided on the issue of the potency of fiscal policy, but Professor Friedman and the architects of the St. Louis Fed's Andersen-Jordan model both appear to occupy the extreme position of denying any significant fiscal effects beyond fleeting changes for no more than six months. The St. Louis model's published fiscal multiplier has drawn an important challenge from Harvard's Professor Benjamin Friedman. In an article entitled "Even the St. Louis Model Now Believes in Fiscal Policy," Friedman presents the results of his reestimation of the St. Louis equation using data through mid-1976. What he finds is that

> the St. Louis equation, reestimated to incorporate the most recent available data, now indicates that fiscal policy unaccompanied by changes in the stock of money *does* matter. Furthermore, the indicated first-year cumulative multiplier of government spending on nominal GNP is about one and one-half—a value not surprising intuitively to believers in fiscal policy, and not very dissimilar to the values reported by familiar nonmonetarist models.[45]

In response, Keith Carlson of the St. Louis Federal Reserve Bank has argued that the inclusion of data from 1975 and 1976 makes "the form in which the St. Louis equation was specified . . . no longer statistically appropriate."[46] Carlson presents a recalculation of the St. Louis equation substituting rate of change for absolute dollar change data and argues that the results reaffirm the original St. Louis conclusions regarding the effects of fiscal policy.

Whatever the St. Louis equation concludes about fiscal policy, however, the majority of post-Keynesians insist that the fiscal multipliers implied by the vast

---

[44]Klein, "Commentary on 'The State of the Monetarist Debate,' " pp. 10–11. For details on the fiscal multipliers of a large number of econometric models, see Gary Fromm and Lawrence Klein, "A Comparison of Eleven Econometric Models," *American Economic Review,* May 1973.

[45]Benjamin M. Friedman, "Even the St. Louis Model Now Believes in Fiscal Policy," *Journal of Money, Credit and Banking,* May 1977, p. 365.

[46]Keith M. Carlson, "Does the St. Louis Equation Now Believe in Fiscal Policy?" *Review,* Federal Reserve Bank of St. Louis, February 1978.

majority of existing econometric models come closer to the true values and, as a result, conclude that fiscal policy, while not so potent as they once believed, possesses significant stabilization potential.[47]

Criticisms of the Statistical Approach of Monetarist Models

The form of the statistical models employed by both Friedman and Meiselman in their earlier work and by Andersen and Jordan in setting up the St. Louis model has come under sharp criticism. Whereas all recognized econometric models of the Keynesian variety are "structural models," which include equations specifically describing "how" monetary, fiscal, and other variables affect aggregate demand, the monetarist models are "reduced form" equations, which make no attempt to explain the underlying interconnections or transmission mechanisms. As Professor Tobin has put it,

> What I mean by a pseudo-reduced-form is an equation relating an ultimate variable of interest, like GNP, to the supposedly causal variables, but one which doesn't come out of any structure at all. Instead, the investigator just says, "Here are the effects and here are the causes, let's just throw them into an equation." The form and content of the equation—the list of variables and the lag structure—are not derived from any structural model. That is what we have presented to us as the main evidence for the supposed superiority of monetary variables in explaining GNP.[48]

Professor Klein has also pointed out that whereas the post-Keynesian structural econometric models of the economy do perform in a manner consistent with the "real world," the same cannot be said for the monetarist models:

> simulations of econometric models built along post-Keynesian lines do show important business cycle characteristics. It is a strong claim on the part of such model builders that these systems are capable of generating the cycle, as it has been historically measured, when the models are subjected to repeated shocks in stochastic simulations. I regard this as a basic validation feature of contemporary econometric model building research, and this is an integral part of my challenge to the monetarists, to see whether they can do as well in reproducing accepted measures of cyclical characteristics from simulations of their models. I am disappointed in their not following this line of econometric research.[49]

---

[47]The post-Keynesians go to pains to point out that their defense of fiscal policy should not be taken to indicate any lack of faith in monetary policy. For example, Professor Tobin has said, "One thing the nonmonetarists should *not* be called is 'fiscalists.' The debate is not symmetrical. Whereas neo-Keynesians believe that both monetary and fiscal policies affect nominal income, monetarists believe that only monetary policies do so." James Tobin, "Friedman's Theoretical Framework," *Journal of Political Economy,* September–October 1972, p. 852.

[48]James Tobin, "The Role of Money in National Economic Policy," *Controlling Monetary Aggregates,* Federal Reserve Bank of Boston, 1969, p. 23.

[49]Klein, "Commentary on 'The State of the Monetarist Debate,' " p. 12.

Monetarist Transmission Mechanism
Must Be More Clearly Explained

The monetarists have charged the post-Keynesian models with requiring money to work its way through to its effect on aggregate demand via a transmission mechanism that is much too narrow. The post-Keynesians respond with the charge that the monetarists have been unable or unwilling to make clear just what the specifics of their own transmissions mechanism are. As Professor Klein has put it, the Keynesian models are all "specific about the channels of monetary influence in a structural way. They stand as challenges to the monetarist points of view."[50]

In short, it is argued, the monetarists have made the claim that the supply of money is the dominant determinant of GNP and have offered considerable empirical evidence in support of the view. But beyond a few very tentative and preliminary descriptions, they have done little to specify exactly *how* and *through what channels* money has such powerful effects on economic activity.[51]

Without such further specification, many post-Keynesians find the logic following from the monetarist propositions quite unacceptable. "How," many ask, "can we accept the proposition that a $100 increase in the money supply will have roughly the same effects on GNP no matter what else happens (changes in technology, changes in consumer and investor psychology) and no matter what the procedure through which the money is created (open-market sale to the public, government borrowing as a result of increased government spending or tax reduction, loans to business, or bank purchases of securities from the public)?" Here, then, lies the heart of much of the debate.

Financial Innovation and the Changing
Meaning of Money

The innovative financial environment of the early 1980s, whatever its other effects, has not been exactly hospitable to the monetarist advocacy of stable, non-discretionary "monetary rules," for to argue that the nation should commit itself to a fixed rate of increase in the money supply requires that the concept of money and components of the money supply stay reasonably fixed. As we have seen earlier, that requirement has not been met in recent years.

Post-Keynesians have been quick to point out the problems financial innovation has created for monetarist policy prescription. As Professor Alan Blinder has put it,

---

[50]Klein, "Empirical Evidence on Fiscal and Monetary Models," p. 49.

[51]This point is granted by a well-known monetarist. "Monetarists must spell out, in greater detail than up to now, the channels by which money influences nominal GNP, the price level, and output." Andersen, "State of the Monetarist Debate," p. 8.

monetarism is now an anachronism. Monetarism simply makes no sense in a world where financial reform and innovation are wreaking havoc upon their demand functions. One result of all these financial innovations . . . is that no one knows what concept of M today corresponds to what we used to think of as M1 or M2 a few years ago.[52]

Where Do We Stand Now in the Monetarist–Post-Keynesian Debate?

Despite continuing differences of major import, substantial progress has been made toward narrowing the gulf between these two groups of economists over the past 15 years. Today, indeed, there appear to be few *theoretical* differences of substance that divide the more moderate monetarists from the more moderate post-Keynesians. As one prominent post-Keynesian put it, "there are no significant differences of analysis between able, intelligent openminded monetarists and nonmonetarists."[53]

This is a far cry from the earlier day of the debate when the acrimonious atmosphere in which it was staged fairly bristled with charge and countercharge. A humorous example of that early atmosphere was recounted a decade ago by Professor Deane Carson regarding a monetary conference being held in the Midwest in the mid-1960s. Carson recalls,

> The sponsor of the conference had chartered two planes to deliver the participants from O'Hare in Chicago to the meeting and it just so happened that all of the neo-Keynesians (except one) were aboard one plane and all the monetarists on the other. As the "monetarist" plane flew over the hot fields of Indiana, it began to pitch and yaw, giving both discomfort and apprehension to its passengers. After a few moments of this, Karl Brunner broke the white-knuckle silence with an apparently rhetorical question: "It would be interesting to speculate on what would be the impact on monetary economics if this plane were to crash and kill us all." After a few further moments of silence, the lone neo-Keynesian leaned across the aisle. "Karl," he said, "I have finished my speculation and I want you to know that I'm prepared to make the supreme sacrifice."[54]

In what areas have the two groups tended to "come together" in recent years? On the one hand, the post-Keynesians appear to have moved measurably toward the monetarist position on the key issue of the role of the money stock as a determinant of aggregate demand. This movement has come in two stages.

[52]Alan S. Blinder, "Monetarism Is Obsolete," *Challenge*, September–October 1981, p. 39.

[53]Franco Modigliani, "The Monetarist Controversy," *Economic Review Supplement*, Federal Reserve Bank of San Francisco, Spring 1977, p. 6.

[54]Deane Carson, "Discussion," *Controlling Monetary Aggregates II: The Implementation*, Federal Reserve Bank of Boston, 1973.

The first stage—a movement largely unrelated to monetarist prodding—constituted a rather general disavowal of the more extreme "money matters hardly at all" position some Keynesians seemed to have adopted in the 1940s and early 1950s. Thus when the monetarist–post-Keynesian debate heated up in the mid-1960s, the majority of post-Keynesians already accepted the money supply as an important determinant of aggregate demand (albeit, not necessarily the *dominant* determinant).

The second stage consisted of a veritable mountain of empirical evidence that has piled up since the battle was really joined in the 1960s, tending to reinforce the importance of the money stock as well as the magnitude of the "crowding out" effects connected with fiscal policy. As a result, the post-Keynesians have adjusted their position further toward the direction of the monetarists. This evidence, as incorporated in the essentially Keynesian M.I.T.–Penn–Social Science Research Council econometric model, implies a relatively steep demand-for-money curve and "pervasive and substantial" interest rate effects on demand. As one economist has recently put it, the "Keynesians have moved to occupy the strategic middle-ground, having been flexible enough to incorporate a major role for money in the Keynesian schema, thus leaving to monetarists the role of defending a more extreme position. The ultimate verdict on the debate *may* well be the victory of a moderate monetarism dressed in Keynesian clothes."[55]

At the same time a significant number of the more moderate monetarists refuse to accept the extreme position vis-à-vis fiscal policy adopted by some of their colleagues. For example, monetarist David Fand has observed that

> to deny any short run stabilization effects to fiscal actions, one must be prepared to argue that surpluses (or deficits), irrespective of magnitude, have no direct effect on spending through changes in disposable income and that they have no indirect effect through changes in desired real balances or desired liquidity, and on velocity. But this can be true only in the exceptional case of a completely (interest) inelastic demand for money.[56]

And monetarists Karl Brunner and Allan Meltzer, in commenting on two of Professor Friedman's papers, observe that

> One of the more striking features of Friedman's analysis is that . . . the fiscal role of government is mentioned only once and only to be dismissed. Changes in government expenditures and taxes, apparently, have so little effect that they can be ignored entirely.
>
> We know of no evidence to support this conclusion. The empirical work done by

---

[55]Thomas Mayer, "Some Reflections on the Current State of the Monetarist Debate," in *Readings in Money, National Income and Stabilization Policy*, 4th ed., ed. Ronald L. Teigen (Homewood, Ill.: Richard D. Irwin, 1978), p. 83.

[56]David I. Fand, "A Monetarist Model of the Monetary Process," *Journal of Finance*, May 1970, p. 286.

Friedman and Meiselman, Keran, Andersen and Jordan, and others frequently identified as "monetarists" provides no evidence that changes in the government expenditure and taxation have no effect on output.[57]

It seems, then, that many post-Keynesians have accepted a very important role for money and have somewhat tempered their claims for fiscal policy while a number of monetarists have granted that the interest elasticity of the demand for money does, indeed, permit some variation in velocity and, consequently, a stabilizing role for fiscal policy. But while the gap between the two groups has been narrowed by these developments, substantive differences on these and other important issues remain.

Perhaps the most fundamental of these is their divergence of views on the government's capacity to moderate cyclical swings via discretionary monetary and fiscal policy. Here the debate continues and the policy implications are profound.

On this issue, the monetarists see the private economy as fairly stable—that is, as not subject to major and continuing disturbance from external shocks (such as large and variable shifts in the MEI curve, the demand-for-money curve, or international trade patterns). To the extent that such external shocks do disturb the economy's stability, monetarists generally see strong and reasonably prompt correction via such neutralizing devices as the interest rate effects that we have labeled the "round 2" effects. As a consequence, they not only see little need for the government to enter in with discretionary stabilization programs to attempt to ameliorate the relatively minor problems caused by such "shocks" but, indeed, see such attempts as likely to make matters worse. This is the case, in their view, because—given the long and variable lags involved before such measures affect aggregate demand—we are unable to apply them at the appropriate time to have the desired effects. On the contrary, monetarists believe that well-intentioned, but ill-advised and badly timed, discretionary stabilization attempts in the past have been a large part of the *cause* of the instability we have suffered.

Post-Keynesians, in the main, view our world quite differently. They do see the potential for serious instability from external shocks and, while granting that the economy does contain built-in stabilizing tendencies that will, in time, lessen the problem, they conclude that "the *interim* response is still of significant magnitude and of considerable duration, basically because the wheels of the offsetting mechanism grind slowly."[58] The post-Keynesian response to the monetarist contention that discretionary stabilization policy can only make matters worse is to contrast the relative stability of the post–World War II era (where discretionary policy has been employed) with the pre–World War II period (where it was not).

One example of a view most post-Keynesians would accept was offered some years ago by Professor Don Patinkin:

---

[57]K. Brunner and A. H. Meltzer, "Friedman's Monetary Theory," *Journal of Political Economy,* September–October 1972, p. 842.

[58]Franco Modigliani, "The Monetarist Controversy, or, Should We Forsake Stabilization Policies?" *American Economic Review,* March 1977.

In brief, even if monetary policy could be depended upon to ultimately restore the economy to full employment, there would still remain the crucial question of the length of time it would need. There would still remain the very real possibility that it would necessitate subjecting the economy to an intolerably long period of dynamic adjustment: a period during which wages, prices, and interest would continue to fall, and—what is most important—a period during which varying numbers of workers would continue to suffer from involuntary unemployment. Though I am not aware that he expressed himself in this way, this is the essence of Keynes' position. This is all that need be established in order to justify his fundamental policy conclusion that the "self-adjusting quality of the economic system"—even when reinforced by central-bank policy—is not enough, and that resort must be had to fiscal policy.[59]

Thus the core of the issue may well be differing views on Keynes's oft-quoted statement "In the long-run we are all dead." The post-Keynesians argue that we can minimize our "short-run illnesses" with appropriate discretionary stabilization policy without jeopardizing the long-run health of the economy. The monetarists feel that the medicine prescribed by the post-Keynesians for short-run ills will make the patient sicker in the short run as well as threaten his long-run welfare.

Review Questions

1. Compare the conclusions of the modern monetarists with those of the "old" quantity theory covered earlier. In what respects do the two differ?
2. Carefully explain how the inclusion of a speculative (or asset) demand for money by Keynes in his interest theory may be said to make it possible for "pure" fiscal policy to affect aggregate demand.
3. How would you characterize the monetarist position on the "crowding out" effects of fiscal policy?
4. The monetarists argue that the use of interest rates as a prime monetary policy target is not only inappropriate but may lead to pro-cyclical monetary policy. Carefully explain this view.
5. Many monetarists would argue that fiscal policy as a stabilization weapon should be eliminated because it is ineffective; they would eliminate discretionary monetary policy not because it is ineffective but because they consider it subject to long and variable time lags. Carefully explain both positions.
6. Explain the "reverse causation" argument.
7. In terms of the four-diagram model employed in Chapter 17, the monetarists might be said to consider the second-round effects to be very powerful. Explain what this means for the slopes of the curves involved and how such slopes would lead to monetarist conclusions.

---

[59]Don Patinkin, "Friedman on the Quantity Theory and Keynesian Economics," *Journal of Political Economy*, September–October 1972, pp. 901–2.

8. To the monetarists, a rise in the supply of money may well lead to a *rise* in interest rates. Explain carefully.

9. What events in the late 1960s gave a major boost to the monetarist case?

10. "One thing the nonmonetarists should *not* be called is 'fiscalists.' The debate is not symmetrical." Explain the point of this quote from Nobel-laureate James Tobin.

11. Carefully outline the major elements of the post-Keynesians' opposition to the monetarist positions and policy prescriptions. What are the implications of financial innovation and the changing definition of money for monetarist policy conclusions?

19

Recent Experience and Theoretical Developments Regarding Inflation and Employment

Introduction

The Keynesian theoretical model presented in Chapter 17 provides an oversimplified, yet reasonably satisfactory, vehicle for analyzing the determinants of the money level of income (i.e., GNP). But GNP, it must be remembered, is the product of two separate components with vastly different implications for economic welfare—price and quantity. An increase in GNP resulting solely from quantity increases, implying as it does lower unemployment and higher real income, would almost universally be judged a favorable development.[1] But a similar increase consisting solely of a rise in the price component would just as universally be condemned as unfavorable. Clearly we need to go further than we have to consider the interconnections between employment and production on the one hand and the price level on the other. Our discussion thus far is particularly misleading as a mechanism for evaluating stabilization policies. Up to this point—largely because we have relied heavily upon a simplified, incomplete version of the Keynesian theory in which the price level has not been included as a specific variable—one might not unreasonably conclude that we have taken the position that (1) if aggregate demand falls short of the full-employment level of production, increases in aggregate demand will have only the "good" effects of raising production, employment, and real income, with no offsetting "bad" effects of price-level increase; (2) if aggregate demand exceeds the full-employment level of production, measures aimed at reducing aggregate demand can have only the "good" effects of eliminating inflation and none of the "bad" effects of eliminating jobs; and (3) there exists some "ideal" level of aggregate demand, which (given the existing level of

---

[1]Some environmentalists may take exception to this view.

productive capacity), once achieved, will assure us of that most desired of situations—full employment with stable prices.

If it only were as simple as that! Unfortunately, however, the policymaker's world is much more complex. Seldom can he or she raise aggregate demand without—to some degree at least—raising prices along with employment. Seldom can demand be restricted without causing (or at least risking) some increase in unemployment along with the desired reduction in upward pressure on prices. And while problems such as these have always been with us, they clearly became much more acute and baffling during the 1970s and 1980s.

This chapter examines the rapidly changing views regarding the optimum use of stabilization policies during the past several decades. First, we shall consider the view of the behavior of employment and prices during the course of a "typical" business cycle that more or less dominated economists' thinking throughout most of the 1950s and 1960s. Then, we shall focus on some of the newer theories developed primarily during the 1970s in an attempt to provide an explanation for that decade's distressing tendency to generate an unprecedented coexistence of high unemployment and high inflation rates. As we shall see, the implications of some of these newer theories for stabilization policy are profound.

The Pre-1970s View of the Business Cycle and the Role for Stabilization Policies

As we have already noted, the idealized world in which policymakers simply pull the appropriate levers to raise aggregate demand when there is unemployment and reverse the dosage when there is inflation never has existed. There have always been phases of the business cycle during which it was known that an expansion of demand aimed at fuller employment would likely raise prices somewhat and other periods where it was to be expected that demand restriction aimed at combating inflation would probably lead to some unemployment also. So some degree of "trade-off" between unemployment and inflation has been a problem confronting policymakers for many years. But prior to the disturbing events of the 1970s, it was generally considered quite manageable.

The Phases of a "Typical" Business Cycle—the Pre-1970s View

From 1945 to 1970, U.S. business cycles, though each was different in cause, length, and amplitude, followed a pattern sufficiently similar to permit one to summarize a "typical" path. This is done in Figure 19-1, where money GNP is measured off on the vertical axis and time on the horizontal axis. The assumption, of course, is that increasing (decreasing) aggregate demand raises (lowers) GNP and that the composition of the GNP change (as between real production and employment on the one hand and prices on the other) varies with the phase of the cycle.

At the initial trough of the typical (pre-1970s) recession (point A in Figure 19-1), one might have expected to find unemployment in the 6 to 7 percent range with the price level essentially stable. Then, when aggregate demand was increased, the initial response (A to B in Figure 19-1) could be expected to be primarily increases in production caused by a callback of laid-off workers with little or no price increase. Thus, no "trade-off" problem existed, for the effects of rising demand were almost entirely the "good" ones of increased production and employment.

After a while, however—possibly as the overall unemployment rate approached 5 percent—further increases in aggregate demand were expected to produce mixed results (from B to C in Figure 19-1). For even though "full" employment for the entire economy had not yet been reached, in certain industries and in the markets for certain skills, capacity had already been reached and the pressure of excess demand in specific sectors began to produce more and more price increases. Indeed, the closer the approach to the overall "full-employment" level, the greater the effect on prices and the less on employment and production.

Often referred to as the "bottleneck inflation" stage, the B to C range was where policymakers encountered their first serious "trade-off" decisions. If unemployment is now at a 5 percent rate and prices are currently rising at 2 percent per year and we *know* (of course, we never are really sure) that the demand increases needed to reduce unemployment to the 4 percent rate then conventionally accepted as full employment will push the inflation rate up to 4 percent per year, should we do it? Are the benefits of reducing the unemployment rate by 1 percent greater than, or less than, the costs of causing a 2 percent increase in the rate of price increase? Here, policymakers generally must rely on their own value judgments, for economists have little to offer them in the way of concrete evaluation of these costs and benefits.

Once full employment has been achieved, further increases in demand can do little, in the short run, but cause price increases. Here we have the classical "demand-pull" inflation case so often described as "too much money chasing too few goods." With full employment having already been reached, production cannot be further raised by adding more workers, so the added spending simply causes inflation.

In this phase (C to D in Figure 19-1), there is no real trade-off problem. With aggregate demand exceeding the full-employment level of aggregate supply, the problem and solution are apparent. Demand must be cut back so as to eliminate the source of the inflation.

While, on the surface at least, no "trade-off" decision need be made in the C to D range, matters are not really that simple for the policymaker. For although he or she may know that an appropriate cut in aggregate demand can eliminate the excess demand, the policymaker must be ever mindful of the possibility that an

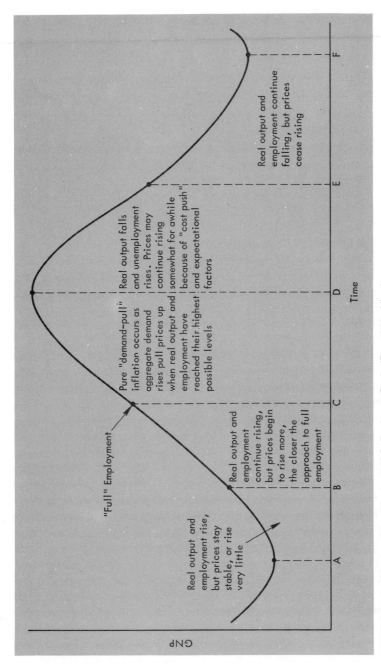

FIGURE 19-1 Stages of the "Typical" U.S. Business Cycle (Pre-1970s View)

excessive cut in demand may not only halt the inflation but also shove the economy over the peak into a new recession.

Whether as a result of overzealous policy, structural dislocations built up within the economy, or demand cutbacks for other reasons, periods of excess demand inflation in the United States have almost invariably been followed by downturn and recession. The first results of such a downturn (D to E in Figure 19-1) have generally consisted of increases in unemployment and cutbacks in production, but very little price relief.

Indeed, even before the 1970 recession, it was widely recognized that prices may continue rising for a time even while employment and production are falling and a full-blown recession is getting underway.

Why might prices continue upward when aggregate demand has fallen off sufficiently to cause rising unemployment? Because of a combination of inequities built up during the preceding boom and expectations, both of which tend to stimulate the development of "cost-push," or "sellers'," inflation.

Cost-push inflation, according to the usual definition, consists of a markup in prices by sellers who possess sufficient market (monopoly) power simply to increase their own prices, *in the absence of an excess of aggregate demand.* This type of inflation, which is a variety not readily controllable by stabilization policies, is generally aided and abetted by inequities and expectations built up during the cycle.

While prices in general have been rising in the preceding boom phase of the cycle, it is inevitable that some wage recipients—perhaps tied in to long-term contracts without escalator clauses—will have suffered real income reductions. If their union contracts then come up for renegotiation during the D to E phase of the cycle, their union can be expected to use its bargaining power—despite developing unemployment—to attempt to at least restore its members' relative purchasing power by demanding wage increases at least equal to the inflation plus productivity increases. And such action, by raising sellers' costs further, will likely trigger further price increases.

And catching up with past cost-of-living increases may not be the end of it. If prices have been rising over some considerable time period, the experience is quite likely to generate expectations that inflation will continue. If so, one should not be surprised to find industry and unions pushing up wages and prices by enough, not only to catch up with perceived past inequities but also to attempt to protect themselves against future erosion of their purchasing power. Expectations thus may reinforce the inflationary process both through generating a (cost-push) wage-price (or price-wage) spiral and through engendering a (demand-pull) buy-now-and-beat-the-price-rise psychology.

In any case, even before the experience of the 1970s, some inflation accompanying falling employment and production in the early portion of the recession phase of the business cycle was a widely recognized phenomenon. It was not, however, considered to be a major source of concern, since, in those days, experience seemed to dictate that the increasing slack in labor markets and the unsold inventories in product markets would fairly expeditiously bring the inflationary forces to heel. And although downward rigidity in wages and prices was recognized as sufficiently strong to prevent actual wage-price declines, the pre-1970 expectation was for roughly stable prices by the time the recession bottomed out.

The Phillips Curve

The general tendency for higher levels of aggregate demand to stimulate rises in prices coupled with declines in unemployment rates would naturally lead one to expect inflation and unemployment rates to be inversely related. In the 1950s, this observation led a British economist, A. W. Phillips, to carry out an empirical study of the British economy over a period of nearly a century aimed at investigating the relationship.[2]

The result of his study was a graphical device called the *Phillips curve,* which sums up neatly the "typical" (indeed, historical, as Phillips's and other similar curves are composed from actual experience with unemployment and inflation in the past) relation between unemployment rates and inflation rates for an economy during a given time period.

Phillips's original curve is shown in Figure 19-2; an early adaptation for the United States, using the rate of change of prices on the vertical axis, is shown in Figure 19-3. Both illustrate the expected negative relationship between unemployment rates and rates of wage (price) change.

It is important to recognize that both these curves are based on experience prior to 1960 and neither claims to represent the available "trade-offs" for the 1970s. With that qualification in mind, let us consider briefly the implications of Figure 19-3.

What it suggests is that, *given the structure of the U.S. economy during the years studied,* government policymakers could—through the use of monetary and fiscal policy to alter aggregate demand—choose among a wide variety of unemployment-inflation combinations. For example, if stable prices are to be achieved, aggregate demand must be low enough to allow 5.5 percent unemployment (point A). Achieving a 4 percent unemployment rate, however, would have required that aggregate demand be raised enough to generate about a 2 percent per annum rate of inflation (point B). If it was desired to push the unemployment rate down to as low as 2 percent (a level only achieved in the United States during World War II), aggregate demand would have had to have been raised sufficiently to cause an inflation rate between 7 and 8 percent.

---

[2]A. W. Phillips, "The Relation Between Unemployment and the Rate of Change of Money Wage Rates in the United Kingdom, 1861–1957," *Economica,* November 1958. As the title of his article indicates, Phillips's work was done with wage rates rather than price-level changes. Because it is normally assumed that money wage rates and price levels tend to move together, it has since become more common to use the so-called "Phillips curve" to relate unemployment rates with rates of price increase.

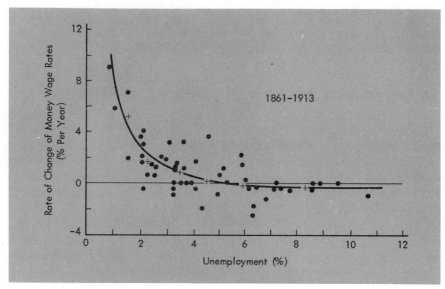

FIGURE 19-2   The Original Phillips Curve

Source: A. W. Phillips, "The Relation Between Unemployment and the Rate of Change of Money Wage Rates in the United Kingdom, 1861–1957," *Economica,* Vol. 25, No. 100, November 1958, p. 285.

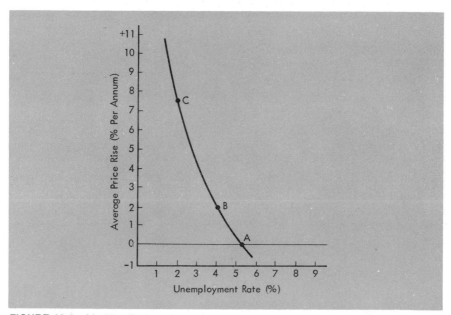

FIGURE 19-3   Modified Phillips Curve for the United States

Source: P. A. Samuelson and R. M. Solow, "Analytical Aspects of Anti-inflation Policy," *American Economic Review,* May 1960.

Conceptually, then, the Phillips curve device implied the existence of a more or less stable menu of unemployment-inflation combinations available to policy-makers. Expansionary monetary-fiscal measures raising aggregate demand would be expected to shift the economy up to the left along its existing curve, reducing unemployment rates but, at the same time, generating more rapid inflation. Contractionary measures would shift us downward to the right, cutting the inflation rate but raising unemployment.

Nor was movement along the curve in response to aggregate demand changes the only way in which government policymakers might affect the nation's economic fate. Since the level (distance from the origin) of any given Phillips curve depends partly upon the structural imperfections of the economy, it seemed entirely possible, *in the long run,* to move toward shifting the curve itself leftward to a position offering a more attractive set of short-run trade-offs. Such measures as manpower training programs and policies aimed at reducing monopolistic restrictions were considered appropriate ways of reducing structural unemployment and minimizing cost-push inflation, thereby—in the long run—tending to shift the Phillips curve leftward to a level closer to the origin.

All in all, the Phillips curve device seemed to constitute a clear as well as a fairly realistic way of summing up the options open to government for influencing employment and prices, and in the 1960s its use spread rapidly. But just as it was gaining widespread acceptance, developments in the late 1960s and early 1970s cast serious doubts on its viability. Let us consider the facts of that period.

Unemployment-Inflation Relationships Since 1965

After a long period of remarkably stable prices but excessive unemployment in the early 1960s, monetary and fiscal policy were brought to bear in the mid-1960s to raise aggregate demand and reduce unemployment. At about the same time, the Vietnam war began to escalate into a major U.S. commitment, which added markedly to the increase in demand. The result was as might well have been expected. Unemployment fell from 5.2 percent in 1964 to 4.5 percent in 1965 and on down to 3.8 percent by 1966. It stayed at or below the 3.8 level through 1969. Concurrently, the consumer price index began to rise. From an annual percentage increase of 1.7 during 1965, it went up by 2.9 percent in 1966, 2.9 percent in 1967, 4.2 percent in 1968, and 5.4 percent during 1969.

All this should not have been surprising. The United States was involved in a lengthy demand-pull inflationary boom, which implied that we had moved to the left and upward on our Phillips curve. The government unwisely postponed action to curb the developing inflation for several years.[3]

---

[3]Although the Federal Reserve did attempt to cool things off with an extremely restrictive monetary policy during part of 1966.

Finally, in late 1968 for fiscal policy and 1969 for monetary policy, a concerted governmental effort was made to cut down on aggregate demand with the aim, of course, of slowing down the accelerating inflation. The result was a rapid increase in unemployment (to 4.9 percent) as the nation slid into the 1970 recession but an astonishing 5.9 percent rise in prices at the same time!

Now, as noted, *some* continuing increase in prices from cost-push and other such factors, as unemployment initially rose, would not have been surprising. But there can be no doubt that virtually everyone—government policymakers and economists alike—was surprised to see inflation continue at such a rapid rate despite the strong action that had been taken to curb demand.

There were explanations after the fact, of course. That long period of unchecked demand-pull inflation, it was pointed out, had undoubtedly generated inflationary expectations that would take some time to subside. And cost-push inflation, it had always been argued, was an inherently short-run phenomenon that could not continue for much longer with aggregate demand held down.

This latter point is a simple one. Certainly, it was granted, monopoly forces *can* raise prices in the absence of excess demand. But when their action (in the absence of a rise in aggregate demand to "sustain" or "accommodate" the inflation) results in large unsold inventories and unemployment, they will reasonably quickly reassess their position and hold back on further price markups. "Just give it time," was the general refrain, "and things will straighten out."

Time passed, but things did not really "straighten out." In 1971, unemployment rose to 5.9 percent while the consumer price index went up another 4.3 percent. This unsettling experience (along with alarming developments in the nation's balance of international payments) led a reluctant President Nixon to implement powers granted him earlier by Congress by instituting a 90-day general price and wage freeze in August 1971 (the so-called Phase I).

The price freeze was followed, starting in November 1971, with "Phase II," a policy under which prices and wages were still directly controlled by governmental authority, but wages were permitted to be increased at a 5.5 percent annual rate and price increases had to be "justified" by cost increases. Phase II was continued throughout 1972, and, for that year, the record showed unemployment averaging 5.6 percent (but falling) and the consumer price index up by only 3.3 percent.

Somewhat encouraged, the administration greatly relaxed controls with the introduction of Phase III in January 1973. Under Phase III, explicit controls over price increases were lifted from all but the food, health, and construction industries, but the federal government retained the power to establish control over others whose price increases were considered "excessive."

What happened during 1973 is a matter of record. Unemployment fell to an average of 4.9 percent during the year, but the consumer price index for the year shot upward by over 6 percent. And all this happened despite another overall 60-day price freeze in mid-1973 and reinstitution of Phase II-type controls for the balance of the year.

Following this brief and relatively unsatisfactory fling at wage and price controls, the federal government, alarmed by the startling resurgence of accelerating inflation, returned to more conventional means for combating it. From mid-1973 to mid-1974, for example, the federal funds interest rate was allowed to rise from just over 7 percent to more than 13 percent as the Fed launched what appeared to be an all-out attack. But the results this time were not only disappointing but spectacularly so.

During 1974 not only did the unemployment rate climb back to an average of 5.6 percent but the consumer price index shot upward by an astonishing 11.0 percent. In 1975 the recession deepened, with the unemployment rate soaring above 9.0 percent and averaging 8.5 percent for the year as a whole. And contrary to the very essence of the Phillips curve analysis, the inflation rate, far from being modified by the excessive slack in the economy, rocketed upward by another 9.1 percent! Clearly something quite new was occurring, and the Phillips curve promise of stable trade-offs between inflation and unemployment was brought into serious question.

There was hope, of course, that one benefit of undergoing what, up to that time was the worst recession since the Great Depression of the 1930s, would be to snuff out the inflationary pressures that had been battering the economy for nearly a decade. The rate of increase in the consumer index did dip sharply to 4.8 percent during 1976, but the respite was only temporary as it shot up again to 6.8 percent in 1977 and 9.0 percent in 1978 before reaching the double-digit level again in 1979 and 1980 with disheartening 13.3 and 12.4 percent performances. And while the economy's unemployment rate did fall steadily from its 1975 average of 8.5 percent to as low as 5.8 percent by 1979, two successive recessions in 1980 and 1982 brought it right back up again to unprecedentedly high rates in the early 1980s. Indeed, by late 1982 the monthly unemployment rate was well over 10 percent for the first time since 1940.

Probably the best way to illustrate the deterioration in performance of the U.S. economy since 1970 is via the Phillips curve–type diagrams in Figures 19-4a and 19-4b. In Figure 19-4a, data for the unemployment rate and the inflation rate (as measured by the implicit GNP deflator) for 1950 to 1969 are plotted and a "Phillips curve" is sketched in to illustrate the relationship.[4]

What stands out here is the fact that (except for the Korean war–price control years of 1952 and 1953) this performance produces a fairly regular pattern quite consistent with the "Phillips curve" hypothesis.

Figure 19-4b then adds observations for the economy's performance from 1970 through 1982. Two things fairly leap out at one from this diagram. First, it dramatically portrays the worsened performance of the economy since 1970. Sec-

---

[4]It should be noted that the curve in Figure 19-4 is not statistically fitted to the data but rather is simply drawn in by "eyeballing" the data.

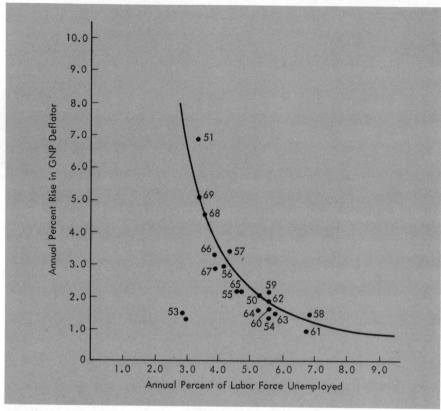

FIGURE 19-4a   Relationship Between Rate of Price Increase and Rate of Unemployment,
1950–1969

Source: U.S. Department of Labor, *Economic Report of the President,* various issues.

ond, it provides ample reason for questioning the concept of a stable Phillips
curve–type "trade-off." How might one explain these startling developments?

Attempts to Explain the Unemployment-
Inflation Experience of the 1970s

Even before the disasters of the 1970s, some economists had begun to doubt the
concept of a stable Phillips curve. For although rising aggregate demand in the
1966–1969 period did reduce the unemployment rate to the 3.5 to 3.8 percent
neighborhood, it became apparent that it stayed there only at the cost of *increasing*
rates of inflation each year. Although one might have explained this experience as
the result of reaching "full" employment and, thus, the essentially vertical (left)

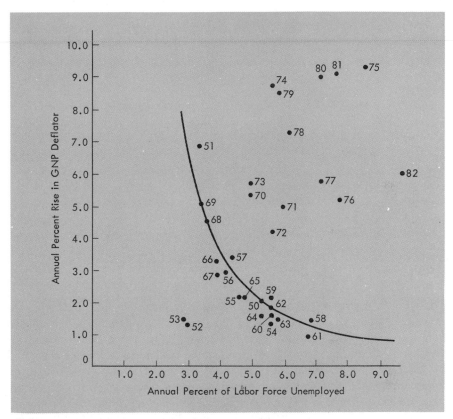

FIGURE 19-4b   Relationship Between Rate of Price Increase and Rate of Unemployment, 1950–1982

Source: U.S. Department of Labor, *Economic Report of the President,* various issues.

portion of an existing Phillips curve, a number of economists took the position that it reflected that the nation's Phillips curve itself had shifted to the right (that is, to a *less* satisfactory position).

The Shifting Phillips Curve View

Whatever the interpretation of the experience of the latter 1960s, it was quite evident that the 1970s and 1980s represented something quite new. Among a number of attempts to explain it was the notion that structural and institutional changes in the economy had combined to shift the U.S. Phillips curve sharply to the right. This view of the situation is depicted in Figure 19-5, where the "1970s curve" implies that a higher level of inflation was associated with each achievable rate of unemployment. There were at least two sets of reasons for this view.

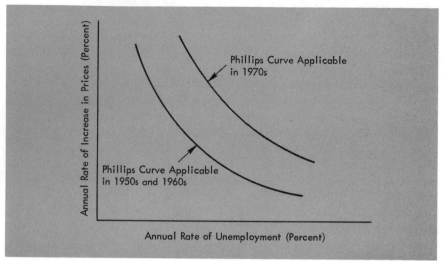

FIGURE 19-5   The Shifting ("Worsening") Phillips Curve View

Changing Structure of Labor Force.   Several economists put forth the view that a changing structure of the U.S. labor force was at least partially responsible for a shift to the right in the nation's Phillips curve and the consequent worsening of "trade-off" terms.[5] It was their position that the nation had undergone changes in the labor force composition such that the achievement of any given overall unemployment rate, say, 4 percent, would require a higher level of demand and therefore a higher rate of inflation than had been the case earlier.

The labor force of the 1970s and early 1980s contained a much larger percentage of teenagers, females, and part-time workers than in earlier years. These are groups of workers who traditionally experience higher unemployment rates than others, but in recent years their employment experience has gotten even worse.[6] Evidence to this effect is contained in Tables 19-1 and 19-2.[7]

A similar view was taken by the President's Council of Economic Advisers in 1977 when changes in labor force structure were cited as the reason for a change in the base on which the "full-employment budget" figures were computed. In

---

[5]See, for example, George L. Perry, "Changing Labor Markets and Inflation," *Brookings Papers on Economic Activity,* Vol. 1, No. 3 (Washington, D.C.: The Brookings Institution, 1970); and Charles L. Schultz, "Has the Phillips Curve Shifted? Some Additional Evidence," *Brookings Papers on Economic Activity,* Vol. 2, No. 2, (Washington, D.C.: The Brookings Institution, 1971).

[6]For example, in 1955 teenage males had unemployment rates 3.7 times as high as those of adult males. By 1969, their unemployment rate was 6.8 times as high as that of older males. See Charles Schultz, "The Inflation-Unemployment Dilemma: Has It Worsened?" in *Charles Schultz on Economics,* December 4, 1972 (New York: Appleton-Century-Crofts, 1972).

[7]For an excellent earlier discussion of the facts of these changes, see Sharon P. Smith, "The Changing Composition of the Labor Force," *Quarterly Review,* Federal Reserve Bank of New York, Winter 1976.

TABLE 19-1

Percentage of Civilian Labor Force Employed, by Sex and Age, 1950–1980

	1950	*1955*	*1960*	*1965*	*1970*	*1975*	*1980*
Males, total	70.6%	68.5%	66.7%	65.1%	62.2%	59.7%	57.6%
Females, total	29.4	31.5	33.3	34.9	37.8	40.3	42.4
Both sexes, 16–19	6.3	5.8	6.1	7.0	7.8	8.3	7.9

Source: U.S. Department of Labor, Bureau of Labor Statistics, *Employment and Earnings,* various years.

effect, the council stated that the same degree of inflationary pressure was now to be expected at a 4.9 percent rate of unemployment as had previously been encountered at a 4.0 percent unemployment rate. In essence, then, the council was attributing unemployment totaling about 1 percent of the labor force to the changed labor force composition.[8]

Undoubtedly there is validity to this position. It has been challenged, however, on two grounds. First, it has been pointed out that other factors affecting the structure of the labor force have worked the other way around.[9] Second, it seems clear that the structural changes in the labor force cited, though important, could not possibly have had sufficient impact to completely explain the nation's dismal "trade-off" situation in the 1970s.

Increased Level of Benefits to the Unemployed.   A second reason that has been cited as working toward a rightward shift in the nation's Phillips curve is the increased level and duration of government benefits currently available to the un-

TABLE 19-2

Unemployment Rates, by Age and Sex, 1950–1980

	1950	*1955*	*1960*	*1965*	*1970*	*1975*	*1980*
Male, 20 and over	4.7%	3.8%	4.7%	3.2%	3.5%	6.8%	5.9%
Female, 20 and over	5.1	4.4	5.1	4.5	4.8	8.0	6.4
Both sexes, 16–19	12.2	11.0	14.7	14.8	15.3	19.9	17.8

Source: U.S. Department of Labor, Bureau of Labor Statistics, *Employment and Earnings,* various years.

---

[8]*Economic Report of the President, 1977* (Washington, D.C.: Government Printing Office, 1977), pp. 48–51. It is interesting (but hardly surprising) to note that while this change was made in the final economic report of the Ford Council, it was subsequently accepted as appropriate and used by the first Carter council. See *Economic Report of the President, 1978,* p. 83.

[9]These include the fact that today's labor force is better educated than that of the 1950s and that a number of governmental manpower training programs have improved the employability of a significant number of workers in recent years. See Edgar L. Feige, "The 1972 Report of the President's Council of Economic Advisers: Inflation and Unemployment," *American Economic Review,* September 1972; and Sylvia S. Small, "Statistical Effect of Work-Training Programs on the Unemployment Rate," *Monthly Labor Review,* September 1972.

employed. This is especially the case for unemployment compensation benefits, but some of the nation's welfare programs have also been singled out for criticism along the same lines.

A distinguished Harvard economist, Professor Martin Feldstein, has presented evidence indicating that increased unemployment compensation benefits have produced additions to the unemployment rolls that may well total .75 percent of the labor force.[10] The point here, of course, is that rising benefit levels—as well as their increased duration—have led some unemployed workers to be a bit more casual and selective in their job search than was previously the case.[11]

Although the estimates are the subject of disagreement, there can be no question that if both Professor Feldstein and those who cite changes in the structure of the labor force as a source of increased unemployment are correct in their judgment, the two factors could account for a substantial shift in the Phillips curve. Taken together, these two factors have been cited as being responsible for unemployment among 1.75 percent of the labor force—a very significant total indeed.

"Supply Shocks" as a Cause of Stagflation

Although the nation's economic performance has been consistently poor ever since 1970, the 1974–1975 years and the 1979–1981 years stand out as exceptionally bad. Is there a way of explaining these unusually bad years?

One common element in both periods was an enormous increase in the price charged for oil imported from the OPEC nations. The oil price increases (along with sharp food price rises during the same periods) have been singled out as solely responsible for much of the exceptional surge of inflation during these two periods.[12]

These factors, as well as others, can be looked upon as generating a special sort of cost-push inflation by reducing the supply of goods available at every price level. Such a situation is depicted in Figure 19-6, where the price level is measured off vertically, the level of real output horizontally, SS represents various possible levels of aggregate supply, and DD represents various possible levels of aggregate demand. Obviously, the aggregate demand curve depicted in Figure 19-6 is a different thing from the aggregate demand lines referred to in Chapters 14 through 17.

The "supply shocks" just referred to would have a tendency to shift the aggregate supply curve from S_1S_1 to S_2S_2, thereby raising the price level as well

---

[10]Martin S. Feldstein, *Lowering the Permanent Rate of Unemployment*, A Study for the Joint Economic Committee, 93rd Cong., 1st sess., 1973.

[11]A somewhat different, but nonetheless related, objection has been raised by others regarding the effects that rising legal minimum-wage levels have on teenage and minority unemployment.

[12]For estimates of the size of their impact, see Charles L. Schultz, "Some Macro Foundations for Micro Theory," *Brookings Papers on Economic Activity*, February 1981; and Alan S. Blinder, "Monetarism Is Obsolete," *Challenge*, September–October 1981.

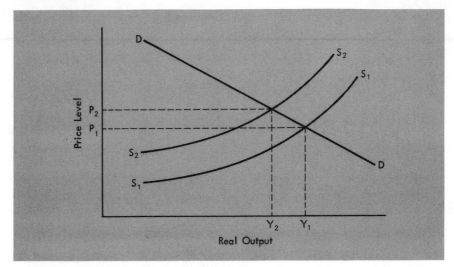

FIGURE 19-6 Short-Run Effects of Supply Shocks on the Economy

as lowering the level of output and employment. Subsequent effects, of course, would depend upon the nature of the government's policy response to these disturbing developments.

It would be foolish to deny that the series of severe supply shocks that befell the U.S. economy in 1974–1975 and again in 1979–1980 had significant effects. Unquestionably they did. But one cannot explain a decade long experience solely on the basis of a number of random (however severe) supply shocks suffered along the way. One factor we have not yet touched upon that, in the opinion of all observers, has played a key role in price-unemployment experience during the 1970s and early 1980s has been that of price expectations. The remainder of the chapter considers this vitally important matter.

The Role of Price Expectations

After a lengthy period of relative stability, the price level began rising alarmingly in the mid-1960s in response to the excess demand generated during the Vietnam war. It was the beginning of an inflationary surge that persisted throughout the next decade and right on into the 1980s. It had long been understood that years of continued inflation could generate price expectations that, in and of themselves, could sustain the process and, indeed, even accelerate it. Buyers, after all, expecting price increases, would tend to buy more now to beat the rise, and price setters such as unions and corporations would attempt to protect themselves against loss of purchasing power by pushing up wages and prices more rapidly. But prior to the end of the 1960s, the implications of these developments for stabilization policy had not been considered in any detail. During the past 15 years, however, much effort has been devoted to that area, and, as a result of these studies, the concept of a "natural" unemployment rate, the so-called "accelerationist" theory, and the newer "rational expectations" argument have arisen to pose a serious challenge to supporters of discretionary stabilization policies.[13]

The Natural Unemployment Rate Hypothesis and the "Accelerationist" View.

Difficulties in relating the Phillips curve concept to the facts of the 1970s have led many economists to the conclusion that Phillips curve–type trade-offs between inflation and unemployment exist only in the short run and only because of transitory differences between the expected and actual rates of inflation. In the longer run, however, when consumers have had sufficient experience to adapt their price expectations fully to the actual rate of inflation, all opportunity for trade-offs via alterations in aggregate demand disappears. To this "accelerationist" group, then, the long-run Phillips curve is a vertical line implying that changes in aggregate demand can only alter the price level with no lasting effect on the employment level.

The accelerationist view is based upon the concept of a "natural" rate of unemployment. The natural rate of unemployment may be defined as *that rate of employment at which the rate of inflation being experienced equals the rate of inflation that was expected*. It is thus an "equilibrium" rate of unemployment, in the sense that, at that rate, everyone is receiving the real wage they expected when they entered into their current wage contract. A rate of unemployment lower than the "natural" rate can be achieved, but only as a result of workers being fooled into working for a lower real wage than they had expected. Such a lower unemployment rate is not an equilibrium because ultimately workers will learn that they have been "fooled" and will readjust their labor offerings accordingly.

This "natural" (or equilibrium) unemployment rate is not considered to be a fixed datum, established by some natural laws for all time, impervious to any efforts to alter it. Rather, it is determined by the number of structural impediments to employment built into an economy. For example, restrictive licensing as an obstacle to entry into a field, minimum wage laws, inadequate employment information, deficiencies in manpower training, and arbitrary restrictions on apprenticeships by unions would all work in the direction of establishing a high "natural" rate of unemployment.[14]

Let us consider this natural rate–accelerationist view in some detail. As noted, its proponents do not deny that, *in the short run,* unemployment can be reduced

---

[13]The following two sections owe much to two excellent articles by Thomas M. Humphrey. See Humphrey, "Changing Views of the Phillips Curve," *Monthly Review,* Federal Reserve Bank of Richmond, July 1973; and "Some Recent Developments in Phillips Curve Analysis," *Monthly Review,* Federal Reserve Bank of Richmond, January–February 1978. For more technical surveys, see Robert J. Gordon, "Recent Developments in the Theory of Inflation and Unemployment," *Journal of Monetary Economics,* April 1976; and Helmut Frisch, "Inflation Theory 1963–1975: A 'Second Generation' Survey," *Journal of Economic Literature,* December 1977.

[14]See Milton Friedman, "The Role of Monetary Policy," *American Economic Review,* March 1968.

below the "natural" rate and the rate of inflation increased by increases in demand. That, is, they grant that there do exist some very short-run Phillips curves along which shifts (and trade-offs between unemployment and inflation) are possible. But, they argue, the price increases resulting from such an effort will quickly generate a higher level of inflationary expectations on the part of the public which, in themselves, will tend to shift the (short-run) Phillips curve up to the right. Consider the graphic illustration in Figure 19-7.

Suppose, for example, that the "natural" rate of unemployment for the economy depicted there is 5 percent and that the country is initially at point A, where unemployment is 5 percent and prices are stable. (By way of example, we might assume that the current price level is $2.00 per unit, while the current money wage rate is $8.00 per hour. This would produce a "real" wage rate—money wage/price level—of $4.00 per hour, which, for equilibrium, we must assume satisfies both employers and employees at the current employment level.)

Now assume that the government decides to raise aggregate demand via monetary-fiscal policies so as to lower unemployment from 5 to 3 percent. Such a rise in demand will, it knows, increase the rate of price increase from its current zero rate to a rate of 4 percent. In Figure 19-7, this means the government action moves the economy along the "short-run Phillips curve" labeled S_1 to point B.

It is worth considering why more workers are hired (97 rather than 95 percent of the labor force) after this governmental measure. From the employers' point of view, it is easy to see. They are now receiving prices for the goods they sell that

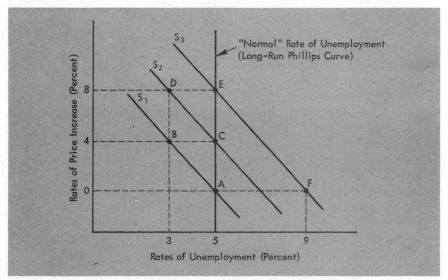

FIGURE 19-7 The Accelerationist View of Unemployment-Inflation Trade-offs

Source: Adapted from similar figure in Thomas M. Humphrey, "Changing Views of the Phillips Curve," *Monthly Review,* Federal Reserve Bank of Richmond, January–February 1978, p. 10.

are rising at 4 percent per year, but (initially, anyway) their money wage costs are hardly rising at all. This means that the real wage they pay has fallen so they can readily *afford* to hire more workers.

And what about the workers? Initially, they are "fooled" into offering more labor by what appears to them as *higher* real wages. Having recently experienced stable prices, they come to expect more of the same. If they now start receiving money wages going up at a rate of, say, 1 percent, that rise, taken together with the expected stability of product prices, appears to them (erroneously, of course) as a higher real wage.

But they are not likely to be fooled this way for long. Once they begin to experience the actual 4 percent rate of price increase, their price expectations will be changed, and they will, of course, act to protect themselves. That is, they will insist on *money* wage increases at a rate of at least 4 percent to keep up with prices and eliminate the cut in real wages they have temporarily undergone.

These changes in price expectations, causing, as they must, increases in money wages at a faster rate, will *shift the nation's short-run Phillips curve to the right*. Indeed, once a 4 percent per annum inflation comes to be fully expected, the short-run Phillips curve will shift to S_2, at which point (because money wages have now risen enough to raise real wages back to their original level) employers will, as at point A, find it worthwhile to hire only 95 percent of the labor force. We are back to the "natural" rate of unemployment once again but find ourselves still experiencing a 4 percent annual inflation rate (point C).

If, however, the government is determined to maintain the level of unemployment at the 3 percent rate, it can do so only at the cost of ever-accelerating price levels. Look again at Figure 19-7. Once the public has come to anticipate an inflation rate of 4 percent, the short-run Phillips curve becomes S_2. From here, unemployment can once again be driven down to 3 percent via aggregate demand increases (along S_2) until we arrive at point D. But we can only stay at point D (with 3 percent unemployment and 8 percent inflation) so long as the public *expects* prices to rise 4 percent per year. As soon as the public adjusts its expectations to the new circumstances and comes to expect 8 percent inflation, the real wage rises once again and the short-run Phillips curve shifts up once more to S_3. And, again, unemployment will rise back to its "natural" level (to point E).

So what is to be done now? The government has attempted to trade off price stability for reduced unemployment but has succeeded in purchasing only brief episodes of fuller employment while people were adapting their price expectations to reality. In the end, it finds itself back at the same old 5 percent unemployment level but saddled with a continuing 8 percent inflation rate. The accelerationist prescription is simple. Since, except briefly, it cannot achieve an unemployment rate below its "natural" 5 percent rate without perpetually accelerating the inflation rate, its optimum course is to accept the inevitable 5 percent of unemployment and do what it can to work its way back to the more desirable S_1 short-run Phillips curve where, at least, prices are stable. This simply requires a reversal of direction of its demand management tools of sufficient magnitude and duration to squeeze out the inflationary expectations built up earlier. It could, for example, enact sufficiently restrictive monetary and fiscal policies to move the economy southeasterly along its current short-run Phillips curve (by assumption, S_3) to point F.

This, of course, will extract a price—a rise in the unemployment rate to 9 percent. But that unhappy situation cannot last. The S_3 short-run Phillips curve implies expectations of 8 percent price rises built up from the past. Since these expectations now *exceed* the actual rate of inflation, the short-run Phillips curve must ultimately shift downward until, when all inflationary expectations have been squeezed out, the nation can return to the best position open to it—point A on short-run Phillips curve S_1.

The accelerationist conclusion, then, is that the "long-run" Phillips curve is the vertical line drawn in at the 5 percent unemployment rate in Figure 19-7. Alterations in demand by those charged with stabilization policy can move us off it, but only temporarily and only because people overestimate or underestimate the inflation rate. In the long run, we are foredoomed to the "natural" unemployment rate, and all that variations in aggregate demand can do is alter the rate of inflation.

The policy implications of the accelerationist view are, of course, of profound importance. Monetary and fiscal policy measures to reduce unemployment below the natural rate through raising aggregate demand are seen as being actually counterproductive because, while they may permanently raise the rate of inflation, they can only temporarily reduce unemployment below its "natural" rate. The only rational course for an economy suffering from the combined ills of inflation and unemployment is intentionally to worsen the latter for a period sufficiently long to eliminate the inflationary expectations underlying the former. And once that is accomplished, we must launch upon the long-run task of reducing the structural impediments to employment—the majority of which are alleged to have been erected by government in any case—which keep the so-called "natural unemployment" rate so high. To the activist, it is an essentially bleak scenario.

The Rational Expectations Hypothesis.   As if the natural unemployment rate and accelerationist thesis were not a sufficient challenge to those favoring an activist government stabilization program, a small but distinguished group of economists has recently gone them one better by denying the possibility of any inflation-unemployment trade-off *even in the short run*. These economists, who have been dubbed the "rational expectationists," have concentrated particularly on the way in which people arrive at their expectations.

In essence they argue that the assumption, implicit in the accelerationist hypothesis, that people's price expectations are formed solely on the basis of past inflation experience is naïve and unrealistic. It will be recalled that according to that hypothesis, increases in demand can have short-run effects on employment only because workers tend to underestimate the degree of price increase, thereby settling for money wage increases that permit a decline in the real wage (because actual product prices rise faster than wages) and therefore provide an incentive to employers to increase hiring. Only after experiencing a given rate of inflation for some time are workers assumed able to adapt their expectations to the true rate of inflation thereby upping their wage demands (or quitting to seek higher pay elsewhere) and wiping out the profit margin that permitted the rise in employment.

According to the rational expectationists, the notion that people form their price expectations solely from past inflation experience is equivalent to assuming that people are irrational. If they start out this way (during a period when, in fact, the rate of price increase is rising), they will soon learn that they were wrong. On learning this, rational people will not slavishly keep committing the same error in the future but, rather, will use all information at their disposal to forecast future inflation more accurately. Assuming that all relevant information is available to them, this should permit them to rapidly improve the accuracy of their price forecasts, thereby minimizing the period during which they underestimate the inflation.

The policy implications of the rational expectations view are indeed extreme. Not only do they envision no long-run trade-off between unemployment and inflation, but they see virtually none in the short run either. If correct, what this means is that governmental monetary and fiscal policies are totally incapable of influencing real magnitudes such as the level of production and employment. And this, in turn, would imply that stabilization policy as we have known it for well over 40 years should be summarily discarded as being unworkable!

Conclusion

When John Maynard Keynes wrote his *General Theory,* it represented an attempt to offer policy solutions to serious economic problems with which the then-dominant theory seemed incapable of coping. His central message was that government could, through judicious use of monetary and fiscal policy, contribute mightily to stabilization, at acceptable levels, of prices, employment, and production. To a generation desperately seeking solutions to the worst economic collapse the nation had ever experienced, it was a heartening message. No longer need we stand by helplessly while forces heretofore thought to be beyond our control buffeted us about. At long last mankind had both the will and the means to control its own economic destiny!

And most of our experience in the following three decades seemed to confirm the validity of Keynes's observations. Business cycles continued in the post–World War II period, but they were relatively mild, short-lived affairs. By the mid-1960s—especially after the 1964 tax cut along with supportive monetary expansion restored the nation to full employment in near-textbook fashion–many economists became convinced that serious unemployment and inflation problems had finally been eliminated.

But by the end of the 1960s, and especially in the 1970s, things began to become unstuck. Not only were we unable to establish full employment with stable prices, but—Professor Phillips notwithstanding—we proved singularly unsuccessful in any efforts to "trade off" unemployment against inflation. Clearly something was amiss, and economic scholars around the country went back to the drawing boards to attempt to uncover explanations.

The preceding sections on the natural rate of unemployment and its corollary, the accelerationist hypothesis, as well as the more recent rational expectations hypothesis, briefly describe the position of some respected members of the economics profession in the 1980s. But it would be less than accurate to say that they as yet form a new consensus. While recognizing the existence of new limitations on stabilization policy via aggregate demand management, most economists still see a substantial role for them. Many, indeed, would readily subscribe to the following statement of Professor Modigliani:

> We must, therefore, categorically reject the Monetarist appeal to turn back the clock 40 years by discarding the basic message of the General Theory. We should instead concentrate our efforts in an endeavor to make stabilization policies even more effective in the future than they have been in the past![15]

Despite their appeal as a way of explaining the role played by expectations in the inflation of the 1970s, the accelerationist and rational expectations hypotheses have been criticized as requiring unrealistic assumptions and as failing, in any case, to "fit the facts" of the U.S. economy.

Based as they are, on a foundation of neoclassical microeconomics, many versions of the accelerationist hypothesis appear to assume competitive markets, to envision downward as well as upward flexibility of wages and prices, and to treat the labor market as an auction market in which a homogeneous product is bought and sold.[16] This leads to a number of peculiarities not the least of which is the position that all unemployment above the natural rate is seen as voluntary. When demand falls in a competitive world, prices and money wages must fall as a consequence. If, however, workers fail to forecast the decline in prices accurately, they will interpret the cut in money wages as a decline in their real wage. And since it is assumed that the quantity of labor they will offer varies positively with the real wage, they will react to the perceived cut in their real wage by cutting back the quantity of labor supplied. In this version of the accelerationist logic we are thus left with the startling conclusion that ". . . output falls not because of the decline in demand but because of the entirely voluntary reduction in the supply of labor, in response to erroneous perceptions."[17] Mindful of the well-documented fact that voluntary quits tend to *fall*, rather than rise, during periods of declining demand and of the demonstrated downward stickiness of wages and prices, many economists find themselves unable to accept this logic.

Further skepticism regarding the accelerationist hypothesis is aroused by the

---

[15]Franco Modigliani, "The Monetarist Controversy or, Should We Forsake Stabilization Policies," *American Economic Review,* March 1977, p. 18.

[16]Ibid., pp. 6–7.

[17]Ibid., p. 4.

fact that its conclusions, especially regarding events during periods of declining demand, appear to be inconsistent with the evidence from U.S. experience. When the actual unemployment rate rises above the "natural" rate, no stimulative boost from the demand side (via expansionary monetary-fiscal policies) is said to be needed because—after some (presumably tolerable) time lag—workers will recognize that prices are no longer rising as fast as before and will modify their wage demands accordingly. Indeed, in the strict logic of the accelerationist hypothesis, "an accelerating deflation should occur when the rate of unemployment increases above the 'natural' rate."[18] But during much of the Great Depression, the long slack period from 1958 to 1964, and the more recent episodes in 1974–1975, and 1981–1982—all of which are surely periods where the unemployment rate rose well above the "natural" rate—little evidence of such a development can be seen.

As might be expected, there is even more opposition to the more extreme rational expectations hypothesis as applied to macroeconomics. Opponents point out that people actually do have imperfect knowledge with which to predict future price levels—less, surely, than the stabilization authorities—and that, in any case, our experience does not confirm the price flexibility and speedy return to the "natural" rate of unemployment than the hypothesis implies.

What seems clear as we struggle through the 1980s is that, while much has been learned from the stagflation of recent years and several plausible hypotheses have been offered, the economics profession is, unhappily, not yet in a position to fully explain it, much less advise policymakers on just how to prevent its recurrence.

Review Questions

1. Define and contrast "demand-pull" and "cost-push" inflation.
2. What does the conventional (short-run) Phillips curve purport to show?
3. The performance of the U.S. economy during the 1970s led some observers to argue that the nation's Phillips curve had shifted to the right. What reasons have been given in support of this view?
4. What are "supply shocks"? How have they tended to affect U.S. economic performance, especially during the 1970s?
5. Define the "natural" rate of unemployment. What factors can cause increases in the natural rate? What must ultimately happen if the actual rate of unemployment is driven down to below the natural rate?
6. According to the "accelerationist" hypothesis, increase in demand to reduce unemployment below the natural rate can only succeed temporarily as a result of workers underestimating the actual rate of inflation Explain carefully why

---

[18]Frisch, "Inflation Theory 1963–1975," p. 1297.

unemployment is reduced in the short run and why this gain will tend to be wiped out in the long run.

7. "In the long run, a nation's Phillips curve is vertical." Explain, making clear in the process, the policy implications of such a viewpoint.

8. What is the major position of the so-called "rational expectationists"? For policy purposes, what does this view imply about the costs, in terms of increased unemployment, of cutting inflation via decreased levels of aggregate demand?

20

The Channels of Monetary Policy and Some Alleged Weaknesses

Introduction

The simplified, essentially Keynesian, income determination model presented in Chapter 17 provides an excellent framework for analyzing many macroeconomic problems of major significance. Partly because of the simplified form in which it was presented, however, it is ill suited for dealing directly with a number of policy issues that must be considered more explicitly.

As we have presented it in this book, for example, the Keynesian model implicitly seems to provide only one channel through which money supply changes can affect spending—that of the changing "cost of capital" (interest cost to borrowers), which raises or lowers the interest cost of financing real investment projects.[1] Such a narrow view of the channels through which monetary policy works is universally considered inadequate, and we shall attempt to broaden our conception of the transmission mechanism of monetary policy in the first part of this chapter.

Following this discussion we shall briefly consider a number of the alleged weaknesses of monetary policy as a stabilization weapon. Here we shall depart from the oversimplification implicit in any purely theoretical discussion to consider the effects of existing structural and institutional imperfections on the "real-world" impacts of monetary policy.

---

[1] It will be recalled that this is an important charge made by the monetarists against reliance on the Keynesian model. Post-Keynesians, however, respond that the *full* post-Keynesian model (not covered in this text) cannot properly be faulted on these grounds.

The Channels of Monetary Policy

Monetary economics and opinion regarding the efficacy of monetary policy are now in a state of flux. But this is hardly a novel situation. Indeed, it is no overstatement to describe the field as having been in such a state for the past half-century.

Time and again since the 1920s, students concerned with *how* monetary policy works and how *well* it works have had to reorient their thinking in response to new theoretical developments, new empirical evidence, and the hard facts of experience. The result has been a whole series of changes in attitude toward monetary policy, some of them approximating 180° turns.

Faith in the powers of the monetary authorities probably reached its zenith in the 1920s. In that period, a near-hypnotic spell cast by a booming economy, along with a firm conviction that all that was required to keep things moving ever onward and upward was a reasonably intelligent handling of the discount rate, convinced many an observer that a new and permanent "plateau of prosperity" had been achieved. Fiscal policy was as yet unknown and, in any case, "unneeded." Monetary policy—indeed a mere fraction of what we now call monetary policy—was sufficient to handle any problems that might crop up. Or, at least, so it was believed at the time.

The 1930s, of course, irreparably shattered the rose-tinted glasses. Not only had we fallen off the prosperity plateau, but monetary policy seemed utterly incapable of doing anything whatever about it! Truly, a reassessment of the potentialities of monetary policy was in order.

As might have been expected, the reaction went too far. The same policy weapon that some had looked upon as a virtual panacea 10 years earlier now appeared next to useless. Not only had the experience of the 1930s seemed to show it incapable of easing a depression, but empirical evidence that began to appear regarding the lack of responsiveness of investors to interest rate changes (the alleged inelasticity of the MEI curve) seemed to cast serious doubt on its usefulness in either direction.

There the matter stood until after World War II. Monetary policy had reached its lowest ebb. To its opponents, it represented an exercise in futility; and even its staunchest defenders admitted to very serious weaknesses.

The Availability Thesis and Credit Rationing

But a revival was already underway. In the late 1940s and early 1950s—well before the monetarist upsurge—the defenders of monetary policy developed a new thesis to explain how monetary restriction could achieve its objectives no matter how unresponsive investors might be to interest rate increases. This new approach, popularly entitled the *availability thesis,* focused on the effects of monetary restriction on lenders, rather than on borrowers.

In essence, the availability thesis argued that monetary restriction by the central bank (the Fed) would lead lenders to not only raise interest rates (and thereby eliminate some potential borrowing and spending via increases in the cost of capital) but also *ration credit to potential borrowers via nonprice devices.*

The main point of the availability thesis was fairly simple. It was argued that lenders, seeing their reserves (and lending capacity) cut by Federal Reserve action, would not necessarily allow the price of credit (the interest rate) to rise to a market-clearing level but rather would rely on *authoritative, nonprice rationing* (via such mechanisms as more stringent collateral requirements, higher compensating balances, or favoritism to old, valued customers) simply to deny credit to prospective borrowers who were perfectly willing to pay the going market interest rate.[2]

The availability thesis was intended primarily as a response to (1) those who felt that the MEI curve was very inelastic and (2) those who felt that monetary restriction "works" only via raising the cost of capital (the interest rate). To the extent that it is valid, it matters little that borrowers (potential spenders) cut back only slightly on the quantity of credit demanded as market interest rates rise (that is, it doesn't really matter if the MEI *is* inelastic), for lenders will simply refuse to lend to many who would be willing to borrow at the going (presumably higher) market rate of interest.[3]

Wealth Effects

A third channel (in addition to the "cost of capital" and "credit rationing" channels) through which monetary policy works to affect aggregate demand is what has come to be called the "wealth effect" of money and credit supply changes.

In essence, the wealth effect channel involves the tendency for money supply increases to increase consumer wealth, which in turn induces a rise in consumer

---

[2]Another important strand of the availability thesis was the argument that rising interest rates, caused by Federal Reserve restraint, would lower the market value of the U.S. securities in bank portfolios and, because they would then allegedly be unwilling to sell them and realize capital losses, "lock in" banks to their present holdings of U.S. securities. This, it was argued, would keep banks from selling U.S. securities to the public (and absorbing largely idle money) to acquire the excess reserves needed to support an expansion of loans to business (which would surely be active money). If the argument is valid, the "locking-in" effect would prevent banks from promoting an increase in velocity via changes in their earning asset portfolios. Data on the behavior of banks during "tight money" periods in the past two decades throw considerable doubt on the potency of the "locking-in" effect.

[3]For an excellent summary of the literature on the availability thesis and credit rationing, see Benjamin M. Friedman, *"Credit Rationing: A Review,"* Staff Economic Studies of the Board of Governors of the Federal Reserve System, 1972. See also Paul S. Anderson and James R. Ostas, "Private Credit Rationing," *New England Economic Review,* Federal Reserve Bank of Boston, May–June 1977.

spending. There are two generally accepted elements of the wealth effect channel—the *real balance effect* and an *equity effect*.

The Real Balance Effect.   The real balance effect (sometimes referred to as the "Pigou effect") emphasizes the real value of the money supply (or monetary base) as a determinant of consumption spending (and of the level of the consumption function).[4] Theoretically, when the government raises the public's supply of currency, such action will, by raising consumer wealth, lessen the need for saving and shift the consumption function upward.

Although this element of the wealth effect has been important in determining whether the less than full-employment equilibrium position proclaimed by Keynes was a theoretical possibility, there is rather general agreement that its practical effect on consumption expenditures is quite minimal.

The Equity Effect.   Of substantially greater impact is the equity effect of money supply changes. This might best be explained as follows.

Suppose that initially society is just satisfied with the relative quantities of money, bonds, stock, and real assets that make up its wealth portfolios. Then assume that the Federal Reserve upsets this equilibrium with an open-market purchase that "inflicts" more money on the public while taking away some bonds.

Clearly the community has no *more* assets or income than before, but the relative proportions have been changed. If the public was "just satisfied" with the proportions of money, bonds, stocks, and real assets before the open-market purchase, it now must have relatively too much money and too few bonds.

Well, that sort of disequilibrium is easily set to rights. The public can simply use the excess money to buy more bonds. But of course there are no more bonds to be had, so their action will raise bond prices and lower interest rates. So far so good and, one may well add, nothing new either.

But note that, although the rise in bond prices may have raised bond values to the level desired to go along with the higher quantity of money, we now have too high a value of bonds and money relative to stocks and real assets. So some more balance sheet reshuffling must go on, with some of the new money spilling over into the stock market and the market for real assets (consumer durables, maybe?). If and when the latter happens, the monetary policy has already raised aggregate demand somewhat.

But that isn't all there is to it. Note that along the way, during all these attempts to reestablish desired proportions of money, bonds, stocks, and real assets, the demand for a fixed quantity of bonds and stock has risen. Necessarily their

---

[4]Actually, the logic of the argument applies to all assets held by customers, but in the case of most of them—aside from the money stock or, possibly, the monetary base only—the inducement to increased consumer spending by the assets' owners tends to be offset by the decline in spending on the part of the corresponding debtors.

prices must have risen in response. And what do these price increases mean to their holders?

Security holders, especially stockholders, will find that the money (market) value of their holdings will have increased. In other words, their net worth—their personal wealth holdings—will be greater than before. Now, of course, wealth is not the same as income and people would not be expected to spend (on consumption) nearly as large a fraction of their increase in wealth as of an equivalent increase in their incomes. Nevertheless, such an improvement in wealth positions has been shown to lead to significant boosts in consumption.[5]

The Relative Importance of the Three Monetary Policy Channels. In econometric studies conducted by the Federal Reserve Board and M.I.T., money supply changes have been estimated to have a significant effect on aggregate demand. For example, a $1 billion increase in excess reserves for the System was predicted to lead to a $3.5 billion increase in spending within one year, a $5.4 billion increase after two years, and $6.8 billion rise by the end of three years.[6]

Of the three "channels" through which monetary changes are expected to work, about 50 percent of the effect is estimated to accrue via the cost-of-capital (falling interest rates as a cost to borrowers) route, 34 to 44 percent (the percentage rising over time) through the wealth effect, and 5 to 17 percent (the percentage falling over time) through the credit-rationing channel.[7]

Problems with Monetary Policy

By now virtually all economists, monetarist and post-Keynesians alike, are convinced that the money supply is a very important determinant of the level of aggregate demand. But not even its staunchest supporters believe that monetary policy, especially given the institutional structure within which it is implemented, is anything close to a panacea for the nation's problems with economic instability. This section considers some of the alleged weaknesses of monetary policy as it is currently constituted.

---

[5]For a more thorough discussion of this area, see Roger W. Spencer, "Channels of Monetary Influence: A Survey," *Review,* Federal Reserve Bank of St. Louis, November 1974. See also Frederic S. Mishkin, "Liquidity, and the Role of Monetary Policy in Consumer Durable Demand," *New England Economic Review,* November–December 1976.

[6]The data in this section are taken from Frank DeLeeuw and Edward M. Gramlich, "The Channels of Monetary Policy," *Federal Reserve Bulletin,* June 1969.

[7]The FRB–M.I.T. researchers found significant effects from credit rationing arising only in the area of residential housing, largely as a result of the disintermediation phenomenon discussed earlier.

Doubts About Expansionary Monetary Policy

For years it was popular to sum up the relative effectiveness of monetary policy in recession and inflation with that overworked cliché: "You can pull on a string but you can't push on it." The obvious inference, of course, was that monetary restriction to counter inflation has ·more chance of success than does monetary ease to combat recession. Some years ago, in fact, there was almost universal agreement on this generality.

In recent years, however, as a result of both theoretical developments and new empirical evidence, there has been a noticeable change of attitude regarding the capacity of money supply changes to generate expansion as well as contraction of demand. And today it is likely that only a relatively few economists still cling to the "nonsymmetrical" view of monetary policy. Nevertheless, since it is a position still held by some, we shall consider it briefly.

Their reasoning runs something like this. There can be little doubt that the Federal Reserve has sufficient power to force a reduction in spending because the impact of substantial money supply reductions surely cannot be *indefinitely* offset by increases in velocity. But the effects of monetary expansion, especially when the economy is mired in a deep recession or depression, may be less certain.

In such a situation the Fed can, of course, provide the banks with sufficient excess reserves to *permit* expansion. But whether and how soon such action will result in substantial increases in spending, it is alleged, is open to question. After all, it is not completely inconceivable that increases in the monetary base might be partially offset by a decrease in the size of the money multiplier caused by a sharp rise in desired excess reserves under such conditions.

True, the interest rate (cost of capital) will be forced down by such action, but if the MEI curve has shifted to the left and become more inelastic (as has been argued typically happens during recession), interest rate reductions may lead to little increase in investment spending. Indeed, if the recession is sufficiently severe and profit prospects sufficiently bleak, even a *zero* rate of interest may be inadequate to call forth sufficient additional investment spending.

And how about monetary policy's so-called "wealth effect"? No doubt it would work in the desired direction, but its magnitude under severe recession conditions is open to question. Given a pessimistic outlook, wealth holders may choose to hold a large proportion of their wealth in idle money form (thereby reducing velocity). And given the typical performance of the stock market during recession, it is difficult to conceive of a very substantial rush to purchase stocks and drive up the market value of equities.

All this must not be carried too far. Those who consider an expansionary monetary policy during recession to be weak (relative to its potential to curb excessive spending during a boom) do not deny that it does work in the desired direction. Their view, rather, is that to achieve recovery, reliance on monetary policy *alone* may require an unacceptably long time period to do the job. Perhaps their attitude could best be summed up as arguing that in such circumstances monetary expansion is "necessary, but by no means sufficient."

The Problem of "Cost-Push" (Sellers') Inflation

As does fiscal policy, monetary policy "works" by affecting aggregate demand. If the problem happens to be demand-pull inflation wherein prices are being pulled up via an excess of aggregate demand at full employment, a reduction in demand via monetary restriction is entirely appropriate, since it gets at the core of the problem—excessive aggregate demand.

But if the source of the inflationary pressure is not excessive demand but rather the exploitation of monopoly power by sellers—that is, cost-push, or sellers', inflation—monetary restraint may not be a viable remedy at all. Let us see why this is so. Cost-push, or sellers', inflation may be defined as *a rise in the price level that is initiated by price (or wage) setters employing monopoly power to simply mark up the prices of the goods or services they sell, in the absence of an excess of aggregate demand.* It may be initiated by unions using their bargaining power to push up wages, which, by raising production costs, leads to a rise in prices; by management employing its market power to increase profit margins; or by outsiders such as the OPEC nations exploiting cartel power to quadruple oil prices.

Whatever the identity of its originators, cost-push inflation constitutes a dilemma for government policymakers. The nature of this dilemma is perhaps easiest to see by using the format of the equation of exchange.

Assume, for purposes of illustration, that initially M equals $200 billion, V' equals 3, P equals $4, and Q equals 150 billion—a full-employment level of output. Obviously this is a favorable situation in which we have equilibrium in the production of goods and services (aggregate demand equals aggregate supply) at the full-employment level. Now suppose that some price setters with sufficient monopoly power to implement it decide to raise their prices to a level sufficiently high to increase the overall average price to $5 per unit. What is the situation now? Clearly,

$$MV' < PQ$$
$$(\$200b \cdot 3) < (\$5 \cdot 150b)$$

That is, aggregate demand now falls short of aggregate supply, since $600 billion will not purchase 150 billion units priced at $5 each. If conditions stay exactly as they are, only 120 billion units will be purchased with the current level of demand and the immediate effect of the unsold inventory of 30 billion is likely to be a layoff of workers. Unemployment, then, will coexist with inflation.

And what can government do about it through monetary (or fiscal) policy?

If it employs the same sort of contradictory policy called for to combat demand-pull inflation, that is, cutting aggregate demand *below* the present $600 level, it will likely *worsen* the unemployment problem while, in the short run at least, accomplishing little toward reducing the inflationary pressure. If, on the other hand, it chooses to combat the rising unemployment by implementing a *rise* in aggregate demand to $750 billion, while all 150 billion units can now be purchased at the $5 price, it will have dealt with the unemployment problem by the dubious method of *ratifying* (or accommodating) the inflation already experienced.[8]

What seems clear is that monetary policy (as well as fiscal policy) is ill equipped to deal with inflation that is not initiated by excess demand. Monetary policy's stabilization potential is effectuated through aggregate demand, and if that is not the source of the problem, the Fed's ability to combat it is, in the short run at least, severely constrained.

The Problem of Time Lags

Among the most serious of the attacks against monetary policy as it is now employed is the charge that, because of time lags involved in its operation, it actually reinforces the business cycle. That is, discretionary monetary policy, aimed at minimizing inflation and unemployment, misses the mark by such a margin that it makes them worse.

There is nothing complicated about the logic involved and, indeed, as we have already seen, it has led to one important monetarist policy position. It starts from the universally recognized fact that monetary policy measures do not affect aggregate demand instantaneously. There is a process involved that takes time to work. Those who believe that discretionary monetary policy is positively destabilizing simply argue that the time required for this process to work itself out is very long—so long, indeed, that policy measures undertaken to combat ongoing inflation are only likely to come to fruition (cut aggregate demand) some months after the inflationary pressure has disappeared and the economy has turned to recession. In that case, of course, the monetary policy will only make the recession worse.

Similarly, in their view, monetary action undertaken to raise aggregate demand to combat recession can also be expected to make matters worse, because by the time aggregate demand is actually increased by monetary measures taken many months previously, the economy may have recovered and be well on the road to inflation. The antirecession measure would thus merely magnify the succeeding inflation.

The relevant time lags have, for purposes of discussion, been divided into three types. The first, the *recognition lag,* is the time between the development of a need for action in the economy and recognition of that need by policymakers.

---

[8] And, indeed, by "bailing out" sellers with unsold inventories, set itself up for further likely rounds of inflation.

Unless and until forecasting techniques provide much more dependable results, this period will be, almost certainly, several months long. Second, there is an *administrative lag*, the time between the recognition of need for action and the action's execution. For monetary policy, with the seven-member semi-independent Board of Governors in the driver's seat, this lag is probably very short.

Finally, there is an additional period, which has been called the *operational lag*, between action by the policy agency and its final effect on demand in the economy. For monetary policy, for example, this would be the time between an actual sale of securities on the open market and its intended reduction in spending.

Everyone agrees that monetary policy involves time lags. Where there is disagreement is on the length and variability of those lags. As we have seen, Professor Friedman sees the lags as both long and variable. This, indeed, is the basic reason for his advocacy of the elimination of discretion in monetary policy in favor of a law requiring a fixed rate of increase in money each year.

The measurement of policy time lags, however, is an extremely difficult task, and, as we have seen, both the St. Louis Federal Reserve Bank and the Federal Reserve–M.I.T.–Penn econometric models conclude that money supply changes tend to begin affecting GNP rather quickly. Other investigators have come up with still different lag measurements.[9]

None of these studies claims to have the last word, the definitive answer, on the length of these lags. But elusive though it is, that answer is of crucial importance. For if the lag *is* relatively short, then discretionary monetary policy can be relied on to make some contribution toward business-cycle stabilization. If, on the other hand, it is as long and variable as some investigators believe, then it follows logically that discretionary monetary policy should be abandoned altogether.

Implementing the Friedman proposal would, of course, require far-reaching changes in the U.S. monetary machinery. The present discretionary power possessed by members of the Board of Governors to employ their tools as they see fit would be abolished in favor of a law requiring the Federal Reserve to take such action as would raise the money supply by a fixed percentage each year, come what may. The present monetary managers would thus become mere technicians instead of policymakers.

Such a change, if it were to be made, could be defended by its advocates as a purely pragmatic act, based solely on the evidence from the past that discretion has not done an adequate job. Yet there would be important philosophical overtones. Long before the evidence cited earlier was developed, Friedman and his illustrious predecessor at the University of Chicago, Professor Henry Simons, had argued for an end to discretion in economic policy on more fundamental and philosophical grounds.

---

[9]See, for example, Thomas Mayer, "The Inflexibility of Monetary Policy," *Review of Economics and Statistics*, November 1958; A. Ando, E. C. Brown, R. Solow, and J. Karaken, "Lags in Fiscal and Monetary Policy," *Stabilization Policies*, Commission on Money and Credit (Englewood Cliffs, N.J.: Prentice-Hall, 1963); and Michael J. Hamburger, "The Lag in the Effect of Monetary Policy," *Monetary Aggregates and Monetary Policy*, Federal Reserve Bank of New York, 1974.

For example, almost 50 years ago Professor Simons said,

> A democratic, free-enterprise system implies, and requires for its effective functioning and survival, a stable framework of definite rules, laid down in legislation and subject to change only gradually and with careful regard for the vested interests of participants in the economic game. It is peculiarly essential economically that there should be a minimum of uncertainty for enterprisers and investors as to monetary conditions in the future—and, politically that the plausible expedient of setting up "authorities" instead of rules, with respect to matters of such fundamental importance, be avoided, or accepted only as a very temporary arrangement. The most important objective of sound liberal policy, apart from the establishment of highly competitive conditions in industry and the narrow limitations of political control over relative prices, should be that of securing a monetary system governed by definite rule.[10]

It thus seems evident that, although part of the steam behind the proposals to eliminate discretion in monetary policy comes from empirical evidence indicating that time lags have kept discretion from working well in the past, part of it is also based on a more fundamental distrust of discretionary policy, in principle.

General Credit Controls Apply Capriciously to Groups of Spenders; The Charge of Unplanned Selectivity

Another major set of criticisms centers not on whether spending is cut or by how much it is cut or when it is cut but rather on *whose* spending is deterred by monetary restraint. To state the issue directly, it is argued that tightening of general credit controls has a disproportionately severe effect on the spending plans of certain groups while leaving other groups of spenders relatively unscathed. The result is, these critics argue, an unplanned, capricious, and, in substantial degree, undesirable selectivity in the impact of general credit restraint.

Let us run through the essence of the argument from the beginning. Credit restraint, if it is to work at all, must have a bite. Some people who would have carried out added spending in the absence of the policy must now find it unwise or impossible to do so. The question with which we are concerned is the identity of those groups whose spending is inhibited.

In a first approximation, this would not seem to be too difficult a problem. General credit restraint reduces the total supply of credit available. This tends to raise its price—in this case, the rate of interest. The prime function of this higher interest rate is to ration out the smaller amount of credit available. If there is a perfect market, those who desire to use credit for purposes that will most satisfy consumer desires will be able to afford the higher interest cost and still obtain it, and those who would have borrowed for less socially desirable purposes will be *rationed out* of the market. Consequently, so the argument runs, it is those who

---

[10]Henry C. Simons, "Rules versus Authorities in Monetary Policy," *Journal of Political Economy*, February 1936.

desired credit for the least socially desirable purposes who will find themselves unable to obtain it. And surely, because for the restrictive policy to work at all, *someone's* spending must be cut, this is the optimum result.

But, say the proponents of the *unplanned selectivity* thesis, this argument grossly oversimplifies the situation. To begin with, the credit market is far from a *perfect* market. It is not just the rise in the price of credit that impersonally rations out the smaller supply but—and this comes from no less avid supporters of monetary policy than the developers of the availability thesis themselves—also a significant amount of authoritative (nonprice) credit rationing by individual lenders. Although both Borrower A and Borrower B may be willing and able to pay the higher interest rate required, the lender may now arbitrarily decide to grant the request of one and refuse that of the other. How can we be sure that this provides an optimum allocation? Then, too, are there not a number of structural imperfections that could have the effect of diverting credit from one sector to another to the detriment of the general welfare?

It is, by now, rather generally accepted that three sectors of the economy have tended to bear disproportionately heavy burdens from general credit restraint. These are the residential construction sector, the state and local government sector, and small and new businesses. Let us consider each of these in turn.

The Residential Home Construction Sector. It has become increasingly apparent that monetary restraint hits the home construction industry with special severity.[11] It requires only a cursory glance at the home construction data for the past 25 years to arouse one's suspicions.

Since the end of the "bond support" program during and immediately after World War II, there have been six well-defined periods of monetary restraint of sufficient duration to be recognized as such. These include 1956–1957, 1959, 1966, 1969, 1974–1975, and 1980–1982. In four of these "tight money" periods, the residential housing industry slumped perceptibly.

From 1955 to 1957, single-family dwelling starts fell off from 1,194,400 to 872,000. Such a decline in an economy with rapidly rising incomes, population, and family formation can hardly be a mere random fluctuation. A closer look at the mid-1950s data reveals that almost the entire decrease in housing starts occurred in homes financed with government-guaranteed mortgages.

Why the special impact on FHA- and VA-financed homes? Almost certainly, it was largely a result of unrealistic interest rate limitations on such mortgages. At the time, lenders financing home building with FHA or VA mortgages were permitted to charge no more than 4.5 percent. As long as alternative opportunities are earning no more than this, a 4.5 percent interest rate ceiling has no effect at all.

---

[11]For a contrary view, see N. M. Bowsher and L. Kalish, "Does Slower Monetary Expansion Discriminate Against Housing?" *Review*, St. Louis Federal Reserve Bank, June 1968.

But 1956–1957 was a tight money period and interest rates generally were rising. Lenders, who had more takers for the available credit than they could accommodate, quite naturally began to back away from taking mortgages on which they could charge only 4.5 percent when numerous alternative opportunities offered them 6 and 7 percent. The result, hardly surprising, was a dramatic cutback in housing starts financed with government-guaranteed mortgages.

In the 1960s, 1970s, and 1980s, as Table 20-1 makes abundantly clear, each of the especially tight money periods, 1966, 1969, 1974–1975, and 1980–1982, exhibited notable decreases in single-family homes started.

In these more recent periods, however, the chief culprit appears to have been *disintermediation*. As interest rates generally rose, governmental authorities, via Regulation Q and its companion pieces applying to savings and loan associations and mutual savings banks, kept interest rates that savings institutions were permitted to pay time depositors well below the alternatives open elsewhere to savers. The result, as might well have been expected, was a sharp decline in the flow of funds to savings and loan associations, savings banks, and commercial banks savings departments, leading to a dramatic restriction in mortgage money available.

The problem, and its relation to monetary policy, was put most succinctly by Professor James S. Duesenberry of Harvard, in his capacity as chairman of the President's Commission on Mortgage Interest Rates:

> if we did not know it before, it is now clear that homebuilding does bear an excessive share of the burden of a restrictive monetary policy. That is so partly because homebuilding is financed mainly with debt and partly because of some special features of our mortgage market.

TABLE 20-1

New Single-Family Housing Starts, 1960–1982
(thousands)

Year	Number of Houses Started	Year	Number of Houses Started
1960	995	1972	1,309
1961	974	1973	1,132
1962	991	1974	888
1963	1,021	1975	892
1964	972	1976	1,163
1965	964	1977	1,451
1966	779	1978	1,433
1967	844	1979	1,194
1968	900	1980	852
1969	814	1981	705
1970	813	1982	661
1971	1,151		

Source: Federal Reserve Bulletin.

Of these special features, the most important are the excessive reliance of the mortgage market on funds raised through thrift institutions and the adverse effects of the ceiling on insured and guaranteed mortgages.[12]

There seems little doubt that reform legislation of the 1980s aimed at phasing out Regulation Q and liberalizing the portfolio restrictions of the savings institutions will ease these problems, but only time will tell how much.

State and Local Government Capital Expenditures. Experience in the mid-1950s and once again in the decade of the 1960s also led to a strong conviction that state and local government capital outlays were disproportionately restricted by monetary restraint.

The essence of this problem was well stated a decade and a half ago by Tilford Gaines, economist for Manufacturers Hanover Trust:

> Almost equally troubling is the impact that tight money and credit conditions in 1969 have had upon the ability of state and local authorities to finance themselves in the municipal bond market. In this case, the fact that credit policy has been centered upon the ability of the commercial banks to increase their loans and investments, and given that banks account for the bulk of all net purchases of such securities, implies that primary responsibility for the shortage of funds in the tax-exempt market does rest with Federal Reserve policy. To the extent that public expenditures that have had to be deferred because they could not be financed would have been on non-essential projects, the market's allocative process has made a useful contribution to restraining spending and restoring price stability. But the market usually allocates money on the basis of credit worthiness not essentiality, and it is more than likely that some essential schools, public health and other facilities have been delayed.[13]

In the tight money period of the mid-1950s, a sharp reduction in the sales of state and local government securities in 1955 and 1956 led to speculation that monetary restriction was playing special havoc with state and local borrowing at that time. As Table 20-2 indicates, the same sort of evidence showed up again in the 1966 and 1969 tight money years. In 1974–1975, however, the data are less persuasive, but a similar pattern reappears in the 1979–1981 period.

As in the case of housing, some significant structural peculiarities of the state and local bond market go a long way toward explaining that sector's apparent sensitivity to credit restraint.

One institutional factor of no small significance in the past was the practice, by most states, of limiting by law the interest rate local governments can pay. For many years, such limits had been set at 5 or 6 percent. At those levels, no real

---

[12]J. S. Duesenberry, testimony on the Mortgage Interest Rate Commission Report, Hearings Before the Committee on Banking and Currency, U.S. Senate, 91st Cong., 1st sess., September 1969, p. 3.

[13]Tilford Gaines, "Federal Reserve Policy Review," *Economic Report* (New York: Manufacturers Hanover Trust Company, November 1969).

TABLE 20-2

New Issues of State and Local Government General Obligations, 1962–1981
(millions of dollars)

Year	New Securities Sold	Year	New Securities Sold
1962	5,582	1972	13,305
1963	5,855	1973	12,257
1964	6,417	1974	13,563
1965	7,177	1975	16,020
1966	6,804	1976	18,040
1967	8,985	1977	18,042
1968	9,269	1978	17,854
1969	7,725	1979	12,109
1970	11,850	1980	14,100
1971	15,220	1981	12,394

Source: Federal Reserve Bulletin.

problem was encountered during the 1930s, 1940s, and early 1950s, as the market interest rates local governments were required to pay were usually well below the legal limits.

As interest rates began rising in the late 1950s, and especially during the 1960s, however, market interest rates began more and more frequently to edge above legal limits for many governments, and this meant real problems. Many local governments, seeking to borrow money within their own legal limits, found no lenders willing to accommodate them. As a result, especially in 1966 and 1969, many local government projects had to be postponed.

A second important factor in the municipal bond market is the fact that interest on state and local government securities is federal income tax exempt. Now normally, of course, the tax-exemption feature is an advantage to these governments, allowing them to borrow at lower interest cost than would be possible without it. But it does create an odd market for municipal securities, which makes it especially susceptible to monetary restraint.

The prime buyers of state and local securities are high-income individuals and commercial banks. High-income individuals have an obvious interest in the tax-exemption feature, and commercial banks, until recent years the most heavily taxed of the financial institutions, have found them attractive for the same reason.

During periods of monetary restraint, however, commercial banks, pressed for reserves, have withdrawn almost completely from the "municipals" market. This means that, at such times, many more state and local securities must be absorbed by individuals. The market for state and local obligations is thus drastically narrowed as a result of credit restriction. The result is that, to entice enough lower-income individuals to purchase the municipal securities seeking placement, very sharp increases in interest yields are necessary. State and local governments, therefore, may find themselves paying rates that are up by 50 percent when other rates have only increased by 25 percent. In the early 1960s, for example, interest rates on state and local securities were about 70 percent of taxable corporate bond yields. By January 1970, they had risen until they were 80 percent as high. Put another way, the average interest yield on state and local bonds more than doubled between 1965 and January 1970, while that on corporate bonds rose by less than 80 percent. And from 1973 to tight money 1975, while corporate bond yields were rising just about 20 percent, municipal bond interest rates shot up by a full 35 percent.

The tendency for commercial banks to reduce their purchases of municipals during periods of rising interest rates is illustrated, for the 1965–1975 period, in Figure 20-1.

All this seems to show quite clearly that state and local government *borrowing* has been noticeably affected by monetary restraint. But borrowing and spending are two different things. Despite the apparent impact on their borrowing, state and local government capital *expenditures* in tight money years do not appear to be cut so sharply. This was true in all recent periods of restraint. For example, the Federal Reserve found that in 1966, although large government borrowing was apparently

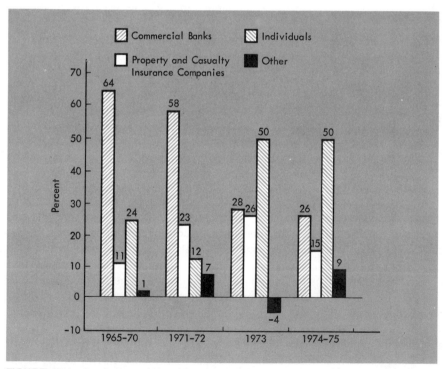

FIGURE 20-1   Purchasers of New Municipal Issues

Source: Rodney Johnson, "A Fresh Look at the Municipal Bond Market," *Business Review,* Federal Reserve Bank of Philadelphia, July–August 1976.

cut by $1.4 billion, the capital spending reduction was estimated at only $250 million.[14] Apparently, by short-term borrowing and using funds borrowed in earlier periods but not yet spent, governments were able to go ahead with spending programs with little reduction.[15]

Conclusions, therefore, are difficult to draw on this point. Monetary restriction surely has notable effects on state and local government borrowing as well as on their interest costs, but the extent to which this carries over to spending is not quite so clear.

Borrowing by Small and New Businesses. Another sector said to be uniquely susceptible to the cutting edge of a tight money policy is that of new and small businesses. The argument here is intuitively appealing, although, once again, we have little reliable quantitative evidence to document it.

When credit is restricted, it is argued, the market power of lenders permits them authoritatively to *ration* credit, granting the credit requests of some while refusing others. It is to be expected, when there is not enough to go around, that the large, well-known, long-established concern will have preference over the small, newly established credit applicant. Thus, in the view of the critics, the larger, well-established firms will suffer little deprivation from credit rationing, while the new, unknown firm will bear the burden. And to make matters worse, the newer firms, having little or no retained earnings, are the ones most urgently in need of external financing.[16]

Although this result may or may not be justifiable from the viewpoint of relative risks, its effect on the nation's economic growth could be undesirable because new products and new ideas, as often as not, are introduced by new firms

---

[14]P. F. McGouldrick, and J. E. Petersen, "Monetary Restraint and Borrowing and Capital Spending by Large State and Local Governments in 1966," *Federal Reserve Bulletin,* July 1968, pp. 522–71.

[15]A survey of smaller governments showed that a larger percentage of borrowing postponements led to expenditure postponements than was the case for the larger governments. See J. E. Petersen and P. F. McGouldrick, "Monetary Restraint, Borrowing, and Capital Spending by Small Local Governments and State Colleges in 1966," *Federal Reserve Bulletin,* December 1968.

[16]Some evidence of this effect is cited by *The Wall Street Journal,* December 10, 1969:

Times are getting uncomfortably difficult for many small companies.

Turning a profit has recently grown harder for business in general. But problems that are only beginning to trouble big corporations already are severely hurting many small firms. The list of woes includes super-tight money, scarce and costly skilled labor and slow payment of bills by some customers. Owners of some small firms, convinced that still more difficult times lie ahead, are reluctantly selling their businesses, usually through exchanges of stock, to big corporations. . . .

A few statistics clearly indicate that small companies are faring worse than their big brothers. Last month a *Wall Street Journal* survey of 436 large corporations found that after-tax profits in the third quarter were 3.7% higher than a year earlier. But a later Commerce Department survey of *all* corporations, small as well as large, found that after-tax profits in the third quarter were no higher than in the 1968 period.

"Obviously, the smaller companies dragged the total down," says a Commerce Department economist.

struggling to establish themselves. If a tight money policy shuts them out, the ultimate cost could be considerable.[17]

Monetary Restraint Does Cut Aggregate Demand, but Its Effect May Be Weak or Hard to Predict

The reputations of some of those who argue that monetary policy is destabilizing and some of those who argue that general credit controls are seriously discriminatory are such as to command solid respect and careful consideration. But respect and consideration do not necessarily imply agreement.

The majority of economists today are neither so pessimistic regarding the time lags involved as to be prepared to eliminate discretion nor so convinced of the capriciousness of quantitative controls as to be willing to abandon them. Judiciously administered monetary policy still seems capable, in the minds of most, of making positive contributions toward stabilization of economic activity.

But among this large group, the degree of faith in monetary policy varies widely. At one end of the spectrum are those whose confidence in the potency of credit control seems almost absolute. Not so for many others, however. For them the record reveals too many disappointing experiences to justify implicit and unreserved faith. "Of course monetary restraint is helpful," they seem to say, "but we need to guard against expecting too much from it. Let us make use of monetary policy, by all means, but let's also be aware of its limitations."

Let us now consider three factors that may operate so as to weaken the effectiveness of monetary restraint.

Increasing Interest Rates May Not Restrict Some Investment Spending Much. The effect of higher interest rates on the investment spending of many firms may be disappointingly small for a number of reasons.

One may be the fact that a very large percentage of investment spending is financed with internal funds rather than those borrowed on the capital market. In 1981, for example, when gross private domestic investment totaled $472 billion, depreciation allowances and corporate retained earnings combined provided over $374 billion of the needed funds. Therefore little more than 20 percent of the funds needed to finance the year's investment spending had to be borrowed from external lenders.

Now, in theory of course, the interest cost involved should be considered roughly the same whether borrowed externally (with a consequent out-of-pocket interest payment) or obtained from internal sources through the firm's own saving.

---

[17]For a survey of this and other aspects of bank nonprice credit rationing, see Paul S. Anderson and James R. Ostas, "Private Credit Rationing," *New England Economic Review,* May–June 1977. Anderson and Ostas conclude that credit rationing "may be characterized as one of the costs of contracyclical monetary policy, with the highest price paid by new and high-risk ventures." (p. 37)

For, as discussed in Chapter 15, there is an implicit interest cost involved in the use of internally generated funds to purchase capital goods directly, which is equal to the interest return given up by not lending them out to someone else at the going market rate.

Despite the airtight logic involved in this argument, there is some room for doubt that all firms *do* maximize profits by recognizing that increases in market interest rates necessarily raise the opportunity cost of internally generated funds.

To the extent that this is the case, a rise in the market rate of interest from 10 to 15 percent, as a result of credit restriction, may not really be looked upon as an increase in investment cost. Certainly, a firm that refuses to use internal funds for any purpose other than financing its own investment outlays, and possesses ample amounts for its needs, will be less responsive to market rate increases than will one forced to rely solely on external funds. And the fact that a preponderance of investment is financed internally may add significantly to the alleged insensitivity to interest rate changes.

Also, the market power of some firms may play a role in explaining borrower insensitivity to interest rate increases. To oligopolistic firms, the rise in credit costs, not unlike a hike in taxes, may provide just the impetus needed to permit a comparable price increase. If this is the case, the burden of the interest rate increase will fall on consumers rather than reducing investors' profit prospects. Such "shifting of the burden" to consumers is even easier for regulated public utilities selling a distinctive service subject to highly inelastic demand. Here the firms need merely show the regulatory agency evidence that their costs have been raised to justify a rate increase. And if consumer demand is sufficiently inelastic, little, if any, cutback in expenditures would be expected.

Shifting Commercial Bank Portfolios May Permit Partially Offsetting Velocity Increases.   Although probably no economists today would expect money supply decreases to be totally offset by equivalent velocity increases, there is a good deal of evidence indicating that, for a variety of reasons, monetary authorities must be prepared for *some* weakening in their effects from this source. A restriction in the supply of money leads quite naturally to ingenious efforts on the part of the public and the financial community to make the smaller money supply "do more work" than before.

No better evidence of this ingenuity exists than the development of the federal funds market, which, after all, is little more than a device to make an existing supply of member bank reserves stretch a bit farther. When the credit restraint screws are tightened, the banking system does not idly accept its fate but rather seeks to make the reserves it has go as far as possible. The effect is to lessen, to some degree, the impact of the restraint policy. The striking pace of financial innovation in the late 1970s and early 1980s serves well to illustrate this phenomenon.

Another example of the banking system's response to a restriction of reserves is the now-familiar practice of unloading U.S. securities during tight money periods to acquire the excess reserves needed to make more business loans. If, for example, a member bank sells U.S. securities to a member of the public who pays by check, the transaction reduces demand deposits and, consequently, required reserves for the system. As total reserves are unaffected, the net effect is a rise in excess reserves. These excess reserves, then, provide the basis for an increase in loans to business.

Note that such a portfolio switch alters neither total bank reserves nor the size of the money supply. But if the old demand deposit given up by the purchaser of the U.S. securities was largely idle money in asset balances or resulted from an effort to economize on transactions balances while the new demand deposit created to lend to the business investor is active money likely to be spent (as is almost certain), then the bank's action has fostered a rise in aggregate demand (MV') by facilitating an increase in velocity.[18]

To what extent do banks actually alter their earning asset portfolios in such a manner and thereby partially offset the intended effect of Federal Reserve policy? Quite a bit, as Table 20-3 makes clear.

Note especially the years 1955–1956, 1965–1966, 1969, and 1973–1974. All were periods of more or less tight money when the Federal Reserve was attempting to restrict demand. In all five periods, banks sharply increased their loans—*partly as a result of excess reserves provided by the sale of U.S. securities*. Glance also at the years 1958–1959, 1966–1967, 1970–1971, and 1975–1976. These were, in general, "easy money" years during which the FRS was providing the banking system with substantial additional reserves. What is striking is the unmistakable impression that banks tend to load up on U.S. securities in easy money years and then sell them off to permit a larger increase in business loans during tight money episodes. When they do so, they tend to facilitate undesired (by the FRS) shifts in velocity.

Increases in Velocity Facilitated by Nonbank Financial Intermediaries: The Gurley-Shaw Thesis.   Another area of weakness of monetary policy, in the view of some, is the absence of direct control over credit expansion by financial intermediaries other than commercial banks. Popularly entitled the *Gurley-Shaw* thesis, after its best known proponents, this argument emphasizes the potential capacity of nonbank financial intermediaries for undermining, through their credit expansion activities, a tight money policy.[19]

---

[18]One part of the "availability thesis" is the argument that increases in interest rates induced by a "tight money" policy will, by driving down the market value of U.S. securities, "lock in" banks to their current security portfolio because they will be reluctant to sell them and realize capital losses on them. The data in Table 20-3 provide some grounds for doubting the effectiveness of this "locking-in" argument.

[19]For the essence of the Gurley-Shaw thesis, see J. G. Gurley and E. S. Shaw, "Financial Aspects of Economic Development," *American Economic Review,* September 1955; Gurley and Shaw, *Money in a Theory of Finance* (Washington, D.C.: The Brookings Institution, 1960); and John G. Gurley, Study Paper No. 14, "Liquidity and Financial Institutions in the Postwar Economy," a part of the *Study of Employment Growth and Price Levels* for the Joint Economic Committee (Washington, D.C., 1960).

TABLE 20-3

Loans and U.S. Securities at Commercial Banks, 1953–1982
(billions)

Year	Loans	U.S. Securities	Change in Loans	Change in Securities
1953	$ 66.2	$ 62.2	—	—
1954	69.1	67.6	+$2.9	+$5.4
1955	80.6	60.3	+11.5	−7.3
1956	88.1	57.2	+7.5	−3.1
1957	91.5	56.9	+3.4	−0.3
1958	95.6	65.1	+4.1	+8.2
1959	110.5	57.7	+14.9	+7.4
1960	116.7	59.9	+6.2	+2.2
1961	123.6	65.3	+6.9	+5.4
1962	137.3	64.7	+13.7	−0.6
1963	153.7	61.5	+16.4	−3.2
1964	172.9	60.8	+19.2	−0.7
1965	198.2	57.1	+25.3	−3.7
1966	213.9	53.5	+15.7	−3.6
1967	231.3	59.4	+17.4	+5.9
1968	258.2	60.7	+26.9	+1.3
1969	279.4	51.2	+21.2	−9.5
1970	292.0	57.8	+12.6	+6.6
1971	320.9	60.6	+28.9	+2.8
1972	378.9	62.6	+58.0	+2.0
1973	460.5	58.5	+81.6	−4.1
1974	520.1	53.6	+59.6	−4.9
1975	517.4	82.2	−2.7	+28.6
1976	555.0	100.8	+37.6	+18.6
1977	632.5	99.8	+77.5	−1.0
1978	747.0	93.8	+114.5	−6.0
1979	849.9	94.5	+102.9	+0.7
1980	915.1	110.0	+65.2	+15.5
1981	974.9	110.9	+59.8	+0.9
1982	1,042.3	130.9	+67.4	+20.0

Source: Federal Reserve Bulletin.

In essence, the Gurley-Shaw thesis argues that nonbank financial intermediaries, such as those discussed in Chapters 2 and 3, can and do contribute to a rise in the velocity of spending, which, despite the monetary authorities' acknowledged ability to hold the money supply stable, permits potentially inflationary increases in effective demand.

Suppose, for example, that the Federal Reserve attempts to combat inflationary pressure by a contractionary monetary policy. This, along with the rising demand for loanable funds, raises interest yields on securities issued by investors. Nonfinancial intermediaries—let us take a savings and loan association as an example—find that their income from financial investment into such direct securities is rising, permitting them to offer higher interest rates to attract savings from prospective shareholders.

Suppose now that a saver, who has been content to hold part of his or her savings in the form of a demand deposit at a commercial bank, finds that the higher return available on a savings and loan share just overcomes the advantage of higher liquidity of the demand deposit. The saver writes a check on his or her checking account and deposits it in a savings and loan association.

Note that the money supply is unchanged. The demand deposit that used to belong to our depositor is now an asset of the savings and loan association. Suppose that the savings and loan association now uses this amount (the demand deposit) to purchase a mortgage. The homebuilder now uses the previously idle demand deposit to purchase building materials, and, without any change in the money supply, spending has risen.

The special role played by the financial intermediary, in this case, is in convincing the original owner of the idle deposit to give it up in return for an asset only slightly less liquid with an attractive return. The original owner might not be willing, independently, to purchase the mortgage, but because the savings and loan association offers a much more liquid alternative, he or she decides to accept the near money.

Still another way of looking at the influence of financial intermediaries in this respect is to consider the possible expansion of credit in two cases—one, where only commercial bank expansion is involved, and the other, where a savings and loan association enters the picture. Suppose that the commercial banking system has $100 of excess reserves, a required reserve ratio of 20 percent, and no other reserve leakage. If commercial banks alone expand to their legal limit, $500 of additional credit can be granted in the form of $500 of new demand deposits created.

But let us suppose that along the way, perhaps at the Bank B level, one of the recipients of new demand deposits transfers them to a savings and loan association. What effect will this have?

If Bank A has all the excess reserves initially, it will lend $100:

Bank A			
Loans	+$100	Demand deposits	+$100

Then, as before, the borrower of the newly created money will write checks payable to his creditor, Mr. Jones, who, we assume, deposits them in Bank B. Bank B, in turn, collects them via the Federal Reserve.

Bank A		Bank B	
Federal Reserve account −$100	Demand deposit of borrower −$100	Federal Reserve account +$100	Demand deposit of Mr. Jones +$100

At this point, let us assume that Mr. Jones succumbs to the attraction of the interest being paid by a savings and loan association and transfers his $100 there. The T-account effects on Bank B and the savings and loan association are

Bank B		Savings and Loan Association	
	Demand deposit of Mr. Jones −$100 Demand deposit of savings and loan association +$100	Demand deposit at Bank B +$100	Deposit (shares) of Mr. Jones +$100

Now the savings and loan association, finding itself with extra liquid funds, uses the $100 to purchase a mortgage.[20]

Bank B		Savings and Loan Association	
	Demand deposit of savings and loan association −$100 Demand deposit of mortgage holder +$100	Demand deposit −$100 Mortgage +$100	

Of course at this point we can expect the mortgage holder to spend his funds to purchase his home, a rise in aggregate demand. But what the reader should especially note is that, throughout all this, the total reserves and demand deposits of the commercial banking system are unaffected. They are still in a position to (in total) extend $500 of credit, even though the savings and loan association has already lent $100. The result, then, is that financial intermediaries facilitate a larger supply of loanable funds (although not of money) than would have been possible in their absence.[21]

---

[20]Although, in fact, the savings and loan association would probably find it necessary to withhold some small part of the $100 as a liquidity reserve against its increased liabilities, we ignore this in our example.

[21]Note, however, that aggregate demand would have been increased only if Mr. Jones had decided to save the $100 he received and had held it as an idle demand deposit if there had been no savings and loan association. If he had cut back his intended consumption spending by $100, to make his savings and loan deposit, the extra spending made possible by the mortgage purchase would have just canceled that which he chose to forgo.

Review Questions

1. Carefully explain the three "channels" through which money supply changes are said to affect aggregate demand.

2. "Cost-push inflation creates a dilemma for policymakers." Explain carefully, making clear your understanding of the nature of cost-push inflation as well as the problems involved in controlling it via monetary and fiscal policy.

3. What are the three time lags associated with monetary and fiscal policy? Which of the lags would you expect would be longer for monetary policy, and which for discretionary fiscal policy? What bearing do the duration and variability of these lags have on monetarist policy prescriptions?

4. How might one defend selective credit controls as, in practice if not in theory, more appropriate than general credit controls? What impact would you expect financial deregulation, such as was included in the Monetary Control Act of 1980, to have on the efficiency of general credit controls?

5. Carefully explain how market imperfections have, in the past, made the housing sector peculiarly susceptible to monetary contraction.

6. Discuss the factors that expose state and local government borrowing to monetary restraint. Do you think tax exemption on the income from municipal securities is a good idea? Why or why not?

7. In what way may changing commercial bank earning assets play a role in modifying the intended effects of monetary policy?

8. Briefly explain the essence of the Gurley-Shaw thesis.

21

Alternatives to Monetary Policy
for Economic Stabilization

Aside from those advocating the most extreme form of the monetarist position, economists generally recognize that monetary policy alone is likely to be inadequate to provide an entirely satisfactory degree of economic stability and growth. This chapter briefly considers the major policy alternatives.

Fiscal Policy

The prime complement to monetary policy is *fiscal policy*. Let us define fiscal policy as *alterations in tax revenue and/or government expenditures that are intended to affect the level of aggregate demand.*

This definition is sufficiently broad to cover both *discretionary fiscal* policy and the nondiscretionary variety, popularly known as the *automatic stabilizers*. Discretionary fiscal policy requires action by the legislature to change tax laws or government expenditure programs with the intent of altering aggregate demand.[1] The automatic stabilizers, on the other hand, are laws already on the books (such as the personal income tax, the corporate profits tax, and the unemployment compensation program) that operate automatically in such a manner as to increase (decrease) the amount of tax revenue collected and/or decrease (increase) the amount spent by government when the nation's income is rising (falling). Before looking into these two types of fiscal policy in more detail, let us attempt to separate fiscal policy from other government actions involving tax/expenditure changes.

---

[1]Properly speaking, discretionary fiscal policy also encompasses action by the executive to speed up or slow down the completion of already authorized programs.

What Is and What Is Not Fiscal Policy

It is important that the student see clearly the distinction between fiscal policy and other activities of government. One source of confusion that sometimes arises is failure to recognize that although discretionary fiscal policy does entail alterations in tax laws or expenditure programs, not every tax or expenditure change should be considered a fiscal policy action.

Discretionary fiscal policy, per se, should be thought of as changes in taxes or government expenditures *that are undertaken primarily for their effect on aggregate demand*. It is entirely possible, for example, for government to launch a new program calling for increased spending, providing at the same time for sufficient added tax revenue to forestall any rise in aggregate demand. Such action would simply represent an attempt to increase the size of the public sector rather than a fiscal policy measure, as the term is customarily used.

In this connection, it is useful to keep in mind the distinction between different economic activities of government drawn by Musgrave.[2] First, there is the allocation branch, which uses taxes, expenditures, and other devices to reallocate resources, both between the public and private sectors and within the private sector itself. Second, there is a distribution branch, which may use taxes and expenditures to alter the distribution of income. Finally, there is the stabilization branch, the function of which is to use taxes and expenditures to achieve the "proper" level of aggregate demand. Fiscal policy, as we are using the term, consists of the activities of the stabilization branch alone.

Another distinction that should be drawn here is that between fiscal and monetary policy. As many activities involve them both and as the aims of both are the same—the pursuit of major economic goals via alterations in aggregate demand—there is sometimes a tendency to confuse them. For purposes of this chapter, we shall define a "pure" monetary policy measure as one carried out by the monetary authorities with the specific intent of altering the *degree of liquidity* of the community's wealth. Most often this would be accomplished by increasing or decreasing the money supply. For example, an open-market purchase from the public would be a "pure" monetary policy measure because its initial effect is simply to substitute money for bonds previously held by the public. The public's wealth is not directly changed in amount, but it has been made more liquid.[3]

On the other hand, as discussed in Chapter 17, a "pure" fiscal policy measure would involve altering taxes or expenditures, *without changing the money supply*. A reduction in taxes, with the resulting budget deficit financed by sale of securities to the public, would be an example, as there is no change in the money supply.

Many stabilization policy measures involve a combination of monetary and fiscal effects. For example, a tax cut creating a budget deficit, with the deficit

---

[2]R. A. Musgrave, *The Theory of Public Finance* (New York: McGraw-Hill, 1959).

[3]Of course, such a policy would, nevertheless, affect aggregate demand through its effects on the cost of capital, consumers' wealth position, and credit rationing.

financed by sale of securities to the banks, involves both. The tax cut by itself would be a fiscal measure, but when it is combined with a sale of securities to the banks, the money supply rises also, adding a monetary element. The same thing would be true of the hypothetical case of increasing the public's money supply by simply running the printing presses and passing out an extra $1,000 to each person. Such an action *sounds* for all the world like pure monetary policy. But it is not. Of course it *does* involve monetary effects because it increases the supply of money. But it also involves fiscal effects because the passing out of such money (without taking away something in exchange) represents a rise in government transfer payments.

How Discretionary Fiscal Policy Works

The potential role of fiscal policy should be clear from the material covered in Part II.[4] If the requirement is to raise production and employment, aggregate demand must be increased. Fiscal authorities can choose any of three methods.[5] They may raise government spending on goods and services without altering taxes; raise government transfer payments without changing taxes; or lower taxes without reducing government spending.

The first approach will raise aggregate demand directly, as government spending on goods and services is a part of aggregate demand. The other two alternatives work (raise aggregate demand) only slightly less directly. In both cases disposable income (plus perhaps business saving) is directly increased with the expectation that a rise in private spending C, and/or I, will be forthcoming.

In all three cases, the initial rise in demand will trigger a multiplier, which will magnify the final effect. On the other hand, if we assume no increase in the supply of money (deficit financed by sale of bonds to the public), the expansionary effects of all three will be tempered by the rise in the rate of interest that must be induced by the increased transactions demand for money.

Let us now briefly consider the chief characteristics of each fiscal device.

Raising Government Spending on Goods and Services, Taxes Unchanged

This approach has an initial advantage over the other two in that aggregate demand will initially go up by the full amount of the increase in government spending. Raising transfer payments or lowering taxes merely gives private spenders more to spend. If their marginal propensity to spend is less than 1, the initial rise in aggregate demand will be less than the amount of the tax cut (or transfer increase).

---

[4]In this chapter we shall overlook the position of some monetarists and assume throughout that fiscal policy *does* alter aggregate demand.

[5]Or, of course, any desired combination of the three.

On the other hand, the time lag involved in this case may be a serious detriment in comparison with the other two. It takes time to organize public works projects (even after Congress has acted), but tax cuts and/or transfer payments programs can be instituted and affect the spending stream almost immediately.[6] Another potential problem with raising government spending is the fact that much of the initial effects may fall on the construction industry and its suppliers. Now if this is one of the industries suffering with excess capacity, the effect is good. If, however, the unemployment is more widespread and the construction industry is near capacity, the initial effects of the government spending may be partly dissipated through raising construction prices and costs.

Raising Transfer Payments, Taxes Unchanged

As just noted, unless the recipients of increased transfer payments happen to have a marginal propensity to spend of 1, $1 billion of added transfers will raise aggregate demand initially (before the multiplier effects are considered) by something less than $1 billion. However, as the average transfer payment recipient is generally in the lower part of the income scale, his or her MPC will probably be quite high. If so, the initial effect on demand will be only slightly less favorable than is the case for goods and services expenditures.

To the degree that the added transfer payments are designed as additions to unemployment compensation, this approach has the additional virtue of reaching, reasonably quickly, those probably in most need of aid.

On the other hand, depending upon the extent and duration of the program, one might object to the possible incentive effects of transfer payments. Public works projects, it might be argued, possess the advantage of requiring the recipient of government paychecks to work for them, thereby avoiding the risk that the government's fiscal policy action will undercut the incentive to work.

Reducing Taxes, Government Expenditures Unchanged

Lowered taxes, by providing households and businesses with enlarged disposable incomes, lead to increased private spending. Of course, the amount of increase depends heavily on whose taxes are cut as well as on taxpayers' perceptions as to the permanence of the cut. If the beneficiaries of tax relief are heavy marginal spenders, the boost given aggregate demand will be significant. If, however, individuals with low MPCs or businesses with little incentive to invest are the affected parties, the fiscal action will be less successful. In addition, the effec-

---

[6]Experience with a tax increase, for example, the income tax surcharge of 1968, has led to doubts about the speed with which tax changes affect aggregate demand.

tiveness of a tax cut would normally be lower if taxpayers perceive it as temporary rather than permanent.

One criticism often made of this variant of fiscal policy is that, if it is the income tax that is cut, the only immediate beneficiaries are those who are still employed and earning sufficient income to benefit from the reduction. The unemployed, currently earning little or no income, derive little or no immediate relief.[7] In addition, as noted, it is likely that it will affect aggregate demand less, per dollar of fiscal action, than would increased expenditures on goods and services.[8]

Government Expenditure Changes versus Tax Changes as Resource Reallocation Devices

One important difference between tax and government expenditure changes not yet discussed is the resource allocation effect.[9] If the problem is recession with unemployed resources, either government expenditure increases or tax cuts can help put those resources back to work. But *where* they will work—on public or private goods—will differ in the two cases.

Suppose, for example, that we have an economy, with an MPC of two-thirds, that is going along at a production level $30 billion short of full employment. The unemployment can be eliminated, we would say, by *either* a $10 billion rise in the level of government spending or by a $15 billion cut in taxes. Either of these two fiscal policy actions will (when the multiplier has worked itself out) raise production by the required $30 billion.[10]

But the additional goods produced in the tax-cut case will be all consumer goods; in the government expenditure increase case, one-third ($10 billion) will be government (social) goods and the remaining two-thirds will be consumer goods. If taxes are cut, in other words, *all* the presently unemployed resources will be allocated toward producing goods in line with voluntarily expressed consumer preferences. If government expenditures are increased, only two-thirds of these resources will react to voluntarily expressed consumer demand; the other one-third will be "allocated" directly by government to the production of social goods.

It has been argued that this difference favors the tax change approach. The "stabilization branch" should not involve itself in decisions that are the proper

---

[7]They do, of course, benefit indirectly via the multiplier effects if the measure has its desired effect.

[8]As long as transfer payment programs are concentrated among the unemployed and lower-income groups, where MPCs can be expected to be high, they too probably raise demand more than tax cuts.

[9]As increased transfer payments are like reduced taxes in that both result in a rise in disposable income (indeed transfer payments are commonly referred to as "negative taxes"), comments in this section referring to tax changes could apply equally well to transfer payment changes.

[10]This, of course, is only the "round 1" effect in the Chapter 17 sense. It ignores offsetting interest rate changes.

province of the "allocation branch."[11] The proportion of resources devoted to producing social (government) goods should be determined by a comparison with marginal benefits from private goods. Stabilization activities aimed at establishing a level of aggregate demand just adequate for full employment with stable prices should not be used in a manner that alters the allocation of resources established by the "allocation branch." Hence, so this argument goes, lowering taxes and allowing consumers to determine the added goods produced has an edge.

"Automatic" Fiscal Policy— The Built-in Stabilizers

Up to this point we have considered only discretionary fiscal policy—where Congress acts to pass a new tax law or new government expenditure program to push aggregate demand in the desired direction. We must now take note that certain laws *already on the books* act in such a manner as to automatically produce budget deficits during recession and surpluses during inflationary booms. These are the built-in or automatic fiscal stabilizers.

Any tax law qualifies as an automatic stabilizer if it automatically (without specific legislative action) collects more tax revenue when GNP is rising (during the expansion phase of the business cycle) and automatically collects less tax revenue when GNP is falling (during the recession phase of the business cycle). Any government expenditure program (law) is an automatic stabilizer if it operates in such a way as to automatically increase the amount spent during recession and to cut back on the amount spent during inflation. The personal income tax and corporate profits tax laws are powerful tax stabilizers. The unemployment compensation program is an important expenditure stabilizer.

In the boom phase of the business cycle, when incomes are rising rapidly, tax revenue from the existing personal income tax law automatically goes up— both because people must pay tax on more income and because, with progressive tax rates, some must pay higher rates of tax. Because corporate profits generally rise more rapidly than GNP in expansion periods and fall more rapidly during recessions, corporate profits tax revenue also increases automatically in booms and falls off sharply in recessions. Both taxes, therefore, act as powerful stabilizers.

The unemployment compensation program calls for tax payments into the unemployment compensation fund by employers, out of which laid-off employees who qualify are paid weekly benefits for specified time periods. Weekly benefit payments to the unemployed are, of course, government transfer payments. As the program is set up, the amount of these government transfers automatically rises dramatically during recession periods when many workers are laid off and automatically is cut back in the expansion phase of the cycle as full employment is approached.

---

[11]The reference, of course, is once again to Musgrave's breakdown of governmental economic activities. See Musgrave, *Theory of Public Finance*.

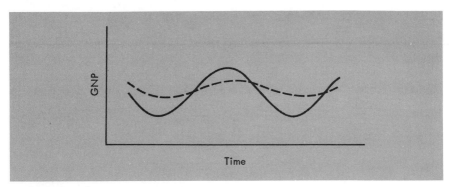

FIGURE 21-1 Effect of Automatic Stabilizers

The role played by the automatic stabilizers is perhaps best described as "shock absorbers." They do not *prevent* recessions and inflations nor do they help the economy to get out of already existing recessions. What they do accomplish is a reduction in the severity of business cycles. Referring, for example, to Figure 21-1, the solid line depicts the movement of GNP over the course of a business cycle if there are no automatic stabilizers combating the movement. The dashed line is intended to show the lesser amplitude of business cycles because of the automatic stabilizers.

It seems clear that, on balance, the effects of the automatic stabilizers are overwhelmingly favorable. They produce deficits in recessions and surpluses in inflations, and they do it automatically, without the long delay often required for Congress to take discretionary action. This is no mean accomplishment.

But despite virtues that have led some to argue that we should dispense with discretionary fiscal policy altogether, the stabilizers are not perfect.[12] In the first place, as noted, they cannot eliminate the business cycle; they simply reduce its severity.

Second, and considerably more objectionable, their effects are not *always* favorable. What the stabilizers do is combat *any* change in the level of income. Over most of the business cycle, such action is obviously in the desired direction and is to be applauded. But this is not so for recovery from existing recession.

Look, for example, at Figure 21-2. The stabilizers' opposition to the changes in income in phase AB and in phase CD deserves unreserved praise. But how about phase BC? At point B, the bottom of the recession has been reached and, over the BC range, the economy is climbing back toward full employment. Clearly this is a movement in income that is desirable, yet the automatic stabilizers—*which automatically combat any change in income*—make this recovery more difficult than it would be in their absence.

---

[12]For a statement favoring sole reliance on the automatic stabilizers, see Committee for Economic Development, *Fiscal and Monetary Policy for High Employment* (New York: Committee for Economic Development, 1962).

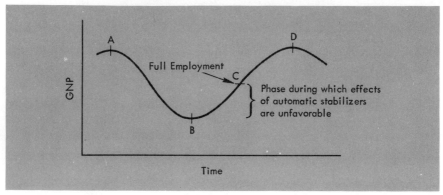

FIGURE 21-2 Deficiencies of Automatic Stabilizers During Recovery from Recession

A case in point was the early 1960s. The economy had been in recession in 1960–1961 and, in 1962 and 1963, was beginning to recover. As income rose, however, tax revenue collected under the personal and corporate tax laws automatically went up too, making further progress toward full employment that much more difficult. It finally became necessary, in 1964, to use *discretionary* fiscal action, in the form of a cut in personal and corporate income tax *rates,* to get back to full capacity.

The Determinants of the Degree of Effectiveness of Discretionary Fiscal Policy

Most economists believe that intelligently administered fiscal policy can play a significant role in achieving economic stability. But we must be on guard against allowing oversimplification to distort our evaluation.

As a first approximation it is often argued that the effects of fiscal policy on the equilibrium level of production and income can be read from the following simple expression[13]:

$$\frac{1}{1 - MPC} \times \begin{array}{l} \Delta \text{ Government} \\ \text{spending on} \\ \text{goods and services} \end{array} = \begin{array}{l} \Delta \text{ Equilibrium level} \\ \text{of production} \\ \text{and income} \end{array}$$

---

[13]Some economists prefer to differentiate between a "tax multiplier" and an expenditure multiplier. For example, if b stands for the MPC, the expenditure multiplier would be as above, $1/(1 - b)$, but the tax (or transfer) multiplier would be $-b/(1 - b)$, which would then be multiplied directly times the tax (or transfer) change. Obviously these are alternative ways of saying the same thing, it being a matter of pedagogical taste whether the multiplier or multiplicand should be altered.

or

$$\frac{1}{1 - MPC} \times (MPC \times \Delta \text{ Taxes}) = \begin{array}{l} \Delta \text{ Equilibrium level} \\ \text{of production} \\ \text{and income} \end{array}$$

or

$$\frac{1}{1 - MPC} \times \left(MPC \times \frac{\Delta \text{ Government}}{\text{transfers}} \right) = \begin{array}{l} \Delta \text{ Equilibrium level} \\ \text{of production} \\ \text{and income} \end{array}$$

Now there is nothing wrong with putting it this way as a simplified first approximation, but the alert student will recognize that this does involve considerable abstraction from reality. Although we cannot, within the scope of this book, exhaustively treat fiscal policy, it does seem in order to carry it a bit further than these expressions permit. What are the determinants of the degree of effectiveness of fiscal policy?

To keep the discussion within manageable proportions, we shall consider only the stabilization effects of fiscal policy. And to avoid unnecessary duplication, let us concentrate on only one side of the stabilization task—fiscal action to deal with unemployment. What will determine *how* effective a given fiscal program will be, in its goal of raising employment?

As the following list indicates, it is convenient to break the discussion down into two major categories. Because the aim is to raise employment through increases in aggregate demand, we must first consider the factors that determine the effect of the fiscal policy on total spending. Then, because the increase in demand is means rather than end, we must go on to discuss the circumstances under which demand increases are likely to cut unemployment.

Factors Determining the Degree of Effectiveness of Antirecession Fiscal Policy.[14]

I. Determinants of the effect of the fiscal policy on aggregate demand
   A. How does the government spend its funds?
      1. On goods and services or transfers?
      2. In an area where the initial recipients of funds spent by government have a higher or lower MPC than the average for the community?
   B. How does the government raise the funds it spends?
      1. By taxing or borrowing?
      2. If by taxing, what is the MPC of the particular taxpayers affected?

---

[14]Obviously this contains a different list of factors than those included in the table back in Chapter 17. In fact, both lists matter, but many included here bear on the slopes of the curves referred to in Chapter 17.

3. If by borrowing,
    a. To what extent, if any, do the lenders cut their consumer spending to lend to government?
    b. To what extent does the government's added use of loanable funds raise the rate of interest and, thereby, indirectly cut private spending (i.e., How much "crowding out" is there?)?
    C. Does the fiscal policy itself cause offsetting cuts in private spending for any other reasons?
    D. If taxes are altered, do those affected view it as a permanent change or a temporary, one-shot affair?

II. Given the rise in aggregate demand, what determines its effectiveness in eliminating unemployment without raising prices?
    A. How near to full employment are we?
    B. How near to full employment are the industries most directly affected by the government policy?
    C. How closely do the areas of unemployment and added government spending coincide geographically?
    D. How long does it take for aggregate demand to be affected?
    E. To what extent does the unemployment result from deficient aggregate demand rather than from structural factors in the economy?
    F. What is the current state of consumer expectations regarding price-level increases?

Regarding the first question—the effect on aggregate demand—the variables are numerous. A given-sized fiscal program will raise demand more, other things being equal, the more government spending is devoted to goods and services expenditures rather than transfers, where there is a possible leakage resulting from the MPS of transfer recipients. In addition, the second round of the multiplier effect may differ somewhat depending on the particular MPCs of those paid by the government. For example, a $10 billion rise in government spending on goods and services raises demand by a full $10 billion in the first instance. Even if the MPC for the "average" citizen is four-fifths, however, there is no guarantee that the rise in consumer spending resulting in the next period will be $8 billion. For the recipients of the money spent by government may not be average. They could conceivably be well-paid contractors and construction workers with an MPC well below the average for the community. If so, the full effect on aggregate demand will be less than the $50 billion the simple formula would predict.[15]

---

[15]If the MPC for the average member of the community is $\frac{8}{10}$, but that of the group initially receiving the $10 billion extra spent by government is only $\frac{1}{2}$, the ultimate rise in the equilibrium income level will be $35 billion rather than $50 billion. Looking at it on a period by period basis, we would expect

Period 1	Period 2	Period 3	Period 4	Period 5	
+ $10 billion	+ $5 billion	+ $4 billion	+ $3.2 billion	+ $2.56 billion	etc.

The increase in period 1 is the rise in government spending; that in period 2 is the added consumer spending done by the group that initially receives the funds spent by government. From period 3 on, it is assumed that new income is dispersed to the community at large, where the average MPC, $\frac{8}{10}$, applies.

If the fiscal action takes the form of added government spending, the ultimate effect on demand depends heavily on the method used to finance the added expenditures. If taxes are increased to pay the tab, the expansionary influence of the rise in government spending will be in large measure (but not entirely) offset by the contractionary effect on private consumer spending of the tax hike. Only if the MPC of the taxpayers were one, implying that all the tax increase (reduction in disposable income) would come out of consumer spending and none of it out of saving, would there be no rise in demand. Nevertheless, financing the government spending by taxes would almost certainly mean a smaller net rise in demand than if the funds were borrowed.

If the government borrows the funds via sale of securities, we must consider the remote possibility that those who lend the money (buy the securities) may cut their consumer spending in order to do so. This hardly seems likely. Unlike taxpayers, whose incomes and private wealth positions are cut when the government takes more, bond buyers simply agree voluntarily to accept government securities in exchange for their loanable funds. Neither their incomes nor their wealth positions are cut, so there is no obvious reason to expect them to reduce their consumption. To argue otherwise is to imply that bond buyers decide voluntarily to save more (consume less) and lend the funds to the government simply because the government is trying to borrow. What seems very much more likely is that the bond buyers decide to divert funds that they had already decided to save away from private borrowers to the government.

But this too has its implications for aggregate demand. Even if we agree that those who lend to the government will not directly cut their spending in order to do so, the fact that government borrowing may reduce the funds available for business may indirectly cut private spending. If, for example, the government finances deficit spending by sale of securities to the nonbank public, the increased demand for loanable securities to the nonbank public, the increased demand for loanable funds—with no rise in the supply—will raise interest rates, cutting back investment spending somewhat. The reader will remember from the theory section that the expansionary effects of a rise in government spending will, assuming no rise in the money supply, be partially offset by a rise in interest rates.

As we noted then, this need not happen if the deficit is financed by sale of securities to the banks. For, in that case, the increase in the demand for money (or for loanable funds) may be just offset by the rise in the supply of money (or loanable funds), so that the interest rate need not rise. The conclusion from all this is that the net increase in aggregate demand will be greatest if increased government spending is financed by borrowing from the banks; less if the funds are borrowed from the nonbank public; and least of all if they are raised via taxation.

In addition, we must recognize the possibility that the expansionary effects of fiscal action could be partially offset by the direct reactions of private spenders to the fiscal policy. For example, if there are investors who (rationally or not) are sufficiently fearful of a rise in the national debt to cut their outlays because of it, their doing so will certainly nullify part of the beneficial effects on aggregate demand.

It does not seem likely, however, that such a negative response to fiscal action would amount to very much. First, the modern business community is, in the main, too knowledgeable to react in this way. Second, there must be set off against such a response the favorable effects of the fiscal policy on the expectations of those investors who understand its purposes and believe in its effectiveness. Those who expect the policy to succeed in raising demand would, on that account, probably increase their investment spending, reinforcing the policy.

Finally, it is generally recognized that the impact of tax changes on spending will be greater if those affected perceive it as a permanent change than if they consider it temporary. This is based on those consumption theories that regard people's so-called "permanent income" as a more reliable predictor of their consumption spending than any given year's income.

So much for the determinants of the effect of the policy on aggregate demand. This takes us half the way. But if the objective is to raise employment, we must go on to consider the conditions under which increased demand will accomplish the objective, instead of spilling over into such undesired results as price increases. This, of course, depends upon a number of factors and is an area about which there is much current debate. First, most economists would argue that the farther from full employment we now are (the greater the "slack" in the economy), the more likely it will be that demand increases will increase employment rather than prices. The distribution of the unemployment matters too. If the industries most immediately affected by the fiscal action (for example, the construction industry) are near capacity, prices there may well be driven up even though there is considerable unemployment in the rest of the economy. Similarly, if the unemployment is geographically concentrated and the fiscal policy raises demand more generally throughout the economy, part of the added spending will be dissipated via undesirable price increases.

Another factor of real significance brought home to us in recent years is the state of consumer expectations regarding future prices. One does not have to subscribe to the "accelerationist" view of the Phillips curve to grant the crucial importance of expectations in determining whether demand increases will raise employment or prices. Without question, a nation that has been experiencing roughly stable prices for some years preceding expansionary fiscal action has more reason for confidence in the success of its policy than one that has been undergoing substantial inflation in the past.

The time factor also matters. There is little benefit to demonstrating that, *if other things remain the same,* a given fiscal policy measure will ultimately raise aggregate demand by x billion dollars if that result would only be achieved after 10 years. If we are attempting to combat the business cycle, it matters little that aggregate demand could be raised by x billion dollars in 10 years, other things being equal, if there is good reason to expect the "other things" to change markedly long before 5 years. Perhaps, for policy purposes, we should concentrate more on the expected rise in demand within a 12- to 18-month period rather than on an equilibrium result that will never be realized anyway.

Finally, we must consider the possibility that the unemployment is not of the sort a rise in demand can easily eliminate. If the unemployment is structural in nature, resulting, for example, from a work force whose training and skills simply do not meet the needs of employers with job openings, increased aggregate demand alone may do little to solve the problem.

The Weaknesses of Fiscal Policy
Relative to Monetary Policy

Fiscal policy, whatever its strengths, is no panacea. Even its most enthusiastic adherents acknowledge that it has weaknesses, although there is, of course, disagreement regarding their severity.

One of the most serious drawbacks to discretionary fiscal policy, given the present institutional structure in the United States, is the time lag involved between the recognition of the need for action and the time when action can be taken. Because discretionary fiscal policy is entirely up to Congress to enact, delays of many months can be expected while the legislature considers action.

In this respect, fiscal policy contrasts sharply with monetary policy. Because monetary policy is in the hands of the seven-person Board of Governors, it can be initiated immediately once the need for action has been determined. Clearly, with the existing U.S. governmental structure, monetary policy is superior to fiscal policy in terms of this particular time lag.[16]

Another disadvantage of the fiscal arm relative to its monetary counterpart is its inflexibility. Monetary policy, especially open-market operations, can easily be reversed when conditions dictate. Fiscal policy, though not totally inflexible, is substantially more difficult to reverse. This is especially true of the public works variant of fiscal policy, which, once turned on, is particularly difficult to stop before completion of the project.

A third problem with fiscal policy appears to be the political problem involved with its use to combat excessive demand. Fortunately, good economics coincides with good politics in a recession. A tax cut or an increase in government expenditure projects makes economic sense as well as being attractive politically. Unhappily, this is not so in the inflation phase, where good economics—a tax increase or a reduction of government services—may be political poison. The result may well be that fiscal action to combat excessive demand may only be taken after even longer lags and in the most extreme cases.

In this respect, monetary policy again has a relative advantage. Although so-called "tight money" policies are by no means free of opposition and political

---

[16]It should be noted that this advantage of monetary policy is not an inherent one. It exists because we have chosen to place the administration of monetary policy with a seven-person board rather than directly with Congress. If fiscal policy should ever be similarly administered, as has been recommended, its time lag problem would be markedly lessened.

pressures, the policymaker, the Federal Reserve Board, is far better insulated from the immediate threat of political retribution than are its fiscal counterparts. The result, almost certainly, is a speedier initial response to inflationary tendencies.

A majority of economists, while granting these deficiencies of discretionary fiscal policy, still feel that it can play a significant role in the nation's stabilization policy. Some others, however, have become so impressed with the problems that they advocate abandoning discretionary fiscal policy altogether, relying only on the so-called "automatic" fiscal stabilizers to supplement monetary policy. It is their feeling that the lags involved in discretionary policy are so long and variable that fiscal action is more likely to reinforce the cycle than to combat it. The most extreme position on fiscal policy, of course, has been taken by the monetarists, some of whom, as we have noted, deny that fiscal policy has *any* significant effects on aggregate demand.

Debt Management

It has become traditional to refer to debt management as a third policy alternative, to be used along with monetary and fiscal policy. Although we shall abide by the strictures of tradition, there is room for questioning the validity of treating debt management as an activity entirely distinct from monetary and fiscal policy, for debt management activities are so closely intertwined with monetary and fiscal actions that they often seem to merge.

Debt Management Defined

For our discussion, we shall accept the definition of debt management employed by the late Warren L. Smith. *Debt management* includes "all actions of the government, including both the Treasury and the Federal Reserve, which affect the composition of the publicly held debt."[17]

By this definition, the *amount* of new debt to be sold by the Treasury is in the fiscal policy province. Only the determination of its *composition* (the types of securities to be sold) involves debt management. Similarly, the amount of securities to be sold (or bought) by the Federal Reserve is a monetary policy decision; the decision about the type of security to be sold (or bought) is one of debt management.

The lion's share of debt management decisions, however, is involved in the Treasury's efforts to refund the national debt. As outstanding securities mature, the Treasury (assuming no tax surplus exists) must sell new ones to raise the money

---

[17]Warren L. Smith, "Debt Management in the United States," Study Paper Number 19, *Study of Employment, Growth and Price Levels* (Washington, D.C.: Joint Economic Committee, 1960), p. 2.

TABLE 21-1

Estimated Ownership of Federal Securities, June 1982
(billions of dollars)

U.S. government agencies and trust funds	$ 211.7
Federal Reserve banks	127.0
Individuals	146.2
Commercial banks	117.0
State and local governments	91.2
Nonfinancial corporations	38.9
Insurance companies	22.2
Mutual savings banks	5.7
Foreigners	141.9
Miscellaneous and all others	177.8
Total federal debt	$1,079.6
Total public held debt	740.9

Source: Federal Reserve Bulletin, October 1982.

to pay off the holders of those coming due.[18] The choice of the type of new issue is, once again, a debt management decision. Some sense of the enormity of this refunding responsibility can be obtained from the fact that, as of July 1982, $361 billion of the $774 billion of marketable federal securities then outstanding were within a year of maturity.

One further comment regarding our definition of debt management appears to be in order before we proceed. We are concerned only with changes in the composition of the publicly held debt. Publicly held debt should be taken to mean federal obligations owned by anyone other than the U.S. government investment accounts and the Federal Reserve banks. As Table 21-1 indicates, only about three-fourths of the total outstanding federal debt is publicly held.

The Objectives of Debt Management

What can and what should be accomplished via debt management? Opinions on this question have varied widely over the years.[19] In the years prior to the 1930s, the major aim of debt management appears to have been simply to keep the then-small federal debt in as long term a form as possible, thereby minimizing the Treasury's refunding difficulties. Then, as now, the prime consideration was protection of the government's credit. Long-term debt, it was felt, was the "soundest" means of accomplishing this end.

---

[18]In fact, refunding usually consists of an "exchange offering" of new securities to the holders of maturing obligations, rather than a sale for cash and then use of the cash to retire the old securities. Because the effect is the same in either case, we shall ignore the distinction.

[19]For a good discussion of these changing attitudes, see the article by William E. Laird, "The Changing Views on Debt Management," *Quarterly Review of Economics and Business,* Autumn 1963.

The Great Depression and World War II changed all this. The former experience markedly intensified concern for economic stabilization; the latter gave us a large federal debt to manage. Debt management had become a major activity, and considerable interest developed in employing it contracyclically, as a stabilization weapon to supplement monetary and fiscal policy.

In general terms, the idea was to shift (in refunding) toward long-term securities in periods of excess demand and then back toward short-term obligations during recessions. Lengthening the maturity of the debt structure during cyclical upswings was expected to help in at least two ways. First, selling more long-term debt would tend to raise long-term interest rates. This, it was hoped, would hold down on investment expenditures somewhat. Second, by replacing highly liquid short-term obligations with less liquid long-term securities, the total liquidity of the public's wealth would be reduced so that, one would hope, further restrictions on demand would be forthcoming. The reverse, of course, follows in recession.

Later, however, the notion that debt management should be employed as a third stabilization weapon encountered increasing opposition.[20] Considerable doubt was expressed regarding the magnitude of the effect on demand of such cyclical switches in the debt's maturity structure. In addition, it was pointed out that whatever can be accomplished through these means to combat the business cycle can probably be done more efficiently through intensification of monetary policy itself. Third, the attempt to lengthen the maturity of the debt during booms runs some risk of undermining Federal Reserve policy, as the Treasury sometimes requires support from the Federal Reserve when it attempts to place long-term issues. Such support, taking as it must the form of Federal Reserve open-market purchases, could require (at least temporarily) abandonment of a policy of restraint. Finally, borrowing long during booms, when interest rates are typically high, and short during recessions, when they are usually low, implies higher borrowing costs to the Treasury.

In the light of all these problems with a contracyclical debt management policy, more and more economists appear to have moved toward the view that it does not really constitute an effective stabilization weapon. There is widespread agreement that the maturity of the debt should be lengthened, but not just during the boom phase of the cycle. Indeed, some would argue that the bulk of the long-term securities should be sold during the recessions, thereby taking advantage of the generally easier market conditions prevailing, and the short-terms during the booms. This would reduce the cost of servicing the debt while generally easing the Treasury's refunding task. It would then be left entirely to the monetary and fiscal policymakers to take whatever action is needed to modify business cycle swings.

---

[20]See, for example, Smith, "Debt Management."

Incomes Policies

For many years economists and government policymakers, while recognizing that the ideal of full employment with stable prices was not fully realizable even with the most skilled use of monetary and fiscal policy, were more or less content to rely solely on these two prime instruments of demand management to produce a roughly satisfactory approximation to the desired results. Events of the 1960s and 1970s, however, shattered much of this complacency and provided an environment within which many governments found it necessary to resort to wide-ranging experimentation with a new set of policies—those that we now call *incomes policies*.

What Are Incomes Policies?

Incomes policies involve direct action by government (as opposed to the indirect thrust of monetary and fiscal policy through aggregate demand) to attempt to hold down excessive rates of inflation. It is almost impossible to provide a specific definition of these policies because they include a vast array of governmental actions varying all the way from mere verbal exhortation to tight-fisted, iron-clad, authoritative, across-the-board price and wage freezes backed up by the threat of heavy fines and/or imprisonment for violators.

For purposes of our discussion, we shall consider incomes policies to include the following sorts of governmental actions:

1. "Jaw-boning." Here the government merely appeals to labor and management to use restraint in raising wages and prices but applies no specific sanctions to the noncooperative. This approach usually implies reliance on the force of public opinion to hold price setters in line and often involves singling out the most "visible" large companies and unions for special verbal admonition.

2. "Arm-Twisting." In this technique the government carries its pressures on key price setters to the point of threats of withdrawals of governmental benefits or other active reprisal. Such actions might include withholding government contracts from offenders, threatening to unload government stockpiles of strategic materials so as to force down the price, reducing subsidies including removing tariff protection, or threatening more intensive antitrust prosecution.

3. Voluntary Price and Wage Controls. This consists of the federal government formally announcing "guidelines" or "standards" specifying maximum acceptable rates of price and wage increase. Such guidelines are voluntary in that the executive has no legal power to enforce them directly. As a result, they are almost invariably accompanied by considerable jaw-boning and arm-twisting to induce compliance. Examples of their use include the guidelines established by the Kennedy administration in the early 1960s and President Carter's program in the late 1970s.

4. Authoritative Price and Wage Controls.   Involved here is a whole range of possible activities whereby government places direct mandatory limits on the rate at which prices and/or wages may be increased. Both the coverage and the degree of authority employed may vary widely. "Phase II" of President Nixon's policy during 1972, wherein wage rates were permitted to increase at a rate of 5.5 percent per year and profits margins in excess of the average of the best two of the three years immediately preceding August 1971 were forbidden, was an example.

5. Price and Wage Freezes.   An across-the-board price and wage freeze is the most extreme form of control wherein prices and wages are—for a specified time period—simply not permitted to rise at all above levels established during a previously designated time period. An example of this for the U.S. was the 90-day Phase I freeze in the fall of 1971.[21]

The Opposition to Incomes Policies

Incomes policies as a means of dealing with inflation are highly controversial. Many economists oppose them altogether on a variety of grounds.

First, there is the charge that such direct governmental involvement in price setting inevitably involves interference with the price system and with the very shifts in relative prices that are relied upon as signals of changes in consumer preferences, in technology, and in resource availability. In short, it is argued, such measures will inevitably lead to a distortion of resource allocation. Most economists oppose *long-run* price freezes on these grounds.

Second, there is the not insignificant matter of time loss through the bureaucracy involved in authoritative price and wage controls. Not only does proper administration of such a program require a considerable administrative hierarchy at the governmental level, but it also causes firms under control to spend substantial amounts of time complying with the regulations.

Third, freezing prices and wages at given levels or allowing them to rise only at some prescribed uniform maximum rate inevitably creates inequities. Workers who got their raises just before imposition of the program are at an advantage as compared with those who did not. Firms whose prices had not previously been raised as rapidly as their costs are similarly disadvantaged. And if the less formal approaches referred to as "jaw-boning" and "arm-twisting" are resorted to, critics point out that, by their very nature, they will apply selectively only to the most "visible" of price setters, thereby discriminating unfairly against certain segments of the business community or of organized labor.

---

[21]This list presents a narrower view of incomes policies than many observers would prefer. A broader definition might include governmental activities to improve labor markets (such as manpower training, job information, and relocation subsidies) and programs aimed at improving the structure and competitiveness of markets (such as more intensive antitrust action, eliminating barriers to entry, lowering tariffs and minimum wage laws).

Fourth, but by no means of least significance, many economists do not believe that incomes policies can succeed in their objectives anyway. Prices and wages held down by fiat can be raised by subterfuge by changing job titles or product quality. Black markets are a distinct threat, especially if controls are applied during a period of excess demand. Excess demand, repressed during a period of controls, is very likely to resurface once they are removed and, in the long run, possibly raise prices to a level just as high as if controls had not been applied in the first place. And, as the clincher, opponents say, incomes policies have been tried in this country and a number of others and the evidence shows they simply have not worked. For example, two researchers who made a careful study of experience with incomes policies in Western Europe conclude that: "In none of the variations so far turned up has incomes policy succeeded in its fundamental objective, as stated, of making full employment consistent with a reasonable degree of price stability."[22]

The Case for Incomes Policies

Despite the still-formidable opposition among economists to attempts at authoritative control of prices, a considerable number support renewed use of incomes policies in the future.[23] Those who support them do not see them as a panacea and do not deny the existence of problems. However, in the troubled times of the 1980s, they see them as capable of making some positive contribution toward the solution of our economic problems.

> Advocates of incomes policies do not deny that such policies are a "second-best" approach to the problem of inflation control. They recognize that restoration of competition in markets would help to reduce inflationary pressures. But they think that such an ideal procompetitive policy would be politically or technologically impossible to achieve in the foreseeable future. Thus, in view of the unavailability of a "first-best" procompetitive policy, a "second-best" incomes policy must be relied upon.[24]

Advocates of incomes policies do not generally favor permanent price and wage controls under any and all circumstances. Most agree that when inflation is being caused by excess demand, the proper solution is not authoritative controls but effective monetary-fiscal restraint on demand. Nor do they differ from their opposition in their support for immediate efforts to remove obstructions to freer

---

[22]Lloyd Ulman and Robert J. Flanagan, *Wage Restraint: A Study of Incomes Policies in Western Europe* (Berkeley: University of California Press, 1971), p. 216.

[23]See, for example, Gardner Ackley, "An Incomes Policy for the 1970s," *Review of Economics and Statistics*, August 1972; John Sheahan, "Incomes Policies," *Journal of Economic Issues*, December 1972; Sidney Weintraub, "Incomes Policy: Completing the Stabilization Triangle," *Journal of Economic Issues*, December 1972.

[24]Thomas M. Humphrey, "The Economics of Incomes Policies," *Monthly Review*, Federal Reserve Bank of Richmond, October 1972. Humphrey's survey article is an excellent source for those who wish to further explore the incomes policy issue.

markets and the improvement of labor markets via retraining, better job information, and the like. And they, like most economists, would countenance across-the-board price freezes only for relatively short periods, as a form of "shock therapy" to, it is hoped, shatter developing inflationary expectations (or during such extreme emergencies as an all-out war).

In the main, however, the incomes policies advocates read the evidence of the 1960s and 1970s as *prima facie* proof that satisfactory performance of market economies now requires something more than the standard monetary-fiscal policy duo can offer. It is their position that serious structural imperfections and the long period of inflationary excesses have now laid the groundwork for a higher level of structural unemployment along with a firmer basis for intolerable cost-push inflation, aided and abetted by inflationary expectations.

And what of the charges that past incomes policy experiments have failed? Incomes policy advocates read the record somewhat differently. For example, in response to the summary judgment of Western Europe's experience by Ulman and Flanagan cited earlier, John Sheahan says,

> [their] judgment seems more negative than the facts warrant. . . . All these attempts broke down eventually because of emerging patterns of excess demand. It seems somewhat arbitrary to emphasize the inability to stop inflation at full employment more than the fact that some of these programs did achieve reductions in the rates of inflation associated with low levels of employment for periods of one to several years.[25]

As for the U.S. experience with incomes policies, some observers argue that inflation during the earlier 1960s was indeed reduced as a result of that period's "Guideposts" program. Despite the high levels of inflation in the United States during the early 1970s, the argument has also been made that the situation would have been even worse had the administration not instituted its control program.[26] The Joint Economic Committee of the Congress, for example, states, "What evidence is available suggests that the Phase I and Phase II controls of 1971–72 reduced the rate of increase in prices and wages as much as one or two percentage points."[27]

In addition, a number of observers have argued that the early 1970s control experiment might well have been more successful had it been better administered. The short duration of the initial price freeze, the fact that spenders were told well in advance when it would end, and the alleged bad timing of the institution of

---

[25]Sheahan, "Incomes Policies," p. 12.

[26]See, for example, Peter Fortune, "An Evaluation of Anti-inflation Policies in the United States," *New England Economic Review,* January–February 1974. The amount of inflation there "would have been" without control programs is, of course, extremely difficult to measure. Opponents of incomes policies offer the 1971–1973 U.S. experience as further evidence of the failure of controls.

[27]The *1974 Joint Economic Report,* Joint Economic Committee of the 93rd Cong., 2d sess., March 24, 1974, p. 37.

Phase III (a significant relaxation of controls) are among the specifics often cited. Then, too, it has been argued, the control policy of the 1970s was initiated and run by an administration whose chief economic advisers had been among the most outspoken opponents of incomes policies. As one former head of the Council of Economic Advisers has put it, "The record is one of political expediency, of an absence of clear plan or firm intention, and unresolved ideological tensions within the Administration."[28]

Proposals for a Tax-Based Incomes Policy

In the early 1980s, it seemed clear that the vast majority of economists, business leaders, and much of organized labor would oppose reinstitution of the more authoritative varieties of incomes policies for the United States. Despite this general atmosphere of disapproval, however, concern about the continuing inflationary environment has generated substantial interest in a recent proposal for an incomes policy based upon the tax system.[29]

In essence, the idea is to attempt to keep wage increases related to the increase in labor's productivity by raising the corporate profits tax rate on employers who grant inflationary wage settlements. It might work as follows.

Suppose that the productivity of labor rises at a rate of 3 percent per year and—assuming ongoing inflation—that it is expected that the average firm will offer wage increases averaging 5 percent. To implement the program, the top-bracket corporate profits tax could be reduced from 46 percent to 40 percent, but then each corporation would have a surcharge added on to the basic 40 percent rate that would be *a multiple of the amount its wage settlement exceeded the 3 percent productivity growth*. If, for example, the multiple chosen was 3, and corporation A agreed to an average 5 percent wage settlement, corporation B settled for an above-average 8 percent wage rise, and corporation C offered only a 3 percent wage boost, the corporate profits tax applying to each firm would be as follows[30]:

Corporation A would pay the basic 40 percent plus a surcharge equal to three times its 2 percent excess, or a total of the same corporate tax it paid at the 46 percent rate.

---

[28]Gardner Ackley, in testimony before the Joint Economic Committee, quoted in the *1974 Joint Economic Report*, p. 38. For an interesting account of the 1971 to 1973 U.S. incomes policy experience, see Arnold R. Weber, *In Pursuit of Price Stability*, Studies in Wage-Price Policy (Washington, D.C.: The Brookings Institution, 1973). See also Robert H. Floyd, "Incomes Policies: A Quick Critique," *Monthly Review*, Federal Reserve Bank of Atlanta, for a brief review of earlier experience in other countries.

[29]See H. Wallich and S. Weintraub, "A Tax-Based Incomes Policy," *Journal of Economic Issues*, June 1971. For a critical review of the Wallich-Weintraub proposal, see Nancy A. Jianakoplos, "A Tax-Based Incomes Policy (TIP): What's It All About?" *Review*, Federal Reserve Bank of St. Louis, February 1978.

[30]The particular multiple chosen could be varied according to how severe a penalty was desired.

Corporation B would pay the basic 40 percent plus a surcharge equal to three times its 5 percent excess, or a sharply increased corporate tax of 55 percent.

Corporation C would be rewarded for its restraint by paying only the basic 40 percent rate, 6 percent less than previously.

Such a plan, once it was initially adopted, would have the advantage of operating automatically, thereby avoiding the administrative bureaucracy that often is necessary to implement other types of incomes policies. In addition, it would put no absolute barrier on any industry. Growing firms and industries would be free to grant wage increases in excess of any arbitrary standard but would be penalized—as far as taxes are concerned—for doing so. But despite this, the plan's authors believe that it would involve less interference with the price system than would other possible plans.

There are, of course, problems. First, success would depend upon the assumption that the corporate profits tax cannot be shifted forward to consumers via increased prices—an assumption about which economists are in disagreement. Second, its success would presuppose an appropriate monetary-fiscal policy so that aggregate demand would not be excessive. And last, but of considerable importance, there would probably be real difficulties in enlisting the support of organized labor for such a plan, since it would directly restrain wages but not prices.

The first official recommendation for a tax-based incomes policy in the United States came from President Carter in late 1978. Recognizing that the cooperation of organized labor was an essential prerequisite to the success of its anti-inflation program, the Carter administration proposed an innovative combination of voluntary wage-price guidelines buttressed by a type of tax-based incomes policy that quickly came to be known as "real wage insurance."

Under this proposal key price setters were asked to keep their rate of price increase down to a level .5 percent less than that during the 1976–1977 period (but in no case, more than 9.5 percent) while wage and salary increases were to be held to a maximum of 7 percent. The unique feature of the plan was the recommendation that Congress enact a tax rebate scheme under which workers whose wage increases were within the 7 percent guideline during fiscal 1979, would be protected from losses in real income should the cost of living increase exceed 7 percent. If, for example, the cost of living should rise by 9 percent in 1979, the proposal was to pay workers who had stayed within the 7 percent wage increase standard a tax rebate equal to the 2 percent difference. The intent, of course, was to forestall another round of inflationary wage increases based upon the premise that larger wage increases were necessary to keep pace with the cost of living. This proposal, however, was flatly rejected by Congress.

Tax-based incomes policies are not, of course, a panacea. But for all their weaknesses, they offer an interesting alternative to dealing with the problem of inflation that seems to merit serious study. The relevant comparison, after all, is not between their admittedly imperfect effects and an "ideal" situation but rather between them and the inequity and misallocation caused by the current degree of inflation.[31]

Review Questions

1. Not all changes in government expenditures and taxes constitute fiscal policy measures. Some are undertaken for allocation purposes and others for distribution purposes. Explain.

2. Carefully distinguish between the three main types of discretionary fiscal policy. How do they compare in terms of their effects on the level of aggregate demand?

3. How do the automatic stabilizers tend to affect the economy? Can you identify any possible unfavorable effects?

4. Aside from the views of the monetarists, what are some of the major weaknesses of fiscal policy in comparison with monetary policy?

5. Explain and evalute debt management as a stabilization weapon.

6. What are incomes policies? What are the fundamental differences in approach between incomes policies and monetary and fiscal policies as means of controlling inflation? Explain.

7. List the pros and cons of incomes policies.

8. Carefully explain how a tax-based incomes policy based on alterations in the corporate profits tax might work. What advantages does a tax-based incomes policy have over other types?

---

[31]A special issue of the *Brookings Papers on Economic Activity,* No. 2 (Washington, D.C.: The Brookings Institution, 1978), contains a series of articles devoted to a thorough discussion of "Innovative Policies to Slow Inflation." The pros and cons of tax-based incomes policies are carefully weighed in this excellent series.

22

Introduction to International Finance

Simplification is the real goal of economic theory. Consequently it was not only acceptable but necessary to proceed within the comfortable confines of an imposing list of simplifying assumptions as we made our way through the income determination model sketched in Part II.

But the luxury of the simplifying assumption carries with it a heavy obligation. The theorist who would say something useful about the world in which we live must be ever mindful of the need to approach reality, even though never really getting there.

The purely domestic aspects of money and banking are, no doubt, of dominant importance, especially for the U.S. economy. But the problems facing an open economy—one involved in trade with other nations—are of great and growing significance. This section of the book considers the complexities and problems of international finance.

The Case for Free Trade

No nation is an island unto itself. Some, it is true, are so lavishly endowed with natural resources and other needed factors of production that they *approach* a state of self-sufficiency. But no nation, however wealthy, can be as well off without trade as it would be with it.

The case for free, unobstructed international trade is, of course, a simple one. Indeed, it can be justified on substantially the same grounds as money itself. Just as the existence of an efficiently operating money system permits fuller exploitation of the advantages of specialization, so too does free, unrestricted international trade.

The reader is no doubt familiar with the time-honored principle of comparative advantage. Given peaceful conditions and ignoring transportation costs, each nation will be better off (that is, have a higher real level of living) by specializing in the production of those goods and services in which it has a comparative advantage while trading for the other things it needs. In its essence, the principle of comparative advantage simply states that a nation should obtain its goods and services wherever they cost least in terms of its own resources. If a nation can obtain more units of Product X from abroad by producing Product Y and trading it to obtain X than it could by using a similar amount of its resources to produce X at home, it clearly gains by specializing in Y and importing X.

Now the real gains available to all nations from the fullest possible exploitation of worldwide specialization in production are unquestionably very large. Unfortunately, however, in the world as it is, these gains are not easily obtainable. We are not "one world," unreservedly committed to the betterment of mankind in general, but a large group of separate nations—all too often given not only to trade warfare but, sadly, to outright military conflict also.

The result has been myriad obstacles to free international exchange and the higher living standards it would make possible. Now, we cannot begin to consider all these obstacles in the short space of three chapters, and in any case, many of them go beyond the normal scope of a money and banking text. One area, however, is not only appropriate but essential. It has to do with the financial side of international trade.

Our prime concern in this section will be with the many problems involved in the use of scores of different national moneys to complete transactions across borderlines. For example, how can an American, who has only dollars, buy a product produced by a German who presumably wants only Deutsche marks? How can the United States sell more to other nations than it buys from them? What institutional structures, private and governmental, have been set up to facilitate the freest possible international exchange? Finally, how effectively do all these international monetary institutions function as mechanisms for the promotion of worldwide specialization? These fundamental questions of international finance will be our concern in this and the following two chapters.

The U.S. Role in International Trade and the Importance of International Transactions to the U.S. Economy

If one were to adopt the parochial viewpoint that the U.S. economy is our only interest, data on international trade might seem to imply that U.S. international transactions are relatively unimportant and that devoting several chapters to this topic overstates its importance to us. For example, it might be noted that, in 1982, the net effect of international trade on U.S. aggregate demand was just over $30 billion—just over 1 percent of the total. Or again, it could be pointed out that *gross* U.S. exports of goods in 1982 totaled about $211 billion, an impressive figure in itself, but one that represented less than 7 percent of the nation's GNP. Figures such as these, however, understate the importance of our current topic—to both the United States and the world economy as a whole.

Although only a relatively small percentage of overall U.S. private sector employment depends on sales to foreigners, the figure is very much higher in specific industries. And on the import side of the ledger, the critical importance to the U.S. economy of certain highly strategic raw materials is suggested by the material depicted in Figure 22-1.

Data such as these and memories of the near havoc created by the oil embargo of 1973 should be sufficient to dispel any notions that even resource-rich America can ignore international trade developments. And if trade is as important as that to

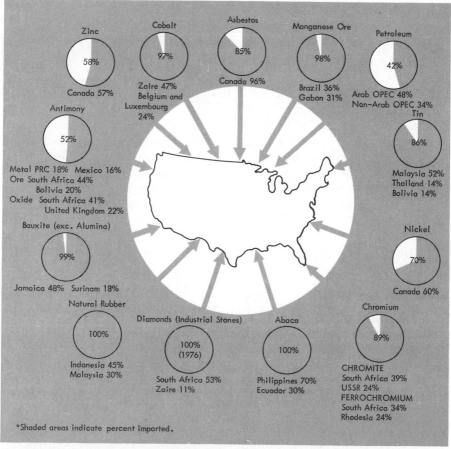

FIGURE 22-1   U.S. Dependence on Imports for 13 Critical Raw Materials, 1977*

Source: The Trade Debate, U.S. Department of State, 1978.

TABLE 22-1

Exports as a Percentage of GNP
for Selected Industrialized
Nations, 1982[a]

Canada	25.4%
West Germany	26.2
Japan	13.4
Netherlands	48.9
United Kingdom	20.1
United States	6.8

[a]Data are estimates of annual rates as of the third quarter of 1982, except for Netherlands, which is for 1981.

Source: U.S. Department of Commerce.

a nation whose exports and imports equal only around 7 percent of its GNP, it requires little imagination to appreciate the vital role it plays in the lives of citizens of the nations listed in Table 22-1, where its relative size is several times as large.

Methods of Making International Payments

For our purposes, the really different aspect of an international transaction is that two different kinds of money are involved. Whereas a transaction between Americans can be simply settled by the buyer handing dollars over to the seller, a transaction between an American and an Englishman is not quite so simple. For in this case, assuming that the American is the buyer, the English seller wants his own currency, pounds, in payment, but the American buyer normally possesses only dollars.

What solution is available? Stripped to its bare essentials, what is required is a mechanism through which dollars can be exchanged for pounds with a minimum of inconvenience to both parties. Such a mechanism exists in the form of the *foreign exchange market.*

The foreign exchange market, not unlike any other market, is made up of buyers, sellers, and middlemen. The object of sale, foreign exchange, consists of foreign currency, demand deposits in foreign banks, and other highly liquid short-term claims payable in foreign money. It is, to put it briefly, the nation's supply of foreign money, plus very short term claims to it. The buyers of foreign exchange (from the American viewpoint) are all those Americans who desire to purchase goods or services or perhaps securities from foreigners—essentially, U.S. importers. The sellers of foreign exchange (still from the U.S. viewpoint) are those Americans who, through the sale of goods or services or securities to foreigners, have acquired foreign money that they would like to convert into dollars—essentially, U.S. exporters.

The middlemen involved in this market are of special concern. It is, of course, their function to bring buyers and sellers together. These middlemen, in the majority of cases, are large commercial banks, located in the nation's financial center (New York, for the United States), acting in the capacity of exchange dealers or brokers.

The commercial banks that perform this vital middleman function in the foreign exchange market arm themselves for their task by establishing a "correspondent" relationship with their counterparts in the financial centers of the other countries of the world. The role of the "correspondent" is an important one. Generally, the American bank will maintain a checking account in its foreign correspondent in the form, of course, of the other country's money. And, in the usual case, the foreign correspondent will reciprocate by maintaining a deposit, in dollars, in the U.S. bank. Besides holding demand deposits for one another, correspondents perform a number of other important services, some of which will be noted in the paragraphs that follow.[1]

So much for the institutional structure of the foreign exchange market. Our major concern is to get some feel for how it works—that is, how international payments are actually made. In what follows, we shall make no attempt to describe all the possible means of making such payments. They are many and varied and, indeed, they change as world trade patterns, competitive conditions, and the like change. What we shall attempt is a description of two of the most prominent mechanisms of payment, leaving greater detail for more specialized treatments. These two will then be relied on as examples for our further consideration of international finance.

Let us consider, for our example, a transaction between an American and a British company where the value involved is $200,000 (or, alternatively, if the exchange rate between the dollar and pound is $2 per £1, £100,000). The mechanism and effects of payment for a U.S. import will be considered in two ways, and then we shall turn everything around for a look at the mechanism and effects of payment for a U.S. export.

Payment for a U.S. Import

Bank Draft. By far the simplest payment instrument in use in international finance is the *bank draft*. A bank draft is merely a special kind of check—an order to pay—that one bank draws on its account at another bank.

---

[1] We shall oversimplify in this chapter in several respects. First, we shall ignore the great and growing significance in the foreign exchange market of branches of U.S. banks located in foreign countries. Second, we shall, for the moment, ignore the dollar's status as an international reserve currency, similar in many respects to gold. Thus, though in fact most transactions with the United States are settled by increasing or decreasing dollar balances owned by foreigners in the United States, we shall proceed in this chapter "as if" adjustments in foreign money balances owned by U.S. banks are equally as important.

Here the American company would go to one of the large New York banks that deals in foreign exchange[2] and "buy a draft" that the New York bank would draw on its account at its correspondent bank in London. The U.S. importer, for example, would write a check for $200,000 (plus a service charge) on its own checking accunt and turn it over to the New York bank in exchange for the draft, which is a check the New York bank makes out for £100,000 on its account at its London correspondent, made payable to the British exporter. The draft is then sent to the exporter, who deposits it in his own account in London.

Let us take a look at the T-account effects of all this. Assuming that the U.S. importer keeps an account at the same New York bank from which the draft is purchased, the effect of its purchase on the New York bank would be as follows:

New York Bank

Due from London correspondent
  − $200,000 (worth of £s)
	Demand deposit of U.S. importer
	  − $200,000

When the draft is received and deposited by the British exporter in the London correspondent bank, the effects on that bank are

London Bank

	Demand deposit of New York
	  correspondent bank − £100,000
	Demand deposit of British export company
	  + £100,000

And that is all there is to it. The U.S. importer has used his dollars to buy pounds from the middleman, the New York bank, and has transferred these pounds to the British exporter to pay his bill. Sometimes such payments are made immediately on receipt of the goods being shipped, but often, especially if the importer is well known, the goods are shipped on a 30-day *open account*. This simply means that payment, by the same means as those just described, does not have to be made until the end of the 30-day period.

Bill of Exchange. The other mechanism of payment is a bit more complicated. In this case the payment process is initiated, not by the importer, but by the exporter. In our example, the British exporter would draw up a *bill of exchange,* a document described by some as a "You owe me." It, in simplest terms, is a paper that states on its face that certain goods are being shipped to a specific U.S. company, for which payment of $200,000 is expected. This bill of exchange can

---

[2]It would not really have to go directly to one of these, as its own local bank may have a "correspondent" relationship with a New York bank. It is simpler, however, for purposes of exposition to assume that the U.S. importer is located in New York.

then be taken by the British exporter to his London bank and "sold" to it for pounds at the going exchange rate (less a discount to account for the fact that the London bank will not be immediately repaid). The exporter thus gets his payment in pounds immediately and his London bank has the bill. The London bank will immediately send the bill to its New York correspondent bank, which will, in turn, present it to the U.S. importer for "acceptance."

The U.S. importer "accepts" the obligation stated in the bill by simply signing "accepted" on the face of it. In the usual case, other documents associated with the shipment, most importantly the bill of lading, are attached to the bill of exchange. Upon his acceptance, the bill of lading, which gives the holder the right to go to the docks and claim the goods that have been shipped, is detached by the bank and is turned over to the importer.

Sometimes the bill will call for immediate payment by the importer, and sometimes it will call for payment 60 or 90 days hence. In the latter case, the New York bank that now holds it can do one of two things, depending on instructions from its London correspondent. It can hold the bill (an "acceptance" now that it has been signed) until maturity, at which time the U.S. importer must meet his obligation for the face value of the acceptance by writing a check for $200,000 and placing it in the account the London bank holds at its New York correspondent.[3] In this case, the London bank is providing the credit involved.

If, on the other hand, the London bank does not choose to finance the transaction, it will instruct its New York correspondent to rediscount the acceptance in the New York money market. This simply involves finding an American lender who will purchase it at its discounted value and hold it for 60 to 90 days to earn the interest involved.

If the U.S. importer is small and not widely known, it may have received advance permission from its own New York bank to have the British exporter draw the bill of exchange on the bank, rather than the importer. Then, when the bank "accepts" it, the acceptance is much more readily salable in the money market because it is the bank's own promise to pay. Such an instrument is typically referred to as a *banker's acceptance*.

What are the T-account effects with the bill of exchange? When the British exporter sells the document to its London bank, the entries would be

London Bank

Discounts and acceptances +£100,000	Demand deposit of British exporter +£100,000

---

[3]The London bank, which paid the British importer £100,000 less a discount, receives the full $200,000, the difference being the interest it earns for financing the 60 or 90 days of credit. It should be pointed out that the original purchase price agreed upon between the two companies would be such that the discounted amount received by the British exporter would fully compensate it. The American importer, who is really getting the 60 or 90 days' credit, bears the interest cost.

If the London bank chooses to remain the owner of the acceptance until its maturity, the effects of final payment by the U.S. importer on the two banks involved would be

New York Bank		London Bank	
	Demand deposit of U.S. importer −$200,000 Demand deposit of London correspondent bank +$200,000	Due from New York correspondent bank +£100,000 (worth of dollars) Discounts and acceptances −£100,000	

Payment for a U.S. Export

Bank Draft. When the United States exports, as might be expected, everything is reversed. If we assume, once again, that a $200,000 sale is involved, the British importer could pay most directly by purchasing a bank draft from his London bank for approximately £100,000 and sending it directly to the U.S. exporter, who deposits it in his New York bank. In this case, the T-account entries are

London Bank		New York Bank	
Due from New York correspondent bank −£100,000 (worth of dollars)	Demand deposit of British importer −£100,000		Demand deposit of U.S. exporter +$200,000 Demand deposit of London correspondent bank −$200,000

Bill of Exchange. If, on the other hand, a bill of exchange is used, the U.S. exporter would draw it up and have it discounted at his New York bank. The New York bank would send it to its London correspondent, who would present it to the British importer for acceptance and, if the New York bank requested, hold it there until maturity. At maturity, the British importer would, of course, pay in pounds, thereby increasing the New York bank's foreign balances. The T-accounts (once again ignoring the interest involved) would look like the following: (1) when the bill is originally discounted at the New York bank,

New York Bank	
Discounts and acceptances +$200,000	Demand deposit of U.S. exporter +$200,000

and (2) when the importer pays at maturity,

New York Bank	London Bank
Due from London correspondent bank +$200,000 (worth of £'s) Discounts and acceptances −$200,000	Demand deposit of British importer −£100,000 Demand deposit of New York correspondent bank +£100,000

The Foreign Exchange Effects of Imports and Exports

Again, the two types of payment just discussed are included only as examples for future reference. Many other payment methods might be described if techniques and instruments of international payment were our prime concern. In fact, of course, they are not.

What is of the greatest importance for the student's understanding of upcoming material is not the details of international payment transactions themselves but the effects of such payments on the quantities of foreign exchange (foreign money) owned by the nations involved and—in turn—the tendency for such changes to affect **exchange rates.**

An exchange rate, of course, is simply *the price of foreign money in terms of your own.* From the U.S. viewpoint, for example, the dollar price of a British pound (as of June 1983) was about $1.57; the price of a German Deutsche mark was just under $0.39; and that of a Japanese yen was well under one-half of a cent.

As with any price, exchange rates tend to move in accordance with supply and demand.[4] Let us make use of the two examples of payment already discussed to trace through the basic exchange rate effects.

When an American imports British goods, as we have seen, the payment process must either reduce the supply of pounds owned by U.S. banks (if a bank draft is used) or increase the supply of dollars owned by British banks (if a bill of exchange is employed). In either case the result will be a tendency for the dollar price of pounds to rise (or, equivalently, the pound price of dollars to fall). For if pound balances owned by U.S. banks fall (the bank draft case), this constitutes a reduction in the supply of pounds and a tendency for their dollar price to rise. Conversely, if dollar balances owned by British banks rise (the bill of exchange case), that rise in the supply of dollars will tend to lower the pound price of dollars.[5]

---

[4]As we shall see, however, government intervention into the foreign exchange market has often been employed to "peg" exchange rates at levels other than the equilibrium rates private supply and demand would have established.

[5]If the exchange rate initially is $1.90 per £1, and an increase in U.S. imports tends to push it to $2.00 per £1, this change (from the U.S. viewpoint) represents a *rise* in the number of dollars required to buy a pound. From the British viewpoint, the same $2.00 per £1 rate represents a *reduction* in the number of pounds needed to buy a dollar.

Consequently, we can conclude that U.S. imports from Britain will

1. **Either lower the supply of pounds owned by U.S. banks or raise the supply of dollars owned by British banks.**
2. **Tend to raise the dollar price of pounds (the same thing as lowering the pound price of dollars).**

American exports have exactly opposite effects. If payment is made by a British importer via a bank draft, the supply of dollars owned by British banks will fall. If a bill of exchange is used, the payment process will result in an increase in the supply of pounds possessed by U.S. banks. In either case, the dollar price of pounds will tend to fall (meaning, of course, that the pound price of dollars rises). As a result, U.S. exports to Britain will

1. **Either raise the supply of pounds owned by U.S. banks or lower the supply of dollars owned by British banks.**
2. **Tend to lower the dollar price of pounds (or, what is the same thing, raise the pound price of dollars).**

The Balance of Payments

In any year, of course, there are many transactions between Americans and foreigners such as those just described. It is obviously useful, for policy purposes, to know something about their total and composition for the nation as a whole. This is the purpose of the *balance of payments,* compiled regularly for the United States by the Department of Commerce.

A thorough understanding of the logic, concepts, and organization of the balance of payments is an indispensable first step to any discussion of international trade problems. And yet, such understanding does not always come easily.

Let us begin at the beginning with a working definition. The U.S. balance of payments can be defined as *a double-entry listing of all economic transactions between American residents and foreign residents during the year, with those transactions grouped according to the direction of payment required.* One way of presenting a balance-of-payments statement is shown in Table 22-2.

Before we look at the various categories of transactions within the balance of payments in somewhat more detail, one point should be stressed. It is an accounting statement, based upon the fundamental premise that there are *two* sides to every transaction. When the balance of payments is presented as in Table 22-2, every transaction between Americans and foreigners will affect it in two places, one on each side, reflecting the two sides of the transaction.

Suppose, for example, that the U.S. exports $100 million worth of goods to foreigners and that payment is made via a bill of exchange increasing American bank holdings of demand deposits in foreign banks. The two sides of this transaction are (1) the shipment of goods from us to them and (2) their payment for these goods by giving our banks increased deposits in their banks. The first side

TABLE 22-2

U.S. Balance of Payments

Export Items—Transactions Requiring Payments to Americans by Foreigners	Import Items—Transactions Requiring Payments by Americans to Foreigners
1. Exports of goods	1. Imports of goods

2. Exports of services
Examples:
  a. U.S. ships transport foreign goods
  b. Foreign tourists spend money in the United States
  c. Value of the services of U.S. capital used by foreigners during the year (equal in amount to interest, dividends, and profits received by Americans on foreign investments)
	2. Imports of services
	Examples:
	  a. Foreign ships transport U.S. goods
	  b. American tourists spend money abroad
	  c. Value of the services of foreign capital used by Americans during the year (equal in amount to interest, dividends, and profits received by foreigners on investments in the United States.

3. Long-term investment (exports of long-term IOUs)
Examples:
  a. Purchase by foreigners of long-term securities issued by U.S. firms and governments
  b. Direct investment by foreigners in U.S. economy
	3. Long-term investment (imports of long-term IOUs)
	Examples:
	  a. Purchase by Americans of long-term securities issued by foreign firms and governments
	  b. Direct investment by Americans in foreign economies

4. Short-term capital movements (export of short-term IOUs)
  a. Foreigners increase ownership of demand deposits in U.S. banks or of other short-term U.S. claims such as U.S. securities
  b. Americans draw down their demand deposits in foreign banks or sell other short-term claims held abroad
	4. Short-term capital movements (import of short-term IOUs)
	  a. Americans increase ownership of demand deposits in foreign banks or of other short-term claims on foreigners
	  b. Foreigners draw down their demand deposits in U.S. banks or sell other short-term claims held here

5. Exports of gold	5. Imports of gold
6. Unilateral transfers—value of gifts from foreigners to Americans	6. Unilateral transfers—value of gifts from Americans to foreigners

of the transaction—the $100 million shipment of goods to foreigners—would clearly be entered on the left-hand side of the U.S. balance of payments as a "Transaction Requiring Payment to Us" (see Table 22-2).[6] We have sent them something of value, and that flow of goods to them establishes an obligation for them to send us something equivalent in return. That "something equivalent in return"—the payment of $100 million in the form of an increase in U.S. banks' holdings of

---

[6]More exactly, it might be described as the *part of* the transaction that gives rise to a liability to us.

deposits in foreign banks—is entered on the right-hand side of the statement under the heading "Short-term capital movements" (see Table 22-2, item 4a). Their payment for our goods, then, is listed separately as a type of "Transaction Requiring Payment by Americans."[7]

The point that merits stress—and also, unfortunately, often creates confusion—is that *each side of every transaction is entered on that side of the balance-of-payments statement that reflects the direction of the obligation incurred.* The fact that we happen to know that in this particular case the right-hand entry merely represents payment for goods we have sent them should not be permitted to obscure the fact that their sending us increased claims on their banks does represent something for which we must pay (and *have* paid, in the form of the goods sent).

In going through the details of the balance-of-payments statement presented in Table 22-2, students will be well advised to ask themselves the following questions about any transaction:

> In this transaction, what are the things of value we are sending foreigners (goods, services, securities, deposits in our banks, gold)? The value of such things is entered on the left-hand side. What are the things of value they are sending us in return (goods, services, securities, bank deposits, gold)? The values of these things are right-hand entries in our balance-of-payments statement.

Let us now consider some of the detail of Table 22-2.

1. Exports and Imports of Goods. There is little problem in understanding and properly locating these. When we export goods, we clearly send out something of value for which we expect payment; and when we import goods, the reverse is true.

2. Exports and Imports of Services. Only slightly greater difficulty is encountered here. If U.S. ships transport foreign goods or if foreign tourists enjoy U.S. hotels, restaurants, and recreation facilities, U.S. citizens are providing valuable services for foreigners for which the U.S. citizens expect payment. Such items will therefore be left-hand entries, representing exports of services. On the other hand, to the extent that foreign ships transport U.S. goods and to the considerable extent that U.S. tourists spend money traveling abroad, foreigners are providing services for U.S. citizens for which the foreigners must be paid. These, then, are right-hand entries.

Students sometimes have difficulties with another item that we list as a part of exports and imports of services—investment income. This represents interest, dividends, and profits earned during the year on investments owned abroad. The *dollar amount* of the payment of interest, dividends, and profits to Americans, earned on securities and branch plants owned abroad, is considered to represent

---

[7]Again, more exactly, it is *that part* of the transaction that accounts for something they do for us.

the value of the services of American capital exported during the year and, as such, appears on the left-hand side of the balance of payments. The dollar amount of interest, dividends, and profits, paid by Americans to foreign owners of U.S. corporate or government securities or branch plants here, is treated as an import of the services of foreign capital, a right-hand entry.

How does this treatment fit in with our prior classification of left-hand entries representing things of value done by Americans for foreigners, requiring payment to Americans, and right-hand entries representing things of value done by foreigners for Americans, requiring payment by Americans? Very simply. The item that goes on the left-hand (export) side represents the *value of the services* U.S. capital invested abroad has performed for foreigners during the year, for which Americans expect payment. This entry is *not* the payment itself (although it is equal to it in amount) but the value of the services rendered for which payment (which will show up elsewhere on the right-hand side) is due. Similarly, the amount of interest, dividends, and profits paid by Americans to foreigners is taken to represent the *value of the services* performed by foreign capital invested in the United States— a service for which Americans must pay.

3. Long-Term Investment. Long-term investment by Americans abroad, a right-hand (import) side entry in our balance of payments, consists of purchases by Americans of securities issued by foreign firms and governments with a maturity date at least one year hence, plus direct investment (outright purchase of productive facilities) abroad by American firms. Its counterpart on the left-hand (export) side of the balance of payments includes purchases during the year by foreigners of long-term securities issued by American firms and governments and direct investment by foreigners in the United States.[8]

As proper handling of these items is sometimes a source of confusion, let us take a closer look. When Americans purchase foreign securities they are, it seems, "exporting" American capital to foreigners. Why, then, have we said that such an activity appears on the right-hand (import) side of the U.S. balance of payments?

To answer this question we need, once again, to emphasize the two-sided nature of all transactions. When Americans buy foreign long-term securities, what are the two sides? On the one hand, Americans are getting something of value from foreigners—the securities themselves, their IOUs—and, on the other, Americans are exporting their capital to pay for these securities. Looked at in this light, it is clear that the entry on the right-hand (import) side is intended to reflect *the value of the securities that Americans get* (import); the actual "capital export"— actual *payment* by Americans for the securities—appears somewhere on the other left-hand (export) side.

Similarly, when foreigners purchase long-term securities issued by American

---

[8]It is interesting to note that U.S. private long-term investment abroad consists primarily of "direct investment," although foreign private long-term investment here consists primarily of "portfolio" investment, or the purchase of securities. As of the end of 1980, $214 billion of the $276 billion of long-term foreign investments owned by Americans was classified as "direct."

firms and governments, the purchase appears on the left-hand (export) side of the U.S. balance of payments because, in truth, Americans are exporting valuable IOUs to foreigners for which they have a right to expect payment. The actual payment, or the "capital import," if that term is desired, will show up somewhere on the right-hand (import) side.

A word of caution before we go on. The reader should take care to avoid confusing interest and dividends earned with investments. The payments for the former, of course, represent *income* from the services of capital invested in past years. Expenditures on the latter, on the other hand, permit an increase in the *stock of capital* that Americans have invested abroad and lay the basis for even greater interest and dividend payments in future years. The two, the volume of U.S. foreign investment and the volume of interest and dividends received, are, over the long run, related. It is, however, important to recognize their fundamental differences.

4. Short-Term Capital Movements. These might equally well be termed "short-term investments" to emphasize their essential similarity to long-term investments. However, the title "short-term capital movements" is the customary one, so we shall use it.

When Americans increase their ownership of short-term (less than one year until maturity) obligations issued by foreign firms and governments, or, significantly, when Americans increase their ownership of deposits in foreign banks, the transaction appears on the right-hand (import) side of the U.S. balance of payments. This treatment is perfectly parallel with that for long-term investments. Such investments represent an "import of short-term IOUs" for which Americans must pay in some form.

Conversely, an increase in foreign ownership of American-issued short-term obligations, including deposits in U.S. banks, affects the left-hand (export) side of the U.S. balance of payments because it represents an "export of American short-term IOUs" to foreigners, in return for which Americans expect payment of some kind.

Decreases in American balances in foreign banks or in U.S. ownership of other short-term foreign claims (item 4b in Table 22-2) show up on the left-hand (export) side because they represent, in effect, Americans sending back ("exporting") claims previously held against foreigners. Decreases in foreign-owned bank balances or short-term securities in the United States go on the import side for the reverse reason.

Suppose, for example, that Americans import $100 worth of goods and pay for them via a draft on foreign bank balances owned by New York banks. The effect will be to reduce American ownership of foreign exchange. The two offsetting effects on the U.S. balance of payments from such a transaction will be

Transactions Requiring Payment to Americans	*Transactions Requiring Payment by Americans*	
Short-term capital movements (decrease in U.S.-owned bank balances abroad) $100	Imports of goods	$100

Similarly, if foreigners buy goods from Americans and pay via a bank draft that reduces their bank's ownership of dollar deposits at their New York correspondents, the U.S. balance of payments would show exports of goods, offset by an equivalent short-term capital movement, on the right-hand side.

5. Exports and Imports of Gold. Prior to 1971 the U.S. government was committed to maintaining parity between gold and the dollar by standing ready to exchange gold for dollars owned by foreign governments at a fixed price. Under that arrangement a significant amount of gold changed hands as foreign nations, equipped with large dollar balances earned through trade with the United States, converted much of it to gold during the years from 1958 through 1970.

When such conversions took place, the treatment of the gold flows in the balance of payments was similar to that of ordinary commodities. That is, the export of gold was entered on the left-hand (export) side of the U.S. statement, while the payment for it—foreign governments drawing down their dollar balances—was a right-hand (import) side entry. When, for instance, the United States sold $100 million of gold under these arrangements, the U.S. balance-of-payments effects were

Transactions Requiring Payment to Americans	Transactions Requiring Payment by Americans
Exports of gold $100 million	Short-term capital movements (item 4b in Table 22-2) $100 million

Although such gold movements were common in earlier years, they have been insignificant since August 1971, at which time President Nixon suspended the convertibility of the dollar. International gold movements have been miniscule since that action.

6. Unilateral Transfers. Finally, we must consider the role of *unilateral transfers,* an area of some new difficulty. The problem here arises out of the fact that, by their very nature, these are not two-sided, *quid pro quo,* transactions. They represent gifts between Americans and the rest of the world.

Because gifts are one sided, but the balance of payments is an accounting statement that must balance, a fictitious "other side" of the transactions called unilateral transfers is employed to keep things straight. Once again, an example may be helpful.

If the U.S. government should make a $1 billion gift to foreign governments in the form of a dollar deposit in New York banks, the effect on the U.S. balance of payments would be

Transactions Requiring Payment to Americans	Transactions Requiring Payment by Americans
Short-term capital movements $1 billion	Unilateral transfers $1 billion

It is, admittedly, pretty farfetched to think of American gifts to foreigners—the unilateral transfers entry on the right-hand side—as being a transaction requiring payment by Americans. What is the thing of value we are getting that requires us to pay foreigners? One could stretch one's imagination a bit and come up with some sort of answer in defense of this treatment, but it is perhaps best to admit that, though the treatment of this entry suggested is perfectly correct, it is difficult to logically fit it in under the tent we have been calling "Transactions Requiring Payment *by* Americans." So let us simply call it a balancing entry and leave it at that.

A gift from foreigners to Americans of $1 billion in the form of deposits in foreign banks would have opposite effects on U.S. balance of payments. The entries, in this case, would be

Transactions Requiring Payment to Americans		*Transactions Requiring Payment by Americans*	
Unilateral transfers	$1 billion	Short-term capital movements	$1 billion

Why the Two Sides of the Balance of Payments Must Balance—Some Further Examples

Having stressed the double-entry nature of the balance of payments, it should be obvious that, when all transactions are considered, the two sides must be equal. This, of course, follows from the fact that every single transaction that affects the statement has offsetting effects on each side. The balance of payments always balances, numerically, by definition. It, like the equation of exchange, is a truism.

This definitional equality of the two sides of the entire balance-of-payments statement does not hold for any single part or parts of the statement, however. That is, there is no reason why exports of goods should necessarily equal imports of goods or that goods and services exports should not exceed or fall short of goods and services imports. Although the sum of *all items* on the left-hand side is defined as equal to the sum of *all items* on the right-hand side, no such equivalence holds for any of the parts of the statement.

We shall conclude this section with a list of examples of the balance-of-payments effects of particular transactions in the hope that (1) they will further illustrate that every transaction has offsetting entries, thereby requiring that the balance of payments must balance and (2) they will help to clarify some of the areas of difficulty in the preceding material.

1. An American company sells $100,000 worth of goods to a British company, payment being made on a bill of exchange that increases the balances owned by New York banks at their London correspondents:

Transactions Requiring Payment to Americans		*Transactions Requiring Payment by Americans*	
Exports of goods	$100,000	Short-term capital movements	$100,000

2. American owners of securities issued by a British firm receive $50,000 of dividend payments, the mechanism of payment raising the balance owned by New York banks at their London correspondents:

Transactions Requiring Payment to Americans		Transactions Requiring Payment by Americans	
Exports of services	$50,000	Short-term capital movements	$50,000

3. Americans purchase $250,000 of the common stock of a British company, the payment process raising the dollar balances of London banks owned at their New York correspondents:

Transactions Requiring Payment to Americans		Transactions Requiring Payment by Americans	
Short-term capital movements	$250,000	Long-term investment	$250,000

4. The U.S. government makes a gift of $500,000 to a foreign government in the form of dollar deposits in New York banks:

Transactions Requiring Payment to Americans		Transactions Requiring Payment by Americans	
Short-term capital movements	$500,000	Unilateral transfers	$500,000

5. The foreign government spends these dollars to buy goods from U.S. companies, thereby reducing its claim on U.S. banks:

Transactions Requiring Payment to Americans		Transactions Requiring Payment by Americans	
Exports of goods	$500,000	Short-term capital movements	$500,000

The U.S. Balance of Payments for 1982

Data for the U.S. balance of payments for 1982 are presented in Table 22-3. We shall use this table as a basis for defining a number of summary relationships that are of significance in evaluating the U.S. performance in international transactions for the year.

The Balance of Merchandise Trade

The difference between a nation's exports of goods and its imports of goods is called its *balance of trade*. If the nation's goods exports exceed its goods imports, it is said to have a balance-of-trade *surplus*. If, however, imports of commodities

TABLE 22-3

U.S. Balance of Payments, 1982
(billions of dollars)

Exports of goods	$211.0	Imports of goods	$247.3
Exports of services	139.0	Imports of services	103.0
Long-term investment,		Short-term capital	
net (here by foreigners)	10.9	movements, net[a]	2.7
		Unilateral transfers, net	7.9

[a]Includes statistical discrepancy of $42 billion.

Source: U.S. Department of Commerce, *Survey of Current Business*, March 1983.

exceed exports of commodities, the nation is said to have incurred a balance-of-trade *deficit*.

As Table 22-3 indicates, the United States ran a large balance-of-trade deficit in 1982—a total of over $36 billion. This was the largest balance-of-trade deficit in U.S. history, topping the previous record of $34 billion established in 1978. The United States regularly ran balance-of-trade surpluses until the enormous increase in OPEC oil prices in the mid-1970s tipped the balance toward deficits.

The Balance on Goods and Services

When the sum of our imports of goods *and* services is subtracted from the sum of our exports of goods *and* services, the result is referred to as the nation's *balance on goods and services*. Despite the fact that U.S. exports of services exceeded U.S. imports of services by about $36 billion in 1982, the nation had a small *deficit* in its balance on goods and services.

The lion's share of the U.S. surplus on international services—about $86 billion—was contributed by interest, dividend, and profit earnings on U.S. investments abroad. Conversely, about $2 billion more was spent by U.S. tourists abroad in 1982 than by foreign tourists in the United States.

The Balance on Current Account

The balance on current account results from adding net unilateral transfers to the balance on goods and services. That is, the sum of U.S. imports of goods and services plus U.S. gifts to foreigners is subtracted from the sum of U.S. exports of goods and services plus foreign gifts to Americans. In 1982, as is clear from the data in Table 22-3, the United States had a *deficit* in its balance on current account of about $8.1 billion.[9]

---

[9]The nation's balance on current account plus any allocations of special drawing rights during the year is equal to "net foreign investment" in the U.S. national income and product accounts. The balance on goods and services is similar, but not quite identical to, "net exports" in the national income accounts. The latter excludes U.S. government interest payments to foreigners, while the balance on goods and services includes them.

TABLE 22-4

U.S. International Trade Performance, 1946–1982
(billions of dollars)

Year	Balance of Trade (deficit = negative)	Balance on Goods and Services	Year	Balance of Trade (deficit = negative)	Balance on Goods and Services
1946	6.7	7.8	1964	6.8	8.5
1947	10.1	11.6	1965	5.0	7.1
1948	5.7	6.5	1966	3.8	4.5
1949	5.3	6.2	1967	3.8	4.4
1950	1.1	1.9	1968	0.6	1.6
1951	3.1	3.8	1969	0.6	1.0
1952	2.6	2.4	1970	2.6	2.9
1953	1.4	0.5	1971	−2.3	−0.3
1954	2.6	2.0	1972	−6.4	−6.1
1955	2.9	2.2	1973	0.9	3.5
1956	4.8	4.1	1974	−5.4	2.2
1957	6.3	5.9	1975	9.0	16.2
1958	3.5	2.4	1976	−9.3	3.6
1959	1.1	0.3	1977	−30.9	−9.5
1960	4.9	4.0	1978	−33.8	−9.8
1961	5.6	5.5	1979	−27.3	5.1
1962	4.5	5.0	1980	−25.3	8.3
1963	5.2	5.9	1981	−27.9	11.1
			1982	−36.3	−0.2

Source: U.S. Department of Commerce, Survey of Current Business, various issues.

The Significance of International Deficit and Surplus Measures

As we have noted, the U.S. incurred unprecedented deficits in most of the major balance-of-payments summary measures during the latter 1970s. So, too, did some European countries as well as many less developed nations heavily dependent on imported oil. On the other side of the ledger, the oil-exporting countries and a few industrialized nations, most notably Japan, recorded large and seemingly persistent surpluses. These developments are depicted in Figure 22-2, for the 1975–1977 period.

Now these facts will hardly be news to anyone who reads the newspapers or watches television. For statistics such as these have been reported, analyzed, and all-too-often sensationalized by the media on a regular basis. But aside from the widespread popular aversion to the term *deficit,* what is the true significance of the deficits and surpluses we have been discussing?

First, it should be recognized that the balance on merchandise trade, while readily available and widely publicized, can be a misleading indicator and, by itself, has relatively little significance. While it does, of course, accurately portray the balance of goods trade, it has the deficiency of tending to "emphasize exces-

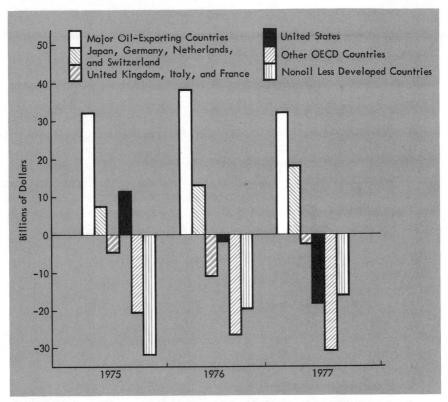

FIGURE 22-2   Current Account Balances for Selected Countries, 1975–1977

Source: Federal Reserve Bank of New York, *1977 Annual Report.*

sively the distinction between goods and services, which is of little economic significance."[10]

The balance on goods and services, however, has the advantage of being very closely related to the "net export" component of the national income and product accounting system and, more fundamentally, provides an accurate measure of the net transfer of real productive resources to or from foreigners as a result of the year's trade. A goods and services surplus, for example, implies that, on balance, a portion of the output of a nation's resources was exported to foreigners, whereas a deficit signifies that, on balance, part of the output of foreign resources was imported during the year.

The balance on current account also closely resembles a key element of the national income and product accounts—"net foreign investment." Conceptually,

---

[10]See "Report of the Advisory Committee on the Presentation of Balance of Payments Statistics," *Statistical Reporter,* June 1976, p. 227.

as the "mirror image of changes in the nation's net financial claims on foreigners," it does show net changes in U.S. investment abroad.

It is easy to comprehend the underlying logic of this statement. If, for example, the United States incurs a goods and services deficit, it is receiving more goods and services from foreigners than it is sending to them. But if that is so—and these excess goods and services were not given to us via unilateral transfers from foreigners—it follows logically that we must still owe for them. That is, we must have borrowed (short term or long term) to finance their purchase. Since the two sides of the entire balance of payments are equal by definition, any net excess of goods and services imports plus gifts to foreigners must be matched by an equivalent amount of borrowing from foreigners (in the form of exports of long-term or short-term IOUs). So current account deficits mean that a country's indebtedness to the rest of the world has risen, and current account surpluses mean that the rest of the world has increased its indebtedness to the surplus country.

Attitudes Toward International Deficits and Surpluses

To understand the meaning of equilibrium in the level of production is to know that it is not necessarily a "good" situation, merely a sustainable or stable one. It may be "bad" or "good" depending, among other things, on the level of employment.

Does the same thing hold for equilibrium (the absence of deficits or surpluses) in a nation's balance of payments? Is it necessarily a good position? The question is a difficult one, not readily subject to a yes or no answer. Nor, for practical purposes, does it really need to be answered because equilibrium is, at best, a transitory phase in the "real world," seldom really reached, retained only momentarily. For most nations, living reality usually consists of either a deficit or a surplus. What of these? Is one good and the other bad, or must we resort to that time-honored hedge, "It all depends"?

We have come a long way since the days when the early British economists devoted themselves to battling the then-dominant philosophy of the mercantilists regarding the goal of international trade. To the mercantilists, the measure of success of an economy was the size of its stock of precious metals, and the prime means of increasing this stock was via the development of a balance-of-payments surplus. In their view, then, a surplus was good and a deficit, bad.

Entrenched though it was, this mercantilist philosophy could not long hold up under the determined onslaught of the earlier classical economists. But although the "free trade" disciples won the day in the minds of the intellectuals of their time, the mercantilist ideas died hard in the minds of the general public. Indeed, it is probably fair to say that these ancient fallacies are still very much alive in some circles.

Of course, as the years went by, the arguments in support of the proposition that surpluses were good and deficits bad took on new sophistication. The emphasis on the accumulation of gold as, in and of itself a major virtue, soon gave way to stress on objectionable employment, wage rate, or other such effects of deficits. But the implications for policy purposes were not much changed.

In more recent years, a simple erroneous analogy may be as responsible as anything else for the popular conception of surpluses as good and deficits, bad. This is the pervasive, yet grossly misleading, habit of identifying the nation and its goals with those of a single business firm. Its simple application to international trade problems is clear and straightforward. "A firm is better off when it sells more (takes in more revenue) than it buys (pays out in costs). Therefore, a nation that is able to sell more to the rest of the world than it buys from it is clearly better off too."

Whatever the appeal of the deceptively simple logic in the preceding quotation and however much it may seem to be in accord with "common sense," it is neither logical nor sensible. The analogy drawn between the firm and the nation is simply faulty, and policy measures based on it are likely to be equally faulty. Indeed, it would be difficult to find a more important single source of economic illiteracy than the tendency to equate the nation and the firm.

Consider, for example, the implications of a current account surplus. The nation that achieves one does so only by sending out to foreigners, through export, more of its own goods and services than it receives from abroad.[11] In return, the surplus country accumulates short- and long-term IOUs. Now this result may very well be fine for a while. But the effects of such a surplus are not "good" in and of themselves. What, after all, is so good about sending useful products out to other countries and receiving back promises to pay? Clearly, the IOUs add to the nation's real economic welfare only if they are used up in later years to finance added imports. And that amounts to saying that the "good" thing about a surplus is the fact that it permits a country to enjoy the fruits of a later deficit. Obviously, a national policy aimed at perpetual balance-of-payments surpluses would be a shortsighted one!

We are forced to the conclusion that it is not really possible to classify surplus and deficit under a "good" or "bad" tag. On the one hand, there is nothing especially good, from a nationalistic economic point of view, about a nation aiming at the perpetual support of other nations (which is what a permanent surplus on current account implies). On the other hand, a nation cannot expect to reap the short-run benefits of a deficit without, sooner or later, having to settle up accounts. Every nation, over a period of time, must experience both surpluses and deficits, and a conscious public policy that aims at the perpetuation of either one must certainly be mistaken.

And yet, entirely aside from erroneous viewpoints based on mistaken analogies or mercantilist reasoning, it is quite clear that in most countries there is more

---

[11]Ignoring, for the moment, unilateral transfers.

worry, more immediate pressure to "do something about it," in the case of a deficit. Indeed, a main focus of the succeeding discussion will be on what can be done to eliminate deficits.

Such an attitude is perfectly natural. A nation with a current account surplus is accumulating other countries' IOUs. As long as it is willing to accept these in exchange for the extra goods and services it is shipping out, it does not have to worry about corrective steps. If, on the other hand, it is operating at a deficit, no such long-run arrangement is possible. For a while, of course, it can get along by using up its current supply of internationally accepted reserves in payment. But this is at best a temporary solution, since no nation possesses an unlimited supply of international reserves. Once they are lost—if the deficit persists—its only option is to issue IOUs payable in its own currency. But this too is likely to be a very limited source of relief, since, except for the case of a "key currency" country whose domestic currency *is* a form of international reserves, such IOUs are likely to be of only limited acceptability.

The certain knowledge that deficits can only be financed for limited periods, and that failure to curb them may ultimately require major readjustments within their domestic economy with serious implications for their citizens' living standards, quite naturally induces most governments to take long-term, chronic deficits quite seriously. In the next chapter we shall consider what mechanisms and measures exist to correct or "adjust" such international payments imbalances.

Review Questions

1. Compare the effects on the financial institutions involved and on the pound/dollar exchange rate of payment for a U.S. export to Britain by a bank draft and by a bill of exchange.
2. Carefully explain why the two "sides" of a nation's balance of payments must always balance.
3. "When Americans invest abroad, the effect on the U.S. balance of payments is similar to that of a U.S. import of goods." Explain.
4. Define and compare
    a. Balance-of-trade deficit.
    b. Balance on goods and services surplus.
    c. Balance on current account deficit.
5. In most recent years, the United States has had heavy deficits in its balance of trade but, with rare exceptions, surpluses in its balance on goods and services. Explain how this can be.
6. Explain why a national policy aimed at a permanent balance of payments surplus would not only be virtually impossible to achieve but probably very foolish.
7. From a strictly nationalistic viewpoint it could be argued that—if either were possible—a perpetual goods and services deficit would be vastly superior to a perpetual goods and services surplus. Comment.

Appendix

The Official U.S. Balance-of-Payments Report

The form of the balance of payments presented in Tables 22-2 and 22-3 is one that is believed to have considerable pedagogical advantages in bringing out the essential double-entry nature of balance-of-payments accounting. It is not, however, the form that the U.S. government currently uses to present its summary of international transactions. For those who may wish to read, interpret, and analyze current international payments developments, therefore, it may be useful to attempt a reconciliation of the two forms of the balance-of-payments statements. Let us begin with the form presented in the body of this chapter.

Transactions Requiring Payment to Us	Transactions Requiring Payment by Us
(A) Exports of goods	(G) Imports of goods
(B) Exports of services	(H) Imports of services
(C) Exports of long-term IOUs	(I) Imports of long-term IOUs
(D) Exports of short-term IOUs	(J) Imports of short-term IOUs
(E) Exports of gold	(K) Imports of gold
(F) Unilateral payments to us	(L) Unilateral payments by us

The basic report currently issued by the U.S. Department of Commerce is entitled "U.S. International Transactions," and for 1977 it was as follows:

(A + B)	Exports of goods and services		176.6
(A)	Merchandise exports	120.5	
(B)	Service exports	56.1	
(G + H)	Imports of goods and services		−192.0
(G)	Merchandise imports	−151.7	
(H)	Service imports	−40.3	
(F − L)	Unilateral transfers, net		−4.8

(I + J)	*U.S. assets abroad, net* [increase/capital outflow (−)]			−26.1
(J)	U.S. official reserve assets, net (Gold, special drawing rights, reserve position in IMF, foreign currencies)		−0.2	
(I)	U.S. government assets, other than official, net		−3.7	
	U.S. private assets, net		−22.2	
(I)	Direct investment abroad	−5.0		
(I)	Foreign securities	−5.4		
(I)	U.S. claims reported by U.S. nonbanking concerns	0.0		
(J)	U.S. claims reported by U.S. banks, not included elsewhere	−11.7		
(C + D + K)	*Foreign assets in the U.S., net* [increase/capital inflow (+)]			49.2
(D + K)	Foreign official assets in U.S., net (U.S. securities, other U.S. gov't liabilities, other liabilities reported by U.S. banks, other foreign official assets)		37.4	
	Other foreign assets in the U.S., net		11.8	
(C)	Direct investment in United States	1.5		
(C)	U.S. gov't and other securities	3.5		
(C)	U.S. liabilities reported by U.S. nonbanking concern	0.1		
(D)	U.S. liabilities reported by banks, not included elsewhere	6.8		
	Statistical discrepancy			−3.0

To relate the balance-of-payments form used in the body of Chapter 22 to the official "U.S. International Transactions" table, we have identified each entry in the former statement by letter and then attempted to indicate its counterparts in the official table. The fact that the official table is presented in vertical fashion in such a manner that (with the statistical discrepancy) it must equal zero rather than in two-sided form where the two sides must be equal should present no conceptual problems to the reader. All that is required for this switch is to enter each "transaction requiring payment by us" with a minus sign, while each "transaction requiring payment to us" is positive.

Some difficulty may well be encountered in separating long-term and short-term capital movements from one another. Note tht U.S. acquisition of official reserve assets, U.S. claims reported by U.S. banks, foreign official assets acquired in the United States, and U.S. liabilities reported by banks are, for purposes of this chapter, treated as short-term capital movements, while all other transfers of IOUs (below unilateral transfers) are categorized as long term. In general, a claim with more than one year to maturity is considered long term.

This distinction is admittedly quite arbitrary and is not entirely satisfactory. Indeed it was in part the blurring of the distinction between short- and long-term capital movements that led the Commerce Department to stop publication of a summary balance-of-payments measure called the "basic balance" in 1976. The basic balance consisted of the current account plus net long-term investment, and it was intended to indicate long-term trends in a nation's international payments by separating out short-term capital movements on the grounds that they were more volatile and merely "balancing" or "settlement" items for other parts of the balance of payments. In addition to problems with distinguishing short- and long-term capital movements it was also felt that, with the abandonment of essentially stable exchange rates in 1973, overall summary balance-of-payments measures such as the basic balance had become less meaningful.[12]

---

[12]On these decisions, see "Report of the Advisory Committee on the Presentation of Balance of Payments Statistics"; and Janice M. Westerfield, "A Lower Profile for the U.S. Balance of Payments," *Business Review,* Federal Reserve Bank of Philadelphia, November–December 1976.

23

International Payments Systems and Their Functions

It is the existence of political boundaries dividing the world into a large number of sovereign nations that makes some sort of *system* to facilitate international exchange a necessity. If all countries used the same type of money and none had the power to obstruct movement of goods or resources across their borders, international economic transactions would be in no significant way different from purely domestic ones. For good or ill, however, our world is not that sort of world, and some sort of international monetary system has been a requirement for generations.

What Is the Function of an "Ideal" International Monetary System?

Just as most purely national economic systems are aimed at maximizing consumer satisfaction in the nation as a whole, the "ideal" international monetary system would be one that promoted allocation of limited world resources in a way that would maximize the satisfaction of all mankind. More specifically, such a system should facilitate the freest possible movement of goods and resources so as to permit (1) the widest possible degree of world specialization of production in accordance with comparative advantage and (2) free flow of capital from the wealthier, better developed countries to the poorer, lesser developed nations.

Achieving this laudable goal, however, would require a system so structured as to (1) encourage producers and consumers around the world to participate freely and willingly in international commerce and (2) make it unnecessary for sovereign national governments to resort to trade barriers and obstructions to the free flow of capital to protect their own national interests. Such a system, in turn, would seem to necessitate the existence of

1. An effective balance-of-payments *adjustment mechanism*.
2. An adequate supply of internationally accepted money, or, to use the more common phrase, *international liquidity*.
3. A sufficiently *stable international economic environment* to minimize the risk of those who might participate in international trade.

Before we discuss several possible types of international monetary systems, let us look at some of the implications of these three requirements.

An Effective Adjustment Mechanism

As we have seen, chronic current account deficits tend almost inevitably to generate governmental action aimed at restoring equilibrium. Such actions, unfortunately, have often taken the form of trade barriers, capital controls, and other measures that seriously hamper free trade and the maximization of world living standards. Consequently it is most important that the international monetary system contain within it some mechanism for promptly and effectively eliminating chronic deficits so that such destructive national measures do not become necessary.

How can a current account deficit be "adjusted"—that is, eliminated? By the creation of conditions under which the deficit nation can reduce its imports and/or raise its exports, of course. And what are the determinants of a nation's imports and exports? Basically, a nation's imports will be larger (1) the higher its income, (2) the lower the level of foreign domestic prices relative to its own, and (3) the lower the cost of the foreign money in terms of its own (the exchange rate). Similarly, its exports will be larger (1) the higher the level of foreign incomes, (2) the lower its own domestic price level relative to its trading partners, and (3) the lower the cost of its money to foreigners.

It should be apparent that the first two determinants of imports and exports just itemized—the level of national income and domestic price levels—are to a considerable degree controllable via appropriate changes in aggregate demand in the deficit and surplus countries. A country's imports can be reduced if its aggregate demand is held down, causing its own income to fall (and thus reducing its ability to buy foreign goods). Its exports can be increased if its domestic price level can be restrained sufficiently to make its goods relatively more attractive, as far as price is concerned, to foreigners.[1]

But note that something quite similar can result from an exchange rate change. The cost of the deficit country's goods to foreigners is dependent on *both* that country's domestic price level and the cost of its money. If the British price of Scotch is £3, and the exchange rate between the dollar and the pound is $3 to £1,

---

[1]At the same time, increases in aggregate demand in countries with balance-of-payments surpluses can raise their incomes, permitting them to buy more from the deficit country and increase their domestic price levels, thereby reducing the attractiveness of their exports (the deficit country's imports).

a bottle of British Scotch costs an American importer $9. If a cut in the British aggregate demand should cut the domestic price to £2, Scotch would cost the American only $6. But the same result could be achieved by depreciation of the pound to $2 per £1. In this case, even if the British price of Scotch stays at £3, the American can obtain it for only $6 because the £3 required to buy it costs only that much.

Therefore, "adjustment" of payments deficits can be accomplished either through a reduction in aggregate demand in the deficit country relative to that of its trading partners or through a reduction in the value of its money relative to that of other nations (that is, a change in its exchange rate). In evaluating the three international monetary systems discussed in the paragraphs that follow, we shall need to consider carefully the effectiveness of the built-in adjustment mechanism in each case.

Sufficient International Liquidity

When a nation incurs a payments deficit, as we have seen, it generally covers the deficit by an appropriate short-term capital movement. If its banks happen to own sufficient deposits in the banks of the nations to which it owes money, it can, of course, use those deposits for payment. If, however, it owes some countries more than the total of its banks' accumulation of their particular currencies, it may have to pay up with a form of money generally accepted by all nations—so-called "international reserves." Gold, of course, has for years been an important part of the world's international reserves. So too, for about three decades, has the U.S. dollar.[2]

Now as there can be no doubt that under any international monetary system, some countries will at all times be incurring deficits, it is essential that there be a sufficient supply of international reserves (or "liquidity") available to let them "get by" until the deficit can be eliminated. And, because the volume of trade grows every year, it must be expected that the volume of deficits that must be covered will grow also. This means—if world trade is not to be hampered by inadequate liquidity—that the international monetary system must include some dependable means of increasing the volume of international reserves at a rate commensurate with the growth of international commerce.

Incidentally, the quantity of international reserves required is directly related to the efficiency of the adjustment mechanism discussed earlier. As we shall see,

---

[2]As the U.S. dollar has been accepted as a form of international reserves, the U.S. has been able to "cover" its long string of deficits by allowing foreign countries to build up short-term dollar claims in this country. This approach, however, has not been open to most other nations. Other forms of international reserves such as IMF borrowing rights and special drawing rights will be considered in the next chapter.

the quantity of international reserves required for the successful operation of a payments system calling for relatively stable exchange rates tends to be much larger than that needed in a system permitting freely floating exchange rates. Under stable exchange rate systems, not only are adequate supplies of international reserves essential for implementation of the mechanism stabilizing exchange rates but relatively inefficient adjustment mechanisms may often lead to longer periods of deficit to be "financed."

A Stable Economic Environment with Minimum Risk

A third requirement for an effective international monetary system, in the eyes of many, is a set of arrangements whereby individual participants in international trade will be protected from unusual risks resulting solely from the fact that their business is international. For many years the chief issue in this area has been the degree of *stability of exchange rates*. Relatively stable exchange rates, it has been argued, have the advantage of lessening risk to traders and international investors, thereby encouraging more international transactions and permitting a fuller exploitation of the advantages that accrue to all from greater worldwide specialization.

It is not difficult to understand the argument here. If an American importer agrees to pay £100,000 for British goods 60 days from the date of sale, a sharp increase in the price of pounds during the 60-day period could turn a potentially profitable deal into a financial disaster. If the cost of pounds was $2.00 per £1 when he made an agreement, he expected his cost to be $200,000. But if the exchange rate jumps up to $2.50 per £1 at the end of the 60 days, he will be required to pay $250,000, a figure that may more than wipe out his expected profit. Now, if our importer is not a speculator, willing to gamble on the possible equal chance that he may gain by a reduction in the cost of pounds, as well as lose by a rise, he may simply shy away from international trading altogether, preferring to concentrate on less risky domestic trade. Consequently the volume of international trade, and its important attendant advantage of fuller specialization, may be impeded.

Whatever the merits of this argument for stability in exchange rates, it must be recognized that—to a degree at least—it tends to conflict with the requirement for an effective adjustment mechanism. As we have seen, the "adjustment" of a balance-of-payments deficit can be aided either through a reduction in aggregate demand in the deficit nation or through a change in its exchange rate. Clearly, then, a system that attempts to provide a "stable economic environment" through arrangements to maintain relatively fixed exchange rates does so at the expense of one of the factors that promotes adjustment. This issue of fixed versus fluctuating exchange rates has long been an area of serious conflict among experts on international finance, and we shall consider it in great depth at a later point.

Three Alternative International Monetary Systems

Although many variations are possible, three distinct types of international monetary systems have been predominant in the past century. These include the full international gold standard, the system in effect from 1945 to 1971, which we shall refer to as the "Bretton Woods" system, and the freely floating exchange rate system. Let us consider the characteristics of each of these in turn.

The Full International Gold Standard

The full international gold standard, under which much of the world operated for many years prior to the 1930s, required a nation to observe certain rules. Specifically, each government was required to

1. Define its monetary unit as being equivalent to a fixed amount of gold (for example, prior to 1933, one U.S. dollar was defined to equal 23.22 grains of gold).
2. Stand ready to exchange its monetary unit for gold, or gold for its monetary unit, in unlimited amounts with anyone, at that price.
3. Allow gold flows out of the country to automatically reduce the nation's money supply and gold flows in to automatically raise the money supply.

Defenders of the gold standard argued that such a system would not only provide the advantage of stable exchange rates but also offer an effective automatic adjustment mechanism. Let us see how it was expected to work.

Stable Exchange Rates Under the Gold Standard. Suppose that the United States has defined the dollar as equivalent to 23.22 grains of gold and that England has defined the pound as being the same as 113 grains of gold.[3] Now, as both monies are defined in terms of a common substance, gold, they are related to one another. This relationship, called the *mint part of exchange,* is obtained by dividing the gold content of the dollar into the gold content of the pound. The result of this operation is approximately 4.87, indicating that the mint par of exchange between the pound and the dollar under these arrangements was $4.87 per £1.[4]

If, for purposes of furthering the example, we assume that the cost of transporting 113 grains of gold across the Atlantic in either direction is 2 cents, we can state definitely that the cost of British pounds can never exceed $4.89 per pound

---

[3]These are the actual relationships set by the two governments during much of the "heyday" of the international gold standard.

[4]It should be noted that this is not, in and of itself, an exchange rate, but simply the arithmetical result arrived at by dividing the statutory gold content of the dollar into the statutory gold content of the pound. It merely said that the British government had defined the pound as being worth as much gold as the American government had said $4.87 was worth.

or be less than $4.85 per pound. The exchange rate, in other words, can fluctuate only within the relatively narrow limits of $4.85 per £1 and $4.89 per £1.

The force that assures this high degree of exchange rate stability is the self-interest of traders. No American importer (needing pounds to make payment) will pay more than $4.89 to obtain a pound because he does not need to. Any tendency for the price of pounds to rise (as a result of a U.S. deficit that makes the U.S. demand for pounds exceed the supply) is limited by the gold standard mechanism itself. No American importer would be willing to pay more than $4.89 to get the pound he needs because he can always take (or, more likely, his bank will take for him) $4.87 to the U.S. Treasury and get 113 grains of gold, ship the gold to England, and exchange it at the British Treasury for one pound. The cost of shipment being 2 cents, our U.S. importer's total expense for his pound is $4.89. Under these gold standard arrangements, he need never pay more to get it.

Similarly, the British importer, if he is a profit maximizer, will never accept anything less than $4.85 for his pound when he uses it to obtain the dollars he needs to make payment. For he too has the option of taking his one pound to the British Treasury, exchanging it for 113 grains of gold, shipping the gold to the U.S. Treasury, and swapping it there for $4.87. As he pays 2 cents transport cost, he realizes a minimum of $4.85 for his pound. He need not accept less.

Thus, with the conditions as stated, the exchange rate between the dollar and the pound can only fluctuate within the narrow limits of $4.85 per £1 and $4.89 per £1. When a U.S. deficit raises our demand for pounds above our supply of them, the price of pounds can only rise to $4.89 per pound, at which point it will be cheaper for American importers to pay by shipping gold to England. The upper limit, the $4.89 per £1 rate, is called the *U.S. gold export point.* On the other hand, when a British deficit (necessarily a U.S. surplus in a two-country world) increases the U.S. supply of pounds above the U.S. demand for them, the price of pounds for Americans will fall toward $4.85 per pound (the cost of dollars to the British will rise to the point where they get only $4.85 for each pound), beyond which it becomes cheaper for British importers to obtain their dollars by shipping gold to the United States. The $4.85 per £1 rate is, thus, the *U.S. gold import point.*

The Adjustment Mechanisms Under the Gold Standard.

The "Indirect, Money Supply" Mechanism. When a country on the full gold standard incurs a balance-of-payments deficit, payment for that deficit will automatically tend to cause both its and the surplus countries' money supplies to change in the direction required to reduce the disequilibrium. Suppose, for example, that the U.S. has developed a trade deficit with Britain. Payment for the excess U.S. imports will (because our demand for pounds exceeds the supply of pounds being provided by our exporters) initially tend to drive up the dollar price of pounds. Under the gold standard, however, the price of pounds can only rise slightly—to the U.S. gold export point— after which gold will flow out of the U.S. to pay, in effect, for the deficit.

Now the loss of gold must have some effects on the economy of the deficit country. It represents, after all, the base of its money supply under the gold standard. When the U.S. Treasury sells gold, not only the money supply but also member bank reserves go down by the amount of the sale. This means, in a fully "loaned-up" banking system, the domestic money supply may be cut by several times the amount of the gold loss.

But that is not all. The money supply reduction that results automatically from the gold loss must, in turn, other things being equal, raise the rate of interest and, in greater or less degree, cut down on aggregate demand.[5] And a reduction in aggregate demand must reflect itself in lowered prices and/or reduced employment, production, and income.

How does all this tend to reduce the deficit that started it all? Very simply. To the extent that the deficit country's prices are cut, it becomes a cheaper market for foreigners (as well as its own citizens) and it may therefore expand its exports. If, as is likely with the "sticky" prices with which we are familiar today, the cut in aggregate demand lowers incomes, the deficit country, having less to spend both at home and abroad, will import less. In either case, the effect is to lessen the deficit.

While all this is going on in the deficit country, the surplus country or countries are feeling the reverse effects. There, gold flows in, bank reserves and the money supply are increased, interest rates tend to be reduced, aggregate demand rises, and prices and/or incomes are raised. As a result of the price and/or income increases, the surplus countries' exports are cut and their imports raised, intensifying the corrective effects both there and in the deficit country. This chain of effects for both countries can be summarized as follows.

Deficit Country	*Surplus Country or Countries*
1. Imports > exports	1. Exports > imports
2. Demand for foreign money > supply of foreign money	2. Demand for foreign money < supply of foreign money
3. Price of foreign money rises to gold export point	3. Price of foreign money falls to gold import point
4. Gold flows out	4. Gold flows in
5. Bank reserves and money supply cut	5. Bank reserves and money supply rise
6. Interest rates rise	6. Interest rates fall
7. Aggregate demand falls	7. Aggregate demand rises
8. Prices and/or incomes fall	8. Prices and/or incomes rise
9. To extent prices fall, exports rise; to extent incomes fall, imports fall	9. To extent prices rise, exports fall; to extent incomes rise, imports rise

---

[5]Indeed, under the unwritten but generally understood "rules of the game" of the gold standard, the central bank was expected to reinforce the effects of the gold loss by raising its discount rate to raise interest rates even more.

The "Direct" Effects on Aggregate Demand.   In addition to the adjustment effects generated automatically through money supply changes, there are certain *direct* effects on aggregate demand that should be noted.

When foreigners spend money to buy currently produced goods and services from a nation's export industries, it is clear that they, no less than the domestic investors, government, and consumers, are adding to the demand for the output of its industry. For an open economy, then, aggregate demand equals not just C + I + G, as we assumed in Part II, but rather C + I + G + X, where X equals a nation's exports of newly produced goods and services.[6]

As an element of aggregate demand, exports are very much like investment and government spending in that their amount is largely unrelated to the domestic level of income. How much a nation is able to sell as exports is pretty much dependent on such "outside" factors as *foreign* tastes and incomes and relative prices and only slightly and indirectly influenced by the domestic income level. Consequently we shall treat it, as we do investment and government spending in the main, as an "autonomously" determined element of the demand for a nation's goods and services.

A nation's imports of goods and services, on the other hand, are, in most essential ways, like saving and taxes. For, like saving and taxes, they are an element of income earned from current production of the nation, which *is not* spent to buy its newly produced goods and services. They represent, that is, an additional "leakage." Consequently, when the theoretical material in Part II is modified to allow international trade into the picture, instead of saying that all income earned from production is split into three parts, C + S + T, we must recognize that it is divided into *four* parts, C + S + T + M, where M stands for imports.

Imports of goods and services are like saving and taxes in still another way. All three are directly related to the level of income. This is especially true to the extent that a country's imported goods are consumer goods, because in this case, just as a country is able to spend more for domestically produced consumer goods when its incomes rises, it also tends to spend more on foreign-produced items.[7]

When exports of goods and services are admitted as an element of aggregate demand for a nation's output, and imports of goods and services are recognized as

---

[6]A word of clarification is in order at this point. The more generally accepted way of defining aggregate demand is C + I + G + (X − M), where C, I and G are defined to include *total* purchase of consumer, investment, and government goods from home and abroad. When defined this way, the imports must be subtracted out somewhere to avoid overstating the demand for domestic production. Our procedure here will diverge from the usual in that C, I, and G will be used to refer to purchases from *domestic producers only*. With this definition, there is no need to subtract expenditures on imports, as they are never included in the first place. Total spending on U.S.-produced goods and services then can be expressed as C + I + G + X, and a shift from buying imported consumer goods to buying domestically produced consumer goods will raise the U.S. consumption function.

[7]Indeed, just as we were able earlier to talk about a marginal propensity to consume and a marginal propensity to save, we could now talk in terms of a marginal propensity to import, defined as $\Delta M/\Delta GNP$.

a leakage from its incomes, we must amend the conditions for stable, rising, and falling production listed in Part II for a closed economy only. Now, we must say

1. Condition for stable production (equilibrium):
    when C + I + G + X = C + S + T + M
2. Condition for rising production:
    when C + I + G + X > C + S + T + M
3. Condition for falling production:
    when C + I + G + X < C + S + T + M

It is these new conditions that reveal most clearly the second automatic corrective mechanism to which we referred as the direct effects. A country that incurs a balance-of-payments deficit (where the deficit is caused by an excess of goods and services imports) is, on that account, leaking more out of its income stream than foreigners are adding to it through their purchases. Consequently, *in addition to the corrective mechanism that works indirectly through affecting the money supply,* we have a direct cut in the nation's aggregate demand through its international trade. Whenever imports of goods and services exceed exports of goods and services, the nation's involvement in international trade directly reduces its aggregate demand. Conversely, an excess of goods and services exports over imports adds to aggregate demand.

Now for our deficit country, this direct cut in aggregate demand puts further downward pressure on its prices and/or income, resulting in even greater increases in its exports and reductions in its imports than the indirect, money supply corrective mechanism alone would produce.

How Effective Were the Gold Standard's Adjustment Mechanisms?   Just how effective were those adjustment mechanisms? In a world with extremely flexible prices, they might well be quite effective, because the reduction in aggregate demand induced by the balance-of-payments deficit would have its impact primarily on domestic prices rather than on income and employment.

In the modern world, however, prices tend to be extremely rigid in the downward direction, so that reductions in aggregate demand initially fall largely on physical output, income, and employment. Although, as we have seen, reductions in a deficit nation's income *will* tend to reduce its deficit, the corrective mechanism involved actually works by requiring the deficit nation to undergo recession and unemployment. This was a prime reason for abandoning the international gold standard in the 1930s. The major countries involved, already reeling under the devastating effects of worldwide depression, decided that the gold standard's "medicine" of unemployment was worse than the "disease" of international payments deficits. We must therefore conclude that in a world in which government policymakers are constrained from condoning periodic recession and excessive unemployment, the gold standard's automatic adjustment mechanisms would be unacceptable.

The Bretton Woods System of Stable, but Adjustable, Exchange Rates—1945 to 1971

Before World War I, the international gold standard served admirably; after that war, however, the reestablished gold standard floundered and finally collapsed amid the chaos of the early 1930s. As a consequence, it was decided, after World War II, to abandon the "discipline of gold" in favor of a new system, which, it was hoped, would retain the gold standard's major advantages while eliminating its most glaring drawbacks.

Under the new system—established at the Bretton Woods Conference in 1944—most of the world's nations bound themselves to the regulations of the newly established International Monetary Fund. IMF member nations were required to define their currencies in terms of a fixed amount of gold (or dollars—the dollar being already defined in terms of gold) to set up initial postwar exchange rates.

Gold, therefore, was still destined to play a key role in international monetary matters. It was, however, no longer a dominant role. The old link between the gold supply and the domestic money supply had been abolished. The fixed commitment to pay out gold for domestic currency in unlimited amounts to anyone had been universally eliminated. Indeed, only the United States agreed to exchange gold for its domestic currency, and even that pledge was not open to everyone. Clearly, many of the features of the old gold standard had disappeared.

The founders of the IMF sought a mechanism that would retain the gold standard's virtue of relatively stable exchange rates but not its vice of requiring deficit nations to periodically abandon their domestic commitment to the maintenance of full employment. The system that emerged—often described as a system characterized by "adjustable pegs"—required that exchange rates be kept quite stable except in cases of chronic deficit. In these cases, *devaluation* of the currency (that is, a once-and-for-all official change in its exchange rate, lowering the value of its money relative to that of other countries), was to be relied on to facilitate "adjustment."

Exchange Rates Under the Bretton Woods System. Exchange rate stability was maintained in the following manner. The United States, which owned about 75 percent of the "free world" gold supply when the system was first introduced, was expected to keep the dollar tied to gold by freely exchanging it for dollars held by foreign governments at a fixed rate of $35 per ounce. Other member nations, having announced an official exchange rate between their currencies and the dollar, were expected to use national *exchange stabilization funds* to "peg" the exchange rate at that level.

The exchange stabilization funds, in theory at last, operated very simply. They were equipped (by their governments) with supplies of gold, foreign exchange, and their own domestic money. When the exchange rate between theirs and another country's currency threatened to exceed the limits set, it was the task of the stabilization fund to enter into the other side of the market and halt the undesired change.

Suppose, for example, that the British government had set the "par value" for the pound at £1 per $2.40.[8] Under the rules of the IMF, the British Exchange Stabilization Fund was required to take action to limit actual variations in the dollar-pound exchange rate to within 1 percent on either side of the stated par value. Roughly speaking, this meant the pound-dollar exchange rate was "pegged" by the British Exchange Stabilization Fund within the limits of £1 per $2.38 and £1 per $2.42.

Within these narrow limits, of course, the exchange rate was subject to the same supply-demand forces as a freely floating rate. If British imports rose, the demand for dollars rose, pushing the price of dollars up (the rate approached the £1 to $2.38 limit). If British exports increased, the supply of dollars rose, lowering the cost of dollars to English citizens (the rate approached the £1 to $2.42 limit).

All this may perhaps best be illustrated by Figure 23-1. Suppose that the par value of the Belgian franc in terms of the dollar has been set at 50 francs per dollar. From the Belgian viewpoint, assume that the initial demand for dollars (on the part of Belgian importers) is D_1D_1. If the initial supply-of-dollars curve (provided by Belgian exports) is S_pS_p, the actual initial exchange rate will be 50 francs = $1.

Now assume that Belgian tastes change in favor of products from the United States, raising the demand-for-dollars curve to D_2D_2. If the Belgian Exchange Stabilization Fund did not intervene, the cost of dollars would rise to the level at which D_2D_2 and S_pS_p intersect—51 francs per dollar. Under its IMF obligation,

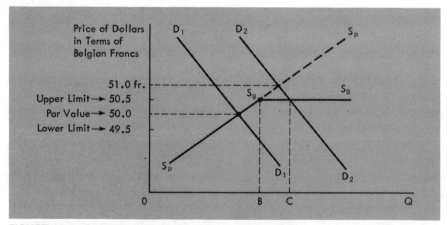

FIGURE 23-1   Stabilization of Exchange Rates under IMF

---

[8]This was the official par value of the pound from 1967 to 1971.

however, the Belgian government could not permit this—a 2 percent rise in the price of dollars—to occur. Its Exchange Stabilization Fund would enter into the foreign exchange market to keep the increase in the price of dollars within 1 percent (no higher than 50.5 francs per dollar).

When the Belgian Exchange Stabilization Fund is brought into the picture, the supply-of-dollars curve becomes the kinked line $S_pS_gS_g$. The S_gS_g portion of the curve depicts dollars coming on to the exchange market from the Belgian government. To keep the exchange rate "pegged" within permissible limits, the Belgian Exchange Stabilization Fund would have to use up BC of its available supply of dollars.

If, on the other hand, the franc price of dollars was tending to fall below 49.5 francs per dollar, the Belgian authorities would enter on the other side of the market—buying dollars with francs—to maintain the required degree of exchange rate stability.

The Adjustment Mechanism Under the Bretton Woods System. As already noted, it was the intention of the framers of the International Monetary fund that countries with chronic balance-of-payments deficits should rely primarily on devaluation of their currencies (lowering their stated par value with respect to the dollar) to provide needed balance-of-payments adjustment. Although the devaluation device was employed quite frequently between 1945 and 1971, it turned out to be something of a disappointment in practice for two main reasons.

First, deficit countries tended to be reluctant to employ it except as a last resort. Defense of the international value of their currency (that is, the current par value with respect to the dollar) was unfortunately permitted to assume domestic political overtones of such significance that governments of deficit countries came to look upon devaluation as a last-ditch, desperation measure accompanied by substantial loss of political face. Second, among the most serious deficit situations was that of the United States, which—because the U.S. dollar was an important part of the world's supply of international reserves and because the United States did not directly control exchange rates between the dollar and other national currencies—did not consider devaluation a measure open to it.[9] The result of all this was that the devaluation device as the basic adjustment mechanism never adequately fulfilled the expectations of the IMF's founders.

What other adjustment mechanisms besides devaluation existed under the Bretton Woods system? The "indirect, money supply" mechanism discussed under the gold standard amounted to very little under the IMF. Even if a payments deficit did, in and of itself, reduce the deficit country's money supply and bank reserves, there was no commitment to avoid "offsetting" those effects with an expansive

---

[9]The United States controlled only the relation between the dollar and gold, whereas *other* countries controlled the exchange rates between their currencies and the dollar. As we shall see, the United States *did* finally devalue the dollar in 1971 and again in 1973, but the essence of the IMF system was markedly changed before this could be accomplished.

discretionary monetary policy. Under the full gold standard, it was clearly understood that the "rules of the game" forbade a domestic monetary policy that offset
the changes in money caused by international disequilibrium. Under the IMF system, there was no such outright commitment.

The same "direct effect" adjustment mechanism discussed under the gold
standard still existed. A nation with a deficit resulting from importing more goods
and services than it exported could expect this to directly reduce its aggregate
demand and, through this, its income and/or prices. It should be stressed, however,
that this mechanism only helped when the deficit showed up in the nation's balance
on goods and services. A deficit such as the United States ran regularly between
1950 and 1970 was accelerated, rather than combated, by these "direct effects."
For, as we have seen, the United States consistently exported more goods and
services than it imported in every post–World War II year prior to 1971, its deficit
being a result of long-term investment abroad and unilateral transfers. Consequently, American involvement in international trade *raised,* rather than lowered,
U.S. aggregate demand for almost 20 years.

In summary, it is generally agreed that the Bretton Woods system contained
automatic adjustment mechanisms that were quite weak—too weak in the opinion
of many critics to do the job of correcting serious and chronic payments imbalances.

The Freely Floating Exchange Rate System

A system of freely floating exchange rates involves the most direct extension
of the institutions of the free market into the settling of international transactions.
Under such a system, exchange rates are determined solely by supply and demand
with, in theory at least, no intervention by government. Unlike the other two types
of systems discussed, it cannot boast of a long history of use, as it has generally
been resorted to only for relatively short periods after a fixed rate system has broken
down. After the downfall of the gold standard in the early 1930s until World War
II, a variant of a floating rate system existed. Similarly, since March 1973, when
the attempt to maintain stable exchange rates under the IMF setup was abandoned,
much of the world has been operating with floating rates. In both cases, however,
national governments have intervened considerably into foreign exchange markets,
producing a "managed" or "dirty" float rather than the "clean" float envisioned
in theory by many of the backers of the freely floating exchange rate system.

Determination of Exchange Rates Under a Freely Floating System.   Under a
freely floating exchange rate system, commercial banks or other foreign exchange
dealers would (as they do now) act as middlemen in the foreign exchange market,
buying foreign money (primarily in the form of deposits in foreign banks) from
those who have it to sell and selling foreign money to those wanting to buy it for
dollars. The price that these banks charge for a unit of foreign money, that is, the
exchange rate, would depend solely on supply and demand.

The demand for foreign money—let us say, pounds—would clearly come from those Americans who need pounds to make payment for goods bought in Britain. U.S. importers then would be the source of the demand for pounds. The supply of pounds, on the other hand, would come largely from British importers who need to get hold of dollars or, what amounts to the same thing, U.S. exporters who earn pounds through their sales to the British.

Given a competitive foreign exchange market and no interference from government, the price of pounds would then continually move toward an equilibrium level, where the demand on the part of importers just equaled the supply coming from exporters. If, at the current exchange rate, the quantity of pounds demanded exceeded the quantity supplied, the dealers (banks) would simply raise the price. If the quantity supplied should exceed the quantity demanded, the price of pounds would tend to fall. Under a freely floating exchange rate system, then, the price of foreign money would tend to rise as imports rise and to fall when exports rise.

The Adjustment Mechanism with Freely Floating Exchange Rates. Opponents of a freely fluctuating exchange rate system object strenuously to the instability that they believe is injected into the international payments scene by rates free to move without limit. Supporters of floating rates, however, see freedom to move as a major virtue. For the change in exchange rates itself constitutes an automatic adjustment mechanism which can quickly and efficiently reestablish international payments equilibrium.

The mechanism in this case is impressively simple. Let us refer to Figure 23-2 to work it through. Suppose, as before, that the initial equilibrium exchange rate between the Belgian franc and the U.S. dollar is 50 francs to 1 dollar, with Belgian importers' demand for dollars being depicted by D_1D_1 and the supply of

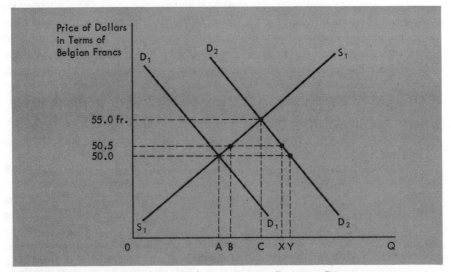

FIGURE 23-2 Reestablishing Equilibrium via Floating Exchange Rates

dollars being earned by Belgian exporters shown as S_1S_1. Note that at this initial equilibrium, the quantity of dollars demanded by importers (OA) exactly equals the quantity of dollars supplied by exporters. An equilibrium exchange rate means that the value of exports equals the value of imports—equilibrium in the balance of payments.

Now, as before, suppose that Belgian tastes change in favor of American goods, raising Belgian imports from the United States and shifting the demand-for-dollars curve out to D_2D_2. Such a development means that initially (at the 50 francs to 1 dollar rate) the quantity of dollars demanded exceeds the quantity supplied by AY. And imports exceed exports by the same amount.

But this is a simple supply and demand case. The sellers of dollars (Belgian banks), facing an excess demand and seeing their inventory of dollars being drawn down, will quite naturally move to raise the franc price of dollars. Under the two systems previously discussed, this rise in the franc price of dollars could only proceed for a short distance before gold flows or exchange stabilization fund activity would stop it. For example, as noted, under the old IMF rules, the exchange rate could only rise to 50.5 francs per dollar before being halted by the government. Accomplishing this would not only drain the stabilization fund's dollar resources by an amount equal to BX but would leave Belgium with imports still exceeding exports.

Contrast this result with the floating exchange rate result. In this case, with no government intervention, Belgian banks will continue raising the franc price of dollars as long as demand exceeds supply. Only when the new equilibrium rate of 55 francs per dollar is reached will the rise stop.

More important, consider what this rise in the exchange rate does to Belgium's balance of payments. As the franc price of dollars rises, American goods, on that account, become more expensive to the Belgians, so their imports are reduced (by an amount equal to CY). Conversely, as an increase in the franc price of dollars means a *decrease* in the dollar price of francs, Belgian goods have been made *less* expensive to Americans who will buy more (in an amount equal to AC). The rise in the exchange rate, therefore, completely and automatically eliminates Belgium's balance-of-payments deficit.

Summary—The Pros and Cons of the Three Types of Systems

What can we say in general summary about the relative merits of the three types of systems just covered?

The full international gold standard does have the advantage of stable exchange rates, but, given the downward rigidity of prices and the general reluctance of modern nations to put up with excessive unemployment, it seems clear that its adjustment mechanisms—whatever their intrinsic merits—would not be permitted to "work." In addition, with gold itself as the sole form of ultimate international reserve, there is considerable question whether such a system would be capable of generating an adequate degree of liquidity to handle expanding world trade. In any case, the full gold standard as described here is currently an issue of only historical and academic importance. There is little interest in returning to it.

The Bretton Woods system in effect from 1945 to 1971 also had the merit of relatively stable exchange rates and appeared—on paper at least—to offer a somewhat better adjustment mechanism than the gold standard. In practice, however, as we have seen, the reluctance of deficit countries to avail themselves of the devaluation weapon more frequently undercut much of its potential for adjustment. The system did adapt itself reasonably well over the years to the international liquidity problem. Not only gold, but billions of U.S. dollars pumped out during years of American deficits, have provided ample liquidity. Also, a third source of international reserves—special drawing rights—was created by international agreement through the IMF. Consideration of special drawing rights will be postponed to the next chapter.

The freely floating exchange rate system, of course, must receive high grades for its adjustment mechanism and—given that advantage—cannot be faulted on grounds of international liquidity. The main bone of contention regarding this system is the complete flexibility of exchange rates themselves. In the concluding chapter we shall return to the fixed versus flexible exchange rate issue.

Discretionary Government Policy Measures to Deal with International Payments Deficits

In the preceding section we have seen that no matter what the institutional arrangement, international payments deficits generate some of the seeds of their own destruction. Unfortunately, however, with the exception of the freely floating exchange rate case, none of the automatic mechanisms is vigorous enough to go all the way and completely wipe out the deficit that triggered them, unless severe unemployment is passively accepted.

The result is that the government in an economy with a chronic deficit, and a limited supply of foreign exchange to finance it, faces enormous pressure to "do something" about it. If automatic forces built into the international monetary system are inadequate to handle the adjustment task, then almost inevitably governments of such deficit-plagued nations turn to authoritative, discretionary policy to deal with it. The remainder of this chapter briefly considers four lines of discretionary action:

1. Erection of trade barriers
2. Reduction of governmental spending abroad and of governmental aid programs to foreign nations
3. Restrictive monetary and fiscal policy at home (coupled with pressure on surplus nations to enact more expansive monetary and fiscal policies)
4. In the case of a stable exchange rate system—devaluation

The Use of Trade Barriers

Trade barriers are as old as nations themselves. They include a wide variety of restrictive devices ranging from tariffs and such nontariff barriers as subsidies to exporters, "health and safety" standards discriminatory toward imported goods, and coerced "voluntary" agreements between governments to limit certain types of internationally traded items to more overt limitations such as explicit import quotas and exchange controls. Most are aimed at reducing imports, but a few constitute attempts to boost exports.

Tariffs are really a special form of excise tax placed upon the importation of foreign goods and services and, in some cases, securities. Quotas can be very much more restrictive in that they involve an absolute barrier to imports beyond a certain point rather than simply a hurdle that can be overcome. Exchange control can be the most extreme of all because, in this case, a governmental agency simply "takes over" all foreign exchange earned by the nation's exporters (by requiring its sale for domestic currency at a fixed exchange rate) and then rations it out to favored importers according to some scale of national priorities, thereby effectively eliminating "excessive" potential importers who would otherwise contribute to the deficit.

The trade barrier method of dealing with a balance-of-payments deficit is held in very low regard by most authorities. It should be, in the opinion of most, employed extensively only as a last resort. Its widespread unpopularity among economists results from the fact that it impedes international specialization and that it is unlikely to succeed in its objective in any case. The more fundamental economic objection to a raising of trade barriers is clear-cut. By interfering with the patterns of trade, such barriers limit the degree of international specialization and thereby lead to a misallocation of resources that reduces world production. On a more practical level, it is even to be doubted whether these objectionable results will, to any significant degree, be counterbalanced by a "favorable" effect on the nation's balance of payments. Trade barriers that "work" by cutting down a nation's imports necessarily reduce another nation's exports. It is extremely unlikely that the "injured" nation will simply sit there and take it; it will almost certainly retaliate quickly by raising its own trade barriers, thereby canceling out whatever balance-of-payments advantage the deficit nation had obtained from its own action. We must conclude that this course is, in general, to be avoided, although, as we shall see, it has not been.

Cutting Foreign Spending by the Government

A second discretionary approach available to cut a balance-of-payments deficit is for the government itself to reduce its foreign spending. To the degree that it imports goods and services, it could cut these; and to the degree that it makes gifts to foreigners, it could reduce these.

But even this apparently more direct approach is not without its problems. In the first place, whatever good effect it would have on the balance of payments might come at quite a cost. If, to solve a balance-of-payments deficit, a nation should sacrifice programs of foreign spending that seem important to its own security, the remedy might well be worse than the disease. In any case, a risk of undetermined magnitude exists.

In the second place, the good effects of this approach on the deficit country's balance of payments may be substantially less than would appear at first glance. When a government spends or gives its money to foreigners, the complete effect of this action on its balance of payments depends partly on what foreigners do with the funds they receive. If foreigners use money acquired in this manner to buy goods and services they would not otherwise purchase, from the deficit country, eliminating the gifts and/or government foreign purchases will reduce the goods and services exports of the deficit country along with the reduction in import items. To the degree that this happens, the deficit would be unchanged and the action, ineffective.

Restrictive Monetary and Fiscal Policy

Given the problems associated with the two discretionary policies already discussed, it would be ideal if the remaining tools could represent all virtue and no vice. Such, however, is not the case for restrictive monetary and fiscal policy.

This classical medicine to cure payments deficits works primarily by reinforcing the automatic mechanisms of fixed exchange rate systems. It consists of a tight money policy and budget surpluses to raise a nation's interest rates and lower its prices and/or incomes. To the extent that short-term interest rates are raised, it is hoped that the nation will be the beneficiary of an inflow of short-term capital. To the extent that the nation's prices are reduced relative to others, it is expected that it will be able to sell more to foreigners. To the extent that its incomes are reduced, it is hoped that it will cut back on its imports.

There can be no doubt that sufficiently restrictive monetary and fiscal policies *can* eliminate a balance-of-payments deficit. But how this is accomplished is a matter of no little concern. If we lived in a world of very flexible prices—prices that would easily and quickly fall as a consequence of a cut in aggregate demand— this policy would have much to recommend it. But, unfortunately, that is not our world. A reduction in aggregate demand resulting from restrictive monetary and fiscal policies would, given the downward inflexibility of prices in the modern world, almost certainly lower employment, production, and income in the deficit country. And that, of course, means that the real price of battling a payments deficit in this way is the creation of a domestic recession.

Recognizing these problems, a more popular approach in recent years has been for deficit countries to try to convince surplus countries to implement more expansive monetary and fiscal policies in the hope that the resultant rise in foreign demand and prices will accomplish the same effect at much less cost to the deficit nation.[10]

Devaluation of the Currency

If the international monetary system is such as to rely upon stable exchange rates pegged at certain levels by governmental action (as under the gold standard or Bretton Woods system), one further discretionary measure is available—devaluation of the currency.

Under any stable rate system, a nation's monetary unit must be defined by law as equivalent to a fixed amount of either some commodity such as gold or some other country's currency that is generally accepted as a form of international reserves. Such legally established "par values" may then be changed by the government involved when circumstances require it.[11] For example, under the Bretton Woods system, the British devalued the pound with respect to the dollar from $2.80 per £ to $2.40 per £ in 1967. And the United States devalued the dollar with respect to gold in both 1971 and 1973, changing the "official" gold price from $35.00 per ounce to $42.22 per ounce.

The purpose of devaluation is clear. By lowering the price of a nation's currency relative to others, it hopes to raise its exports. At the same time, because devaluation makes foreign money (and therefore foreign products) more expensive to its citizens, the devaluating nation hopes to cut its own imports.[12]

There is, however, no guarantee that it would work that way. In the first place, this action, as is true of an increase in trade barriers, is subject to retaliation on the part of the nation's trading partners—a development that could render it totally ineffective. Nor is this the only problem. Even in the absence of retaliation, devaluation will only succeed in reducing the deficit if demand elasticities are favorable.[13]

---

[10]The reluctance of the United States to attack its 1977 current account deficit via restrictive aggregate demand policies was explicitly expressed in the 1978 *Economic Report of the President:* "Especially for large countries like the United States, where the economic cost of changing domestic growth is large relative to the improvement in the current account that would result, it is not appropriate to modify domestic objectives for economic growth in order to reduce the current account deficit" (p. 125).

[11]When the stated par value of a currency is reduced relative to other currencies (or gold) by a specific act of that nation's government, the currency is said to have been *devalued*. When the value of a currency falls relative to others as a result of supply and demand market pressures (as under a floating exchange rate system), the currency is said to have *depreciated*.

[12]The term *revaluation* has often been used to describe the reverse action—where a country *raises* its currency's value relative to others. This action would normally be undertaken by a country with substantial balance-of-payments surpluses and, perhaps, inflationary pressure.

[13]Elasticity of supply in the affected countries is also a factor that is relevant in determining the effectiveness of devaluation. To simplify as much as possible, we shall ignore this added complication in our discussion.

The point here is complicated, but important. Assume that the United States has a deficit and that Great Britain represents its sole trading partner. If the United States should devalue the dollar so that the exchange rate rises from $2 per £1 to $3 per £1, the action would certainly reduce the number of pounds Americans purchase to pay for imports from Britain. So long as the U.S. demand for British imports were anything other than *perfectly inelastic* (in which highly unlikely case, Americans would purchase the same number of pounds at the higher price), the devaluation would reduce the quantity of pounds (and, therefore, the quantity of imports) demanded by Americans and help to reduce the U.S. deficit.

On the other side, however, things are not so clear-cut. American goods are now cheaper for Britons because dollars cost less. But whether this would lead them to spend more pounds on American goods depends upon the degree of elasticity of the British demand for U.S. goods.

If their demand were of greater than unit elasticity, they would spend more pounds on U.S. goods than before and the U.S. deficit would be further reduced. If their demand were of unit elasticity, they would spend the same number of pounds as before the devaluation and, although this would not help to cut the U.S. deficit, the fact that Americans were buying fewer pounds from the British would reduce it. If, however, the British demand for U.S. goods were of less than unit elasticity, the devaluation would lead them to spend fewer pounds to buy U.S. goods, which would, in and of itself, tend to worsen the U.S. deficit.

Under circumstances of highly inelastic demands in both countries, it would be possible for devaluation to worsen the U.S. deficit. Because, if the American demand were highly inelastic, the favorable effects of cutting the American demand for British goods would be small. If the British demand for U.S. goods were highly inelastic, the unfavorable effects of cutting their demand for U.S. goods would be large. In such a situation, devaluation would not only not work, but it would worsen the U.S. deficit.

Summary of Discretionary Policies to Deal with International Payments Deficits

Perhaps the best way of summarizing the points made in this section is to restate the central lesson of economics. As *long as resources are scarce, getting more of one thing requires giving up something else*. The same general point can be made about any economic policy measures. *As long as our economic goals are in partial conflict with one another, we may be able to achieve one only by losing some ground in our progress toward another*.

A balance-of-payments deficit might be ended by trade barriers, but to do so would impair the worldwide allocation of resources. It might be ended by reducing foreign spending by government, but to do so might jeopardize the national security. It might be countered by devaluation of the currency, but then again this might not work. Or finally, it could be fought with restrictive monetary and fiscal policy, but only at the likely cost of increasing unemployment.

The economic arena, it seems, is not one of blacks and whites, but one of grays. Economic policy measures are not classifiable into good and bad in any absolute sense, but almost all require a delicate balancing of the good effects against the bad. We must recognize that there are few policy measures that advance us toward one of our goals without, to some degree, conflicting with another.

Review Questions

1. "Ultimately, adjustment of a goods and services deficit can be accomplished either through lowering the external value of the deficit nation's currency or through reducing the rate of growth in the deficit nation's domestic prices and income." Explain.
2. Carefully explain why international liquidity tends to be more important with a stable exchange rate system than with a flexible exchange rate system.
3. Explain how, under a full international gold standard system,
   a. Exchange rates were kept stable.
   b. Payments deficits generate changes that automatically tend to reduce the deficit.
4. Explain how, under the Bretton Woods system,
   a. Exchange rates were kept stable.
   b. Nations with chronic payments deficits were expected to eliminate the deficits.
5. Explain how, under a freely floating exchange rate system,
   a. Exchange rates are determined.
   b. Adjustment of a payments deficit would occur.
6. List and evaluate the discretionary measures available to policymakers to attempt to deal with international payments deficits.

24

Recent History and Current Problems in International Finance

The past century's experience in organizing and managing international monetary affairs provides painfully clear evidence indicating that there is no one perfect international monetary system ideally suited for all time and all situations. As patterns of trade, techniques of payment, degree of industrialization, and the like have changed over the years, international monetary institutions have been forced to adapt. The result has been a continuing evolutionary process that provided us with some experience with each of the types of systems described in the preceding chapter. If perfection in this complex area exists, the world has not yet found it. But the search goes on, right into the mid-1980s.

In this concluding chapter, we shall attempt to trace through the highlights of this process of change. The first section—as background—briefly comments on developments from 1870 to the end of World War II, during most of which the international gold standard played the central role. The second section reviews the 1945–1973 period, during which the Bretton Woods system—implemented by the International Monetary Fund—withstood, with varying degrees of success, a seemingly unending series of challenges and monetary crises. The concluding section deals with the massive upheavals that led to the abandonment of the Bretton Woods system in 1973 in favor of the current system of "managed" floating exchange rates.

The Past—Midnineteenth Century Through World War II

The Golden Era: 1870–1914

The period from about 1870 to 1914 has often been characterized as the *golden era*. During most of those years the world was untroubled by the vast upheavals associated with major wars, and the full international gold standard held the center of the stage.

It was in many ways an idyllic era, and the gold standard seemed to many to be the ultimate in sane and stable economic arrangements. Although such faith in the now-discarded system may seem, with the invaluable aid of hindsight, to have been overdone, one can hardly deny that it worked amazingly well.

The unquestioned financial center of the world at the time was that staunch citadel of free trade, Great Britain. She played her key role well. As a developed industrial giant, Britain permitted less fully developed nations to finance trade deficits by making long-term loans abroad. As the heart of the financial world, she played an important role in fostering the development of freer trade with a minimum of trade barriers and restrictions. And, along with most other nations, her monetary authorities obeyed, reasonably faithfully, the "rules" of the gold standard game whereby monetary policy was tightened in the face of a payments deficit and eased to combat a surplus.

But it took more than skillful management to make the system work so well. Other conditions favored it greatly. In the first place, wages and prices were considerably more flexible than they are today. This had the important effect of permitting the drop in demand associated with payments deficits to lower prices rather than income and employment—a much preferred result. In addition, public and official attitudes had not yet reached the point where "doing something about unemployment" was considered a proper area for governmental action. Hence the policy conflict that has worried us so much since—between policy to deal with inflation and a payments deficit and policy to deal with unemployment—was largely absent.

One does less than justice to the international gold standard if one does not recognize its solid record of accomplishment prior to World War I. And yet one does a certain violence to history if one does not recognize that the "ideal" conditions for its efficient operation largely evaporated under the extreme pressures of World War I and its aftermath.

The Unsettled Years: 1918–1930

Not that an attempt was not made to return to the "good old days" of the prewar gold standard after that conflict. Most major countries went back "on gold" as soon as possible. But the conditions of the nineteenth century, fortunately or unfortunately, were gone forever. The institutional trappings of the gold standard were restored, but the conditions necessary to make it a viable, efficient system of world financial order had simply disappeared.

A full discussion of the problems of the between-the-wars gold standard is not permitted by the scope of this book. We can, however, mention some of the chief causes of difficulty: unrealistic reparation demands imposed on vanquished Germany; an attempt by the British to reestablish their pound at the same relationship with gold as that maintained in prewar days—a clear overevaluation; excessive use of the protective tariff by the emerging industrial giant, the United States; and, finally, the growing recognition, especially after the experience of mass unemployment in the 1920s and 1930s, that the strict discipline of the gold standard required the sacrifice of what was rapidly emerging as the major domestic policy goal—restoring and maintaining full employment.

The combination of all these factors produced, if not a hostile climate, at least a less than ideal environment for a smoothly functioning gold standard. And when, in the early 1930s, the public's confidence in the ability of its governments to honor their pledge to pay gold on demand to all comers dipped sharply, country after country, drained of its gold supply through payments deficits, public hoarding demands, and speculative short-term capital movements, was forced to abandon the standard.[1]

The Chaotic 1930s

The decade of the 1930s was indeed a turbulent period in international finance. This period was marked not only by the abandonment of the gold standard by most nations but also by a wild scramble of unilateral devaluations, increased tariff barriers, and a whole range of actions calculated to impede the restoration of normal, free international exchange. It was an economically sick world that girded itself for the second all-out war of the century in 1939.

U.S. actions during the interwar period were, at times, deplorable; at other times, exemplary. The nation at first enabled the post–World War I reparations arrangements to work by, in essence, lending Germany sufficient amounts to enable the Germans to pay reparations to England and France, which countries, in turn, used these proceeds to pay off part of their war debts to the United States. U.S. lending to permit this triangular deal, however, was made necessary partly by its own greatly increased tariff barrier in the 1920s, which made it all but impossible for the Germans to earn the reparation payment through exports.

When the U.S. stock market crash in 1929 put a virtual end to long-term U.S. lending, and when the United States followed up this calamity with the new Smoot-Hawley tariff bill, establishing the highest tariff rates in its history, the Germans were simply unable to meet their obligations. And, in turn, the British and French were unable to keep up with scheduled repayments on their war debts to the United States. The result was that the United States had no choice but to declare a *moratorium* on payment of inter-Allied war debts, and, of course, the Germans were forced to default on much of their reparation burden.

Only in the latter 1930s did the United States begin to demonstrate its awareness of the futility of unilateral competitive trade restrictions. During this period the historic Reciprocal Trade Agreements Act was passed, providing for substantial

---

[1]It would be incorrect, however, to say that the U.S. decision to go "off gold" in 1933 was forced by any immediate shortage of gold reserves.

reductions in U.S. tariff barriers; the Tri-Partite Agreement with England and France was signed, forming the basis for an end to competitive devaluation; and the Export-Import Bank was established to provide long-term loans to some of the trading partners of the United States.

These more enlightened, constructive policies were followed up during and after World War II with all-out efforts to avoid the mistakes of unilateralism of the 1920s and 1930s. No heavy reparations were demanded of the defeated Axis powers; no large inter-Allied debts were built up during the war, largely as a result of the U.S. Lend-Lease Program; the basis for large-scale international monetary cooperation after the war in the form of the International Monetary Fund was established in the historic 1944 conference at Bretton Woods; and the rebuilding of the economies of the war-ravaged Western Allies was speeded up immeasurably by the unprecedented, far-sighted Marshall Plan. The lessons learned at such heavy cost in the interwar period had provided the basis for the far more enlightened multilateral approach of the late 1940s and 1950s.

The Bretton Woods System and the "Gold Exchange" Standard: 1945–1971

The international monetary system that emerged in the quarter-century following World War II was shaped primarily by two fundamental institutional developments—the implementation of the Bretton Woods agreement and the emergence of a "gold exchange" standard. Let us consider the essence of both these developments before taking a look at how well they worked out in practice.

The Original Bretton Woods System and the International Monetary Fund

As already noted, the heart of the Bretton Woods agreement was the establishment of the *International Monetary Fund*. Its initial purposes, as clearly stated in its *Articles of Agreement* promulgated in 1944, were to (1) promote the growth of world trade through international cooperation; (2) work toward eliminating the widespread network of exchange controls in existence in the late 1940s; (3) establish a system whereby exchange rates could be kept relatively stable without returning to the shackles of the old full gold standard; and (4) provide a new source of loans of foreign exchange to assist member nations undergoing temporary or cyclical balance-of-payments deficits. The system is perhaps best described by the steps taken to implement the last of these two objectives.

The "Stable, but Adjustable," Exchange Rate System Established by the IMF.   As we saw in the preceding chapter, exchange rates were to be kept stable primarily by the "pegging" activities of governmental exchange stabilization funds. The United States (possessor of a majority of the world gold supply in the late

1940s) was committed to maintaining a fixed relationship between the dollar and gold by standing ready to convert all dollars obtained by foreign governments to gold at a fixed ($35 per ounce of gold) price. Other member nations, then, were formally to announce a "par value" for their currencies with respect to the dollar (thereby setting up an official exchange rate with the dollar) and to intervene directly into the foreign exchange market to keep fluctuations in that exchange rate within 1 percent on either side.

The IMF's framers were not so naïve as to believe that a fixed and rigid set of exchange rates could be maintained for all time regardless of changes in productivity, resources availability, inflation rates, and the like. Rather, as we have seen, they set up a system whereby nations suffering from chronic deficits caused by a "fundamental disequilibrium" could, upon consultation with IMF authorities, devalue their currencies in an effort to restore payments equilibrium. It was, then, a system under which exchange rates were "pegged" by governmental action, but the pegs were adjustable over time in response to changing circumstances.

IMF "Drawing Rights"—Loans to Assist Member Nations with Short-Term Deficits.　While devaluation was considered an appropriate way to combat a chronic, long-term payments deficit, those deficits that arose from random or seasonal factors or as a result of the business cycle were expected to be dealt with by other measures. For example, a "cyclical" payments deficit resulting from excess demand in the deficit nation was thought to be most effectively combated by more appropriate (i.e., restrictive) domestic monetary-fiscal measures.

To help member nations withstand deficits of this sort while corrective measures were taking effect, the IMF established a loan facility offering members so-called "drawing rights" under carefully specified conditions. To set up the loan fund, the IMF originally assessed each member nation a "quota" (based roughly on the relative size of the country in the world economy), 25 percent of which was to be paid in the form of gold and the rest in the form of its own domestic currency. Payment of its quota entitled a country to "drawing rights" (the right to borrow) on the foreign exchange held in the IMF loan fund.

　As originally established, any member country could borrow any other country's currency (by exchanging an equivalent amount of its own domestic currency for it) in an amount up to 25 percent of its own quota (often referred to as its *gold tranche*) at any time and without question. Beyond that, it could borrow (or, more correctly, buy with its own currency) additional yearly amounts not exceeding 25 percent of its own quota until the fund had accumulated its domestic currency in an amount equivalent to 200 percent of its quota. These added amounts, however, were *not* automatically available on simple request and were made available only with sufficient justification to IMF authorities.

Over the years the national quotas (and therefore the size of the loan fund) have been raised several times and the conditions for borrowing have been altered, but the "drawing rights" facility still exists in essentially its original form. Also, in the most recent change, no gold payments are required to meet the quota. It should be noted, however, that it is a fund of limited size, intended only to help with temporary deficit problems. Nations with large, chronic deficits were expected to deal with their problems through more fundamental alterations in their competitive status.

The Rise of the "Gold Exchange" Standard

While the Bretton Woods system was the result of carefully thought-out international planning, another main feature of the post–World War II international monetary structure—the so-called "gold exchange" standard—simply evolved naturally without any preconceived planning. The basic structure of the International Monetary Fund, along with the earlier predominance and strength of the U.S. economy, provided the foundation for this development. Perhaps the most fruitful way to go about explaining the emergence of the gold exchange standard is to comment briefly on the balance-of-payments experience of the United States during the late 1940s and the 1950s.

Developments in the 1940s and the 1950s. In the immediate post–World War II years the United States, already the possessor of about 70 percent of the free world's gold supply, ran heavy balance-of-payments surpluses while the leading nations of Western Europe had to contend with substantial deficits. From 1946 through 1949, for example, the U.S. surplus on goods and services averaged over $8 billion, an enormous amount in terms of the prices of that earlier period. It was a situation that many felt would continue indefinitely, and, indeed, methods of dealing with what was assumed to be a very-long-term dollar shortage problem dominated discussion.

A look back at the events of the late 1940s and early 1950s, however, provides a much better perspective of what was happening than was possible at the time. The *dollar gap,* which was the cause of so much concern, was rapidly being bridged by developments all around. The role of Marshall Plan aid has already been mentioned in this regard. Not only did it permit a temporary bridging of Western Europe's balance-of-payments gap but it also aided the rebuilding and modernization of European industry to the point where it could better compete in world markets. And when the Marshall Plan ended, the intensification of the cold war provided justification for continuance, on a long-term basis, of heavy, U.S. foreign aid to its allies abroad.

In the meantime, Western Europe was acting on its own to recover its share of world trade. Not only was it modernizing its productive equipment, but it acted firmly and boldly to achieve a degree of economic integration through the Schuman Plan, the European Economic Community, and the Common Market, which gave it trade advantages it had never before possessed. Finally, the nations of Western Europe acted, in 1948 and 1949, to devalue their currencies sharply with respect to the dollar to curtail their then-heavy deficits.

While the United States was occupied with the Korean war and then, later, a postwar boom in the first half of the 1950s, vast changes in its international economic position were taking place almost without notice. What had been considered a dollar gap had already disappeared. But the relatively small U.S. payments deficits that had begun to show up caused no alarm whatsoever because foreigners were quite content to hold the bulk of their excess dollar earnings in dollar form. This, in turn, was a consequence of the rapid development of the *gold exchange standard* for which the pound and the dollar were the key currencies.

As we have seen, the gold exchange standard was not the result of any worldwide planning. Rather, it spread as a result of decisions on the part of individual nations to hold part of their international reserves in dollar form (or pounds, for the sterling bloc) as well as in gold.

That this should have happened is hardly surprising. The rapidly expanding volume of trade in the period required greatly increased international reserves to finance it (i.e., to enable deficit nations to continue pegging their exchange rates). Clearly some method had to be found for making the too-small and maldistributed world gold supply stretch farther. One partial answer to the problem was for many nations to begin counting their dollar holdings (which were, after all, readily convertible into gold) as an additional form of international reserve. And that is what a gold exchange standard is—a system whereby a strong national currency, adequately backed by, and convertible into, gold, permits an otherwise inadequate world gold supply to support a much larger supply of internationally accepted reserves.

The advantages to other countries from this arrangement are obvious. Instead of tying up all their monetary reserves in the nonincome-earning form of gold, they could hold substantial portions in the form of short-term dollar assets, which not only earned interest but were, as long as the U.S. honored its promise to make them convertible into gold, "as good as gold" itself. For the United States, on the other hand, it meant that its deficits during the early and middle 1950s led only to a piling up of more short-term dollar obligations to foreigners who were, in the main, more desirous of expanding the dollar-asset portion of their monetary reserves than of taking out gold.

During this period, therefore, the dollar became a true world currency in the sense that it performed, for all nations of the world, the three basic functions of money. It was then, and is still, widely used as a "vehicle" currency in that a very large percentage of world trade is actually transacted with the use of dollars. Thus it acted as a *medium of exchange* for most international transactions. Second, it served as a *unit of account* as all other IMF member nations expressed the value of their currencies in terms of U.S. dollars.[2]

---

[2]Specifically, these "par values" were expressed in terms of the U.S. dollar *with a gold content as of 1944*. When the United States finally devalued in the early 1970s (by lowering the gold content of the dollar below that of 1944), the other nations had to decide whether to allow their currencies' relationship to the dollar to stay the same (thereby changing it with respect to the dollar's 1944 content).

Experience Under Bretton Woods: 1958–1970

The almost unnoticed U.S. deficits of the mid-1950s mushroomed suddenly in 1958 to a scale that seemed to demand not only attention but action from responsible authorities. It was a combination of two developments that rang the warning bell.

First, the reasonably comfortable surplus on goods and services the United States had enjoyed in the mid-1950s fell precipitously. Indeed, when net long-term investment abroad by Americans was added to the U.S. current account balance, it was clear that in both 1958 and 1959, foreigners acquired some $3.5 billion to $4.0 billion in short-term dollar claims from their transactions with the United States.

Second, foreign nations that had been willing, in the past, to accept the proceeds of their surpluses with the United States almost entirely in the form of increased holdings of short-term dollar claims suddenly switched tactics and withdrew over $2 billion of gold. This sudden change in foreign attitudes undoubtedly resulted from a combination of two factors. On the one hand, some of them, having already built up their dollar reserves to the tolerable limits, felt obliged to take gold to keep a balanced proportion of gold and dollars in their monetary reserves. Others, however, probably reacted to the sharply expanded U.S. deficit as a danger sign and, on the chance that the United States might be forced to devalue, took the defensive speculative action of withdrawing gold. Note, in Table 24-1, that the

TABLE 24-1

U.S. Balance-of-Payments Performance, 1959–1971
(billions of dollars)

Year	Balance on Goods and Services	Current Account Plus Net Long-Term Capital Movements	Liquid Liabilities Owed to Foreign Governments	Gold Stock
1959	0.3	−4.1	10.6	19.5
1960	4.1	−1.2	11.9	17.8
1961	5.6	0	12.6	17.0
1962	5.1	−1.0	13.6	16.1
1963	5.9	−1.3	15.2	15.6
1964	8.5	0	16.2	15.5
1965	7.1	−1.8	16.2	14.1
1966	5.2	−1.7	14.6	13.2
1967	5.1	−3.3	16.7	12.1
1968	2.5	−1.4	13.6	10.9
1969	1.9	−3.0	13.0	11.9
1970	3.6	−3.0	20.6	·11.1
1971	0.8	−9.6	48.2	11.1[a]

[a]Value of gold stock raised via devaluation of dollar.

Source: Federal Reserve Bank of St. Louis and Federal Reserve Bulletin.

U.S. gold stock, which had been almost $23 billion as late as 1957 (with only a little over $8 billion of liquid liabilities owed to foreign governments), fell steadily throughout most of the 1960s.

The U.S. reaction to this balance-of-payments experience and its attendant gold drain was many faceted. In accordance with its commitment to the IMF, the United States regularly reaffirmed its pledge to maintain the convertibility of foreign-government-held dollars into gold. Early in the period this was an eminently credible promise, since the U.S. gold stock was larger (until 1964) than the short-term dollar claims of foreigners. But as the "gold drain" continued and the volume of foreign-owned short-term dollar claims grew, it became clear that some sort of discretionary action would be needed.

Throughout the 1960s, the U.S. government employed every discretionary measure available with the exception of devaluation. For example, there can be little doubt that governmental spending abroad was held down and that domestic monetary and fiscal policy were kept less expansive than the unemployment levels in the early 1960s might otherwise have dictated.[3]

In addition, it instituted a whole range of measures that properly belong under the heading of trade barriers. These included cutting the duty-free allowance for American tourists abroad from $500 to $100; restricting Defense Department purchases to U.S. firms only unless the U.S. price was more than 50 percent higher than the foreign price; more stringent action to require recipients of U.S. foreign aid to spend it on U.S.-produced goods; levying a 15 percent tax (called the "interest equalization" tax) on purchase of foreign securities by Americans; limiting direct lending to foreigners by U.S. financial institutions; and controlling the amount and method of financing direct investment abroad.

How well did all this work? As Table 24-1 indicates, it did reduce the size of U.S. deficits and—through the 1960s at least—held down on the foreign accumulation of short-term dollar claims. But these successes were not sufficient to restore full confidence in the dollar, and the "gold drain" continued. And as the 1960s drew to a close, the acceleration of the Vietnam war and ever more serious inflation combined to almost wipe out the accustomed surplus on goods and services, pushing the entire U.S. balance of payments into heavy deficit and paving the way for an extremely rapid buildup of foreign-held short-term dollar claims. The result was that by 1971, with foreign government short-term dollar claims approaching five times the level of the U.S. gold stock, it was obvious to all that the American

---

[3]Evidence of this is the following observation on President Kennedy's view of the balance-of-payments problem by one of his chief advisers:

> The balance of payments remained a constant worry to Kennedy. . . . He used to tell his advisors that the two things which scared him most were nuclear war and the payments deficit. . . . He had acquired somewhere, perhaps from his father, the belief that a nation was only as strong as the value of its currency; and he feared that, if he pushed things too far, "loss of confidence" would descend and there would be a run on gold.

Arthur M. Schlesinger, Jr., *A Thousand Days: John F. Kennedy in the White House* (Boston: Houghton Mifflin, 1965), pp. 654–55.

promise to maintain the convertibility of the dollar had become an essentially empty pledge.

Why, one might reasonably ask, did the United States take so long before resorting to devaluation? The answer is rather complex but worth our consideration.

In the first place, under the Bretton Woods rules, the United States on its own actually lacked the power to devalue the dollar *with respect to other currencies*. It could devalue the dollar in terms of gold (raise the dollar price of gold), but, it will be recalled, it was other nations (and their exchange stabilization funds) that established and maintained exchange rates between the dollar and other national currencies. And since the only way devaluation could help restore equilibrium to the American balance of payments was by lowering the value of the dollar relative to other national currencies, cooperation from U.S. trading partners was essential.

But there were more fundamental barriers to a dollar devaluation than mere mechanics. The dollar, after all, was an international reserve currency, and its relationship to gold was the cornerstone of the Bretton Woods system. The United States not only had formally committed itself to converting dollars held by foreign countries into gold at a $35-per-ounce price but had publicly pressured friendly governments to do their bit to keep the Bretton Woods system afloat by forgoing their option to conversion. Some had acquiesced, opting to retain their short-term dollar claims rather than take out gold, but others had rejected the American plea and had taken out large quantities of gold. Devaluation under these circumstances (raising the dollar value of gold) would consequently reward those who had refused to cooperate at the expense of those who had gone along and kept the bulk of their reserves in dollar form. For all these reasons, devaluation of the dollar was considered a last-ditch alternative, to be resorted to only in the most critical of circumstances. Therefore, it was not until December 1971, four months after the suspension of the convertibility of the dollar, that the first devaluation came about.

An Aside—The Authorization of Special Drawing Rights

Long before the events of 1971 brought about the suspension of the dollar's convertibility signaling the eventual demise of Bretton Woods' stable exchange rate system, international monetary authorities were wrestling with a dilemma of a different sort—how to maintain an adequate flow of international reserves after the United States eliminated its chronic deficits.

Despite official concern over the string of U.S. deficits in the 1950s and 1960s, they did have one important redeeming feature. During a period when world trade was expanding rapidly but official gold stocks were hardly rising at all, there was a pressing need for an expansion of international reserves. This need was met during these years primarily by the outpouring of U.S. dollars in consequence of this nation's deficits.

But helpful though it was, this method of enlarging international reserves was a hazardous one. Its continuance depended solely on continuance of American deficits. And continuance of those deficits seemed certain, eventually, to undermine foreign nations' *confidence* in the dollar as an appropriate international reserve asset. Clearly, the longer the United States continued to incur large deficits, pumping out more and more short-term dollar claims, the less credible would be its promise to convert those dollars to gold on demand. As short-term dollar claims owned by foreigners mushroomed while the U.S. gold stock dwindled, it seemed inevitable that the U.S. would eventually be forced to suspend the convertibility of the dollar and/or devalue it (both of which, of course, it did in 1971).

Given this situation, it was apparent that a new form of international liquidity was needed. After much study, the International Monetary Fund authorized the creation of *special drawing rights,* first issued in 1970.

Special Drawing Rights. Special drawing rights (or SDRs) are claims on the IMF that have been issued to member countries in proportion to their quotas but separate and *additional* to those quotas. A total of $9.3 billion worth of such claims were created and distributed from 1970 through 1972, the U.S. share being just about 25 percent of the total.[4] Since that time, the IMF has sharply increased the amount of SDRs authorized.

Countries receiving these added claims against the IMF incur no added liability. The IMF simply created new international money in establishing them.

A country with a balance-of-payments deficit may use its SDRs to "purchase" convertible currencies from other participant nations. Participant nations are obligated to accept such increases in their SDR accounts until their total holdings equal three times their original SDR allocation. For those nations who acquire additions to their SDR accounts in this manner, the IMF pays interest.

Suppose, for example, that the United States finds it necessary to acquire $500 million worth of Deutsche marks to settle a deficit. It could transfer $500 million of its SDR account to Germany, in return for which it would receive an equivalent value in marks. Germany, now holding its original allotment of SDRs plus the $500 million obtained from the United States, would receive interest on the $500 million.

At the time of their authorization, it was expected that SDRs might eventually become the dominant type of international reserve, supplanting both gold and such foreign exchange reserves as the dollar. However, while the *absolute* amount of SDRs has increased sharply in recent years, they still constituted only about 5 percent of total reserves (excluding gold) held by all nations in early 1982.

---

[4]When the SDRs were first authorized, one SDR equaled one dollar. Since then the dollar has been devalued (and depreciated) with respect to the SDR, so that while there were a total of SDR 21.4 billion outstanding in 1981, their dollar value had risen to well above that figure.

The Transition to a New Exchange Rate System: 1971–1973

When the United States suspended the convertibility of the dollar in August 1971, the cornerstone of the "stable, but adjustable," exchange rate systems established at Bretton Woods was removed. In the immediate aftermath, most industrial countries suspended their efforts to peg their exchange rate to the dollar. "By the end of August, all major currencies except the French franc were floating, but exchange controls were in widespread use and central bank intervention was substantial."[5]

There was at the time a widespread desire to return to a stable exchange rate system as soon as possible. All recognized, however, that any new exchange rate structure set up must involve a substantial devaluation of the dollar—especially relative to the Japanese yen and the German mark—if the United States was to be able to curb its burgeoning balance-of-payments deficits. There were, however, sharp differences, especially between the United States and France, as to how this should be accomplished.

The American position was for the world's major surplus nations to *re*value their currencies with respect to the dollar but to leave the dollar price of gold unchanged. The French, on the other hand, insisted that any realignment of exchange rates include a devaluation of the dollar with respect to gold. After months of debate, a compromise was reached in the Smithsonian Agreement of December 1971.

In that document it was agreed that most industrialized countries would revalue their currencies with respect to the dollar. For example, relative to the U.S. dollar, the Japanese yen was raised 16.7 percent, the German mark 13.6 percent, and the French franc 8.6 percent. In return, the United States agreed to devalue the dollar with respect to gold by 8.57 percent, thereby raising the dollar price of gold from $35 to $38 per ounce.[6]

The raising of the "official" gold price represented a political compromise by the United States, but its economic significance was really minimal. Since the dollar remained inconvertible into gold in any case, it is difficult to see what was gained by the action aside from the purely political accomplishment of forcing the Americans to swallow the same devaluation medicine that its Western European trading partners had had to accept in the past. After all, as one observer put it, "it made no real difference whether the U.S. was not buying or selling monetary gold at $35 per ounce or whether it was not buying or selling it at $38 per ounce."[7]

[5]Robert Solomon, *The International Monetary System, 1945–1976* (New York: Harper & Row, 1977), p. 189. This section relies heavily upon Solomon's excellent account as well as on Gerald M. Meier's *Problems of a World Monetary Order* (New York: Oxford University Press, 1974).

[6]Other parts of the Smithsonian Agreement included removal of a temporary 10 percent surcharge on imports by the United States and agreement that exchange rates would be permitted to fluctuate above and below the newly established levels by 2.25 percent rather than the old 1 percent limit.

[7]Ernest Olson, "Devaluation of the Dollar," *Monthly Review*, Federal Reserve Bank of San Francisco, June 1972, p. 7.

Nevertheless, hopes were high that the realignment of exchange rates between world currencies would permit a long-term return to a stable exchange rate system. Indeed, in what turned out to be a classic overstatement, President Nixon hailed the Smithsonian Agreement as "the most significant monetary achievement in the history of the world."

With the aid of hindsight, it would be an almost equally classic understatement to point out that it turned out to be no such thing. By early 1973, just a little over a year after the signing of the Smithsonian Agreement, international monetary markets were once again in chaos. Accelerating U.S. inflation and discouraging balance-of-trade reports led to renewed speculation against the dollar. Italy, France, and Belgium broke away from the Smithsonian agreements to allow their currencies to float for capital transactions. Switzerland also floated its franc. And the West German government was forced to absorb billions of U.S. dollars to maintain the mark-dollar exchange rate agreed upon at Smithsonian.

In the face of all this, the United States announced a second dollar devaluation—this one by 10 percent—in February 1973.[8] The action helped little to stay the immediate crisis. The following day the Japanese yen was allowed to float. The flow of dollars to Germany accelerated at such a rate that on March 1 alone the West German government had to absorb almost $3 billion! Amid these chaotic conditions, European foreign exchange markets were closed and an emergency meeting among major industrial countries was called in Paris in early March. Out of that Paris meeting came an agreement to scrap the remnants of the Smithsonian guidelines and turn to general floating. Not only Smithsonian but the long-cherished stable exchange rate system had been abandoned for the indefinite future.

The exchange rate system adopted in the spring of 1973 (and retained to the present) was not a pure floating system wherein exchange rates fluctuate solely in accordance with private demand and supply factors. Rather, it was (and is) a "managed" floating system wherein private supply and demand (by exporters and importers) are the dominant exchange rate determinants but in which governments feel free to intervene directly any time they consider a nudge to the exchange rate appropriate.

Efforts at Reform Since 1973

Even before the Smithsonian Agreement broke down in early 1973, the International Monetary Fund had set into action a group charged with planning a thorough reform and overhaul of the international monetary system. The members of this group, popularly known as the *Committee of Twenty,* were chosen to represent all segments of the world community and instructed to report back to the IMF Board of Governors with their recommendations by July 1974. Singled out as critical

---

[8]This action raised the "official" price of gold from $38.00 per ounce to the current $42.22.

areas requiring study were the exchange rate mechanism, a means of restoring worldwide convertibility of currencies, the proper role in the revised system for foreign exchange reserves, gold, and SDRs, the appropriate steps to control disequilibrating capital movements, and techniques for providing more aid to lesser developed nations.

In its early deliberations it seems clear that the Committee of Twenty considered the "managed" floating exchange rate system resorted to in March 1973 as a temporary arrangement to be superseded, when plans were completed, by a return to a stable rate system. For example, in an interim report issued in September 1973, the committee recommended that reform should include measures aimed at "establishing an exchange rate system based on stable but adjustable par values, with temporary floating to be considered an acceptable method of changing par values."

Whatever the merits or demerits of this professed intent to return to a stable rate system, it has since been all but abandoned in the wake of a series of international economic upheavals of sufficient severity to convince even the most adamant of stable rate proponents that, at least for the foreseeable future, we must learn to live with floating.

The major developments that convinced world monetary leaders that the managed floating system in effect since 1973 must remain for the indefinite future were the extraordinary hikes in OPEC oil prices beginning in late 1973 and the continuing acceleration of worldwide inflation. With unprecedented international payments imbalances caused by widely differing dependence on imported oil and major differences in the rates of inflation of various nations, it has become clear to all that the adjustment potential of floating rates is currently an indispensable ingredient for the maintenance of reasonably free international commerce.

In recognition of all this, agreement was reached in 1976 on a proposed change in the IMF's Articles of Agreement, which specifically authorizes member countries to adopt any exchange rate system for their currency they choose so long as they "avoid manipulating exchange rates on the international monetary system in order to prevent effective balance-of-payments adjustment or to gain an unfair advantage over other members." Under this new article, which was ratified by the required number of member nations in early 1978, the IMF proposes to exercise "firm surveillance over the exchange rate policies of members" and to "adopt specific principles for the guidance of all members with respect to those policies." So as we proceed through the 1980s, the exchange rate procedures first established in the early 1970s remain much the same. Some currencies are floating with only occasional interventions by their governments to influence their movement; many (by the individual choice of their governments rather than by IMF rules) are pegged at a stable rate with the dollar (especially the developing countries); and some (such as most of the nations in the European Economic Community) are held roughly stable among one another but float as a group with respect to the dollar. This is what has come to be called the current "managed floating" system, and it is likely to be with us for some time.

How Well Has the "Managed Floating" System Worked?

The current exchange rate system, as we have seen, was adopted more or less out of necessity in the wake of the breakdown of the "stable, but adjustable, peg system" instituted initially by the Bretton Woods agreement. Although it seems clear that momentous changes in underlying conditions forced the abandonment of the "stable rate" system, the current "managed floating" system has since been officially sanctioned by the International Monetary Fund through a change in its Articles of Agreement that currently approves virtually any exchange rate system that does not involve "manipulating exchange rates . . . in order to . . . gain an unfair competitive advantage over other members."

In effect, then, the 1970s featured a dramatic turnaround from a "stable rate" to a more or less "flexible rate" system. It therefore seems appropriate that we conclude this chapter by first considering the alleged pros and cons of stable and flexible rate systems and then briefly discussing how the new system has "worked" in terms of U.S. international payments experience.

The Case for Stable Exchange Rates

Stable exchange rate advocates, while recognizing the effectiveness of exchange rate flexibility as a balance-of-payments adjustment mechanism, argue that (1) this benefit is more than offset by a number of potentially unfavorable side effects from fluctuating rates and (2) it is possible to develop quite satisfactory alternative mechanisms for adjustment without accepting the risks inherent in a market-determined exchange rate system.

One of their major points, noted in the preceding chapter, is the fear that exchange rate flexibility may impose so much *added risk* that some prospective traders will avoid international transactions altogether. While they recognize that it is possible to hedge against this risk by purchasing forward exchange (buying foreign exchange for delivery at a specified future time at a currently guaranteed exchange rate), they point out that such hedging itself might be quite expensive and that forward commitments might conceivably be impossible to obtain for such very-long-term transactions as long-term investments.

Second, there is the alleged risk of *destabilizing speculation*. What is envisaged here is the possibility that a movement of exchange rates in any one direction will generate expectations that a further move in that direction is likely, leading to actions that fulfill the expectation. Exchange rates movements, then, might become self-generating in the same sense that prices are during hyperinflation or the stock market is during a crash.

With completely flexible exchange rates, it may well also be that short-term capital movements will cause wide swings in exchange rates that are entirely inappropriate in dealing with the nation's current account. Such a possibility might be especially damaging to a nation whose dependence on imports is such as to expose it to major changes in its cost of living as a result. Such "hot money" movements are said to pose a particular threat to the United States because of the hundreds of billions of dollars of U.S. money already held by foreigners.

And advocates of stable exchange rates point to experience with floating rates in the 1970s as evidence in support of their conviction that flexible exchange rates may contribute heavily to *worldwide inflation*. One point here is that, whereas with a stable rate system domestic inflation causes a loss of reserves that serves as a signal that the inflation must be arrested, with flexible rates the only international result of inflation is exchange rate depreciation. In other words, a flexible rate system may undermine the discipline required to combat inflation.

Another part of the argument that flexible exchange rates may contribute to inflation involves the potential "feedback" on the cost of living in a deficit country whose currency is undergoing rapid depreciation. Depreciation of the currency, it is argued, will necessarily make imported goods more expensive in the deficit country, which will not only raise the cost of those items still imported but—in so doing—shelter domestic producers of goods that are also imported from competition which would otherwise hold down on their prices. And, so the argument runs, those cost-of-living increases may, in turn, trigger a further "wage-price" spiral as labor and management attempt to protect themselves from inflation-induced reductions in their living standards.

Such an inflationary result, it is argued, is all the more likely in a world in which wages and prices are highly resistant to downward changes. What is to be expected, then, is a rise of prices in the deficit country (whose currency is depreciating) but no equivalent fall in prices in the surplus country (as a result of currency appreciation).[9]

The Case for Flexible Exchange Rates

Without question, the most fundamental advantage claimed for a flexible exchange rate system is its alleged capacity to adjust or eliminate international payments imbalances automatically through market-induced alterations in the external value of the currency.

As the flexible exchange rate advocates see it, the "adjustable peg" system established at Bretton Woods (or, indeed, any feasible system relying on stable exchange rates) contains some serious deficiencies that are an inevitable result of the exchange rate stability itself.

If, for example, a nation develops a chronic payments deficit under a stable exchange rate system, it is likely to react as follows:

---

[9]Another argument that receives some support is the possibility that, due to potentially highly inelastic supply and demand for traded goods and services, depreciation of the currency could even increase a deficit.

1. Initially, in the short run, it will be forced to use up part of its precious supply of international reserves to "finance" the deficit and keep its currency "pegged" at the current level. This means, as noted, that such a system requires far more concern for the development of procedures for generating large and growing supplies of international reserves than is the case for a flexible rate system.

2. If the deficit is truly chronic, the use of international reserves to finance it can do no more than buy time until more fundamental corrective measures can be taken. And experience has shown that these measures are very likely to consist of (a) the erection or intensification of trade barriers and (b) the use of contractive monetary-fiscal measures at home to hold down on both the domestic demand for imports and domestic export prices, as well as to raise short-term interest rates in the hope of attracting foreign capital. Trade barriers (even if they do succeed in reducing the deficit) constitute a clear-cut impediment to the maximization of world living standards, while contractive monetary-fiscal policies are almost certain to result in an undesired rise in unemployment.

3. Therefore, devaluation of the currency is likely to become the only viable solution. But, as we have seen, this step is likely to be postponed until "defense of the currency" has been allowed to become a major political issue. And the delay plays directly into the hands of speculators who, recognizing the need for, and eventual certainty of, devaluation are presented with a "can't lose" situation. They can sell their supplies of the deficit country's currency with a strong likelihood of a profit (when the devaluation does occur) but no chance (given a rate pegged within narrow limits) of loss. And this speculative activity only makes matters worse for the deficit nation. With it all, when the devaluation finally comes, the devaluing government will have no clear-cut indication as to *how much* to lower the international value of its currency, and it is more likely than not—to be sure that the painful action does the job—that they will overshoot the mark.

How much simpler and more sensible it is, say the flexible rate advocates, to let market forces guide the rate down automatically to the appropriate market-clearing (equilibrium) level!

And what about the stable rate adherents' charge that a flexible rate system may introduce an added element of uncertainty into the picture that will cause risk averters to back away from international transactions? The flexible rate advocates point out that it is perfectly possible for a trader to protect himself against the risk of an exchange rate change by hedging. And as to the longer-run international transactions, they note that under a stable rate system, the risk of the imposition of exchange controls and of devaluation itself produces at least as much uncertainty as anticipated rate changes under a flexible system.

The charge that a flexible rate system may break down under the pressure of destabilizing speculation is also denied by the flexible rate camp. Pointing out that such a development (where speculators expect a currency to depreciate and sell it—thereby not only contributing to the depreciation but fostering the expectation that it will continue, requiring even further sales and even more depreciation) implies that speculators must lose money. For the only way that speculation *can* be destabilizing is if the participants, on average, sell when the currency is low in price and buy when it is high.

Finally, it is pointed out that the Bretton Woods stable rate system tended to spread the disease of worldwide inflation. According to this view, the United States allowed overly expansive monetary-fiscal policies in the late 1960s to generate excessive price rises in the United States, which, in turn, contributed to heavy American payments deficits. This, in turn, required surplus nations, under their IMF commitment to maintain stable exchange rates with the dollar, to buy up billions of excess dollars with their domestic currencies. But the very act of doing so inflated their own domestic money supplies and subjected them to inflation also! Thus, it is argued, the stable rate system acted as a mechanism whereby inflation was spread from one nation to another. To resort to an old cliché, it was simply one more example of a case where "when Uncle Sam sneezed, the rest of the world caught pneumonia."

The "Managed Floating" System and the
U.S. Balance of Payments in Recent Years

In light of the claims of flexible exchange rate advocates, it seems appropriate to take a brief look at how effective a job the new, more flexible system launched in 1973 has done in terms of U.S. balance-of-payments performance. In assessing the evidence available, it is important to bear in mind that the world does not now have a *perfectly* flexible exchange rate system. As noted, many countries (by their own choice) still keep their exchange rates stable with respect to the dollar. In addition, among those that do not, direct governmental intervention into the foreign exchange market to—at least—prevent "disorderly markets" has been commonplace.[10] But despite all this, there can be no doubt that the current system contains exchange rates that are much more flexible than those of past systems, so for evaluative purposes it seems reasonable to take a look at the record.

In Table 24-2 the U.S. balance on goods and services for 1972–1982 is compared with a weighted index of the value of the U.S. dollar with respect to the currencies of 10 major foreign nations with which the United States trades. The weights assigned to each foreign currency in constructing the index are based upon that country's proportionate role in total U.S. trade. For example, the 116.57 figure for December 1982 indicates that, on average in comparison with the 10 other currencies, the dollar had appreciated by about 16.6 percent between March 1973 and December 1982.

---

[10]The definition of disorderly markets is, at best, vague. The congressional Joint Economic Committee has offered the following interpretation:

> Disorderly markets are characterized by an unusually low volume of transactions and abnormally wide spreads between bid and asked prices for at least some currencies, i.e., there is a heavy supply of some currencies but virtually no purchasers, while other moneys are in strong demand but only small amounts are offered. When markets are disorderly, exchange rates are likely to fluctuate erratically.

"Living with the Trade Deficit," Report of the Subcommittee on International Economics of the Joint Economic Committee (Washington, D.C.: Government Printing Office, November 18, 1977), p. 8.

TABLE 24-2

U.S. Balance on Goods and Services and Exchange
Rate Changes, 1972–1982

	Balance on Goods and Services (billions of dollars)	End-of-Year Weighted Average Exchange Value of U.S. Dollars (March 1973 = 100)
1972	−6.1	110.06
1973	3.5	101.48
1974	2.2	98.59
1975	16.2	103.51
1976	3.6	105.33
1977	−9.5	98.36
1978	−9.8	88.52
1979	5.1	88.09
1980	8.3	87.39
1981	11.1	102.94
1982	−0.2	116.57

Source: U.S. Department of Commerce, *Survey of Current Business,* various issues, and *Federal Reserve Bulletin,* various issues.

Although figures such as these are very crude for purposes of drawing conclusions, they do permit some tentative observations. The United States ran a heavy $6.1 billion goods and services deficit in 1972. Partially in response to that, the dollar depreciated by about 10 percent by the end of 1973. One result (although many other factors were also involved) was the elimination of the U.S. deficit, just as one would expect. In this earlier period, the exchange rate fluctuation seems to have worked reasonably well, and in the desired direction. By 1975, a year of severe recession in the United States, the American surplus on goods and services had risen to over $16 billion. As might have been predicted, this surplus resulted in an appreciation of the dollar of over 7 percent through 1976.

But then came 1977 and 1978 and their unprecedented near $10 billion goods and services deficits. The oversupply of dollars from this episode would be expected to lead, once again, to a depreciation. As Table 24-2 reveals, it did, this time by 7 percent during 1977 and another 10 percent during 1978. Such a large depreciation, other things being equal, would be expected to contribute mightily to a turnaround in the balance on goods and services. Once again, as the 1979–1981 figures show, the balance moved in the expected direction.

It is more difficult to explain the 1982 result. With the serious recession in this country, one might normally have expected an increase in our goods and services surplus. However, as indicated, it disappeared. This result seems to have resulted partly from equally serious recessions abroad and partly from an extraordinarily sharp appreciation of the dollar during 1982.

It must be recognized that significant time lags are to be expected between an exchange rate change and its impact upon the nation's balance of payments. It takes time for imports to be cut back and for export industries to gear up to take advantage of a better competitive position. But beyond that, both changes in exchange rates and their impact on the U.S. goods and services balance are subject to myriad complex influences that make simple cause-and-effect predictions extremely hazardous.

This is primarily because exchange rates between the dollar and other currencies depend upon far more than goods and services transactions. Capital flows—American investing abroad and foreigners investing here—also heavily influence the demand for, and supply of, dollars. And with foreigners currently possessing hundreds of billions of U.S. dollars, those capital flows could, at any time, totally dominate the effects of trade transactions. One would normally expect that the sharp appreciation experienced during 1982 would tend to produce deficits in the near future—other things unchanged. But those "other things" in the case of the United States are not only enormous but quite unpredictable. As of this point, we shall just have to wait and see how well the "managed floating" system handles them.

Review Questions

1. How did the "gold exchange" standard arise during the 1950s?
2. What is the purpose of IMF "drawing rights"?
3. "Under Bretton Woods, the United States really was not in a position to devalue the dollar with respect to other currencies in order to deal with its payments deficits." Explain carefully.
4. What are SDRs? Why were they initially issued by the IMF?
5. "The early 1970s devaluations of the U.S. dollar with respect to gold, taken by themselves, were of very little significance." Do you agree? Explain.
6. Carefully explain the case for and against flexible exchange rates.

Index